WOMEN AND SUBSTANCE ABUSE

WOMEN AND SUBSTANCE ABUSE

edited by
Edith S. Lisansky Gomberg
and
Ted D. Nirenberg

ABLEX PUBLISHING
NORWOOD, NEW JERSEY

Library of Congress Cataloging-in-Publication Data

Women and substance abuse / edited by Edith S. Lisanky Gomberg, Ted D. Nirenberg.
    p.   cm.
    Includes bibliographical references and index.
    ISBN 1-56750-065-X.—ISBN 1-56750-066-8 (pbk.)
    1. Substance abuse—United States. 2. Women—United States—Substance use. 3. Drug abuse—United States. 4. Women—United States—Drug use. 5. Smoking—United States. 6. Women—United States—Tobacco use. I. Gomberg, Edith Lisansky, 1920-
II. Nirenberg, Ted D., 1952-
HV4999.2.W66 1993
362.29′1′082—dc20   93-23065
                                             CIP

Ablex Publishing Corporation
355 Chestnut Street
Norwood, New Jersey 07648

Contents

Foreword   vi

1 Women and Alcohol: Gender Differences in Metabolism   1
and Susceptibility
  Charles S. Lieber

2 Alcoholic Beverage Consumption and Estrogenization   18
in Normal Postmenopausal Women
  Judith S. Gavaler

3 Genetic Vulnerability to Alcoholism in Women   42
  Shirley Y. Hill

4 Epidemiological Research on Women's Drinking: 62
Recent Progress and Directions for the 1990s
  Sharon C. Wilsnack and Richard W. Wilsnack

5 Cross-Cultural Perspectives on Women and Alcohol   100
  Dwight B. Heath

6 Antecedents and Consequences   118
  Edith S. Lisansky Gomberg and Ted D. Nirenberg

7 Depression and Antisocial Personality Disorder   142
in Alcoholism: Gender Comparison
  Michie N. Hesselbrock and Victor M. Hesselbrock

8 Women and Illicit Drugs: Marijuana, Heroin,   162
and Cocaine
  Barbara W. Lex

9   The Effects of Maternal Drinking in the Reproductive   191
     Period: An Epidemiologic Review
          Ruth E. Little and Judith K. Wendt

10 Substance Abuse by Special Populations of Women   214
          Michael R. Liepman, Roberta E. Goldman,
          Alicia Monroe, Karen W. Green, Ann Sattler,
          James Broadhurst, and Edith S. Lisansky Gomberg

11 Women and Smoking: Toward the Year 2000   258
          Barbara A. Berman and Ellen R. Gritz

12 The Relationship of Eating Disorders   286
     and Substance Abuse
          Dean D. Krahn

13 Women and Substance Abuse: Treatment Modalities   314
     and Outcomes
          Barbara S. McCrady and Helen Raytek

14 Prevention of Alcohol and Drug Problems   339
     Among Women
          Ted D. Nirenberg and Edith S. Lisansky Gomberg

Author Index   361

Subject Index   384

FOREWORD

The editors, having collaborated on a special issue of the *Journal of Substance Abuse* dealing with female substance abuse issues (Gomberg & Nirenberg, 1991), found it a natural expansion that the contributors be asked to report on the state of their art. Work on female drinking and female drug and alcohol abuse is proliferating, partly because of federal interest in research on women, but mainly because interest and productivity in alcohol research has expanded. The literature is expanding so rapidly, it behooves us to draw a breath every now and again and say, "Where are we and what have we accomplished?"

We have tried to make this a multidisciplinary work. Since we are both psychologists, the behavioral and social aspects of substance use and abuse get more attention, but we have included seminal discussion of alcohol metabolism, hormonal status, and the role of genetics in female alcohol abuse and its consequences. There are more chapters dealing with alcohol as the drug of use and abuse than chapters dealing with other drugs. This is inevitable, since most of the research activity deals with alcohol: its biological effects, behavioral effects, abuses, problems, etc. An attempt is made to be more inclusive so that there are chapters on illicit drug use, smoking, and eating disorders.

Clearly we assume that alcohol and drug use and abuse is a biopsychosocial issue, and we have made an attempt to include both epidemiological and clinical reports. With the computer and the refinement of general population survey techniques, much epidemiological work has been produced, often as a byproduct of national surveys on health, morbidity, and the like. Knowledge, we believe, lies in both epidemiological and clinical research. It is true that those who are in treatment constitute only a limited percentage of those in the general population who would be diagnosable as drug or alcohol abusers. Nonetheless, there is a sizable industry devoted to rehabilitation, much of it government-sponsored, and those who give treatment and receive treatment must also be served. Although clinical research is sometimes dismissed as involving only, "a selected sample," it is important to know as much as possible about that sample. How do those who get into the treatment system differ from those who do not? What proportion of the drug-abusing population at any given point in time manifests "spontaneous recovery"? What are treatment outcome studies telling us about those who are more or less successful in treatment programs? Epidemiology and clinical research may be serving different masters: So-called policy decisions need the information about population trends—look at the role of polling information in recent American elections—but the study of problem behavior, whether it is the role of alcohol in automobile accidents, workplace problems, or family disruption is quite germane. Researchers have two roles: to influence policy and to improve health care.

It is a very positive experience to watch the field of alcohol/drug studies grow in sophistication. The beginning of wisdom is more than newer and better methodologies, it is also the posing of questions. We would point out that there are at least four ways in which we have made progress over the last decades.

First, we have recognized that behavior (and people) change over time and longitudinal or follow-up research is one way of studying such change. Change over time has been recognized by some contributors to alcohol studies. Jellinek's (1952) "phases" emphasized a distinction between earlier alcoholic behaviors and later behaviors. An early discussion of the family's adjustment to the "crisis of alcoholism" (Jackson, 1954) pointed to the different stages an alcoholic family passes through. We believe, too, that the population of alcohol abusers is a shifting population, and as Cahalan, Cisin, and Crossley (1969) pointed out in an early report of drinking survey research, people may present problems at one time and not at the next. People move in and out of the alcoholic subpopulation.

Second, while most researchers would support a biopsychosocial approach, the enormity of the task and the complexity of etiology seem to encourage univariate explanations. We have moved to multivariate awareness, usually confined to multivariate analyses within a given problem or discipline. Is the day coming when research will be both multivariate and multidisciplinary?

Third, when a finding is reported about female drinking or female alcohol or drug problems, the finding needs to be qualified in terms of the *subgroup* studied. Women are no more homogeneous a sample of humankind than are men, and the women we study will differ by age or cohort or generation, by socioeconomic status, by education and occupation, by ethnicity and religion, and by marital status. They will be rural or urban, more or less healthy, more or less adequate as problem solvers, more or less emotionally labile, and so on.

Fourth, we have separate federal institutes for study of different drugs, but that does not reflect the real world. Most persons, whether they are using a substance within normal limits or abusing, use more than a single substance. Female alcohol abusers have been known for decades to be users/abusers of bromides, barbituates, minor tranquilizers, and antidepressants, to say nothing of marijuana and other illicit substances. Persons who abuse other drugs, such as heroin or cocaine, frequently resort to alcoholic beverages. There is some awareness of this issue in the alcoholism treatment field's growing sensitivity to issues about smoking.

This book is an update of where we are at this moment. The first five chapters deal with basic issues of biology, epidemiology, and anthropology. The next five chapters deal with substance abuse, and this includes antecedents, consequences, comorbidity, fetal effects, special populations, and illicit drug use. Two chapters which follow are concerned with related disorders, that is, smoking and eating disorders. The final chapters deal with treatment and prevention. This is the state of our knowledge in the particular areas covered by each contributor, and this is as good a place as any to thank our contributors for their expertise, hard work, and patience.

Many years ago, a wise philosopher opined that there was no such thing as "a definitive work" in science. Indeed, research activity is of such a nature, it often challenges the accepted wisdom. So we prefer to think of this book as a statement of current knowledge, subject to modification and change with time, but presented here by contributors who are the best in their chosen areas.

Edith S. Lisansky Gomberg
Ted D. Nirenberg

REFERENCES

Cahalan, D., Cisin, I. H., & Crossley, H. M. (1969). *American drinking practices* (Monograph No. 6) New Brunswick, NJ: Rutgers Center of Alcohol Studies.

Gomberg, E. S. L., & Nirenberg, T. D. (1991). Special Issue: Women and substance abuse. *Journal of Substance Abuse, 3,* 131–267.

Jackson, J. K. (1954). The adjustment of the family to the crisis of alcoholism. *Quarterly Journal of Studies on Alcohol, 15,* 562–586.

Jellinek, E. M. (1952). Phases of alcohol addiction. *Quarterly Journal of Studies on Alcohol, 13,* 673–684.

Chapter 1

Women and Alcohol: Gender Differences in Metabolism and Susceptibility*

Charles S. Lieber, M.D.

Alcohol Research and Treatment Center and G.I.-Liver and Nutrition Program Bronx VA Medical Center and Mt. Sinai School of Medicine, New York, NY

INTRODUCTION

Until recently, most studies concerning the adverse effects of alcohol focused mainly on men because, on the average, men drink much more than women and therefore bear the brunt of the adverse effects. However, drinking levels of women have been increasing and may soon be approaching those of men (Mercer & Khavari, 1990). This trend is particularly significant since it apparently selectively affects young women (Corti & Ibrahim, 1990). Therefore, it behooves us at the present time to focus a greater attention on possible consequences of

* This chapter has been supported by the Department of Veterans Affairs and DHHS grant #AA03508.

heavy drinking in women, particularly since some of the evidence accumulated in recent years indicates a greater susceptibility of women to the development of somatic complications of alcoholism, such as liver disease (Van Thiel, 1991; Parrish, Higuchi, & Dufour, 1991). The latter aspect is the focus of this article, with a brief review of some gender difference in terms of the metabolism of alcohol which might have an impact on the differential susceptibility.

GENDER DIFFERENCES IN THE DISTRIBUTION AND METABOLISM OF ETHANOL

Women have higher blood ethanol concentrations than men after an equivalent oral dose (Jones & Jones, 1976; Arthur, Lee, & Wright, 1984). This difference has been attributed to a smaller volume of distribution of ethanol because of a lower water content in the body in women than in men (Marshall, Kingstone, Boss, & Morgan, 1983). We (Frezza, Di Padova, Pozzato, Terpin, Baraona, & Lieber, 1990) confirmed that the volume of ethanol distribution is lower in women. However, the apparent volume of distribution, calculated from intravenous curves, was only 12% larger in normal men than in normal women (767 ± 4 ml per kilogram in the men and 686 ± 6 in the women; $p < 0.05$) (Frezza et al., 1990). We wondered, therefore, whether other factors might contribute to the higher blood alcohol levels in women. We focused on the role of gastric alcohol dehydrogenase activity and first-pass metabolism because we had found recently that the stomach represents some kind of "protective" barrier against the penetration of alcohol into the body by retaining and breaking down part of the alcohol consumed orally.

Although it is generally recognized that the liver is the main site of ethanol metabolism (Lieber, 1992), extrahepatic metabolism occurs: Ethanol oxidation in the digestive tract of the rat has been previously reported (Lamboeuf, De Saint Blanquat, & Derache, 1981; Lamboeuf, La Droitte, & De Saint Blanquat, 1983) and has been related to the alcohol dehydrogenase (ADH) present in this tissue (Hempel & Pietruszko, 1979; Pestalozzi, Buhler, von Wartburg, & Hess, 1983). In the rat, the ability of the stomach to oxidize ethanol has been demonstrated *in vitro* (Carter & Isselbacher, 1971), and *in vivo* (Lamboeuf et al., 1983). However, the magnitude of gastrointestinal ethanol metabolism was assumed to be small (Lamboeuf et al., 1981, 1983). Some authors (Lin & Lester, 1980) could not demonstrate any significant gastrointestinal ethanol oxidation when they gave an acute high dose to rats and they, as well as more recently Wagner (1986), concluded that this process was of negligible quantitative significance. The issue was reopened when it was shown that a significant fraction of alcohol ingested in doses in keeping with usual "social drinking" does not enter the systemic circulation in the rat and is oxidized mainly in the stomach (Julkunen, Di Padova, & Lieber, 1985; Julkunen, Tannenbaum, Baraona, & Lieber, 1985). This process also was shown to occur in a man with a small (0.15 g/kg) (Figure 1.1) (Di Padova, Worner,

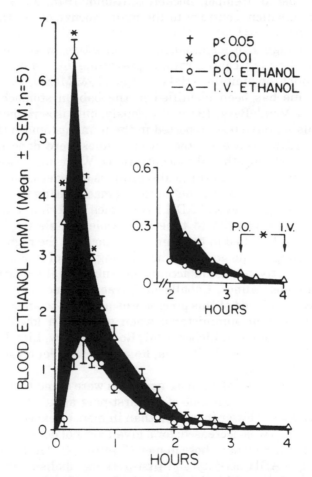

Figure 1.1. Bioavailability of ethanol in five normal subjects after a small dose of ethanol (0.15 g/kg body weight). Ethanol was administered in a 5% dextrose solution (5 g/100 ml) perorally or intravenously 1 hour after a standard breakfast. Drinking time was 10 minutes and that of the intravenous infusion 20 minutes. The black area in the figure reflects the amount of ingested alcohol that did not enter the systemic circulation and gives an indication of the magnitude of the first-class metabolism of ethanol.

"Effects of Fasting and Chronic Alcohol Consumption on the First-Pass Metabolism of Ethanol," by C. Di Padova, T.M. Worner, R.J.K. Julkumen, & C.S. Lieber, 1987, *Gastroenterology, 92,* p. x. Reprinted by permission.

Julkunen, & Lieber 1987; Julkunen, Di Padova, & Lieber, 1985), as well as a moderate (0.3 g/kg, Figure 1.2) dose of alcohol. Moreover, gastrectomy was associated with an abolition of the first-pass metabolism (Caballeria et al., 1989).

In the rat stomach, an ADH isoenzyme has been described (Cederbaum, Pietruszko, Hempel, Becker, & Rubin, 1975; Julia, Farres, & Parés, 1987), which, contrary to the main isoenzymes of the liver, is not inhibited by high ethanol concentrations. Although this gastric ADH has a high Km for ethanol, it is effective in the oxidation of ethanol at the high concentrations prevailing in the gastric lumen during alcohol consumption (Halsted, Robles, & Mezey, 1973). A similar isoenzyme has been identified in the baboon stomach (Holmes, Courtney, & VandeBerg, 1986). Previously, only isoenzymes with low Km for ethanol have been reported in the human stomach (Hempel & Pietruzko, 1979). However, the latter studies were done in autopsy material and at low ethanol concentrations. When we reassessed gastric ADH activity in fresh surgical specimens using ethanol concentrations similar to those prevailing in the stomach during the drinking of alcoholic beverages, several ADH isoenzymes (differing in their affinity for ethanol, sensitivity to 4-methylprazole and electrophoretic migration) were identified in the human stomach. At the high concentrations prevailing in the gastric lumen during alcohol consumption, the sum of their activities could account for substantial oxidation of ethanol (Hernandez-Munoz, Caballeria, Baraona, Greenstein, & Lieber, 1990). The magnitude of this process was assessed to amount to about 20% of the ethanol administered when given at a low dose to rats (Caballeria, Baraona, & Lieber, 1987; Roine, Gentry, Lim, Baraona, & Lieber, 1991) or to men (Di Padova, Roine, Frezza, Gentry, Baraona, & Lieber, 1992).

Gastric alcohol dehydrogenase activities were found to correlate significantly with the magnitude of the first-pass metabolism and, since the activities were lower in women than in men, as expected, first-pass metabolism also was decreased; for a given alcohol dose, blood levels of women were higher than those in men (Figure 1.2). Alcoholism further decreased the ADH activity and first-pass metabolism, with a corresponding rise in blood levels of alcohol. Those effects were more striking in alcoholic women (Figure 1.2). In alcoholic women, blood levels of alcohol were virtually the same whether the alcohol was given orally or intravenously, and thus alcoholic women have lost this "gastric protective mechanism." Thus, it is understandable that for a given dose of alcohol, blood levels achieved are higher in women than in men. This effect is particularly striking in alcoholic women, but it is also of great significance for social drinking in normal women. Indeed, for a

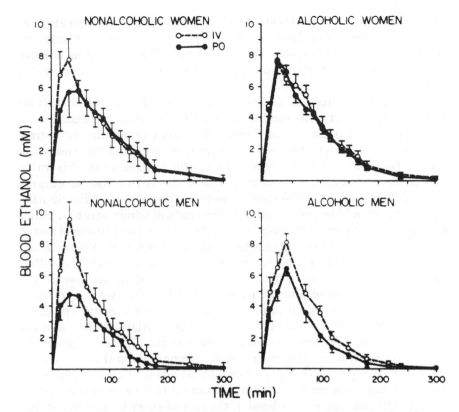

Figure 1.2. Effects of gender and chronic alcohol abuse on blood ethanol concentrations. Ethanol was administered orally (solid lines) or intravenously (dashed lines) in a moderate dose (0.3 g/kg body weight). The shaded area represents the difference between the curves for the two routes of administration.

From "High Blood Alcohol Levels in Women: The Role of Decreased Gastric Alcohol Dehydrogenase Activity and First-Pass Metabolism," by M. Frezza et al., 1990, *New England Journal of Medicine, 322,* p. x. Reprinted by permission.

given dose of alcohol, normal women develop higher blood levels than men for at least three reasons. First, women are usually smaller than men, but the amounts of alcohol offered to them in social settings do not take this gender difference into account. Second, the alcohol consumed is distributed in a smaller water space (*vide supra*). Finally, less of the alcohol will be broken down in the stomach and more will reach the peripheral blood. These differences are obvious at levels of social drinking (Figure 1.2). It is therefore clear that what is considered a moderate dose for men is not necessarily moderate for women. These gender differences are now being taken into account in recently published guidelines for moderate drinking, which define moderate consumption as not more than two drinks per day in men, but only one drink per day in women (Dietary Guidelines, 1990). Count as a drink 12 ounces of regular beer, 5 ounces of wine, or 1½ ounces of distilled spirits (80 proof).

The largest sex-related differences in blood ethanol concentrations were observed after oral administration. These results were consistent with those of Marshall et al. (1983): The area under the BAC-time curve values were greater in women than in men, and the volume of distribution was markedly decreased in the women when this value was calculated with the assumption that the entire dose of ethanol reached the systemic circulation. However, the volume of distribution for ethanol should be independent of the route of administration. Since we found a much smaller sex-related difference in the volume of distribution after intravenous than after oral administration (Frezza et al., 1990), a more likely explanation for these results is that the differences in volume of distribution were overestimated, because only a fraction of the dose of ethanol ingested reaches the systemic circulation. We found that this fraction was higher in the women. The question has been raised whether the differences in ADH activity and the gastric mucosa between men and women could, in fact, explain the relatively striking difference in blood ethanol levels (Figure 1.2). It should be pointed out that peripheral blood levels of alcohol represent the difference between the amount of ethanol that reaches the circulation and the amount metabolized. If the rate of entry is close to the rate of oxidation, even moderate differences in the bioavailability of ethanol may result in striking blood-level changes, with consequently substantial effects on the brain and other tissues. The lower rate of first-pass metabolism in normal women as compared with normal men (Frezza et al., 1990) and the lower rate in alcoholic women as compared with normal women (Frezza et al., 1990) or in alcoholic men as compared with nonalcoholic men (Di Padova et al., 1987; Frezza et al., 1990) and the differential effect of H_2 blockers on first-pass metabolism (Caballeria et al., 1989; Di Padova et al., 1992) all paralleled changes in gastric ADH activities that were consistent with the role of gastric ethanol oxidation.

Women differ from men not only in terms of gastric ethanol metabolism. According to some (Cole-Harding & Wilson, 1987; Mishra, Sharma, Potter, & Mezey, 1989) but not to others (Marshall et al., 1983), women have a more rapid elimination of alcohol as compared to men. Individual variabilities are great, however. The fact that Mishra et al. (1989) observed a difference which escaped Marshall et al. (1983) is probably due to the fact that the former studied natural siblings (to reduce genetic variability), rather than subjects taken at random. One explanation of this finding is the fact that the hepatic ADH activity is suppressed by testosterone and its derivatives, both *in vivo* (Teschke & Wiese, 1982) and at least at high concentrations *in vitro* (Mezey, Potter, & Diehl, 1980). ADH activity in the livers of women is significantly higher than in men, but after the age of 53 in men and 50 in women, the difference, including the sex specificity of the intralobular distribution profiles is no longer apparent. ADH activity in men under 53 years of age showed a maximum in the intermediate zone, whereas in women less than 50 years of age, an increase in the gradient toward the perivenous zone was observed (Maly & Sasse, 1991). Furthermore, the fact that estradiol induces class I ADH activity and mRNA in the kidneys of female rats (Qulali, Ross, & Crabb, 1991) also may contribute to the faster blood ethanol clearance in the female gender. Moreover, ADH activity was found to be greater in female rat kidneys than in males (Buttner, 1965). It should be pointed out, however, that only small increases in liver ADH activity have been observed in female rats treated with estrogens, contrasting with a marked increase of ADH activity and mRNA in the kidney. Since the enzyme activity is much lower in the kidney than the liver, the effect of a change in ADH activity in kidney on overall ethanol metabolism is limited.

Of course ADH activity measured *in vitro* is only one of the determinants of ethanol metabolism *in vivo* and discrepancies between the two are not uncommon (Zorzano & Herrera, 1990). Some studies reported decreased elimination times, reduced areas under the BAC-time curve, and faster disappearance rates during the midluteal menstrual phase, associated with increased levels of progesterone, elevated progesterone-to-estradiol ratios, and decreased FSH levels (Sutker, Goist, & King, 1987). The hormonal response to ethanol in terms of prolactin and cortisol also may be gender dependent (Lex, 1991; Schuckit, Gold, & Risch, 1987a; Schuckit, Gold, & Risch, 1987b). The gender effect is further complicated by the impact of hormones on the stimulatory and sedative effects of ethanol. With regard to all the experiments quoted above, a word of caution is needed concerning the possible variability caused by species and strain differences. In spontaneously hypertensive rats, rates of ethanol metabolism appear to be modulated by ADH activity, which in turn is strikingly affected by sex hormones, with inhibition by testosterone and stimulation by estradiol (Rachmamin, MacDonald, Wahid, & Clapp, 1980). In conventional rats as well, a number of studies have shown hormonal influences, as discussed before and elsewhere (Lieber, 1984, 1987). Interaction between sex hormones and ethanol-metabolizing enzymes was tested in detail by Teschke, Wannagat, Löwendorf, and Strohmeyer (1986). Estradiol

increased the hepatic activities of ADH and catalase in both ovariectomized and sham-operated female rats on a control diet, whereas this
enhancing property was virtually lost in animals on an alcohol diet.
The hepatic activities of the microsomal ethanol-oxidizing system remained unaffected under these experimental conditions, irrespective
of the diet used. Testosterone increased the hepatic activities of the
microsomal ethanol-oxidizing system and decreased the ADH activity
in female rats on a control diet, but these changes were either not
clear-cut or markedly reduced in similarly treated female rats fed an
alcohol-containing diet. According to Lumeng and Crabb (1984),
changes in alcohol elimination rates produced by fasting and castration mainly reflected changes in the V_{max} of liver ADH. It has been
shown that a decrease in the rate of degradation is the principal cause
for the increase liver ADH following castration (Mezey & Potter,
1985). As discussed elsewhere (Lieber, 1992), chronic ethanol consumption has a profound interaction with testosterone metabolism,
including a castration-like effect.

One observation of interest is the fact that the menstrual cycle
affects the rate of gastric emptying of women (Cripps & Williams,
1975; Datta, Hay, & Pleuvry, 1974; Scott, Lester, & Van Thiel, 1983;
Van Thiel, Gavaler, & Stremple, 1976; Van Thiel, Gavaler, & Joshi,
1977; Van Thiel, Gavaler, & Stremple, 1979; Wald, Van Thiel, &
Hoechstetter, 1982). Gastric emptying is delayed during the luteal
phase of the menstrual cycle, which is characterized by high estradiol
and progesterone levels. As discussed before, gastric emptying is one of
the factors which determines the rate of first-pass metabolism of ethanol in the stomach and the speed of intestinal absorption. Other
studies on the pharmacokinetics of ethanol administration during different phases of the menstrual cycle were discussed recently in detail
by Van Thiel (1991).

One confounding variable, not always fully taken into account in
the gender studies, is the superimposed effect of age, affecting both the
response to ethanol (Engel, 1985) and possibly its metabolism. In experimental animals, it was observed that the ethanol metabolic rates
decreased linearly with advancing age, associated with a linear decrease in hepatic ADH activity (Hahn & Burch, 1983), whereas no such
effect was seen in men (Vestal, McGuire, Tokin, Andres, Norris, &
Mezey, 1976). The latter study revealed, however, an age-related decrease in the volume of distribution of ethanol. Preliminary results
indicate that only younger women (under 50 years of age) seem to have
significantly lower gastric ADH activities in biopsy specimens from
the antrum and corpus of the stomach than men; with advanced age
this difference was no longer detectable (Table 1.1). Older women

Table 1.1.   Effect of Age and Sex on Gastric Alcohol Dehydrogenase Activity

Site	Alcohol Dehydrogenase Activity				
	Age 17–49 nmol/mg of protein min	No. of Subjects	Age 50–83 nmol/mg of protein min	No. of Subjects	P Value
Antrum					
Women	6.0 ± 1.3*	9	7.1 ± 0.6*	14	NS
Men	9.5 ± 1.3	11	3.7 ± 0.4	9	$p < 0.001$
Corpus					
Women	6.4 ± 0.7*	14	6.2 ± 0.7*	19	NS
Men	8.8 ± 0.6	15	4.7 ± 0.6	14	$p < 0.001$

*$p < 0.001$ for the comparison with men in the same group.
From "High Blood Alcohol Levels in Women (Letter to the Editor)," by H.K. Seitz, G. Egerer, & U.A. Simanowski, New England Journal of Medicine, 323, p. 58. Reprinted 1990, by permission.

probably have even higher gastric ADH activities than men of similar age, because gastric ADH activity decreased with age only in men. Although like Frezza et al. (1990), Seitz, Egerer, and Simanowski (1990) found significantly elevated blood ethanol concentrations in younger (21 to 37 years of age) nonalcoholic women as compared to younger (27 to 37 years) nonalcoholic men, these results were reversed in subjects over 50 years of age and the highest blood ethanol levels were observed in men over 60.

In contemporary social settings, women are commonly served amounts of alcohol comparable to those given to men. Making women aware of their increased vulnerability may strengthen their resolve to resist the social pressures that may lead to inappropriate levels of consumption, possibly resulting in impairment of the ability to drive and to perform other similar tasks. In addition, the increased bio-availability also may influence the severity of medical problems related to drinking (vide infra).

GENDER DIFFERENCES IN ALCOHOL-INDUCED LIVER DISEASE

The male-to-female ratio of mortality has been more than 2:1 for all cases of cirrhosis, and it is even greater when restricted to alcoholic cirrhosis (Hällen & Krook, 1963; Jolliffe & Jellinek, 1941). But, as discussed in the introduction, convergence of the genders is occurring. There also is evidence that the progression to more severe liver injury is accelerated in women (Rankin, 1977). Indeed, Wilkinson, Santamaria, and Rankin (1969) found women to be more susceptible than men to the development of alcoholic cirrhosis. Other studies also found the incidence of chronic advanced liver disease to be higher among women than among men for a similar history of alcohol abuse (Maier, Haag, Peskar, & Gerok, 1979; Morgan & Sherlock, 1977; Nakamura, Takezawa, Sato, Kera, & Maeda, 1979). Pequignot, Chabert, Eydoux, and Corcowl (1974), and Pequignot, Tuyns, and Berta (1978) also have shown that a daily intake of alcohol as low as 40 g in men and only 20 g in women resulted in a statistically significant increase in the incidence of cirrhosis in a well-nourished population.

The mechanism whereby the female gender potentiates alcohol-induced liver damage is not known. It could obviously relate to the hormonal status since both endogenous and exogenous (i.e., contraceptive) female hormones have been shown to result in some impairment of liver function in a significant number of women (Allan & Tyler, 1967; Kappas, 1967; Larsson-Cohn, 1967; Pihl, Rais, & Zeuchner, 1968; Saleh & Abd-el-Hay, 1977). It is conceivable that an interaction between some of these hormone-related changes and those induced by ethanol may result in more severe liver damage. Alternatively, or in addition, some gender-dependent biochemical differences may contribute in some different ways to further enhance the vulnerability to the hepatotoxicity of ethanol. For instance, it was recently found that the response, to ethanol, of the hepatic fatty acid-binding protein differs in male and female rats. We previously reported that the feeding of alcohol-containing diets to rats (Baraona, Leo, Borowsky, & Lieber, 1975; Baraona, Leo, Borowsky, & Lieber, 1977) and baboons (Savolainen, Baraona, Pikkarainen, & Lieber, 1984) increases the amount of protein in the liver. Part of this increase is due to retention of export proteins, which occurs in the Golgi, microsomal, and cytosolic fractions (Baraona et al., 1977; Volentine, Tuma, & Sorrell, 1986). However, the measured increase in albumin and transferrin accounted for only a small fraction of the total increase in cytosolic protein. This raised the possibility that other export or constituent proteins of the cytosol could also contribute to the increase. More recently, we found that fatty acid-binding protein is a major contributor to the ethanol-induced increase in liver cytosolic proteins in the rat (Pignon, Bailey, Baraona, & Lieber, 1987). This increase in liver fatty acid-binding protein (L-FABP) may obviously play a role in protecting the liver against the excess accumulation of free fatty acids by binding them and thereby making them less reactive. These initial results were all observed in male rats. We now find a much smaller increase of cytosolic fatty acid-binding capacity in females (58%) than in males (161%) (Shevchuk, Baraona, Ma, Pignon, & Lieber, 1991). Whereas the ethanol-induced increase in fatty acid-binding capacity provided an ample excess of binding sites for the fatty acids in the males, the increase in females was barely sufficient for the binding of the large increase of fatty acids produced by ethanol in the females. The protein responsible for this binding, the liver fatty acid-binding protein of the cytosol (L-FABPc), also promotes esterification of the fatty acids. In keeping with the postulated role of this protein, the ethanol-induced increases in hepatic triacylglycerols, phospholipids, and cholesterol esters were smaller in females than in males. The gender difference in cholesterol esters was associated with parallel changes in acyl-CoA transferase activity. A possible implication of the relatively small and most likely inadequate increases in liver fatty acid-binding capacity and fatty acid esterification during alcohol consumption in the females is that under these circumstances the risk for development of a potentially deleterious accumulation of fatty acids in the liver is increased, thereby potentially contributing to the enhanced vulnerability of females to alcohol-induced hepatotoxicity. Of course, several factors are involved, including increased bioavailability of ethanol in the females (Frezza et al., 1990) (*vide supra*).

ATPase is an important membrane enzyme reported to be affected by ethanol and gender. When the two hepatic plasma membrane ATPases—Na^+, K^+–ATPase and Mg^{2+}–ATPase—were investigated over concentrations ranging from 8 to 90 mM, ethanol did not cause significant inhibition in male rats (Yamada, Mak, & Lieber, 1985), although in female rats an eightfold decrease of NA^+, K^+–ATPase activity was reported (Pascale et al., 1989).

In addition to the liver, gender affects pathologic response to ethanol in different other tissues. This may involve breast cancer (Longnecker, Berlin, Orza, & Chalmers, 1988; Lowenfels & Zevola, 1989), and gastric ulcer (Rabinovitz, Van Thiel, Dindzans, & Gavaler, 1989). Hormones also have an obvious interaction with the behavorial effects of alcohol (Jones & Jones, 1976).

In conclusion, gender differences in response to alcohol, suspected for centuries, are now beginning to be objectively documented. One of the most striking differences is the increased bioavailability of alcohol in women. This basic gender difference has an impact not only in terms of pathology, but perhaps even more importantly, it also affects that large segment of our population engaged in social drinking. It is now clear that an alcohol intake that may be considered moderate and innocuous in men is not necessarily so in women. A broader dissemination of this information is needed, especially since gender affects the metabolism of ethanol in some other ways as well, as alluded to here and also reviewed elsewhere (Van Thiel, Tarter, Rosenblum, & Gavaler, 1989). Gender also influences some of the pathologic actions of ethanol. The greater susceptibility of women to alcohol in terms of liver injury were discussed in detail here, as an example, but obviously other tissues may also display a gender difference in their response to ethanol. Further studies are now required to investigate and document such possibilities and to unravel the mechanisms involved.

REFERENCES

Allan, J.S., & Tyler, E.T. (1967). Biochemical findings in long-term oral contraceptive usage. I. Liver function studies. *Fertility and Sterility, 18,* 112–123.

Arthur, M.J., Lee, A., & Wright, R. (1984). Sex differences in the metabolism of ethanol and acetaldehyde in normal subjects. *Clinical Science, 67,* 397–401.

Baraona, E., Leo, M.A., Borowsky, S.A., & Lieber, C.S. (1975). Alcoholic hepatomegaly: Accumulation of protein in the liver. *Science, 190,* 794–795.

Baraona, E., Leo, M.A., Borowsky, S.A., & Lieber, C.S. (1977). Pathogenesis of alcohol-induced accumulation of protein in the liver. *Journal of Clinical Investigation, 60,* 546–554.

Buttner, H. (1965) Acetaldehyde and alcohol dehydrogenase activities in liver and kidney of the rat. *Biochemische Zeitschrift, 341,* 300–314.

Caballeria, J., Baraona, E., & Lieber, C.S. (1987). The contribution of the stomach to ethanol oxidation in the rat. *Life Sciences, 41,* 1021–1027.

Caballeria, J., Frezza, M., Hernandez, R., Di Padova, C.; Korsten, M.A., Baraona, E., & Lieber, C.S. (1989). The gastric origin of first-pass metabolism of ethanol in man: Effect of gastrectomy. *Gastroenterology, 97,* 1205–1209.

Carter, E.A., & Isselbacher, K.J. (1971). The metabolism of ethanol to carbon dioxide by stomach and small intestinal slices. *Proceedings of the Society of Experimental Medicine and Biology 138,* 817–819.

Cederbaum, A.I., Pietruszko, R., Hempel, J., Becker, F.F., & Rubin, E. (1975). Characterization of a nonhepatic alcoholic dehydrogenase from rat hepatocellular carcinoma and stomach. *Archives of Biochemistry and Biophysics (New York), 171,* 348–360.

Cole-Harding S., & Wilson, J.R. (1987). Ethanol metabolism in men and women. *Journal of Studies on Alcohol, 48,* 380–387.

Corti, B., & Ibrahim, J. (1990). Women and alcohol—trends in Australia. *The Medical Journal of Australia, 152,* 625–632.

Cripps, A.W., & Williams, V.J. (1975). The effect of pregnancy and lactation on food intake, gastrointestinal anatomy and the absorptive capacity of the small intestine in the albino rat. *British Journal of Nutrition, 33,* 17–25.

Datta, S., Hay, V.M., & Pleuvry, B.J. (1974). Effects of pregnancy and associated hormones in mouse intestine *in vivo* and *in vitro*. *Pluegers Archives, 346,* 87–93.

Dietary Guidelines. (1990). *Nutrition and your health: Dietary guidelines for Americans*. (3rd ed.) Washington, DC: U.S. Department of Agriculture, U.S. Department of Health and Human Services.

Di Padova, C., Roine, R., Frezza, M., Gentry, R.T., Baraona, E., & Lieber, C.S. (1992). Effects of ranitidine on blood alcohol levels after ethanol ingestion: Comparison with other H_2-receptor antagonists. *Journal of the American Medical Association, 267*, 83–86.

Di Padova, C., Worner, T.M., Julkunen, R.J.K., & Lieber, C.S. (1987). Effects of fasting and chronic alcohol consumption on the first-pass metabolism of ethanol. *Gastroenterology, 92*, 1169–1173.

Engel, J.A. (1985). Influence of age and hormones on the stimulatory and sedative effects of ethanol. In U. Rydberg et al. (Eds.), *Alcohol and the developing brain* (pp. 57–67). New York: Raven Press.

Frezza, M., Di Padova, C., Pozzato, G., Terpin, M., Baraona, E., & Lieber, C.S. (1990). High blood alcohol levels in women: The role of decreased gastric alcohol dehydrogenase activity and first-pass metabolism. *New England Journal of Medicine, 322*, 95–99.

Hahn, H.K.J., & Burch, R.E. (1983). Impaired ethanol metabolism with advancing age. *Alcoholism: Clinical and Experimental Research, 7*, 299–301.

Halsted, C.H., Robles, E.A., & Mezey, E. (1973). Distribution of ethanol in the human gastrointestinal tract. *American Journal of Clinical Nutrition, 26*, 831–834.

Hällen, J., & Krook, H. (1963). Follow-up studies on an unselected ten-year material of 360 patients with liver cirrhosis in one community. *Acta Medica Scandinavica, 173*, 479–493.

Hempel, J.D., & Pietruszko, R. (1979). Human stomach alcohol dehydrogenase: Isoenzyme composition and catalytic properties. *Alcoholism: Clinical and Experimental Research, 3*, 95–98.

Hernandez-Munoz, R., Caballeria, J., Baraona, E., Greenstein, R., & Lieber, C.S. (1990). Human gastric alcohol dehydrogenase: Its inhibition by H_2-receptor antagonists, and its effect on the bioavailability of ethanol. *Alcoholism: Clinical and Experimental Research, 14*, 946–950.

Holmes, R., Courtney, Y.R., & VandeBerg, J.L. (1986). Alcohol dehydrogenase isoenzymes in baboons: Tissue distribution, catalytic, properties and variant phenotypes in liver, kidney, stomach, and testis. *Alcoholism: Clinical and Experimental Research, 10*, 623–630.

Jolliffe, N., & Jellinek, E.M. (1941). Vitamin deficiencies and liver cirrhosis in alcoholism. Part VII: Cirrhosis of the liver. *Quarterly Journal of Studies on Alcohol, 2*, 544–583.

Jones, B.M., & Jones, M.K. (1976). Male and female intoxication levels for three alcohol doses or do women really get higher than men? *Alcohol Technical Report, 5*, 11–14.

Julia, P., Farres, J., & Parés, X. (1987). Characterization of three isoenzymes of rat alcohol dehydrogenase: Tissue distribution and physical and enzymatic properties. *European Journal of Biochemistry, 162*, 179–189.

Julkunen, R.J.K., Di Padova, C., & Lieber, C.S. (1985). First-pass metabolism of ethanol—A gastrointestinal barrier against the systemic toxicity of ethanol. *Life Science, 37,* 567–573.

Julkunen, R.J.K., Tannenbaum, L., Baraona, E., & Lieber, C.S. (1985). First-pass metabolism of ethanol: An important determinant of blood levels after alcohol consumption. *Alcohol, 2,* 437–441.

Kappas, A. (1967). Estrogens and the liver. *Gastroenterology, 52,* 113–116.

Lamboeuf, Y., De Saint Blanquat, G., & Derache, R. (1981). Mucosal alcohol dehydrogenase–and aldehyde dehydrogenase–mediated ethanol oxidation in the digestive tract of the rat. *Biochemical Pharmacology, 30,* 542–545.

Lamboeuf, Y., La Droitte, P., & De Saint Blanquat, G. (1983). The gastrointestinal metabolism of ethanol in the rat: Effect of chronic alcohol intoxication. *Archives Internationales de Pharmacodynamie et de Therapie, 261,* 157–169.

Larsson-Cohn, U. (1967). The 2-hour sulfobromophtalein retention test and the transaminase activity during oral contraceptive therapy. *American Journal of Obstetrics and Gynecology, 98,* 188–193.

Lex, B.W. (1991). Prolactin and cortisol levels following acute alcohol challenges in women with and without a family history of alcoholism. *Alcohol, 8,* 383–387.

Lieber, C.S. (1984). Alcohol and the liver. In I.M. Arias, M.S. Frenkel, & J.H.P. Wilson. (Eds.), *Liver Annual-IV* (pp. 130–186). Amsterdam, The Netherlands: Excerpta Medica.

Lieber, C.S. (1987). Alcohol and the liver. In I.M. Arias, M.S. Frenkel, & J.H.P. Wilson. (Eds.), *Liver Annual-VI* (pp. 163–240). Amsterdam, The Netherlands: Excerpta Medica.

Lieber, C.S. (1992). *Medical and nutritional complications of alcoholism: Mechanisms and management* New York: Plenum Press.

Lin, G.W.J., & Lester, D. (1980). Significance of the gastrointestinal tract in the *in vivo* metabolism of ethanol in the rat. *Advances in experimental medicine and biology, 132,* 281–286.

Longnecker, M.P., Berlin, J.A., Orza, M.J., & Chalmers, T.C. (1988). A meta-analysis of alcohol consumption in relation to risk of breast cancer. *Journal of the American Medical Association, 260,* 652–656.

Lowenfels, A.B., & Zevola, S.A. (1989). Alcohol and breast cancer: An overview. *Alcoholism: Clinical and Experimental Research, 13,* 109–111.

Lumeng, L., & Crabb, D.W. (1984). Rate-determining factors for ethanol metabolism in fasted and castrated male rats. *Biochemical Pharmacology, 33,* 2623–2628.

Maier, K.P., Haag, S.G., Peskar, B.M., & Gerok, W. (1979). Forms of alcoholic liver diseases. *Klinische Wochenschrift, 57,* 311–317.

Maly, P.I., & Sasse, D. (1991). Intraacinar profiles of alcohol dehydrogenase and aldehyde dehydrogenase activities in human liver. *Gastroenterology, 101,* 1716–1723.

Marshall, A.W., Kingstone, D., Boss, M., & Morgan, M.Y. (1983). Ethanol elimination in males and females: Relationship to menstrual cycle and body composition. *Hepatology, 3,* 701–706.

Mercer, P.W., & Khavari, K.A. (1990). Are women drinking more like men? An empirical examination of the convergence hypothesis. *Alcoholism: Clinical and Experimental Research, 14,* 461–466.

Mezey, E., & Potter, J.J. (1985). Effect of castration on the turnover of rat liver alcohol dehydrogenase. *Biochemical Pharmacology, 34,* 369–371.

Mezey, E., & Potter, J.J., & Diehl, A.M. (1980). Depression of alcohol dehydrogenase activity in rat hepatocyte culture by dihydrotestosterone. *Biochemical Pharmacology, 35,* 335–339.

Mishra, L., Sharma, S., Potter, J.J., & Mezey, E. (1989). More rapid elimination of alcohol in women as compared to their male siblings. *Alcoholism: Clinical and Experimental Research, 13,* 752–754.

Morgan, M.Y., & Sherlock, S. (1977). Sex-related differences among 100 patients with alcoholic liver disease. *British Medical Journal, 1,* 939–941.

Nakamura, S., Takezawa, Y., Sato, T., Kera, K., & Maeda, T. (1979). Alcoholic liver disease in women. *Tohoku Journal of Experimental Medicine, 129,* 351–355.

Parrish, K.M., Higuchi, S., & Dufour, M.C. (1991). Alcohol consumption and the risk of developing liver cirrhosis: Implications for future research. *Journal of Substance Abuse, 3,* 325–335.

Pascale, R., Daino, L., Garcea, R., Frassetto, S., Ruggiu, M.E., Vannini, M.G., Cozzolino, P., & Feo, F. (1989). Inhibition of ethanol of rat liver plasma membrane (Na^+, K^+) ATPase: Protective effect of S-Adenosyl-L-Methionine, L-Methionine, and N-Acetylcysteine. *Toxicology and Applied Pharmacology (New York), 97,* 216–229.

Pequignot, G., Chabert, C., Eydoux, H., & Corcowl, M.A. (1974). Increased risk of liver cirrhosis with intake of alcohol. *Revue de l'alcoolisme, 20,* 191–202.

Pequignot, G., Tuyns, A.J., & Berta, J.L. (1978). Ascitic cirrhosis in relation to alcohol consumption. *International Journal of Epidemiology (London), 7,* 113–120.

Pestalozzi, D.M., Buhler, R., von Wartburg, J.P., & Hess, M. (1983). Immunohistochemical localization of alcohol dehydrogenase in the human gastrointestinal tract. *Gastroenterology, 85,* 1011–1016.

Pignon, J-P., Bailey, N.C., Baraona, E., & Lieber, C.S. (1987). Fatty acid-binding protein: A major contributor to the ethanol-induced increase in liver cytosolic proteins in the rat. *Hepatology, 7,* 865–871.

Pihl, E., Rais, O., & Zeuchner, E. (1968). Functional and morphological liver changes in women taking oral contraceptives: A clinical and ultrastructural study with special reference to the occurrence of cholestasis. *Acta Chirurgica Scandinavica, 134,* 639–650.

Rabinovitz, M., Van Thiel, D.H., Dindzans, V., & Gavaler, J.S. (1989). Endoscopic findings in alcoholic liver disease: Does gender make a difference? *Alcohol, 6,* 465–468.

Rachmamin, G., MacDonald, J.A., Wahid, S., & Clapp, T.A. (1980). Modulation of alcohol dehydrogenase and ethanol metabolism by sex hormones in the spontaneously hypertensive rat: Effect of chronic ethanol administration. *Biochemical Journal (London), 186,* 483–490.

Qulali, R., Ross, R.A., & Crabb, D.W. (1991). Estradiol induces class I alcohol dehydrogenase activity and mRNA in kidney of female rats. *Archives of Biochemistry and Biophysics (New York), 288,* 406–413.

Rankin, J.G. (1977). The natural history and management of the patient with alcoholic liver disease. In M.M. Fisher & J.G. Rankin (Eds.), *Alcohol and the liver* (pp. 365–381). New York: Plenum Press.

Roine, R.P., Gentry, R.T., Lim, R.T., Jr., Baraona, E., & Lieber, C.S. (1991). Effect of concentration of ingested ethanol on blood alcohol levels. *Alcoholism: Clinical and Experimental Research, 15,* 734–738.

Saleh, F.M., & Abd-el-Hay, M.M. (1977). Liver function tests after the use of long-acting progestational contraceptives. *Contraception, 16,* 409–416.

Savolainen, M.J., Baraona, E., Pikkarainen, P., & Lieber, C.S. (1984). Hepatic triacylglycerol synthesizing activity during progression of alcoholic liver injury in the baboon. *Journal of Lipid Research, 25,* 813–820.

Schuckit, M.A., Gold, E.O., & Risch, S.C. (1987a). Serum prolactin levels in sons of alcoholics and control subjects. *American Journal of Psychiatry, 114,* 854–859.

Schuckit, M.A., Gold, E.O., & Risch, S.C. (1987b). Plasma cortisol levels following ethanol in sons of alcoholics and controls. *Archives of General Psychiatry, 44,* 942–945.

Scott, L.D., Lester, R., & Van Thiel, D.H. (1983). Pregnancy-related changes in small intestinal myoelectric activity in the rat. *Gastroenterology, 84,* 301–307.

Seitz, H.K., Egerer, G., & Simanowski, U.A. (1990). High blood alcohol levels in women (Letter to the Editor). *New England Journal of Medicine, 323,* 58.

Shevchuk, O., Baraona, E., Ma, X-L., Pignon, J-P., & Lieber, C.S. (1991). Gender differences in the response of hepatic fatty acids and cytosolic fatty acid-binding capacity to alcohol consumption in rats. *Proceedings of the Society for Experimental Biology and Medicine, 198,* 584–590.

Sutker, P.B., Goist, K.C., Jr., & King, A.R. (1987). Acute alcohol intoxication in women: Relationship to dose and menstrual cycle phase. *Alcoholism: Clinical and Experimental Research, 11,* 74–79.

Teschke, R., & Wiese, B. (1982). Sex-dependency of hepatic alcohol metabolizing enzymes. *Journal of Endocrinological Investigation, 5,* 243–250.

Teschke, R., Wannagat, F-J., Löwendorf, F., & Strohmeyer, G. (1986). Hepatic alcohol-metabolizing enzymes after prolonged administration of sex hormones and alcohol in female rats. *Biochemical Pharmacology, 35,* 521–527.

Van Thiel, D.H. (1991). Gender differences in the susceptibility and severity of alcohol-induced liver disease (RSA Presidential Address). *Alcohol and Alcoholism Supplement, 1,* 9–18.

Van Thiel, D.H., Gavaler, J.S., & Stremple, J.R. (1976). Lower esophageal sphincter pressure in women using sequential oral contraceptives. *Gastroenterology, 71,* 232–241.

Van Thiel, D.H., Gavaler, J.S., & Joshi, S.H. (1977). Heartburn of pregnancy. *Gastroenterology, 72,* 666–671.

Van Thiel, D.H., Gavaler, J.S., & Strempler, J.F. (1979). Lower esophageal sphincter pressure during the normal menstrual cycle. *American Journal of Obstetrics and Gynecology, 134,* 64–69.

Van Thiel, D.H., Tarter, R.E., Rosenblum, E., & Gavaler, J.S. (1989). Ethanol, its metabolism and gonadal effects: Does sex make a difference? *Advances in Alcohol and Substance Abuse, 7,* 131–169.

Vestal, R.E., McGuire, E., Tokin, J.D., Andres, R., Norris, A.H., & Mezey, E. (1976). Aging and ethanol metabolism. *Clinical Pharmacology and Therapeutics, 21,* 343–354.

Volentine, G.D., Tuma, D.J., & Sorrell, M.F. (1986). Subcellular location of secretory proteins retained in the liver during the ethanol-induced inhibition of hepatic protein secretion in the rat. *Gastroenterology, 90,* 158–165.

Wagner, J.G. (1986). Lack of first-pass metabolism of ethanol at blood concentrations in the social drinking range. *Life Sciences, 39,* 407–414.

Wald, A., Van Thiel, D.H., & Hoechstetter, L. (1982). Effect of pregnancy on gastrointestinal transit. *Digestive Diseases and Sciences, 27,* 1015–1018.

Wilkinson, P., Santamaria, J.N., & Rankin, G. (1969). Epidemiology of alcoholic cirrhosis. *Australian Annals of Medicine, 18,* 222–226.

Yamada, S., Mak, K.M., & Lieber, C.S. (1985). Chronic ethanol consumption alters rat liver plasma membranes and potentiates release of alkaline phosphatase. *Gastroenterology, 88,* 1799–1806.

Zorzano, A., & Herrera, E. (1990). *In vivo* ethanol elimination in man, monkey and rat: A lack of relationship between the ethanol metabolism and the hepatic activities of alcohol and aldehyde dehydrogenases. *Life Sciences, 46,* 223–230.

Chapter 2

Alcoholic Beverage Consumption and Estrogenization in Normal Postmenopausal Women*

Judith S. Gavaler, Ph.D.

Division of Women's Research
Oklahoma Transplant Institute
Baptist Medical Center
and
Oklahoma Medical Research Foundation

INTRODUCTION: ALCOHOLIC BEVERAGE ABUSE AND USE

Very few data exist related to the endocrine effects of *moderate* alcoholic beverage consumption in any population group, be it men,

* This work has been supported by grant AA06772 from the National Institute on Alcohol Abuse and Alcoholism. The author thanks Nicola Powell and Mary Ann Klaus for the preparation of the manuscript.

women during the reproductive years, or postmenopausal women. In population groups of individuals who drink, the majority consume alcoholic beverages moderately. It is, however, the alcohol-abusing minority on which studies of the endocrine effects of alcoholic beverage consumption have been performed. From the standpoint of being able to detect effects, it makes perfect sense to start by studying individuals at the highest end of the spectrum of alcoholic beverage consumption. In reality, studies of endocrine status were first performed in alcoholic individuals who had come to the attention of physician investigators because of the clinical complications of their alcohol-induced liver disease. As a result, most of what is known about the endocrine effects of alcoholic beverage abuse may be "contaminated" by the presence of liver disease in the study subjects. Be that as it may, there is much to be learned from the investigations which have been performed on alcoholic individuals of both genders with liver disease.

Given the current level of attention and concern for the realization that much federally funded biomedical research has systematically not included women, it is not surprising that fewer studies have been performed in alcoholic beverage-abusing women than in men. Fortunately, such women have not been entirely ignored. An early study (Lloyd & Williams, 1948) reported endocrine changes associated with alcohol-induced liver disease in both men and women. In women, these findings included sterility, menstrual disturbances, and amenorrhea (the absence of menstrual cycles), which when sustained becomes early natural menopause.

ALCOHOL ABUSE: EFFECT ON POSTMENOPAUSAL ESTROGEN LEVELS

The bulk of what is known about the effects of alcoholic beverage consumption on postmenopausal estrogen status has come from studies performed in postmenopausal women with alcohol-induced cirrhosis (Hugues, Coste, Perret, Jayle, Sebaoun, & Modigliani, 1980; James et al., 1982; Jasonni et al., 1983). The study populations of these reports were often small (Hugues et al., 1980; James et al., 1982), were not always composed exclusively of postmenopausal women with alcohol-induced liver disease (James et al., 1982), and sometimes included alcoholic women who were not postmenopausal (Jasonni et al., 1983). In spite of these shortcomings, these reports found estrogen levels to be increased either statistically (Hugues et al., 1982, as reworked by Gavaler, 1985) or arithmetically (James et al., 1982; Jasonni et al., 1983). A more recent study, which was able to improve the study design by taking advantage of these earlier studies, reported severe disruptions of hormonal relationships in addition to statistically significant differences in a variety of hormones, including estradiol, between alcoholic cirrhotic postmenopausal women and normal controls (Gavaler & Van Thiel, 1992). This collection of studies of estrogen levels in postmenopausal women with alcohol-induced liver disease provided encouragement to investigators interested in endocrine effects of moderate alcoholic beverage consumption by providing data to show that alcoholic beverage consumption, at least at abusive levels, was associated with detectable effects on estrogen levels.

MODERATE ALCOHOLIC BEVERAGE CONSUMPTIONS: BENEFICIAL EFFECTS ON CORONARY HEART DISEASE RISK

Interest in the health effects of *moderate* alcoholic beverage consumption started with reports that the risk of myocardial infarction was statistically reduced among ordinary men and women who consumed alcoholic beverages (Klatsky, Friedman, & Siegelaub, 1974). Risk estimates are shown in Table 2.1. In examining the data, the reader needs to remember that the confidence interval for a relative risk estimate must exclude unity (a value of one, which is indicative of no risk), in order for the risk to be declared statistically significantly increased or decreased. As may be seen in Table 2.1, the major report by Klatsky and coworkers was soon followed by others in which the original observation was confirmed. Specifically, the risk of myocardial infarction was reported to be significantly reduced among drinkers in a cohort of 16,759 women (Petitti, Wingerd, Pellegrin, & Ramcharan, 1979). Similarly, the risk of death due to ischemic heart disease was reported to be reduced in alcohol users, as compared with alcohol abstainers in a case/control study of elderly women (Ross, Paganini-Hill, Mack, Arthur, & Henderson, 1981), while the death rate from cardiovascular disease was also decreased among alcohol users in a cohort of 1,105 women followed for 13 years (Cullen, Stenhouse, & Wearne, 1982). As may be seen in Table 2.1, the beneficial effect of moderate alcoholic beverage consumption on cardiovascular disease risk was at least of the same magnitude as that provided by the use of postmenopausal estrogen-replacement therapy (Colditz, Willett, Stampfer, Rosner, Speizer, & Hennekens, 1988; Criqui, Suarez, Barrett-Conner, McPhillips, Wingard, & Garland, 1988; Ross et al., 1981).

The question of how much alcohol needs to be consumed to confer the benefit was not addressed until 1983, when a report using the

Table 2.1. Heart Disease Risk in Women
Effects of Estrogen Replacement Therapy (ERT) and Moderate Alcohol Beverage Consumption

Risk Variable	Relative Risk (95% CI)	Modulating Factor	Cohort Characteristics	Authors (year)
MI incidence	0.48 (0.29, 0.82)*	drinking yes/no	120 cases and 120 controls, mean age 59 matched for age and skin color	Klatsky et al. (1974)
MI incidence	3.1 (1.6, 6.0)*	abstaining yes/no	16,759 women age 18 to 54; 6.5 years of follow-up	Petitti et al. (1979)
MI death	0.38* 0.43 (0.24, 0.75)	drinking yes/no ERT use yes/no	133 cases and 133 controls matched for age (73 years) and race	Ross et al. (1981)
CVD death	percent death rates: 10.9 vs. 18.7* 5.8 vs. 8.6	drinking versus abstaining	1,105 women; age ≥ 40 13 years of follow-up	Cullen et al. (1982)
CHD death	0.41 (0.23, 0.71)* 0.47 (0.25, 0.86)* 0.56 (0.23, 0.98)*	0.7–1.4 daily drinks 1.4–2.1 daily drinks 2.1–4.2 daily drinks	2,599 women, 22 years of follow-up	Gordon & Kannel (1983)
CHD incidence	compared to premenopausal women 2.2 (1.2, 4.2)*	in ovariectomized women: ERT never	121,700 women, age 30 to 55; 6 years of follow-up	Colditz et al. (1988)
CVD death CHD death all cause death	0.81 (0.61, 1.08) 0.75 (0.45, 1.24) 0.69 (0.55, 0.87)*	ERT use yes/no	1,869 women, age 50 to 79; 12 years of follow-up	Criqui et al. (1988)
MI incidence (fatal or non-fatal)	0.5 (0.4, 0.8)* 0.5 (0.5, 0.8)* 0.6 (0.3, 1.1) 0.6 (0.3, 1.0)	0.1 to 0.4 daily drinks 0.4 to 1.4 daily drinks 1.5 to 2.3 daily drinks ≥ 2.4 daily drinks	87,526 women, age 34 to 59; 334,382 person-years follow-up	Stampfer et al. (1988)

Abbreviations used: CI = confidence interval; MI = myocardial infarction; CHD = coronary heart disease; CVD = cardiovascular disease
*Statistically significant difference in risk

Framingham data for 2,599 women who had been followed for 22 years was published (Gordon & Kannel, 1983). In this report, the risk of death from coronary heart disease was statistically reduced among women consuming at least 0.7 drinks daily but fewer than 4.3 drinks daily. As investigators in alcohol consumption research well know, be it psychosocial or biomedical, accurate quantitation of alcoholic beverage ingestion continues to be problematic. Thus it is no surprise that the next big epidemiologic study examining alcoholic beverage intake and risk of coronary heart disease reported different consumption levels at which the benefit was detected (Stampfer, Colditz, Willett, Speizer, & Hennekens, 1988). In this second study, among 87,526 women with 334,382 person-years of follow-up, the age-adjusted risk of nonfatal or fatal myocardial infarction was reported to be statistically reduced among women consuming at least 0.1 drinks daily but fewer than 1.5 drinks daily.

Prevalence of Moderate Alcoholic Beverage Consumption Among Normal Postmenopausal Women: The Potential for Benefit

When all of these studies are considered as a group, it is clear that there is a striking relationship between a statistically significant reduction in coronary heart disease risk and moderate ingestion of alcoholic beverages, whatever the exact alcohol consumption window of benefit may be. Given these findings, what proportion of normal postmenopausal women might be eligible to experience this benefit? Granted, a low proportion of postmenopausal women can be described as being alcohol abusers based on self-reported alcoholic beverage consumption. Depending upon the definition of heavy drinking, 12.5% of alcohol users is the highest proportion reported (Wechsler, 1980). Alcoholic beverage consumption patterns in menopause-aged women are summarized in Table 2.2. There are two important observations to be made from these data. First, it is not uncommon for postmenopausal women to consume alcoholic beverages: The proportions of alcohol users range from as low as 39% in the more elderly to as high as 75% in groups 50 to 59 years of age. The second observation to be made has to do with the criteria used to define heavy drinking, and how these intake levels relate to the alcohol consumption levels reported in the studies which have examined a dose effect for cardiovascular disease risk. Specifically, heavy drinking is defined as consumption of five or more drinks nearly every day on most occasions in two of the studies in Table 2.2 (Cahalan & Cisin, 1968; Wechsler, 1980), or as four or more drinks per day (O'Connell, Hudson, & Graves, 1979). In contrast, the

Table 2.2. Alcoholic Beverage Consumption Patterns in Normal Postmenopausal Women

Authors (year)	N	Age Group	Alcohol Users (%)	Heavy Drinkers* (%)	Definition of Heavy Drinkers
Cahalan & Cisin (1968)	265	50–59	50	3	Nearly every day with 5 or more drinks on most occasions
	367	≥ 60	44	2	
O'Connell et al. (1979)	141	50–59	75	2.8	4 or more drinks per day
	103	60–69	58	1.7	
	66	≥ 70	59	0	
Wechsler (1980)	88	55–64	73	12.5	Nearly every day with 5 or more drinks on most occasions
	100	≥ 65	63	4.8	
NIAAA (1981)	7,586	≥ 55	56	8	More than 2 drinks per day
Clark & Midanik (1982)	**	50–64	49	3	More than 2.3 drinks per day
	**	≥ 65	40	2	
Gomberg (1982)	143	51–60	50	8	More than 2 drinks per day
	102	61–70	39	3	
	103	≥ 71	39	0	
Goodwin et al. (1987)	145	≥ 65	40	NA	More than 3 drinks per day
Hilton & Clark (1987)	141	50–59	62	7	More than 1.5 drinks per day and more than 5 drinks per occasion at least once in a while
	258	≥ 60	49	2	

*Percentages of those who drink
**Not stated

remaining reports describe alcoholic beverage consumption as being heavy at intake levels ranging from two to three drinks daily (Clark & Midanik, 1982; Gomberg, 1982; Goodwin, Sanchez, Thomas, Hunt, Garry, & Goodwin, 1987; Hilton & Clark, 1987; NIAAA, 1981). These consumption levels encompass those found to be associated with decreased cardiovascular risk (as do the lower alcohol beverage consumption levels).

STEROID ESTROGEN LEVELS IN NORMAL POSTMENOPAUSAL WOMEN NOT RECEIVING ESTROGEN REPLACEMENT THERAPY

Already-Identified Factors Which Influence Postmenopausal Estrogen Levels

Coming back to the subject of the effects of moderate alcoholic beverage consumption on the estrogenization of normal postmenopausal women not receiving estrogen replacement therapy, it is now clear that there are two distinctly different sets of findings to prod investigation. First, both moderate alcoholic beverage consumption and menopausal estrogen-replacement therapy have been reported to reduce the risk of cardiovascular disease in postmenopausal women. Second, estrogen levels have been found to be increased in alcoholic postmenopausal women with alcohol-induced liver disease. The question to be addressed now is whether or not *moderate* alcoholic beverage consumption has the ability to influence menopausal estrogen levels. In order to adequately evaluate such a hypothesis, it is necessary to design a study so that the factors already known to modulate estrogen levels in postmenopausal women can be taken into account (Gavaler, 1988).

There are two such factors: the first is body fat mass, and the second is the presence of the postmenopausal ovaries. Body fat mass as estimated by weight, Body Mass Index (BMI), or some other variable, is of substantial importance because the major source of estrogen in postmenopausal women is the conversion of androgens to estrogens. This conversion occurs primarily in adipose tissue where the enzyme aromatase converts androstenedione to estrone, and testosterone to estradiol. In normal postmenopausal women, estradiol levels are statistically higher in obese women (49.0 ± 7.3 pg/ml) than in thin women (34.1 ± 6.4 pg/ml) (Gavaler, 1992). The presence of postmenopausal ovaries is important because, although they no longer produce estrogens, they do continue to produce androgens which then can be converted to estrogens. In normal postmenopausal women, estradiol levels are significantly higher in women with intact ovaries (42.5 ± 2.9) than in women whose ovaries have been surgically removed (28.5 ± 4.5) (Gavaler, 1992).

The Potential for Interaction of Alcoholic Beverages With the Known Determinants of Postmenopausal Estrogen Levels

Clearly, factors which influence either the conversion of androgens to estrogen, or the availability of androgens which can be aromatized to estrogens, may also detectably modulate the actual levels of circulating estrogens in normal postmenopausal women. In this context, several studies which have been performed in males are instructive. With respect to androgen conversion/aromatization to estrogens, it has been demonstrated that alcoholic men with cirrhosis have higher aromatization rates than controls (Gordon, Olivo, Fereidoon, & Southren, 1975; Longcope, Pratt, Schneider, & Fineberg, 1984). Further, in experimental male animals fed 36% of total calories as ethanol, hepatic aromatase activity is increased (Gordon, Southren, Vittek, & Lieber, 1979). Of particular relevance, in studies performed in normal male volunteers administered ethanol for up to 25 days, the percent of testosterone substrate converted to estradiol was increased (Gordon, Altman, Southren, Rubin, & Lieber, 1976). With respect to availability of androgens for conversion to estrogens, it has been demonstrated in male experimental animals using an isolated adrenal perfusion system that ethanol increases adrenal production of steroids, including the androgen androstenedione (Cobb, Van Thiel, & Gavaler, 1981).

The Reality of Moderate Alcoholic Beverage Consumption as a Factor Which Influences Postmenopausal Estrogen Levels

Given that we already know that estrogen levels are increased in alcoholic cirrhotic postmenopausal women, that alcohol itself influences the aromatization of androgens to estrogens, and that aromatization per se is the major source of estrogens in postmenopausal women, it is not particularly surprising that moderate alcoholic beverage consumption can be demonstrated to increase estrogen levels in normal postmenopausal women (Gavaler et al., 1991; Gavaler & Van Thiel, 1992). What is surprising is how long it has taken for the observation to be made.

Table 2.3. Characteristics of the 4 Study Populations of Healthy Postmenopausal Women

	Pittsburgh (n = 128)	Copenhagen (n = 62)	Lisbon (n = 34)	Madrid (n = 20)
Age (years)	57.7 ± 0.4	64.0 ± 1.0	58.2 ± 1.3	57.1 ± 1.4
Menopause duration (years)	8.8 ± 0.5	14.8 ± 1.2	10.9 ± 1.6	8.2 ± 1.6
Weight (pounds)	144.0 ± 2.2	138.2 ± 2.2	135.6 ± 4.0	142.2 ± 5.1
Body Mass Index (BMI)	24.9 ± 0.4	23.5 ± 0.3	24.6 ± 0.7	25.1 ± 0.9
Obesity (BMI≥30)	11%	2%	6%	15%
Ovariectomy	27%	5%	26%	20%

Table 2.4. The Relationship Between Alcoholic Beverage Consumption and Estradiol Levels in Healthy Postmenopausal Women

	Pittsburgh	Copenhagen	Lisbon	Madrid
Alcohol users	79%	95%	31%	75%
Self-reported total weekly drinks (among drinkers)	5.7 ± 0.6	6.9 ± 0.8	12.4 ± 26.8	5.4 ± 1.3
Prevalence of alcohol consumption among drinkers at a level greater than:				
2 daily drinks	9.9%	15.2%	18.1%	13.3%
3 daily drinks	4.0%	3.4%	18.1%	0.0%
4 daily drinks	0.0%	1.7%	0.0%	0.0%
Spearman correlation of estradiol with total weekly drinks	r = 0.309*	r = 0.473*	r = 0.450*	r = 0.146

*Statistically significant

The seminal study was performed in a group of 128 normal post-menopausal women. In this study population, 78.8% reported that they consumed alcoholic beverages. For the women in this study sample, data were available so that their self-reported usual consumption of alcoholic beverages could be verified by comparison with their three-day food record information. Although the number of women who used alcohol did not change when the two quantitation methods were compared, total weekly drinks among the drinkers were 5.7 ± 0.6 based on self-report, but 4.8 ± 0.6 based on the three-day food record (Gavaler & Love, 1992). The estradiol data in relation to alcoholic beverage consumption in this study were analyzed using a variety of statistical approaches. Using multivariate linear regression, the independent determinants of estradiol levels were found to be body weight and the

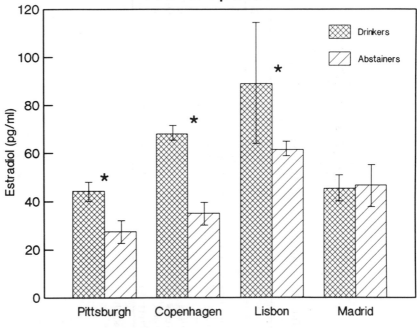

Figure 2.1.   Estradiol levels in four study populations of normal postmenopausal women. The height of the bar represents the mean, and the bracket represents the standard error of the mean. An asterisk indicates a statistically significant difference between alcohol users and alcohol abstainers.

presence of postmenopausal ovaries—as would have been predicted—as well as total weekly drinks. These three variables together explained 19.9% of the variation in estradiol levels. Keeping in mind that estradiol is produced by the aromatization of testosterone, when testosterone was added to the equation containing total weekly drinks, body weight, and the presence of postmenopausal ovaries, 28.9% of the variation in estradiol concentrations was explained (Gavaler & Van Thiel, 1992).

Whether or not this relationship between moderate alcoholic beverage consumption and a statistically significant increase in estradiol levels was a reproducible rather than an isolated finding was addressed by repeating the study in three additional study populations of normal postmenopausal women. The characteristics of all four groups of normal postmenopausal women are summarized in Table 2.3. As can be seen, there was variability in the major menopausal estrogen determinants: fat mass, as estimated by the BMI, and ovariectomy prevalence. The pattern of alcoholic beverage consumption in each of these four study groups is shown in Table 2.4. In spite of the variability in estrogen determinants and alcoholic beverage ingestion, as may be seen in Figure 2.1, a relationship between self-reported alcoholic beverage consumption and estradiol levels was detected in three of these four study populations.

CONSIDERATION OF THE POSSIBILITY OF DELETERIOUS EFFECTS OF MODERATE ALCOHOLIC BEVERAGE CONSUMPTION WHICH MIGHT OFFSET THE BENEFICIAL EFFECTS ON CORONARY HEART DISEASE AND ESTROGEN LEVELS

The Liver

Thus far, we have been viewing moderate alcoholic beverage consumption solely from the standpoint of beneficial effects with respect to coronary heart disease risk. For balance, we need to evaluate the possibility of deleterious effects at these moderate consumption levels. The issue of the potential for alcohol-induced liver injury has been examined in the large study group of 128 normal postmenopausal women (Gavaler et al., 1988). Compared to the alcohol-abstaining women, there were no differences in two markers of liver injury—gamma glutamyl transpeptidase and aspartate aminotransferase—nor in a measure of liver function, albumin. Thus, at the moderate consumption level of approximately five weekly drinks in this study group of normal postmenopausal women, there appears to be no detectable deleterious effect on the liver.

Breast Cancer

There are two additional areas with the potential for adverse effects: osteoporosis and breast cancer. A great deal of investigative attention has been directed at the association between breast cancer and alcoholic beverage consumption. The issue has been and continues to be that of alcohol dosage. Several large epidemiologic studies with alcoholic beverage dose data are summarized in Table 2.5. In addition, for purposes of comparison, a large cohort study of breast cancer risk with estrogen-replacement therapy is included. As before, the reader must keep in mind the requirement that the confidence interval around the relative risk estimate excludes the value of one in order to be able to speak to a statistically significant change in risk. While investigators have shown that alcoholic beverage consumption at a level of three or more daily drinks is associated with a statistically increased risk of breast cancer (Hiatt & Bawol, 1984), at lower consumption levels, no statistical change in risk can be detected even in large cohorts in which sample size inadequacy cannot be invoked as a reason for failure to demonstrate an effect (Schatzkin et al., 1987; Willett, Stampfer, Colditz, Rosner, Hennekens, & Speizer, 1987). It is worth noting that the alcoholic beverage risk estimates and their confidence intervals are essentially identical to those reported for estrogen-replacement therapy (Buring et al., 1987).

Osteoporosis

Studies in which alcoholic beverage consumption by postmenopausal women has been evaluated with respect to measures of osteoporosis are summarized in Table 2.6. The most interesting aspect of this table is the absence of any symbol used to denote statistical significance. Whether for fracture risk (Davidson, Ross, Paganini-Hill, Hammond, Silteri, & Judd, 1982; Felson, Kiel, Anderson, & Kannel, 1988; Hemenway, Colditz, Willett, Stampfer, & Speizer, 1988; Paganini-Hill, Ross, Gerkins, Henderson, & Mack, 1981) or for measures of bone mineralization (Black-Sandler et al., 1982; Cauley, Gutai, Black-Sandler, La Porte, Kuller, & Sashin, 1986; Slemenda, Hui, Longcope, Wellman, & Johnston, 1990), moderate alcoholic beverage consumption has no discernable deleterious effect.

Table 2.5. Breast Cancer Risk in Women: Effects of Estrogen-Replacement Therapy (ERT) and Moderate Alcoholic Beverage Consumption

Breast Cancer Risk Variable	Relative Risk (95% CI)#	Modulating Factor	Cohort Characteristics	Authors (years)
Age-adjusted incidence	1.63 (1.26, 2.11)*	≥ 3 daily drinks vs. abstainers	96,565 women, age >15; 8 years of follow-up	Hiatt & Bawol (1984)
Incidence	1.1 (0.7, 1.6)	ERT current	33,335 postmenopausal women; 4 years of follow-up	Buring et al. (1987)
	1.4 (0.9, 2.0)	ERT past		
		daily drinks:		
Age-adjusted incidence	1.4 (0.9, 2.3)	0.1	7,188 women, age 25 to 74; 10 years of follow-up	Schatzkin et al. (1987)
	1.5 (0.9, 2.6)	0.1–0.4		
	1.6 (1.0, 2.7)	≥ 0.5		
		daily drinks:		
Incidence	1.04 (0.74, 1.47)	0.1–0.4	33,561 women, age 50–59; 4 years of follow-up	Willett et al. (1987)
	1.35 (0.98, 1.87)	0.5–1.4		
	1.30 (0.98, 1.73)	≥ 1.5		
	1.16 (0.88, 1.47)	any use		

#CI = confidence interval
*Statistically significant difference in risk

Table 2.6. Moderate Alcoholic Beverage Consumption and Osteoporosis in Normal Postmenopausal Women

Risk Variable	Relative Risk (95% CI)#	Modulating Factor	Cohort Characteristics	Authors (year)
Hip fracture	1.36 (0.74, 2.50) 1.92 (0.78, 4.73)	shots of liquor/wk 1–7 ≥ 8	83 cases, 166 controls: all postmenopausal	Paganini-Hill et al. (1981)
Radius bone mass	not a significant predictor in multivariate analyses	daily alcohol intake	59 postmenopausal women; mean age 61.1 years	Black-Sandler et al. (1982)
Hip fracture	1.64 (0.53, 3.10)	alcohol on a daily or almost daily basis	25 cases and 25 controls; mean age 76 years	Davidson et al. (1982)
Radius bone density	not significantly correlated (r = 0.03)	alcohol consumption (mean: 5 weekly drinks)	77 postmenopausal women; mean age 57 years	Cauley et al. (1986)
Hip fracture (age-adjusted)	1.34 (0.91, 1.95) 1.54 (0.92, 2.58)	weekly drinks: 4 to 12 ≥ 12	Framingham cohort; 117,224 person-years of follow-up; ? women	Felson et al. (1988)
Hip and forearm fractures	0.95 (0.74, 1.16) 1.06 (0.88, 1.27) 0.98 (0.81, 1.14) 1.16 (0.95, 1.41)	weekly drinks: < 1 1 to 3 3 to 10 > 10	96,508 women age 30 to 55; 10,000 person-years follow-up	Hemenway et al. (1988)
Bone mineral content	highest vs lowest mineralization tertile: radius lumbar spine femoral neck	weekly drinks: 4.7 vs 3.5 4.5 vs 3.2 3.6 vs 4.1	124 perimenopausal women; mean age 51 years	Slemenda et al. (1990)

#CI = confidence interval

Summary

In summary, it may be concluded that for normal postmenopausal women, at alcoholic beverage consumption levels of two or fewer drinks per day, there is no significant increase in risk of osteoporosis, breast cancer, or liver injury. Further, at this moderate alcoholic beverage consumption level, there is a clearly beneficial decrease in risk of various manifestations of heart disease. The magnitude of the diminution in heart disease risk associated with moderate ingestion of alcoholic beverages is similar to that afforded by the use of menopausal estrogen-replacement therapy. Coincidentally or mechanistically, such moderate alcoholic beverage consumption by normal postmenopausal women results in detectable increases in circulating estradiol levels. The obviousness of this connection between moderate alcoholic beverage consumption and both increased estrogen levels and decreased cardiovascular disease risk is sufficiently satisfying that it is tempting to let the story end with these findings.

MODERATE ALCOHOL BEVERAGE CONSUMPTION: A SOURCE OF INVISIBLE ESTROGENIC SUBSTANCES

The story, however, is not yet finished. Although the author has been careful to use the phrase "alcoholic beverages" rather than the term "alcohol" throughout the above discussion, the reader may have been thinking only "alcohol" instead. Use of the more cumbersome phrase "alcoholic beverages" has been intentional. The consumption of alcoholic beverages entails more than ingestion of ethanol; such beverages contain a plethora of congener substances (Kahn, 1969; Pirola, 1978). Some of these come from the plants and grains from which the alcoholic beverages are made.

Plant Estrogens in Nature

It has been hypothesized that alcoholic beverages might contain phytoestrogens, substances of plant origin with estrogenic activity. Such compounds might be contained in the plants from which the beverages are made. Such a hypothesis is not as far-fetched as it may initially seem to be. A variety of substances present in plants have been shown to possess estrogenic activity, and have thus been termed phytoestrogens (Biggers & Curnow, 1954; Curnow, 1954). It is of particular interest that preparations of hops, rice, and corn have been shown to possess estrogenic activity (Bhandari, 1964; Booth, Bickoff, & Kohler, 1960; Fenselau & Talalay, 1973; Zenisek & Bednar, 1960). The phytoestrogenic compounds which have been isolated from the plants themselves, as well as from plant byproducts such as oils, include β-sitosterol, coumestrol, and the isoflavones: daidzein, formononetin, genistein, and biochanin A (Bickoff, Booth, Lyman, Livingston, Thompson, & De Eds, 1957; El Samannoudy, Shareha, Ghannudi, Gillaly, & El Mougy, 1980; Guggolz, Livingston, & Bickoff, 1961). Although of lesser potency, these compounds possess measurable estrogenic activity (Bickoff, Livingston, Hendrickson, & Booth, 1962; Shutt & Cox, 1972). The metabolism of these phytoestrogenic isoflavones has been studied extensively in animals (Chang, Robinson, & Common, 1975; Lindsay & Kelly, 1970; Nilsson, Hill, & Davies, 1967). Of greater interest perhaps are studies in which these isoflavones have been isolated from human urine specimens (Adlercreutz et al., 1991; Bannwart, Fotsis, Heikkinen, & Aldercreutz, 1984).

Plant Estrogens in Certain Alcoholic Beverages

Two alcoholic beverages have been seriously investigated: the whiskey bourbon which is made from corn, and beer which is made from hops. Both biochanin A and β-sitosterol have been isolated and identified in bourbon (Gavaler et al., 1978; Gavaler, Imhoff, Pohl, Rosenblum, & Van Thiel, 1987; Rosenblum, Van Thiel, Campbell, Eagon, & Gavaler, 1987; Rosenblum, Van Thiel, Campbell, & Gavaler, 1991), while daidzein and genisten have been similarly found in beer (Rosenblum, Van Thiel, Campbell, & Gavaler, 1988). Experimental work has shown the bourbon congener preparation to be capable of eliciting an estrogenic response as demonstrated by an increase in uterine mass and a decrease in levels of luteinizing hormone in overiectomized rats (an animal equivalent for ovariectomized postmenopausal women). Further, this bourbon congener preparation has been demonstrated to be able to compete for cytosolic estrogen receptor binding sites (Gavaler et al., 1987a).

Detectable Effects of Plant Estrogens in Postmenopausal Women

Although the above studies in experimental animals are of interest, the real question is whether or not phytoestrogens are capable of producing a clinically relevant response. Such responses might include increases in sex hormone binding globulin (SHBG) and high-density lipoprotein (HDL), two proteins of hepatic origin known to be elevated in response to estrogen exposure. In postmenopausal women not being treated with estrogen-replacement therapy, an estrogenic response would include a decrease in the gonadotropins—luteinizing hormone (LH) and follicle stimulating hormone (FSH)—as well as in changes in vaginal cytology, or even a reduction in postmenopausal bone mineral loss. Several reports provide indirect evidence using data obtained in vegetarian postmenopausal women. In alcohol-abstaining women, vegetarian women had higher levels of both SHBG and HDL compared to nonvegetarian women. Further, among the nonvegetarian postmenopausal women, the women reporting consumption of alcoholic beverages had higher levels of these two estrogen-responsive hepatic proteins than the alcohol-abstaining women (Armstrong et al., 1981). Even more interesting, in a large study of postmenopausal bone mineralization, lactoovovegetarian women demonstrated significantly less mineral bone loss over a period of 20 years that did omnivorous women (Marsh, Sanchez, Michelsen, Chaffee, & Fagal, 1988).

A recent study has directly examined the possibility that the administration of certain plant foods known to contain phytoestrogens to normal postmenopausal women could result in detectable estrogenic responses (Wilcox, Wahlqvist, Burger, & Medley, 1990). Three foods were chosen, based on reports that they could induce vaginal estrus in experimental animals: soya flour, red clover sprouts, and linseed (Farnsworth, Bingel, Cordell, Crane, & Fong, 1975). In this study, decreases in gondotropin levels were observed, as were changes in vaginal cytology indicative of estrogenization.

Clinical Responses to the Plant Estrogens of the Alcoholic Beverage Bourbon

Returning to the hypothesis that the phytoestrogens contained in alcoholic beverages may be of clinical importance, two reports are instructive (Van Thiel, Galvao-Teles, Monteiro, Rosenblum, & Gavaler, 1991; Gavaler, Galvao-Teles, Monteiro, Van Thiel, & Rosenblum, 1991). The first is a case report in which a preparation of bourbon congeners was administered over a four-week period to a single normal postmenopausal woman. This bourbon congener preparation contained an unquantified amount of biochanin A and approximately 12 ug of β-sitosterol per daily dose, the equivalent of the congener content of two shots of bourbon. Consistent with exposure to biologically active estrogenic substances, LH and FSH both decreased while SHBG and HDL both increased during the period of phytoestrogen administration, and all returned to pretreatment levels within one week after cessation of congener administration. The second report is an extension of the first. In it, three additional normal postmenopausal women were treated identically. In this small sample, LH decreased and SHBG increased in three of the four subjects, while HDL and the ratio of total cholesterol to HDL cholesterol increased in all four. As before, levels returned to baseline within a week of discontinuing administration of the phytoestrogen-containing bourbon congener preparation (Gavaler, Galvao-Teles, Montiero, Van Thiel, & Rosenblum, 1991). These two reports are the first to directly evaluate the hypothesis that the phytoestrogens contained in at least one type of alcoholic beverage are capable of producing a significant clinical response.

CONCLUSIONS

Simply put, it is now possible to assert that moderate consumption of alcoholic beverages by normal postmenopausal women results in clinically relevant estrogenization via two distinct mechanisms. On the one hand, the biologically active phytoestrogens consumed may be viewed as acting directly; on the other hand, the ethanol consumed may be viewed as acting to increase the aromatization of androgens, thereby increasing endogenous levels of estrogen. When alcoholic beverages are consumed moderately (i.e., no more than 2 drinks per day), based on available data, it seems to be reasonable to say that there may indeed be a beneficial effect via modulation of the estrogenization of normal postmenopausal women.

REFERENCES

Adlercreutz, H., Honjo, H., Higashi, A., Fotsis, T., Hamalainen, E., Hasegawa, T., & Okada, H. (1991). Urinary excretion of lignans and isoflavonoid phytoestrogens in Japanese men and women consuming a traditional Japanese diet. *American Journal of Clinical Nutrition, 54*, 1093–1100.

Armstrong, B.K., Brown, J.B., Clarke, H.T., Crooke, D.K., Hahnel, R., Masarei, J.R., & Ratajczak, T. (1981). Diet and reproductive hormones: A study of vegetarian and nonvegetarian postmenopausal women. *Journal of the National Cancer Institute, 67*, 761–767.

Bannwart, C., Fotsis, T., Heikkinen, R., & Aldercreutz, H. (1984). Identification of the isoflavonic phytoestrogen daidzein in human urine. *Clinica Chemica Acta, 136*, 165–172.

Bhandari, P.R. (1964). Identification of flavonoids in hops (humulus lupulus linne) by thin-layer chromatography. *Journal of Chromatography, 16*, 130–135.

Bickoff, E.M., Booth, A.N., Lyman, R.I., Livingston, A.L., Thompson, C.R., & DeEds, F. (1957). Coumestrol, a new estrogen isolated from forage crops. *Science, 126,* 969–970.

Bickoff, E.M., Livingston, A.L., Hendrickson, A.P., & Booth, A.N. (1962). Relative potencies of several estrogen-like compounds found in forages. *Journal of Agriculture and Food Chemistry, 10,* 410–412.

Biggers, J.D., & Curnow, D.H. (1954). Oestrogenic activity of subterranean clover. 1. The oestrogenic activity of genistein. *Journal of Biochemistry, 58,* 278–282.

Black-Sandler, R., LaPorte, R.E., Sashin, D., Kuller, L.H., Sternglass, E., Cauley, J.A., & Link, M. (1982). Determinants of bone mass in menopause. *Prevention Medicine, 11,* 269–280.

Booth, A.N., Bickoff, E.M., & Kohler, G.O. (1960). Estrogenlike activity in vegetable oils and mill byproducts. *Science, 131,* 1807–1808.

Buring, J.E., Hennekens, C.H., Lipnick, R.J., Willett, W., Stampfer, M.J., Rosner, B., & Peto, R. (1987). A prospective cohort study of postmenopausal hormone use and breast cancer in U.S. women. *American Journal of Epidemiology, 125,* 939–947.

Cahalan, D., & Cisin, I.H. (1968). American drinking practices: Summary of findings from a national probability sample. I. Extent of drinking by population subgroups. *Quarterly Journal of Studies on Alcohol, 29,* 130–151.

Cauley, J.A., Gutai, J.P., Black-Sandler, R., LaPorte, R.E., Kuller, L.H., & Sashin, D. (1986). The relationship of endogenous estrogen to bone density and bone area in normal postmenopausal women. *American Journal of Epidemiology, 128,* 606–614.

Chang, H.H.S., Robinson, A.B., & Common, R.H. (1975). Excretion of radioactive daidzein and equol as monosulfates and disulfates in the urine of laying hens. *Canadian Journal of Biochemistry, 53,* 223–230.

Clark, W.B., & Midanik, L. (1982). Alcohol use and alcohol problems among U.S. adults: Results of the 1979 national survey. In National Institute on Alcohol Abuse and Alcoholism. Alcohol Consumption and Related Problems. *Alcohol and Health Monograph No. 1* (DHHS Publication No. (ADM) 82–1190, pp. 3–52). Washington, DC: U.S. Government Printing Office.

Cobb, C.F., Van Thiel, D.H., & Gavaler, J.S. (1981). Isolated rat adrenal perfusion: A new method to study adrenal function. *Journal of Surgical Research, 31,* 347–353.

Colditz, G.A., Willett, W.C., Stampfer, M.J., Rosner, B., Speizer, F.E., & Hennekens, C.H. (1987). Menopause and the risk of coronary heart disease in women. *New England Journal of Medicine, 316,* 1105–1110.

Criqui, M.H., Suarez, L., Barrett-Conner, E., McPhillips, J., Wingard, D.L., & Garland, C. (1988). Menopausal estrogen use and mortality: Results from a prospective study in a defined, homogeneous community. *American Journal of Epidemiology, 128,* 606–614.

Cullen, K., Stenhouse, N.S., & Wearne, K.L. (1982). Alcohol and mortality in the Busselton study. *International Journal of Epidemiology, 11,* 67–70.

Curnow, D.H. (1954). Oestrogenic activity of subterranean clover. 2. Isolation of genistein from subterranean clover and methods of quantitative estimation. *Journal of Biochemistry, 58,* 283–287.

Davidson, B.J., Ross, R.K., Paganini-Hill, A., Hammond, G.D., Siiteri, P.K., & Judd, H.L. (1982). Total and free estrogens and androgens in postmenopausal women with hip fractures. *Journal of Clinical Endocrinology and Metabolism, 54,* 115–120.

El Samannoudy, F.A., Shareha, A.M., Ghannudi, S.A., Gillaly, G.A., & El Mougy, S.A. (1980). Adverse effects of phytoestrogens. 7. Effects of β-sitosterol on follicular development, ovarian structure and uterus in the immature female sheep. *Cellular and Molecular Biolology, 26,* 255–266.

Farnsworth, N.R., Bingel, A.S., Cordell, G.A., Crane, F.A., & Fong, H.H.S. (1975). Potential value of plants as sources of new antifertility agents. II. *Journal of Pharmacology and Science, 64,* 717–754.

Felson, D.T., Kiel, D.P., Anderson, J., & Kannel, W.B. (1988). Alcohol consumption and hip fracture: The Framingham Study. *American Journal of Epidemiology, 128,* 1102–1110.

Fenselau, C., & Talalay, P. (1973). Is oestrogenic activity present in hops? *Food and Cosmetic Toxicology, 11,* 597–603.

Gavaler, J.S. (1985). Effects of alcohol on endocrine function in postmenopausal women: A review. *Journal of Studies on Alcohol, 46,* 495–516.

Gavaler, J.S. (1988). Effects of moderate consumption of alcoholic beverages on endocrine function in postmenopausal women: Bases for hypotheses. In M. Galanter (Ed.), *Recent developments in alcoholism* (Vol. 6, pp. 229–251). New York: Plenum Publishing.

Gavaler, J.S. (1992). Alcohol effects in postmenopausal women: Alcohol and estrogens. In J. Mendelson & N. Mello (Eds.), *Diagnosis and treatment of alcoholism* (3rd ed., pp. 623–638). New York: McGraw-Hill.

Gavaler, J.S., Galvao-Teles, A., Monteiro, E., Van Thiel, D.H., & Rosenblum, E.R. (1991). Clinical responses to the administration of bourbon phytoestrogens to normal postmenopausal women. *Hepatology, 14,* 193.

Gavaler, J.S., Imhoff, A.F., Pohl, C.R., Rosenblum, E.R., & Van Thiel, D.H. (1987). Alcoholism beverages: A source of estrogenic substances. In K.O. Lindros, R. Ylikhari, & K. Kilanmaa (Eds.), *Advances in biomedical alcohol research* (pp. 545–549). Oxford: Pergamon Press.

Gavaler, J.S., Kelly, R.H., Wight, C., Sanghvi, A., Cauley, J., Belle, S., & Love, K. (1988). Does moderate alcoholic beverage consumption affect liver function/injury tests in postmenopausal women? *Alcoholism: Clinical and Experimental Research, 12,* 337.

Gavaler, J.S., & Love, K. (1992). Detection of the relationship between moderate alcoholic beverage consumption and serum levels of estradiol in normal postmenopausal women: Effects of alcohol consumption quantitation and sample size adequacy. *Journal of Studies on Alcohol, 53,* 1992.

Gavaler, J.S., Love, K., Van Thiel, D.H., Farholt, S., Gluud, C., Monteiro, E., Galvao-Teles, A., Conton-Ortega, T., & Cuervas-Mons, V. (1991). An international study of the relationship between alcohol consumption and postmenopausal estradiol levels. In H.J. Kalant, J.M. Khanna, Y. Israel (Eds.), *Advances in biomedical alcohol research* (pp. 327–330). New York: Pergamon Press.

Gavaler, J.S., Rosenblum, E.R., Van Thiel, D.H., Eagon, P.K., Pohl, C.R., Campbell, I.M., & Gavaler, J. (1987). Biologically active phytoestrogens are present in bourbon. *Alcoholism: Clinical and Experimental Research, 11,* 399–406.

Gavaler, J.S., & Van Thiel, D.H. (1992a). The association between moderate alcoholic beverage consumption and serum estradiol and testosterone levels in normal postmenopausal women: Relationship to the literature. *Alcoholism: Clinical and Experimental Research, 16,* 87–92.

Gavaler, J.S., & Van Thiel, D.H. (1992b). The hormonal status of postmenopausal women with alcohol-induced cirrhosis: Further findings and a review of the literature. *Hepatology, 16,* 312–319.

Gomberg, E.S.L. (1982). Alcohol use and alcohol problems among the elderly. In: National Institute on Alcohol Abuse and Alcoholism. Special Population Issues. *Alcohol and Health Monograph No. 4* (DHHS Publication No. (ADM) 82-1193, pp. 263–290). Washington, DC: U.S. Government Printing Office.

Goodwin, J.S., Sanchez, C.J., Thomas, P., Hunt, C., Garry, P.J., & Goodwin, J.M. (1987). Alcohol intake in a healthy elderly population. *American Journal of Public Health, 77,* 173–177.

Gordon, G.D., Altman, K., Southren, A.L., Rubin, E., & Lieber, C.S. (1976) Effect of alcohol (ethanol) administration on sex-hormone metabolism in normal men. *New England Journal of Medicine, 295,* 793–797.

Gordon, G.G., Olivo, J., Fereidoon, F., & Southren, A.L. (1975). Conversion of androgens to estrogens in cirrhosis of the liver. *Journal of Clinical Endocrinology and Metabolism, 40,* 1018–1026.

Gordon, G.G., Southren, A.L., Vittek, J., & Lieber, C.S. (1979). The effect of alcohol ingestion on hepatic aromatase activity and plasma steroid hormones in the rat. *Metabolism, 28,* 20–24.

Gordon, T., & Kannel, W.B. (1983). Drinking habits and cardiovascular disease: The Framingham Study. *American Heart Journal, 105,* 667–673.

Guggolz, J., Livingston, A., & Bickoff, E.M. (1961). Detection of daidzein, formononetin, genistein, and biochanin A in forages. *Journal of Agriculture and Food Chemistry, 9,* 330–332.

Hemenway, D., Colditz, G.A., Willett, W.C., Stampfer, M.J., & Speizer, F.E. (1988). Fractures and lifestyle: Effect of cigarettes, alcohol intake and relative weight on the risk of hip and forearm fractures in middle-aged women. *American Journal of Public Health, 78,* 1554–1558.

Hiatt, R.A., & Bawol, R.D. (1984). Alcohol beverage consumption and breast cancer incidence. *American Journal of Epidemiology, 120,* 676–683.

Hilton, M.E., & Clark, W.B. (1987). Changes in American drinking patterns and problems, 1967–1984. *Journal of Studies on Alcohol, 48,* 515–522.

Hugues, J.N., Coste, G., Perret, T., Jayle, M.F., Sebaoun, J., & Modigliani, E. (1980). Hypothalamo pituitary ovarian function in thirty women with chronic alcoholism. *Clinical Endocrinology, 12,* 543–551.

James, V.H.T., Green, J.R.B., Walker, J.B., Goodall, A., Short, F., Jones,

D.L., Noel, C.T., & Reed, M.J. (1982). The endocrine status of postmenopausal cirrhotic women. In M. Langer, L. Chiandussi, I.J. Chopra, & L. Martini (Eds.), *The endocrines and the liver* (pp. 417–419). New York: Academic Press.

Jasonni, V.M., Bulletti, C., Bolelli, G.F., Franceschetti, F., Bonavia, M., Ciotte, P., & Flamigni, C. (1983). Estrone sulfate, estrone, and estradiol concentrations in normal and cirrhotic postmenopausal women. *Steroids, 41,* 569–573.

Kahn, J.H. (1969). Compounds identified in whiskey, wine, and beer: A tabulation. *Journal of the Association of Analytic Chemistry, 52,* 1166–1178.

Klatsky, A.L., Friedman, G.D., & Siegelaub, A.B. (1974). Alcohol consumption before myocardial infarction: Results from the Kaiser-Permanente epidemiologic study of myocardial infarction. *Annals of Internal Medicine, 81,* 294–301.

Lindsay, D.R., & Kelly, R.W. (1970). The metabolism of phytoestrogens in sheep. *Australian Veterinary Journal, 46,* 219–222.

Lloyd, C.W., & Williams, R.H. (1948). Endocrine changes associated with Laennec's cirrhosis of the liver. *American Journal of Medicine, 4,* 315–330.

Longcope, C., Pratt, J.H., Schneider, S., & Fineberg, E. (1984). Estrogen and androgen dynamics in liver disease. *Journal of Endocrinology Investigation, 7,* 629–634.

Marsh, A.G., Sanchez, T.V., Michelsen, O., Chaffee, F.L., & Fagal, S.M. (1988). Vegetarian lifestyle and bone mineral density. *American Journal of Clinical Nutrition, 48,* 837–841.

National Institute on Alcohol Abuse and Alcoholism (NIAAA). (1981). *First Statistical Compendium on Alcohol and Health* (DHHS Publication No. (ADM) 81-1115). Washington, DC: U.S. Government Printing Office.

Nilsson, A., Hill, J.L., & Davies, H.L. (1967). An in vitro study of formononetin and biochanin A metabolism in rumen fluid of sheep. *Biochemica et Biophysica Acta, 148,* 92–98.

O'Connell, B., Hudson, R., & Graves, G. (1979). Alcohol and tobacco use. In J. Krupinsky, & A. Mackenzie (Eds.), *The Health and Social Survey of the Northwest Region of Melbourne* (pp. 96–111). Melbourne, Australia: Health Commission of Victoria, Mental Health Division, The Institute of Mental Health Research and Post-Graduate Training.

Paganini-Hill, A., Ross, R.K., Gerkins, V.R., Henderson, B.E., & Mack, A.M. (1981). Menopausal estrogen therapy and hip fractures. *Annals of Internal Medicine, 95,* 28–31.

Petitti, D.B., Wingerd, J., Pellegrin, F., & Ramcharan, S. (1979). Risk of vascular disease in women: Smoking, oral contraceptives, noncontraceptive estrogens and other factors. *Journal of the American Medical Association, 242,* 1150–1154.

Pirola, R.C. (1978). Congeners of alcoholic beverages. In *Drug metabolism and alcohol* (pp. 123–129). Baltimore: University Press.

Rosenblum, E.R., Van Thiel, D.H., Campbell, I.M., Eagon, P.K., & Gavaler, J.S. (1987). Separation and identification of phytoestrogenic compounds isolated from bourbon. In K.O. Lindros, R. Ylikhari, & K. Kilanmaa (Eds.), *Advances in biomedical alcohol research* (pp. 551–555). Oxford: Pergamon Press.

Rosenblum, E.R., Van Thiel, D.H., Campbell, I.M., & Gavaler, J.S. (1988). Isolation of phytoestrogens from beer. *Alcoholism: Clinical and Experimental Research, 12,* 316.

Rosenblum, E.R., Van Thiel, D.H., Campbell, I.M., & Gavaler, J.S. (1991). Quantitation of β-sitosterol in bourbon. *Alcoholism: Clinical and Experimental Research, 15,* 205–206.

Ross, R.K., Paganini-Hill, A., Mack, T.M., Arthur, M., & Henderson, B.E. (1981). Menopausal oestrogen therapy and protection from death from ischemic heart disease. *Lancet, 1,* 858–860.

Schatzkin, A., Jones, D.Y., Hoover, R.N., Taylor, T.P., Brinton, L.A., Ziegler, R.G., Harvey, E.B., Carter, C.L., Licitra, L.M., Dufour, M.C., & Larson, D.B. (1987). Alcohol consumption and breast cancer in the epidemiologic follow-up study of the First National Health and Nutrition Examination Survey. *New England Journal of Medicine, 316,* 1169–1173.

Shutt, D.A., & Cox, R.I. (1972). Steroid and phyto-oestrogen binding to sheep uterine receptors in vitro. *Journal of Endocrinology, 52,* 299–310.

Slemenda, C.W., Hui, S.L., Longcope, C., Wellman, H., & Johnston, C.C. (1990). Predictors of bone mass in perimenopausal women. *Annals of Internal Medicine, 112,* 96–101.

Stampfer, M.J., Colditz, G.A., Willett, W.C., Speizer, F.E., & Hennekens, C.H. (1988). A prospective study of moderate alcohol consumption and the risk of coronary heart disease and stroke in women. *New England Journal of Medicine, 319,* 267–273.

Van Thiel, D.H., Galvao-Teles, A., Montciro, E., Rosenblum, E.R., & Gavaler, J.S. (1991). The phytoestrogens present in deethanolized bourbon are biologically active: A preliminary study in a postmenopausal woman. *Alcoholism: Clinical and Experimental Research, 15,* 822–823.

Wechsler, H. (1980). Introduction: Summary of the liver. [I. Epidemiology of male/female drinking over the last century.] In National Institute on Alcohol Abuse and Alcoholism. *Alcoholism and Alcohol Abuse Among Women: Research Issues* (Research Monograph No. 1, DHEW Publication No. (ADM) 80-835, pp. 3–31). Washington, DC: U.S. Government Printing Office.

Wilcox, G., Wahlqvist, M.L., Burger, H.G., & Medley, G. (1990). Oestrogenic effects of plant foods in postmenopausal women. *British Medical Journal, 301,* 905–906.

Willett, W.C., Stampfer, M.J., Colditz, G.A., Rosner, B.A., Hennekins, C.H., & Speizer, F.E. (1987). Moderate alcohol consumption and risk of breast cancer. *New England Journal of Medicine, 316,* 1174–1180.

Zenisek, A., & Bednar, I.J. (1960). Contribution to the identification of the estrogen activity of hops. *American Perfumes and Cosmetics, 75,* 61–64.

Chapter 3

Genetic Vulnerability to Alcoholism in Women

Shirley Y. Hill, Ph.D.

University of Pittsburgh School of Medicine
Department of Psychiatry
Western Psychiatric Institute and Clinic
Alcoholism and Genetics Research Program

The focus of this chapter concerns what is currently known about the etiology of alcoholism in women. While there have been a number of reviews that have addressed possible etiological factors in the development of alcoholism, those concerning alcoholism in women are rare (Hill, 1981). A separate review of putative etiological factors by gender appears to be needed based on both empirical and logical considerations. From an empirical perspective, we now know that even in our modern society, men and women are socialized to perform different roles: What is acceptable behavior in one gender is not in another. Therefore, some factors leading to abusive drinking in men may not apply to women. Still others may be shared in common, for example, a genetic vulnerability factor leading to increased rates of illness among related individuals. The existence of a genetic vulnerability to alcoholism continues to be debated by some in the alcoholism research field (Murray, Clifford, & Gurling, 1983; Peele, 1986). However, most observers would support the notion that some genetic mediation occurs. The real question is how much of the variance is explained by genetic factors and to what degree are they moderated by personal factors (gender, age, and psychiatric comorbidity) and environmental ones (cultural milieu, shared familial environment).

From a logical perspective, we recognize that the clinical heterogeneity one sees among alcoholics by gender may represent two separate genetic diatheses, or alternatively, there may be a single genetic diathesis with variable expression by gender. The difficulty lies in untangling which of these alternatives represents the true state of affairs. One approach is to compare concordance rates in monozygotic (MZ) and dizygotic (DZ) twin pairs. Pickens et al. (1991) compared MZ and DZ twins and found alcoholism (alcohol dependence) to be moderately heritable for both males and females ($h^2 = .595$ for males; $h^2 = .420$ for females) suggesting a largely genetic etiology for both genders.

Thus, if alcoholism is a heterogeneous disorder with some forms exhibiting greater or lesser genetic mediation, particularly when gender is considered, then the need for a separate review of etiological factors in alcoholism by gender is clear. The intent of the present review is to fill an existing gap in the theoretical literature concerning alcoholism in women. The review is organized with respect to: (a) evidence for the existence of multiple types of alcoholism in women, one more genetic than the other, (b) genetic models that take gender into account, (c) further discussion of the genetic heterogeneity of alcoholism as it relates to gender, and (d) presentation of data obtained from the Pittsburgh family study.

EVIDENCE FOR HETEROGENEITY
OF ALCOHOLISM IN WOMEN:
EPIDEMIOLOGICAL SURVEY DATA

The last decade has provided a unique opportunity to assess changing patterns of alcohol consumption in women. Prior to the initiation of community surveys in the 1980s, estimates of the rates of alcoholism and alcohol abuse among women were made on the basis of treated cases alone. With the advent of community surveys, age and sex-specific rates of particular psychiatric illnesses became available. It is now well known that women are less likely to develop alcohol problems than men, a fact that has recently been substantiated by the Ecological Catchment Area (ECA) project (Robins et al., 1984).

Wilsnack, Wilsnack, and Klassen (1984) in collaboration with the National Opinion Research Center (NORC) conducted a national survey of drinking practices, noting rates of heavy drinking by age group among women. They found the highest levels of heavy drinking to be for women between the ages of 35 and 49 (9%), with those 21–34 showing slightly lower rates (6%). At approximately the same time that the survey was being conducted, the Epidemiologic Catchment Area (ECA) program was engaged in a national survey of specific psychiatric disorders including alcoholism in the community. The ECA project used trained interviewers to assess the number and variety of symptoms reported by the respondents and compared these with established DSM-III criteria. This study (Myers et al., 1984; Robins et al., 1984) reported rates of Alcohol Abuse and Alcohol Dependence by sex and age, allowing comparison with the Wilsnack data gathered at approximately the same time (1980–1982). What is striking (see Figure 3.1) is that while the peak for heavy drinking appears to be between the ages of 35–49 in the NORC survey, the peak of Alcohol Abuse and Alcohol Dependence reported by the ECA authors is between the ages of 18–24 (see Figure 3.1). Only 1.8% of women in the 25–44 age group were alcoholic and even fewer women are alcoholic after the age of 45.

Cloninger, Bohman, and Sigvardsson (1981) have described the characteristics of male Type I alcoholics in contrast to Type II alcoholics as those whose likelihood of drinking depends much more heavily on the environmental milieu in which the individual resides. The latter or Type II males tend to be of the familial form and display earlier onset. Because every alcoholic woman must first pass through a heavy drinking stage, combining the results from the ECA and NORC surveys suggests that those young women who become alcoholic early (between 18 and 24) are atypical of the female drinking population as a whole. Could this group of women represent a familial form? Quite possibly there exist two forms of alcoholism in women: one which is largely the result of environmental pressures and which grows out of late-onset heavy drinking (peak 35–49) and another early-onset form that occurs between the ages of 18 and 24 and is much more likely to be genetically mediated.

In addition to the theoretical prediction of at least two types of alcoholism which can be made utilizing epidemiological data, results of two recent studies also support the existence of two types of alcoholism in women. Lex, Sholar, Bower and Mendelson (1991) examined a sample of women who came to the attention of the courts because of

Drinking Patterns For Women by Age

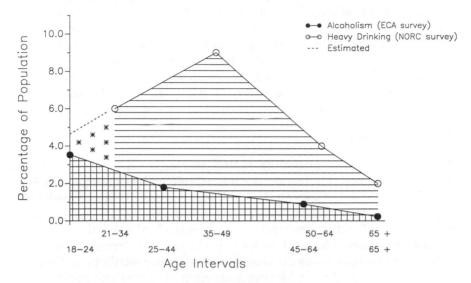

Figure 3.1. **Drinking Patterns For Women by Age**

multiple DUI offenses, finding that a majority of these women had family histories of alcoholism. Similarly, Glenn and Nixon (1991) classified 51 female alcoholics by age of onset (< 25 or > 25), finding a number of significant differences in the two types ("late alcoholism onset" and "early alcoholism onset") with regard to severity and familial density of alcoholism. In general, the early alcoholism onset group displayed greater severity of symptoms and more affected relatives. In conclusion, these two studies suggest that the familial form of alcoholism when seen in women may resemble that seen in men (e. g., early onset, multiple affected relatives, relative independence from environmental antecedents). Epidemiological data appear to confirm the existence of these two forms of the disorder in women.

GENETIC MODELS OF ALCOHOLISM IN WOMEN

Even though differences in the prevalence of alcoholism between men and women appear to be decreasing over time (Reich, Cloninger, Van Eerdewegh, Reiss, & Mullaney, 1988), the fact that women are less likely to develop alcohol problems raises the question of whether or not alcoholism is equally heritable in men and women. To examine this question, behavioral geneticists typically construct models of familial transmission in an attempt to understand the empirical data.

Construction of models to describe the transmission of alcoholism within families has been carried out using three types of data: family history data, data from adoption studies, and twin data. The data available for analysis have been limited because of relatively rarer occurrence of data sets involving female as opposed to male alcoholics. At any rate, the review summarizes what is currently known by focusing on data resulting from each of these methodologies.

Family History Data

The first attempt to model alcoholism transmission using empirical data that included rates by gender was completed by Cloninger, Christiansen, Reich, & Gottesman (1978). Using the multifactorial model of Falconer (1965), in which the collective influence of all genetic and environmental factors that influence an individual's risk for developing a disorder are subsumed under a single variable termed "liability," Cloninger and colleagues considered the relative contribution of these factors by gender. In considering both environmental and genetic influences, further delineation of the environmental influences were made: those arising from cultural or ecological variables, and those originating within the family.

Using predictions from the more general multifactorial model, three specific models were tested: the independent model, isocorrelational, and the environmental. Testing of these models requires the availability of nuclear families. Nuclear families are usually selected through a proband, and individual who is selected under some selection procedure (e. g., male treated alcoholic). The proband is so designated because the individual draws the attention of the investigator to a particular pedigree because the proband has a particular trait. When diagnostic information is available for the proband and his first-degree relatives, testing for transmission of the disorder can be achieved. To briefly describe the models:

1. The independent model predicts a reduction in transmission across gender (e. g., father to daughter or mother to son) on the assumption that familial factors relevant to the etiology of alcoholism are different by gender.
2. The isocorrelational model assumes that alcoholism in women is a more severe disorder and is tested by looking at the proportion of relatives (both male and female) of female probands to determine if a greater proportion of relatives of female probands are affected than that of male probands.

3. The environmental model assumes that differences in prevalence of alcoholism in men and women are due entirely to nonfamilial environmental influences. In this model it is assumed that one gender is exposed to greater pressure to drink (or not drink) as a function of their gender.

Utilizing information from 365 first-degree relatives of 259 alcoholics who were consecutive admissions to a psychiatric hospital in St. Louis, Cloninger and colleagues (1978) observed that alcoholism among women is less common than it is among men in the general population, though equal numbers of affected relatives are found among both male and female probands. Therefore, they concluded that differences in prevalence were due entirely to nonfamilial environmental factors. Both genders have an equal likelihood that if they become alcoholic, the etiology of their disorder is genetically mediated.

The salience of the earlier finding (Cloninger, Christiansen, Reich, & Gottesman, 1978) from the St. Louis group has been overlooked in more recent discussions. If the observed differences in alcoholism rates by gender are due entirely to environmental factors, then one can presume that genetic factors are equally relevant to the etiology of alcoholism in women as is men. The report which was based on more recent analyses of family data coming out of the St. Louis group implies that alcoholism in women may be of a milder form, and less likely to be genetically mediated. The term "female-like" has been used to describe a less severe and less genetically mediated form of alcoholism in men (Type I alcoholism), presumably on the assumption that alcoholism in women less often requires involvement of genetic factors in its etiology (Gilligan, Reich & Cloninger, 1987).

Gilligan, Reich, and Cloninger (1987), studying male and female probands and their respective first-degree relatives, have concluded that alcoholism in women fits a multifactorial model, while alcoholism in men fits a mixed model with a recessive major locus. Because the latter model more strictly implies a genetic factor operating than does the multifactorial model, it may be concluded that the Gilligan study implies greater genetic involvement in male alcoholism than female alcoholism.

However, some limitations have been noted for analyses presented in that study (Aston & Hill, 1990). First, nuclear families rather than extended families were classified as "male-like" and "female-like." Second, the testing for heterogeneity within the sample may have been problematic (Aston & Hill, 1990). Third, there was an assumption of no heterogeneity among the 55 families of female probands (heterogeneity was not directly tested).

48   HILL

With respect to the first issue, a nuclear family consists of a proband, siblings, and parents, whereas an extended family includes multigenerational information. To perform their analyses, Gilligan and colleagues classified nuclear families as "male-like" if their likelihood under the recessive mixed model (seen in male proband families) exceeded their likelihood under the multifactorial model (seen in female probands). All others were classified as "female-like." When segregation analysis was applied to the data to determine the best fit for each subset of families (male-like or female-like), a different mode of transmission was found for each: The male-like demonstrated a dominant gene mode of inheritance, whereas the female-like followed a multifactorial mode of transmission. Had extended pedigrees been used for classification, a different result might have been obtained.

With respect to the question of genetic heterogeneity, Gilligan, Reich, and Cloninger (1987) contrasted the male and female families for the presence or absence of heterogeneity. Genetic heterogeneity may be defined as quantitative evidence that more than one type of inheritance explains the transmission of a disease within families. Geneticists commonly use statistical tests to evaluate the likelihood of homogeneity relative to heterogeneity by evaluating the observed sample relative to a theoretical one using a chi-square distribution. Gilligan, Reich, and Cloninger (1987) may have incorrectly concluded that heterogeneity existed for the male families because of improper nesting of alternative hypotheses (for details see Aston & Hill, 1990). Furthermore, no formal tests of heterogeneity were applied to the female families, although the authors stated that they were not heterogeneous.

The alcoholism field appears to have bought the notion of two types of male alcoholism (one more severe and derived more clearly from a genetic predisposition, and the other more environmentally based), while assuming that only one type of alcoholism exists in females. Moreover, it has been assumed without scientific evidence that this single form does not have a genetic etiology. Because the assumption is based on incomplete information, it may not be correct. Thus, based on currently available family history data, we conclude that there is every reason to believe that the etiology of female alcoholism (at least one form of it) has as much likelihood of being mediated through genetic factors as it does in men.

Adoption Studies

Female samples of adoptees have been studied, including Danish (Goodwin, Schulsinger, Knop, Mednick, & Guze, 1977), Swedish (Bohman, Sigvardsson, & Cloninger, 1981), and American (Cardoret, O'Gorman, Troughton, & Heywood, 1985) groups (see Table 3.1). The goal of adoption studies is to determine the relative contribution of genes and environment to the etiology of alcoholism. In many cases, the results fall far short of this goal because of methodological difficulties. In the Goodwin study, 49 daughters of alcoholics were compared to 47 daughters of nonalcoholics, all of whom had been adopted away by nonrelatives at an early age. Due to the relatively low rates of reported problems with alcohol among women in this sample and the small sample size, too few alcohol-abusing women were available to warrant comparison (four alcoholic women were found among the high-risk group and two among the controls).

The Bohman, Sigvardsson, and Cloninger (1981) study concluded that daughters of alcoholic fathers who had extensive treatment for alcoholism and criminality did not have an excess of alcohol abuse, though daughters of men with mild alcohol abuse (no criminality) did. Thus, Bohman and colleagues concluded that their data confirmed the existence of a patrilineal form of inheritance of alcoholism. In this form, transmission is observed to occur only from father to son, with women seldom expressing the trait. Although this study is now more than a decade old, its conclusions are widely quoted as supportive of a male-limited form of alcoholism that is presumably more severe than that seen among women. For this reason, it is useful to examine the data presented from this study to determine the validity of their conclusions. First, all of the women studied were born out of wedlock between 1930 and 1949 in Stockholm. Given the cultural milieu of that time period, it may be assumed that one or both parents of such adoptees were relatively deviant for their time. Having children as a single parent was not common at that time, so that it may be reasonable to assume that women who did so would be more likely to have

Table 3.1. Adoption Studies in Women:
High-Risk—Daughters of Alcoholics Versus Low-Risk—Daughters of Controls

	High-Risk		Low-Risk		Author's Conclusions
Goodwin et al., 1977	2 daughters 49 fathers	(4.1)	2 daughters 47 fathers	(4.3)	Inconclusive
Bohman et al., 1981	3 daughters 29 mothers	(10.3)	16 daughters 577 parents	(2.8)	Female to female transmission only
	10 daughters 285 fathers	(3.5)	16 daughters 577 parents	(2.8)	
Cadoret et al., 1985	4 daughters 12 parents	(33.3)	4 daughters 75 parents	(5.3)	1° relatives with alcoholism increases female's risk

antisocial tendencies than women in similar circumstances today. This fact, coupled with the extensive criminality reported for the fathers of these offspring suggests that the offspring were at extremely high risk for antisocial behavior. It may be assumed, therefore, that the alcoholic cases that were detected arose out of a comorbidity for antisocial personality and not because of a diathesis for alcoholism, per se. Two subtypes of alcoholism, one with antisocial personality and one without, have long been recognized in male alcoholics (Guze, Wofgram & McKinney, 1967). Also, the absence of this subtype (alcoholism/sociopathy) in women has been recognized for some time (Schuckit, Pitts, Reich, King, & Winokur, 1969). Thus, the conclusion of this report which assumes a patrilineal form of transmission of alcoholism may be incorrect. The authors have only studied sociopathic alcoholism and not alcoholism, per se. Secondly, the number of available female alcoholic mothers with similarly affected daughters was too small to warrant definitive conclusions (only five such pairs were available).

Cadoret and colleagues (1985) compared the influence of genetic and environmental factors in the etiology of alcoholism in a sample of male and female adoptees, finding genetic effects operating for both males and females. Log-linear models were constructed using information about both the adoptive parents and the biological first-degree relatives. This information included information on whether or not the relative met criteria for antisocial personality or alcoholism. Results of the log-linear analyses revealed three main points. First, there was a demonstrated specificity of inheritance. The presence of biological first-degree relatives with antisocial problems did not increase the risk for alcohol abuse in either men or women. Second, environmental factors were found to contribute to risk. Adoptees reared with parents who abused alcohol had a greater risk of becoming alcoholic. Third, the model that predicted alcohol abuse in men appeared to fit that for women, and demonstrated that genetic effects were operating in female alcohol abuse.

In conclusion, the adoption studies do not give a definitive answer to the question of whether or not the etiology of alcoholism is mediated by genetic factors that contribute a significant proportion of variance. This is due largely to the extremely small number of cases of alcoholism among female adoptees, whether or not they are from high- or low-risk parents (Bohman, Sigvardsson, & Cloninger, 1981; Goodwin, Schulsinger, Knop, Mednick, & Guze, 1977). Cadoret, O'Gorman, Troughton, and Heywood (1985) employed a reasonable sample size and more sophisticated data analytic techniques, concluding that genetic factors operate in the etiology of alcoholism in both men and women.

Twin Studies

Some insights into the genetic aspects of alcoholism in women can be
gained from studies that have utilized adult female twin pairs. Although there are particular limitations to the twin data design, including the special environment that may be created by having a twin,
there are clear advantages to this design, including the ability to
control for cohort effects (both have the same age and social milieu).
Most of the twin studies have emphasized concordance of alcohol use
rather than alcohol dependence (Jonsson & Nilsson, 1968; Kaprio,
Koskenvuo, & Sarna, 1981; Partanen, Brunn, & Markkanen, 1966).
Moreover, all of these were concerned with male twin pairs.

One large scale study of twins was conducted in Australia which
included 1,690 pairs of female twins who used alcohol to some degree
(Heath, Jardine, & Martin, 1989). While this study was not specifically
concerned with concordance for alcoholism per se, concordance in
drinking habits was studied both among MZ and DZ twin pairs to
determine the percentage of variance in drinking that could be attributed to genetic factors. The highest degree of concordance was found
for unmarried twins, with 76% of the variance being accounted for by
genetic factors in the unmarried twins, versus 46% to 59% of the variance among married twins. Although married twins are influenced by
the drinking habits of their spouses, resulting in a reduction in similarity with their co-twin, the explained variation accounted for by
genetic factors is noteworthy. While these results suggest that sociodemographic variables greatly modify the impact of the inherited
liability, it also underscores the fact that there is little reason to
believe that genetic factors are less important for drinking in women
than they are in men.

While these results are intriguing, they do not speak to the issue of
heritability of alcoholism or alcohol dependence. The genetic factors
which might lead to the initiation of alcohol use and its maintenance
may be different than those which lead to alcohol dependence. There
are four twin samples that have been concerned with alcohol dependence among male twin pairs (Gurling, Murray, & Clifford, 1981;
Hrubec & Omenn, 1981; Kaij, 1960; McGue, Pickens, & Svikis, in
press; Pickens & Svikis, 1988; Pickens et al., 1991), which appear to
have obtained mixed results. Three showed the expected increase in
similarity in MZ twins over DZ twins, while one (Gurling et al., 1981)
did not. Only two of these investigations contained a sample of female
twins (see Table 3.2).

The Gurling, Murray, and Clifford (1981) study found similar pair-
wise concordance for MZ and DZ pairs within each gender: 33% and

Table 3.2.   Female Twin Studies of Alcohol Abuse and Alcohol Dependence

Authors	Males		Females	
	MZ	DZ	MZ	DZ
Gurling et al., 1981	33%	30%	8%	13%
Pickens et al., 1991	79%	44%	53%	17%
Kaij, 1960	71%	32%		
Hrubec and Omenn, 1981	26%	12%		

30%, respectively, for the males and 8% and 13% respectively, for the females. The samples were small, with only 35 male twin pairs and 21 female pairs in all. Pickens and Svikis (1988) reported on DZ and MZ pairs of twins (93 male and 46 female), finding higher concordance ratios (MZ:DZ) for male than female twin pairs (1.6:0.8, respectively). Moreover, the MZ:DZ ratio was statistically significant for the males but not the females, suggesting that at least in men a genetic component was operating in development of DSM-III defined Alcohol Abuse and Alcohol Dependence. Similar conclusions were drawn from this research group's more recent analysis of data (Pickens et al., 1991), which was based on a slightly enlarged sample (114 male and 55 female twin pairs). However, the more recent study also found evidence for moderate heritability in women.

Taken together, these three investigations (four separate samples) of female twins provide inconsistent results. On the one hand, concordance in MZ and DZ twins was found to be comparable for each gender, with MZ and DZ pairs approximately equal in the study reported by Gurling et al. (1981), suggesting no genetic variance operating for either men or women. On the other hand, one study (Pickens & Svikis, 1988) suggested a genetic mechanism operating for alcoholism in males but not females. In a later study (Pickens et al., 1991), alcohol dependence was found to be moderately heritable in both men and women. In summary, no definitive conclusions can be drawn regarding genetic mediation of alcoholism in women based on twin data alone. However, two of the three studies reviewed did not rule out the possibility of equal genetic mediation for men and women. Moreover, the one study that failed to find evidence for genetic mediation in women also failed to find evidence for genetic factors in men.

GENETIC HETEROGENEITY IN ALCOHOLISM
AMONG WOMEN

For some time there has been an attempt to describe more homogeneous subtypes of alcoholism (Horn & Wanberg, 1969; Jellinek, 1952)

based on the recognition that there is considerable variability in the alcoholic phenotype. In general, the clinical heterogeneity seen in common psychiatric disorders has proven to be a difficult problem in understanding the etiology of these disorders. Even when one can adequately define the phenotype by setting forth clear clinical criteria for the disorder to be studied (alcoholic or nonalcoholic), problems arise in searching for genetic factors relevant to the emergence of the phenotype. A single clinical phenotype may be the result of multiple genotypes. Alternatively, multiple phenotypes are possible that are the result of a single genotype. This phenomenon, known as pleiotropy, occurs commonly for many traits. In the case of alcoholism, one might speculate that the same genes are responsible both for male and female alcoholism, but the phenotypic variation is gender-specific. For example, alcoholism in men is more often seen with sociopathy accompanying it. This may be due to the fact that sociopathy is a relatively rare disorder in women, so the likelihood of it occurring with alcoholism is greatly reduced among women. This reduced rate of sociopathy in women, which leads to lower rates of comorbidity between alcoholism and sociopathy, will undoubtedly alter the symptom expression. Because of the lesser likelihood of sociopathic behavior, in general, it might be expected that women would show less sociopathic behavior while drinking than men. As one example, women might be less likely to exhibit behavior while drinking that gets them in trouble with the law (e.g., arrests for peace disturbance, fighting in bars). Because these symptoms are used in making a diagnosis of alcoholism using the Feighner Criteria (Feighner et al., 1972), a woman with alcoholism may be judged to be less severe than a man with a similar history.

Also, it is possible that symptoms which appear as a single phenotype may, in fact, be the merging of symptoms from two different psychiatric disorders, each with their own genetic underpinning. More than 20 years ago, Winokur, Reich, Rimmer, and Pitts (1970) suggested that the increased rate of depression seen among sisters of male alcoholic probands might be an example of the former situation. More recently, Cloninger, von Knorring, Sigvardsson, and Bohman (1986) have suggested that somatization disorder, which occurs both in men and women, is associated with an excess of biological fathers who are alcoholic in the case of female, but not male, somaticizers. Through the use of discriminate function analysis, they have demonstrated that there is both a genetic and environmental independence of somatization disorder in women and men. This gender-specific association between somatization disorder and alcoholism could be of either form: (a) a single genotype manifested as different phenotypic disorders (alcoholism or somatization disorder); or (b) multiple genotypes leading to similar phenotypic expression but conditioned by the gender of the individual. In summary, consideration of clinical and genetic heterogeneity in alcoholism has special relevance to the accurate diagnosis of alcoholism and appropriate treatment. This can best be achieved by considering the gender of the alcoholic individual for whom diagnosis and an appropriate treatment plan is being considered. Alcoholism is clearly not a homogeneous disorder in men, and certainly no less so in women.

Pittsburgh Family Study

A consideration of the data gleaned from a number of family history studies indicates that when one compares rates of alcoholism among first-degree relatives of male proband alcoholics and female proband alcoholics, the rates appear higher among relatives of the females than the males (McKenna & Pickens, 1981; Midanik, 1983). When rates of other psychiatric disorders are considered for proband male alcoholics, two disorders appear prominently in the discussions: depression and somataform disorder (Cloninger, von Knorring, Sigvardsson, & Bohman, 1986; Goodwin, Schulsinger, Knop, Mednick, & Guze, 1977; Sigvardsson, Bohman, von Knorring, & Cloninger, 1986). Modeling the genetic transmission of alcoholism has often included the assumption that observation of similar phenotypes across gender implies a common genotype. If this is so, rates of other specific psychiatric illnesses might be expected to be similar, controlling for the gender of the first-degree relative. If, on the other hand, the same biological entity (genotype) has variable expression by gender, then uncovering these differences would be important in terms of future modeling of transmission within families. Therefore, with the opportunity to assess rates of psychiatric illness in female relatives of male alcoholic probands, we began to compare the rates of psychiatric disorders in this sample with those seen in our control sample.

Ascertainment of families in Pittsburgh study. Families were selected for study if they contained at least two brothers who were alcoholic. Ascertainment of families through a pair of probands provided families with greater loading for the disorder than would have occurred if we had chosen families based on the presence of a single alcoholic proband.

The high-risk families were part of a larger family study of alcoholism initiated in 1984 (The Cognitive and Personality Factors Family Study [CPFS]—NIAAA - AA-005909) that includes multiple extended pedigrees with multigenerational alcoholism, largely uncontaminated by other psychopathology. The male probands included in this study were Caucasian, born in western Pennsylvania, and were predominantly residents of the Pittsburgh area. In order for a family to be included in the study, there had to be an absence of comorbidity in the parents and male first-degree relatives of the proband selected. Both the alcoholic proband and his alcoholic brother were required to meet Feighner et al. (1972) criteria for definite alcoholism and not meet DSM-III criteria for affective disorder, schizophrenia, or drug dependence before being included in the study. Similarly, the nonalcoholics in these families did not meet even probable Feighner Criteria for alcoholism. However, all were social drinkers. Female siblings also were interviewed and a variety of assessments performed. The diagnosis of the female siblings was free to vary (alcoholic or nonalcoholic), so long as other psychopathology was not found in the proband. In this way, the level of comorbidity within these families was reduced, and the density of alcoholic individuals increased.

Data also were analyzed for control probands who, along with their male first-degree relatives, were free of all psychiatric disorders including alcoholism (none met even probable Feighner Criteria for alcoholism). All subjects were interviewed directly by a trained clinician and assessed for absence of Axis I psychiatric disorders.

Clinical assessment. The clinical assessment included administration of a comprehensive diagnostic interview that included questions needed to meet both Feighner et al. (1972) and DSM-III criteria for major psychiatric disorders. The clinical assessment also included a battery of psychological tests including both personality dimensions and cognitive functioning. A brief summary of our findings to date are presented here because of their relevance to the preceding theoretical discussion. Data were analyzed from the diagnostic interviews conducted with 51 sisters (26 high-risk and 25 low-risk) from the CPFS pedigrees that had been selected through a pair of proband alcoholic brothers. The evaluations of these sisters of men who were selected because of their membership in either the control or alcoholic families included administration of the Premenstrual Assessment Form (PAF). This instrument was developed by Endicott, Nee, Cohen, and Halbreich (1986) and was used with a subsample of the women receiving the clinical interviews.

We chose to look at the prevalence of psychiatric disorders in the sisters, along with accompanying premenstrual conditions, as a way of determining whether or not the sisters of male alcoholic probands were showing elevated rates of dysfunction. In order to determine if the rates of depression and anxiety were higher among the female siblings of our male alcoholic probands, we completed a consensus diagnosis which was based on evaluations of two clinicians using DSM-III and Feighner Criteria. As shown in Table 3.3, the rate of depression in the

Table 3.3. Frequency of Depression, Anxiety Disorder
and Alcoholism in Sisters of Male Alcoholic Probands

	High-Risk N = 26	Low-Risk N = 25
Alcoholism	4*	2
Depression	10	10
Anxiety	3	1
No Diagnosis	12	12

*Diagnosis Count–Some individuals made criteria for more than one disorder.
Alcoholism: $X^2 = 0.15$, df = 1, $p = 0.70$
Depression: $X^2 = 0.03$, df = 1, $p = 0.86$
Anxiety Disorder: $X^2 = 0.23$, df = 1, $p = 0.23$

two groups was identical. Although none of the women studied would
meet criteria for recurrent depression (all had a single episode), there
was a significant number of women who had a lifetime diagnosis of
depression (two or more weeks of low mood accompanied by five or
more specific symptoms). The prevalence of anxiety disorders among
sisters from the affected families also appears higher. Obviously, too
few cases were available to come to any definitive conclusion. Additionally, there was twice as much alcoholism among these sisters from
the affected families than there was in the control group. Finally, these
results suggest that when male alcoholic probands are selected for
absence of affective disorder in themselves and their male first-degree
relatives, the risk for depression in sisters is no higher than in the
general population. However, the male alcoholic probands were at exceptionally high risk for developing alcoholism based on the early
onset of the disorder observed, coupled with the presence of multiple
relatives similarly affected (Aston & Hill, 1990; Hill, in press). These
results suggest that there is an underlying liability for alcoholism that
is expressed in both genders which is most clearly observed in families
exhibiting a severe form of alcoholism characterized by a high density
of alcoholism.

Cloninger, von Knorring, Sigvardsson, and Bohman (1986) have
pointed to the increased prevalence of somataform disorder among
female relatives of alcoholic males. The present series of female subjects were sisters of male alcoholics who were part of the CPFS pedigrees. Therefore, it was of interest to determine if sisters in our series
had higher rates of somataform disorder. Reproductive and endocrinological changes have been reported to be prominent features of
the somataform disorders (Cloninger, von Knorring, Sigvardsson, &
Bohman, 1986; Cohen, Robins, Purtell, Altmann, & Reid, 1953).
Therefore, an assessment of premenstrual changes was completed for

the two groups, to determine if women who were from high-risk families were afflicted by greater premenstrual difficulties. As may be seen in Table 3.4, six symptoms of a total of 53 symptoms tested from the Premenstrual Assessment Form were found to be significantly different. However, adjustment by Bonferroni correction resulted in only one symptom, "less desire to talk," distinguishing the high- and low-risk women. This indicates that, on the whole, the high-risk women were no more likely to report somatic complaints related to their menstrual cycles than the low-risk women, though there was a tendency for the high-risk women to show increased social withdrawal during the premenstrual phase of their cycles. The women in the present investigation were not evaluated specifically for the presence of somataform disorder as it is currently defined in DSM-III-R. However, we expected that rates of premenstrual problems among sisters of male alcoholics might be higher than among sisters of male controls, but they were not.

In summary, the sisters of male proband alcoholics from these high-density, high-risk families appear to be at greater risk for developing alcoholism, but are not at higher risk for developing depressive disorders or somataform complaints. This may be due to the ascertainment strategy that was used to acquire these families, namely, a strategy that reduced the variability by excluding families in which affective disorder appeared to be segregating. Further, it suggests that the earlier results by the St. Louis group, indicating a higher rate of depression among sisters of male alcoholics, may have been due to the fact that the families ascertained in St. Louis could have had higher rates of comorbidity for these two disorders than was allowed in our present series.

Some comment is in order regarding the failure to find increased somatization among the sisters of these male proband alcoholics. First, the sample ascertained in Sweden by Cloninger et al. (1986) was rampant with sociopathy. Moreover, previous reports of assortative mating

Table 3.4. Comparison of the Frequency of Premenstrual Assessment Form Endorsements by Family Type (Affected or Control)

Variable	Chi-Square Value	DF	P
Insecure	6.71	2	.035
Depressed	7.15	2	.028
Less Desire to Talk	8.10	1	.004
Feel Under Stress	6.52	2	.038
Bites Fingernails	4.23	1	.040
Lacks Inspiration	4.05	1	.044

between sociopathy in men and Briquet's Syndrome in women (Guze, Woodruff, & Clayton, 1971) would also tend to elevate rates of somataform disorder among female relatives of alcoholics having sociopathy as well. Therefore, if one assumes that the rate of sociopathy seen in the sample studied by Cloninger and colleagues (Bohman et al., 1981; Cloninger et al., 1981; Cloninger et al., 1986) exceeds the population values, as surely it did, then it would be expected that somatization would occur at a higher rate among the female relatives as well. Unlike the Swedish adoption sample, the Pittsburgh pedigree series has been ascertained with the absence of other psychopathology, though sociopathy was free to vary. Although the ascertainment strategy allowed sociopathy to be free to vary, it should be noted that the majority of subjects came from intact families. This may have been due to the ascertainment strategy used which required that there be three or more siblings available for the study. The fact that the families remained intact tended to mitigate against selection of families with excessive sociopathy.

In conclusion, female alcoholism is a heterogeneous disorder with both early and late onset subtypes. Much of the confusion surrounding whether or not there is a single genotype expressed as multiple phenotypes, particularly across gender, or whether there are, indeed, different genotypes producing these disorders, is largely the result of different ascertainment strategies being utilized by different research groups. If one does not take steps to reduce the comorbidity within a sample of families collected, then the rate of psychiatric disorder in first-degree relatives, whether they be of the same or different gender, will be similarly affected. At this point in time, it would be premature to conclude that alcoholism in women is any less influenced by genetic factors than it is in men. Further work is needed with samples of families of female probands to uncover those factors which may be operating in the development of alcoholism in women that may be genetically mediated.

REFERENCES

Aston, C.E., & Hill, S.Y. (1990). Segregation analysis of alcoholism in families ascertained through a pair of male alcoholics. *American Journal of Human Genetics, 46,* 879–887.

Bohman, M., Sigvardsson, S., & Cloninger, C.R. (1981). Maternal inheritance of alcohol abuse: Cross-fostering analysis of adopted women. *Archives of General Psychiatry, 38,* 965–969.

Cadoret, R.J., O'Gorman, T.W., Troughton, E., & Heywood, E. (1985). Alcoholism and antisocial personality: Interrelationships, genetic and environmental factors. *Archives of General Psychiatry, 42,* 161–167.

Cloninger, C.R., Bohman, M., & Sigvardsson, S. (1981). Inheritance of alcohol abuse: Cross-fostering analysis of adopted men. *Archives of General Psychiatry, 38,* 861–868.

Cloninger, C.R., Christiansen, K.O., Reich, T., & Gottesman, I.I. (1978). Implication of sex differences in the prevalences of antisocial personality, alcoholism, and criminality for familial transmission. *Archives of General Psychiatry, 35,* 941–951.

Cloninger, C.R., von Knorring, A-L, Sigvardsson, S., & Bohman, M. (1986). Symptom patterns and causes of somatization in men: II. Genetic and environmental independence from somatization in women. *Genetic Epidemiology, 3,* 171–185.

Cohen, M.E., Robins, E., Purtell, J.J., Altmann, M.W., & Reid, D.E. (1953). Excessive surgery in hysteria. *Journal of the American Medical Association, 151,* 977–986.

Endicott, J., Nee, J., Cohen, J., & Halbreich, U. (1986). Premenstrual Changes: Patterns and correlates of daily ratings. *Journal of Affective Disorders, 10,* 127–135.

Falconer, D.S. (1965). The inheritance to certain diseases, estimated from the incidence among relatives. *Annals of Human Genetics, 29,* 51–76.

Feighner, J.P., Robins, E., Guze, S.B., Woodruff, R., Winokur, G., & Munoz, R. (1972). Diagnostic criteria for use in psychiatry research. *Archives of General Psychiatry, 26,* 57–63.

Gilligan, S.B., Reich, T., & Cloninger, C.R. (1987). Etiologic heterogeneity in alcoholism. *Genetic Epidemiology, 4,* 395–414.

Glenn, S.W., & Nixon, S.J. (1991). Applications of Cloninger's subtypes in a female alcoholic sample. *Alcoholism: Clinical and Experimental Research, 15,* 851–857.

Goodwin, D.W., Schulsinger, F., Knop, J., Mednick, S., & Guze, S.B. (1977). Alcoholism and depression in adopted-out daughters of alcoholics. *Archives of General Psychiatry, 34,* 751–755.

Gurling, H.M.D., Murray, R.M., & Clifford, C.A. (1981). Investigations into the genetics of alcohol dependence and into its effects on brain function. In L. Gedda, P. Parisi, & W.E. Nance (Eds.), *Twin research 3: Epidemiological and clinical studies.* New York: Alan R. Liss.

Guze, S.B., Wofgram, E., & McKinney, J. (1967). Psychiatric illness in the families of convicted criminals: A study of 519 first-degree relatives. *Diseases of the Nervous System, 28,* 651–659.

Guze, S.B., Woodruff, R.A., Jr., & Clayton, P.J. (1971). Hysteria and antisocial behavior: Further evidence of an association. *American Journal of Psychiatry, 127,* 957–960.

Heath, A.C., Jardine, R., & Martin, N.G. (1989). Interactive effects of genotype and social environment on alcohol consumption in female twins. *Journal of Studies on Alcohol, 50,* 38–48.

Hill, S.Y. (1981). A vulnerability model for alcoholism in women. Focus on Women. *Journal of Addictions and Health, 2,* 68–91.

Hill, S.Y. (1992). Absence of paternal sociopathy in the etiology of severe alcoholism: Is there a type III alcoholism? *Journal of Studies on Alcohol, 53,* 161–169.

Horn, J.L., & Wanberg, K.W. (1969). Symptom patterns related to excessive use of alcohol. *Quarterly Journal of Studies on Alcohol, 30,* 35–58.

Hrubec, Z., & Omenn, G.S. (1981). Evidence of genetic predisposition to alcoholic cirrhosis and psychosis: Twin concordances for alcoholism and its biological end points by zygosity among male veterans. *Alcoholism: Clinical and Experimental Research, 5,* 207–215.

Jellinek, E.M. (1952). Phases of alcohol addiction. *Quarterly Journal of Studies on Alcohol, 13,* 573–584.

Jonsson, E., & Nilsson, T. (1968). Alcoholkonsumtion hos monozygota och dizygota tvillinpar (Alcohol consumption in monozygotic and dizygotic pairs of twins). *Nordsk Hygienisk Tidskrift, 49,* 21–25.

Kaij, L. (1960). Studies on the etiology and sequels of abuse of alcohol. In Almquist & Wiksell (Eds.), *Alcoholism in twins.* Stockholm, Sweden: University of Lund.

Kaprio, J., Koskenvuo, M., & Sarna, S. (1981). Cigarette smoking, use of alcohol, and leisure-time physical activity among same-sexed adult male twins. In L. Gedda, P. Parisi, & W.E. Nance (Eds.), *Twin research 3: Epidemiological and clinical studies.* New York: Alan R. Liss.

Lex, B.W., Sholar, J.W., Bower, T., & Mendelson, J.H. (1991). Putative type II alcoholism characteristics in female third DUI offenders in Massachusetts: A pilot study. *Alcohol, 8,* 283–287.

McGue, M., Pickens, R.W., & Svikis, D.S. (in press). Sex and age effects on the inheritance of alcohol problems: A twin study. *Journal of Abnormal Psychology.*

McKenna, T., & Pickens, R. (1981). Alcoholic children of alcoholics. *Journal of Studies on Alcohol, 42,* 1021–1029.

Midanik, L. (1983). Familial alcoholism and problem drinking in a national drinking practices survey. *Addictive Behaviors, 8,* 133–141.

Murray, R.M., Clifford, C.A., & Gurling, H.M.D. (1983). Twin and adoption studies: How good is the evidence for genetic role? In M. Galliter (Ed.), *Recent developments in alcoholism, Vol. I. Genetics, behavioral treatment, social mediators and prevention: Current concepts in diagnosis.* New York: Plenum Press.

Myers, J.K., Weissman, M.M., Tischler, G.L., Holzer, C.E., Leaf, P.J., Orvaschel, H., Anthony J.C., Boyd, J.H., Burke, J.D., Kramer, M., & Stoltzman, R. (1984). Six-month prevalence of psychiatric disorders in three communities. *Archives of General Psychiatry, 41,* 959–967.

Partanen, J., Brunn, K., & Markkanen, T. (1966). *Inheritance of drinking behavior.* Helsinki: The Finnish Foundation for Alcohol Studies.

Peele, S. (1986). Implications and limitations of genetic models of alcoholism and other addictions. *General Studies on Alcohol, 47,* 63–73.

Pickens, R.W., & Svikis, D.S. (1988). The twin method in the study of vulnerability to drug abuse. In *Biological vulnerability to drug abuse* (Research Monograph Vol. 89, pp. 41–51).

Pickens, R.W., Svikis, D.S., McGue, M., Lykken, D.T., Heston, L.L., & Clayton, P.J. (1991). Heterogeneity in the inheritance of alcoholism: A study of male and female twins. *Archives of General Psychiatry, 48,* 19–28.

Reich, T., Cloninger, C.R., VanEerdewegh, P., Reiss, J.P., & Mullaney, J. (1988). Secular trends in familial transmission of alcoholism. *Alcoholism: Clinical and Experimental Research, 12,* 458–464.

Robins, L.N., Helzer, J., Weissman, M.N., Orvaschel, H., Gruenberg, E., Burke, J.D., & Reiger, D.A. (1984). Lifetime prevalence of specific psychiatric disorders in three sites. *Archives of General Psychiatry, 41,* 949–958.

Schuckit, M., Pitts, F.N., Reich, T., King, L.J., & Winokur, G. (1969). Alcoholism. *Archives of General Psychiatry, 20,* 301–306.

Sigvardsson, S., Bohman, M., von Knorring, A-L, & Cloninger, C.R. (1986). Symptom patterns and causes of somatization in men: I. Differentiation of two discrete disorders. *Genetic Epidemiology, 3,* 153–169.

Wilsnack, R.W., Wilsnack, S.C., & Klassen, A.D. (1984). Women's drinking and drinking problems: Patterns from a 1981 national survey. *American Journal of Public Health, 74,* 1231–1238.

Winokur, G., Reich, T., Rimmer, J., & Pitts, F.N. (1970). Alcoholism III: Diagnosis and familial psychiatric illness in 259 alcoholic probands. *Archives of General Psychiatry, 23,* 104–111.

Chapter 4

Epidemiological Research on Women's Drinking: Recent Progress and Directions for the 1990s*

Sharon C. Wilsnack, Ph.D.
Richard W. Wilsnack, Ph.D.

Department of Neuroscience
University of North Dakota School of Medicine

The epidemiology of women's drinking has been the subject of considerable scientific and popular interest in the past two decades. A particular focus of this interest has been the question of whether drinking
and/or drinking problems in women are increasing. It is not uncom-

* This chapter is updated and adapted from "Epidemiology of Women's Drinking" by
Sharon C. Wilsnack and Richard W. Wilsnack, 1991, *Journal of Substance Abuse, 3,*
133–157. The 1981, 1986, and 1991 national surveys of women's drinking reported in
this chapter were supported by Research Grant #AA04610 from the National Institute
on Alcohol Abuse and Alcoholism.

mon, even today, to find statements in both scholarly articles and popular media to the effect that alcohol problems in women are increasing dramatically and that female and male problem-drinking rates are "converging," despite the lack of empirical support for either of these ideas (Berkowitz & Perkins, 1987; Fillmore, 1984; Wilsnack, Wilsnack, & Klassen, 1986). This chapter provides an overview of epidemiological research conducted during the past 10 years. We highlight major findings of this research and suggest directions for future work. Because of length limitations, our review is selective, focusing primarily on adult women (rather than female adolescents or college students) and omitting such special topics as epidemiological studies of alcoholic women in treatment, surveys of drug use other than alcohol, and surveys of health consequences of women's drinking.

GENDER DIFFERENCES IN DRINKING LEVELS

Hilton (1988a) compared levels of alcohol consumption for women and men in 11 U.S. national surveys conducted between 1964 and 1984. For the most part, drinking patterns over the 20-year period were stable. Although the abstention rate for women was significantly lower (36%) in 1984 than in previous surveys (where it ranged from 39% to 47%), in all age groups men were still considerably more likely than women to be drinkers and to drink heavily.

More recent surveys, including the 1985–1991 National Household Surveys on Drug Abuse (e.g., National Institute on Drug Abuse, 1991; Robbins, 1989) and the 1989 Canadian National Alcohol and Other Drugs Survey (Health & Welfare Canada, 1990), also found that men in all age and ethnicity categories exceeded women in levels of alcohol use. Adjustment for male–female differences in body weight and total body water reduced but did not eliminate males' higher rates of heavier drinking among respondents in the 1988 National Health Interview Survey (Dawson & Archer, 1992); the excess of male heavier drinkers was greatest at the highest levels of consumption. Although these later surveys used different measures than the 11 surveys compared by Hilton, the studies taken as a whole contain no consistent evidence of convergence in female and male rates of drinking or heavier drinking across the 25-year period represented.

These findings from the United States and Canada are consistent with findings from an international collaborative research project that conducted meta-analyses of data from 38 longitudinal general population surveys from 16 different countries (Fillmore et al., 1991). In almost every age group and country represented, female drinkers drank less frequently and consumed smaller amounts per occasion than male drinkers. One exception was that late adolescent *drinking* girls in central Europe and in the United States drank more frequently than their male counterparts, possibly because such girls are likely to have older male partners who drink more heavily.

Despite the general pattern of stability of drinking levels between 1964 and 1984, Hilton (1988a) found changes within certain *age groups* of women. For example, there were increases in light drinking (less than 0.22 ounces ethanol per day) among young women aged 18–20, and in drinking (nonabstention) among women aged 50–64. There was also a modest but statistically significant increase in *heavy* drinking among both female and male respondents aged 21–34. Between 1964 and 1984, the proportion of 21–34-year-old women who reported drinking 60 or more drinks per month increased from 4% to 7% (from 15% to 23% for men); women in this age group who reported drinking five or more drinks on a drinking occasion at least once a week increased from 3% to 8% (from 19% to 31% among men). Despite the increase in young women's drinking, Hilton's findings do not demonstrate male-female "convergence": Rates of heavy drinking increased for *both* young women *and* young men, and a gender gap remained.

Recent findings by Williams and Debakey (1992) suggest a possible shift toward increased abstention and decreased heavy drinking in the *later* 1980s. Using data from the 1983 and 1988 National Health Interview Surveys, these authors found significant increases in abstention and/or decreases in heavy drinking among both women and men in a number of population subgroups defined by gender and selected demographic characteristics. Female subgroups showing one or both of these changes included all age groups, black women, white women, better-educated and higher-income women, and employed, never-married, and divorced/separated women. Williams and Debakey used slightly different measures and definitions of drinking levels than Hilton, and thus the 1983 and 1988 surveys cannot be simply appended to the series of 11 surveys discussed earlier. In addition, the 1983 survey had unusually *high* levels of drinking (nonabstention) compared to the 1981 and 1984 surveys in Hilton's series, for reasons that are not clear (Debakey & Williams, personal communication, 1992). Nonetheless, their findings are consistent with other data (including estimates of per capita consumption based on alcohol sales (e.g., National Institute on Alcohol Abuse and Alcoholism, 1993)) that suggest a trend toward declining alcohol consumption since the early 1980s.

Studies of young adults in the late 1980s have not consistently supported the pattern reported by Hilton of increased heavy drinking among 21–34-year-old women and men. For example, the annual surveys of high school seniors, college students, and noncollege young adults aged 19–30 conducted for the National Institute on Drug Abuse found a stabilization or decline in most drinking measures for both women and men between 1980 and the late 1980s (e.g., Johnston, O'Malley, & Bachman, 1989). To the extent that the prevalence of alcohol and other drug use among late adolescents and young adults peaked at the end of the 1970s, Hilton's comparison of 1964 and the early 1970s with the early 1980s might have missed a leveling off or downturn of high-risk drinking in younger cohorts. Wechsler and Isaac (1992) report that intoxication and drinking to get drunk were more common among both female and male college students in 1989 than in 1977, but this contrast may have been affected by multiple differences between their two regional samples. Additional data points from future national surveys are needed to determine whether heavy or hazardous drinking is increasing among young women as suggested by Hilton's findings and by Wechsler and Isaac, or stabilizing or declining as suggested by Williams and Debakey and others.

GENDER DIFFERENCES IN DRINKING PROBLEMS

As in earlier surveys, men in general population surveys in the 1980s reported higher levels of drinking-related problems than did women, again with little evidence of convergence between genders (Clark & Hilton, 1991; Health & Welfare Canada, 1990; Hilton, 1988b).

Although men in the 1985 National Household Survey on Drug Abuse were more likely than women to report each of 17 psychosocial problems related to alcohol or drug use, the *types* of problems most strongly related to substance use differed for women as compared with men (Robbins, 1989). Women were more likely to report alcohol- and drug-related psychological problems (e.g., becoming depressed or losing interest in things) whereas men were more likely to report problems of social functioning (e.g., job or school problems, impaired driving, or problems with police). Robbins interpreted these differences in terms of feminine and masculine "styles of deviance," with women being more likely to internalize distress and men being more likely to express deviance outwardly. Robbins' interpretation is consistent with recent findings by Perkins (1992): In four surveys conducted at the same liberal arts college between 1979 and 1989, male students considerably exceeded female students on rates of drinking problems that were more public and that involved legal repercussions or damage to others (e.g., fighting, impaired driving, property damage, and offensive behavior), while gender differences were small or nonexistent on less public problems that involved damage to relationships or to oneself (e.g., unintended sexual activity, damaged friendships, or physical injury to self). A relatively stronger intrapsychic component of alcohol problems among women also may explain a gender difference in the 1989 Canadian National Survey (Health & Welfare Canada, 1990): The only drinking-related problem on which women who had consumed any alcohol in the week before the survey exceeded their male counterparts (consistently across three levels of consumption) was self-reports that the respondent's alcohol consumption had caused problems with her "outlook on life."

One reason for the higher rates of drinking problems among men is clearly the higher rate of heavier drinking among men, with three to five times as many men as women being classified as heavy drinkers in most drinking surveys. Among persons with the same high level of consumption, however, women may experience as many or more problem consequences as men (Clark & Midanik, 1982; Knupfer, 1982). For example, in our 1981 national survey of 917 women and 396 men, men exceeded women in rates of all drinking problems (Wilsnack, Wilsnack, & Klassen, 1986). However, among drinkers at the highest level of alcohol consumption (2 or more ounces of ethanol per day), women equalled or exceeded men on a number of drinking problems. The three problems reported *more* often by the heaviest drinking women than by the heaviest drinking men were starting fights with a spouse, starting fights with someone outside the family, and drinking-related problems with children. A similar finding was reported from the 1985 National Household Survey on Drug Abuse, in which women were significantly more likely to report drinking-related arguments and fights than would have been predicted from their level of alcohol use (Robbins, 1989). Heavy drinking may allow women to express anger that is typically suppressed. Furthermore, women's heavy drinking is likely to occur in the context of heavy drinking by companions, especially husbands or partners, who may be unusually likely to provoke or participate in drinking-related fights.

In the same analyses of the 1981 survey data, we were surprised by the relatively low rates of several problem consequences thought to be particularly relevant to women. For example, only 3% of female drinkers (and only 20% of the heaviest drinking women) reported that drinking had interfered with their housework or chores. Even lower proportions reported drinking-related accidents in the home or drinking-related problems with children. Interestingly, a number of *men* also acknowledged these "women-specific" drinking problems.

It is possible that even surveys designed to be sensitive to women's drinking behavior have not yet adequately covered the full range of drinking-related problems experienced by women, particularly problems experienced by women in nontraditional roles. This possibility is presently being explored in a study employing both ethnographic and survey methods. Based on a comprehensive review of the literature on women and alcohol, a review of existing survey measures, interviews with specialists in the field, and in-depth interviews with 65 women in treatment, Ames and colleagues (Klee, Schmidt, & Ames, 1991; Schmidt, Klee, & Ames, 1990) identified a set of "novel indicators" of women's alcohol problems that do not appear in standard clinical or survey instruments. These indicators—among them lethargy or fatigue, frequent illness, neglect or deterioration of general appearance, and various forms of "excessive behavior"—were included in a 1991 county survey in California, where their success in identifying early-stage problem drinking in women can be compared with that of more established survey questions. Results may help identify drinking-related problems that can be added to existing instruments to maximize their coverage of women's alcohol problems.

ALCOHOL ABUSE AND ALCOHOL DEPENDENCE

Moving from individual drinking-related problems to clusters of problems and symptoms diagnosed clinically as alcohol abuse and alcohol dependence, surveys of drinkers in the general population continue to find that more men than women meet diagnostic criteria for these alcohol disorders. However, the *magnitude* of the male–female ratio varies considerably across studies. Williams, Grant, Harford, and Noble (1989) used data from a 1984 national survey conducted by the Alcohol Research Group to approximate DSM-III criteria for alcohol abuse and dependence. The prevalence of alcohol abuse and dependence in males 18 and older was estimated to be 12.47%. The prevalence in females 18 and older was 5.11%, a male-female ratio of 2.4 to 1. Applying DSM-III-*R* criteria to data from the 1988 National Health Interview Survey, Grant et al. (1991) estimated that 13.35% of males and 4.36% of females 18 and older met diagnostic criteria for alcohol abuse or dependence, a male-female ratio of 3.1 to 1.

Male-female ratios were considerably higher than 2 or 3 to 1 in the five sites of the Epidemiological Catchment Area (ECA) study (Myers et al., 1984; Robins, Helzer, Przybeck, & Regier, 1988). Male–female ratios ranged from 4:1 to 8:1 for the total sample of men and women, and showed considerable variation by age, with the lowest gender ratios in the youngest age groups. Reasons for the higher male-female ratios in the ECA surveys than in the 1984 and 1988 U.S. national surveys are not completely clear. In part, the high ratios may reflect a masculine bias in some of the interview questions, for example, using very high cut points for defining pathological drinking, or including many drinking problems more characteristic of men (e.g., legal difficulties). Additionally, the ECA surveys were conducted in only five geographic sites, and findings may not be broadly representative of the total U.S. population.

ARE ALCOHOL DISORDERS INCREASING?

Cross-Sectional Studies

Several types of evidence reported in the 1980s were interpreted as suggesting that alcohol disorders may be becoming more prevalent in the U.S. general population, particularly among younger persons. In all five ECA sites, for example, persons under age 45 reported higher lifetime rates of alcohol abuse/dependence than did older persons, despite the fact that younger persons had had less time to develop alcohol problems (Robins et al., 1988). In four of the five sites, these age differences were most pronounced in women, leading Robins to suggest that alcohol disorders "may be rising particularly rapidly for women" (p. 18). Reich, Cloninger, van Eerdewegh, Rice, and Mullaney (1988) found similar patterns in the first-degree relatives of St. Louis-area alcoholics, among whom younger cohorts reported higher lifetime rates of alcoholism and earlier ages of onset than did older cohorts, with these differences again more pronounced in female than in male relatives. Finally, Grant et al. (1991) found that rates of alcohol abuse and dependence in the 1988 National Health Interview Survey were highest—and male to female ratios were lowest—in the youngest age groups. Although alternative explanations are possible (see below), these patterns could be interpreted as suggesting increased prevalence of alcohol disorders among younger persons, particularly younger women.

Time Trends

Other evidence that may suggest increasing prevalence of alcohol disorders comes from comparisons of several cross-sectional surveys over time. Mulford and Fitzgerald (1988) found "upward trends" in most alcohol problems across three surveys in Iowa between 1961 and 1985. Our U.S. national survey in 1981 found that both women and men reported higher rates of alcohol dependence symptoms in 1981 than in four previous surveys conducted between 1973 and 1979 (Wilsnack, Wilsnack, & Klassen, 1986). Comparing U.S. national surveys conducted in 1979 and 1984, Hilton (1988b) found an increase in alcohol dependence symptoms reported by men but not by women.

Hasin, Grant, Harford, Hilton, and Endicott (1990) compared rates of 11 drinking problems and alcohol dependence symptoms in four national surveys between 1967 and 1984. The investigators found substantial upward trends in both the lifetime and current prevalence of experiencing three or more alcohol problems. These trends were present for both women and men, although the lower rate of problems among women reduced the statistical significance of some of the patterns among women.

What can we conclude about recent time trends in drinking problems among women? There does appear to be evidence from a number of sources that younger persons—both female and male—are reporting higher lifetime prevalence of alcohol disorders than are older persons, and that respondents in surveys through the mid-1980s were more likely to report drinking-related problems than respondents in surveys two decades earlier. Reasons for these findings may be partly methodological. In cross-sectional studies, differential mortality may be involved (alcoholics dying at earlier ages and thus being underrepresented in the older samples), and older respondents may be less likely than younger ones to recall or report alcohol problems. In this regard, however, Robins et al. (1988) noted that the higher prevalence of alcoholism in younger persons is observed in whites more often than in blacks (similar age x ethnicity patterns were present in the 1988 NHIS; Grant et al., 1991), and there is no reason to think that biases in recall or reporting would operate differently for blacks as compared with whites.

Other possible explanations include increased recognition of alcohol problems, and greater willingness to report them, perhaps reflecting the effects of public education campaigns in recent years. Increased rates of drinking problems also may reflect a harsher *social reaction* to, and decreased social tolerance for, heavy drinking or intoxicated behavior. This view receives some support from Hilton's (1988b) finding that social attitudes toward alcohol became less permissive between 1979 and 1984, especially among the youngest respondents, and from Room's (1989) finding of a 50% increase between 1979 and 1987/1988 in northern California respondents' reports that others have ever said anything (critical) about their drinking. Some writers (e.g., Hammer &

Vaglum, 1989) have suggested that broader social changes, such as changes in women's employment and in female and male roles, have contributed to an increased prevalence of alcohol problems. Here, it seems important to remember that the apparent increases are not specific to women (a gender gap still remains), and that several studies (e.g., Wilsnack & Cheloha, 1987) failed to find any simple relationship between women's drinking problems and their "liberation" from traditional female roles. One other possibly relevant social change is the increased availability of *other drugs* during the 1970s, contributing to increased rates of polysubstance abuse, especially among younger persons. Whatever reasons underlie the apparent increase in alcohol problems, it will clearly be important to continue to monitor rates of heavy drinking and drinking problems throughout the 1990s, with a particular focus on younger drinkers.

SUBGROUP VARIATIONS IN WOMEN'S DRINKING AND DRINKING PROBLEMS

Age

Cross-sectional surveys have found quite consistently that younger persons, both females and males, report higher rates of heavy drinking and drinking-related problems than do older persons. For example, in our 1981 national survey (Wilsnack, Wilsnack, & Klassen, 1984), women aged 21–34 were more likely than women in older age groups to report drinking problems, alcohol dependence symptoms, heavy episodic drinking (six or more drinks in a day), and intoxication. The younger women were *not* more likely than women aged 35–64 to report *heavier* consumption (1 ounce or more of ethanol per day). Their higher rates of drinking problems and dependence symptoms may relate to heavy episodic drinking. The young woman who drinks six or eight drinks on an occasion (e.g., at a weekend party) is likely to experience more negative social and behavioral consequences than the older woman who consumes the same number of drinks spaced over a period of several days. One such consequence is alcohol-impaired driving and alcohol-related crashes, which have shown striking increases among young women in recent years (Popkin, 1991). As in earlier studies, women aged 65 and older in the 1981 survey had substantially lower rates of drinking and adverse drinking consequences than women in any other age group.

Age-related patterns were quite similar in the 1984 national survey conducted by the Alcohol Research Group (Clark & Hilton, 1991;

Hilton, 1988a). Percentages of drinkers and heavy drinkers were highest in women aged 18–49 and decreased after age 50; rates of drinking-related problems followed the same general pattern. Like drinking levels and drinking-related problems, rates of alcohol abuse and dependence are also lower among women (and men) in older age groups. In the 1988 National Health Interview Survey (Grant et al., 1991), for example, DSM-III-R alcohol abuse and dependence were most common among women aged 18–29 (10.10%), with rates falling steadily across age groups to 0.37% in women aged 65 and older.

Unlike all measures of heavy drinking and adverse drinking consequences, which were lowest among women aged 60 and older, *daily drinking* in the 1984 national survey was as common in women aged 60 and over (5%) as in women aged 30–49, and more common than in women aged 18–29 (2%) and women aged 50–59 (3%). It appears that a pattern of daily light or moderate drinking, with few apparent problem consequences, is characteristic of a modest number of U.S. women aged 60 and older.

As in U.S. surveys, findings from the 1989 Canadian National Survey (Health & Welfare Canada, 1990) showed increasing rates of abstention with age, for both women and men. Among current drinkers, however, Canadian women aged 65 and older were the most likely of any age group (11%) to report drinking four or more times a week, paralleling U. S. findings that rates of frequent drinking do not decline with age among older women who drink.

Caution is needed in interpreting cross-sectional survey data, because differences between age groups may reflect a specific cohort effect rather than, or in addition to, the effects of aging. Indeed, persons presently over age 65 have had some unique historical experiences, including Prohibition and the Great Depression of the 1930s, which may have contributed to lower rates of drinking within the current elderly population (Gomberg, 1990). Two *longitudinal* studies that included women have produced conflicting findings. Gordon and Kannel (1983) failed to confirm a decrease in alcohol consumption with age among respondents in the Framingham study, where alcohol use in all age groups of drinkers increased between 1950 and 1970, and the proportion of women over 60 who consumed any alcohol increased slightly. In contrast, Adams, Garry, Rhyne, Hunt, and Goodwin (1990) found a significant decline between 1980 and 1987 in the percentage of healthy elderly persons who drink, although mean alcohol intake did not change over time among those elderly who continued to drink.

In meta-analyses of longitudinal data from the Collaborative Alcohol-Related Longitudinal Project, Fillmore et al. (1991) found that, *among drinkers* in the United States, women in their 60s drank as much per drinking occasion as women in their 20s. The meta-analyses also indicated that U.S. women drinkers drink more frequently after age 40 than before. Like the cross-sectional findings discussed earlier, these longitudinal patterns suggest that any age-related decline in drinking among U.S. women is primarily the result of women becoming abstainers, because those who continue to drink do not show much age-related moderation of drinking behavior. This conclusion is supported by two additional findings. Among women in the 1982–84 National Health and Nutrition Examination Survey Followup Study (Colliver, Grigson, Barbano, Dufour, & Malin, 1989), abstention increased with age, but heavy drinking did not decrease among older women who drank. Interestingly, older white women who drank showed a slight increase in consumption, while older black women drinkers drank somewhat less. In Williams and Debakey's (1992) comparisons of 1983 and 1988 national data, women aged 65 and older had higher rates of abstention in 1988 than in 1983, but heavy drinking did not decrease among women drinkers in this age group. The latter finding suggests that whatever historical or cohort effect may be contributing to increased abstention among older women is not simultaneously reducing the likelihood that older women drinkers will drink heavily.

We recently analyzed 5-year changes in problem-drinking indicators (heavy consumption, drinking problems, and alcohol dependence symptoms) among two groups of women initially interviewed in 1981: 157 women who reported no problem-drinking indicators in 1981, and 143 women who reported at least two problem-drinking indicators in 1981 (Wilsnack, Klassen, Schur, & Wilsnack, 1991). Women in the youngest age group (21–34) were the most likely to develop signs of problem drinking over the 5-year period (27% of young women with no problem-drinking indicators in 1981 reported the onset of at least one indicator by 1986). Women in this age group were also the most likely to move *out* of problem drinking: Of 21–34-year-old women who reported at least two problem-drinking indicators in 1981, 38% reported no such indicators in 1986—significantly higher than rates of remission among women in older age groups. Younger women's greater movement both into and out of problem drinking may relate to changes in drinking contexts and drinking partners, as well as to transitions in employment, marriage, and parenthood common in this age group.

In the same longitudinal analyses, women aged 35–49 showed the greatest chronicity of problem drinking (i.e., were least likely of any age group to show remission of 1981 problem-drinking indicators), whereas women aged 50 and older were nearly as likely as women aged 21–34 to show reductions in drinking problems. Reductions in problem drinking among women aged 50 and older may relate to loss of a spouse and drinking partner, changes in drinking contexts accompanying retirement (own or husband's), and health-related reductions in alcohol consumption.

Because most data suggesting age-related declines in women's drinking are cross-sectional, and because cohort-specific historical influences may have reduced the drinking of the current generation of elderly persons, it will be particularly important to examine aging and cohort effects on women's drinking in *longitudinal* surveys wherever possible. We are presently addressing these issues with data from a 10-year follow-up of our full 1981 national female sample, which was conducted in the fall and winter of 1991.

Employment

Hazards or benefits of paid employment and multiple roles? The prevailing view about employment and women's drinking through the 1970s was that employment outside the home had negative effects on women's mental health and drinking behavior, particularly when combined with marital or family roles. Johnson's (1982) finding, from a 1975 national survey, that married women who were also employed outside the home had higher rates of heavier drinking and drinking problems than either single employed women or married women not employed outside the home, was widely cited in support of this view. Explanations for the increased drinking associated with employment and/or with multiple roles for women included stress-related interpretations involving role conflict (conflicting demands of work and family roles) and role overload (too much to do, whether or not roles conflict), as well as environmental explanations involving increased drinking opportunities and more permissive drinking norms outside the home.

The idea that paid employment is hazardous for women's drinking behavior was not consistently supported by surveys in the 1980s. Employed women in the 1989 Canadian National Survey (Health & Welfare Canada, 1990) were more likely to be drinkers than were women "keeping house." However, rates of drinking and heavier drinking among employed women varied considerably with the type of employment (e.g., managerial/professional vs. blue collar), suggesting that there was not a single, simple effect of employment per se (see later discussion of nontraditional employment).

In our 1981 U.S. national sample, women employed full time had slightly higher rates of heavier drinking and drinking problems than did full-time homemakers, but women employed *part time* were significantly higher than *both* groups on rates of drinking problems and alcohol dependence symptoms (Wilsnack, Wilsnack, & Klassen, 1986). In longitudinal analyses of 5-year followup data gathered in 1986 (Wilsnack & Wilsnack, 1992), among married women showing no signs of problem drinking in 1981, full-time employment in 1981 or in 1986 had no significant associations with 1986 drinking patterns. Among married women reporting at least two problem-drinking indicators in 1981, full-time employment in 1981 predicted significantly *lower* levels of alcohol dependence symptoms and lower scores on a problem-drinking index in 1986, and full-time employment in 1986 was associated with lower average consumption in 1986.

Findings such as these support a newer hypothesis that multiple roles, including paid employment, can be *beneficial* for women, in ways that may reduce their risks of physical or mental health problems (e.g., Adelmann, Antonucci, Crohan, & Coleman, 1989; Froberg, Gjerdingen, & Preston, 1986; Verbrugge, 1986). Consistent with this view, in our 1981 survey, employment was a part of age-specific configurations of social roles that were associated with lower risks of problem drinking (Wilsnack & Cheloha, 1987). Reasons for possible beneficial effects of employment and multiple roles may include the increased self-esteem and social support associated with meaningful employment roles, as well as increased performance demands and social monitoring that could discourage excessive alcohol consumption.

Nontraditional employment and women's drinking. The beneficial or adverse effects of employment on women's drinking may depend in part on the type of job a woman holds. Several recent studies, in different cultural settings, suggest that the gender balance of women and men in particular occupations may affect women's drinking and drinking-related problems. In analyses of our 1981 national survey data, we used 1980 U.S. Census data to estimate the percentages of female workers in each occupation reported by respondents (Wilsnack & Wright, 1991). We found that women employed in occupations that had more than 50% male workers had higher scores on a problem-drinking index (which summed intoxication, drinking problems, and alcohol dependence symptoms in the past 12 months) than did women in occupations with more than 50% female workers. There was no relationship between the gender balance of occupations and the drinking or drinking problems of *men* in our 1981 male comparison sample.

Employment in male-dominated occupations (e.g., banking, insurance, male-dominated industry) was associated with greater frequency of drinking among 3,997 Norwegian women in a 1985 national health survey (Hammer & Vaglum, 1989). Having a nontraditional occupation accounted for 3% of additional variance in women's drinking frequency after controlling for such possible explanatory variables as age, socioeconomic status, and full-time versus part-time employment status.

Employment in a nontraditional occupation also was associated with women's drinking in a 1987 community survey of 718 adult women residing in Prague, Czechoslovakia (Kubicka, Csemy, & Kozeny, 1991). In this interview study, masculinity of a respondent's occupation (as classified by the researchers, based on predominance of male employees) was significantly associated with women's frequency of wine and liquor consumption and with their total average daily consumption of all alcoholic beverages combined.

A 1987 study used mailed questionnaires to gather data on health practices of 545 U.S. women executives in high-ranking business and professional positions (LaRosa, 1990). Compared with employed women controls matched on age and education, the women executives were more likely to be drinkers (72% vs. 45%) and, among drinkers, to drink either moderately (39% vs. 27%) or heavily (3% vs. 0.6%). The executives studied reported excellent health and greater life satisfaction than the controls, and their overall wellness and health risk assessment scores were similar to those of the controls. Compared with the controls, the executive women exercised more regularly and were less likely to smoke or overeat.

Finally, Haavio-Mannila (1991) reported findings from a 1989 general population sample of more than 3,000 adult women in Helsinki. In this Finnish sample, there was a positive monotonic relationship between women's frequency of drinking and the gender composition of the respondent's workplace as measured by a 4-point scale: having *only women as colleagues, mostly women as colleagues, both women and men as colleagues, or mostly or only men as colleagues*. This relationship between gender composition of the workplace and frequency of drinking remained statistically significant when effects of respondents' education, socioeconomic status, and income were taken into account. In an earlier study by the same author, women in male-dominated occupations consumed more alcohol than women in traditional female occupations, but men in occupations dominated by women did not consume less alcohol than men in traditional male occupations (Haavio-Mannila, 1987).

The most common interpretations of relationships between nontraditional employment and heavier drinking by women involve peer influence and women's imitation of higher-status male drinking models, increased drinking opportunities in nontraditional settings, and specific stresses experienced by women in male-dominated work environments (which Haavio-Mannila terms "token stress"). However, the available studies have not directly measured these possible explanatory variables. One exception is Hammer and Vaglum's (1989) report that neither women's ratings of stress at work nor their self-reported feelings of nervousness were related to their alcohol consumption. LaRosa's (1990) findings that female executives, despite being more likely to drink and to drink heavily, were in good health and unlikely to engage in other negative stress-reduction activities such as smoking or overeating, also seem to contradict any simple job-stress interpretation.

Analyses of our own data on nontraditional employment suggest that traditionally feminine values and attitudes (which surprisingly did not differ between women who were employed in female-dominated occupations and those in male-dominated occupations) had considerably less effect on the drinking behavior of women in male-dominated occupations than those in female-dominated occupations (Wilsnack & Wright, 1991). It may be that predominantly male occupations have a *culture* or climate that weakens any influence of women's traditional gender-related values and attitudes (Bradley, 1989), with the result that women's drinking and its consequences are affected more by conditions that are not gender-specific (e.g., drinking opportunities or emotional distress) or that are associated with traditional masculine values.

The convergence of findings from four different countries suggests that linkages between nontraditional employment and women's drinking may be a particularly fruitful area for further research. One question is whether nontraditional employment increases women's risks of *problem* drinking (as seemed to be the case in our 1981 sample), or simply makes it more likely that they will drink or drink heavily. Studies that evaluate possible explanations for the influence of nontraditional work on women's drinking also would be valuable (e.g., the possibility that women engage in collegial, companionate drinking with male colleagues that increases the frequency of drinking but is not necessarily associated with adverse drinking consequences). Also worth exploring (though difficult to operationalize and measure) is the hypothesis that women in nontraditional occupations drink more, in part, as a symbolic expression of power and gender equality (Morrissey, 1986; Wilsnack, Klassen, & Wright, 1986).

Marital Status

Relationships between drinking behavior and marital status have been quite consistent across most U.S. surveys, with never-married and divorced or separated persons generally having the highest rates of heavier drinking and drinking problems, married persons intermediate, and widowed persons the lowest (e.g., Cahalan, Cisin, & Crossley, 1969; Clark & Midanik, 1982; Wilsnack et al., 1984). These simple bivariate relationships are confounded by age differences (never-married persons are more likely to be young; widowed persons to be older) and may differ in nonwhite populations (e.g., Darrow, Russell, Cooper, Mudar, & Frone, 1992; Taylor & Jackson, 1990b).

Cohabitation and women's drinking. One marital status category neglected in many surveys is cohabitation: living with a partner to whom one is not married. Some drinking surveys (e.g., the Alcohol Research Group's 1984 national survey) combined cohabiters with married respondents for purposes of data analysis, whereas others distributed them among the never-married, divorced/separated, or widowed categories as appropriate. When we analyzed cohabiting women as a separate category in the 1981 national survey, this group had the highest rate of drinking (100%) and heavier drinking (18%) of any marital status category, and among drinkers, cohabiting women exceeded all other marital status groups on rates of problem consequences, alcohol dependence symptoms, and intoxication (Wilsnack, Wilsnack, & Klassen, 1986).

In longitudinal analyses of the 1981 and 1986 surveys, 1981 nonproblem drinkers who were cohabiting in 1981 were significantly more likely than other nonproblem drinkers to report episodes of heavy episodic drinking in 1986, and 1981 nonproblem drinkers who began cohabiting between 1981 and 1986 reported higher average consumption, more intoxication, and higher scores on a problem-drinking index in 1986 than did other 1981 nonproblem drinkers (Wilsnack et al., 1991). We speculate that cohabiting may be associated with greater freedom from traditional moral constraints that have restricted both sexual behavior and drinking in women. In addition, some cohabiting relationships, lacking institutional protection or support, may involve uncertainties, stresses, and tensions which alcohol may seem to relieve. If cohabiters are particularly at risk for problem drinking, it would be wise for future surveys of drinking behavior to record and analyze these respondents as a separate group, distinct from married respondents.

Divorce and separation: Is the risk changing over time? Drinking surveys in the 1960s and 1970s typically found that divorced or separated women had higher rates of drinking, heavy drinking, and/ or adverse drinking consequences than did married or widowed women (Cahalan et al., 1969; Clark & Midanik, 1982; Johnson, 1982). In our 1981 national sample, rates of drinking-related problems and alcohol dependence symptoms were nearly twice as high among divorced and separated women drinkers as among married women drinkers (Wilsnack et al., 1984).

Two surveys in the mid- to late 1980s found what appear to be weaker relationships between divorce/separation and women's drinking than those reported in earlier surveys. Rates of heavier drinking and drinking problems among divorced or separated women in the 1984 national survey (Hilton, 1991) were quite similar to rates among married women, with both groups' rates lower than those for never-married women. Drinking patterns of divorced or separated men, on the other hand, continued to exceed those of married men and to resemble those of never-married men, as in earlier surveys. In the 1989 Canadian National Survey (Health & Welfare Canada, 1990), divorced women, separated women, and married women had virtually identical rates of drinking. Among drinkers, divorced women and separated women averaged a slightly higher number of drinks per week (2.6 for each group) than married women (1.8 drinks per week), but divorced women were also more likely to report having had *no* drinks in the 7 days prior to the survey (62%) than were separated women (54%) or married women (56%).

Because national drinking surveys have used different ways of classifying both drinking levels and marital status, it is difficult to make precise comparisons of relationships between divorce/separation and drinking over time. However, the possibility that divorce is less strongly associated with women's drinking now than in the past seems worth pursuing in future studies. If true, the weaker association might reflect some decline in the stigma of divorce for women, perhaps making this experience less stressful or less damaging to a woman's self-esteem and thus less of a risk factor for self-medicative drinking. Horwitz and White (1991) have offered a similar speculation to explain the absence of predicted differences in mental health and alcohol disorders between married and never-married young adults, that is, a possible recent cohort effect in which differences between single and married persons may have declined.

Divorce: Risk, remedy, or both? The associations between divorce and women's drinking discussed so far have been based on cross-sectional survey data, which are clearly inadequate for inferring time order. A number of temporal/causal sequences could produce positive cross-sectional associations between being divorced and drinking heavily, including the following: (a) a woman's heavy drinking precedes and increases the risks of divorce; (b) a woman begins or increases heavy drinking in response to the stress of an impending or completed divorce; and (c) some third factor (e.g., stress related to a dysfunctional marriage) increases the chances of both heavy drinking and divorce.

The few studies of drinking and marital dissolution that have used time-ordered data have produced mixed results. A macroeconomic analysis of U.S. divorce rates and alcohol consumption between 1933 and 1984 (Magura & Shapiro, 1988) concluded that divorce rates influence alcohol consumption but not the reverse, although the study's methodology did not permit gender-differentiated analyses. Using data from the National Longitudinal Study of Youth for the years 1982 through 1988, Hanna, Faden, and Harford (1993) found that women aged 24–32 who divorced or separated during the study interval showed increased drinking, while those who married or remarried showed decreased drinking. In contrast, a study using longitudinal data from a large British sample (Power & Estaugh, 1990) found that rates of partnership dissolution (including marriage and cohabitation) were higher among both female and male young adults who had been heavier drinkers at age 16, particularly if heavy drinking had been maintained between ages 16 and 23. Although drinking change and partnership dissolution could not be precisely time-ordered in this longitudinal study, the findings suggest a sequence in which heavy drinking contributes to relationship dissolution. Finally, using data from 1965 and 1974 surveys in Alameda County, California, Romelsjo, Lazarus, Kaplan, and Cohen (1991) found that among respondents whose drinking *increased* during the study period, divorce predicted a 32% increase in consumption for men and a 17% increase in consumption for women. Among respondents whose drinking *decreased* during the study period, being divorced in 1965 predicted a 19% decrease in drinking for women respondents aged 20-44 but did not affect the consumption of women aged 45 and older or men of any age.

We recently analyzed relationships between divorce/separation and drinking change in our U.S. national sample of women (Wilsnack et al., 1991). In multiple regression analyses of women reporting no problem-drinking indicators in 1981, neither being divorced or separated in 1981 nor becoming divorced or separated during the follow-up interval predicted the onset of problem-drinking indicators by 1986, although there were near-significant trends for divorce or separation during the follow-up interval to predict the onset of several 1986 indicators. In other analyses, nonproblem drinkers who reported higher average consumption and more frequent intoxication in 1981 were more likely than other 1981 nonproblem drinkers to become divorced or separated between 1981 and 1986. Thus, in our sample of women with no signs of problem drinking in 1981, divorce and separation were more likely to *follow* than to precede heavy drinking.

Among women already identified as problem drinkers in 1981, divorce and separation predicted a *reduction* in problem drinking. After controlling for the effects of other predictors, becoming divorced or separated between 1981 and 1986 predicted significantly lower rates of 1986 alcohol dependence symptoms among 1981 problem drinkers, and showed near-significant tendencies to predict less frequent intoxication in 1986 and lower scores on the 1986 problem-drinking index. Rather than being a risk factor as expected, becoming divorced or separated seemed to increase the chances of remission of at least some problem-drinking indicators.

To explain this unexpected finding, we speculated that the marriages or quasimarital relationships of problem-drinking women might be characterized by certain sources of conflict or distress that women attempt to lessen by drinking (Klassen, Wilsnack, Harris, & Wilsnack, 1991). If divorce or separation removes a woman from these sources of distress, her drinking may decrease or even cease. We selected four hypothetical sources of relationship distress for which self-report measures were available in our data: (a) lack of emotional intimacy; (b) primary sexual dysfunction (an index summing lack of sexual interest, low frequency of orgasm, and vaginismus); (c) lack of sexual balance (disparity between partners in sexual expectations and functioning); and (d) frequent drinking by one's partner. When we compared 1981 problem drinkers who remained in their 1981 relationships with those who had separated or divorced by 1986, 1981 frequent-drinking partners and sexual dysfunction tended to be positively associated with 1986 problem drinking among the women who remained with their partners, and negatively associated with 1986 problem drinking among those 1981 problem drinkers who had subsequently divorced or separated. These findings suggest that, for some problem-drinking women, leaving a frequent-drinking partner or a sexually dysfunctional relationship can be a positive life change increasing the woman's chances of problem-drinking remission.

To answer the question of whether divorce is a "risk" or a "remedy," it may be both. The small number of 1981 nonproblem drinkers in our sample who subsequently divorced or separated ($n = 11$) showed near-significant tendencies to report more problem-drinking indicators in 1986. A risk effect would be consistent with clinical and anecdotal evidence that women's drinking often increases following a divorce, with Hanna et al.'s (in press) finding that drinking among women aged 24–32 increased following divorce or separation, and with preliminary findings from a study of recently divorced/separated women, who reported that they more often drank alone at home and more often drank to "feel better about themselves" following their divorce/separation than before (Cheitman, 1991).

If divorce does place *non*-problem-drinking women at risk for increased drinking, it also may provide a remedy for *problem*-drinking women whose distressed relationships and excessive drinking may form a mutually reinforcing system. We plan to pursue this possibility further in our 10-year follow-up survey, where larger numbers of divorced and separated women will be available for analysis. At that time, it may also be feasible to test additional hypotheses, including the possibility that some women reduce their drinking following divorce or separation in order not to jeopardize their performance of new role responsibilities, such as single parenthood.

Ethnicity

Knowledge about racial and ethnic variations in women's drinking has come primarily from two types of studies: surveys of drinking behavior within specific ethnic communities or subpopulations; and larger national surveys not designed primarily to study drinking behavior, but including some measures of alcohol use.

Studies of the first type have examined correlates of drinking and drinking problems in such special populations as black inner-city women (Taylor & Jackson, 1990a, 1990b), immigrant and later-generation Mexican-American women (Gilbert, 1987), Mexican-American married couples (Corbett, Mora, & Ames, 1991), Native American settlements composed of one or two tribal groups (Leland, 1984), and Chinese, Japanese, and Korean residents of Los Angeles (Chi, Lubben, & Kitano, 1989). Other studies have used larger community samples for comparisons among black and white women and men (Darrow et al., 1992; Russell, Mudar, Cooper, & Frone, 1992) and between Mexican Americans and non-Hispanic whites (e.g., Golding, Burnam, & Wells, 1990). Generalizations from these studies are made difficult by the limited sample sizes in many studies, questions about how representative a given ethnic community sample is of the larger ethnic group or category, the inclusion of only one or two racial/ethnic groups in most studies, and intra-ethnic-group heterogeneity (e.g., within Asian-American, Hispanic, or Native American samples).

Studies of the second type include several national health surveys that have asked questions about drinking behavior, among them the 1983 and 1988 National Health Interview Surveys (Grant et al., 1991; Williams & Debakey, 1992; Wilson & Williams, 1989) and the National Health and Nutrition Examination Surveys (e.g., Colliver et al., 1989). In general, these surveys have found that of the three largest racial/ethnic groups, white non-Hispanic women and men are most likely to be drinkers, black non-Hispanic women and men are least likely to drink, and Hispanic women and men are intermediate. (In the 1983 NHIS, Native American women were second only to white women in rates of drinking, while Asian-American women were least likely of all groups to be drinkers, although the Native American and Asian-American subsamples included fewer than 50 women each.) Within all age x ethnicity categories, men exceed women in rates of drinking, heavier drinking, and drinking-related problems. With some exceptions, sociodemographic characteristics such as age, marital status, and employment have generally related similarly to drinking within gender x ethnicity subgroups, although the surveys typically have too few black and Hispanic *heavy*-drinking women for analysis of most demographic correlates of heavier drinking.

With regard to alcohol *disorders*, whites and nonwhites in the 1988 National Health Interview Survey (Grant et al., 1991) showed quite different age-related patterns of DSM-III-R alcohol abuse/dependence. For both females and males, the 1-year prevalence of alcohol abuse and dependence in the youngest age group (18-29) was considerably higher among whites than among nonwhites (11.45% for young white women vs. 3.86% for young nonwhite women). The nonwhite-to-white ratio increased steadily with increasing age, with nonwhites slightly exceeding whites in the oldest age group (0.62% of nonwhite women aged 65 and older vs. 0.34% of white women that age). Thus, while both whites and nonwhites show declines from youthful abuse/dependence rates over time, whites show higher rates of alcohol disorders in youth than nonwhites, and the white age trajectory is steeper than the nonwhite trajectory. It is possible that ethnic or cultural differences in age-specific social roles and role expectations (e.g., earlier assumption of marital and family roles in nonwhites) contribute to different age trajectories for risks of alcohol-related problems.

The first national study of drinking behavior to systematically oversample black respondents and Hispanic respondents was conducted in 1984 by the Alcohol Research Group (Caetano, 1989, 1991; Herd, 1989, 1991). The 1984 sample included nationally representative subsamples of 1,947 blacks and 1,433 Hispanics, in addition to 1,841 ("white") respondents from all other racial/ethnic groups. Findings from the 1984 survey confirmed earlier reports of higher rates of abstention among black and Hispanic women than among white women, and also confirmed that any pattern of exceptionally heavy drinking among black women who do drink (Herd, 1988; Wilsnack et al., 1984) had largely disappeared by 1984. Black and white women drinkers did not differ on rates of frequent heavy drinking.

As in earlier community studies (e.g., Corbett et al., 1991; Gilbert, 1987), Hispanic women who were highly acculturated or of Mexican descent, or who were breaking tradition by being employed outside the home, were more likely than others to drink heavily. The relationship between acculturation and heavier drinking was stronger for Hispanic women than for Hispanic men. In one analysis, highly acculturated women had nine times the chance of being frequent heavy drinkers as women in the low acculturation group (Caetano, 1987; Caetano & Medina-Mora, 1988). These acculturation effects—presumably reflecting a weakening of the strict gender-segregation and strong sanctions against women's drinking in traditional Latin cultures—may have important implications for prevention and treatment of alcohol problems in younger Hispanic women (Mora & Gilbert, 1991).

Rates of drinking *problems* in the 1984 national survey were generally low among black and Hispanic women, relative both to black and Hispanic men and (to a lesser extent) to white women. Among both whites and Hispanics, drinking problems were more common among single women and younger women; neither age nor marital status related to drinking problems among black women. A weaker relationship between marital status and drinking among black women than among white women has also been reported in other studies of community samples (Darrow et al., 1992; Taylor & Jackson, 1990b).

Because the 1984 survey was not able to oversample heavier-drinking women within the ethnic subsamples, the actual numbers of black and Hispanic women with drinking-related problems are small. In addition, as in other national probability samples, numbers of Native American women and Asian-American women are too small for reliable statistical analysis. Despite these limitations, the survey is a significant contribution to understanding ethnic variations in women's drinking. A follow-up survey of the 1984 sample conducted in 1992 will provide important longitudinal data on cross-ethnic similarities and differences in the patterns and predictors of drinking changes over time.

OTHER FINDINGS FROM THE NATIONAL LONGITUDINAL STUDY OF WOMEN'S DRINKING

Predicting Onset and Chronicity of Women's Problem Drinking

Many of the studies discussed in preceding sections have been limited by their cross-sectional design, which does not allow temporal sequences to be specified. The longitudinal design of our national study of women's drinking has allowed us to select variables that related to heavier drinking and/or adverse drinking consequences cross-sectionally, and to test the predictive power of these variables in longitudinal analyses. Wilsnack et al. (1991) reported results of multiple regression analyses of the individual and combined effects of a large number of demographic, personality, social-environmental, and life-experience variables as predictors of 5-year changes in women's drinking behavior. Dependent variables were 1986 average consumption, heavy episodic drinking (six or more drinks in a day), intoxication, drinking-related problems, alcohol dependence symptoms, and scores on a problem-drinking index which summed the occurrence in the past 12 months of: (a) any intoxication, (b) any drinking problem, and (c) any alcohol dependence symptom.

Among the 157 women who reported no problem-drinking indicators in 1981, 11% reported the onset of at least one problem-drinking indicator by 1986. Variables that predicted significantly higher levels on two or more 1986 drinking variables included younger age, cohabiting in 1981, entering a cohabiting relationship between 1981 and 1986, number of drugs used up to 1981, and experiencing a depressive episode between 1981 and 1986. In addition, nontraditional sexual behavior (an index composed of premarital sexual experience and masturbation prior to age 21) and low self-esteem in 1981 predicted higher frequency of heavy episodic drinking in 1986.

Among the 143 women who reported at least two problem-drinking indicators in 1981, 36% continued to report at least two indicators in 1986, 31% reported only one indicator, and 33% no longer reported any indicators. The most consistent predictor of continued (chronic) problem drinking was 1981 sexual dysfunction, which predicted higher levels of four of the six 1986 drinking variables. Other predictors of chronicity included depressive episodes (both before 1981 and during the follow-up interval), never having been married, working part time in 1981 or becoming unemployed between 1981 and 1986, having nontraditional gender traits or a frequent-drinking partner in 1981, using drugs other than alcohol in 1981, and experiencing infertility during the 1981–1986 follow-up interval.

These findings suggest that reasons for the onset of women's problem drinking are not the same as the reasons why problem drinking may then persist. Cohabiting and nontraditional sexual behavior may be indicators of a relatively nontraditional or nonconventional lifestyle. The increased drinking opportunities and greater freedom from traditional moral constraints associated with such a lifestyle may increase women's risks of hazardous drinking behavior. Low self-esteem or a lifetime pattern of using drugs to feel good or deal with problems may increase these risks further.

Whether problem drinking, once begun, will continue may depend on a different set of influences. Experiencing sexual dysfunction or depression seems to increase a woman's chances of continuing in problem drinking, perhaps because her use of alcohol to cope with these problems may only make the problems worse (Klassen & Wilsnack, 1986). Being never-married, unemployed, or employed only part time may represent forms of "role deprivation"—a lack of stable employment or family roles—which may maintain problem drinking by reducing self-esteem, social support, and social feedback about excessive drinking behavior (Wilsnack & Cheloha, 1987). Having a frequent-drinking partner may create drinking opportunities and alcohol-related conflicts that encourage further drinking, whereas concurrent use of alcohol and other drugs may have synergistic effects that reduce a woman's chances of problem-drinking remission.

Childhood Sexual Abuse and Women's Drinking

One potentially important antecedent of problem drinking in women is the experience of incest or other childhood sexual abuse (Hurley, 1991; Miller, Downs, Gondoli, & Keil, 1987; Miller, Downs, & Testa, 1990; Rohsenow, Corbett, & Devine, 1988; Russell & Wilsnack, 1991). The 1986 survey added new questions about experiences in which "someone tried to make you have sexual activity that you *really did not want*." With this as our basic definition of sexual abuse, additional questions asked about the ages at which such experiences occurred, with whom the experiences occurred (from a list that included both intra- and extrafamilial perpetrators), and the respondent's emotional reactions to the experience.

Initial analyses of these measures indicated that more than twice as many 1981 problem drinkers (23%) as 1981 nonproblem drinkers (10%) reported experiencing at least one incident of sexual abuse before age 18. Childhood sexual abuse predicted the onset of problem-drinking indicators over a 5-year period: 1981 nonproblem drinkers who reported any child sexual abuse ($n = 16$) were significantly more likely than 1981 nonproblem drinkers with no child sex abuse history ($n = 141$) to obtain scores of one or more on the 1986 problem-drinking index (51% vs. 19%, $p < .01$). Histories of childhood sexual abuse also were associated with some lifetime experience of depressive moods and feelings of worthlessness among 1981 problem drinkers; with lifetime experience of suicidal thoughts among both 1981 nonproblem drinkers and problem drinkers; and with use of drugs other than alcohol and involvement in violent or conflicted relationships in 1986 among both 1981 nonproblem drinkers and problem drinkers (Russell, Wilsnack, Klassen, & Deitz, 1988; Wilsnack, 1991). These findings clearly support earlier clinical reports that associate childhood sexual abuse with a variety of long-term adverse consequences, including alcohol abuse.

Because the rates of childhood sexual abuse reported in the 1986 survey were lower than those found in several community surveys designed specifically to study sexual abuse (Russell, 1983; Wyatt, 1985), the 1991 follow-up survey included a revised and expanded set of questions designed to increase the valid self-reporting of these sensitive experiences. Initial analyses indicate that the 1991 questions elicited substantially higher rates of reported abuse than did the more abbreviated questions in the 1986 survey. Using definitions adapted from earlier surveys of childhood sexual abuse, rates of reported abuse for the total 1991 sample ranged from 30% to 35% (Wilsnack & Klassen, 1992). As in the 1986 survey, preliminary analyses of 1991 data indicate strong relationships between reported histories of childhood sexual abuse and problem drinking in adulthood.

Drinking Partnerships Between Wives and Husbands

Both clinical investigations (e.g., Dahlgren, 1979; Jacob & Bremer, 1986) and general population surveys (e.g., Corbett et al., 1991; Hammer & Vaglum, 1989; Kolonel & Lee, 1981) have consistently reported strong positive relationships between women's levels of alcohol consumption and those of their husbands or partners. Until recently, however, there has been relatively little attention paid to the dynamics of these "drinking partnerships," or to ways in which partners' drinking patterns affect the consequences of alcohol consumption and other aspects of marital relationships.

Analyses using our 1981 national sample of 917 women and a smaller comparison sample of 396 men (Wilsnack & Wilsnack, 1990a) showed that husbands' self-reported problem drinking was not strongly associated with their perceptions of their wives' drinking frequency, but that wives' self-reported frequency of intoxication, drinking problems, and alcohol dependence symptoms were associated with their perceptions that their husbands drank frequently. This apparently stronger influence of husbands' drinking on wives' drinking than the reverse is consistent with interpretations by Haavio-Mannila (1991) and others that women are more likely to imitate the drinking behavior of higher status males, whether in the family or in the workplace, than men are to imitate female drinking behavior. We wonder whether a stronger effect of men's drinking on women's drinking also might help explain the provocative finding reported by Gomberg (1990) from the ECA data on problem drinkers aged 60 and older, in which older female problem drinkers were more likely to be married (and thus potentially part of a drinking partnership), whereas older male problem drinkers were predominantly divorced or widowed, and living alone.

Analyses of our 1981 and 1986 data for all continuously married women indicated that *discrepancies* in the drinking frequencies of marital partners (e.g., an infrequent-drinking wife with a frequent-drinking husband, or the reverse) were associated with more frequent heavy drinking and more adverse drinking consequences for the wife than would otherwise be expected. In other analyses (Wilsnack & Wilsnack, 1990b), discrepancies between spouses' drinking frequencies also were associated with several indicators of poorer marital functioning, including the wife's self-dissatisfaction and the husband's perceived dissatisfaction with the wife. In three-way analyses of variance, there was some suggestion that a history of problem drinking (or lack of it) interacted with drinking partnership type to influence marital quality: In both cross-sectional and longitudinal analyses, marriages of 1981 non-problem-drinking women showed more negative qualities (including wife's self-dissatisfaction and marital aggression) where both spouses drank frequently—a pattern consistent with our initial hypothesis that spouses' drinking would have additive or multiplicative effects on adverse marital consequences. Marriages of 1981 problem drinkers, on the other hand, showed more negative qualities where spouses' drinking patterns were *incongruent*. It is possible that in marriages with a history of problem drinking, drinking behavior is especially salient, and thus discrepancies between spouses' drinking patterns are particularly likely to express marital conflicts and/or to function as a source of conflict. In marriages without a history of problem drinking, partners' drinking may interact in a simpler way, involving modeling or "contagion" of spouses' drinking behavior and its consequences.

SOME IMPLICATIONS AND RECOMMENDATIONS

Time Trends in Women's Drinking

One conclusion of this review is that despite the absence of large changes in the drinking behavior of women *in general*, it is possible that drinking behavior may be changing within certain subgroups of women, and that relationships between drinking and other variables may be changing. Furthermore, some evidence suggests that drinking problems and clinically diagnosable alcohol disorders may be increasing, perhaps especially among younger women. For these reasons, it will be important to continue to monitor time trends in women's drinking, with a focus on possible changes within specific age groups. One question is whether surveys in the 1990s will support the increase in heavy drinking among women in their 20s and early 30s noted by Hilton (1988a) in surveys conducted between 1964 and 1984, or whether they will replicate the pattern of stabilization or decline in young adults' drinking noted in NIDA surveys conducted during the 1980s (Johnston et al., 1989) and in comparisons of 1983 and 1988 U.S. adult surveys (Williams & Debakey, 1992).

Attention to possible changes in younger women's drinking should not mean that women in older age groups are neglected. If the low rates of drinking and drinking problems among women currently over 60 reflect a specific cohort effect (related to these women's experiences of Prohibition, economic depression, or other unique historical influences), surveys may reveal lower rates of abstention among women entering their 60s in the 1990s. Surveys also should monitor the stability or change in the frequency of alcohol consumption among older women *drinkers*, and in the quantity consumed per drinking occasion, which may be less influenced by aging and/or cohort effects than are rates of drinking versus abstention.

Questions regarding demographic variations include possible changes in relationships between marital status or ethnicity and women's drinking. Will the apparent risks of divorce and cohabitation decrease as these statuses become more normative in American society? Will the weakening of previously reported differences between drinking patterns of black and white women drinkers continue? Will the presently low rates of heavy drinking and drinking problems among Hispanic women increase in younger, more acculturated women of Hispanic descent? An additional challenge will be to find ways of obtaining valid, representative data from smaller ethnic subgroups, including Asian-American women, for whom data are quite limited (e.g., Chi et al., 1989; Wong, 1992), and Native American women, whose risks of adverse drinking consequences appear high (Leland, 1984; Weibel-Orlando, 1986).

Social Contexts of Women's Drinking

Frequent or heavy drinking by her husband or partner may increase a woman's risks of problem drinking by providing a heavy-drinking model, increasing the availability of alcohol, and contributing to relationship conflict or violence. However, *discrepancies* between partners' drinking patterns also may reflect or create relationship conflict that can increase women's risks of adverse drinking consequences.

Women's drinking may be influenced not only by the drinking behavior of their husbands, partners, or other family members and close friends, but also by that of their co-workers. Although recent studies have linked nontraditional employment with heavier drinking and/or more adverse drinking consequences for women, the mechanisms underlying these associations are not clear. Longitudinal studies measuring characteristics of both the female drinker and her work environment could help evaluate the simpler hypotheses that nontraditional employment (a) increases opportunities for drinking; (b) provides heavier-drinking (male) models, which women imitate due to men's higher social status; and (c) creates stress that women attempt to reduce by drinking; as well as the more complex hypotheses that (d) the "culture" of male-dominated occupations involves values, norms, and attitudes that weaken the influence that women's own values and attitudes would normally exert on their drinking behavior; and (e) women's drinking serves to symbolize and reinforce gender equality and female power in traditionally male-dominated occupational settings.

A question relevant to both the relationship/family sphere and the work setting is to what extent women's drinking is a *reaction* to the drinking behavior of persons in their social environments, and to what extent women themselves *influence* the drinking behavior of their significant others and co-workers. Analyzing age and cohort differences in the relationships between women's drinking and that of their co-workers and significant others may indicate: (a) whether effects of nontraditional employment on women's drinking will decrease as employment in traditionally male-dominated occupations becomes more common, and (b) whether directions of influence will become more "egalitarian" and reciprocal (women influencing as well as being influenced) with succeeding generations of younger women.

Risk Factors for Problem Drinking in Women

A major goal of epidemiological research is to identify risk factors for specific diseases or disorders, and recent epidemiological research on women's drinking has made progress in this area. For example, longitudinal data suggest that involvement in a nontraditional lifestyle (including cohabitation and nontraditional sexual behavior) may increase the chances that women will begin to drink in hazardous ways, as may low self-esteem, a history of childhood sexual abuse, and prior use of drugs other than alcohol. Risk factors for continuing problem drinking once begun may include sexual dysfunction, depression, and a lack of stable social roles.

Future epidemiological research may be able to replicate these findings with other samples, as well as discover additional risk factors for problem drinking in women. Once established, knowledge of risk factors for problem-drinking onset and chronicity can be used to design primary and secondary prevention strategies for women. For example, confirming that low self-esteem or a history of childhood sexual abuse increases the risk of problem-drinking onset might suggest primary prevention approaches that examine personal and societal sources of women's low self-esteem and provide experiences that strengthen feelings of self-worth, as well as programs that target sexually abused female adolescents as a high-priority group for support, alcohol and sex education, and other early intervention. If sexual dysfunction and depression are replicated as predictors of problem-drinking chronicity, prevention implications might include the need for education of caregivers (including alcohol counselors, marital and sex therapists, mental health personnel, and physicians) regarding the reciprocal interactions between these experiences and women's drinking. If "role deprivation" is confirmed as a risk factor for women's problem drinking, prevention implications may be at least as much societal as individual-psychological, including the need to increase women's access to stable, meaningful employment roles.

In addition to educating professional caregivers and gatekeepers about risk factors for women's problem drinking, information about established risk factors can be disseminated to women themselves. As with lists of risk factors and warning signs for cancer, heart disease, or diabetes, knowledge of personal and social factors that increase the probability of alcohol abuse can allow women to assess their own chances of experiencing problems with alcohol, and to make informed decisions about changing their drinking behavior, and/or their exposure to risk factors, to minimize these risks.

Epidemiological Research on Women's Drinking in the 1990s: Complexity and Consolidation

The past decade has seen considerable progress in epidemiological research on women's drinking. Several large-scale surveys focused specifically on women have been undertaken in the United States and Europe, at least three of which (Kubicka et al., 1991; Spak & Hallstrom, 1986, 1992; Wilsnack et al., 1991) are longitudinal in design. Although heavier-drinking women are generally not oversampled in national alcohol and drug surveys, increasing attention is being paid to gender similarities and differences in analyzing and reporting these surveys, and some recent surveys (e.g., NIAAA's National Longitudinal Alcohol Epidemiologic Survey) are large enough to generate substantial numbers of heavier-drinking women for analysis. A large data set combining longitudinal drinking surveys from 16 countries is now available (Fillmore et al., in press), allowing gender-relevant hypotheses to be tested across differing historical periods and cultural settings.

Perhaps the strongest general impression from this accumulating research is that the epidemiology of women's drinking is more complex than was previously appreciated. Rather than looking for general increases (or decreases) in women's drinking or drinking problems, we need to look for possible changes within specific age groups (e.g., younger women and women over age 65). Furthermore, certain demographic variables such as ethnicity or marital status may relate to drinking differently—or show different patterns of change—within different age groups.

Complexity also characterizes relationships between employment and women's drinking. Although employment per se does not seem to be a simple risk factor for women's problem drinking, certain *types* of employment (including part-time jobs and traditionally male-dominated occupations) may pose risk. Similarly, relationships between women's drinking and that of their significant others may not be as simple as once thought. Women's problem drinking may be affected not only *directly* by partners' drinking, but also by *discrepancies* between their own and their partners' drinking patterns.

This complexity is one sign of the growing maturity of epidemiological research on women's drinking. Ten years ago, a major focus was the relative neglect of problem-drinking women in epidemiological studies, and the need for greater sensitivity to special characteristics of women's drinking in survey sampling and measurement (e.g., Fillmore, 1988; Wilsnack, Wilsnack, & Klassen, 1986). Given the limited knowledge about the distribution and correlates of women's drinking at that time, substantive questions posed were relatively simple (Is there an "epidemic" of problem drinking in women? Are multiple roles risky for women's drinking?). As research attention to women's drinking has grown in recent years, a larger number of studies have generated findings and questions that are increasingly diverse and differentiated. A major task for the next decade will be to consolidate this emerging knowledge about women's drinking while respecting the complexity of the relationships being studied. Indeed, the increasing complexity of recent findings may mean that we are coming one step closer to a valid description of women's drinking behavior, which (like men's drinking behavior) is undoubtedly determined by an intricate, dynamic interaction among biological, psychological, interpersonal, and sociocultural influences.

REFERENCES

Adams, W.L., Garry, P.J., Rhyne, R., Hunt, W.C., & Goodwin, J.S. (1990). Alcohol intake in the healthy elderly: Changes with age in a cross-sectional and longitudinal study. *Journal of the American Geriatrics Society, 38*, 211–216.

Adelmann, P.K., Antonucci, T.C., Crohan, S.E., & Coleman, L.M. (1989). Empty nest, cohort, and employment in the well-being of midlife women. *Sex Roles, 20*, 173–189.

Berkowitz, A.D., & Perkins, H.W. (1987). Recent research on gender differences in collegiate alcohol use. *Journal of American College Health, 36*, 123–129.

Bradley, H. (1989). *Men's work, women's work: A sociological history of the sexual division of labour in employment.* Cambridge, UK: Polity Press.

Caetano, R. (1987). Acculturation and drinking patterns among U.S. Hispanics. *British Journal of Addiction, 82*, 789–799.

Caetano, R. (1989). Drinking patterns and alcohol problems in a national sample of U.S. Hispanics. In National Institute on Alcohol Abuse and Alcoholism, *The epidemiology of alcohol use and abuse among U.S. minorities* (NIAAA Monograph No. 18, Department of Health and Human Services Publication No. ADM 89-1435; pp. 147–162). Washington, DC: U.S. Government Printing Office.

Caetano, R. (1991). Findings from the 1984 National Survey of Alcohol Use among U.S. Hispanics. In W.B. Clark & M.E. Hilton (Eds.), *Alcohol in America: Drinking practices and problems* (pp. 293–307). Albany: State University of New York Press.

Caetano, R., & Medina-Mora, M.E. (1988). Acculturation and drinking among people of Mexican descent in Mexico and the United States. *Journal of Studies on Alcohol, 49*, 462–471.

Cahalan, D., Cisin, I.H., & Crossley, H.M. (1969). *American drinking practices: A national study of drinking behavior and attitudes.* New Brunswick, NJ: Rutgers Center of Alcohol Studies.

Cheitman, E.A. (1991, March). *First-year progress report: Project Transition (alcohol abuse prevention for divorced/separated women).* Winthrop, ME: Light Work, Unlimited.

Chi, I., Lubben, J.E., & Kitano, H.H.L. (1989). Differences in drinking behavior among three Asian-American groups. *Journal of Studies on Alcohol, 50*, 15–23.

Clark, W.B., & Hilton, M.E. (Eds.). (1991). *Alcohol in America: Drinking practices and problems.* Albany: State University of New York Press.

Clark, W.B., & Midanik, L. (1982). Alcohol use and alcohol problems among U.S. adults: Results of the 1979 national survey. In National Institute on Alcohol Abuse and Alcoholism, *Alcohol consumption and related problems* (Alcohol and Health Monograph No. 1, Department of Health and Human Services Publication No. ADM 82-1190; pp. 3–52). Washington, DC: U.S. Government Printing Office.

Colliver, J. Grigson, M.B., Barbano, H., Dufour, M., & Malin, H. (1989).

NHANES I Epidemiologic Followup Study: Methodological issues and preliminary findings. In National Institute on Alcohol Abuse and Alcoholism, *The epidemiology of alcohol use and abuse among U.S. minorities* (NIAAA Monograph No. 18, Department of Health and Human Services Publication No. ADM 89-1435; pp. 411–423). Washington, DC: U.S. Government Printing Office.

Corbett, K., Mora, J., & Ames, G. (1991). Drinking patterns and drinking-related problems of Mexican-American husbands and wives. *Journal of Studies on Alcohol, 52*, 215–223.

Dahlgren, L. (1979). *Female alcoholics: A psychiatric and social study.* Stockholm: Karolinska Institute.

Darrow, S.L., Russell, M., Cooper, M.L., Mudar, P., & Frone, M.R. (1992). Sociodemographic correlates of alcohol consumption among African-American and white women. *Women and Health, 18* (4), 35–51.

Dawson, D.A., & Archer, L. (1992). Gender differences in alcohol consumption: Effects of measurement. *British Journal of Addiction, 87*, 119–123.

Debakey, S.F., & Williams, G.D. (1992, June). Personal communication (unpublished analyses of 1983 and 1988 NHIS data using same drinking categories as Hilton (1988a) and Wilsnack et al. (1984)).

Ferrence, R.G. (1980). Sex differences in the prevalence of problem drinking. In O.J. Kalant (Ed.), *Research advances in alcohol and drug problems. Vol. 5: Alcohol and drug problems in women* (pp. 69–124). New York: Plenum.

Fillmore, K.M. (1984). "When angels fall": Women's drinking as cultural preoccupation and as reality. In S.C. Wilsnack & L.J. Beckman (Eds.), *Alcohol problems in women: Antecedents, consequences, and intervention* (pp. 7–36). New York: Guilford Press.

Fillmore, K.M. (1988). *Alcohol use across the life course: A critical review of 70 years of international longitudinal research.* Toronto: Addiction Research Foundation.

Fillmore, K.M., Hartka, E., Johnstone, B.M., Leino, E.V., Motoyoshi, M., & Temple, M.T. (1991). A meta-analysis of life course variation in drinking. *British Journal of Addiction, 86*, 1221–1268.

Fillmore, K.M., Golding, J.M., Leino, E.V., Motoyoshi, M., Shoemaker, C., Terry, H., Ager, C.R., & Ferrer, H.P. (in press). Patterns and trends in women's and men's drinking. In R.W. Wilsnack & S.C. Wilsnack (Eds.), *Gender and alcohol.* New Brunswick, NJ: Rutgers Center of Alcohol Studies.

Froberg, D., Gjerdingen, D., & Preston, M. (1986). Multiple roles and women's health: What have we learned? *Women and Health, 11*(2), 79–96.

Gilbert, M.J. (1987). Alcohol consumption patterns in immigrant and later generation Mexican American women. *Hispanic Journal of Behavioral Sciences, 9*, 299–313.

Golding, J.M., Burnam, M.A., & Wells, K.B. (1990). Alcohol use and depressive symptoms among Mexican Americans and non-Hispanic whites. *Alcohol and Alcoholism, 25*, 421–432.

Gomberg, E.S.L. (1990). Drugs, alcohol, and aging. In L.T. Kozlowski, H.M.

Annis, H.D. Cappell, F.B. Glaser, M.S. Goodstadt, Y. Israel, H. Kalant, E.M. Sellers, & E.R. Vingilis (Eds.), *Research advances in alcohol and drug problems* (Vol. 10, pp. 171–213). New York: Plenum.

Gordon, T., & Kannel, W.B. (1983). Drinking and its relation to smoking, BP, blood lipids, and uric acid. *Archives of Internal Medicine, 143*, 1366–1374.

Grant, B.F., Harford, T.C., Chou, P., Pickering, R., Dawson, D.A., Stinson, F.S., & Noble, J. (1991). Epidemiologic Bulletin No. 27: Prevalence of DSM-III-R alcohol abuse and dependence: United States, 1988. *Alcohol Health and Research World, 15* (1), 91–96.

Haavio-Mannila E. (1987). *Alkohol, arbete och familj—en jamforelse mellan man och kvinnor [Alcohol, work and family—A comparison between men and women]* (Publication No. 15). Helsinki: Nordic Council for Alcohol and Drug Research.

Haavio-Mannila, E. (1991, March). *Impact of colleagues and family members on female alcohol use.* Paper presented at the Symposium on Alcohol, Family and Significant Others, Social Research Institute of Alcohol Studies and Nordic Council for Alcohol and Drug Research, Helsinki, Finland.

Hammer, T., & Vaglum, P. (1989). The increase in alcohol consumption among women: A phenomenon related to accessibility or stress? A general population study. *British Journal of Addiction, 84*, 767–775.

Hanna, E., Faden, V., & Harford, T. (1993). Marriage: Does it protect young women from alcoholism? *Journal of Substance Abuse, 5*, 1–14.

Hasin, D., Grant, B., Harford, T., Hilton, M., & Endicott, J. (1990). Multiple alcohol-related problems in the United States: On the rise? *Journal of Studies on Alcohol, 51*, 485–493.

Health and Welfare Canada. (1990). *National Alcohol and Other Drugs Survey (1989): Highlights report* (Catalogue No. H39-175/1990E). Ottawa: Health and Welfare Canada.

Herd, D. (1988). Drinking by black and white women: Results from a national survey. *Social Problems, 35*, 493–505.

Herd, D. (1989). The epidemiology of drinking patterns and alcohol-related problems among U.S. blacks. In National Institute on Alcohol Abuse and Alcoholism, *The epidemiology of alcohol use and abuse among U.S. minorities* (NIAAA Monograph No. 18, Department of Health and Human Services Publication No. ADM 89-1435; pp. 3–50). Washington, DC: U.S. Government Printing Office.

Herd, D. (1991). Drinking problems in the black population. In W.B. Clark & M.E. Hilton (Eds.), *Alcohol in America: Drinking practices and problems* (pp. 308–328). Albany: State University of New York Press.

Hilton, M.E. (1988a). Trends in U.S. drinking patterns: Further evidence from the past 20 years. *British Journal of Addiction, 83*, 269–278.

Hilton, M.E. (1988b). Trends in drinking problems and attitudes in the United States: 1979–1984. *British Journal of Addiction, 83*, 1421–1427.

Hilton, M.E. (1991). The demographic distribution of drinking patterns in 1984. In W.B. Clark & M.E. Hilton (Eds.), *Alcohol in America: Drinking practices and problems* (pp. 73–86). Albany: State University of New York Press.

Horwitz, A.V., & White, H.R. (1991). Becoming married, depression, and alcohol problems among young adults. *Journal of Health and Social Behavior, 32,* 221–237.

Hurley, D.L. (1991). Women, alcohol and incest: An analytical review. *Journal of Studies on Alcohol, 52,* 253–268.

Jacob, T., & Bremer, D.A. (1986). Assortative mating among men and women alcoholics. *Journal of Studies on Alcohol, 47,* 219–222.

Johnson, P.B. (1982). Sex differences, women's roles and alcohol use: Preliminary national data. *Journal of Social Issues, 2,* 93–116.

Johnston, L.D., O'Malley, P.M., & Bachman, J.G. (1989). *Drug use, drinking, and smoking: National survey results from high school, college, and young adults populations, 1975–1988* (Department of Health and Human Services Publication No. ADM 89–1638). Washington, DC: U.S. Government Printing Office.

Klassen, A.D., & Wilsnack, S.C. (1986). Sexual experience and drinking among women in a U.S. national survey. *Archives of Sexual Behavior, 15,* 363–392.

Klassen, A.D., Wilsnack, S.C., Harris, T.R., & Wilsnack, R.W. (1991, March). *Partnership dissolution and remission of problem drinking in women: Findings from a U.S. longitudinal survey.* Paper presented at the Symposium on Alcohol, Family and Significant Others, Social Research Institute of Alcohol Studies and Nordic Council for Alcohol and Drug Research, Helsinki, Finland.

Klee, L., Schmidt, C., & Ames, G. (1991). Indicators of women's alcohol problems: What women themselves report. *International Journal of Addictions, 26,* 885–901.

Knupfer, G. (1982). Problems associated with drunkenness in women: Some research issues. In National Institute on Alcohol Abuse and Alcoholism, *Special population issues* (Alcohol and Health Monograph No. 4, Department of Health and Human Services Publication No. ADM 82-1193; pp. 3–39). Washington, DC: U.S. Government Printing Office.

Kolonel, L.N., & Lee, J. (1981). Husband-wife correspondence in smoking, drinking, and dietary habits. *American Journal of Clinical Nutrition, 34,* 99–104.

Kubicka, L., Csemy, L., & Kozeny, J. (1991, March). *The sociodemographic, microsocial, and attitudinal context of Czech women's drinking.* Paper presented at the Symposium on Alcohol, Family and Significant Others, Social Research Institute of Alcohol Studies and Nordic Council for Alcohol and Drug Research, Helsinki, Finland.

LaRosa, J.H. (1990). Executive women and health: Perceptions and practices. *American Journal of Public Health, 80,* 1450–1454.

Leland, J. (1984). Alcohol use and abuse in ethnic minority women. In S.C. Wilsnack & L.J. Beckman (Eds.), *Alcohol problems in women: Antecedents, consequences, and intervention* (pp. 66–96). New York: Guilford Press.

Magura, M., & Shapiro, E. (1988). Alcohol consumption and divorce: Which causes which? *Journal of Divorce, 12*, 127–136.

Miller, B.A., Downs, W.R., Gondoli, D.M., & Keil, A. (1987). The role of childhood sexual abuse in the development of alcoholism in women. *Violence and Victims, 2*, 157–172.

Miller, B.A., Downs, W.R., & Testa, M. (1990, August). *Relationship between women's alcohol problems and experiences of childhood violence.* Paper presented at the Annual Convention, American Psychological Association, Boston, MA.

Mora, J., & Gilbert, M.J. (1991). Issues for Latinas: Mexican American women. In P. Roth (Ed.), *Alcohol and drugs are women's issues. Vol. 1: A review of the issues* (pp. 43–47). New York: Women's Action Alliance.

Morrissey, E.R. (1986). Power and control through discourse: The case of drinking and drinking problems among women. *Contemporary Crises, 10*, 157–179.

Mulford, H.A., & Fitzgerald, J.L. (1988). Per capita alcohol sales, heavy drinker prevalence and alcohol problems in Iowa for 1958–1985. *British Journal of Addiction, 83*, 265–268.

Myers, J.K., Weissman, M.M., Tischler, G.L., Holzer, C.E., Leaf, P.J., Orvaschel, H., Anthony, J.C., Boyd, J.H., Burke, J.D., Kramer, M., & Stoltzman, R. (1984). Six-month prevalence of psychiatric disorders in three communities. *Archives of General Psychiatry, 41*, 959–967.

National Institute on Alcohol Abuse and Alcoholism (1993). Epidemiology of alcohol use and alcohol-related consequences. In *Eighth Special Report to the U.S. Congress on Alcohol and Health* (Chap. 1). Washington, DC: U.S. Government Printing Office.

National Institute on Drug Abuse (1991). *National Household Survey on Drug Abuse: Population estimates 1991* (Department of Health and Human Services Publication No. ADM 92-1887). Washington, DC: U.S. Government Printing Office.

Perkins, H.W. (1992). Gender patterns in consequences of collegiate alcohol abuse: A 10-year study of trends in an undergraduate population. *Journal of Studies on Alcohol, 53*, 458–462.

Popkin, C.L. (1991). Drinking and driving by young females. *Accident Analysis and Prevention, 23*, 37–44.

Power, C., & Estaugh, V. (1990). The role of family formation and dissolution in shaping drinking behaviour in early adulthood. *British Journal of Addiction, 85*, 521–530.

Reich, T., Cloninger, C.R., van Eerdewegh, P., Rice, J.P., & Mullaney, J. (1988). Secular trends in the familial transmission of alcoholism. *Alcoholism: Clinical and Experimental Research, 12*, 458–464.

Robbins, C. (1989). Sex differences in psychosocial consequences of alcohol and drug abuse. *Journal of Health and Social Behavior, 30*, 117–130.

Robins, L.N., Helzer, J.E., Przybeck, T.R., & Regier, D.A. (1988). Alcohol disorders in the community: A report from the Epidemiologic Catchment Area. In R.M. Rose & J. Barrett (Eds.), *Alcoholism: Origins and outcome* (pp. 15–29). New York: Raven.

Rohsenow, D.J., Corbett, R., & Devine, D. (1988). Molested as children: A hidden contribution to substance abuse? *Journal of Substance Abuse Treatment, 5,* 13–18.

Romelsjo, A., Lazarus, N.B., Kaplan, G.A., & Cohen, R.D. (1991). The relationship between stressful life situations and changes in alcohol consumption in a general population sample. *British Journal of Addiction, 86,* 157–169.

Room, R. (1989, August). *Worries, concerns, suggestions: Informal processes in the social control of drinking.* Paper presented at the Annual Meeting, Society for the Study of Social Problems, Oakland, CA.

Russell, D.E.H. (1983). The incidence and prevalence of intrafamilial and extrafamilial sexual abuse of female children. *Child Abuse and Neglect: The International Journal, 7,* 133–146.

Russell, M., Mudar, P.J., Cooper, M.L., & Frone, M.R. (1992, June). *Correlates of drinking problems among blacks and whites.* Poster presented at the Annual Meeting, Research Society on Alcoholism, San Diego, CA.

Russell, S.A. (1991). *Childhood sexual abuse as an antecedent of problem drinking and sexual dysfunction in women.* Unpublished doctoral dissertation, Department of Psychology, University of North Dakota, Grand Forks.

Russell, S.A., & Wilsnack, S.C. (1991). Adult survivors of childhood sexual abuse: Substance abuse and other consequences. In P. Roth (Ed.), *Alcohol and drugs are women's issues. Vol. 1: A review of the issues* (pp. 61–70). New York: Women's Action Alliance.

Russell, S.A., Wilsnack, S.C., Klassen, A.D., & Deitz, S.R. (1988, November). *Consequences of childhood sexual abuse among problem drinking and nonproblem drinking women in a U.S. national survey.* Paper presented at the Annual Meeting, American Society of Criminology, Chicago, IL.

Schmidt, C., Klee, L., & Ames, G. (1990). Review and analysis of literature on indicators of women's drinking problems. *British Journal of Addiction, 85,* 179–192.

Spak, F., & Hallstrom, T. (1986). WAG (Women and Alcohol in Gothenburg). *Nordic Council for Alcohol and Drug Research (NAD) Publication No. 14,* pp. 127–132.

Spak, F., & Hallstrom, T. (1992, June). *Validation of a screening instrument for use with female populations.* Paper presented at the 18th Annual Symposium of the Kettil Bruun Society for Social and Epidemiological Research on Alcohol, Toronto, Ontario, Canada.

Taylor, J., & Jackson, B. (1990a). Factors affecting alcohol consumption in Black women: Part I. *International Journal of the Addictions, 25,* 1287–1300.

Taylor, J., & Jackson, B. (1990b). Factors affecting alcohol consumption in Black women: Part II. *International Journal of the Addictions, 25,* 1415–1427.

Verbrugge, L.M. (1986). Role burdens and physical health of women and men. *Women and Health, 11,* 47–77.

Wechsler, H., & Isaac, N. (1992). "Binge" drinkers at Massachusetts colleges:

Prevalence, drinking style, time trends, and associated problems. *Journal of the American Medical Association, 267,* 2929–2931.

Weibel-Orlando, J. (1986). Women and alcohol: Special populations and cross-cultural variations. In National Institute on Alcohol Abuse and Alcoholism, *Women and alcohol: Health-related issues* (Research Monograph No. 16, Department of Health and Human Services Publication No. ADM 86–1139; pp. 161–187). Washington, DC: U.S. Government Printing Office.

Williams, G.D., & Debakey, S.F. (1992). Changes in levels of alcohol consumption: United States, 1983–1988. *British Journal of Addiction, 87,* 643–648.

Williams, G.D., Grant, B.F., Harford, T.C., & Noble, J. (1989). Epidemiologic Bulletin No. 23: Population projections using DSM-III criteria: Alcohol abuse and dependence, 1990–2000. *Alcohol Health and Research World, 13,* 366–370.

Wilsnack, R.W., & Cheloha, R. (1987). Women's roles and problem drinking across the lifespan. *Social Problems, 34,* 231–248.

Wilsnack, R.W., & Wilsnack, S.C. (1990a, June). *Husbands and wives as drinking partners.* Paper presented at the 16th Annual Alcohol Epidemiology Symposium of the Kettil Bruun Society for Social and Epidemiological Research on Alcohol, Budapest, Hungary.

Wilsnack, R.W., & Wilsnack, S.C. (1992). Women, work, and alcohol: Failures of simple theories. *Alcoholism: Clinical and Experimental Research, 16,* 172–179.

Wilsnack, R.W., Wilsnack, S.C., & Klassen, A.D. (1984). Women's drinking and drinking problems: Patterns from a 1981 national survey. *American Journal of Public Health, 74,* 1231–1238.

Wilsnack, R.W., & Wright, S.I. (1991, August). *Women in predominantly male occupations: Relationships to problem drinking.* Paper presented at the Annual Meeting of the Society for the Study of Social Problems, Cincinnati, OH.

Wilsnack, S.C. (1991). Sexuality and women's drinking: Findings from a U.S. national study. *Alcohol Health and Research World, 15,* 147–150.

Wilsnack, S.C., & Klassen, A.D. (1992, September). *Childhood sexual abuse and problem drinking in a U.S. national sample of women.* Paper presented at the Women's Issues Related to Alcohol Abuse and Violence Conference, University of Illinois at Chicago, College of Nursing.

Wilsnack, S.C., Klassen, A.D., Schur, B.E., & Wilsnack, R.W. (1991). Predicting onset and chronicity of women's problem drinking: A five-year longitudinal analysis. *American Journal of Public Health, 81,* 305–318.

Wilsnack, S.C., Klassen, A.D., & Wright, S.I. (1986). Gender-role orientations and drinking among women in a U.S. national survey. In *Proceedings of the 34th International Congress on Alcoholism and Drug Dependence* (pp. 242–255). Calgary, Alberta: International Council on Alcohol and Addictions.

Wilsnack, S.C., & Wilsnack, R.W. (1990b, June). *Marital drinking and the quality of marital relationships: Patterns from a U.S. longitudinal survey.*

Paper presented at the 35th International Institute on the Prevention and Treatment of Alcoholism, International Council on Alcohol and Addictions, Berlin, Federal Republic of Germany.

Wilsnack, S.C., Wilsnack, R.W., & Klassen, A.D. (1986). Epidemiological research on women's drinking, 1978–1984. In National Institute on Alcohol Abuse and Alcoholism, *Women and alcohol: Health-related issues* (NIAAA Research Monograph No. 16, Department of Health and Human Services Publication No. ADM 86–1139; pp. 1–68). Washington, DC: U.S. Government Printing Office.

Wilson, R.W., & Williams, G.D. (1989). Alcohol use and abuse among U.S. minority groups: Results from the 1983 National Health Interview Survey. In National Institute on Alcohol Abuse and Alcoholism, *The epidemiology of alcohol use and abuse among U.S. minorities* (NIAAA Monograph No. 18, Department of Health and Human Services Publication No. ADM 89-1435; pp. 399–410). Washington, DC: U.S. Government Printing Office.

Wong, T.H. (1992). Female Chinese problem drinkers. *British Journal of Addiction, 87,* 1205–1206.

Wyatt, G.E. (1985). The sexual abuse of Afro-American and white women in childhood. *Child Abuse and Neglect: The International Journal, 9,* 507–519.

Chapter 5

Cross-Cultural Perspectives on Women and Alcohol*

Dwight B. Heath

Brown University
Department of Anthropology

In recent years, increasing popular and scientific attention has been paid to alcohol use by women and its results, although the phenomena have been systematically studied in only a few countries. Predictably, the bulk of the literature deals with the United States (e.g., Blume, 1991; Engs, 1990; Greenblatt & Schuckit, 1976; National Institute on Alcohol Abuse & Alcoholism, 1980, 1982, 1986; Stimmel, 1986; Wilsnack & Beckman, 1984). Other reviews were done in the United Kingdom (Camberwell Council on Alcoholism, 1980), Canada (MacLennan, 1976), and Scandinavia (Haavio-Mannila, 1989); a series of volumes is

* My friend and colleague, A.M. Cooper, provided an appropriate context and encouragement for writing, as well as teaching me the positive aspects of what I know about women. Clyde Kluckhohn sparked my original interest in anthropology, George Murdock got me started in cross-cultural studies, and Mark Keller prompted an academic concern for alcohol.

This is a revised and expanded version of "Women and Alcohol: Cross-Cultural Perspectives," 1991, *Journal of Substance Abuse, 3*, 175–185.

projected on women's drinking in New Zealand (J. Park, personal communication, July 27, 1988). A concise but thorough review of the subject written in lay terms is also available (Youcha, 1986). Although the emphasis was never on women's drinking, the widely scattered corpus of ethnographic descriptions of cultures throughout the world is a surprisingly rich source of relevant information (Heath & Cooper, 1981), and it provides the basis for many of the cross-cultural observations.

The scientific literature just cited has not yet succeeded in dispelling a number of popular stereotypes that persist, even though these stereotypes do not stand up under close scrutiny. The major thrust of this article is to offer historical and cross-cultural evidence to correct many widely held beliefs about women and alcohol that are distorted or inaccurate.

EVIDENCE IS NOT LACKING

One fundamental misunderstanding about women and alcohol has to do with the availability of data on the subject. There is a widespread presumption that virtually nothing is known about drinking by women prior to the mid-1960s. One reason given is that the overwhelming majority of researchers were men, who paid no special attention to what women were doing, and who would have ignored it as unimportant even if they had seen it. Another explanation is that preconceptions about sex roles were so compelling (even if largely unconscious) that few scientists would have been able to report accurately on women's drinking, with a strong bias toward underreporting to be expected from the presumption of male dominance in this field of human endeavor, as in many others.

The facts are very different from the presumptions. Occasional studies comparing male and female alcohol use appeared in scientific journals early in this century, and a few specifically about women began to appear by the 1950s (e.g., Berner & Solms, 1953; Curran, 1937; Karpman, 1948; Lisansky, 1957; Wall, 1937). Ethnographic descriptions around the world showed that women's drinking was widespread and that many societies were relatively permissive.

SIMILARITIES AND DIFFERENCES
BETWEEN THE SEXES

Among those who think at all about cross-cultural similarities and differences, it is widely assumed that men tend to monopolize access to alcohol, often forbidding women to drink. The reality is otherwise.

When Child, Barry, and Bacon (1965) carefully analyzed data on alcohol use from 139 societies, they found adequate information on 113; all but 4 allowed both sexes to drink, and only 1 accepted drunkenness on the part of men but not women. Clearly, women's drinking was not nearly so rare as most people imagined. One anthropologist was correct in recently offering as 1 of only 16 "important generalizations about alcohol and humanity," the proposition that: "Typically, alcoholic beverages are used more by males than by females" (Marshall, 1979, p. 454).

Even that generalization is not without exception. In recent years, a couple of interesting cases have come to light in which women drink more than men. In a multitribal study among Native Americans in the western United States, Weibel-Orlando (1966) reported that "rural Sioux women drink more frequently than do the rural Sioux men" (p. 178). Furthermore, "the rural Sioux women actually consume more alcohol per session than do the rural Sioux and Five Tribes men" (pp. 179–180). Another interesting interethnic study, in Malaysia, included findings that similarly differ from predominant worldwide patterns:

> Most participants [of both sexes] reported using alcohol for special occasions only. . . . An exception to this were the 7 Malay female users of alcohol with daily consumption of wine in quantity being the common pattern. Daily use was also more common among Chinese females (21%) than among Chinese males (5%). (Armstrong, 1985, p. 1,804)

Although the samples were small in each of these cases, such findings contradict what has long been thought to be a universal pattern.

Although it is true that men tend to drink more, more often, and in more varied circumstances than do women, this does not mean that women's drinking is necessarily just token sipping, hedged about with much stricter limits concerning time, place, quantity, and so forth. In fact, when the same large worldwide sample of drinking cultures was reexamined in terms of 49 alcohol-related variables (dealing with quantity, frequency, ritualization, hospitality, etc.), "the majority of societies showed no sex differences in quantitative rating" (Bacon, 1976, p. 30).

It's not so much that men monopolize drinking, or even that they drink more often. The major difference seems to be that men more often drink large quantities and become intoxicated. The double standard may have less to do with the act of drinking than with the allowance of "time out," that socially acceptable disinhibition during intoxication (MacAndrew & Edgerton, 1969) that is typically accorded to males but only rarely to females. Some implications of this difference are discussed below.

The familiar pattern of drinking as an integral part of life on skid row is replicated among women (Bahr & Garrett, 1976); their participation in English pub culture is not unlike that of men (Hunt & Satterlee, 1987); and bars are inappropriately linked with alcoholism among lesbians just as they are among gay men (Woods, 1981). Both sexes adjust their pace of drinking (apparently unconsciously) to approximate that of the fastest drinker in a group (Billings, Weiner, Kessler, & Gomberg, 1976). When ritual drunkenness is prescribed as an appropriate aspect of the religious experience, women often take part on an equal footing with men (e.g., Allen, 1988), and when drinking is an integral part of communal work projects, women as well as men participate (e.g., Kennedy, 1978).

It may be surprising to some that drinking patterns are not more different between the sexes, especially in view of the fact that the results of drinking are so different, both in the short- and long-term perspectives. To be sure, there are some respects in which any biological organism is similarly affected by high concentrations of ethanol in the system, but at levels consonant with customary human usage, there is a wide range of variation. This is true among individuals of either sex, but there are a few patterned differences between the sexes that have been noted in the literature and deserve cross-cultural scrutiny. Unfortunately, there is little detailed information available on many of these points from societies other than those of Western Europe. Nevertheless, in a quest for identifying regularities in the human experience with alcohol, the following factors deserve to be mentioned.

The presumed link between alcohol and aggression is not nearly so strong as many believe: There is no physiological or pharmacological evidence for a "triggering action" (Heath, 1983). Furthermore, we should be concerned about the "tendency to accept the disinhibition theory as a self-evident truth despite the lack of conclusive empirical data to support it" (Wilsnack, 1984, p. 191). Using broadly cross-cultural data, McClelland, Davis, Kalin, and Wanner (1972) emphasized men's need for power as the primary motivation for drinking, and the feeling of power as the most important outcome of men's drinking. Wilsnack (1976), however, reported just the opposite motive and effect in American women's drinking. Child et al. (1965) found only a few non-Western societies in which women acted out hostility after drinking, but among those, the women were more hostile in terms of quarreling and fighting than the men.

Data on sexual arousal are equivocal. In small doses, alcohol does appear to have some aphrodisiac qualities for men, although the depressant effect of high doses often overcomes that, as was aptly immortalized by Shakespeare: "it provokes, and unprovokes; it provokes the desire but it takes away the performance" (*Macbeth*, Act II, Scene 1). However, in double-blind balanced placebo experiments, expectancy has been demonstrated to have a more potent effect than ethanol. Wilsnack (1984) made the point that women show no physiological arousal from alcohol, although they often subjectively report having been stimulated by drink (or by the belief that they had drunk). Leigh (1990) offered a specifically sociocultural interpretation for such apparent gender differences in terms of sexual arousal, emphasizing that cues are differentially interpreted in ways consistent with sex-role socialization. Thus, a woman may become more anxious (rather than more disinhibited), knowing that her male partner may become more aggressive (stereotypically interpreting her drinking as signaling sexual availability).

The "double-standard," which generally holds women to a stricter level of morality, has influenced scientific writing as well as popular lay stereotypes. Ridlon (1988) approached such differential judgments from the perspective of sociological labeling theory. Ridlon wrote of "status insularity" as the quality of a status that decreases the likelihood of being labeled deviant, but an individual who is so labeled then becomes more heavily stigmatized. This interpretation also may help to explain why, once a woman does start habitual heavy drinking, problems compound rapidly, so that the trajectory of her suffering is "telescoped" in comparison with a more gradual accumulation of drinking problems, such as men normally encounter (Beckman, 1976), even though men are more publicly visible. This contrast may not be as great as is often suggested, however. Schuckit and Morrissey (1976) made the point that many of the supposed differences between male and female alcoholics had to do with differences in socioeconomic status, and that the apparent progression of alcoholism in both sexes was quite similar if one controlled for that variable.

PHYSIOLOGY IS ONLY PART OF THE PICTURE

It has long been recognized that a given dose of ethanol will produce a significantly higher blood-alcohol level (BAL) in women than in men. The differential impact of alcohol holds even when amount is adjusted in proportion to body weight. Because alcohol is distributed throughout the body in proportion to the water content of tissues, and there are differences between sexes in muscle mass and adipose distribution even with the same weight, a woman gets more concentrated ethanol

from a drink than a man. Another reason appears to be that significantly smaller quantitites of the enzyme alcohol dehydrogenase—
important for the metabolism of ethanol—are found in the gastrointestinal tracts of women (Frezza et al., 1990).

Changes in water distribution and hormone status related to the
menstrual cycle make for marked differences in alcohol potency, even
within the same individual during a month's time (Jones & Jones,
1976). There appears to be some linkage between menstruation and
drinking problems, but the exact nature of that linkage is not yet clear.
Some women drink more with the onset of menstruation; even if they
suffer no physical discomfort, many cite mood changes and emotional
stress, often using the term "depression" in a clearly nonclinical sense
(Belfer & Shader, 1976).

From the viewpoint of society, a woman's ability to become pregnant
is a major consideration that sometimes outweighs her importance as
an autonomous human being. There are some who insist that the
impact of a mother's drinking is so grave that it was recognized in the
folk wisdom of the ancients. As evidence, they cite the Old Testament
account of an angel's advising Samson's mother: "thou shalt conceive
and bear a son. Now therefore beware, I pray thee, and drink not wine
nor any strong drink" (Judg. 13:7).

Others emphasize that fetal alcohol syndrome (FAS)—widely invoked to prohibit drinking among women in childbearing age—occurs
at rates that vary markedly among different populations. When Rosett
and Weiner (1984) reviewed the scientific literature, they found just
"over 400" adequately documented cases throughout the world, all
involving long-term heavy drinking on the part of the mother. A more
recent study replicates the finding that no case has been reported of
FAS to a moderate drinker (Ernhart, Sokol, Ager, Morrow-Tlucak, &
Martier, 1989). A major effort by the U.S. Indian Health Service to
study FAS among Native Americans (generally agreed to be the population at highest risk) in several northwestern states recently floun-
dered for the simple reason that they could find no such births during a
full year (C. Duimstra, personal communication, May 8, 1990). Although there are some Indian communities that suffer dramatically
from FAS and FAE (fetal alcohol effects), they do not constitute a
characteristically ethnic phenomenon, with rates ranging from 4.59–
30.49 per 1,000 women of childbearing age among various Indian
populations. Even those figures can appear misleadingly inflated, however, in view of the fact that fully one-fourth of those women produce
more than one FAS- or FAE-injured baby (Heath, 1989). Researchers
make the point that, for unknown reasons, women almost always
drink less during pregnancy than they do otherwise, "a powerful but

unexplained phenomenon" (Little & Ervin, 1984). Some questions which remain inadequately explored in connection with birth defects and learning disabilities are possible teratogenic effects of paternal drinking and the roles of a host of other drugs, as well as vitamin A and other legal substances known to be harmful.

It is striking that, even in an article explicitly focused on the biological aspects of drinking, Hill (1982) made the point that "the relatively smaller likelihood that women in a given population will develop alcoholism appears to be due to factors which may be considered to be cultural and which may mitigate against heavy drinking among women" (p. 66).

CONTROL OF ALCOHOL BY WOMEN

With all of the attention being paid to women as consumers of alcohol in recent years, their traditional roles as producers and distributors have been relatively neglected. In that connection, a cross-cultural perspective is especially salient. It is a reminder that, contrary to stereotypical expectations, women often have greater access to alcoholic beverages than men.

Eames (1992) makes much of the fact that female deities are credited with having brought the benefits of beer to humankind, as in Egypt, Sumeria, Aztec Mexico, Incan Peru, and elsewhere. It is also noteworthy that brewing and serving tended to be monopolized by women for millennia, and still are in many parts of the world. Throughout Latin America and sub-Saharan Africa, it is almost always women who manufacture and distribute the grain- or vegetable-based homebrews that are both staple foods and intoxicants. Chicha, kaffir beer, pulque, and related fermented drinks made from maize, millet, barley, yuca, and maguey, among other bases, are usually produced by women, and it often is the same women who sell them at retail in recognized public-drinking establishments that they own and manage. The South African *shebeen*, the Andean *chichería*, the Mexican *pulquería*, and related establishments elsewhere, are outlets where women dispense to men the wares that they have made. In that respect, they are like wineshops in Babylon more than 4,000 years ago, which were the subject of considerable regulation in the earliest known codification of law (Harper, 1904). In fact, many governments issued licenses for sale of alcoholic beverages only to women, often strictly to widows, and sometimes even more narrowly to widows of a recent war. Such practice may have been a crude antecedent of Social Security for a vulnerable segment of the population. Another aim might have been to create public drinking establishments that might be less likely to become customary sites for sedition, prostitution, political agitation, or other activities that the incumbent leaders hoped to minimize.

In a tribal society in Ghana, for example, maize beer made by women is "the focus of the economy, as well as the necessary element in virtually all ritual activities. It is the most important thread in the loose fabric of LoBir life" (Hagaman, 1980, p. 205). Similar observations have been made with respect of various fermented beverages in many other regions. Brewing is a major activity on the part of women in much of the developing world, providing them with social status, and often, a significant source of independent income. It is especially important because it is one of the few ways women can earn money in such societies, particularly in those instances where they are heads of households. It is not only a source of income for widows and unwed mothers, but also for wives who remain in villages while their husbands migrate for long periods to work in distant mines, factories, or plantations.

An early detailed study by Hellmann (1934) of such brewing in urban South Africa stressed both the positive economic and social functions and the symbolic political dysfunctions at a time of prohibition for natives. A recent account, which traced 30 years of change with a focus on beer in a Zambian culture, pointed out how the shift toward industrially produced beer has undercut not only women's economic and social status but even age grading, views about sorcery, sacred and secular concepts, and many other areas of concern (Colson & Scudder, 1988).

It is noteworthy that none of the societies in which women produce alcoholic beverages has shown any sign of major problem drinking among women. Although the British alewife, the German barmaid, an international airline stewardess, or a U.S. cocktail waitress do not produce the drinks they dispense, no one can doubt that these women also have easy and inexpensive access. Clearly, easy availability of beer and wine is not a stimulus to alcoholism or any other alcohol-related problems. This contradicts assertions by World Health Organization (1991), National Institute on Alcohol Abuse and Alcoholism (1987), and many others who advocate the imposition of stricter controls on the availability of alcohol as the best means of preventing or reducing problems.

CONTROL *BY* AND *OF* WOMEN, USING ALCOHOL

In a broadly theoretic sense, the question of women and alcohol is revealing as an interface between biology and culture. It is apparent in terms of drinking, as in terms of many other realms of human behavior that the distinctions between men and women are at least as salient in sociocultural terms as they are in biological terms.

Even focusing on social and cultural aspects of gender differences, symbolic considerations often appear to be as important as more concrete ones. Interpretations of past events are recast in ways that reflect the social structure, with meanings and values affecting what seems like an objective question: Has there been an "epidemic" of problem drinking among women in recent years? Some would reply that there certainly has been, because of stresses on women who are newly competitive and working away from home. Others suggest that female problem drinkers are not a new phenomenon but that, as stigma lessened, more have identified themselves or been labeled by physicians or counselors. In practical terms, women's long and widespread experience with easy access to alcohol raises questions about the policies for prevention most popular today. The following vignettes illustrate those points about the relevance of male–female similarities and differences vis-á-vis alcohol use and its outcomes.

When we examine the many and diverse meanings and functions that alcohol has with respect to relations between the sexes, it is noteworthy that two other very different kinds of control also feature prominently. That most often criticized in recent writings has to do with control *of* women, the widespread occurrence of differential norms and customs that express male dominance and power (including hegemonies of politics, wealth, and other realms, as well as sheer physical strength, and the converse female subordination). Another very different kind of control is that exercised *by* women, through which they often use alcohol as a medium to achieve ends that are often strikingly "liberating" and in contrast to their stereotyped and more usual role as dominated.

Control *of* Women, Using Alcohol

Fillmore (1986) tellingly noted that recent expressions of alarm over a supposed "epidemic" of drinking among women actually related to behavioral patterns that changed fully half a century ago. The irony that society at one time plays down drinking problems among women and at another time maximizes them may relate more to political and symbolic factors than to the pharmacologic impact of alcohol (Fillmore, 1984). Fillmore's reminder that drinking is often a social marker of full citizenship gives focus to feminist complaints that men may be criticizing female drinking now in order to "keep women in their place."

With all of the public clamor about alcohol-related problems and alcoholism, it would be easy to lose sight of the fact that per capita consumption of distilled beverages has been falling markedly in the United States for a decade, whereas that of beer and wine at first leveled off and now also has begun to decline. Even before this overall pattern emerged, knowledgeable researchers straightforwardly asserted that "There is no evidence over the past decade of a dramatic increase or 'epidemic' of heavy drinking or drinking problems among American women" (Wilsnack, Wilsnack, & Klassen, 1986, p.59).

In comparing male and female drinking and its outcomes, much has been made of the "double standard" in Western culture that implies women should drink less, and certainly not become drunk in public. A similar and even more stringent double standard, which holds women to a stricter code of public conduct than men, is especially notorious in the circum-Mediterranean area of *machismo* and in the honor-and-shame complex of cultures that also predominates in much of Latin America.

Simplistic functional interpretations of such cultural institutions can be misleading if they are misconstrued as causal explanations, but they also can be highly suggestive if they are viewed in that limited light. For example, the old view that men prevented women from drinking because they wanted to monopolize the powerful and symbolic substance of alcohol loses plausibility when one recognizes that it is usually women who provide men with alcohol in the first place. Nevertheless, Morrissey (1986, p. 248) may have hit on a profound truth by asserting that "One problem for female drinkers, it seems, is the acceptance of male definitions of the functions of alcohol," citing health warnings that caution against drinking during pregnancy, which are phrased in terms of protecting the unborn at the expense of women's rights. Access to alcohol as a symbol of equality in gender-status politics was notable during the prefeminist flapper days of Prohibition, but obviously it still makes some men uneasy two generations later.

There is another meaning of the double standard that weighs heavily on some of those women who choose to drink. In some groups, even where drinking by women is not closely restricted, there is an implicit belief that it is slightly improper, and any woman who does so runs the risk of being presumed wanton or sexually promiscuous. Many authors have made brief mention of this pattern; it has even been suggested that female heavy drinkers in the United States (Youcha, 1986) and in England (Camberwell Council, 1980) have been hesitant to seek help because of that stigma. This pattern is more fully described with reference to urban Irish Catholics (Ablon, 1985), Cuban expatriates in the United States (Page, Rio, Sweeney, & McKay, 1985), and New

Zealanders (Park, 1990). The fact that women tend more often to drink at home—their own or a friend's—rather than in public, is probably closely linked with such thinking, as among Mexican Americans (Gilbert, 1985), Navaho Indians (Topper, 1985), Greek farmers (Gefou-Madianou, 1992), and others. It is noteworthy that women accompanied by their husbands, and post-menopausal women, are often not subject to the restriction against drinking in public.

Another simplistic interpretation of the double standard is that men, as "providers" who work long and hard to "bring home the bacon," have earned and deserve the relaxing and sociable values of drinking as kind of "time out." Detailed economic and ecological studies of subsistence among hunting-and-gathering populations have repeatedly shown that women tend to work longer than men and to contribute more to the food supply, apart from their major efforts in unpaid sorts of work that too often are ignored, such as housekeeping, child rearing, cooking, and fuel or water gathering. The social roles traditionally assigned to women are not necessarily lighter or less exacting; on the contrary, they are often precisely those tasks that cannot safely be postponed or done haphazardly, such as caring for children, carrying water, tending the fire, or preparing meals. In short, in most cultures, women are less often afforded the luxury of time out, which may, in large part, account for the relative rareness of female intoxication (Child et al., 1965).

In case anyone assumes that the supposedly "weaker constitution" of women militates against their using alcohol as much as men, the pattern of consumption of prescription psychotropic drugs should be considered. Several studies have reported that women use psychotropics more often than men, and stereotyping of women by male physicians is usually cited as the primary reason. Women more often go to the doctor with nonspecific complaints, which, often are dismissed as as psychosomatic, with the prescription of a psychotropic drug as a routine, but not innocuous, response. However, "a sociocultural approach to this problem rejects the concept of the immutability of the 2:1 female-male ratio of use, unless one accepts the immutability of the social structure of society" (Cooperstock, 1976, p. 106). In fact, Hansen (1989) reported that in another society (Finland), the ratio is only 1.4:1, an illustration of cultural variability in a pattern of drug prescription and usage that had been posited as universal.

Controls *by* Women, Using Alcohol

A different kind of control is that exercised informally among friends, relatives, and peers in the social network that characterizes each individual's fields of sentiment and interaction. Women have traditionally played a major—even if largely unstated—role in moderating the amount and kind of drinking that men do, and in preventing or minimizing the disruptive behaviors that sometimes ensue. A classic ethnographic example was noted as early as the 16th century. The Tupinamba Indians of Brazil enjoyed periodic binges in which all of the men in a community drank copiously; accusations and acrimony often flared briefly but aggression never went beyond verbal exchanges because the women supposedly "hid the weapons" (Staden, 1928). Similar recent accounts are given of Australian aborigines (Brady, 1989), and Quechua women in the Andes often take great pains to protect their drunken husbands from falls, thieves, being run over, and other risks (Allen, 1988).

In contrast, Scandinavian social scientists have written extensively about the striking degree to which women there control men's drinking, by discreetly—or sometimes forcefully—seeing to it that the times, places, and extent of drinking conform to their wishes (Holmila, 1988; Järvinen, 1991). In a similar manner, women who dominated both the production and distribution of native beers usually kept strict order in their informal sales outlets, whether in the Andes, Central America, or sub-Saharan Africa. In all those regions, the recent identification of "problem drinking" tends to be associated with factorymade beverages, sold by males in more impersonal settings.

An unusual illustration of female control through alcohol is the degree to which women in rural Greece can regulate the frequency and often even the time and place of sexual intercourse by their apportionment of sweet wine to their husbands. And this is in a society where another kind of wine (retsina) is wholly made by men and is jealously hoarded by them, to be shared with only a few close friends (Gefou-Madianou, 1992).

The folklore of many cultures provides innumerable instances in which women exert control by using alcohol, soliciting and exacting gifts, services, and valuable promises from men whom they have caused to be intoxicated. The biblical account of Judith's luring Holofernes to his own beheading is perhaps an extreme example. To the extent that European and American drama and fiction reflect reality, alcohol appears similarly to be a tool some women use in gaining at least temporary power they might not otherwise be able to exert over men.

It is important to keep in mind that, however inequitable a culture may be in terms of gender norms, not all women have been victimized before collective consciousness raising, and that alcohol, with its powerful symbolism, can be used in a variety of ways that are extremely liberating, even as it is sometimes used as a tool of oppression.

WHY DOES IT MATTER?

Another stereotype which deserves to be reexamined with respect to alcohol and control is the presumption of a direct correlation between easy availability of alcoholic beverages and a wide range of so-called "alcohol-related problems." This simplistic view has gained almost axiomatic status, as a pseudoscientific misinterpretation of fragmentary data from a few countries with unusual drinking patterns (Heath, 1990). Because it also fits well with intuitive "common sense," it has become the intellectual cornerstone of "the control model" of prevention, which emphasizes increased taxation, limited hours of sale, and a variety of other legal and regulatory restrictions on the availability of alcoholic beverages as the most effective way of preventing drinking problems.

If sheer availability of drink were a major risk factor, women would be drinking much more than men and would have far higher rates of drinking problems, for the simple reason that they have greater access to alcohol. This would certainly be true in those many societies where women are the sole producers and distributors of drink. The ethnographic evidence is overwhelming to the contrary. This contradiction of the "control model" suggests that an alternative "sociocultural model" (Heath, 1992) may be more helpful, a combination of education about alcohol, and recognition of the values of moderate drinking, within appropriate cultural contexts, as the better way to avoid problems with alcohol use.

The time has come to mount studies of women and alcohol that will deal with age cohorts, so that changes in individuals over the life cycle can be disaggregated from changes in cultural norms (Fillmore, 1986). Similarly, studies of women and alcohol should be designed with more attention to subcultures, not only ethnic minority populations, but various socioeconomic, educational, occupational, and other levels (Knupfer, 1982). On survey and screening instruments, the lists of problems that respondents are asked to identify should be revised to include more women-specific concerns (Gomberg, 1986). As always, more attention should be paid to ascertaining what anthropologists call the emic perspective, that is, the viewpoint of the people being studied.

REFERENCES

Ablon, J. (1985). Irish-American Catholics in a west coast metropolitan area. In L.A. Bennet & G.M. Ames (Eds.), *The American experience with alcohol: Contrasting cultural perspectives* (pp. 395–409). New York: Plenum Press.

Allen, C.J. (1988). *The hold life has: Coca and cultural identity in an Andean community*. Washington, DC: Smithsonian Institution Press.

Armstrong, R.W. (1985). Tobacco and alcohol use among urban Malaysians in 1980. *International Journal of the Addictions, 20*, 1803–1808.

Bacon, M.K. (1976). Cross-cultural studies of drinking: Integrated drinking and sex differences in the use of alcoholic beverages. In M.W. Everett, J.O. Waddell, & D.B. Heath (Eds.), *Cross-cultural approaches to the study of alcohol* (pp. 23–33). The Hague: Mouton.

Bahr, H., & Garrett, G.R. (1976). *Women alone: The disaffiliation of urban females*. Lexington, MA: D.C. Heath.

Beckman, L.J. (1976). Alcoholism problems and women: An overview. In M. Greenblatt & M.A. Schuckit (Eds.), *Alcoholism problems in women and children* (pp. 65–96). New York: Grune & Stratton.

Belfer, M.L., & Shader, R.I. (1976). Premenstrual factors as determinants of alcoholism in women. In M. Greenblatt & M.A. Schuckit (Eds.), *Alcoholism problems in women and children* (pp. 97–102). New York: Grune & Stratton.

Berner, P., & Solms, W. (1953). Alkoholismus bei Frauen [Alcoholism in women]. *Wiener Zeitschrift für Nervenheilkunde und deren Grenzgebeite, 6*, 275–301.

Billings, A.G., Weiner, S., Kessler, M., & Gomberg, C.A. (1976). Drinking behavior in laboratory and barroom settings. *Journal of Studies on Alcohol, 37*, 85–89.

Blume, S.B. (1991). Women, alcohol, and drugs. In N.S. Miller (Ed.), *Comprehensive handbook of drug and alcohol addiction*. New York: Marcel Dekker.

Brady, M. (1989). Alcohol use and its effects upon aboriginal women. In J. Vernon (Ed.), *Alcohol and crime* (pp. 135–147). Canberra: Australian institute of Criminology.

Camberwell Council on Alcoholism (Ed.). (1980). *Women and alcohol*. London: Tavistock.

Child, I.L., Barry, H., & Bacon, M.K. (1965). A cross-cultural study of drinking: III. Sex differences. *Quarterly Journal of Studies on Alcohol Supplement, 3*, 49–61.

Colson, E., & Scudder, T. (1988). *For prayer and profit: The ritual, economic, and social importance of beer in Gwembe District, Zambia, 1950–1982*. Stanford, CA: Stanford University Press.

Cooperstock, R. (1976). Women and psychotropic drugs. In A. MacLennan (Ed.), *Women: Their use of alcohol and other legal drugs* (pp. 83–111). Toronto: Addiction Research Foundation.

Curren, F.I. (1937). Personality studies in alcoholic women. *Journal of Nervous and Mental Disorders, 86*, 645–667.

Eames, Alan (1992). *Blood, sweat, and beer*. Los Angeles: Milk and Honey Press.

Engs, R.C. (Ed.), (1990). *Women: Alcohol and other drugs*. Dubuque, IA: Kendall/Hunt.

Ernhart, C.B., Sokol, R.J., Ager, J.W., Morrow-Tlucak, M., & Martier, S. (1989). Alcohol-related birth defects: Assessing the risk. *Annals of the New York Academy of Sciences, 562*, 159–172.

Fillmore, K.M. (1984). "When angels fall": Women's drinking as cultural preoccupation and as reality. In S.C. Wilsnack & L.J. Beckman (Eds.), *Alcohol problems in women: Antecedents, consequences, and intervention* (pp. 7–36). New York: Guilford Press.

Fillmore, K.M. (1986). Issues in the changing drinking patterns among women in the last century. In National Institute on Alcohol Abuse and Alcoholism (Ed.), *Women and alcohol: Health-related issues* (pp. 69–77). Rockville, MD: National Institute on Alcohol Abuse and Alcoholism.

Frezza, M., DiPadova, C., Pozzato, G., Terpin, M., Baraona, E., & Lieber, C.S. (1990). High blood-alcohol levels in women: The role of decreased gastric alcohol dehydrogenase activity and first-pass metabolism. *New England Journal of Medicine, 322,* 95–99.

Gefou-Madianou, D. (1992). Exclusion and unity, retsina and sweet wine: Commensality and gender in a Greek agrotown. In D. Gefou-Madianou (Ed.), *Alcohol, gender and culture.* New York: Routledge, Chapman, & Hall.

Gilbert, M.J. (1985). Mexican-Americans in California: Intracultural variation in attitudes and behavior related to alcohol. In L.A. Bennett & G.M. Ames (Eds.), *The American experience with alcohol: Contrasting cultural perspectives* (pp. 255–277). New York: Plenum Press.

Gomberg, E.S.L. (1986). Women and alcoholism: Psychosocial issues. In National Institute on Alcohol Abuse and Alcoholism (Ed.), *Women and alcohol: Health-related issues* (pp. 78–120). Rockville, MD: National Institute on Alcohol Abuse and Alcoholism.

Greenblatt, M., & Schuckit, M.A. (Eds.). (1976). *Alcoholism problems in women and children.* New York: Grune & Stratton.

Haavio-Mannila, E. (Ed.). (1989). *Women, alcohol, and drugs in the Nordic countries* (NAD Publication 16). Helsinki: Nordic Council for Alcoholism and Drug Research.

Hagaman, B.L. (1980). Food for thought: Beer in a social and ritual context in a west African society. *Journal of Drug Issues, 10,* 203–214.

Hansen, E.H. (1989). Sex differences in the use of psychotropic drugs: An annotated review of Danish studies. In E. Haavio-Mannila (Ed.), *Women, alcohol, and drugs in the Nordic countries* (pp. 97–132). Helsinki: Nordic Council for Alcoholism and Drug Research.

Harper, F.F. (1904). *The Code of Hammurabi, King of Babylon.* London: Luzac.

Heath, D.B. (1983). Alcohol and aggression: A "missing link" in worldwide perspective. In E. Gottheil, K.A. Druley, T.E. Skoloda, & H.M. Waxman (Eds.), *Alcohol, drug abuse and aggression* (pp. 89–103). Springfield, IL: Charles C. Thomas.

Heath, D.B. (1989). American Indians and alcohol: Epidemiological and sociocultural relevance. In D.L. Spiegler, D.A. Tate, S.S. Aitkin, & C.M. Christian (Eds.), *Alcohol use among U.S. minorities* (NIAAA Research Monograph 18, pp. 207–222). Rockville, MD: National Institute on Alcohol Abuse and Alcoholism.

Heath, D.B. (1990). Flawed policies from flawed premises: Pseudoscience about alcohol and drugs. In R.C. Engs (Ed.), *Controversies in the addictions field* (Vol. 1, pp. 78–83). Dubuque, IA: Kendall/Hunt.

Heath, D.B. (1992). Prohibition or liberalization of alcohol and drugs: A sociocultural perspective. In M. Galanter (Ed.), *Recent developments in alcoholism* (Vol. 10, pp. 129–145). New York: Plenum Press.

Heath, D.B., & Cooper, A.M. (1981). *Alcohol use and world cultures: A comprehensive bibliography of anthropological sources.* Toronto: Addiction Research Foundation.

Hellmann, E. (1934). The importance of beer brewing in an urban native yard. *Bantu Studies, 8,* 38–60.

Hill, S.Y. (1982). Biological consequences of alcoholism and alcohol-related problems among women. In National Institute on Alcohol Abuse and Alcoholism (Ed.), *Special population issues* (pp. 43–73). Rockville, MD: National Institute on Alcohol Abuse and Alcoholism.

Holmila, M. (1988). *Wives, husbands and alcohol: A study of informal drinking control within the family.* Helsinki: Finnish Foundation for Alcohol Studies.

Hunt, G., & Satterlee, S. (1987). Darts, drinks and the pub: The culture of female drinking. *The Sociological Review, 35,* 575–601.

Járvinen, M. (1991). The controlled controllers: Women, men, and alcohol. *Contemporary Drug Problems, 18,* 389–406.

Jones, B.M. & Jones, M.K. (1976). Women and alcohol: Intoxication, metabolism, and the menstrual cycle. In M. Greenblatt & M.A. Schuckit (Eds.), *Alcoholism problems in women and children* (pp. 103–136). New York: Grune & Stratton.

Karpman, B. (1948). *The alcoholic woman.* Washington: Linacre Press.

Kennedy, J.G. (1978). *Tarahumara of the Sierra Madre: Beer, ecology, and social organization.* Arlington Heights, IL: A H M Publishing.

Knupfer, G. (1982). Problems associated with drunkenness in women: Some research issues. In National Institute on Alcohol Abuse and Alcoholism (Ed.), *Special population issues* (pp. 3–39). Rockville, MD: National Institute on Alcohol Abuse and Alcoholism.

Leigh, B.C. (1990). "Venus gets in my thinking": Drinking and female sexuality in the age of AIDS. *Journal of Substance Abuse, 2,* 129–145.

Lisansky, E.S. (1957). Alcoholism in women: Social and psychological concomitants: I. Social history data. *Quarterly Journal of Studies on Alcohol, 18,* 588–623.

Little, R.E., & Ervin, C.H. (1984). Alcohol use and reproduction. In S.C. Wilsnack & L.J. Beckman (Eds.), *Alcohol problems in women: Antecedents, consequences, and intervention* (pp. 155–188). New York: Guilford Press.

MacAndrew, C., & Edgerton, R.B. (1969). *Drunken comportment: A social explanation.* Chicago: Aldine.

MacLennan, A. (Ed.). (1976). *Women: Their use of alcohol and other legal drugs.* Toronto: Addiction Research Foundation.

Marshall, M. (Ed.). (1979). *Beliefs, behaviors, and alcoholic beverages: A cross-cultural survey.* Ann Arbor: University of Michigan Press.

McClelland, D.C., Davis, W.N., Kalin, R., & Wanner, E. (1972). *The drinking man.* New York: Free Press.

Morrissey, E.R. (1986). Of women, by women, or for women? Selected issues in the primary prevention of drinking problems. In National Institute on Alcohol Abuse and Alcoholism (Ed.), *Women and alcohol: Health-related issues* (pp. 226–259). Rockville, MD: National Institute on Alcohol Abuse and Alcoholism.

National Institute on Alcohol Abuse and Alcoholism. (Ed.). (1980). *Alcoholism and alcohol abuse among women: Research issues* (Research Monograph 1). Rockville, MD: Author.

National Institute on Alcohol Abuse and Alcoholism. (Ed.). (1982). *Special population issues* (Alcohol and Health Monograph 4). Rockville, MD: Author.

National Institute on Alcohol Abuse and Alcoholism. (Ed.). (1986). *Women and alcohol: Health-related issues* (Research Monograph 18). Rockville, MD: Author.

National Institute on Alcohol Abuse and Alcoholism. (Ed.). (1987). *Sixth special report to the U.S. Congress on alcohol and health* (D.H.H.S. Publication (ADM) 87–1519). Rockville, MD: Author.

Page, J.B., Rio, L., Sweeney, J., & McKay, C. (1985). Alcohol and adaptation to exile in Miami's Cuban population. In L.A. Bennett & G.M. Ames (Eds.), *The American experience with alcohol: Contrasting cultural perspectives* (pp. 315–332). New York: Plenum Press.

Park, J. (1990). Only "those" women: Women and the control of alcohol in New Zealand. *Contemporary Drug Problems, 17,* 221–250.

Ridlon, F.V. (1988). *A fallen angel: The status insulary of the female alcoholic.* London: Associated University Presses.

Rosett, H.L., & Weiner, L. (1984). *Alcohol and the fetus: A clinical perspective.* New York: Oxford University Press.

Schuckit, M.A., & Morrissey, E.R. (1976). Alcoholism in women: Some clinical and social perspectives with an emphasis on possible subtypes. In M. Greenblatt & M.A. Schuckit (Eds.), *Alcoholism problems in women and children* (pp. 5–35.). New York: Grune & Stratton.

Staden, Hans (1928). *The true history of his captivity. . . .* London: Broadway Travelers. (Original work published 1557)

Stimmel, B. (Ed.). (1986). *Alcohol and substance abuse in women and children.* New York: Haworth Press.

Topper, M.D. (1985). Navajo "alcoholism": Drinking, alcohol abuse, and treatment in a changing cultural environment. In L.A. Bennett & G.M. Ames (Eds.), *The American experience with alcohol: Contrasting cultural perspectives* (pp. 227–251). New York: Plenum Press.

Wall, J.H. (1937). A study of alcoholism in women. *Journal of Psychiatry, 93,* 943–952.

Weibel-Orlando, J. (1986). Women and alcohol: Special populations and cross-cultural variations. In National Institute on Alcohol Abuse and Alcoholism (Ed.), *Women and alcohol: health-related issues* (pp. 161–187). Rockville, MD: National Institute on Alcohol Abuse and Alcoholism.

Wilsnack, S.C. (1976). The impact of sex roles and women's alcohol use and abuse. In M. Greenblatt & M.A. Schuckit (Eds.), *Alcoholism problems in women and children* (pp. 37–63). New York: Grune & Stratton.

Wilsnack, S.C. (1984). Drinking, sexuality, and sexual dysfunction in women. In S.C. Wilsnack & L.J. Beckman (Eds.), *Alcohol problems in women: Antecedents, consequences, and intervention* (pp. 189–227). New York: Guilford Press.

Wilsnack, S.C. & Beckman, L.J. (Eds.). (1984). *Alcohol problems in women: Antecedents, consequences, and intervention*. New York: Guilford Press.

Wilsnack, S.C., Wilsnack, R.W., & Klassen, A.D. (1986). Epidemiological research on women's drinking, 1978–1984. In National Institute on Alcohol Abuse and Alcoholism (Ed.), *Women and alcohol: Health-related issues* (pp. 1–68). Rockville, MD: National Institute on Alcohol Abuse and Alcoholism.

Woods, C.P. (1981). *Alcohol abuse among lesbians: An investigation of possible contributing factors* (Dissertation No. DDJ 81–27512). Ann Arbor, MI: University Microfilms.

World Health Organization. (1990). *Health for all by the year 2000*. Geneva: W.H.O.

Youcha, G. (1986). *Women and alcohol: A dangerous pleasure*. New York: Crown Publishers.

Chapter 6

Antecedents and Consequences

Edith S. Lisansky Gomberg

Department of Psychiatry
Alcohol Research Center
University of Michigan

Ted D. Nirenberg

Department of Psychiatry and
Human Behavior
Center for Alcohol and
Addiction Studies
Brown University
and
Roger Williams Medical Center
Providence, RI

Although several discussions of alcohol use and abuse theories have emerged (Blane & Leonard, 1986; Chaudron & Wilkinson, 1988), the theorists rarely raise the question of relevance of their theory to *female* alcohol use and abuse. As is true in many areas of research, the assumption is that having theorized about male alcoholism, the same theoretical constructs explain female alcoholism as well. Although there are many theoretical approaches, such as social learning theory, systems theory, neurobiological theory, theories about expectancy or stress response dampening, a review of theories as they relate to female alcohol and drug use and abuse has yet to be written.

That many differences have surfaced in the years of research on male and female drinking goes without saying, but it is questionable whether women's behavior in relation to drinking and alcoholism should be called "theoretical anomalies" (Blane & Leonard, 1986):

When the research has been conducted with women, it is not unusual to find theoretical anomalies . . . . Some of the factors posited to influence drinking do not seem to apply to females in quite the same way as they apply to males. (pp. 392–393)

A useful theoretical approach seems to be an interactional one (Sadava, 1985, 1986, 1988). Based historically on the theorizing of Lewin (1935) with its description of the interaction of person and "environmental forces," and brought up to date by Sadava, behavior is conceived as a function of the interaction of person, environment, and behavior. Behavior "X" may be predicted with knowledge of the relevant variables describing the person, environment, and other behaviors. Principles include the conception of personality as a multivariate system; personality variables may be grouped into different patterns or dimensions. Relevant environmental features are characteristics of the environment which are reasonably consistent over time and across different situations. Variables studied may be distal or proximal, past history or recent events. Such an interactional approach is at the base of developmental models, such as Zucker's (1987) developmental model, and also at the base of the Jessors's problem behavior viewpoint (1977). The interactional approach leads to models which involve multivariate analyses and longitudinal study.

Antecedents and consequences are discussed in separate sections, recognizing the fact that there is no simple, sequential cause–effect relationship which goes from antecedents to onset to continued heavy drinking to consequences. Depression, for example, may run like a thread through all of these. It may be antecedent to abusive drinking for both men and women, but the heavy alcohol intake and the inevitable consequences produce deepening of depression. This is the place to note the fallacy of *post hoc, ergo propter hoc* reasoning: Behaviors noted in people presenting themselves for treatment are not necessarily behaviors which existed antecedent to the heavy alcohol/drug use. It is useful in treatment to know about such behaviors, but they cannot be assumed etiological. Furthermore, there is cycling: Negative consequences may produce relapse with a cycling back in the sequence of events and often it is difficult to discriminate between cause and effect. Etiology is never simple, indeed it represents "a convergence of causal influences" (Sadava, 1988). Ours is a developmental approach, that is, many antecedent conditions and states will contribute at different points in the life course to the onset of alcohol and drug abuse.

ANTECEDENTS

Events and states which are antecedent to alcohol and drug problems may be viewed as multivariate in at least two ways. First, antecedents

Table 6.1.   Antecedents of Female Alcohol/Drug Problems

	Childhood	Adolescence	Young Adulthood
Biological/ genetic	Positive family history	Menses, pregnancies	Metabolism of alcohol/ gynecological and obstetrical events
Personality	Irritability, tantrums, "nervousness"	Impulse control problems	Depression, inadequate coping mechanisms
Sociocultural	SES, neighborhood, region, family norms	School, peers, religious group	Availability, user who is a significant other
Drinking/drug behavior	Of parents, sibs, relatives	Early use of alcohol, marijuana, nicotine	Social contexts of drug/alcohol use

are biopsychosocial, and second, the antecedents may occur during childhood, adolescence, young adulthood, and in fact, throughout the lifespan. Since the largest proportion of female alcohol and drug abuse occurs during early and middle-aged adult life, we present those antecedents, those events, states, conditions, and influences which occur in the earlier parts of the lifespan.

Table 6.1 presents in tabular form the complex and multivariate nature of antecedents. Biological/genetic and personality variables may be considered as person variables and sociocultural and drinking and drug use behaviors as social-environmental. In a sense, all of the antecedents listed under childhood continue on through adolescent and adult life. For example, positive family history remains a major influence throughout the lifespan. The same is true of personality variables. For example, childhood depression is reported by significantly more alcoholic women in treatment (39%) then by matched controls (18%) (Gomberg, 1989a). For most female substance abusers, depression is an issue throughout the lifespan. Sociocultural and drinking and drug use behavior in the social environment are significant influences among antecedents, although it may be different groups (i.e., family, peers, spouse, or friends) which influence one's drinking or drug use at different stages of life.

Biological/Genetic Variables

The relevance of genetic mediation in the development of female alcoholism is discussed in Chapter 3. The discussion of genetic mediation contains the old question of nature versus nurture. People who grow up with an alcoholic parent, sibling, or other relative are not only biologically linked to alcoholism, but they have also grown up with a model of alcoholic behavior. The role of positive family history has been well-studied in designs which compare children of alcoholic biological parents who are adopted and raised by nonalcoholic parents (Goodwin, Schulsinger, Hermanson, Guze, & Winokur, 1973; Goodwin, Schulsinger, Knop, Mednick, & Guze, 1977). The role of genetic endowment in female alcoholism has been unclear, the consensus being that although an important etiological variable, such genetic endowment was less of a risk factor for women than for men. This has been called into question by Hill and Smith's work (Chapter 3, this volume) and by a recent twin study of women (Kendler, Heath, Niele, Kessler, & Eaves, 1992). Using female twin sets in the general population, all in their twenties, and three definitions of lifetime prevalence of alcoholism based on the criteria in DSM IIIR (*Diagnostic and Statistical Manual*, 1987), the authors conclude that the role of genetic factors among women is "similar" for both narrow and broad definitions of alcoholism. These definitions included alcoholism with tolerance or dependence, alcoholism with or without tolerance or dependence, and alcoholism with or without tolerance, dependence, or problem drinking. Differences between male and female alcoholics are minimal. Estimates for the heritability of liability to alcoholism in women in this sample ranged from 50% to 61% (Kendler et al., 1992). They conclude that genetic factors play a "major role" in the etiology of female alcoholism which is similar to the contribution of genetic factors in male alcoholism. The remaining 40-50% of the total variance in vulnerability to alcoholism is attributed by Kendler et al. to "environmental factors," which may include socioeconomic class status, parental drinking, parental discipline, friends' drinking, and so on.

The onset of menses and subsequent pregnancies are biological facts of life, and while hormonal cycles and pregnancies are quite within normal range, there may be associated biopsychological stresses. For a brief period, the role of premenstrual syndrome (PMS) in triggering heavy drinking bouts among alcoholic women was speculated on, discussed, and researched. There is surprisingly little work reported about the effects of alcohol during different stages of the menstrual cycle. Parturition has had a good deal of research attention, but such attention has been focused on fetal effects, and little work has been devoted to alcohol and the pregnant woman. A serendipitous finding in the Michigan Alcoholism in Women Study (described below) is of interest (Gomberg, 1986). Alcoholic women in treatment, 184 of whom have had at least one child, were asked about drinking during pregnancies. Responses indicated that daily drinking was reported by no women during the *first* pregnancy, 1.3% during the second pregnancy, and 3.0% during the third pregnancy. Drinking "often" during pregnancy was reported by 2.7% for the first pregnancy, by 5.8% for the second pregnancy, and by 5.9% for the third pregnancy. Surely, there is more to be explored in alcohol and drinking during pregnancy by women than the fetal alcohol syndrome.

Gender differences in the metabolism of alcohol are discussed in Chapter 1. Such differences clearly are related to female alcoholics' greater vulnerability to hepatic disorder then male alcoholics, and the establishment of such differences may be a valuable tool in prevention.

As for sexual and reproductive antecedents of female alcoholism, Wilsnack (1984) reviewed studies which show rather high levels of sexual dysfunction among alcoholic women. With a general population sample, a retrospective analysis of changes in female drinking behavior over the lifetime (Wilsnack, Klassen, & Wilsnack, 1986) led to the conclusion that heavy drinking was more likely to *follow* experience with "reproductive problems." This suggests that events like miscarriage, premature delivery, and hysterectomy are more likely to occur *before* the heavy drinking of women. The unhappiness which often accompanies impairment of the reproductive role may then be viewed as antecedent. The negative influence of heavy alcohol intake on gynecological/obstetrical health is clear as well, and heavy drinking— as well as smoking, marijuana use, and other drug behaviors— produces reproductive health problems.

Personality Variables

Patterns of behavior may be evident as early as infancy (e.g., irritability and "nervousness" are observed in newborns). As the child grows, one fundamental task of socialization is impulse control, and difficulties in impulse control may surface early in life. In a classic follow-up study, Robins (1966) followed up a sample of children, median age 13, who were referred to and seen at a psychiatric clinic. Thirty years later, these "deviant children grown up" demonstrated that those who presented with antisocial behavior and conduct disorders as children were likely to be "problem adults." Women and men who were antisocial as children experienced similar problems as adults. As for alcohol problems:

> Patients referred for antisocial behavior had a very high rate of excess alcohol intake as adults. . . . Alcohol problems, like arrests, are much more common in men than in women. . . . Although the rates in women were lower, the excess of alcohol problems in women who had antisocial referrals was as marked as for men. (Robins, 1966, p. 61)

The same linkage between acting-out behaviors and poor impulse control in early life and later development of alcohol/drug problems has been found by others. Block, Block, and Keyes (1988), studying longitudinal foretelling of drug usage in adolescence, report that at ages 3 and 4 years "subsequent adolescent drug usage in girls related to both undercontrol and lower ego resiliency" (p. 336). Marijuana use in girls at age 14 was related to rebelliousness, inability to delay gratification, unconventional behavior, and hostility. For both boys and girls, the personality characteristics persisted over time and led to later involvement with drugs, and for both sexes, the behaviors were conceptualized as ego undercontrol.

A comparison of alcoholic women in treatment with an age-matched, social class-matched, nonalcoholic control group, showed the alcoholic women reporting significantly more often a history of childhood temper tantrums, enuresis, running away, and behavior difficulties in school (Gomberg, 1989a). While it is true that these comparisons are based on retrospective self-report, it is significant that the alcoholic and nonalcoholic women show very little difference in childhood "neurotic" behaviors, while they show very large differences in problem behaviors related to impulse control. Also of some relevance is the clear association of such difficulties in impulse control with the earlier onset of alcohol problems in this sample.

There is some evidence to support a hypothesis linking inadequate coping mechanisms in early life with later development of alcohol/drug abuse. The alcoholic women in the sample described above did not differ from the control women in the report of negative *events* during childhood and adolescence (e.g., a parent absent because of death or desertion, economic deprivation, illness in the family). The description of *affective response* to events in early life does distinguish the alcoholic and nonalcoholic women. From childhood on, the women who have developed alcohol problems report feeling unloved and unwanted, a good deal of unhappiness, and a lack of closeness to their mothers. Clearly, what distinguishes female alcoholics and a matched control group is not the events per se in childhood, but the way in which those events are responded to.

Female alcoholics often have dealt with their depressions and family tensions by engaging in problematic behaviors. The female alcoholics in the Michigan study left school earlier, made unsatisfactory marriages, and worked at relatively low occupational levels (Gomberg, 1991). Inevitably, these attempts at solving problems produce more depression. Depressive affect frequently precedes the onset of problem drinking, is dealt with by alcohol intake, and the coping technique (i.e., the drinking) compounds and deepens the depression.

Sociocultural Variables

Children are born to mothers and fathers and into families which are defined socially by income, religion/ethnicity, parental occupation and education, and the community in which they live. These social definitions of family determine the pattern of socialization and the content, which includes attitudes and behavior relating to alcohol and drugs. The drinking and drug use behaviors of significant others, extended family, and peers and friends communicate the norms and model the behavior. There has been a fair amount of work in the alcohol literature reporting the normative behaviors relating, for example, to drinking in different ethnic groups. Such normative behavior relating to alcohol and drugs is part of a broader socialization:

> Current information about linkages between nationality and cultural differences and differences in patterns of drinking is . . . available. Although knowledge of ethnicity may be useful in developing a predictive etiologic equation, it is essential to remember that ethnic differences relate not only to norms about child and adult alcohol use and intoxication but . . . (also to) differences in educational and occupational aspiration, cohesiveness of kinship networks, and cultural values about sexuality, marriage, and other elements of socialized behavior. (Zucker & Gomberg, 1986, p. 789)

The *availability* of alcohol and other drugs may be included as a relevant sociocultural variable. The reported easy availability of alcohol and other drugs in high schools, and even in many junior high schools, produces more experimentation with alcohol and drugs than would be the case if availability was limited.

A user or abuser who is a significant other is a major influence in determining alcohol and drug abuse among women. Starting with early family members in the family of origin, and moving on to the boyfriend, husband, and/or lover, the impact of an abuser who is a significant other is great, and must be considered a major antecedent.

Generally, surveys have found the largest proportion of heavy drinkers among divorced/separated women, with single women ranking second (Cahalan, Cisin, & Crossley, 1969; Clark & Midanik, 1982; Johnson, 1982; Wilsnack, Wilsnack, & Klassen, 1984). Women who were cohabiting also showed heavier drinking and more adverse consequences (Wilsnack, Wilsnack, & Klassen, 1984). It is probably on that basis that an assumption has been made that divorce is a stress and a trauma and, as a negative event, is somehow associated with heavier drinking. Hanna, Faden, and Harford (in press) in an analysis of drinking data of women 24 to 32 years of age who were respondents in the National Longitudinal Survey of Youth, also found that women who become separated or divorced increased alcohol consumption. In addition, they found that women who married or remarried decreased their consumption. They concluded that "instability created by a change in social position, viz. marital status, led to changes in drinking patterns during the study interval in the direction of those associated with the new social position." Further, recent analyses of epidemiological, longitudinal data have suggested that divorce may be "a remedy" as well as a risk factor for heavy drinking (Wilsnack & Wilsnack, 1991). The dissolution of an unhappy marriage may lead to *less* rather than more drinking (see Chapter 4).

Drinking and Drug Using Behaviors

One of the best predictors of future behavior with alcohol and drugs is current behavior with substances. This is supported by a number of research reports. Fillmore, Bacon, and Hyman (1975) followed the respondents in an early survey of college drinking and reported that the best predictor for female problem drinking in later life was "frequent heavy drinking" reported during the college years. The predictive value of early drinking and drug-use behaviors was borne out in a study of 301 alcoholic women (Gomberg, 1988a). Attempting to predict the age of onset among these alcoholic women in treatment, many variables were examined. The best model included three variables: age at first intoxication, use of marijuana and other drugs between ages 13 and 15, and childhood temper tantrums. It was concluded that while some predictors, such as temper tantrums during childhood, have some merit, early behaviors relating to alcohol and drugs are probably the strongest predictors of later abusive use. It is of relevance, too, that twice as many alcoholic women respondents began smoking at or before age 15 than matched-control women respondents: 43% and 21%, respectively (Gomberg, 1989b).

It is not only the fact of early use and abuse of substances which is predictive of later problems, but the *social contexts* in which such early use and abuse occurs. The alcoholic women who constituted the study sample (Gomberg, 1986) were asked about the social contexts in which adolescent drinking occurred. Of the early-onset alcoholic women, in their twenties, 9% reported adults present during early-life drinking; 27% of the alcoholic women in their thirties reported adults present;

and among the oldest group, 43% of the alcoholic women in their forties did their earliest drinking with adults present.

Other Antecedents

A review of the state of knowledge about antecedents (Gomberg & Lisansky, 1984) includes a discussion of cause and effect sequences, and a definition of antecedents as "life events and responses" that lead to the onset of heavy, problematic drinking. One approach is the study of risk factors. Another is the study of vulnerabilities. There is also an approach through the study of motivation to drink, but there is a significant limitation to such an approach. The functional autonomy of motives (i.e., the reasons that women *maintain* their heavy, abusive use of alcohol) may not be the same as the motivations that led to *onset*. Most writers agree that the etiology of female alcoholism is "multifactorial" (Shaw, 1980), and after a good deal of path analyses of epidemiological survey data, Wilsnack, Wilsnack, and Klassen (1987) concluded that the pathway to female alcoholism is not simple. Shaw (1980) includes not only physiological, psychological, and social variables, but economic variables as well (e.g., greater or lesser availability of alcoholic beverages, prices, and advertising).

For a long time, it was accepted that female alcoholism was "more intimately associated with a definite life situation" than male alcoholism (Wall, 1937), although there was speculation that such report of traumatic precipitants could be a defensive maneuver (Lisansky, 1957). The *definition* of such precipitating situations was undetermined: Sometimes, it involved a traumatic event, and other times, a prolonged negative mood state. The idea of concrete precipitants was questioned by Allan and Cooke (1985), who argued cogently that some of the negative events cited as causes could as easily be argued as consequences. As noted earlier, for example, in terms of depression, women may start heavy drinking to deal with depression, but there is no question that the alcohol intake compounds the depression. The *nature* of so-called traumatic events also may be called into question. The process of divorce may be stressful, but Wilsnack and Wilsnack's (1991) data question whether divorce is a "risk" or a "remedy" and conclude that it is both. Finally, there is some evidence that it is not stress per se, but the affective response to stress which is a relevant etiological variable.

One "definite life situation" which has received some recent research attention is the antecedent of childhood physical and sexual abuse. Epidemiological study of women's drinking and reported early childhood sexual abuse indicates that a relationship between a history of abuse and heavy episodic drinking, frequency of intoxication,and problem consequences exists (Wilsnack & Klassen, 1992). A relationship between childhood sexual abuse and the development of alcoholism in women has also been reported (Miller, Downs, Gondoli, & Keil, 1987). What is needed is further study of families in which physical and sexual abuse occurs and does not occur. Although the abuse occurs more frequently in families where one or both parents are alcoholic, later onset of alcohol or drug abuse may be both a byproduct of neglect and poor protection of the child, and a result of direct parental abuse.

Integration

There is general agreement that the etiology of female alcoholism, like the etiology of male alcoholism, is complex and multivariate. A useful concept is Sadava's (1988) description of a "convergence of causal influences." A major task of science is prediction and the search for reliable antecedents is part of the search for a sound predictive equation. Such an equation would have not one but several components: biological, psychological, and social. Furthermore, some of the components appear at one life stage and others at different life stages. The task is a large one, encompassing both epidemiological and clinical research.

CONSEQUENCES

The study of consequences of female problem drinking usually appears as one of the following: problems presented by women in treatment, reasons for entering treatment, comparisons of male and female alcoholism, and, in the biomedical field, the effect of alcohol intake on different bodily systems. A book by Estes and Heineman (1986) deals with the "pathophysiologic" effects of alcohol in chapters on intoxication and withdrawal, malnutrition, disorders of the gastrointestinal system, neurologic disorders, hematologic disorder, and disorders of the heart and skeletal muscles. Wartenberg and Liepman (1987) provide a comprehensive review of the medical consequences of substance abuse. Wilsnack and Beckman (1984) describe consequences in two chapters dealing with "marital violence" and effects on the family. In another chapter they list some of the characteristics of women seeking treatment, including health-related problems, difficulties on the job, financial difficulties, family problems, and stigma.

Consequences also may act to maintain the problem drinking. Stresses and unhappy events may precipitate more drinking bouts which, in turn, compound the problems. When alcoholic women in treatment facilities are asked about their entry into treatment, the reason for seeking treatment cited most often (see Table 6.2) is deepening depression. Allan and Cooke (1985) have written about the probability that heavy drinking produces "an increased frequency of stressful life events." It seems obvious to view the life problems presented by alcoholics as linked to their drinking, as well as to antecedent events.

What are some of the biopsychosocial factors which may influence the nature and intensity of consequences for the problem-drinking women?

1. Comorbidity (see Chapter 7) is one variable which contributes to consequences. Clinical research consistently indicates that female alcoholics present with more comorbidity than male alcoholics, and it appears that alcoholics with comorbid psychiatric conditions have poorer prognosis.

2. Socioeconomic status may play a major role in determining the nature and intensity of consequences. An early study noted that the "social repercussions" of alcoholism among women seemed determined primarily by social status (Fort & Porterfield, 1961). A review of sex roles and psychiatric labeling noted that upper-income persons gave men "much greater tolerance for drug and alcohol abuse than women" (Coie & Costanzo, 1977). Most of the epidemiological work which has noted SES has compared the proportion of light, moderate, and heavy drinkers in different income groups. There is more light and moderate drinking in upper-middle and upper-income groups, but the proportion of heavy drinkers does not show significant social class differences.

Table 6.2.   Early Stage Behaviors Reported by Female Alcoholics
Q: When you first started drinking regularly, did you experience:

| | | Ages | |
	Total (%)	20–29 (%)	30–39 (%)	40–49 (%)
Hangover	60	74	62	44
Driving while drunk	46	68	45	22
Drinking alone	45	58	46	31
Drunk in public places more than once	45	72	40	23
Blackouts	34	61	29	12
Beginning to drink in the morning	23	33	21	15
Taking pills in the morning to get going	23	42	17	9

Note. All age comparisons yield significant *p* values, ranging from .0000 to .0080

Nor are sex, age, and social class differences clear (Cahalan, Cisin, & Crossley, 1969).

3. Age of the problem drinker is also a factor. There are clear indications that societal consequences may be heavier for younger female problem drinkers (Gomberg, 1988b). The intervening variable here may be the public versus the private nature of the heavy drinking. While all age groups of alcoholic women tend to do much of their drinking at home, the youngest group studied, those 20 to 29, did much more drinking than older alcoholic women in bars and other public places (Gomberg, 1986). Consequences are likely to relate to visibility of the drinker.

4. One may list the severity of drinking as related to the consequences, but this is circular. Severity is usually defined, in tests and clinical interviews, by the consequences.

Some Male/Female Comparison of Consequences

A review of the literature on female problem drinking from 1970 to 1986 by Schmidt, Klee, and Ames (1990) led to the conclusion that the consequences of alcohol problems may be greater for women than for men. These authors distinguished two sets of consequences: physiological and marital/familial consequences. They noted that health problems appear earlier in women's drinking histories and that women experience more marital and familial disruption, intensifying the effects on children and the workplace.

Other reports deal with different patterns of male or female consequences of problem drinking. Robbins (1989), examining the data of the 1985 National Institute on Drug Abuse National Household Survey, concluded that drug abuse is related more strongly to "intrapsychic problems" in women and to problems in "social functioning " among men. Intrapsychic problems include depression, irritability,and anxiety, while difficulties in social functioning include trouble at work, money problems, and difficulty with the police. Worner and Delgado (1991), using the Addiction Severity Index, found male alcohol is reporting more problems with legal authorities and female alcoholics reporting more family and "psychiatric" problems. Orford and Keddie (1985) also compared male and female problem drinkers in reported effects of their drinking. Interestingly enough, women were not more likely than men to report interpersonal effects. Males were more likely to report negative consequences relating to work, finances, leisure, and fitness.

We have argued that consequences are related to the age and social status of the problem drinker and there is no reason to doubt that consequences are related to gender as well. Clearly, the problem of sexual impotence is primarily a male effect and fetal alcohol effects are primarily a female consequence. Some consequences (e.g., drunk driving or problems at work) can be adjusted for the different proportion of men and women involved. However, when we get to issues of guilt, neglect of obligations, effects on children, and psychiatric diagnoses, we are into study of consequences with difficult measurement problems.

A Clinical Study of Female Alcoholics

In an attempt to examine the consequences of problem drinking, 301 women enrolled in alcoholism treatment facilities were asked questions about their behaviors when they first started drinking heavily and during the entire period they were drinking heavily,and recent consequences of their drinking.

The women reported that when they first started drinking regularly (early-stage behaviors) consequences frequently included hangovers, driving while drunk, drinking alone, being drunk in public places, blackouts, and so on. Table 6.2 includes the frequency of these behaviors across the different age groups. All early-stage behaviors associated with drinking are reported significantly more often by younger alcoholics.

Table 6.3 shows the problems and behaviors as the drinking continues (middle-stage behaviors). Problems with family and friends are

Table 6.3.   Middle Stage Behaviors Reported by Female Alcoholics
Q: During the period while you were drinking . . .

	Total (%)	Ages		
		20–29 (%)	30–39 (%)	40–49 (%)
Family/friends became angry and critical	71	70	74	70
Sometimes you wouldn't leave the house at all except to buy liquor	59	56	65	55
Saw few people, mostly those you drank with	59	74	57	46
Cut yourself off from old friends	57	70	51	51
There was gossip about your being immoral	27	44	22	14

Age differences yield significant p values, .0000 to .009.

Table 6.4.   Consequences Reported by Female Alcoholics
Q: Things that may have happened to you because of your drinking . . .

	% Reporting
A. Effects on self	
You started to dislike yourself	94
Felt increasingly depressed and drank even more	93
Felt increasingly lonely and drank even more	86
Lost the ability to concentrate	72
Felt as if you were going out of your mind	69
Trouble making a decision about anything	69
Felt very suspicious and distrustful	63
B. Physical/Medical effects	
Couldn't account for some periods of time	81
Felt sick/crummy most of the time	76
Found bruises/couldn't remember how you got them	77
Noticed that your hands shook when you tried to pick something up	72
You began to look awful	70
Began needing a drink when you got up in the morning	57
Became more and more unbearable when you were hung over	53
C. Interpersonal/Social/Familial consequences	
People you knew asked you to stop drinking	77
Began having serious family quarrels	68
Began avoiding friends who didn't drink much	56
Communication with parents or other relatives decreased	53

Significant age differences. Youngest group reporting most.

reported most frequently and consistently across all ages. The other items deal with increasing isolation and withdrawal.

Table 6.4 shows three major areas of consequences as reported by the women in treatment: effects on the self (psychological effects), physical/medical effects, and interpersonal/social/familial consequences. Interestingly, when the women were asked about what was going on in their lives just before entering treatment, the responses were parallel. The reason for entering into treatment given most frequently is a psychological consequence, for example, deepening depression. The physical/medical effects of alcohol rank as the second most frequent reason for entry into treatment (e.g., blackouts, DTs), and the third is problematic relationships.

The consequences that existed during the months before entrance into treatment are listed in Table 6.5. Two sets of the consequences relate to age grouping. First in noting problems with children, it is important to note that less than a quarter of the younger women and 95% of the older women had children. Second, "trouble with police" seemed linked to the public nature of younger persons' drinking.

Table 6.5.   Later Stage Behaviors Reported by Female Alcoholics
Q: During the months before you stopped drinking and got into treatment
    this time . . .

| | | Ages | | |
	Total (%)	20–29 (%)	30–39 (%)	40–49 (%)
Deepening depression	88	91	90	83
Increasing trouble with blackouts, DTs, shakiness, passing out	67	77	60	66*
Problems with husband/ relationship	66	62	72	62
Problems with one of your children	33	10	35	44**
Trouble with police	21	33	14	17**

*$p = .05$
**$p = .001$

Differences in drinking-related consequences were explored in a factor analysis study (Turnbull & Gomberg, 1991). A series of exploratory principal component analyses yielded nine factors: social withdrawal, sexuality, early effects, maternal role, accidents, symptoms, work, illness, and relationship conflict. The authors note the differences in "the structure of consequences" among the different age groups of women. The prevalence of the various consequence items varied significantly for many of the items among the three age subgroups.

Specific Consequences

Medical/Physical. Women are more vulnerable to the physiological consequences of heavy drinking. Female alcoholics have death rates 50% to 100% higher than male alcoholics, and a greater percentage of them die from alcohol-related accidents, suicide, and circulatory disorders. Women are vulnerable to alcoholic liver disease and they develop liver pathology after a comparatively shorter duration of heavy drinking and at lower levels of daily drinking than men (Alcohol Alert, 1990). One of the major variables which contribute to the sex difference in liver disease is lesser female activity of gastric alcohol dehydrogenase in first-pass metabolism (see Chapter 1). Other possible contributing factors include differences in body weight and fluid content, the combination of estrogen and alcohol intake, and more steady daily drinking (albeit in a lesser quantity) by women. Gender comparison on the effect of heavy drinking on cognitive status is unclear. When studies are done which take into consideration the amount of alcohol consumed, the pattern of consumption, the number of years of heavy drinking, and so on, we will be more ready than now to make gender comparisons in cognitive impairment.

Comorbidity. Although many investigators have reported that depression is a frequent concomitant of female alcoholism and the antisocial personality of male alcoholism (see Chapter 7), these psychiatric diagnoses are *not*, as a rule, the consequence or effect of heavy drinking. They precede and accompany the heavy drinking, but heavy drinking is not usually the antecedent of a major psychiatric disorder with the exception of end-product diseases such as Korsakoff syndrome, Wernicke's disease and other neurological disturbances. Women often present themselves for treatment with a good deal of transient psychiatric symptomatology but these symptoms are likely to diminish as recovery progresses (Corrigan, 1980).

Effects on the family. When effects on the family are examined, discussion almost invariably is of marriage and children. Cohabitational relationships and lesbian relationships get far less attention, and relationship with parents and others in the family of origin is seldom mentioned. In a study of female alcoholics in different age groups (Gomberg, 1986), a question about difficulties with parents over drinking elicited a positive response from 75% of the women in their 20s. Among women in their 30s, 55% reported problems with their parents, as did 29% of women in their 40s. It is also true that a much larger proportion of young women reported their marital status as single; the percentage of single women in their twenties, thirties, and forties was 59%, 15%, and 2%, respectively. For younger problem drinkers, it is more likely that there will be family problems in the family of origin for a simple reason: This age group is more likely to be involved in the family of origin and less likely to be married.

When male and female alcoholics are compared, the women report more marital disruption (Perodeau, 1984). This always has seemed logical: The wife of an alcoholic husband is apparently more reluctant to end a marriage than the husband of an alcoholic wife for many reasons that probably have to do with financial support and with social support of the spouse of an alcoholic. Nonetheless, it is an unfortunately widespread myth that 90% of alcoholic women and 10% of alcoholic men are divorced.

When the drinking status of the spouse of the alcoholic man or woman is studied, a consistent difference emerges: More female than male alcoholic patients report heavy/problem drinking by the spouse.

It is a widely held belief that maternal heavy drinking has a worse effect on the children than paternal heavy drinking. Even among alcoholic women, two-thirds hold such a belief, although faith in that belief varies with age; only half of younger women alcoholics believe that "fact" but 79% of middle-aged alcoholic women do (Gomberg, 1988b). Williams and Klerman (1984) reviewed the available studies of the effects of maternal heavy drinking and alcoholism on children. They concluded that:

> Not enough research has been conducted on the specific effects of an alcoholic mother on her children to be able to draw definitive conclusions. Since children report feeling unloved, rejected by, and angry with their parents as well as rejecting of them, it can be assumed that the parent-child bond has been seriously impaired. (Williams & Klerman, 1984, p. 302)

If we vary the question and ask about the effect of children and family responsibilities on the treatment behavior of alcoholic women, there is general agreement that such family responsibilities are "barriers to treatment" more often for women than for men (Beckman & Amaro, 1984). In a review of studies dealing with female alcoholism and family therapy, Gomberg, Nelson, and Hatchett (1991) questioned the accepted wisdom that families always facilitate treatment for women alcoholics.

Effects on employment and economic status. Although a sizable percentage of women of all ages work outside the home, the proportion of employed men is larger than employed women in alcoholic populations. There is mixed evidence about the effectiveness of employee assistance programs in reaching women employees, but there are data which suggest that such programs work at least as well for women (Milne, Blum, & Roman, 1990).

On economic status, the evidence is clear and consistent. Female alcoholics have fewer economic resources than male alcoholics. Female alcoholics include single heads of families and the lower economic status of one-parent families headed by women is well documented. Even with middle-class families, nonpayment of child support remains a major problem. Beckman and Amaro (1984) report that female alcoholics are more likely than men to drop out of treatment "because of economic considerations."

Social supports and social networks. One should distinguish between social supports and networks of primary relationships, such as family, friends and significant others, and those networks and supports which are institutional/community, such as coworkers, fellow students, neighbors, members of the same church, or other organizations. In a comparison of alcoholic women in treatment and a matched nonalcoholic group, Schilit (1984) found the alcoholic women reporting less social support as children and adolescents and significantly less current support than the control group. Existing relationships were described as less happy and less supportive.

There are, on the other hand, the reports of Orford and Keddie (1985) and Makela and Simpura (1985). In the first report, interpersonal consequences of alcoholic drinking are defined in terms of these behaviors: argumentative, aggressive, breaking off relationships, making enemies, destructive, and violent. Neither gender reported greater interpersonal consequences; 56% of men and 53% of women reported such consequences. In the second study, "social reactions" are defined in terms of response from family, physician, workplace, police, and friends. Men reported "control reactions by significant others" more frequently than did women, and such comparison includes heavy/ problem drinkers.

In addressing the effects of problem drinking on social networks and social supports, several points need to be made. First, as men or women continue problematic drinking, the initiative often is taken by the drinker himself/herself in narrowing social interactions to drinking companions (Gomberg & Schilit, 1985). Second, it is usually the family or the people with whom the drinker lives who know about the problem and make objections earlier than others. Third, there is little research attention to the changes in social networks and social supports in alcoholic progression and recovery.

Trouble with the law. Male problem drinkers get into difficulties with legal authorities more often than do female problem drinkers. Considering that many male problem drinkers may be dually diagnosed as antisocial personalities, it is to be expected that many will have a record of fighting and arrests. The fact that males tend to drink more publicly than females also contributes to the gender differences. If one adds an antisocial history to greater visibility when intoxicated, the fact of more male trouble with the law follows. In a study of a college-aged population (Perkins, 1991), negative consequences which included property damage, injury to others, fighting, and impaired driving are reported "substantially more often" by male heavy drinkers than female heavy drinkers.

Sexuality and sexual dysfunction. Sexual dysfunction may precede and contribute to female problem drinking (Wilsnack, 1984). It also may be the other way around: Heavy drinking may contribute to sexual dysfunction. The problem is complicated because some women may use alcohol to cope with sexual dissatisfaction while others may have sexual problems which are a consequence of the heavy drinking. A study of alcoholic women in treatment (Gomberg, 1986) included several questions about sexuality. Asked if they were more "willing or eager to have sex" when drinking, 73% of the women in their 20s, 51% of the women in their 30s and 34% of the women in their 40s responded that they were. Asked whether they enjoyed sex more when drinking, the percentages responding affirmatively were 36%, 34%, and 21%, respectively. Studies which analyze alcoholic women's sexual attitudes and beliefs and their sexual behaviors during the prealcoholic and alcoholic periods in their lives have not been done. There is a fair amount of published research about the effects of alcohol on male sexuality and the issues in treating impotence. In addition to issues of sexual dysfunction, problems associated with high-risk behavior should be noted. Under the influence of alcohol, both men and women are less likely to be cautious in use of contraception and are more likely to risk sexually transmitted disease (Leigh, 1990).

Reproduction. Although there have been some reports about the effect of male drinking and alcoholism on offspring (Abel, 1989; Abel & Moore, 1987; Klassen & Persaud, 1976), there is a vast literature on fetal alcohol effects of female drinking (Little & Wendt, 1991). Such effects have been noted for centuries and a recent paper (Jones, Smith, Ulleland, & Streissguth, 1973) reintroduced the topic. The response was intense. Fetal alcohol effects have figured in U.S. government policy, in warning labels, and in many campaigns directed toward pregnant women.

Stigma and social attitudes. More negative attitudes toward female alcoholics than toward male alcoholics prevail. Earlier work and more recent work show the stereotyped belief that women who drink are more available sexually and that heavy-drinking women neglect their nurturing roles. Whatever the reasons, there is more negative feeling about female alcoholics. When 438 women were asked whether they agree that people think less of female problem drinkers (Gomberg, 1988b), 91% of the alcoholic subjects and 88% of the nonalcoholic women agreed that people do. When the same women were asked whether they believe that female intoxication is "more obnoxious and disgusting" than male intoxication, 51% of the alcoholic women and 36% of the control women agreed. In addition, more than half of the women believe that maternal alcoholism has "a worse effect" on children than paternal alcoholism.

The issue of stigma becomes more complicated when one considers that the greater social isolation of female alcoholics is related to more drinking at home alone, to social rejection, and to narrowing social contacts. More attempts at "control" of the heavy drinker, noted by Makela and Simpura (1985), seem to be linked to keeping the male drinker working and supporting the family. Female alcohol problems seem to produce more negative effect and resultant condemnation. It is interesting that in spite of the feminist movement, women in the workplace, the sexual revolution, and all the other changes of the late 20th century, so many stigmatizing stereotypes persist.

Integration. Health problems which follow from heavy drinking differ among men and women. Occupational, job-related consequences and difficulties with the law show gender differences when male and female alcoholics are compared. Many of these differences are related to social role. Males are more likely to be in the workplace, to drink in public places, and to act out belligerence, while women show more marital disruption and more concern about parenting.

Consequences differ among female problem drinkers depending on social class status, minority status, age, the public or private nature of their drinking, and other factors. Consequences often depend on whether the female problem drinker is drinking alone, with a spouse, or with drinking friends. Consequences depend on whether the woman is married, cohabiting, in a lesbian relationship, living alone, and so on.

When one considers the complexity of human lives, it takes a display of hubris to attempt to define the antecedents and consequences of problem drinking among women. But while recognizing the incomplete state of our knowledge, it is also important to sum up, to review, and to see where matters stand at particular moments. We have, therefore, summarized under Antecedents some of the recent work which illuminates some of the biological/genetic, personality and sociocultural variables, and those drinking/drug behaviors which seem to antecede problems. In discussing Consequences, we are aware of the variations which exist and relate to age, income, comorbid conditions, etc. We have summarized some of the male/female comparisons of consequences, most of which have stood up well with continuing study. The state of our knowledge is a vast improvement over what was known and thought about female alcohol problems only a decade or two ago, but there is still a long way to go.

REFERENCES

Abel, E.L. (1989). Paternal and material alcohol consumption: Effects on offspring in two strains of rats. *Alcoholism: Clinical & Experimental Research. 13*, 533–541.

Abel, E.L., & Moore, C. (1987). Effects of paternal alcohol consumption in mice. *Alcoholism: Clinical & Experimental Research, 11*, 533–535.

Alcohol Alert. (1990). Washington, DC: National Institute on Alcohol Abuse and Alcoholism, No. 10 PH 290.

Allan, C.A., & Cooke, D.J. (1985). Stressful life events and alcohol misuse in women: A critical review. *Journal of Studies on Alcohol, 46*, 147–152.

Beckman, L.J., & Amaro, H. (1984). Patterns of women's use of alcohol treatment agencies. In S.C. Wilsnack & L.J. Beckman (Eds.), *Alcohol problems in women* (pp. 319–348). New York: Guilford Press.

Blane, H.T., & Leonard, K.E. (Eds.) (1986). *Psychological theories of drinking and alcoholism.* New York: Guilford Press.

Block, J., Block, J.H., & Keyes, S. (1988). Longitudinally foretelling drug usage in adolescence: Early childhood personality and environmental precursors. *Child Development, 59,* 336–355.

Broadening the base of treatment for alcohol problems. (1990). Washington, DC: National Academy Press.

Cahalan, D., Cisin, I.H., & Crossley, H.M. (1969). *American drinking practices* (monograph 6). New Brunswick, NJ: Rutgers Center of Alcohol Studies.

Chaudron, C.D., & Wilkinson, D.A. (Eds.). (1988). *Theories on alcoholism.* Toronto: Addiction Research Foundation.

Clark, W., & Midanik, L. (1982). Alcohol use and alcohol problems among U.S. adults: Results of the 1979 national survey. *Alcohol consumption and related problems* Alcohol and Health Monograph No. 1, DHHS Publ. No. (ADM) 82-1190, pp 3–54). Washington, DC: National Institute of Alcohol Abuse and Alcoholism.

Coie, J.D., & Costanzo, P.R. (1977). *Sex role and mental illness labeling: A subcultural study.* Presentation at the 1977 American Psychological Association Meeting, San Francisco, CA.

Corrigan, E.M. (1980). *Alcoholic women in treatment.* New York: Oxford University Press.

Diagnostic and Statistical Manual of Mental Disorders (3rd. ed., Rev.). (1987). Washington, DC: American Psychiatric Association.

Estes, N.J., & Heinemann, M.E. (1986). *Alcoholism, development, consequences and interventions.* St. Louis, MO: Mosby.

Fillmore, K.M., Bacon, S.D., & Hyman, M. (1979). *The 27-year longitudinal panel study of drinking by students in college, 1949–1976* (Final report. Report No. PB 300–302, vi + 530 pp.). Springfield, VA: US National Tech. Information Services.

Fort, T., & Porterfield, A.L. (1961). Some backgrounds and types of alcoholism among women. *Journal of Health and Human Behavior, 2,* 283–292.

Gomberg, E.S.L. (1986). Women and alcoholism: Psychosocial issues. In *Women and alcohol: Health-related issues.* Research Monograph 16, DHHS Publ. No. ADM 86-1139, pp. 78–120). Washington, DC: National Institute on Alcohol Abuse and Alcoholism.

Gomberg, E.S.L. (1988a). Predicting age at onset for alcoholic women. *Alcoholism: Clinical & Experimental Research, 12,* 337.

Gomberg, E.S.L. (1988b). Alcoholic women in treatment: The question of stigma and age. *Alcohol and Alcoholism, 23,* 507–514.

Gomberg, E.S.L. (1989a). Alcoholic women in treatment: Early histories and early problem behaviors. *Advances in Alcohol and Substance Abuse, 8,* 113–132.

Gomberg, E.S.L. (1989b). Alcoholism in women: Use of other drugs. *Alcoholism: Clinical and Experimental Research, 13,* 338.

Gomberg, E.S.L. (1991). Women and alcohol: Psychosocial aspects. In D.J. Pittman & H.R. White (Eds.), *Society, culture and drinking patterns reexamined* (pp. 263–284). New Brunswick, NJ: Rutgers Center of Alcohol Studies.

Gomberg, E.S.L., & Lisansky, J.M. (1984). Antecedents of alcohol problems in women. In S.C. Wilsnack, & L.J. Beckman (Eds.), *Alcohol problems in women* (pp. 233–259). New York: Guilford Press.

Gomberg, E.S.L., Nelson, B.W., & Hatchett, B.F. (1991). Women, alcoholism, and family therapy. *Family and Community Health, 4,* 61–71.

Gomberg, E.S.L., & Schilit, R. (1985). Social isolation and passivity of women alcoholics. *Alcohol and Alcoholism, 20,* 313–314.

Goodwin, D.W., Schulsinger, R., Hermansen, L., Guze, S.B., & Winokur, G. (1973). Alcohol problems in adoptees raised apart from alcoholic biological parents. *Archives of General Psychiatry, 28,* 238–243.

Goodwin, D.W., Schulsinger, R., Knop, J., Mednick, S., & Guze, S.B. (1977). Psychopathology in adopted and nonadopted daughters of alcoholics. *Archives of General Psychiatry, 34,* 1005–1008.

Hanna, E., Faden, V., & Harford, T. (in press). Marriage: Does it protect young women from alcoholism? *Journal of Substance Abuse.*

Jessor, R., & Jessor, S.L. (1977). *Problem behavior and psychosocial development: A longitudinal study of youth.* New York: Academic Press.

Johnson, P.R. (1982). Sex differences, women's role and alcohol use: Preliminary national data. *Journal of Social Issues, 38,* 93–116.

Jones, K.L., Smith, D.W., Ulleland, C.N., & Streissguth, A.P. (1973). Pattern of malformation in offspring of chronic alcoholic mothers. *The Lancet, 1,* 1267–1271.

Kendler, K.S., Heath, A.C., Neale, M.C., Kessler, R.C., & Eaves, L.J. (1992). A population based twin study of alcoholism in women. *Journal of the American Medical Association, 268*(14), 1877–1882.

Klassen, R.W., & Persaud, T.V.N. (1976). Experimental studies on the influence of male alcoholism on pregnancy and progeny. *Experimental Pathology, 12,* 38–45.

Leigh, B.C. (1990). "Venus gets in my thinking:" Drinking and female sexuality in the age of AIDS. *Journal of Substance Abuse, 2,* 129–145.

Lewin, K. (1935). *A dynamic theory of personality.* New York: McGraw-Hill.

Lisansky, E.S. (1957). Alcoholism in women: Social and psychological concomitants. I. Social history data. *Quarterly Journal of Studies on Alcohol, 18,* 588–623.

Little, R.E., & Wendt, J.K. (1991). The effects of maternal drinking in the reproductive period: An epidemiological review. *Journal of Substance Abuse, 3,* 187–204.

Makela, K., & Simpura, J. (1985). Experiences related to drinking as a function of annual alcohol intake and by sex and age. *Drug and Alcohol Dependence, 15,* 389–404.

Miller, B.A., Downs, W.R., Gondoli, D.M., & Keil, A. (1987). The role of childhood sexual abuse in the development of alcoholism in women. *Violence and Victims, 2,* 157–182.

Milne, S.H., Blum, T., & Roman, P.M. (1990, October). *Managerial and super-*

visory propensity to use an EAP: Facilitating and inhibiting factors. Research presentation, 19th Annual EAPA conference, New Orleans.

Orford, J., & Keddie, A. (1985). Gender differences in the functions and effects of moderate and excessive drinking. *British Journal of Clinical Psychology, 24*, 265–279.

Perkins, H.W. (1991). Gender patterns in consequences of collegiate alcohol abuse: A 10-year study of trends in an undergraduate population. *Journal of Studies on Alcohol, 52*, 458–462.

Perodeau, G.M. (1984). Married alcoholic women: A review. *Journal of Drug Issues, 14*, 703–719.

Robbins, C. (1989). Sex differences in psychosocial consequences of alcohol and drug abuse. *Journal of Health and Social Behavior, 30*, 117–130.

Robins, L.N. (1966). *Deviant children grown up: A sociological and psychiatric study of sociopathic personality.* Baltimore, MD: Williams and Wilkins.

Sadava, S.W. (1985). Problem behavior theory and consumption and consequences of alcohol use. *Journal of Studies on Alcohol, 46*, 392–397.

Sadava, S.W. (1986). Interactional theory. In H.T. Blane & K.E. Leonard (Eds.), *Psychological theories of drinking and alcoholism.* New York: Guilford.

Sadava, S.W. (1988). Problem drinking and alcohol problems: Widening the circle of covariation. In M. Galanter (Ed.), *Recent developments in alcoholism* (Vol. 8). New York: Plenum.

Schilit, R. (1984). *Social support structures of women in treatment for alcoholism.* Doctoral dissertation, University of Michigan.

Schmidt, C., Klee, L., & Ames, G. (1990). Review and analysis of literature on indicators of women's drinking problems. *British Journal of Addiction, 85*, 179–192.

Shaw, S. (1980). The causes of increasing drinking problems amongst women: A general etiological theory. In Camberwell Council on Alcoholism, *Women and alcohol.* London: Tavistock.

Turnbull, J.E., & Gomberg, E.S.L. (1991). The structure of drinking-related consequences in alcoholic women. *Alcoholism: Clinical & Experimental Research, 15*, 29–38.

Wall, J.H. (1937). A study of alcoholism in women. *American Journal of Psychiatry, 93*, 943–952.

Wartenberg, A.A., & Liepman, M.R. (1987). Medical consequences of addictive behaviors. In T.D. Nirenberg & S.A. Maisto (Eds.), *Developments in the assessment and treatment of addictive behaviors.* Norwood, NJ: Ablex.

Williams, C.N., & Klerman, L.V. (1984). Female alcohol abuse: Its effects on the family. In S.C. Wilsnack & L.J. Beckman (Eds.), *Alcohol problems in women.* New York: Guilford.

Wilsnack, R.W., Klassen, A.D., & Wilsnack, S.C. (1986). Retrospective analysis of lifetime changes in women's drinking behavior. *Advances in Alcohol and Substance Abuse, 5*, 9–28.

Wilsnack, R.W., Wilsnack, S.C., & Klassen, A.D. (1984). Women's drinking and drinking problems: Patterns from a 1981 survey. *American Journal of Public Health, 74*, 1231–1238.

Wilsnack, R.W., Wilsnack, S.C., & Klassen, A.D. (1987). Antecedents and consequences of drinking and drinking problems in women: Patterns from a U.S. national survey. In P.C. Rivers, (Ed.), *Alcohol and addictive behavior* (Nebraska Symposium on Motivation, Vol. 34, pp. 85–158). Lincoln: University of Nebraska Press.

Wilsnack, S.C. (1984). Drinking, sexuality and sexual dysfunction in women. In S.C. Wilsnack & L.J. Beckman (Eds.), *Alcohol problems in women.* New York: Guilford.

Wilsnack, S.C., & Beckman, L.J. (Eds.). (1984). *Alcohol problems in women.* New York: Guilford.

Wilsnack, S.C., & Klassen, A.D. (1992, September). *Childhood sexual abuse and problem drinking in a U.S. national sample of women.* Presentation at Women's Issues Related to Alcohol Abuse and Violence Conference, University of Illinois at Chicago, College of Nursing.

Wilsnack, S.C., & Wilsnack, R.W. (1991). Epidemiology of women's drinking. *Journal of Substance Abuse, 3,* 133–157.

Worner, T.M., & Delgado, I.M. (1991). Addiction Severity Index: Comparison between men and women undergoing alcohol detoxification. *Alcoholism: Clinical and Experimental Research, 15*(ASAM abstracts No. 21).

Zucker, R.A. (1987). The four alcoholisms. In P.C. Rivers (Ed.), *Alcohol and Addictive Behavior* (Nebraska Symposium on Motivation, Vol. 34). Lincoln: University of Nebraska Press.

Zucker, R.A., & Gomberg, E.S.L. (1986). Etiology of alcoholism reconsidered: The case for a biopsychosocial process. *American Psychologist, 41,* 783–793.

Chapter 7

Depression and Antisocial Personality Disorder in Alcoholism: Gender Comparison*

Michie N. Hesselbrock,
Ph.D.

School of Social Work
University of Connecticut
West Hartford, CT

Victor M. Hesselbrock,
Ph.D.

Department of Psychiatry
School of Medicine
University of Connecticut
Health Center
Farmington, CT

INTRODUCTION

Individuals who are diagnosed as "alcoholics" often have additional comorbid psychiatric disorders. The National Institute of Mental

---

* This work was supported in part by NIAAA grant #P 50 AA03510.

Health Epidemiologic Catchment Area (ECA) study sample derived from five different communities in the United States found that 37% of the sample with an alcohol disorder had at least one additional co-morbid mental disorder (Regier et al., 1990). Among hospitalized alcoholics, as many as 75% have one or more coexisting psychiatric disorders (Hesselbrock, Meyer, & Keener, 1985; Penick, Powell, Liskow, Jackson, & Nickel, 1988). A number of studies of comorbid psychiatric disorders among persons with alcoholism have been conducted over the past several years and the severity of psychiatric symptoms is often predictive of poor treatment outcome for substance abusers (La Porte, McLellan, O'Brien, & Marshall, 1981; McLellan, Luborsky, Woody, O'Brien, & Druley, 1983). However, relatively little is known about the problems and treatment needs of dually diagnosed persons.

It is difficult to accurately assess the prevalence of additional psychiatric disorders among persons with alcoholism since the rates vary according to the source of the sample studied (i.e., clinical vs. community samples) and the methods used to assess psychiatric problems. The types and rates of additional psychopathology identified also differ between male and female subjects. For example, the prevalence rate of antisocial personality disorder (ASP) is very common among male alcoholics, while major depressive disorder is a frequent comorbid psychiatric condition among female alcoholics (Gomberg, 1974; Hesselbrock, Meyer, & Keener, 1985).

Studies of the genetic and clinical implications of affective disorder and alcoholism have found that the two disorders may be independent diseases with some overlap in their clinical symptoms (Cadoret & Winokur, 1974; Schuckit, 1986). In order to make an appropriate treatment decision, it is important to differentiate affective symptoms that may directly result from the chronic, heavy consumption of alcohol versus symptoms that are part of the major affective disorder. Similarly, alcoholism and antisocial personality disorder often occur together, and distinguishing alcoholism from antisocial personality disorder can be difficult and may lead to diagnostic confusion (Hesselbrock, Hesselbrock, Tennen, Weidenman, & Meyer, 1983; Schuckit, 1973). By differentiating the source of these different types of symptoms, it is possible to make an appropriate diagnosis.

Alcoholic persons with an additional psychiatric disorder are difficult to treat because the philosophy and the focus of alcohol treatment programs and of psychiatric programs often differ. The primary goal of alcoholism treatment is to help the client cease drinking and remain sober, while an assumption is sometimes made in psychiatric settings that the psychiatric disorder causes the co-occurring alcoholism. These assumptions may lead to incomplete intervention in both instances. Alcohol treatment programs often treat only the alcoholism and ignore the coexisting psychiatric disorders of their alcoholic clients. On the other hand, clinicians in psychiatric settings may mistakenly presume that the treatment of the psychiatric disturbance will ameliorate the alcohol problem (Mulinski, 1989). Hesselbrock, Meyer, and Keener (1985) suggest the importance of considering psychiatric symptoms in alcoholism as indicative of a true coexisting psychiatric disorder and that these disorders need to be considered in the development of individualized treatment plans.

These findings indicate that further efforts are necessary to systematically review existing studies to clarify the treatment implications for those individuals with alcoholism and a coexisting psychiatric disorder who seek treatment. This chapter reviews the literature on alcoholism and other comorbid psychiatric conditions (particularly the diagnoses of antisocial personality disorder and depression) and the influence of gender.

Although studies of alcoholism among women are increasing, the majority of clinical studies are still conducted using male samples. Studies of treated samples and samples drawn from the general population have found gender differences with respect to prevalence rates, types and the effects of psychiatric disorders on the course and outcome of alcoholism. With the increase in the prevalence rate of alcoholism among women, it is important to address the possible differential assessment and treatment needs for both men and women with alcohol-related problems.

DEPRESSION AND GENDER IN ALCOHOLISM

Affective disorder is one of the most frequent comorbid psychiatric disorders associated with alcoholism. The rates of depression among alcoholics vary depending on the types of subjects studied, the types of assessment instruments utilized, and the definition of depression. The prevalence rate of depressive disorder in alcoholism ranges from 30% to 70% (Schuckit & Monteiro, 1988). Studies comparing male and female alcoholics consistently have found higher rates of depression among women. Hesselbrock, Meyer, & Keener (1985) found that among hospitalized alcoholics more than half of women (52%) and one-third of men (32%) met the DSM-III criteria for major depressive disorder in their lifetime. Further, more than half of those with a lifetime diagnosis of depression reported symptoms of depression at the time they were hospitalized for the treatment of alcoholism.

In a study of DWI offenders, Windle and Miller (1989) found no significant differences between men and women in terms of the rates of global depression, depressive mood, or depressive features. However, for those females who met criteria for alcohol dependence, consistently higher levels of global depression, depressive mood and ideation, and depressive features were reported than for the men.

Epidemiological studies of alcoholics in the general population also have found gender differences with regard to the diagnosis of depression. In the ECA study, Helzer and Pryzbeck (1988) reported that female alcoholics are more likely to have a diagnosis of depression than nonalcoholic women, while alcoholic men and nonalcoholic men reported similar rates of depression.

While studies conducted in the U.S. generally agree that depression is more common among alcoholic women than alcoholic men, similar rates of reported depression were found in Toronto, Canada for men and women who sought help for substance abuse problems (Ross, Glaser, & Stiasny, 1988). Using the National Institute of Mental Health Diagnostic Interview Schedule (NIMH-DIS), nearly one-third of the sample (29% for men and 30% women) were found to have met criteria for a lifetime diagnosis of depression. Sample characteristics may account for the difference between the Ross et al., study and the studies conducted in the U.S. (cf. Hesselbrock, Meyer, & Keener, 1985). The Hesselbrock et al. sample included a relatively homogeneous group of hospitalized alcoholics who met criteria of alcohol abuse/ dependence, while Ross et al.'s study included both inpatients and outpatients who sought assistance for alcohol and drug problems (not just those who met criteria for either alcohol or other substance abuse/ dependence). However, Windle and Miller (1989) also found similar rates of depressive symptoms among male and female DWI offenders, some of whom did not meet the criteria for alcohol abuse. The higher rates of depression found among hospitalized female alcoholics may result from the higher rates of psychiatric treatment utilization among women. Weissman, Myers, and Hading (1980), in their longitudinal household survey of a New Haven, CT community mental health center catchment area, reported similar rates of major depression for men and women who were diagnosed as having alcoholism.

The high rates of depression among clinical samples of alcoholics may reflect help-seeking behavior among alcoholics with depression in general (Vaglum, Vaglum, & Larsen, 1987). Weissman et al. (1980) found that the combination of alcoholism and depression made a person particularly vulnerable to suicidal behavior. Often, alcoholics are brought to a treatment facility because of such behavior.

Differentiating Alcoholism and Affective Disorders

Differentiating affective symptoms attributable to an affective disorder from those likely to result from the pharmacological effects of chronic alcohol use is often difficult. Many symptoms of depression can result from the pharmacological/toxicological effects of alcohol. Further, various forms of dysphoric mood and social and psychological problems often result from prolonged periods of heavy drinking. The feelings of sadness can be potentiated by a combination of the pharmacological effects of alcohol and the social and psychological problems resulting from heavy alcohol consumption.

As a typical CNS depressant, the ingestion of alcohol can produce sadness in both alcoholics and nonalcoholics. Birnbaum, Taylor, and Parker (1983) found that relatively low levels of alcohol consumption increased depression and anger in female social drinkers, while other investigators have found an association between alcohol consumption and low mood in samples of alcoholics (Nathan & Lisman, 1976; Tamerin, Weiner, & Mendelson, 1970). The severity of the depressive symptoms reported appears to be positively associated with higher blood-alcohol concentrations, the duration of heavy drinking (Schuckit & Monteiro, 1988), the mood state before alcohol consumption, and the circumstances of drinking (Schuckit, 1979).

Furthermore, feelings of sadness may also result from the social and psychological problems experienced by the persons who maintain chronic, heavy drinking patterns. A repetitive pattern of relapse, abstinence, and brief periods of controlled drinking often requires readjustment of those persons associated with the alcoholic that may result in increased difficulties in family interaction, job performance, and financial problems for the alcoholic and his/her family. Alcoholics often seek treatment when their alcohol-related problems become overwhelming and their ability to cope with these problems is compromised (Schuckit & Monteiro, 1988). Alcoholics seeking treatment often report severe difficulty in coping with their life situation and demonstrate a depressive mood consistent with their difficulties (Schuckit & Monteiro, 1988). Fowler, Liskow, and Tanna (1980) compared alcoholic male veterans diagnosed with and without secondary depression. More of the alcoholics with secondary depression reported undesirable life events within one year of admission than those alcoholics without depression. The undesirable life events experienced by the men included divorce, legal difficulties, sexual difficulties, and personal injury or illness. Their findings are consistent with the life problems and difficulties in coping often experienced by alcoholics seeking treatment.

Another reason for the difficulty in distinguishing alcoholism and depression is that many depressive-like symptoms (e.g., feeling guilty or worthless, sleep disturbance, loss of appetite, lack of concentration, irritability) are also reported by alcoholics when they drink. Further, recovering alcoholics often report dysphoric mood and symptoms during the withdrawal phase from alcohol. Hershon (1977) examined a variety of assessed "subclinical" withdrawal symptoms that alcoholics might experience between bouts of drinking, including physical and affective disturbances. The affective disturbance associated with "subclinical" withdrawal symptoms was greater among female than male alcoholics during the month prior to hospitalization and included problems such as depression, irritability, anxiety, paranoia, anger, inability to face the day, and guilt (Herson, 1977; Hesselbrock, Meyer, & Keener, 1985). However, these depressive symptoms seemed to be transient. Other investigators have also observed that the presence of depressive symptoms decreases markedly as patients progress from active drinking to abstinence (Dackis, Gold, Pottash, & Sweeney, 1986; Dorus, Kennedy, Gibbons, & Ravi, 1987).

Schuckit and Monteiro (1988) suggest making the distinction between primary and secondary alcoholism according to the age of onset of alcoholism in relation to the other psychiatric disorder. "Primary alcoholism" is defined as the presence of an alcohol-use disorder occurring in the absence of any other psychiatric disorder, while "secondary alcoholism" develops once one or more psychiatric disorder(s) already exist. Schuckit (1983a, 1986) demonstrated the importance of identifying a primary diagnosis among substance abusers in terms of phenomenology and treatment outcomes. Weissman et al. (1977) compared groups of patients with primary and secondary depression and found that the primary depressives reported more severe symptomatology as compared to the secondary depressives, even though the two groups reported similar symptom patterns.

Gender differences have been found in terms of the age of onset of alcoholism and affective disorder. While depressive affective disorder tends to develop prior to the onset of alcoholism among women, it tends to be secondary to the development of alcoholism in men. Schuckit, Pitts, Reich, King, and Winokur (1969) studied 70 female alcoholics and found that 31 subjects (44%) were secondary alcoholics. Other investigators also have found that female alcoholics with depression were more likely to have a diagnosis of primary affective disorder than male alcoholics (Winokur, Reich, Rimmer, & Pitts, 1970; Winokur, Rimmer, & Reich, 1971) Hesselbrock, Meyer, and Keener (1985) found that among hospitalized alcoholics, primary alcoholism was more common among men, while primary depression was more common among women. Alcoholism may be more reactive or secondary to other psychiatric problems in clinical (Jacobson, 1987; Schmidt, Klee, & Ames, 1990) and nonclinical samples (Helzer & Pryzbeck, 1988).

Several explanations have been offered about the high prevalence of primary affective disorders among female alcoholics. Winokur et al. (1971) suggested that some cases of alcoholism might be variations of unipolar, primary affective disorder and that alcohol abuse might serve as a manifestation of depressive symptoms. However, most studies have failed to explain the exact nature of the relationship between alcoholism and depression (Berner, Lesch, & Walter, 1986). Schuckit and Monteiro (1988) reexamined the commonly held belief regarding "self-medication," that a person experiencing depressive symptoms may increase alcohol intake in order to medicate herself. However, they found that most patients with major depressive disorder either decreased their alcohol intake or did not change their level of consumption after beginning to experience depressive symptoms. Vaglum et al. (1987) found no general dose-response relationship between level of depression and level of alcohol use among alcoholic women, but found an inverse relationship between depression scores and the amount of alcohol consumed among nonalcoholic subjects.

Other investigators have suggested that the reason depression precedes the development of alcoholism among females is that alcoholism develops at a later age among women, which may give them more time to become depressed (Goodwin, Schulsinger, Knop, Mednick, & Guze, 1977; Solomon, 1983). However, no differences in depression scores of young and older alcoholic women were reported by other investigators (Gomberg, 1986). The relationship between the absence of affective disorder and the delay in the onset of alcoholism in women is not clear.

A comparison of alcoholics with and without affective disorder found gender differences on several alcohol-related characteristics. Several studies have noted an association between the presence of affective disorder in alcoholic men and a longer and more severe course of alcoholism, a higher number of alcohol related problems, and more suicide attempts (McMahon & Davidson, 1986; O'Sullivan et al., 1983b; Schuckit, 1983b; Yates, Petty, & Brown, 1988).

The effect of depression on the course of alcoholism among women, however, is not clear. A study of 301 alcoholic women, interviewed in 21 inpatient and outpatient treatment facilities, found high rates of depressive symptoms among those with alcoholism. Increasing levels of depressive symptoms were the most frequently reported pretreatment stressful life event (Gomberg & Turnbull, 1990). The level of depressive mood was also associated with an earlier age of onset, loss of control, and binge drinking, indicting an association between depressive symptoms and a severe, chronic course of alcoholism in women (Turnbull & Gomberg, 1988). Further, high levels of depressive symptoms were associated with negative consequences of alcoholism including social withdrawal, problems with sexuality, accidents, work problems, illness, and relationship conflicts (Turnbull & Gomberg, 1988). Similar findings have been reported in some studies of men with affective disorder as noted above, but not all (cf. Hesselbrock, Hesselbrock, & Workman-Daniels, 1986).

ALCOHOLISM, DEPRESSION, AND SUICIDE

A high rate of suicide attempts and suicides is associated with alcoholism and affective disorder (Lippmann, Manshadi, Christie, & Gultekin, 1987; Pitts & Winokur, 1966; Solomon, 1983; Yates et al., 1988). High rates of completed suicide have been reported only among persons with alcoholism and affective disorder (Pitts & Winokur, 1966), while nearly half (45%) of male alcoholics with secondary depression reported previous suicide attempts, as compared to 8% of men without depression (Yates et al., 1988). Hesselbrock, Hesselbrock, Syzmanski, and Weidenman (1988) compared hospitalized male and female alcoholics with a history of suicide attempts to those who did not. Suicide attempts were associated with a lifetime diagnosis of major depressive disorder in both male and female alcoholics, but the prevalence of a lifetime diagnosis of major depression was higher among the women than for the men in both the suicide-attempt and nonattempt groups.

Gomberg (1989) found that alcoholic women under 40 years of age were nearly five times more likely to attempt suicide as compared to nonalcoholic women. Alcoholic women who reported suicide attempts reported significantly more tension, indecisiveness, anxiety, and nervousness than the women who did not attempt suicide (Gomberg, 1989).

Relationship of Depression, ASP, and Alcoholism

A greater frequency of behaviors characteristic of conduct problems have also been reported among depressed alcoholic men than nondepressed men. Fowler et al. (1980) found that depressed alcoholic men reported more fights and nontraffic arrests than nondepressed men with alcoholism did. Woodruff and his colleagues also reported that depressed alcoholics had more sociopathic symptoms (Woodruff, Guze, Clayton, & Carr, 1973). Hesselbrock et al. (1986) examined the effects of a history of major depressive disorder and antisocial personality disorder on the course of alcoholism in male and female patients. They found that neither a history of major depression nor the interaction of antisocial personality disorder and depression altered the course of alcoholism for either gender.

ALCOHOLISM, AFFECTIVE DISORDER, AND TREATMENT OUTCOME

Conflicting results have been reported concerning the treatment outcome of male and female alcoholics with affective disorder. While several studies have reported better treatment outcomes for female alcoholics with a coexisting affective disorder, other studies have been inconclusive. MacDonald (1987) found that a combination of life problems—not depression or emotional problems alone—was associated with poor treatment outcomes. At the 1-year follow-up of 93 alcoholic women, a high rate of major life problems was found. While "depression" was not a separate variable, the most frequently cited problem was emotional or nervous difficulty as a predictor of poor treatment outcomes. Schuckit and Winokur (1972) examined 21 primary alcoholic females with secondary affective disorder and 21 female alcoholics with primary affective disorder. At the 3-year follow-up, the alcoholics with primary affective disorder reported much better treatment outcomes than the primary alcoholics.

Affective disorder appears to impact differentially on male and female alcoholics in terms of the treatment outcomes. At the 1-year posttreatment follow-up, male alcoholics diagnosed as having a lifetime diagnosis of depression tended to relapse to drinking. However, women with a lifetime diagnosis of depression tended to have a lower rate of relapse than women without a diagnosis of depression (Rounsaville, Dolinsky, Babor, & Meyer, 1987). Female alcoholics with depression reported higher rates of affective disturbance than those without depression at the 1-year follow-up evaluation. Furthermore, the diagnosis of depression remained higher among female alcoholics than male alcoholics at the one-year posthospital discharge (Hesselbrock, 1991a). The persistence of depression in alcoholics long after the completion of treatment for alcoholism has been frequently reported (cf. Bander, Rabinowitz, Turner, & Grunberg, 1983; Behar, Winokur, & Berg, 1984; Pottenger et al., 1978). Interestingly, however, concurrent alcoholism does not seem to affect the treatment outcome of persons with primary depression (Hirschfield, Kosier, Keller, Lavori, & Endicott, 1989). Time to recovery, time to relapse into another episode, and cross-sectional clinical ratings did not vary over the two years posttreatment between the primary depressives with and without concurrent alcoholism.

ANTISOCIAL PERSONALITY DISORDER AND GENDER IN ALCOHOLISM

Antisocial personality disorder (ASP) is also common among persons with alcoholism. However, as with affective disorder, it can be difficult to distinguish between alcoholism and ASP on the basis of phenomenology alone. Thus, the differential diagnosis of alcoholism and antisocial personality disorder can be difficult (Hesselbrock, Stabenau, & Hesselbrock, 1985; Meyer, 1986; Schuckit, 1973). Persons who are suffering from alcoholism often display a variety of antisocial behaviors (e.g., fights, lying, employment problems, difficulty in interpersonal relationships, and the neglect of family obligations), while persons with ASP often abuse alcohol (Cadoret, Troughton, & Widmer, 1984; Hesselbrock, Stabenau, & Hesselbrock, 1985; Penick, Powell, Othmer, Bingham, & Rice, 1984).

It is difficult to distinguish ASP from early-onset alcoholism. Alcohol abuse at an early age is a criterion for ASP, while heavy alcohol consumption may produce behavior problems among youth (Gerstley, Alterman, McLellan, & Woody, 1990; Meyer, 1986). In order to separate the two disorders, the psychiatric assessment needs to consider the individual's lifetime history of psychiatric problems (including childhood behavior problems and alcohol abuse/addiction), as well as a family history of ASP and alcoholism rather than focusing only on the time period immediately prior to entering treatment (Hesselbrock, in press).

A higher prevalence of ASP has generally been reported for alcoholic men than for women with alcoholism. Hesselbrock et al. (1985) found that 49% of men and 20% of women hospitalized for alcoholism received an additional lifetime diagnosis of ASP. Similarly, Ross et al. (1988) found that 52% of men and 29% of women in their sample of persons who sought treatment for substance abuse in Canada had ASP. Among medical and surgical inpatients referred for psychiatric consultation, the prevalence of ASP was reported to be higher for males than for females. However, no gender difference was found in the rate of ASP among those who were diagnosed as having alcohol abuse/alcoholism (Lewis, Rice, & Helzer, 1983).

ASP, Gender, and Consequences of Alcoholism

The importance of comorbid ASP for the course and consequences of alcoholism among both male and female alcoholics has been shown in a number of studies. Both male and female alcoholics with ASP have been characterized by an earlier onset of regular drinking, regular drinking to intoxication, and problem drinking than non-ASP alcoholics (Hesselbrock et al., 1984; Hesselbrock, Stabenau, & Hesselbrock, 1985; Hesselbrock et al., 1986). Further, both male and female ASP alcoholics had a more severe course of the disorder and were likely to relapse sooner and at a higher rate following treatment than non-ASP alcoholics (Hesselbrock, 1991b).

However, ASP, like alcoholism, may not be a homogeneous disorder. Loeber and Schmaling (1985) were able to identify four types of antisocial behaviors in a sample of boys. They divided the boys into four groups based on two factors: fighting and stealing. Differences were found between the groups with respect to disobedience, hyperactivity, irritability, negativism, alcohol/drug use, police contacts, and multiple-offender status. The "fighting-only" group tended to score high on a range of antisocial behaviors but not delinquent behaviors, while the "stealing-only" group scored high on some overt antisocial behaviors with some involvement in delinquency. The boys in both the "stealing" and "fighting" group were involved in a variety of overt and covert antisocial and delinquent acts. A number of studies support the persistence of the more severe types of conduct disorder from childhood into adulthood (Farrington, 1991), including a study of aggressive/nonaggressive ASP alcoholics conducted by Jaffe, Babor, and Fishbein (1988). This study found that violent behavior by alcoholics was greatest among those with a childhood history of aggressive behavior.

While ASP in alcoholism has been widely studied, most studies have examined only samples of men. Few studies of alcoholism and ASP have included women in their samples. However, the existence of ASP female problem drinkers has been documented by Gomberg (1974) in a review of studies conducted in penal institutions and drinking problems of delinquent girls. Lewis, Rice, and Helzer (1983) studied 412 (131 men and 281 women) medical and surgical inpatients referred for psychiatric consultation. The subjects were evaluated by psychiatric residents using a structured psychiatric screening interview. The 34 men and 47 women who met the criteria for ASP were compared with those who were not diagnosed as ASP. Antisocial men and women were more likely to be at risk for alcoholism, with the risk for alcoholism greater among the ASP men than the ASP women. Among those diagnosed as having alcoholism, the ASP men and women reported an earlier age of onset of heavy drinking and a shorter duration of heavy drinking, indicating a faster progression to alcoholism among the ASP subjects. The age of onset of heavy drinking and duration of heavy drinking for the men and women subjects within the ASP and within the non-ASP groups were similar. However, a higher proportion of the men (both ASP and non-ASP) reported loss of control and problems limiting intake than the women. Among the male subjects, ASP alcoholics had a higher prevalence of loss of control and of trying to limit alcohol intake, but did not have a higher rate of alcohol-related job difficulties, arrests, or fighting. Hesselbrock et al. (1984) compared ASP and non-ASP, hospitalized, alcoholic men and women in terms of their history and the consequences of alcohol abuse. Both men and women with ASP had an early onset of alcoholism followed by a more chronic and severe course of alcoholism. Alcoholics with ASP were found to have taken their first drink and to begin regular drinking and drunkenness much earlier than their non-ASP counterparts. While the alcoholic ASP men and women were, on average, 10 years younger than the non-ASP alcoholics when assessed at the current hospitalization, the ASP alcoholics had a drinking problem as long as the older subjects without ASP. Further, ASP alcoholics reported physical, psychological, and social problems at a similar rate to non-ASP subjects. In terms of gender differences, ASP women tended to have a more accelerated progression from regular drinking to problem drinking than did ASP men. The progression was similar for non-ASP men and women.

Expression of ASP by Gender

Family studies and family pedigree studies of the relationship between ASP and alcoholism suggest that the expression of ASP may differ by gender (Cadoret, O'Gorman, Troughton, & Heywood, 1985; Cloninger, Christiansen, Reich, & Gottesman, 1978; Cloninger & Reich, 1983; Cloninger, Reich, & Guze, 1978). A pattern of transmission of alcoholism and ASP, based on these family study data, suggests that ASP may be a spectrum disorder expressed as sociopathy in males and expressed as somatization/Briquet's disorder expressed in females. This distinction is supported by a longitudinal study (Windle, 1990) of boys and girls with conduct disorder which found that antisocial behavior in early adolescent boys was predictive of conduct problems and alcohol/substance abuse problems in later adolescence. For girls, however, only the number of property offenses (not criminal offenses or aggressive behaviors against others) during early adolescence was marginally associated with the adolescent's alcohol/substance abuse problems. Windle (1990) suggests that internalizing symptoms (e.g., somatic complaints, depression) rather than externalizing symptoms (e.g., conduct disorder, delinquency) may be more predictive of alcohol/drug use in girls. A similar conclusion has been reached by Ensminger, Brown, & Kellam (1982). ASP, then, appears to be a heterogeneous disorder that may vary in expression both within and across gender. For males, there appear to be at least two types—aggressive and nonaggressive ASP—while for females the expression of "ASP" may vary due to its severity. Severe ASP among females may closely resemble the male type of ASP, while less severe cases may be expressed by a more internalizing form (e.g., a histrionic, borderline, or somatoform disorder).

However, there is evidence suggesting a possible bias due to gender in the assignment of the ASP diagnosis. Ford and Widiger (1985) found that the differential prevalence of ASP and Histrionic Disorder (also a member of DSM-III-R Cluster B Personality Disorders) varied with respect to the gender of the patient rather than to criteria. The diagnosis of ASP was assigned more frequently to example cases when the patient was identified as male, while histrionic disorder was more frequently diagnosed in those cases identified as female.

The Influence of ASP and Gender on the Transmission of Alcoholism

The relationship of alcoholism and antisocial behavior in men and women has been linked differentially to the pattern of genetic transmission of alcoholism. Two types of alcoholism in men have been proposed, based on the genetic transmissibility of alcoholism and personality traits from a sample of Swedish adoptees (Cloninger, 1987; Cloninger, Bohman, & Sigvardsson, 1981). Type 1 alcoholism ("milieu-limited") was associated with recurrent alcohol abuse without criminality in the biological parents. The personality features of the Type 1 alcoholics included being high on reward dependence (social approval), high on harm avoidance (cautious), and low on novelty seeking (preference for nonrisk-taking situations). Thus, the Type 1 alcoholism resembles the non-ASP type of alcoholism found in clinical samples in the United States. The Type 2 alcoholism ("male-limited") is thought to be transmitted from father to son and was associated with criminality and severe alcohol use in the biological fathers. The Type 2 alcoholic was characterized by personality traits opposite those of the Type 1: being low on reward dependence, low on harm avoidance, and high on novelty seeking. Thus, the Type 2 alcoholism appears to be similar to the ASP alcoholism often reported in the literature. In terms of alcohol-related symptoms, Type 1 is characterized by a later age of onset (after age 25), psychological dependence, and guilt and fear about alcohol dependence. Spontaneous alcohol seeking behavior, fights and arrests when drinking were infrequent. On the other hand, Type 2 alcoholism is characterized by an early age of onset (before age 25), frequent alcohol-seeking behavior, and fighting and arrests when drinking. Psychological dependence, guilt, and fear about alcohol dependence are infrequent in Type 2 alcoholism.

An attempt to replicate the classification proposed by Cloninger and colleagues in the female counterparts of the Swedish adoptee sample produced only one type. Bohman, Sigvardsson, and Cloninger (1981) examined women in Sweden who were adopted at an early age. Daughters were found to inherit alcoholism from their biological mothers and the alcoholism in female adoptees was characterized by only the Type 1, milieu-limited form of alcoholism. Bohman et al. (1981) concluded that alcoholism in women was relatively homogeneous. The classifications of alcoholism proposed by Cloninger et al. (1981) and Bohman et al. (1981), however, have been criticized due to the small sample size (n = 31 for female alcohol abusers), sample selection methods, and the indirect measurement of the proband and father variables (Vanclay & Raphael, 1990). Glenn and Nixon (1991) examined the presence of the Type 2, male-limited alcoholism in women. They examined 51 female alcoholics by dividing them into early versus late onset of alcoholism groups. While they were unable to distinguish the Type 1 and Type 2 alcoholism in terms of alcohol-related symptoms, the early-onset group more closely resembled the characteristics of male Type 2 alcoholics, including having a high rate of paternal and familial alcoholism. Their findings indicate that Type 2 alcoholism may not be limited to males in the U.S. Hesselbrock (1991b) also examined a sample of alcoholic women and men in terms of the present/absence of ASP. While the number of women who were diagnosed as ASP was small, ASP women resembled the Type 2 alcoholism. Babor et al. (1992) employed an empirical clustering technique to subtype hospitalized alcoholics and found two subgroups resembling the Type 1 and Type 2 alcoholism in both male and female alcoholics. While the findings of the U.S. studies failed to confirm the Swedish adoptee study, this could be due to differences in the samples, methodology, culture, and other variables. Further research efforts are needed to compare gender and ASP in association with the Type 1 and Type 2 alcoholism.

SUMMARY

This chapter reviewed gender differences regarding the relationship of affective disorder, ASP, and alcoholism. The differential diagnoses of alcoholism and depression and alcoholism and antisocial personality disorder based on phenomenology alone can be difficult. The pharmacological effects of chronic alcohol use can produce depressive-like symptoms, while chronic alcohol abusers often display a variety of conduct problems. Studies of both clinical and nonclinical samples have confirmed a striking level of comorbidity of depression among alcoholic women and antisocial personality disorder among alcoholic men. The co-occurrence of antisocial personality disorder and alcoholism is associated with an earlier onset and a more severe course of alcoholism for both males and females. The effect of depression on the development of alcoholism is less clear. Some studies have found a high frequency of depressive symptoms to be associated with a more severe form of alcoholism among females, while other studies have found that major depressive disorders do not affect the course of alcoholism for either males or females.

Implications for Future Research

While a number of research efforts have been devoted to the area, several methodological concerns have been identified. First, the diagnostic criteria used to identify affective disorder and ASP are not consistent across studies, making direct comparisons difficult. For example, the diagnosis of affective disorder utilizing a diagnostic screening interview may not agree with "depression" identified using psychometric methods that focus only on symptom counts (e.g., Beck Depression Scale, Hesselbrock et al., 1983). The presence of a psychiatric disorder should be distinguished from the occurrence of psychiatric symptoms occurring over a long period of time.

More studies of women with dual diagnoses are needed since the majority of published studies of alcoholism have employed only samples of men. While some studies include women in the sample, gender comparisons are not always presented. With an increase in the incidence of alcoholism among women, more knowledge of dual diagnoses in women would assist clinicians to provide more appropriate interventions.

REFERENCES

Bander, K., Rabinowitz, E., Turner, S., & Grunberg, H. (1983). Patterns of depression in women alcoholics. *Alcoholism: Clinical and Experimental Research, 7,* 105.

Babor, T.F., Hofmann, M., DelBoca, F.K., Hesselbrock, V.M., & Meyer, R.E. (1992). Types of alcoholics II: Evidence for an empirically derived typology based on indicators of vulnerability and severity. *Archives of General Psychiatry, 49,* 599–608.

Behar, D., Winokur, G., & Berg, C.J. (1984). Depression in the abstinent alcoholic. *American Journal of Psychiatry, 141,* 1105–1107.

Berner, R., Lesch, O.M., & Walter, H. (1986). Alcohol and Depression. *Psychopathology, 19* (Suppl. 2), 177–186.

Birnbaum, I.M., Taylor, T.H., & Parker, E.S. (1983). Alcohol and sober mood state in female social drinkers. *Alcoholism: Clinical and Experimental Research, 7,* 362–368.

Bohman, M., Sigvardsson, S., & Cloninger, C. (1981). Maternal inheritance of alcohol abuse: Cross-fostering analysis of adopted women. *Archives of General Psychiatry, 38*, 965–969.

Cadoret, R., & Winokur, G. (1974). Depression in alcoholism. *Annals of New York Academy of Science, 233*, 34–39.

Cadoret, R., Troughton, E., & Widmer, R. (1984). Clinical differences between antisocial and primary alcoholics. *Comprehensive Psychiatry, 25*, 1–8.

Cadoret, R., O'Gorman, T.W., Troughton, E., & Heywood, E. (1985). Alcoholism and antisocial personality. *Archives of General Psychiatry, 42*, 61–67.

Cloninger, C.R. (1987). Neurogenetic adaptive mechanisms in alcoholism. *Science, 236*, 410–416.

Cloninger, C.R., Bohman, M., & Sigvardsson, S. (1981). Inheritance of alcohol abuse: Cross-fostering analysis of adopted men. *Archives of General Psychiatry, 38*, 861–868.

Cloninger, C.R., Christiansen, R.C., Reich, T., & Gottesman, I. (1978). Implications of sex differences in the prevalence of antisocial personality, alcoholism, and criminality of familial transmission. *Archives of General Psychiatry, 35*, 941–951.

Cloninger, C.R., & Reich, T. (1983). Genetic heterogeneity in alcoholism and sociopathy. In S. Kety, L. Rowland, R. Sidman, & S. Matthysse (Eds.), *Genetics of neurological and psychiatric disorders* (pp. 145–167). New York: Raven Press.

Cloninger, C.R., Reich, T., & Guze, S.B. (1978). Genetic-environmental interactions and antisocial behavior. In R.D. Hare & D. Schalling (Eds.), *Psychopathic behavior* (pp 225–237). New York: Wiley.

Dackis, C.A., Gold, M.S., Pottash, A.L.C., & Sweeney, D.R. (1986). Evaluating depression in alcoholics. *Psychiatry Research, 17*, 105–109.

Dorus, W., Kennedy, J., Gibbons, R.D., & Ravi, S.D. (1987). Symptoms and diagnosis of depression in alcoholics. *Alcoholism: Clinical and Experimental Research, 11*, 150–154.

Ensminger, M., Brown, C.H., & Kellam, S. (1982). Sex differences in antecedents of substance use among adolescents. *Journal of Social Issues, 38*, 25–42.

Farrington, D.P. (1991). Antisocial personality from childhood to adulthood. *Psychologist, 4*, 389–394.

Ford, R., & Widiger, T.A. (1985). Sex bias in the diagnosis of histrionic and antisocial personality disorders. *Journal of Consulting and Clinical Psychology, 57*, 301–305.

Fowler, R.C., Liskow, B.I., & Tanna, V.L. (1980). Alcoholism, depression, and life events. *Journal of Affective Disorders, 2*, 127–135.

Gerstley, L.J., Alterman, A.I., McLellan, A.T., & Woody, G.E. (1990). Antisocial personality disorder in patients with substance abuse disorder. A problematic diagnosis? *American Journal of Psychiatry, 147*, 173–178.

Glenn, S.W., & Nixon, S.J. (1991). Application of Cloninger's subtypes in a female alcoholic sample. *Alcoholism: Clinical and Experimental Research, 15*, 851–857.

Gomberg, E.S. (1974). Women and alcoholism. In V. Franks & V. Burtle (Eds.), *Women in therapy* (pp. 169–190). New York: Brunner/Mazel.

Gomberg, E.S. (1986). Women and alcoholism: Psychosocial issues. In *Women and Alcohol: Health Related Issues* (NIAAA Research Monograph No. 16, pp. 86–111). Washington DC: U.S. Department of Health and Human Services.

Gomberg, E.S.L. (1989). Suicide risk among women with alcohol problems. *American Journal of Public Health, 79,* 1363–1365.

Gomberg, E.S., & Turnbull, J.E. (1990). Alcoholism in women: Pathways to treatment. *Alcoholism: Clinical and Experimental Research, 14,* 312.

Goodwin, D., Schulsinger, F., Knop, J., Mednick, S., & Guze, S.B. (1977). Alcoholism and depression in adopted-out daughters of alcoholics. *Archives of General Psychiatry, 34,* 751–755.

Helzer, J., & Pryzbeck, T. (1988). The co-occurrence of alcoholism with other psychiatric disorders in the general population and its impact on treatment. *Journal of Studies on Alcohol, 49,* 219–224.

Hershon, H.I. (1977). Alcohol withdrawal symptoms and drinking behavior. *Journal of Studies on Alcohol, 38,* 953–971.

Hesselbrock, M.N. (1991a). Gender comparison of antisocial personality disorder and depression in alcoholism. *Journal of Substance Abuse, 3,* 205–219.

Hesselbrock, M.N. (1991b). *Dual diagnosis in alcoholism: Gender comparison.* Paper presented at the Symposium on Alcoholism in Women: Research Updates, Annual Meeting of the Research Society on Alcoholism, Marco Island, FL.

Hesselbrock, M.N. (in press). Genetic determinants of alcoholic subtypes. In H. Begleiter & B. Kissin (Eds.), *Genetics of alcoholism.* New York: Plenum Press.

Hesselbrock, M.N., Meyer, R.E., & Keener, J. (1985). Psychopathology in hospitalized alcoholics. *Archives of General Psychiatry, 42,* 1050–1055.

Hesselbrock, M., Hesselbrock, V., Babor, T., Stabenau, J., Meyer, R., & Weidenman, M. (1984). Antisocial behavior, psychopathology and problem drinking in the natural history of alcoholism. In D. Goodwin, K. Van Dusen, & S. Mednick (Eds.), *Longitudinal research in alcoholism* (pp. 197–213). Boston, MA: Kluwer-Nijhoff.

Hesselbrock, M.N., Hesselbrock, V.M., Syzmanski, K., & Weidenman, M.A. (1988). Suicide attempts and alcoholism. *Journal of Studies on Alcohol, 49,* 436–442.

Hesselbrock, M., Hesselbrock, V., Tennen, H., Weidenman, M., & Meyer, R. (1983). Methodological considerations in the assessment of depression of alcoholics. *Journal of Consulting and Clinical Psychology, 51,* 399–405.

Hesselbrock, V.M., Hesselbrock, M.N., & Workman-Daniels, K.L. (1986). Effect of major depression and antisocial personality on alcoholism: Course and motivational patterns. *Journal of Studies on Alcohol, 47,* 207–212.

Hesselbrock, V., Stabenau, J., & Hesselbrock, M. (1985). Alcoholism in men patients subtyped by family history and antisocial personality. *Journal of Studies on Alcohol, 46,* 59–64.

Hirschfeld, R.M.A., Kosier, T., Keller, M.B., Lavori, P.W., & Endicott, J. (1989). The influence of alcoholism on the course of depression. *Journal of Affective Disorders, 16,* 151–158.

Jacobson, G. (1987). Alcohol and drug dependency problems in special populations: women. In R.E. Herrington, C.R. Jaconson, & D. Benzer (Eds.), *Alcohol and drug abuse handbook* (pp. 385–404). St. Louis, MO: Warren H. Green.

Jaffe, J.H., Babor, T.F., & Fishbein, D.H. (1988). Alcoholics, aggression, and antisocial personality. *Journal of Studies on Alcohol, 49,* 211–218.

Keeler, M.H., Taylor, C.J., & Miller, W.C. (1979). Are all recently detoxified alcoholics depressed? *American Journal of Psychiatry, 136,* 586–588.

LaPorte, D.J., McLellan, A.T., O'Brien, C.P., & Marshall, J.R. (1981). Treatment response in psychiatrically impaired drug abusers. *Comprehensive Psychiatry, 22,* 411–419.

Lewis, C., Rice, J., & Helzer, J. (1983). Diagnostic interactions: Alcoholism and antisocial personality. *Journal of Nervous and Mental Disease, 171,* 105–113.

Lippmann, S., Manshadi, M., Christie, S., & Gultekin, A. (1987). Depression in alcoholics by the NIMH-Diagnostic Interview Schedule and Zung Self-Rating Depression Scale. *The International Journal of the Addictions, 22,* 273–281.

Loeber, R., & Schamaling, D.B. (1985). The utility of differentiating between mixed and pure forms of antisocial child behavior. *Journal of Abnormal Child Psychology, 18,* 215–316.

MacDonald, J.G. (1987). Predictors of treatment outcome for alcoholic women. *The International Journal of the Addictions, 22,* 235–248.

McLellan, A.T., Luborsky, L., Woody, G.E., O'Brien, C.P., & Druley, K.A. (1983). Predicting response to alcohol and drug abuse treatments: Role of psychiatric severity. *Archives of General Psychiatry, 40,* 620–625.

McMahon, R.C., & Davidson, R.S. (1986). An examination of depressed vs. nondepresed alcoholics in inpatient treatment. *Journal of Clinical Psychology, 42,* 177–184.

Meyer, R.E. (1986). How to understand the relationship between psychopathology and addictive disorders: Another example of the chicken and the egg. In R.E. Meyer (Ed.), *Psychopathology and addictive disorders* (pp. 3–16). New York: The Guilford Press.

Mulinski, P. (1989). Dual diagnosis in alcoholic clients: Clinical implications. *Social Casework, 70,* 333–339.

Nathan, P.E., & Lisman, S.A. (1976). Behavioral and motivational patterns of chronic alcoholics. In R.E. Tarter & A.A. Sugarman (Eds.), *Alcoholism: Interdisciplinary approaches to an enduring problem* (pp. 470–522). Reading, MA: Addison-Wesley.

O'Sullivan, K., Whillans, P., Daly, M., Carroll, B., Clare, A., & Cooney, J. (1983). A comparison of alcoholics with and without coexisting affective disorder. *British Journal of Psychiatry, 143,* 133–138.

Penick, E., Powell, B., Othmer, E., Bingham., S., & Rice, A. (1984). Subtyping alcoholics by coexisting psychiatric syndromes: Course, family history and outcome. In D. Goodwin, D. Van Dusen, & S. Mednick (Eds.), *Longitudinal research in alcoholism* (pp. 167–196). Boston, MA: Kluwer-Nijhoff.

Penick, E., Powell, B., Liskow, B., Jackson, J.O., & Nickel, E.J. (1988). The stability of coexisting psychiatric syndromes in alcoholic men after one year. *Journal of Studies on Alcohol, 49*, 395–405.

Pitts, F.N., & Winokur, G. (1966). Affective disorders VII. Alcoholism and affective disorder. *Journal of Psychiatric Research, 4*, 37–50.

Pottenger, M., McKernon, J., Petrie, L., Weissman, M., Ruben, H., & Newberry, P. (1978). The frequency of persistence of depressive symptoms in the alcohol abuser. *Journal of Nervous and Mental Disease, 166*, 562–569.

Regier, D.A., Marmer, M.E., Rae, D.S., Locke, B.Z., Keith, S.J., Judd, L.L., & Goodwin, F.K. (1990). Comorbidity of mental disorders with alcohol and other drug abuse: Results from the Epidemiologic Catchment Area (ECA) Study. *JAMA, 264*, 2511–2518.

Ross, H., Glaser, F., & Stiasny, S. (1988). Sex differences in the prevalence of psychiatric disorders in patients with alcohol and other drug problems. *Archives of General Psychiatry, 45*, 1023–1031.

Rounsaville, B., Dolinsky, Z., Babor, T., & Meyer, R. (1987). Psychopathology as a predictor of treatment outcome in alcoholics. *Archives of General Psychiatry, 44*, 505–513.

Shuckit, M.A. (1973). Alcoholism and sociopathy-diagnostic confusion. *Journal of Studies on Alcohol, 34*, 157–164.

Schuckit, M.A. (1979). Alcoholism and affective disorder: Diagnostic confusion. In D.W. Goodwin & C.K. Erickson (Eds.), *Alcoholism and affective disorders* (pp. 9–20). New York: Spectrum Publications.

Schuckit, M.A. (1983a). Alcoholic patients with secondary depression. *American Journal of Psychiatry, 140*, 711–714.

Schuckit, M.A. (1983b). Alcoholism and other psychiatric disorders. *Hospital and Community Psychiatry, 34*, 1022–1027.

Schuckit, M.A. (1986). Genetic and clinical implications of alcoholism and affective disorder. *American Journal of Psychiatry, 143*, 140–147.

Schuckit, M.A., & Monteiro, M.G. (1988). Alcoholism, anxiety and depression. *British Journal of Addiction, 83*, 1373–1380.

Schuckit, M., Pitts, F.N., Jr., Reich, T., King, L.J., & Winokur, G. (1969). Alcoholism, I. Two types of alcoholism in women. *Archives of General Psychiatry, 20*, 301–306.

Schuckit, M.A., Rimmer, J., Reich, T., & Winokur, G. (1971). The bender alcoholic. *British Journal of Psychiatry, 119*, 183–184.

Schuckit, M.A., & Winokur, G. (1972). A short term follow-up of women alcoholics. *Diseases of the Nervous System, 33*, 672–678.

Schmidt, C., Klee, L., & Ames, G. (1990). Review and analysis of literature on indicators of women's drinking problems. *British Journal of Addiction, 85*, 179–192.

Solomon, J. (1983). Psychiatric characteristics of alcoholics. In B. Kissin & H. Begleiter (Eds.), *The Pathogenesis of Alcoholism: Psychosocial Factors* (pp. 67–112). New York: Plenum Press.

Tamerin, J.S., Weiner, S., & Mendelson, J.H. (1970). Alcoholics' expectancies and recall of experiences during intoxication. *American Journal of Psychiatry, 126,* 1697–1704.

Turnbull, J.E., & Gomberg, E.S.L. (1988). Impact of depressive symptomatology on alcohol problems in women. *Alcoholism: Clinical and Experimental Research, 12,* 374–381.

Vaglum, S., Vaglum, P., & Larsen, O. (1987). Depression and alcohol consumption in nonalcoholic and alcoholic women. *Acta Psychiatrica Scandanavia, 75,* 577–584.

Vanclay, F.M. & Raphael, B. (1990). Type I and Type 2 alcoholics: Schuckit and Irwin's negative findings (Letter to the Editor). *British Journal of Addiction, 85,* 683–688.

Weissman, M., Myers, J., & Harding, P. (1980). Prevalence and psychiatric heterogeneity of alcoholism in a United States urban community. *Journal of Studies on Alcohol, 41,* 672–681.

Weissman, M., Pottenger, M., Kleber, H., Ruben, H.L., Williams, D., & Thompson, W.D. (1977). Symptom patterns in primary and secondary depression. *Archives of General Psychiatry, 34,* 854–862.

Windle, M. (1990). Longitudinal study of antisocial behaviors in early adolescence as predictors of late adolescent substance use: Gender and ethnic group differences. *Journal of Abnormal Psychology, 99,* 86–91.

Windle, M., & Miller, B.A. (1989). Alcoholism and depressive symptomatology among convicted DWI men and women. *Journal of Studies on Alcohol, 50,* 406–413.

Winokur, G., Reich, T., Rimmer, J., & Pitts, F. (1970). Alcoholism III, Diagnosis and familial psychiatric illness in 259 alcoholic probands. *Archives of General Psychiatry, 23,* 104–111.

Winokur, G., Rimmer, J., & Reich, T. (1971). Is there more than one type of alcoholism? *British Journal of Psychology, 118,* 525–531.

Wood, H.P., & Duffy, E.L. (1966). Psychological factors in alcoholic women. *American Journal of Psychiatry, 123,* 341–345.

Woodruff, R.A., Guze, S.B., & Clayton, P.J., & Carr, D. (1973). Alcoholism and depression. *Archives of General Psychiatry, 28,* 97–100.

Yates, W.R., Petty, F., & Brown, K. (1988). Factors associated with depression among primary alcoholics. *Comprehensive Psychiatry, 29,* 28–33.

Chapter 8

Women and Illicit Drugs: Marijuana, Heroin, and Cocaine*

Barbara W. Lex

Department of Psychiatry
Harvard Medical School
Alcohol and Drug Abuse Research Center
McLean Hospital
Belmont, MA

INTRODUCTION

In the United States, more than half (57.8% and 52.8%, respectively) of all women ages 18 to 25 and 26 to 34 years responding to the National Household Survey in 1991 (NIDA, 1991) reported that they had used alcohol during the previous month, and more than one in ten women

* Preparation of this manuscript was supported in part by Grant Nos. AA 06794-07 and AA 06252, from the National Institute on Alcohol Abuse and Alcoholism, and DA 04870 from the National Institute on Drug Abuse. Judith Lawrence, Carol Buchanan, and Janice R. Norris assisted with literature search and preparation of this manuscript.

surveyed in these age groups (13.4% and 11.2%, respectively) had used some illicit drug during the same interval. Roughly 10% of women 18 to 25 and 26 to 34 years reported marijuana use, and slightly over 1% of women in each of these age groups reported cocaine use during the previous month. About 15% of women ages 18 to 34 (approximately 5,161,000) reported that they had used alcohol at least once per week during the previous year, and about 1,100,000 women (4.2% and 2.5%, respectively), had used marijuana at least once per week during the previous year. Slightly under 1% of women in both of these age groups (0.7% and 0.6%, respectively), or about 217,000 women, reported that they had used cocaine at least once per week during the previous year. More men than women use heroin, and until recently (Kozel, 1990) heroin use was considered relatively rare, practiced by an aging group whose tendency to remain hidden makes use and related factors difficult to measure. Drug use also can be assessed in the criminal justice system. As is true for men, drug use and crime are associated for women. Of all female inmates in state prisons in 1986, 34% said they were under the influence of a drug at the time of their offense, 39% had used drugs daily in the month before committing that offense, and 24% used a "major" drug daily (cocaine, heroin, methadone, LSD, or PCP) during that month (BJS National Update, 1991).

Several factors engender caveats regarding our ability to identify causes and risk factors for women which can be used to design prevention and intervention programs. Various definitions of substance abuse confound the literature. Over time, marijuana, cocaine, and heroin "abuse" have become synonymous with "use," because all are illegal. Further, epidemiological data derived from cross-sectional studies of drug use are often aggregated, not only by gender, but also by age and race or ethnicity. In addition, few investigators or clinicians have examined the impact of substance abuse on women's reproductive function, although all of these substances are known to affect the female reproductive system at some juncture in the hypothalamic-pituitary-gonadal axis. Perhaps most important is that typical behavior of those using illicit substances (e.g., marijuana, cocaine or heroin) is to prefer one while concurrently using other substances—the most common being alcohol (Chan, 1991). In the United States, concurrent alcohol dependence with other drug abuse or dependence is an established clinical reality in women as well as in men, and is of increasing concern. Interestingly, in a study of 114 Irish women in alcoholism treatment in the Dublin area, 58% also used tranquilizers, 55% used "sleeping pills," and 13% used marijuana (Corrigan & Butler, 1991). Thus, women with alcohol problems are at increased risk for polydrug use, including cocaine, marijuana, opiates, and psychotropic prescription medications (Clayton, Voss, Robbins, & Skinner, 1986). Accordingly, description of the use of one substance is too restrictive in focus. Instead, discussing women's *polysubstance use* is most clinically relevant.

POLYSUBSTANCE USE PREVALENCE

A combination of environmental, familial, and genetic factors also are important for polysubstance use (Clayton et al., 1986; Griffin, Weiss, Mirin, & Lange, 1989; Lex, Sholar, Bower, & Mendelson, 1991; Lex, Teoh, Lagomasino, Mello, & Mendelson, 1990). For example, it has been asserted that consumption patterns are converging for women and men. This hypothesis has been controversial for more than a decade (Ferrence & Whitehead, 1980), and is related to an ideological debate (Lex, 1985). Epidemiological data for alcohol and other drug consumption patterns in recent years yield little support for the idea that consumption behavior by all women and men is similar. However, there is evidence that younger age groups exhibit less gender difference in consumption patterns. Robbins (1989) contended that the appearance of increased prevalence of drinking by women currently stems from fewer female abstainers rather than more numerous female heavy drinkers. "Convergence" also can be seen in the *consequences* of substance abuse that now may exhibit greater similarity for men and for women in certain sectors of society. However, popular opinion has not accepted greater alcohol and drug consumption by women. Instead, changes in the policies of societal institutions, such as the criminal justice system, employee assistance programs, and the social welfare system have altered the swiftness and severity with which arrests, jeopardy of employment, or referral for child abuse have become more common for women with substance abuse problems (Argeriou, McCarty, Potter, & Holt, 1986; Shore, McCoy, Toonen, & Kuntz, 1988; Herskowitz et al., 1989; Canestrini, 1991).

Some have hypothesized that the differential psychosocial consequences of substance use for women derive in part from biological factors, especially alcohol metabolism (Robbins, 1989). Since more women than men use psychoactive prescription drugs, some of which are cross-tolerant with alcohol, vulnerability to alcohol-drug interactions is likely to stem from liver clearance rates. Behaviorally, differences in performance of gender-related social roles are also thought to have greater adverse consequences for women, since substance use is commonly believed to be more stigmatizing for women (Underhill, 1986). Indeed, some have alleged that the potential compromise of

women's sexual chastity or nurturing childcare responsibilities under-
lies the greater stigma that accords to females who use substances,
especially because similar observations have been noted historically,
as well as cross-culturally (Lex, 1985).

It also has been argued that men and women have different styles of
deviant behavior (Robbins, 1989). Male deviance is said to be antisocial and directed towards others. In contrast, deviance as expressed by
women is thought to be channeled into internalized distress and manifested in emotional upset. There is some evidence that women use
substances at the behest of or in the company of a male partner, make
stronger efforts to hide substance use, curtail alcohol and drug use
except when caretaking expectations are in abeyance, and strive to
behave in "feminine" social roles despite drug or alcohol effects (Robbins, 1989). It is possible that for these reasons, women who use alcohol
and other drugs report greater depression, anxiety, and guilt, whereas
a greater number of men report alcohol- and drug-related belligerence,
employment problems, and legal problems. These generalizations also
are reflected in the greater frequency of referrals for treatment that
follow alcohol-related legal, financial, or job problems among men.

A highly comprehensive study by Robbins (1989) examined gender
differences in psychosocial problems associated with alcohol and other
drug use to test these three hypotheses. Data were drawn from the
1985 National Household Survey on Drug Abuse (National Institute
on Drug Abuse, 1985). Factor analysis grouped 17 drug- (marijuana
and cocaine) or alcohol-related symptoms and behaviors into three
factors. *Intrapsychic problems* associated with substance use included:
feeling depressed or losing interest in activities, feeling alone and
isolated, feeling anxious, feeling irritable, feeling suspicious and mis-
trustful, and having increased difficulty in contending with personal
problems. *Difficulties in social functioning and carrying out role expectations*, the second factor, included: having trouble at school or on the
job, having trouble with the police, having serious financial problems,
failure to consume four or more regular daily meals, and needing to
obtain emergency medical help. The third factor reflected *consequences
of substance use episodes*, including: disputes with family or friends,
driving unsafely, memory lapses (blackouts), and confused thinking.

Data in Robbins's study generally supported the "styles of pathology" hypothesis. Of the 17 problems, 12 showed gender differences,
although not all were statistically significant. Proportionately more
women reported themselves more diffusely affected by intrapsychic
factors, such as feeling depressed, suspicious, distrustful, or irritable.
On the other hand, men had more serious external problems with
trouble at school or on the job, impaired driving, financial difficulties,

criminal justice encounters, and need for emergency medical help. Interestingly, more men reported feeling unable to contend with their personal problems. Unanticipated findings included greater vulnerability in women to belligerence associated with alcohol, marijuana, and cocaine use. Missing four or more regular meals, purportedly related to uncontrolled or binge drug consumption, was more frequent among women and associated with cocaine use, suggesting that some women may use cocaine to limit food intake.

It was concluded that *intrapsychic problems* are strongly associated with alcohol abuse among women, and that problems in *social functioning* are strongly associated among men. Gender differences could be explained by men's greater consumption and frequency of intoxication. Alcohol, marijuana, and cocaine use explained nearly 80% of the gender differences in social problems. Men used more alcohol and other drugs, which explained their higher frequency of problems in social functioning.

However, it should be noted that a cross-sectional survey of persons residing in households may underrepresent the effects of marijuana and cocaine on individuals not living in conventional domestic settings. Studies of incarcerated or hospitalized populations of both men and women might have yielded different results. Thus, the sociological interpretation may be correct, insofar as conclusions were drawn from observations of a less deviant or severely impaired population. Robbins (1989) also wondered whether women's greater vulnerability to disputes with their family and friends reflected a gender difference in expected behavior, or reflected greater stigma and social disapproval directed towards women who abuse substances. However, another factor could be that women who abuse alcohol and other drugs are more likely to have families that include other substance abusers (Lex et al., 1990; Midanik, 1983), thus generating greater family conflict and dysfunction, if not a genetic vulnerability. Women also are more likely to use substances in the company of substance-abusing spouses or mates (Kandel, 1984; Kandel, Davies, Karus, & Yamaguchi, 1986; Robbins, 1989), which also may contribute to domestic discord.

Gomberg (1989) interviewed 301 alcoholic women (ages 20 to 50) after detoxification in 21 treatment facilities in Michigan. Data about their drug use were obtained, and their responses were compared with those of a matched control group. Polydrug use was a more common behavior among female alcoholics. Compared with their nonalcoholic age peers, all alcoholic women reported more experience with cocaine (29% versus 16%), heroin (8% versus 1.5%) and marijuana (53% versus 50%). It was younger alcoholic women, however, who were more likely to report using combinations of alcohol and other drugs. Older alcoholic women were significantly more likely to use medications, mainly prescribed minor tranquilizers.

A recent study (Ross, Glaser, & Stiasny, 1988) of drug use and intercurrent psychological disorders investigated comorbidity in 260 male and 241 female patients with alcohol and drug problems. Diagnoses were made using the NIMH Diagnostic Interview Schedule (DIS) (Robins, Helzer, Croughan, & Ratcliff, 1981). Individuals with polysubstance dependence had higher rates of intercurrent psychiatric disorders. Women and men did not differ in overall rates for cognitive impairment, schizophrenia, *or* affective disorders. Women had higher rates of anxiety, bulimia, and psychosexual disorders, an unexpected finding. In all likelihood, these findings reflect use of the DIS, since disorders such as bulimia have only been recognized within the past decade.

Marijuana

Kandel and coworkers (Kandel, 1984; Kandel et al., 1986) conducted longitudinal studies of substance use among individuals who were first identified in high school during 1971 and 1972. In 1980 and 1981, 83% of the original 1,651 adolescents were reinterviewed at ages 24 to 25. The majority of respondents had used marijuana—78% of men and 69% of women. Furthermore, 37% of the males and 24% of the females had used cocaine; 32% of the males and 19% of the females had used psychedelics; 30% of the males and 19% of the females had used stimulants; and 20% of the males and 15% of the females had used minor tranquilizers (such as benzodiazepines). Overall, 90% of individuals in this cohort who had used marijuana at least 1,000 times in their lives had also used other illicit drugs. In addition, 79% who had used marijuana more than 100 times (but less than 1,000 times) reported use of illicit drugs, 51% of those who had used marijuana less than 100 times but more than 10 times used illicit drugs, 16% of those who had used marijuana between 1 and 9 times used other illicit drugs, and only 6% of adolescents who had *never* used marijuana reported use of illicit drugs. This relationship was strongly log-linear, yielding a correlation of .995 between increasing marijuana use and use of other illicit drugs. Consequently, it was difficult to disentangle marijuana effects from effects of other substance use, including alcohol and cigarettes.

Job instability was associated with marijuana and other illicit drug use for both men and women. The amount of marijuana use reported in the initial survey predicted an increased number of unemployment intervals at follow-up. Illicit drug use also affected performance of adult family roles, predicting lower rates of marriage for women and yielding positive correlations with divorce or separation among both women and men and with abortions among women. By age 15 or 16, women's use of illicit drugs, other than marijuana, predicted subsequent use of prescribed psychoactive medications. It was concluded that use of illicit drugs other than marijuana during adolescence may palliate feelings of depression (Paton, Kessler, & Kandell, 1977).

Marijuana users were found to be heavily involved in social relationships where marijuana use was common. Men's marijuana consumption within the last 12 months was associated with divorce, separation, or never being married. Male marijuana users also were more likely to report having automobile accidents. Of women who had used marijuana four or more times per week during the past year, 96% reported that most or all of their friends used marijuana (Kandel, 1984). Among women living with a spouse or partner, one could observe the "husband effect"; that is, a male spouse or partner's use had a strong main effect on women's marijuana use. This effect was greater than peer use and the use of other illicit drugs.

Kandel (1984) concluded that interpersonal factors are more significant for women's marijuana use. She proposed that men are likely to be involved in several different types of social networks and in friendships where prevailing behaviors and values are different from those favored by their spouses or partners. In contrast, women may be engaged in more circumscribed and less variable social activities. Marijuana use requires a permissive social context in both adolescence and young adulthood. For women involved with a partner, not only the partner but friends provide important influences on continued marijuana smoking.

Kantor and Strauss (1989) studied marijuana use in battered women's spouses. They found a sixfold increase in marijuana use in the previous year among battering victims appearing in an emergency room compared with nonvictims. Consistent findings regarding abuse of pregnant women and use of marijuana (and cocaine and alcohol) are reported by Amaro, Fried, Gabral, and Zuckerman (1990).

Two laboratory studies investigated marijuana self-administration in young men (Babor, Mendelson, Greenberg, & Kuehnle, 1975) and women (Babor, Lex, Mendelson, & Mello, 1984). Subjects were classified as either "moderate" or "heavy" users based on drug-use histories and self-report questionnaires. Moderate smokers had used marijuana more than five times per month but less than daily during the previous year, while heavy smokers had used marijuana five or more times per week during the previous year.

Subjects were studied on a research unit for 35 days in groups of three or four that included both moderate and heavy smokers. Study protocols included three phases: A 7-day drug-free baseline phase; a 21-day drug acquisition period during which marijuana cigarettes could be purchased on a free-choice basis; and a 7-day post-drug phase. During all study phases, subjects could work for points at a simple operant task that earned 50 cents per one-half hour of effort. During the 21-day acquisition period, points earned could either be exchanged directly for marijuana ($.50 per cigarette) or accumulated until the conclusion of the study, added to points earned during the baseline periods, and exchanged for money. If subjects had sufficient points for purchase, there was no limit on the amount of marijuana they could smoke.

Male heavy smokers consumed about four cigarettes per day at the beginning of the 21-day marijuana smoking interval and their use increased by one-half to about 6.5 cigarettes a day by day 20, while male moderate smokers consumed about two cigarettes per day at the beginning and use increased by one-half to about 3 cigarettes a day (Babor et al, 1975). In sharp contrast, daily marijuana use by female heavy smokers averaged 3.5 cigarettes per day and female moderate smokers, 1.4 cigarettes per day (Babor et al, 1984). There was no significant linear increase in marijuana smoking for women. Although heavy-smoking women used significantly more marijuana than moderate-smoking women, their smoking patterns showed more fluctuation. Over 21 days, marijuana consumption showed a negligible decrease for heavy smokers and a negligible increase for moderate smokers. Average daily marijuana use by female heavy smokers fluctuated because no subject smoked on all 21 days. Female moderate marijuana smokers also did not smoke every day, but their average daily use hovered around the overall mean.

Thus, there may be distinct factors influencing marijuana use for men and women. Men's marijuana smoking appears influenced by drug availability. Women's marijuana smoking patterns, however, may reflect social influences, such as the temporal pattern of weekday versus weekend smoking (Lex, Palmieri, Mello, & Mendelson, 1987) or influence of male partners (Kandel, 1984; Kandel et al., 1986). However, fluctuations also could be related to the greater amount of lipid tissue in females which can store and gradually release Δ^9-THC. To further complicate interpretations, data for women also showed that moderate smokers increased their smoking on days when they reported heightened unpleasant moods, such as anger (Babor et al., 1984).

Another study series used daily diaries to obtain prospective reports of marijuana and alcohol consumption by female marijuana smokers, and alcohol and marijuana consumption by female social drinkers, while they were residing in the community for three consecutive menstrual cycles (Lex, Griffin, Mello, & Mendelson, 1986; Lex, Lukas, Greenwald, & Mendelson, 1988). A study of 30 female marijuana smokers (mean age 26.4 years) obtained questionnaires for roughly 90 days per subject, with a 98% completion rate. Subjects recorded the quantities and times of their alcohol and marijuana use, episodes of sexual activity, and occurrence of self-defined unusual life events (our definition of "stress") (Lex et al., 1986). Temporal variables significantly affected both marijuana and alcohol consumption. On weekdays, marijuana use occurred earlier in the day, but significantly more marijuana use and more concordant alcohol and marijuana use occurred on weekends. Older women (ages 26 to 30) reported more concordant alcohol and marijuana use than younger women (ages 21 to 25). Significant differences in alcohol use also differentiated heavy from light marijuana smokers, but neither sexual activity nor unusual events were associated with concordant alcohol and marijuana consumption in all subjects (Lex et al., 1986).

Female marijuana smokers were divided into two consumption categories. On days of marijuana use, heavy smokers consumed between 1.8 to 7.6 marijuana cigarettes, while light smokers consumed between 0.4 to 1.5 marijuana cigarettes. Heavy marijuana smokers were slightly younger than light smokers, but significantly younger when they had begun to smoke marijuana. Interestingly, light marijuana smokers were four times more likely to attribute a search for insight and understanding as a reason for their marijuana use. Heavy smokers reported more daily alcohol use, more days of concordant alcohol and marijuana use, greater frequency of morning marijuana smoking, and higher frequency of smoking in the morning, afternoon, and evening on a single day. Heavy marijuana smokers smoked marijuana more frequently on days when unusual events occurred, but showed no weekday versus weekend effect. More heavy marijuana smokers also had a history of tobacco cigarette smoking (Lex et al., 1986). No significant differences were found for age at first alcohol use, age at first sexual intercourse, years of regular alcohol or marijuana use, years of education, or reported lifetime use of hallucinogens, tranquilizers, or cocaine. Patterns of concordant consumption and sexual activity were similar for heavy and light marijuana smokers (Lex et al., 1986).

A study of female social drinkers (Lex et al., 1988) used a similar prospective method to examine consumption patterns and mood states for roughly 90 days per subject (98% completion rate). Heavy drinkers (mean ≥ 1.80 drinks per day) were significantly more likely to smoke marijuana than moderate drinkers (mean ≤ 1.75 drinks per day). Heavy drinkers also smoked significantly more marijuana. In this sample of social drinkers, neither age nor frequency of sexual activity were related to patterns of alcohol or marijuana consumption (Lex et al., 1988).

Analysis of mood state data examined for potential predictors of eight mood ratings from 30 female marijuana smokers (Lex, Griffin, Mello, & Mendelson, 1989) also found differences between heavy and light users. Questionnaires were submitted daily during three consecutive menstrual cycles. Heavy users smoked a mean of 2.1 marijuana cigarettes per day across the three menstrual cycles, while light users smoked a mean of 0.6 marijuana cigarettes per day. Marijuana and alcohol were consumed on the same day by heavy users on 41% of study days, and by light users on 29% of study days. Unusual events occurred on 22% of all study days for 29 subjects. Sexual activity was recorded on 28% of all study days by 24 subjects. No difference in sexual activity frequency was found for heavy versus light users.

Multiple regression analysis examined interaction of mood states with effects of six variables: heavy use, consumption of both marijuana and alcohol, occurrence of unusual events (self-defined by subjects), sexual activity, menses, and weekdays versus weekends. The strongest predictor was heavy smoking. Heavy marijuana smokers had lower scores on friendliness, elation, and vigor, and higher scores on tension, anger, fatigue, and confusion. Thus, being a heavy marijuana smoker influenced *all* mood ratings except depression. Days of both smoking marijuana and consuming alcohol co-occurred with increased scores for friendliness and vigor and decreased scores for tension and fatigue. Days of sexual activity did not affect negative moods, but did increase friendliness, elation, and vigor. In contrast, on days of unusual events, increased tension, depression, anger, and confusion, but not fatigue, were unrelated to changes in positive moods. Only elation was significantly lower on weekdays than weekends and only menstruation influenced moods by increasing fatigue (Lex et al., 1989).

Decreased elation scores reported by female heavy marijuana smokers may indicate that, for women who smoke marijuana heavily, marijuana smoking becomes associated with decreased euphoria (Lex et al., 1989). Similar findings for young men were reported by Mirin and coworkers (Mirin, Shapiro, Meyer, Pillard, & Fisher, 1971). However, absence of changes in depression scores for female heavy marijuana users was an unanticipated finding that differed from increased depression reported by male heavy marijuana users (Mirin et al., 1971). Unusual events were significantly associated with increased tension, depression, anger, and confusion, but unrelated to positive moods (Lex et al., 1989). Bruns and Geist (1984) reported that stress, inherent in unusual events labeled "good" or "bad," may differentially affect adolescent females and males, as females generally assigned significantly higher scores to the acute effects of stressors (Bruns & Geist, 1984).

Opiates

A series of reports examined gender differences in addiction careers for 546 male and female clients in methadone maintenance programs in Southern California (Anglin, Hser, & Booth, 1987; Anglin, Hser, & McGlothlin, 1987; Hser, Anglin, & Booth, 1987; Hser, Anglin, & McGlothlin, 1987). At admission, women were approximately 26 years of age, versus 29 years for men. Both women and men averaged about 10.5 years of education. Roughly 90% of men and women had been arrested, with their first arrest at approximately 16.5 and 18.5 years, respectively. About 80% of men and women were married and about 85% had lived with a partner in consensual union, with an average number of 2.5 children. Significantly, about 15% of women, but no men, reported initiation into heroin use by a spouse or common law partner. Instead, men were more likely to initiate use within a group context. More women reported that they were initiated by a daily user. However, no man reported living with an addicted woman prior to his initial heroin use.

In this sample, approximately 60% of men used marijuana, and 40% drank daily. White men were more likely to deal drugs than white women, but Hispanic women were more likely to be involved in drug dealing than Hispanic men. Overall, more men than women reported having been a gang member and having school problems. Male addicts also were arrested at younger ages, were more frequently incarcerated for more than 30 days, and were more likely to be on probation.

Over 25% of the sample began daily heroin use within three weeks after initiation, and about 25% became dependent within one month of their first use. Overall, women took less time to develop dependence, and many became dependent within one month. The mean number of total months from initiation into opiate use to opiate dependence was 14 months for women and 21 months for men.

During the interval between initiation of use to physiologic dependence, women were likely to sharply curtail nonopiate drug use and slightly decrease alcohol use. It was conjectured that women replace use of other drugs with heroin, while men continue to experiment simultaneously with many drugs. Women and men seemed to follow similar opiate use patterns, but for women, addiction careers seemed "compressed" into a shorter cycle (Hser, Anglin, & McGlothlin, 1987). This pattern of differential time to dependence is consistent with findings from other studies (Kosten, Rounsaville, & Kleber, 1985).

Women in this sample (Hser, Anglin, & McGlothlin, 1987) reported shorter durations of consistent daily use (23 months vs. 32 months). Women were abstinent for shorter intervals (approximately 3.5 months) than men (approximately 8 months), but men were incarcerated more frequently. Female opiate users entered treatment after significantly less time, averaging about 5 years from first drug use to admission to a methadone maintenance program, versus about 8 years for men.

Women were most likely to attribute their use to social reasons, especially use by a partner (36%), but about 10% of men and women reported social use by friends as a major social reason for using opiates. For about 50% of men and 30% of women, other sustaining factors were "liking the high" and developing tolerance. Men also cited the ready availability or cheap price of heroin, while women were less likely to obtain their own heroin (Hser, Anglin, & McGlothlin, 1987). Influence of an opiate-using partner is a strong factor perpetuating opiate use for women, most likely because opiate use becomes intimately involved with sexual activity (Lex, 1990b).

Kosten, Rounsaville, and Kleber (1985) studied 522 treated opiate addicts, including 126 women (24%). Both men and women had first used opiates at approximately age 18 and had similar duration of opiate use (9 years). The majority of men and women were in the age group 26 through 35 (55% and 63%, respectively), followed by the 18- to 25-year age range (25% and 28%, respectively). Most had completed high school and roughly 20% had education beyond high school. Men were more likely to have full-time employment, but also were more likely to be unmarried. In contrast to 30% of men, 15% of women had experienced school failure, although rates for school behavior problems were 50% for men and women. With regard to other problems, males had approximately double the arrest rate (11%) for women (6%), and women were slightly more likely (40%) than men (32%) to have experienced severe family disruption. On the Addiction Severity Index (McLellan, Luborsky, Woody, & O'Brien, 1980), the rating for legal problems was similar for men and for women (3.3). Ratings for family and social problems (3.4) and substance abuse problems also were comparable (5.4). However, women had a severity rating of 4.0 for intercurrent psychological problems, whereas men averaged 3.3. Women also had higher scores for medical problems (2.5 vs. 1.5), but employment problems were comparable, averaging 3.3.

Using RDC criteria (Spitzer, Endicott, & Robins, 1978), intercurrent psychiatric diagnoses differed by gender, with women having more dysphoric and anxiety disorders (64% vs. 49%), and more men having antisocial personality disorders (30% vs. 17%). Women were twice as likely to have received their first psychiatric treatment by age 15 (10%). The alcoholism rate for the 522 addicts was 35%.

This study (Kosten et al., 1985) also investigated whether parental alcoholism was associated with addict alcoholism, with 17.6% of fathers and 5.8% of mothers alcoholic. The maternal alcoholism rate was higher (9.7%) in alcoholic addicts than among nonalcoholic addicts (3.8%). Overall, approximately 16% of men and about 20% of women reported that their father had a history of alcoholism. Women were less likely (about 3%) than men (7%) to report alcoholism in a sibling. The rate of drug dependence of siblings, however, was about 25% for both men and women. Some generalized vulnerability for substance abuse may be transmitted from alcoholic parents to their offspring (Kosten et al., 1985).

Family history of paternal depression was approximately double (10%) for women. Family history of psychological disorders in mothers was about 7% for males and females and a history of depression in mothers was around 10% for both men and women. Interestingly, parental alcoholism was more strongly associated with proband's alcoholism in the case of antisocial personality in female addicts and with affective disorder in alcoholic male addicts.

Cocaine

There are comparatively few direct comparisons of male and female cocaine users in treatment. Wallace (1991) provided a brief literature review to preface discussion of the need for treatment for the pregnant crack addict, pointing out that while cocaine-related deaths are declining, arrests, admissions for treatment, and births of infants affected by cocaine are rising. A recent article (Phibbs, Bateman, & Schwartz, 1991) documented the exorbitant costs of maternal cocaine use. Babies delivered at Harlem Hospital in New York between September 1985 and August 1986 were studied. During that interval, urine specimens for all newborn infants were tested for cocaine, opiates, amphetamines, barbiturates, and methadone. A total of 355 cocaine-exposed infants were compared with a random sample of infants not exposed to cocaine ($n = 199$). Cocaine-exposed infants were more likely to be born to black mothers who were older, who had more previous pregnancies, and who had received no prenatal care. Mothers of cocaine-exposed infants also were more likely to smoke tobacco cigarettes and to use alcohol. Infants exposed to cocaine had significantly lower birth-weights (31.3% less than 2,500 gm, and 3.7% less than 1,500 gm). At birth, cocaine-exposed infants also were an average of one less week gestational age (38.1 weeks versus 39.2 weeks), and almost 20% had a gestational age less than 37 weeks. One-fourth (24.6%) were admitted to the neonatal intensive care unit.

Fetal cocaine exposure increased both neonatal hospital costs and length of stay. These effects of prenatal substance use were especially strong for offspring of women who had used crack or who had histories of multiple-drug use. Exposure to cocaine versus exposure to multiple drugs generated significant differences. For babies exposed to multiple drugs, hospital costs were $8,450 versus $1,283 for babies exposed to cocaine alone, a fivefold increase. Babies exposed to multiple drugs also had lengths of stay averaging 10 days (versus 2.7 days), remaining in the hospital 3.7 times longer than babies exposed to cocaine alone (Phibbs et al., 1991).

The authors attempted to estimate the national cost of cocaine-exposed infants for the year 1990. Estimating that 158,400 cocaine-exposed infants were born during 1990 in the United States, and assuming an average hospital cost of $3,182 per cocaine-exposed infant results in an overall cost of $504,000,000 for 1990. It should be noted that this estimate specifically pertains to medical costs and did not include the cost of "boarder" babies in hospitals awaiting placement.

Also, many women who use crack exchange sex to obtain it. A recent study of prostitution in New York assessed the impact of crack cocaine use (Maher & Curtis, 1991). One unforeseen outcome was to deflate the standard fees for sex acts, and to increase the level of violence associated with these exchanges. The cost of a cocaine "rock" dropped to about $2. Ethnographic fieldwork disclosed that the conventional charges for sex acts also decreased, in some instances to $2 to $3 per episode, from what had been $10 or more.

It is suggested that the increase in the numbers of females participating in more traditionally male criminal activities, such as assault or robbery, also reflects the deflation of the fees for sexual favors, as well as the climate of violence in which these behaviors occur (Maher & Curtis, 1991). Women's participation in the drug trade has been further marginalized, and movement into more violent activity can be seen as opportunistic rather than deliberate and calculated.

Data from the New York State Department of Correctional Services (Canestrini, 1991) indicate a high prevalence of inmates with self-reported drug use during the six months prior to their incarceration, or MAST scores of 9 or greater. Information was available for 46,646 males and 2,611 females, of whom 80% and 73%, respectively, were identified as substance abusers on April 6, 1991. Of all women found to be substance abusers, 12% were alcoholic, 22% used drugs and alcohol, and 66% used drugs alone.

Half of the incarcerated women (51%) admitted to cocaine use, including crack, 28% used heroin, 5% used marijuana, and 4% used other drugs. Interestingly, almost one-half of incarcerated men (48%) reported cocaine or crack use. Two-thirds of women (67%) had committed drug offenses, 10% had committed robbery, and 8% had committed homicide. The proportion of men committing drug offenses (35%) was approximately half the percentage for women, while slightly more than double the proportion of men (22%) had committed robbery, and 13% had committed homicide. Age distributions were similar for men and women, with 54% ages 29 years or less, and equal proportions of males and females were black (48%). Almost the same percentage of men (58%) and women (56%) had committed at least one previous felony (Canestrini, 1991).

One recent study of cocaine users in treatment (Griffin et al., 1989) compared sociodemographic characteristics, reasons for cocaine use, drug effects, depressive symptoms, and psychiatric diagnoses in 95 men and 34 women. Women were significantly younger than men at time of first drug use (mean age 15.6 vs. 18.5 years) and age of first substance abuse treatment (mean 24.6 vs. 29.1 years) and had used cocaine for a significantly shorter period of time (mean 3.7 vs. 5.4 years). Men and women were similar in their mean total years of drug use (10.2 vs. 9.0 years), years of heavy drug use (5.2 vs. 4.3), number of different drugs used during the previous 30 days (3.5 vs. 4.4), and amount of cocaine used during the past six months (106.3 vs. 107.5), but differed in the amount of money that they had spent on cocaine during the past six months ($9,375 vs. $3,050). More men were married (40% vs. 21%), but more women lived with a drug-dependent partner (36% vs. 21%). More men were employed (78% vs. 50%) and had professional, executive, or sales jobs (61% vs. 20%).

Women were more likely to have an Axis I DSM-III-R (APA, 1987) diagnosis in addition to substance abuse, especially depression, while only men had antisocial personality disorder. Of patients with depression, women reported more depression than men on the Hamilton Depression Rating Scale (HDRS) at admission, at two weeks after admission, and at four weeks after admission. For patients who had no diagnosis of major depression at admission, HDRS scores were similar for men and women at admission, but women had persistent elevated scores at two and at four weeks post-admission.

Women gave four reasons for cocaine use: depression, feeling unsociable, family and job pressures, and health problems. Overall, men cited more intoxication effects from cocaine and were more likely to report that cocaine decreased libido (67% vs. 38%). For men and women, cocaine had similar effects on aggression, appetite, anxiety, and mood. However, women reported significantly less guilt as a cocaine effect (47% vs. 23%). Most men and women (57%) reported they used cocaine to increase sociability.

Involvement with a drug-dependent partner may have contributed to the more rapid development of addiction in some women (Griffin et al., 1989), as cohabiting with a cocaine-using partner was more frequently reported by women. This observation also was made for female opioid addicts (Kosten, Rounsaville, & Kleber, 1986), and alcoholics (Hesselbrock, Meyer, & Keener, 1985).

SOCIAL AND BIOLOGICAL CONSEQUENCES
OF DRUG USE

A pioneering study that investigated the effects of race on the association between physical abuse of pregnant women and substance use (Berenson, Stiglich, Wilkinson, & Anderson, 1991) was based on 501 white (nonhispanic), black, and Hispanic women who attended a prenatal clinic. They reported that battered pregnant women reported using drugs more often than women who were not physically abused. They further noted an increased risk of cocaine use (especially for white nonhispanics) and marijuana use (especially for blacks) among battered pregnant women. However, there is no attempt to distinguish the temporal related order of physical abuse and substance abuse.

It is generally reported that 1 out of every 6 couples experiences an infertility problem, and women seeking help for obstetric and gynecologic problems appear to have a higher than expected rate of substance abuse problems. Results from a 1988 cross-sectional survey found that 9% of women of childbearing age (15 to 44 years) had used marijuana or cocaine during the month before the study (National Institute on Drug Abuse, 1989). Busch and colleagues (Busch, McBride, & Benaventura, 1986) conducted a mail questionnaire study of two groups of women diagnosed with infertility problems or pelvic pain. Items in the questionnaire included type and amount of alcohol and drug consumption and patterns of use, the Michigan Alcoholism Screening Test (MAST) (Selzer, 1971), and a comparable inventory for drug dependence that included 21 questions. Subjects also identified the date of onset of use of various substances as well as dates of onsets of the pelvic pain or infertility problems.

A total of 23 women (31%) in the study had either a potential or probable alcohol and/or drug use problem. On the basis of alcohol use and MAST scores, 16 (or 70%) were identified as having an alcohol problem. In the total sample, 11 other women (15%) had potential or probable drug dependence problems, and an additional 5% had combined alcohol *and* drug dependency problems. More than one psychoactive drug was used by the women with drug dependence problems, including marijuana, cocaine, narcotic analgesics, tranquilizers and hypnotics, or stimulants. Marijuana was the most frequently consumed substance, and four patients reported smoking marijuana one or more times per day. Most of the women who reported using mood-altering drugs used several types of drugs. Analgesic drug use was reported by more pelvic pain subjects than infertility subjects, and many reported use of analgesics during menses. A higher rate of infertility was associated with a larger percentage reporting alcohol problems (23%). More importantly, 13 out of 74 (18%) reported that use of alcohol and/or mood-altering substances increased after onset of pelvic pain or infertility (Busch et al., 1986).

Related findings were obtained in a 5-year follow-up study (Wilsnack, Klassen, Schur, & Wilsnack, 1991) of women first interviewed in 1981 (Wilsnack, Wilsnack, & Klassen, 1984). Both sexual dysfunction and use of other psychoactive drugs in 1981 predicted onset of drinking problems by 1986. Wilsnack and colleagues also found nontraditional lifestyles to have an important influence on outcome (Wilsnack et al., 1991).

Alcohol disrupts the hypothalamic-pituitary-gonadal axis in both men and in women (Mello, Mendelson, & Teoh, 1989). Postmortem studies of alcoholic women have found evidence of ovarian atrophy. Derangements of female reproductive function also are reported for cocaine, marijuana, and opiate users. Cocaine, marijuana, and opiates have been associated with amenorrhea, anovulation, and spontaneous abortion, while cocaine and opiates are linked to hyperprolactinemia, and marijuana and opiates with luteal phase dysfunction (Mello et al., 1989).

One pioneering study examined endocrine profiles of 18 women ages 17 to 58 receiving court-ordered treatment for alcohol or polysubstance dependence under civil commitment in a Massachusetts hospital (Teoh, Lex, Cochin, Mendelson, & Mello, 1990). According to DSM-III-R criteria, 12 women were diagnosed as alcohol-dependent or abusers, and their alcohol consumption ranged from 42–324 grams per day, while six women were diagnosed as polysubstance dependent. Besides alcohol (84–830 g/day), cocaine was the most frequently abused drug, followed by tranquilizers, sedatives, marijuana, amphetamines, and opiates. All women received a thorough physical examination and laboratory studies including blood hemogram and chemistry. All were detoxified and showed no abstinence signs when samples were obtained for LH, FSH, prolactin, estradiol, progesterone, and cortisol analysis.

No single profile of derangements was observed. Independent of amount and duration of alcohol use, 50% of the alcoholic women had hyperprolactinemia, and one patient had secondary amenorrhea with a normal prolactin level and low levels of LH and estradiol. Two polysubstance dependent women had hyperprolactinemia, and one had secondary amenorrhea with normal prolactin but low LH, FSH, and estradiol. Although specific mechanisms of alcohol and drug effects on reproductive dysfunction have yet to be determined, hyperprolactinemia may cause amenorrhea and disruptions of the menstrual cycle. In another report of this sample (Lex et al., 1990), polysubstance-dependent women recalled beginning sexual activity at an earlier age (mean = 15.7 years ± 2.6) than alcohol-dependent women (mean = 18.6 years ± 3.3). Although 50% of alcohol-dependent women had had no live births, one polysubstance-dependent woman reported 12 conceptions, resulting in 6 live births, 1 stillbirth, and 5 spontaneous abortions.

Thus, the effects of substance use on reproductive capacity are far from clear and, in all likelihood are influenced by other environmental factors, such as nutrition or trauma. There is a vast literature on fetal effects of psychoactive substances. The contribution of any drug, which must also take dose-response factors into consideration, has yet to be completely investigated (Coles, Platzman, Smith, James, & Falek, 1992; Maynes, Granger, Bornstein, & Zuckerman, 1992; Phibbs et al., 1991).

TREATMENT AND PREVENTION

Treatment

In September 1990, the Institute of Medicine of the National Academy of Sciences issued a report on drug treatment programs (Gerstein & Harwood, 1990). The committee charged with developing the report deemed that the ability to function in society is an *appropriate* treatment goal, whereas complete abstinence from using illicit drugs is desirable. It should be noted that cocaine, rather than heroin, predominated as the primary substance of choice.

Four major treatment methods were identified: Methadone maintenance, residential therapeutic communities, outpatient nonmethadone treatment, and chemical-dependency programs. Regarding their effectiveness, methadone maintenance appears to be the most rigorously studied method of treatment and has yielded the most consistently positive results—regardless of judgmental concerns that methadone maintenance perpetuates dependence. Therapeutic treatment communities, typically requiring residence for 9 to 18 months, are designed for drug-dependent persons with serious behavioral and social problems including criminal behavior. Abstinence from drugs and steady employment were compared with preadmission rates and with persons referred who did not participate. Heterogeneous outpatient methadone-treatment approaches with diverse clients yielded results similar to therapeutic communities. Finally, the combination of 28-day inpatient chemical dependency programs and with two-year participation in self-help groups have been largely assessed for alcohol dependence rather than other drug problems, and outcome results were unclear.

With regard to treatment programs, the committee found such major differences between the public and private sector that separate recommendations were issued. Of relevance to this chapter is that among the four priorities for public expansion was the recommendation that increased outreach programs and services be tailored to pregnant women and young mothers, particularly by providing childcare and related services and increased research on treating these women.

Goldstein and coworkers (Goldstein, Surber, & Wilner, 1984) summarized outcome evaluations for substance abuse treatment, including studies of programs designed primarily for alcohol-dependence treatment and programs designed primarily for other drug abuse treatment. Information was drawn from a data bank of program evaluations. The major criterion for inclusion was reported findings for a minimum of ten patients. A total of 2,231 studies were included, with 18.2% ($N = 182$) focused on alcoholism treatment and 10.5% ($N = 234$) focused on drug abuse. All studies included information about both intervention and outcome variables.

Few studies focused on program quality such as therapist training, appropriateness of technique, or the importance of the program in a community. In comparison with results from alcohol abuse treatment programs and treatment programs for other psychological disorders, roughly 50% of the 234 studies of drug abuse treatment had weak designs, including absence of control subject comparisons. Roughly 40% of alcohol treatment studies used both random and matched control groups, and analyses beyond descriptive statistics were most frequently used for alcoholism studies (45%), and least frequently used in drug abuse treatment research (26.5%). One-third of *all* studies in the data bank did not specify gender. In almost half (49.5%) of the alcohol studies all patients were male, and 20.5% of drug abuse treatment programs reported data from men alone. With regard to ethnicity, drug abuse treatment programs were more likely to report the proportion of black patients in their populations (15.9%, as opposed to 2.2% of alcohol studies).

In a test-retest design examining follow-up six months after admission, McLellan and colleagues (McLellan, Luborsky, & O'Brien, 1986) assessed efficacy of treatment using the Addiction Severity Index (ASI) (McLellan et al., 1980). Information was obtained from three treatment sites: A Veterans Administration outpatient clinic sample ($N =$ 57 males), 15 male and 22 male alcohol-dependent patients and 15 female and 8 male drug-dependent patients at a private clinic, and 11 male and 10 male alcohol-dependent patients and 24 female and 19 male drug-dependent patients from a rehabilitation facility. Follow-up interviews at six months postadmission used the ASI. However, only 84% ($N = 151$) of the patients could be contacted for follow-up interviews. The best predictor of a patient's overall status at follow-up was the ASI psychiatric severity rating at treatment admission. It should be noted, however, that these findings were generalized to both male and female patients in both the alcohol and drug abuse treatment samples.

Beck and colleagues (Beck, Steer, & Shaw, 1984) used the Beck Hopelessness Scale (a 20-item self-report instrument that evaluates negative future expectancies) to assess hopelessness for 20 alcoholic and 20 heroin-addicted women in outpatient treatment. Total scores (yes = 1, no = 0) range from 0 to 20. Classification estimates in this study correctly assigned 18 out of 20 women to their type of substance abuse.

The mean hopelessness score for alcohol-dependent women was 7.3, and 8.3 for heroin-dependent women, indicating moderate levels of hopelessness in both groups. Five items distinguished between alcohol-dependent women and heroin-addicted women, including expected quality of life 10 years hence, accomplishments, future success, inability to attain goals, and anticipation of future pleasant events. Alcohol-dependent women were more hopeful about events in the next decade and generally expected greater success in the future (Beck et al., 1984). Although the authors interpreted these results as an argument for cognitive therapy focused toward rectifying dysfunctional thoughts, it is also possible that heroin-dependent women may have experienced more adverse consequences of substance abuse and, accordingly, made a realistic appraisal of their possible futures.

Brunswick and Messeri (1986) studied response to treatment in 43 male and 26 female black young adult heroin users. As measured by abstinence, treatment had a significantly greater effect on women, although women had entered treatment later than men, and had higher rates of fertility, school dropout, and resorted to "hustling" to support their addiction. One possible interpretation of women's more favorable treatment outcome may stem from helpful social supports provided by therapeutic relationships.

Underhill (1986) identified numerous factors relevant to treatment programs for women. According to Underhill, the greater social stigma attached to women with alcohol problems manifests itself in lower self-esteem, a factor that persists as women recover. For this reason, highly confrontative techniques are likely to be counterproductive. Information about the concept of learned helplessness, assertiveness and recognition of negative affect (such as anger), should be a portion of education for women in alcohol treatment programs. Other relevant topics include sexual abuse (including incest), physical abuse, and sexual assault, since the prevalence of these events in the histories of women seeking treatment for substance abuse dependence may range from 40% to 74%.

Some have argued that women's unique experiences are best treated in the context of same-sex groups, while others contend that the shared experienced of substance abuse can be effectively handled in groups including both men and women. Others also have suggested that men are more expressive of emotional problems in mixed groups and accordingly receive nurturing support from women, the net result being that men improve while women do not. This topic requires additional consideration.

Prevention

Numerous associated factors emerge from the multiplicity of problems related to substance abuse. These can be categorized as sociocultural factors, biological factors, and pharmacologic effects of substances. All factors interact to exacerbate substance abuse problems.

1. *Predisposing cultural factors*: There is evidence both for and against cause-and-effect relationships between life crises and substance use. Accordingly, women experiencing stress should be made aware of their increased risk for substance abuse. Preventative strategies would include education about human tendencies to palliate psychological distress with alcohol or drugs, and provide realistic and readily accessible ways of solving problems. It is also important to examine the social influence of male partners, to consider the cognitive

and affective distortions that can occur within a family affected by alcoholism or other substance abuse, and to assess the impact of life stressors. Socioeconomic factors and social-class status also are important impinging factors.

2. *Predisposing biological risk factors*: Biological factors, which include effects of family history of alcoholism and other substance abuse, comorbidity with other psychological disorders, such as depression, anxiety, and eating disorders, and reproductive dysfunctions, have a role in promotion and perpetration of women's substance abuse. For example, when dysphoria accompanies heavy consumption, it can have a significant impact on interpersonal relationships. Derangements of reproductive function associated with excessive drug intake also are a stressful burden. Socioeconomic status can affect nutritional status, which also can exert an influence on biological factors as well as pharmacologic effects.

3. *Predisposing pharmacological factors*: While pharmacologic effects of substances may appear to be more clear-cut than sociocultural or biological factors, all intersect. Reproductive dysfunction may be preexisting, as in some cases of infertility, but also may be exacerbated by substance abuse (Mello, Mendelson, & Teoh, 1989). Family history of alcoholism may affect perception of sensitivity to alcohol and other substances (Lex et al., 1988; Schuckit, 1984), and also may alter mood states associated with consumption (Lex, 1990a). In one key study, (Birnbaum, Taylor, & Parker, 1983) it was found that even social drinkers who became abstinent during a 90-day study reported improved moods after they stopped drinking. Comorbidity with other psychological disorders is also important (Griffin et al., 1989; Mello, 1983a, 1983b; Ross et al., 1988; Turnbull, 1988).

With all of these interacting factors, it is important to choose appropriate junctures for intervention. One salient issue pertains to family history of alcoholism. It has been asserted that close to 28 million individuals in the United States (Russell, Henderson, & Blume, 1985; Woodside, 1988), slightly more than half of whom may be female (Midanik, 1983), constitute a large population at risk for alcohol and substance abuse. Since this legacy can include domestic violence, and is believed by some to foster associations with men who also have substance abuse problems, the sheer magnitude of this population invites educational initiatives.

Cloninger and coworkers (Cloninger, Sigvardsson, Reich, & Bohman, 1986) argued that in the recent past, the prevalence of family history of alcoholism has increased in response to a secular trend that has been facilitated by greater overall alcohol consumption and drug use in American society. Reich and coworkers (Reich, Cloninger,

Van Eerdewegh, Rice, & Mullaney, 1988) suggested there is increasing prevalence of Type II (early onset with antisocial behavior) alcoholism in young women. There may be a relationship between inheritance of Type II alcoholism and reproductive dysfunction, since daughters of Type II alcoholic men have increased abdominal pain (Cloninger, Bohman, & Sigvardsson, 1981; Cloninger, Bohman, Sigvardsson, & von Knorring, 1985; Cloninger, Sigvardsson, Reich, & Bohman, 1986). Characteristics of Type II alcoholism, especially early onset of legal problems, were identified in a sample of female third DUI offenders (Lex et al., 1991). Assessments of women civilly committed to receive treatment (Lex et al., 1990; Teoh et al., 1990) found a substantial number of women with concurrent family history of alcoholism, polysubstance dependence, hormonal disruption and reproductive dysfunction, lower socioeconomic status, and encounters with the criminal justice system. Some of them also had been victims of violence, including rape and incest, and all had experienced heavy consumption and accompanying dysphoria. It is an understatement to say that the optimal time to intervene was much earlier in their lives.

Strategies for prevention of child abuse related to substance abuse include strengthening the system of prenatal care delivery that is targeted to high-risk communities. Moreover, reproductive dysfunction (Lex et al., 1990; Mello, Mendelson, & Teoh, 1989; Teoh et al., 1990) accompanies use of marijuana, opiates, and cocaine, as well as alcohol. Consequently, additional efforts needed include increased access to prenatal care, especially for minority women, as well as ongoing healthcare, social services, day care, employment, and financial assistance services. Further, there may be positive benefits of school-based alcohol and drug prevention programs targeted to eleventh and twelfth graders. However, since young women who drop out of school earlier may be at higher risk, special attention through outreach should be addressed to their needs.

RESEARCH NEEDS

Suggested topics indicate work that could further illuminate gender differences in substance abuse.

1. It is fundamentally important to establish a comprehensive body of information about substance abuse. Differentiation of subjects by gender in cross-sectional, point-prevalence, treated-prevalence, longitudinal, and outcome studies is a basic need.

2. Effects of substances on the neuroendocrine systems of both women and men must be studied to address a poorly explored topic that is likely to prove integral in treatment.

3. More individuals are presenting for treatment with dual diagnoses, either polysubstance use and/or another Axis I disorder, or an Axis II disorder, especially Antisocial Personality Disorder. Substance use by patients with other DSM-III-R categories of psychological disorders will continue to require greater attention, and use of illicit substances or alcohol to self-medicate psychological distress requires further study. These patients require thorough comprehensive evaluation and treatment. Basic epidemiological and laboratory research can examine efficacy of various treatment modalities via analysis of outcome data.

4. Both familial/genetic and environmental variables are important factors in promotion and persistence of illicit drug use. However, "nature-nurture" discussions generate needless debate since substance abuse is multidetermined. Major strategies for analysis should examine a broad spectrum of interacting factors.

5. Substance use affects all life areas, and its costs to individuals and society are almost beyond calculation. Contributions to knowledge about primary prevention should be a goal for both basic and applied scientists and treatment specialists. Cooperation among clinicians and scientists is a prerequisite, since their work interprets and guides research and treatment needs.

6. It is unlikely that the substances used, substance consumption patterns, research strategies, or treatment approaches will remain constant. Changing patterns of substance use will present a continual challenge to clinicians that can be met in part by ongoing epidemiological and laboratory research.

REFERENCES

Amaro, H., Fried, L.E., Gabral, H., & Zuckerman, B. (1990). Violence during pregnancy and substance use. *American Journal of Public Health, 80,* 575–579.

American Psychiatric Association. (1987). *Diagnostic and statistical manual of mental disorders*, DSM-III-R (3rd ed., revised). Washington, DC: American Psychiatric Association.

Anglin, M.D., Hser, Y.I., & Booth, M.W. (1987). Sex differences in addict careers. 4. Treatment. *American Journal of Drug and Alcohol Abuse, 13,* 253–280.

Anglin, M.D., Hser, Y.I., & McGlothlin, W.H. (1987). Sex differences in addict careers. 2. Becoming addicted. *American Journal of Drug and Alcohol Abuse, 13,* 59–71.

Argeriou, M., McCarty, D., Potter, D., & Holt, L. (1986). Characteristics of men and women arrested for driving under the influence of liquor. *Alcoholism Treatment Quarterly, 3,* 127–137.

Babor, T.F., Lex, B.W., Mendelson, J.H., & Mello, N.K. (1984). Marijuana, effect and tolerance: A study of subchronic self-administration in women. In L.S. Harris (Ed.), *Problems of drug dependence, 1983* (pp. 199–204; NIDA Res. Monograph No 49. DHHS Pub. No. (ADM) 84-1316). Washington, DC: U.S. Government Printing Office.

Babor, T.F., Mendelson, J.H., Greenberg, I., & Kuehnle, J.C. (1975). Marihuana consumption and tolerance to physiological and subjective effects. *Archives of General Psychiatry, 32,* 1548–1552.

Beck, A.T., Steer, R.A., & Shaw, B.F. (1984). Hopelessness in alcohol- and heroin-dependent women. *Journal of Clinical Psychology, 40,* 602–606.

Berenson, A., Stiglich, N.J., Wilkinson, G.S., & Anderson, G.D. (1991). Drug abuse and other risk factors for physical abuse in pregnancy among white non-Hispanic, black, and Hispanic women. *American Journal of Obstetrics and Gynecology, 164,* 1491–1499.

Birnbaum, L.M., Taylor, T.H., & Parker, E.S. (1983). Alcohol and sober mood state in female social drinkers. *Alcoholism: Clinical and Experimental Research, 7,* 362–368.

BJS National Update. (1991). *Nearly half of the women in state prisons for a violent crime in 1986 were under sentence for a homicide.* Washington, DC: U.S. Government Printing Office.

Bruns, C., & Geist, C. (1984). Stressful life events and drug use among adolescents. *Journal of Human Stress, 10,* 135–139.

Brunswick, A.F., & Messeri, P.A. (1986). Pathways to heroin abstinence: A longitudinal study of urban black youth. *Advances in Alcohol and Substance Abuse, 5,* 103–122.

Busch, D., McBride, A.B., & Benaventura, L.M. (1986). Chemical dependency in women: The link to ob/gyn problems. *Journal of Psychosocial Nursing, 24,* 26–30.

Canestrini, K. (1991). *Identified substance abusers, New York State Department of Correctional Services, April 1991.* Albany, NY: New York State Department of Correctional Services Division of Program Planning, Research and Evaluation.

Chan, A.W. (1991). Multiple-drug use in drug and alcohol addiction. In N.S. Miller (Ed.), *Comprehensive handbook of drug and alcohol addiction* (pp. 87–113). New York: Marcel Dekker.

Clayton, R.L., Voss, H.L., Robbins, C., & Skinner, W.F. (1986). Gender differences in drug use: An epidemiological perspective. In B.A. Ray & M.C. Braude (Eds.), *Women and drugs: A new era for research* (pp. 80–99; NIDA Res. Monograph No. 65. DHHS Publication No. (ADM) 86-1447). Washington, DC: U.S. Government Printing Office.

Cloninger, C.R., Bohman, B., & Sigvardsson, S. (1981). Inheritance of alcohol abuse cross-fostering analysis of adopted men. *Archives of General Psychiatry, 38,* 861–868.

Cloninger, C.R., Bohman, M., Sigvardsson, S., & von Knorring, A.L. (1985). Psychopathology in adopted-out children of alcoholics: The Stockholm adoption study. In M. Galanter (Ed.), *Recent developments in alcoholism* (Vol. 3, pp. 37–51). New York: Plenum Press.

Cloninger, C.R., Sigvardsson, S., Reich, T., & Bohman, M. (1986). Inheritance of risk to develop alcoholism. In M.C. Braude & H.M. Chao (Eds.), *Genetic and biological markers in drug abuse and alcoholism* (pp. 86–96; NIDA Res. Monograph No. 66. DHHS Publication No. (ADM) 86-1444). Washington, DC: U.S. Government Printing Office.

Coles, C.D., Platzman, K.A., Smith, I., James, M.E., & Falek, A. (1992). Effects of cocaine and alcohol use in pregnancy on neonatal growth and neurobehavioral status. *Neurotoxicology and Teratology, 14,* 1–11.

Corrigan, E.M., & Butler, S. (1991). Irish alcoholic women in treatment: Early findings. *The International Journal of the Addictions, 26,* 281–292.

Ferrence, R.G., & Whitehead, P.C. (1980). Sex differences in psychoactive drug use: Recent epidemiology. In O.J. Kalant (Ed.), *Alcohol and drug problems in women* (pp. 125–201). New York: Plenum Press.

Gerstein, D.R., & Harwood, H.J. (1990). *Treating drug problems.* Washington, DC: National Academy Press.

Goldstein, M.S., Surber, M., & Wilner, D.M. (1984). Outcome evaluations in substance abuse: A comparison of alcoholism, drug abuse and other mental health interventions. *The International Journal of the Addictions, 19,* 479–502.

Gomberg, E.S.L. (1989). Alcoholism in women: Use of other drugs. (Poster presented at the Research Society on Alcoholism Meeting, Beaver Creek, CO, June 14, 1989. Abstract 215.) *Alcoholism: Clinical And Experimental Research, 13,* 338.

Griffin, M.L., Weiss, R.D., Mirin, S.M., & Lange, U. (1989). A comparison of male and female cocaine abusers. *Archives of General Psychiatry, 46,* 122–126.

Herskowitz, J., Seck, M., Fogg, C., Osgood, S., Powers, J., & Makin, D. (1989). *Substance abuse and family violence. Part I. Identification of drug and alcohol usage during child abuse investigations in Boston.* Boston: Commonwealth of Massachusetts Department of Social Services.

Hesselbrock, M.N., Meyer, R.E., & Keener, J.J. (1985). Psychopathology in hospitalized alcoholics. *Archives of General Psychiatry, 42,* 1050–1055.

Hser, Y.I.,Anglin, M.D., & Booth, M.W. (1987). Sex differences in addict careers. 3. Addiction. *American Journal of Drug and Alcohol Abuse, 13,* 231–251.

Hser, Y.I., Anglin, M.D., & McGlothlin, W. (1987). Sex differences in addict careers. 1. Initiation of use. *American Journal of Drug and Alcohol Abuse, 13,* 33–57.

Kandel, D.B. (1984). Marijuana users in young adulthood. *Archives of General Psychiatry, 41,* 200–209.

Kandel, D.B., Davies, M., Karus, D., & Yamaguchi, K. (1986). The consequences in young adulthood of adolescent drug involvement. *Archives of General Psychiatry, 43,* 746–754.

Kantor, G.K., & Strauss, M.A. (1989). Substance abuse as a precipitant of wife abuse victimizations. *American Journal of Drug and Alcohol Abuse, 15,* 173–189.

Kosten, T.R., Rounsaville, B.J., & Kleber, H.D. (1985). Parental alcoholism in opioid addicts. *Journal of Nervous and Mental Disease, 173,* 461–469.

Kosten, T.R., Rounsaville, B.J., & Kleber, H.D. (1986). Ethnic and gender differences among opiate addicts. *International Journal of Addictions, 20,* 1143–1162.

Kozel, N.J. (1990). Epidemiology of drug abuse in the United States: A summary of methods and findings. *Bulletin of PAHO, 24,* 53–62.

Lex, B.W. (1985). Alcohol problems in special populations. In J.H. Mendelson & N.K. Mello (Eds.), *The diagnosis and treatment of alcoholism* (2nd ed., pp. 89–187). New York: McGraw-Hill.

Lex, B.W. (1990a, November). *Anthropological insights on substance abuse.* Paper presented at Annual Meeting of the American Anthropological Association, Washington, DC.

Lex, B.W. (1990b). Male heroin addicts and their female mates: Impact on disorder and recovery. *Journal of Substance Abuse, 2,* 147–175.

Lex, B.W., Griffin, M.L., Mello, N.K., & Mendelson, J.H. (1986). Concordant alcohol and marihuana use in women. *Alcohol, 3,* 193–200.

Lex, B.W., Griffin, M.L., Mello, N.K., & Mendelson, J.H. (1989). Alcohol, marijuana, and mood states in young women. *International Journal of Addictions, 24,* 405–424.

Lex, B.W., Lukas, S.E., Greenwald, N.E., & Mendelson, J.H. (1988). Alcohol-induced changes in body sway in women at risk for alcoholism: A pilot study. *Journal of Studies on Alcohol, 49,* 346–356.

Lex, B.W., Palmieri, S.L., Mello, N.K., & Mendelson, J.H. (1987). Alcohol use, marijuana smoking, and sexual activity in women. *Alcohol, 5,* 21–25.

Lex, B.W., Sholar, J.W., Bower, T., & Mendelson, J.H. (1991). Putative Type II alcoholism characteristics in female third DUI offenders in Massachusetts: A pilot study. *Alcohol, 8,* 283–287.

Lex, B.W., Teoh, S.K., Lagomasino, I., Mello, N.K., & Mendelson, J.H. (1990). Characteristics of women receiving mandated treatment for alcohol or polysubstance dependence in Massachusetts. *Drug and Alcohol Dependence, 25,* 13–20.

Maher, L., & Curtis, R. (1991). Women on the edge of crime: Crack cocaine and the changing contexts of street level sex work in New York City. *International Journal of the Sociology of Law.*

Maynes, L.C., Granger, R.H., Bornstein, M.H., & Zuckerman, B. (1992). The problem of prenatal cocaine exposure. *Journal of the American Medical Association, 267,* 406–408.

McLellan, A.T., Luborsky, L., & O'Brien, C.P. (1986). Alcohol and drug abuse treatment in three different populations: Is there improvement and is it predictable. *American Journal of Drug and Alcohol Abuse, 12,* 101–120.

McLellan, A.T., Luborsky, L., Woody, G.E., & O'Brien, C.P. (1980). An improved diagnostic evaluation instrument for substance abuse patients: The addiction severity index. *The Journal of Nervous and Mental Disease, 168*, 26–33.

Mello, N.K. (1983a). A behavioral analysis of the reinforcing properties of alcohol and other drugs in man. In B. Kissin & H. Begleiter (Eds.), *The pathogenesis of alcoholism, biological factors* (Vol. 7, pp. 133–198). New York: Plenum.

Mello, N.K. (1983b). Etiological theories of alcoholism. In N.K. Mello (Ed.), *Advances in substance abuse* (Vol. 3, pp. 271–312). Greenwich, CT: JAI.

Mello, N.K., Mendelson, J.H., & Teoh, S.K. (1989). Neuroendocrine consequences of alcohol abuse in women. *Annals of the New York Academy of Sciences, 562*, 211–240.

Midanik, L. (1983). Familial alcoholism and problem drinking in a national drinking practices survey. *Addictive Behavior, 8*, 133–141.

Mirin, S., Shapiro, L., Meyer, R., Pillard, R., & Fisher, S. (1971). Casual versus heavy use of marijuana: A redefinition of the marijuana problem. *American Journal of Psychiatry, 127*, 1134–1140.

National Institute on Drug Abuse. (1985). *National household survey on drug abuse: Main findings, 1985*. Washington, DC: U.S. Government Printing Office.

National Institute on Drug Abuse. (1989). National household survey on drug abuse: 1988 cross-sectional data. In *HHS News, August, 1989*. Washington, DC: U.S. Department of Health and Human Services.

National Institute on Drug Abuse. (1991). *National household survey on drug abuse: Population Estimates, 1989*. Washington, DC: U.S. Department of Health and Human Services.

Paton, S., Kessler, R., & Kandell, D. (1977). Depressive mood and illicit drug use: A longitudinal analysis. *Journal of Genetic Psychology, 131*, 267–289.

Phibbs, C.S., Bateman, D.A., & Schwartz, R.M. (1991). The neonatal costs of maternal cocaine use. *Journal of the American Medical Association, 266*, 1521–1526.

Reich, T., Cloninger, C.R., Van Eerdewegh, P., Rice, J.P., & Mullaney, J. (1988). Secular trends in the familial transmission of alcoholism. *Alcoholism: Clinical and Experimental Research, 12*, 458–464.

Robbins, C. (1989). Sex differences in psychosocial consequences of alcohol and drug abuse. *Journal of Health and Social Behavior, 30*, 117–130.

Robins, L.N., Helzer, J.E., Croughan, J., & Ratcliff, K.S. (1981). National Institute of Mental Health diagnostic interview schedule. *Archives of General Psychiatry, 38*, 381–389.

Ross, H.E., Glaser, F.B., & Stiasny, S. (1988). Sex differences in the prevalence of psychiatric disorders in patients with alcohol and drug problems. *British Journal of Addiction, 83*, 1179–1192.

Russell, M., Henderson, C., & Blume, S.B. (1985). *Children of alcoholics: A review of the literature*. New York: Children of Alcoholics Foundation.

Schuckit, M.A. (1984). Subjective responses to alcohol in sons of alcoholics and control subjects. *Archives of General Psychiatry, 42*, 879–884.

Selzer, M.L. (1971). The Michigan Alcoholism Screening Test: The quest for a new diagnostic instrument. *American Journal of Psychiatry, 127,* 1653–1658.

Shore, E.R., McCoy, M.L., Toonen, L.A., & Kuntz, E.J. (1988). Arrests of women for driving under the influence. *Journal of Studies on Alcohol, 49,* 7–10.

Spitzer, R.L., Endicott, J., & Robins, E. (1978). *Research diagnostic criteria (RDC) for a selected group of functional disorders.* New York: New York State Psychiatric Institute.

Teoh, S.K., Lex, B.W., Cochin, J., Mendelson, J.H., & Mello, N.K. (1990). Anterior pituitary gonadal and adrenal hormones in women with alcohol and polydrug abuse. In L.S. Harris (Ed.), *Problems of drug dependence 1989* (pp. 481–482; NIDA Res. Monograph No. 95. DHHS Publication No. (ADM)90-1663). Washington, DC: U.S. Government Printing Office.

Turnbull, J.E. (1988). Primary and secondary alcoholic women. *Social Casework: The Journal of Contemporary Social Work, 69,* 290–297.

Underhill, B.L. (1986). Issues relevant to aftercare programs for women. *Alcohol and Health Research World, 11,* 46–48.

Wallace, B. (1991). Chemical dependency treatment for the pregnant crack addict: Beyond the criminal-sanctions perspective. *Psychology of Addictive Behavior, 5,* 23–35.

Wilsnack, S.C., Klassen, A.D., Schur, B.E., & Wilsnack, R.W. (1991). Predicting onset and chronicity of women's problem drinking: A five-year longitudinal analysis. *American Journal of Public Health, 81,* 305–318.

Wilsnack, R.W., Wilsnack, S.C., & Klassen, A.D. (1984). Women's drinking and drinking problems: Patterns from a 1981 national survey. *American Journal of Public Health, 74,* 1231–1238.

Woodside, M. (1988). Research on children of alcoholics: Past and future. *British Journal of Addiction, 83,* 785–792.

Chapter 9

The Effects of Maternal Drinking in the Reproductive Period: An Epidemiologic Review*

Ruth E. Little, Sc.D.

Epidemiology Branch
National Institute of
Environmental Health Sciences
Research Triangle Park, NC

Judith K. Wendt, M.P.H.

Texaco, Inc.
Houston, TX

Each year in the United States, at least 30,000 infants are born with alcohol-related birth defects (based on Russell, 1980). Some of the defects are mild, but many are severe. They range from subtle behavioral alterations, through the full fetal alcohol syndrome, to death. The incidence and prevalence of most types of these defects are unknown,

* Part of this chapter appeared in the *Journal of Substance Abuse* (1991), *3*, 187–204. This work was supported in part by the National Institute of Environmental Health Sciences.

but they are not rare. Fetal alcohol syndrome, for example, has a reported birth prevalence in the United States and Canada that varies from 1.3 per thousand in an urban area (Hanson, Streissguth, & Smith, 1978) to 121 per thousand in an isolated native Indian tribe (Robinson, Conry, & Conry, 1987). At the lower prevalence, its frequency is comparable to Down syndrome and spina bifida. Clarren and Smith (1987) described alcohol as the "most frequent known teratogenic cause of mental deficiency in the Western world."

In this chapter, epidemiologic studies of alcohol-related birth defects that use population-based samples are selectively reviewed, concentrating on the pregnancy outcomes that are associated most strongly with alcohol use. Studies of representative samples of alcoholic women that address these outcomes are also considered. (The large number of studies and variety of reported effects preclude a detailed review of the literature in these pages.) We then discuss drinking before and after pregnancy, and the presence of a J-shaped risk curve for birthweight is considered. We close with suggestions for further research.

STUDIES OF THE EFFECTS OF ALCOHOL USE DURING PREGNANCY

The full fetal alcohol syndrome (FAS) was described by Jones and coworkers in 1973, although its features had been delineated earlier in medical reports that had only local circulation. The initial shock and disbelief that alcohol was a teratogen has been superseded by concern over the broad spectrum of effects secondary to maternal drinking and their frequency in the population. The diagnosis of FAS requires deficits in growth and CNS functioning, accompanied by a characteristic facial dysmorphology (Sokol & Clarren, 1989). It appears that full FAS results only from very heavy or alcoholic drinking. (For a full review of the FAS literature, please see Abel, 1990.)

In the 19 years since the initial description of FAS in this country, hundreds of studies of the children of alcoholic women have appeared. Based on these studies, fetal alcohol effects have generally been grouped into three categories: reduced somatic growth, morphologic abnormalities (including the characteristic facial dysmorphology of FAS), and CNS impairment. The alcohol-related effects may occur singly or in clusters. One or some combination of these three types is often the dependent variable in epidemiologic studies of maternal drinking and fetal development, and subsequent discussion will concentrate on these effects.

The exposure in population-based studies frequently is the average ethanol consumed, possibly coupled with an indicator of massed consumption. Average daily ethanol is computed by determining the frequency of drinking in the period and the usual amount of each alcoholic beverage consumed on a drinking occasion, to obtain a weighted average (e.g., Jessor, Graves, Hanson, & Jessor, 1968). An average of 30 ml of ethanol daily is sometimes used as the dividing line for "regular" or "heavier" drinking during pregnancy. (One standard-sized drink of any beverage contains about 15 ml [0.5 oz] of ethanol, so an average ethanol intake of 30 ml is about two drinks per day.) Frequency of massed consumption, or a "binge," reflects how often drinking to intoxication occurs. Sometimes problems related to alcohol use are also assessed (e.g., Russell & Bigler, 1979; Sokol, Miller, & Reed, 1980). Since population-based cohorts seldom contain enough alcoholics for study, representative samples of alcoholic women may be used; then the exposure may be a diagnosis of alcoholism by some criterion.

Fetal Growth

If drinking is very heavy in the sample under study, or if drinking problems accompany consumption, decreased fetal growth is usually observed. There is greater controversy about the relationship of lower levels of drinking to size at birth. Several studies have reported significant decreases in birthweight associated with two to three drinks daily (Kaminski, Rumeau-Rouquette, & Schwartz, 1976; Kuzma & Sokol, 1982; Little, 1977; Little, Asker, Sampson, & Renwick, 1986; Mills, Graubard, Harley, Rhoads, & Berendes, 1984; Wright et al., 1983). The lowest amount of alcohol at which birthweight decreases have been reported is a daily average of one drink, which was related to a drop of 225 gm in birthweight (Little et al., 1986). All women in this study were nonsmokers, so the decrease was not due to maternal smoking. In another study, women having 10 drinks or more weekly had a doubled risk for birthweight below the tenth percentile (Wright et al., 1983). Other investigators find no significant change in birthweight with moderate maternal alcohol use (Grisso, Roman, Inskip, Beral, & Donovan, 1984; Gusella & Fried, 1984; Hingson et al., 1982; Marbury et al., 1983; Sulaiman, Florey, Taylor, & Ogston, 1988; Tennes & Blackard, 1980).

Anomalies

Studies exploring the risk of anomalies have produced mixed results, depending on the anomalies selected and the level of maternal alcohol use. The birth prevalence of FAS, which depends on a diagnosis of certain facial features, has been rather consistent across prospective studies, generally 2 to 3 per 1000 live births (Hanson et al., 1978; Larsson, Bohlin, & Tunell, 1985; Rosett, Weiner, Zuckerman, McKinlay, & Edelin, 1980; Sokol et al., 1986). Birth prevalence is a function of the amount of drinking in the target population, and populations with higher rates of heavy drinking will clearly have a higher birth prevalence of FAS (May, Hymbaugh, Aase, & Samet, 1983). FAS may be overdiagnosed (Abel & Sokol, 1991), or underdiagnosed (Chavez, Cordero, & Becerra, 1989), depending on the training of the diagnostician (if any) and methodology of the investigation. Rates based on surveillance records or on studies in which no systematic attempt was made to identify FAS cases are misleading, and their use will lead to a biased estimate (Chavez et al., 1989; Abel & Sokol, 1991).

Anomalies suggestive (but not diagnostic) of FAS have been associated with two or more drinks daily (Hanson et al., 1978) and with maternal alcohol problems (Ernhart et al., 1985). There is evidence for a dose-response relationship between maternal alcohol use in the first trimester and morphologic abnormalities associated with alcohol exposure (Day et al., 1989). Others have failed to replicate these findings (Hingson et al., 1982; Tennes & Blackard, 1980), although there were small numbers of heavier drinkers in the samples. An excess of congenital malformations that are not specific to FAS have been reported in infants of heavy and problem drinkers (Ernhart et al., 1985; Ernhart et al., 1987; Graham, Hanson, Darby, & Streissguth, 1988; Jones, Smith, Streissguth, & Myrianthopoulous, 1974; Rosett et al., 1983). Day and coworkers (1989) have reported an association between increased alcohol consumption and increased number of minor physical anomalies. Kaminski and coworkers (1981), in France, obtained conflicting results in three studies of major congenital malformations carried out by her team. Werler and colleagues (1991) found an association between cleft lip, with or without cleft palate, with five or more drinks per drinking day; the increased risk was not apparent for other malformations of the cranial neural crest. Similarly, in a large study of HMO patients, Mills and Graubard (1987) found an association between increasing alcohol use and malformations of the genitourinary tract or the sex organs, but no association between alcohol use and total malformations or all major malformations. Other studies also have been unable to detect an association between drinking and total malformations or major malformations, or those not recognized as associated with alcohol exposure (Halmesmaki, Raivio, & Ylikorkara, 1987; Hingson et al., 1982; Marbury et al., 1983). These confusing results reflect several difficulties inherent in studies of morphologic abnormalities associated with a potential teratogen. The large number

of anomalies that exist and the difficulty of diagnosing them, especially at birth, increases the probability that two investigations will
not be in agreement. Furthermore, only specific anomalies may be
increased as a result of the exposure (as is often the case with a
teratogen) so that very large samples are necessary to obtain the power
to detect a true association if it exists.

CNS

A plethora of abnormal responses and altered behaviors have been
observed in neonates exposed to varying amounts of alcohol during
gestation. There are frequent accounts of increased tremulousness
(Coles, Smith, Fernhoff, & Falek, 1985; Landesman-Dwyer, Keller, &
Streissguth, 1978; Ouellette, Rosett, Rosman, & Weiner, 1977). Decreasing sucking also is present in some infants (Martin, Martin,
Streissguth, & Lund, 1979; Ouellette et al., 1977), a sign reminiscent
of the more serious failure-to-thrive seen in the full FAS. Abnormalities on the Brazelton Neonatal Behavior Assessment Scale have
been noted (Coles et al., 1985; Smith, Coles, Lancaster, Fernhoff, &
Falek, 1986; Streissguth, Barr, & Martin, 1983), though not all studies
find the same abnormalities, and a large prospective study in Cleveland was unable to find any abnormalities (Ernhart et al., 1985). In
general, lesser neurological impairment is reported with lower doses of
alcohol. In some cases, the dose associated with abnormal responses on
the Brazelton scale is consistent with doses that could be classed as
"social" or nonabusive drinking. Many abnormalities are reportedly
present in the absence of any physical sign of alcohol effect. Joffe and
coworkers (1984) have found evidence of hypersynchrony of the neonatal encephalogram in 4- to 6-week-old infants whose mothers have had
four or more drinks daily, indicating potentially serious prolonged
effects on brain function. A large prospective study in Pittsburgh
(Scher, Richardson, Coble, Day, & Stoffer, 1988) has also found abnormal sleep encephalograms in neonates. The large body of literature on
neurological deficits secondary to alcohol exposure has been extensively reviewed by Streissguth (1986).

Other Outcomes

In addition to the classic triad of signs suggestive of FAS, other types of
outcomes have been reported in neonates exposed to alcohol. These
include lowered Apgar scores, altered state regulation, and complications of pregnancy and delivery, especially abruptio placenta (e.g.,

Kaminski, Franc, Lebouvier, du Mazaubrun, & Rumeau-Rouquette, 1981; Little et al., 1985; Lumley, Correy, Newman, & Curran, 1985; Rossett et al., 1980; Sander et al., 1977; Sokol et al., 1980; Streissguth et al., 1984; Sulaiman et al., 1988), though not all studies are in agreement. A large prospective study of 30,000 HMO prenatal patients found no effect of alcohol use on gestation time (Shiono, Klebanoff, & Rhoads, 1986), contrary to other reports (Berkowitz, 1981; Halmesmaki et al., 1987; Hingson et al., 1982; Sulaiman et al., 1988; Tennes & Blackard, 1980).

Increased frequency of spontaneous abortion has been noted in several studies (Harlap & Shiono, 1980; Kline, Shrout, Stein, Susser, & Warburton, 1980; Sokol et al., 1980; Vitez & Czeizel, 1982). One very large epidemiologic investigation found a twofold risk for spontaneous abortion in the second trimester with only one to two drinks daily (Harlap et al., 1980), with a dose-response relation evident. This finding was supported by a later, smaller study in Oklahoma (Ankoute, 1986). A study in New York City also revealed a dose-response relationship between alcohol consumption and spontaneous abortion, with risk apparent at drinking twice weekly (Kline et al., 1980). There has been no epidemiologic investigation specifically focused on perinatal or neonatal mortality, but some studies with large numbers of heavy drinkers or alcohol abusers have reported increased (but not necessarily "statistically significant") relative risks, many in the range of 1.8 to 2.5 (Kaminski et al., 1978; Kaminski et al., 1981; Rosett et al., 1983; Sokol, 1980).

Longitudinal Studies

Follow-up of the children in some of the large prospective epidemiologic studies has begun. The Seattle longitudinal study (Streissguth, Martin, Martin, & Barr, 1981) has provided data on the children at 8 months, 4 years, and 7 years of age. At 8 months, the Bayley Mental and Motor Development Scales were administered. Significant decreases in both MDI (mental) and PDI (motor) scores were evident among alcohol-exposed infants, with a possible threshold effect at four drinks daily (Streissguth, Barr, Martin, & Herman, 1980). The significant relationship between alcohol use and Bayley MDI scores also has been found by others (Graham et al., 1988; Gusella & Fried, 1984; O'Connor, Brill, & Sigman, 1986; Staisey & Fried, 1983), sometimes at very moderate levels of drinking. Infant height, weight, and head circumference at 8 months were related to maternal alcohol use in the Seattle study, especially if binging was taken into account (Barr, Streissguth, Martin, & Herman, 1984). Day's group in Pittsburgh also found reduced somatic growth at 8 months in infants exposed to alcohol in utero in early pregnancy (Day et al., 1989). In subjects at four years of age, the Seattle investigators found lower IQ, poor attention, longer reaction time, and other nonoptimal behaviors in the alcohol-exposed children (Landesman-Dwyer, Ragozin, & Little, 1981; Streissguth, Barr, Sampson, Darby, & Martin, 1989; Streissguth et al., 1984), even though many of the mothers had drunk at "social" levels (about two drinks daily) during pregnancy. At age 7, alcohol use, especially that occurring in binges before recognition of pregnancy, was predictive of compromised neuropsychological function, including decrements in short-term memory and problems with quantitative functioning, perceptual motor skills, and sustained attention (Streissguth, Bookstein, Sampson, & Barr, 1989). Others have noted the decreased growth and development in children of alcoholic mothers (e.g., Aronson, Kyllerman, Sabel, Sandin, & Olegard, 1985; Aronson & Olegard, 1985; Golden, Sokol, Kuhnert, & Bottoms, 1982; Kyllerman et al., 1985; Larsson et al., 1985). Most studies of children of heavier drinkers support clinical reports that fetal alcohol effects in humans do not generally improve with time (Graham et al., 1988; Streissguth & LaDue, 1985).

Limitations of Studies

The studies reviewed above are in substantive—but not unanimous—agreement that heavy or alcoholic drinking by the mother affects offspring growth, morphology, CNS integrity, and a host of other indicators of health. The evidence that moderate drinking during pregnancy is harmful is also extensive, but there are a greater proportion of conflicting results. There are several reasons why study results could be discrepant.

First, the period in which exposure takes place will influence the measure of growth and development that is affected. For example, drinking early in gestation would be expected to influence organogenesis, while drinking in the last trimester would affect somatic growth and brain development. However, few studies attempt longitudinal drinking assessments, which are expensive and difficult; even those that do trace drinking over time must deal with problems of validity and subject recall. In virtually every study, measurements of the timing and dose of the exposure are inexact to some degree, and this is especially true for cross-sectional assessments where there is only a single measurement.

Using retrospective estimates of alcohol consumption gathered after delivery also could affect study results (Little, Mandell, & Schultz,

1977). In one study of patients interviewed twice, fewer women who reported regular drinking during pregnancy reported it again after delivery (Weiner, Rosett, Edelin, Alpert, & Zuckerman, 1983). On the other hand, retrospective studies can also yield *higher* reports of pregnancy drinking (Ernhart, Morrow-Tlucak, Sokol, & Martier, 1988). Perhaps the safest way is to obtain both current and retrospective reports and take the higher.

Another reason for the conflicting findings in studies of moderate drinking could be the difficulty of separating smoking and drinking effects in samples where almost all drinkers smoke. Adjusting for smoking first can obliterate any alcohol effect. Highly correlated variables must be dealt with in the design, rather than relying on statistical methods to pull apart the effects after the study is conducted. Fortunately, almost all studies of fetal alcohol effects *do* take smoking and use of other drugs into account (unlike many studies of fetal smoking effects, which must frequently omit alcohol use as a confounding variable because the data are not available).

Many population-based studies of "moderate" drinking suffer from low statistical power, or an insufficient number of heavier drinkers in the sample. In the birthweight studies, for example, some of the studies which found no relationship had fewer than ten women who drank at least two drinks daily (Gusella & Freid, 1984; Tennes & Blackard, 1980). The problem is exacerbated by the decrease in drinking after recognition of pregnancy that occurs in many women. Although two drinks daily may seem moderate, three percent of subjects at most in several population-based samples reported drinking this much (e.g., Ankoute, 1986; Kwok, Correy, Newman, & Curran, 1983; Little, Schultz, & Mandell, 1976; Little, Worthington-Roberts, & Lambert, 1990; Mills & Graubard, 1987; Streissguth, Darby, Barr, Smith, & Martin, 1983; Sulaiman et al., 1988). Of course, drinking at this level was more common in other unselected samples (e.g., Russell & Bigler, 1979; Weiner et al., 1983), especially if the study was done before the wide awareness of alcohol as a teratogen that now exists. In any case, one cannot detect the risk of having two drinks daily during pregnancy if very few in the sample are doing so. If heavier drinking is rarely reported, the sample must be enriched with heavier drinkers in order to detect any true association between drinking and fetal welfare.

Finally, we are coming to appreciate that the expression of fetal alcohol effects is influenced by race/ethnic origin and by socioeconomic status. American Indians have the highest rate of FAS in the Birth Defects Monitoring Program supported by the Centers for Disease Control (Chavez et al., 1989). The rate for FAS in newborn black infants is more than six times greater than for white infants. These discrepant rates may reflect differential patterns of diagnosis or inherent susceptibility; the true reasons for the excess of cases are unknown. However, there is increasing evidence of an interaction of socioeconomic status with the relationship between maternal drinking and fetal effect. Poor women appear to have a higher risk of fetal alcohol effects than middle-class women (Streissguth & LaDue, 1985). Since the race and socioeconomic status of subjects varies widely across the major longitudinal studies of drinking and pregnancy, it is not surprising that the results do not always agree.

In spite of the discrepancies in the results of the studies of drinking and pregnancy, some conclusions appear clear. Heavy or alcoholic drinking is associated with significantly increased risks of fetal loss and compromised growth, morphology, and CNS function. Lower doses of alcohol have been implicated in these outcomes, too, and a dose-response relationship appears evident in humans and animals. Many discrepancies in the human studies of maternal drinking and pregnancy outcome can be attributed to the myriad difficulties that exist in such investigations. We believe that this does not invalidate the conclusion that alcohol use, even at levels that can be considered "social" or harmless to nonpregnant females, can have teratogenic effects on the developing child.

DRINKING BEFORE PREGNANCY AND THE J-SHAPED RISK CURVE

Russell has written that "of all the substances voluntarily consumed by humans, alcohol is one of the most toxic" (Russell, 1981, p. 120). The toxicity of alcohol is shown by the cessation of fetal breathing movements with a single drink by the mother (Fox et al., 1978). Given a dose of alcohol, the blood alcohol levels of the fetus and mother are approximately the same as a result of it. However, fetal metabolism of alcohol is at best half of the adult levels, so it is not surprising to find that large doses can be devastating to the developing child. But could the toxic effects of alcohol on the *mother*, possibly from drinking even before conception, result in compromised reproductive performance? There is suggestive (but not conclusive) evidence that they could.

Studies relating fetal development to drinking *before* conception frequently find an association, even if drinking that clearly occurs *after* conception is not associated with decrements in fetal development. For example, the work of O'Connor and colleagues (1986) cited above shows a significant linear relationship for drinking *prior* to pregnancy (only) and infant mental development. Others (Hanson et al., 1978; Little, 1977; Little et al., 1986; Wright et al., 1983) also found drinking "before pregnancy" or before recognition of pregnancy to be more predictive of size at birth and fetal alcohol effects than consumption "during pregnancy." Russell and Skinner (1989) present data showing that reported drinking prior to pregnancy is associated with lower Apgar scores and increased risk of spontaneous abortion. The Seattle longitudinal study has reported that the strongest predictor of compromised neuropsychological function at 7 years is occasional episodes of "binge" drinking prior to recognition of pregnancy (Streissguth, Bookstein, et al., 1989).

If these results are correct, they imply that abstinence *prior* to conception may be prudent. However, there is some reason to think that the results are an artifact of measurement. Mothers tend to lump the period before awareness of pregnancy together with the preconception period, so that very early drinking is classified as occurring before conception. Thus, drinking in the period immediately before conception, or drinking "prior to recognition of pregnancy" could be any time in the periconceptional period. Very careful measurements for each week or month have been made by some investigators (e.g., Day et al., 1989; Ernhart et al., 1988). Even though the measurement depends on the accuracy of the subject's memory and the veracity of her report, new information on critical periods is emerging.

There is also reason to suspect a residual effect of preconception consumption, however. An early study of alcoholic women who had recovered and were abstinent during pregnancy indicated that their infants were smaller than infants of women who had never been alcoholic (Little, Streissguth, Barr, & Herman, 1980). The children also did less well on developmental tests given when they were recruited into the study (Streissguth, Little, Herman, & Woodell, 1979). Other investigators have noted improvement in infant condition when very heavy-drinking or alcoholic women moderated their consumption (Larsson et al., 1985; Rossett et al., 1980), but the improvement did not necessarily result in infants comparable to those from nonalcoholic pregnancies.

Examination of the relationship between drinking before pregnancy and fetal development sometimes reveals a paradoxical increase in risk among infants whose mothers are either total abstainers or very light drinkers *before* pregnancy. This results in a J-shape for the risk curve, and hence its name. The J-shaped risk curve with alcohol use has been reported for several types of morbidity in adults. Here the risk of morbidity is slightly higher for abstainers than for light drinkers, rising sharply as drinking increases to heavy levels. Colsher and Wallace (1989) have discussed the evidence for this J-curve in heart disease, hypertension, accidents and injuries, obesity, various cancers, and general indicators of morbidity and mortality. They comment on the "biobehavioral precedent for a biphasic effect of alcohol" but indicate that inflections in the risk curve are "typically small, not always statistically evaluated or significant if tested, and sometimes difficult to replicate" (p. 206). Aside from coronary disease, they conclude that there is little evidence that moderate drinkers have lower morbidity and mortality than abstainers. Yet a recent report presents evidence that age- and smoking-stratified relative risks of total mortality have a J-shape, being lowest for men having one drink per day, with abstinence the reference category (Boffetta & Garfinkel, 1990).

Evidence for the J-shaped risk curve for drinking before pregnancy (or prior to recognition of pregnancy) has frequently been reported, but to our knowledge, never explored. In data for one early study (Little, 1977), women who abstained *before* pregnancy appeared to bear infants who were slightly smaller than women who drank two to five drinks weekly; however, numbers of subjects were too small to pursue the result. The J-shaped curve is also apparent with early-pregnancy drinking in some studies, although it is difficult to separate one period from another in practice. Streissguth has reported a similar problem in her large longitudinal study in Seattle (personal communication, 1992), and her statistical models for neonatal growth parameters include an abstainer term (Streissguth et al., 1981). For birthweight, Grisso and coworkers (Grisso, Roman, Inskip, Beral, & Donovan, 1984) have noted that "women who reported drinking every day before pregnancy was diagnosed had heavier babies than those who did not drink at all, but there were no differences in mean birthweight according to alcohol use at the first antenatal visit" (p. 232). The same finding for abstinence in the week before the first prenatal visit was seen among nonsmokers at St. George's Hospital in London (Brooke, Anderson, Bland, Peacock, & Stewart, 1989). Lumley and colleagues (1985) found that "total abstainers fared very slightly worse than those who drank occasionally" (p. 33) in malformation rate, low birthweight, and low Apgar scores. Shiono and coworkers (1986) show a J-shaped curve of odds ratios for drinking in the first three months of pregnancy and both preterm and very preterm birth; they comment that because of this "the evidence of an alcohol effect on preterm births seems unconvincing" (p. 84). In most of these studies, the disadvantage of abstainers cannot be ascribed to a greater proportion of smokers in the group.

We have examined three data sets to determine if the shape of the birthweight curve shows an inflection at low levels of reported drinking prior to conception. (In this case, the J would be inverted.) The data sets are very different. The first two, collected in the United States about 10 years ago, used similar alcohol variables and permit computation of average daily ethanol consumption. These are described together. The third data set is from the current Avon County Longitudinal Study of Pregnancy and Childhood (ALSPAC) conducted by the Institute of Child Health of the University of Bristol, England (Golding, 1990). Findings from this study are presented separately since the country, time of data collection, and alcohol variables are different from the first two.

The first U.S. sample was drawn from the 1980 National Neonatality Survey (NNS) (Placek, 1984). The NNS was based on a probability sample of all registered live births in the United States in 1980, enriched with low birthweight infants. Information was gathered initially from the birth records, hospitals, and health care providers. Married women were also followed up, either by mail or telephone. All women provided information on their drinking and smoking during pregnancy, and the mail responders also provided information about these variables for the period prior to conception. We selected from this sample all live singletons who had information on maternal drinking before pregnancy and birthweight, whose gestational age was 28 weeks or more, and who weighed at least 1000 gm at birth. (In preparation for a study of fetal death, live births from Michigan were excluded to establish comparability with the National Fetal Mortality sample.) The second sample of U.S. single live births was drawn from a pool of subjects who were members of a Seattle health maintenance organization (Group Health Cooperative of Puget Sound, or GHC). The subject pool has been described elsewhere (Little, Anderson, Ervin, Worthington-Roberts, & Clarren, 1989). Briefly, a consecutive sample of prenatal patients was supplemented with all women who reported regular drinking or smoking before or during pregnancy. All were contacted in their sixth month of pregnancy, and interviewed again at one month postpartum. Data presented below are based on the subsample of all women who had valid information on drinking in the month before conception and on infant birthweight.

Table 9.1 compares the maternal and infant characteristics in the two U.S. studies. The data reflect the way in which the samples were selected: the NNS sample was enriched with low birthweight infants, and the GHC sample was enriched with heavier drinkers and smokers. Table 9.2 shows the mean birthweights by reported drinking before conception and smoking status. In both samples, smokers who drank .25 to .49 ounces of ethanol daily (about three to seven drinks weekly on the average) before pregnancy had infants who weighed more than the infants of women drinking less than this. For nonsmokers, the

Table 9.1. Characteristics of Two Samples of U.S. Mothers and Their Live Singleton Infants

	GHC (N = 1057)	NNS (N = 3839)
Mean age	28	26
Mean education (yr)	14	13
Mean usual weight (lb)	147	132
Mean weight gain during pregnancy	34	29
Mean parity	1.8	2.0
(Percent primapara)	(48%)	(41%)
Percent non-black	93%	94%
Percent smoking in 12 months before delivery*	41%	30%
Average daily oz ethanol before pregnancy*		
0 – .24	55%	92%
.25 – .49	8	5
.50 – .99	10	2
1.00 or more	27	2
Mean infant birthweight (g)	3534	3294
Percent preterm (< 37 weeks)	5.1%	11.8%

*"GHC" refers to the study of a sample drawn from Group Health Cooperative of Puget Sound. "NNS" refers to the National Neonatality Survey. For GHC, drinking and smoking questions covered the period from a month before conception, the first 6 months of pregnancy, and the last three months of pregnancy, or about ten months before delivery. For NNS, the first question asked about drinking/smoking in the 12 months before delivery, and then broke down the period by "before" and "during" pregnancy.
Numbers may not add to 100% due to rounding.

maximal weight was seen in infants of women having a daily average of .50 to .99 oz ethanol (7 to 14 drinks weekly) before pregnancy. The relationship between birthweight and the preconception drinking category was essentially unchanged when birthweight was first adjusted for maternal age, usual weight, pregnancy weight gain, parity, education, and race. It also persisted when the adjustment variables included reported drinking *during* pregnancy. When drinking during pregnancy was used instead of drinking before conception, the alcohol-birthweight relationship was still apparent, but attenuated.

Alcohol use was described by frequency of drinking in the English (ALSPAC) study. ALSPAC is a prospective investigation of all clinically recognized pregnancies in three health districts of Avon County, England, over a 12-month period in 1991–1992. The sample used here is all participants to date for whom demographic information, birthweight, and smoking status are available. Table 9.3 shows mean birthweight of 434 live singletons, adjusted for parity, maternal age and height, amount smoked, and coffee consumption. Infants whose moth-

Table 9.2.   Mean Birth Weight by Mean Maternal Ethanol Comsumption
Before Pregnancy in Smokers and Nonsmokers* in Two Samples of U.S.
Women Bearing Live Singleton Infants

	Mean Birthweight	
Average Daily Ethanol Before Pregnancy (oz)	GHC	NNS
SMOKERS		
0 – .24	3501	3102
.25 – .49	3629	3263
.50 – .99	3366	3131
1.00 or more	3399	2934
(N)	(435)	(1150)
NONSMOKERS		
0 – .24	3595	3374
.25 – .49	3512	3374
.50 – .99	3610	3494
1.00 or more	3533	3111
(N)	(621)	(2686)

*"Smokers" are all women who reported smoking in the 12 months before delivery (10 months before delivery for GHC). Smoking data are missing for one GHC subject and three NNS subjects.

ers reported drinking less often than once a week prior to conception were slightly lighter in weight than infants whose mothers drank once or more a week but less than daily. The results are unchanged if one considers only women who reported abstinence *both* before conception and in the first trimester of pregnancy. Infants of both smokers and nonsmokers showed the same pattern, except the birthweight curve for nonsmokers continued to rise slightly with daily drinking. The unadjusted data are consistent with the adjusted data shown in Table 9.3.

Table 9.3.   Mean Adjusted Birthweight* of 434 Live Singletons in England by Maternal Frequency of Drinking Before Pregnancy and Smoking Status

Frequency of Drinking (N1/N2) #	Mean Birthweight (g)		Total
	Smokers	Non-smokers	
Less than once a week (40/182)	3234	3374	3350
At least once a week but not daily (31/142)	3297	3398	3383
Daily (13/26)	3100	3411	3334

*Data adjusted for parity, maternal height and age, and number of cigarettes and number of cups of coffee reported at 20 weeks gestation.
#(N1/N2) shows the number of smokers in the group (N1) and the number of nonsmokers (N2).

How could it be that "moderate" drinking before pregnancy has a salutory effect on fetal growth and possibly pregnancy outcome? We suggest that it does not. If it appears to, this may reflect some of the reasons for abstinence rather than the beneficial effects of regular alcohol use. Eward and coworkers (Eward, Wolfe, Moll, & Harburg, 1986) have pointed out the psychosocial and behavioral factors that differentiate "past drinkers" and "life-long abstainers," and they suggest that these may indeed be two different populations. Abstainers could include past problem drinkers or recovering alcoholics; the decrement in birthweight seen in infants of recovering alcoholics has been noted earlier. Neither the NNS nor the GHC study collected information on alcohol problems or alcoholism from the mothers, and the ALSPAC data on alcoholism are uninformative as yet. Preconception abstainers also may be refraining from drinking because they have a medical condition that precludes alcohol consumption and possibly affects pregnancy outcome. Abstainers may be of lower socioeconomic status; in the GHC study, drinking before pregnancy was associated with higher income and education, a finding noted by others (Heller et al., 1988). We have remarked earlier on the interaction between SES and the alcohol-pregnancy outcome relationship. The abstainer category also contains those who wish to deny heavy alcohol use, in our experience. More than once, subjects with documented recent alcohol abuse have declared themselves "abstainers" in a research interview. What easier way to sidestep the many questions about quantity, frequency, and period than simply to deny any drinking? Some of these arguments also apply to persons who report very light drinking before pregnancy.

Of course, there are valid reasons for abstinence or very light drinking before pregnancy that are unrelated to pregnancy outcome. However, those who study maternal drinking and pregnancy outcome should be aware of the possibility that there is a subtle bend in the risk curve, and perhaps avoid choosing persons who report abstaining or very light drinking *before* pregnancy as their unexposed cohort.

OTHER RESEARCH QUESTIONS

There are several important research questions about drinking and reproduction that are well suited to epidemiologic studies, but have hardly been addressed. One of these is the effect of maternal drinking in the lactation period. A recent study (Little et al., 1989) suggests that ethanol in breast milk, consumed regularly in the first three months of life, is associated with a decrease in motor skills at one year of age.

There is animal literature to support this finding, and a new study in humans indicates that milk intake is reduced when the mother consumes as little as 0.3g of ethanol per kg of body weight (Mennella & Beauchamp, 1991). If, indeed, moderate levels of alcohol use are detrimental to the nursing infant, this information has important public health implications.

Another research question that is not being answered is the role of the drinking father in pregnancy outcome. There is no clear biological mechanism whereby the father's drinking before and during the periconceptional period can be responsible for some of the fetal effects observed. Nevertheless, there is a growing animal literature and one human study (Little & Sing, 1986) to indicate that this question should not be ignored.

There are open research frontiers in the area of change in drinking during pregnancy, and variables that predict success in this venture. Several investigators have given strong evidence that decreasing one's drinking even as late as the third trimester of pregnancy can result in substantial benefits for the newborn (Larsson et al., 1985; Little, Young, Streissguth, & Uhl, 1984; Rosett et al., 1980; Smith et al., 1986). The question is extremely important if the mother is alcoholic. Possibly alcoholic women who can moderate their drinking are different in some essential way that in turn affects the outcome of their pregnancy. Majewski (1981) was the first to suggest that the stage of alcoholism may be more important than its duration, or the dose of alcohol taken by the woman who suffers from it. Coles and coworkers (1985) found that heavy drinkers who were able to decrease drinking had fewer symptoms of alcoholism and fewer alcohol-related illnesses in their histories, while others have noted that in heavy drinkers, the severity of the alcohol problem is more predictive of the pregnancy outcome than the dose taken (Ernhart et al., 1985). Rosett (Rosett, Weiner, & Edelin, 1983) wrote that women who reduced drinking with counseling were lighter users of alcohol initially than those who continued to drink at the same level. Our own experience is that the less developed the drinking problem, the greater the treatment success and the better the pregnancy outcome. Women in the late stages of alcoholism are at very high risk and have the most severely affected children (Little et al., 1984; Majewski, 1981). Epidemiologic and experimental studies need to consider routinely the severity of alcoholism as well as the amount of drinking. Predictors of decreased drinking during pregnancy should be a high priority on the research agenda.

Finally, the offspring of mothers and fathers who themselves have fetal alcohol effects are now being identified. The careful description of these parents and their offspring should lend additional depth to our knowledge of this tragic and preventable condition.

REFERENCES

Abel, E.L. (1990). *Fetal alcohol syndrome*. Oradell, NJ: Medical Economics Books.

Abel, E.L., & Sokol, R.J. (1991). A revised conservative estimate of the incidence of FAS and its economic impact. *Alcoholism: Clinical and Experimental Research, 15*, 514–524.

Ankoute, C.C. (1986). Epidemiology of spontaneous abortions: The effects of alcohol consumption and cigarette smoking. *Journal of the National Medical Association, 78*, 771–775.

Aronson, M., Kyllerman, M., Sabel, K.-G., Sandin, B., & Olegard, R. (1985). Children of alcoholic mothers: Developmental, perceptual, and behavioural characteristics as compared to matched controls. *Acta Paediatrics Scandinavia, 74*, 27–35.

Aronson, M., & Olegard, R. (1985). Fetal alcohol effects in pediatrics and child psychology. In U. Rydberg, C. Alling, J. Engel, P. Jorgen, L.A. Pellborn, & S. Rossner (Eds.), *Alcohol and the developing brain* (pp. 135–145). New York: Raven Press.

Barr, H.M., Streissguth, A.P., Martin, D.C., & Herman, C.S. (1984). Infant size at 8 months of age: Relationship to maternal use of alcohol, nicotine, and caffeine during pregnancy. *Pediatrics, 74*, 336–341.

Berkowitz, G.S. (1981). An epidemiologic study of pre-term delivery. *American Journal of Epidemiology, 113*, 81–92.

Boffetta, P., & Garfinkel, L. (1990). Alcohol drinking and mortality among men enrolled in an American Cancer Society prospective study. *Epidemiology, 1*, 342–348.

Brooke, O.G., Anderson, H.R., Bland, J.M., Peacock, J.L., & Stewart, C.M. (1989). Effects on birth weight of smoking, alcohol, caffeine, socioeconomic factors, and psychosocial stress. *British Medical Journal, 298*, 795–801.

Chavez, G.F., Cordero, J.F., & Becerra, J.E. (1989). Leading major congenital malformation among minority groups in the United States, 1981-1986. *Journal of the American Medical Association, 261*, 205–209.

Clarren, S.K., & Smith, D.W. (1987). The fetal alcohol syndrome. *New England Journal of Medicine, 298*, 1063–1067.

Coles, C.D., Smith, I., Fernhoff, P.M., & Falek, A. (1985). Neonatal neurobehavioral characteristics as correlates of maternal alcohol use during gestation. *Alcoholism: Clinical and Experimental Research, 9*, 454–460.

Colsher, P.L., & Wallace, R.B. (1989). Is modest alcohol consumption better than none at all? *Annual Review of Public Health, 10*, 203–219.

Day, N.L., Jasperse, D., Richardson, G., Robles, N., Sambamoorthi, U., Taylor, P., Scher, M., Stoffer, D., Jasperese, D., & Cornelius, M. (1989). Prenatal exposure to alcohol: Effect on infant growth and morphologic characteristics. *Pediatrics, 84*, 536–541.

Ernhart, C.B., Abraham, W.W., Linn, P.L., Sokol, R.J., Kennard, M.J., & Filipovich, H.F. (1985). Alcohol-related birth defects: Syndromal anomalies, intrauterine growth retardation, and neonatal behavior assessment. *Alcoholism: Clinical and Experimental Research, 9*, 447–453.

Ernhart, C.B., Morrow-Tlucak, M., Sokol, R.J., & Martier, S. (1988). Under-reporting of alcohol use in pregnancy. *Alcoholism: Clinical and Experimental Research, 12,* 506–511.

Ernhart, C.B., Sokol, R.J., Martier, S., Moron, P., Nadler, D., Ager, J.W., & Wolf, A. (1987). Alcohol teratogenicity in the human: A detailed assessment of specificity, critical period, and threshold. *American Journal of Obstetrics and Gynecology, 156,* 33–39.

Eward, A.M., Wolfe, R., Moll, P., & Harburg, E. (1986). Psychosocial and behavioral factors differentiating past drinkers and life-long abstainers. *American Journal of Public Health, 76,* 68–70.

Fox, H.E., Steinbrecher, M., Pessel, D., Inglis, J., Medvid, L., & Angel, E. (1978). Maternal ethanol ingestion and the occurrence of human fetal breathing movements. *American Journal of Obstetrics and Gynecology, 132,* 354–358.

Golden, N.L., Sokol, R.J., Kuhnert, B.R., & Bottoms, S. (1982). Maternal alcohol use and infant development. *Pediatrics, 70,* 931–934.

Golding, J. (1990). Children of the nineties: A longitudinal study of pregnancy and childhood based on the population of Avon (ALSPAC). *West of England Medical Journal, 105,* 80–82.

Graham, J.M., Jr., Hanson, J.W., Darby, B.L., & Streissguth, A.P. (1988). Independent dysmorphology evaluations at birth and 4 years of age for children exposed to varying amount of alcohol in utero. *Pediatrics, 81,* 772–778.

Grisso, J.A., Roman, E., Inskip, H., Beral, V., & Donovan, J. (1984). Alcohol consumption and outcome of pregnancy. *Journal of Epidemiology and Community Health, 38,* 232–235.

Gusella, J.L., & Fried, P.A. (1984). Effects of maternal social drinking and smoking on offspring at 13 months. *Neurobehavioral Toxicology Teratology, 6,* 13–17.

Halmesmaki, E., Raivio, K.O, & Ylikorkara, O. (1987). Patterns of alcohol consumption during pregnancy. *Obstetrics and Gynecology, 69,* 594–597.

Hanson, J.W. Streissguth, A.P., & Smith, D.W. (1978). The effects of moderate alcohol consumption during pregnancy on fetal growth and morphogenesis. *Journal of Pediatrics, 92,* 457–460.

Harlap, S. & Shiono, P.H. (1980). Alcohol, smoking, and incidence of spontaneous abortions in the first and second trimester. *Lancet, 2,* 173–176.

Heller, J., Anderson, H., Bland, J.M., Brooke, O.G., Peacock, J.L., Stewart, C.M. (1988). Alcohol in pregnancy: Patterns and associations with socioeconomic, psychological and behavioural factors. *British Journal of Addiction, 83,* 541–551.

Hingson, R., Alpert, J.J., Day, N., Dooling, E., Kayne, H., Morelock, S., Oppenheimer, E., & Zuckerman, B. (1982). Effects of maternal drinking and marijuana use on fetal growth and development. *Pediatrics, 70,* 539–546.

Jessor, R., Graves, T.D., Hanson, R.C., & Jessor, S. (1968). *Society, personality, and deviant behavior: A study of a tri-ethnic community.* New York: Holt, Rinehart & Winston.

Joffe, S., Childiaeva, R., & Chernick, V. (1984). Prolonged effects of maternal alcohol ingestion on the neonatal electroencephalogram. *Pediatrics, 74,* 330–332.

Jones, K.L., Smith, D.W., Streissguth, A.P., & Myrianthopoulous, N.C. (1974). Outcome in offspring of chronic alcoholic women. *Lancet, 1,* 1076–1078.

Kaminski, M., Franc, M., Lebouvier, M., du Mazaubrun, C., & Rumeau-Rouquette, C. (1981). Moderate alcohol use and pregnancy outcome. *Neurobehavioral Toxicology Teratology, 3,* 173–181.

Kaminski, M., Rumeau-Rouquette, C., & Schwartz, D. (1976). Consommation d'alcool chez les femmes enceintes et issue de la grossesse. Revue Epidemiology. *Sante Publication, 24,* 27–40. (English translation by Little, R.E., & Schinzel, A. (1978). Alcohol consumption in pregnant women and the outcome of pregnancy. *Alcoholism: Clinical and Experimental Research, 2,* 155–163.)

Kline, J., Shrout, P., Stein, Z., Susser, M., & Warburton, D. (1980). Drinking during pregnancy and spontaneous abortion. *Lancet, 2,* 176–180.

Kuzma, J.W., & Sokol, R.J. (1982). Maternal drinking behavior and decreased intrauterine growth. *Alcoholism: Clinical and Experimental Research, 6,* 396–402.

Kwok, P., Correy, J.F., Newman, N.M., & Curran, J.T. (1983). Smoking and alcohol consumption during pregnancy: An epidemiological study in Tasmania. *Medical Journal of Australia, 1,* 220–223.

Kyllerman, M., Aronson, M., Sabel, K.-G., Karlberg, E., Sandin, B., & Olegard, R. (1985). Children of alcoholic mothers: Growth and motor performance compared to matched controls. *Acta Paediatrics Scandinavia, 74,* 20–26.

Landesman Dwyer, S., Keller, L.S., & Streissguth, A.P. (1978). Naturalistic observations of newborns: Effects of maternal alcohol intake. *Alcoholism: Clinical and Experimental Research, 2,* 171–177.

Landesman-Dwyer, S., Ragozin, A.S., & Little, R.E. (1981). Behavioral correlates of prenatal alcohol exposure: A four-year follow-up study. *Neurobehavioral Toxicology Teratology, 3,* 187–193.

Larsson, G., Bohlin, A.-B., & Tunell, R. (1985). Prospective study of children exposed to variable amounts of alcohol in utero. *Archives of Diseases in Childhood, 60,* 316–321.

Little, R.E. (1977). Moderate alcohol use during pregnancy and decreased infant birthweight. *American Journal of Public Health, 67,* 1154–1156.

Little, R.E., Anderson, K.W., Ervin, C.H., Worthington-Roberts, B., & Clarren, S.K. (1989). Maternal alcohol use during breast-feeding and infant mental and motor development at one year. *New England Journal of Medicine, 321,* 425–430.

Little, R.E., Asker, R.L., Sampson, P.D., & Renwick, J.H. (1986). Fetal growth and moderate drinking in early pregnancy. *American Journal of Epidemiology, 123,* 270–278.

Little, R.E., Mandell, W., & Schultz, F.A. (1977). Consequences of retrospective measurement of alcohol consumption. *Journal of Studies on Alcohol, 38,* 1777–1780.

Little, R.E., Schultz, F.A., & Mandell, W. (1976). Drinking during pregnancy. *Journal of Studies on Alcohol, 37,* 375–379.

Little, R.E., & Sing, C.F. (1986). Association of father's drinking and infant's birthweight. *New England Journal of Medicine, 314,* 1644–1645.

Little, R.E., Streissguth, A.P., Barr, H.M., & Herman, C.S. (1980). Decreased birthweight in infants of alcoholic women who abstained during pregnancy. *Journal of Pediatrics, 96,* 974–976.

Little, R.E., Streissguth, A.P., Guzinski, G.M., Uhl, C.N., Paulozzi, L., Mann, S.L., Young, A., Clarren, S.K., & Grathwohl, H.L. (1985). An evaluation of the Pregnancy and Health Program. *Alcohol Health & Research World, 10,* 44–53.

Little, R.E., Worthington-Roberts, B., & Lambert, M.D. (1990). Drinking and smoking at three months postpartum: Differences by lactation history. *Paediatric and Perinatal Epidemiology, 4,* 290–302.

Little, R.E., Young, A., Streissguth, A.P., & Uhl, C.M. (1984). Preventing fetal alcohol effects: Effectiveness of a demonstration project. In CIBA Foundation, *Mechanisms of Alcohol Damage in Utero* (Monograph 105). London: Pitman.

Lumley, J., Correy, J.F., Newman, N.M., & Curran, J.T. (1985). Cigarette smoking, alcohol consumption and fetal outcome in Tasmania 1981-82. *Australia New Zealand Journal of Obstetrics and Gynaecology, 25,* 33–40.

Majewski, F. (1981). Alcohol embryopathy: Some facts and speculations about pathogenesis. *Neurobehavioral Toxicology and Teratology, 3,* 129–144.

Marbury, M.C., Linn, S., Monson, R., Schoenbaum, S., Stubblefield, P.G., & Ryan, K.J. (1983). The association of alcohol consumption with outcome of pregnancy. *American Journal of Public Health, 73,* 1165–1168.

Martin, D.C., Martin, J.C., Streissguth, A.P., & Lund, C.A. (1979). Sucking frequency and amplitude in newborns as a function of maternal drinking and smoking. In M. Galanter (Ed.), *Currents in alcoholism* (Vol. 5). New York: Grune and Stratton.

May, P.A., Hymbaugh, K.J., Aase, J.M., & Samet, J.M. (1983). Epidemiology of fetal alcohol syndrome among American Indians of the Southwest. *Social Biology, 30,* 374–387.

Mennella, J.A., & Beauchamp, G.K. (1991). The transfer of alcohol to human milk. *New England Journal of Medicine, 325,* 981–985.

Mills, J.L., & Graubard, B.I. (1987). Is moderate drinking during pregnancy associated with an increased risk for malformations? *Pediatrics, 80,* 309–314.

Mills, J.L., Graubard, B.I., Harley, E., Rhoads, G.G., & Berendes, H.W. (1984). Maternal alcohol consumption and birth weight: How much drinking during pregnancy is safe? *Journal of the American Medical Association, 252,* 1875–1879.

O'Connor, M.J., Brill, N.J., & Sigman, M. (1986). Alcohol use in primiparous women older than 30 years of age: Relation to infant development. *Pediatrics, 78,* 444–450.

Olsen, J., Rachootin, P., & Schiodt, A.V. (1983). Alcohol use, conception time, and birthweight. *Journal of Epidemiology Community Health, 37,* 63–65.

Ouellette, E.M., Rosett, H.L., Rosman, N.P., & Weiner, L. (1977). Adverse effects on offspring of maternal alcohol abuse during pregnancy. *New England Journal of Medicine, 297,* 528–530.

Placek, P.J. (1984). The 1980 National Natality Survey and National Fetal Mortality Survey: Methods used and PHS agency participation. *Public Health Reports, 99,* 111–117.

Robinson, G.C., Conry, J.L., & Conry, R.F. (1987). Clinical profile and prevalence of fetal alcohol syndrome in an isolated community in British Columbia. *Canadian Medical Association Journal, 137,* 203–207.

Rosett, H.L., Weiner, L., & Edelin, K.C. (1983). Treatment experience with pregnant problem drinkers. *Journal of the American Medical Association, 249,* 2029–2033.

Rosett, H.L., Weiner, L., Lee, A., Zuckerman, B., Dooling, E., & Oppenheimer, E. (1983). Patterns of alcohol consumption and fetal development. *Obstetrics and Gynecology, 61,* 539–546.

Rosett, H.L., Weiner, L., Zuckerman, B., McKinlay, S., & Edelin, K.C. (1980). Reduction of alcohol consumption during pregnancy with benefits to the newborn. *Alcoholism: Clinical and Experimental Research, 4,* 178–184.

Russell, M. (1977). Intrauterine growth in infants born to women with alcohol-related psychiatric disorders. *Alcoholism: Clinical and Experimental Research, 1,* 225–231.

Russell, M. (1980). The impact of alcohol-related birth defects (ARBD) on New York State. *Neurobehavioral Toxicology, 2,* 277–283.

Russell, M. (1981). The epidemiology of alcohol-related birth defects. In E.L. Abel (Ed.), *Fetal Alcohol Syndrome* (Vol. 2: Human Studies, pp. 89–126). Boca Raton, FL: CRC Press.

Russell, M., & Bigler, L. (1979). Screening for alcohol-related problems in an outpatient obstetric-gynecologic clinic. *American Journal of Obstetrics and Gynecology, 134,* 4–12.

Russell, M., & Skinner, J.B. (1989). Early measures of maternal alcohol misuse as predictors of adverse pregnancy outcomes. *Alcoholism: Clinical and Experimental Research, 12,* 824–830.

Sander, L.W., Snyder, P., Rosett, H.L., Lee, A., Gould, J.B., & Ouelette, E. (1977). Effects of alcohol intake during pregnancy on newborn state regulation: A progress report. *Alcoholism: Clinical and Experimental Research, 1,* 233–241.

Scher, M., Richardson, G., Coble, P., Day, N.L., & Stoffer, D.S. (1988). The effects of prenatal alcohol and marijuana exposure: Disturbances in neonatal sleep cycling and arousal. *Pediatric Research, 24,* 101–105.

Shiono, P.H., Klebanoff, M.A., & Rhoads, G.G. (1986). Smoking and drinking during pregnancy. *Journal of the American Medical Association, 255,* 82–84.

Smith, I.E., Coles, C.D., Lancaster, J., Fernhoff, P.M., & Falek, A. (1986). The effect of volume and duration of prenatal ethanol exposure on neonatal physical and behavioral development. *Neurobehavioral Toxicology and Teratology, 8,* 375–381.

Sokol, R.J., Ager, J., Martier, S., Debanne, S., Ernhart, C., Kuzma, J., & Miller, S.I. (1986). Significant determinants of susceptibility to alcohol teratogenicity. *Annals of the NY Academy of Sciences, 63,* 87–100.

Sokol, R.J., & Clarren, S.K. (1989). Guidelines for use of terminology describing the impact of prenatal alcohol on the offspring. *Alcoholism: Clinical and Experimental Research, 13,* 597–598.

Sokol, R.J., Miller, S.I., & Reed, G. (1980). Alcohol abuse during pregnancy: An epidemiological model. *Alcoholism: Clinical and Experimental Research, 4,* 135–145.

Staisey, N.L., & Fried, P.A. (1983). Relationships between moderate maternal alcohol consumption during pregnancy and infant neurological development. *Journal of Studies on Alcohol, 44,* 262–270.

Streissguth, A.P. (1986). The behavioral teratology of alcohol: Performance, behavioral, and intellectual deficits in prenatally exposed children. In J. West (Ed.), *Alcohol and brain development* (pp. 3–44). New York: Oxford University Press.

Streissguth, A.P., Barr, H.M., & Martin, D.C. (1983). Maternal alcohol use and neonatal habituation assessed with the Brazelton scale. *Child Development, 54,* 1109–1118.

Streissguth, A.P., Barr, H.M., Martin, D.C., & Herman, C.S. (1980). Effects of maternal alcohol, nicotine and caffeine use during pregnancy on infant mental and motor development at 8 months. *Alcoholism: Clinical and Experimental Research, 4,* 152–164.

Streissguth, A.P., Barr, H.M., Sampson, P.D., Darby, B.L., & Martin, D.C. (1989). IQ at age 4 in relation to maternal alcohol use and smoking during pregnancy. *Developmental Psychology, 25,* 3–11.

Streissguth, A.P., Bookstein, F.L., Sampson, P.D., & Barr, H.M. (1989). Neurobehavioral effects of prenatal alcohol: Part III. PLS analysis of neuropsychologic tests. *Neurotoxicology and Teratology, 11,* 493–507.

Streissguth, A.P., Darby, B.L., Barr, H.M., Smith, J.R., & Martin, D.C. (1983). Comparison of drinking and smoking patterns during pregnancy over a six-year interval. *American Journal of Obstetrics and Gynecology, 145,* 716–724.

Streissguth, A.P., & LaDue, R.A. (1985). Psychological and behavioral effects in children prenatally exposed to alcohol. *Alcohol and Health Research World, 10,* 6–12.

Streissguth, A.P., Little, R.E., Herman, C., & Woodell, S. (1979). IQ in children of recovered alcoholic mothers compared to matched controls. *Clinical and Experimental Research, 3,* 197.

Streissguth, A.P., Martin, D.C., Barr, H.M., Sandman, B.M., Kirchner, G.L., & Darby, B.L. (1984). Intrauterine alcohol and nicotine exposure: Attention and reaction time in 4-year-old children. *Developmental Psychology, 20,* 533–541.

Streissguth, A.P., Martin, D.C., Martin, J.C., & Barr, H.M. (1981). The Seattle longitudinal prospective study on alcohol and pregnancy. *Neuro-behavioral Toxicology Teratology, 3,* 223–233.

Sulaiman, N.D., Florey, C.D., Taylor, D.J., & Ogston, S.A. (1988). Alcohol consumption in Dundee primigravidas and its effects on outcome of pregnancy. *British Medical Journal, 296,* 1500–1503.

Tennes, K., & Blackard, C. (1980). Maternal alcohol consumption, birth weight, and minor physical anomalies. *American Journal of Obstetrics and Gynecology, 138,* 774–780.

Vitez, M., & Czeizel, E. (1982). Az iszakos-alkoholista nok termekenysege [Fertility of Female Alcoholics]. *Alkohologia, 13,* 79–83.

Vitez, M., Koranyi, G., Gonczy, E., Rudas, T., & Czeizel, A. (1984). A semi-quantitative score system for epidemiologic studies of fetal alcohol syndrome. *American Journal of Epidemiology, 119,* 301–308.

Weiner, L., Rosett, H.L., Edelin, K.C., Alpert, J.J., & Zuckerman, B. (1983). Alcohol consumption by pregnant women. *Obstetrics and Gynecology, 61,* 6–12.

Werler, M.M., Lammer, E.J., Rosenberg, L., & Mitchell, A.A. (1991). Maternal alcohol use in relation to selected birth defects. *American Journal of Epidemiology, 132,* 691–698.

Wright, J.T., Barrison, I.G., Lewis, I.G., Waterson, E.J., Toplis, P.J., Gordon, M.G., MacRae, K.D., Morris, N.F., & Murray-Lyon, I.M. (1983). Alcohol consumption, pregnancy, and low birthweight. *Lancet, 1,* 663–665.

Chapter 10

Substance Abuse by Special Populations of Women*

Michael R. Liepman, MD[1,2,3]
Roberta E. Goldman, PhD[2]
Alicia D. Monroe, MD[2]
Karen W. Green, MD[1,4]
Ann L. Sattler, MD, MEd[1]
James B. Broadhurst, MD, MHA[1]
Edith S. L. Gomberg, PhD[5]

* We acknowledge funding support from the U.S. Center for Substance Abuse Prevention awarded to the University of Massachusetts Medical School and Brown University School of Medicine. Thanks also to Lucy C. Sasser and Francine M. Woodcock for manuscript preparation.

[1] Departments of Psychiatry, Obstetrics & Gynecology, Pediatrics, and Family & Community Medicine, respectively, University of Massachusetts Medical School, Worcester

[2] Department of Family Medicine, Brown University School of Medicine, Providence, RI and Memorial Hospital of Rhode Island, Pawtucket, RI

[3] Chief, Chemical Dependency Service, Department of Psychiatry, Medical Center of Central Massachusetts, Worcester, MA

[4] Chief, Maternal-Fetal Medicine, Department of Reproductive Medicine, Medical Center of Central Massachusetts, Worcester, MA

[5] Department of Psychiatry & Alcohol Research Center, University of Michigan, Ann Arbor, MI

214

INTRODUCTION

This chapter addresses some of the issues implicit in understanding certain special subgroups of women (and girls). We focus on several ethnic groups (i.e., African-American, Hispanic, and Native American), two age groups (adolescents and elderly), plus pregnant women and female athletes.

When studying substance use and abuse among different ethnic groups in the United States, it is important to consider not only current patterns of use but how these patterns have changed historically. Familiarity with the social, political, and cultural context in which substance use and abuse occurs can enhance our understanding of attitudes and behavior. Many ethnic groups actually represent a variety of cultural subgroups lumped together for the convenience of the researcher. For instance, Hispanic groups may be subdivided by the country of origin, as well as by religious groups, socioeconomic factors, urban versus rural, and extent of Native American, African, and European background. Such aggregations may blur our understanding of cultural patterns. There also are problems in defining cultural groups for research purposes (see Hahn, 1992).

Cultures prescribe both drug use patterns and control rituals to protect the society and the individuals from disruptive effects (Andrew Weil, personal communication, 1980). When cultures mix, drug use patterns and protective rituals may become dissociated (Wolin, Bennett, Noonan, & Teitelbaum, 1980).

Biological Factors

The contribution of genetic factors may be substantial in alcoholism, and perhaps in other drug abuse as well (alcoholism: see Dinwiddie, 1992; Hill, Steinhauer, Smith & Locke, 1991; Johnson, 1985; smoking: see Swan, Carmelli, Rosenman, Fabsitz, & Christian, 1990; other drug abuse: see Cadoret, Troughton, O'Gorman & Haywood, 1986). Hereditary pharmacogenetic factors can alter the metabolism of drugs and may affect drug action, and there may be gender-specific genetic factors (e.g., Frezza et al., 1990) as well as specific genetic factors that occur more often in one particular group than another. The research on genetics is beyond the scope of this chapter. Suffice it to say that genetic polymorphisms in the world populations are not evenly distributed and follow migratory patterns, much like religion and other cultural characteristics. Until we have a better understanding of genetic factors that influence vulnerability to substance abuse, we will not be able to differentiate genetic influences on addictive behaviors from environmental ones.

Acculturation

Immigrant groups have been known to bring their cultural mores, including drinking and drug-use practices, with them from their country of origin. As subsequent generations acculturate, the substance use patterns tend to become more similar to that of the host culture (Markides, Krause, & Mendes de Leon, 1988; Parrish et al., 1992). When cultural groups are discriminated against, wherein their cultural acceptance may seem greatest within drug cultures, they may increase substance use to gain acceptance. Unfortunately, most studies do not differentiate the degree of acculturation of cultural subgroups, or degree of discrimination obscuring our understanding of the contribution of these factors.

Social Class

Socioeconomic factors have been implicated as an important determinant of substance abuse. Some believe that lower socioeconomic status is associated with substance abuse, but research shows that there is more alcohol abuse among those who can better afford it (Cahalan, Cisin, & Crossley, 1969). Wilsnack (1992) has shown that increased drinking can be associated with role dissatisfaction. For men, the only significant predictor of excessive drinking was job-related role dissatisfaction, whereas for women, all sorts of role dissatisfactions (e.g., marital, parental, socioeconomic, job) were predictive. Since women, particularly minority women, may be forced to settle for unsatisfactory roles in life, they may be particularly at risk of developing excessive drinking (or drug use). In particular, those women who have been victimized sexually during childhood, usually by an alcoholic adult or older sibling, are at risk of developing substance abusing lifestyles. As many as two-thirds of women in substance abuse treatment programs report sexual abuse histories. Women may be at greater risk if raised in deprived environments by parents who have not been able to succeed in their goals, and who rely on substance use to cope with such dissatisfaction.

Limitations of the Literature

We were limited by the available literature on women, which is still quite sparse. While many recent studies include women as subjects, it is difficult to locate studies that report interesting findings in women (Toneatto, Sobell, & Sobell, 1992). To date, our understanding of the interrelationships between substance abuse and gender, race, age, and ethnicity, as well as biological, psychological, and socioeconomic variables, is incomplete.

AFRICAN-AMERICAN WOMEN

Historical Perspectives

The patterns of substance use and the health and social consequences of substance abuse have changed significantly among African-American women (hereafter called blacks) during the 19th and 20th centuries. Herd's (1989) analysis of epidemiologic trends in liver cirrhosis mortality in blacks with a focus on the impact of migration and cultural transformation shows that during the 19th century, and up until 1950, blacks had low rates of liver cirrhosis mortality. This is attributed to their strong support of abstinence (reinforced by the Southern Baptist tradition) and the American temperance movement, which had appeal to blacks due to its support of antislavery reform.

In the 19th century, while the nation was preoccupied with protecting women and keeping them at home, black women were unprotected by the law and relegated to field and domestic work. Although some black women retired from field work after emancipation, the number of black women in the work force was, and continues to be, proportionately higher than the number of white women (White, 1985). Although black and white women have shared some similarities in work, childrearing, and family roles, disparate cultural and historical experiences have contributed to the widely different sociodemographic profiles of black and white women.

During the early 20th century, the politics of the prohibition movement shifted to align with white supremacy. Massive migration of blacks from the rural "dry" south to the "wet" north occurred simultaneously with alienation of blacks from the antialcohol movement (Herd, 1989). The nightclub culture, increased alcohol use at social gatherings, and the economic benefits of "bootlegging" were associated with increased alcoholization and urbanization of black communities (Herd, 1989). In the 1920s, the rate of hospital admissions for blacks with alcoholic psychosis (presumably withdrawal delirium) began to increase. By 1950, the cirrhosis mortality rate for black men and women began to rise, doubling between 1950 and 1973 (Herd, 1989). Average age-adjusted death rates for chronic liver disease and cirrhosis from 1979-1981 data (expressed as cases/100,000) were 6.9 for white females, 13.5 for black females, 15.4 for white males, and 29.4 for black males (Ronan, 1986-1987).

Few studies have focused exclusively on substance use/abuse in black women. Many of the studies providing such information have used small sample sizes and have tended to focus on populations in high-density, low socioeconomic areas. The applicability of these studies to black women in other settings may be limited (Herd, 1989).

Alcohol

Some previous surveys have shown that black women are more likely to abstain from alcohol (Knupfer & Lurie, 1961; Russell, 1989), but if they do drink they are more likely to drink heavily and to have alcohol-related problems (Caetano, 1984; Johnson, Armor, Polich, & Stambul, 1977; Wecshler, Demone, & Gottlieb, 1980), resulting in overall prevalence rates of heavy drinking, and indicators of problem drinking being comparable for black and white women. Rates of abstinence among black and white women increase with age; however, there are some racial differences. In a study of alcohol use in gynecologic patients, black women were more likely to abstain than whites at every age except 35–39 (Russell, 1989). A 1984 national survey of drinking patterns of women found approximately one-third of black women (versus 22% of whites) under 30 abstained, and 56–69% of black women over 40 abstained (USDHHS, 1991). This concurs with the low rates of alcohol use and heavy drinking reported for black female youth (Harford & Lowman, 1989). For age 18–39, approximately 20% of white women, compared to 10% of black women, are likely to be heavy drinkers as measured by the combined categories of frequent high maximum and frequent heavy drinking (USDHHS, 1991).

The patterns of onset of heavy drinking appear to differ for black and white women. The proportion of heavy drinkers among black women peaks at a later age (45–59) compared to white women (25–44) (Lillie-Blanton, Mackenzie, & Anthony, 1991; Russell, 1989; USDHHS, 1991). One possible reason for the high prevalence of alcohol-related problems among blacks could be a later onset of prolonged, sustained high consumption (Herd, 1989). Among whites there may be more experimentation in the younger years, some of which matures out, whereas for blacks, the pattern may be more hidden and less subject to social sanctions.

Rates of heavier drinking among women in the 1981 National Survey did not vary significantly with marital status and employment (Wilsnack, Wilsnack, & Klassen, 1984). However, Russell (1989) found that black and white women who were married and worked part time, and those who were never married or widows drank more heavily than women in the national survey. The highest rates of heavier drinking were seen in black and white women who were unemployed and looking for work (Russell, 1989). Household income of less than $6,000 a year is shown to correlate with heavy drinking (Lillie-Blanton et al., 1991). This is consistent with the observation that women who drink heavily are likely to be dissatisfied with their current situation (Wilsnack, 1992). Heavier drinking is less common among black women who work full time than among their white counterparts. White housewives have lower rates of heavier drinking than black housewives. Divorced or separated black women drink less heavily than comparable whites in the national sample (Russell, 1989). This suggests that black women may be more likely to drink at home, in contrast to white women who may be more likely to drink with work associates.

In an analysis of the black female respondents of the 1977–1980 San Francisco study, age, marital status (being married or living together), and religious fundamentalism were negatively associated with drinking. There was a positive association between employment and drinking. The study asserted that internalized norms such as religious beliefs and attitudes toward women's roles and conduct may be more important influences on black drinking patterns than socioeconomic factors (Caetano & Herd, 1984). Marital status and race interact significantly in their relationship to highest usual number of drinks per occasion and abstinence: black married women were most likely and white married women were least likely to abstain (Russell, 1989).

The relationship between the likelihood of heavy drinking and education differs for black and white women. For black women, education appears inversely related to heavy drinking. Black women with 12 or more years of education are less likely than their white counterparts to be heavy drinkers. This observation may be important in developing culturally competent preventive interventions for black youth (Lillie-Blanton et al., 1991).

The relationship between a positive family history of problem drinking (FHP) and alcohol abuse/dependence in offspring appears to vary by race, gender, and age. Russell, Cooper, and Frone (1990) reported twice the rates of alcohol abuse/dependence in FHP white women and black men compared to black women and white men. The risk was a direct function of age for whites and was an inverse function of age for blacks.

A regression analysis of Baltimore ECA data for black and white women showed that after other sociodemographic variables were taken into account, race was not associated with a history of alcohol use disorder or a current alcohol use disorder. Current rates of alcohol dependence or abuse for black and white women were strongly associated with age (18–59 years) or being separated, divorced or widowed (Lillie-Blanton et al., 1991). Black female respondents to the 1984 survey who were classified as current drinkers (women who drank at least one alcoholic beverage over the past year) reported fewer alcohol-related problems. Fewer black women report driving while drunk, belligerence, and financial problems (Herd, 1989). Black and Hispanic women were more likely to report spouse or family member problems due to drinking than white women (Caetano, 1984).

Smoking

Survey data from the civilian population show that rates of current smoking between 1965–1987 dropped from 33% to 28% in black women and from 35% to 27% in white women (National Center for Health Statistics, 1989). In a survey of black adults in Oakland and San Francisco between 1985–1986, adults reporting high levels of stress were more likely to smoke, and black women with poor social networks were more likely to smoke than those with optimal networks (Romano, Broom, & Syme, 1991).

Other Drug Abuse

NIDA household survey data show overall use rates to be comparable for blacks, whites, and Hispanics. Blacks and Hispanics are more likely to be current users of cocaine and crack, and whites are more likely to be current users of inhalants. Blacks are significantly more likely to have used crack and heroin than whites. Heroin use is a more serious problem among blacks and Hispanics, compared to whites. Household surveys exclude the homeless and incarcerated populations that are disproportionately black and have high rates of drug abuse. Blacks seem to be more likely than whites to administer drugs by injection or freebasing and to use several drugs in combination (USDHHS, 1991). Epidemiologic evidence shows that IV drug use (IVDU) is a prominent factor in the prevalence of HIV infection in black women and children. Black female IVDUs report more sex partners, more frequent involvement in exchange of sex for money or drugs, and a greater percentage of their partners being non-IVDUs compared to white female IVDUs (Brown, 1990).

Treatment

Cultural factors are important to integrate into treatment planning for black women. Cultural values common to black American families include flexibility in family roles, strong kinship bonds, commitment to religious values and church participation, humanistic orientation, strong education and work-achievement orientation, and endurance of suffering (Ho, 1987). Blacks tend to rely on extended family networks (including adopted relatives such as godparents) and church organizations in times of crisis and may distrust institutional medicine and view mental health therapy to be for the strange or crazy (McAdoo, 1977). They are unlikely to easily form a trusting relationship with a therapist of another race (Womble, 1990). In one study of help-seeking behavior, only 9% of black respondents with self-reported serious personal problems sought help within the mental health sector. Of the 49% who used professional help, ministers and traditional healthcare providers were used most often (Neighbors, 1985). There are ongoing concerns about barriers to substance abuse treatment which included financial, institutional, provider, and patient factors. Outreach efforts do increase the likelihood of bringing black women into treatment.

For those who present for mental health (as opposed to primary care) treatment, NIMH data provide some information about minority experiences with mental health services. In 1986 NIMH data on inpatient admissions, minority women were represented at a rate of nearly 1.5 times greater than white women. Minority women had a shorter length of stay in all types of facilities other than state and multistate facilities. Between 1982–1986 minorities had much higher utilization rates for mental disorders and alcoholism, but shorter lengths of stay. Outpatient utilization rates show lower rates of admissions for minority women compared to white women. These outcomes may reflect differences in socioeconomic status and thus insurance coverage.

In a 1987 survey of public and private substance abuse treatment programs, blacks comprised 18.3% of all clients, and 14.6% of all alcohol clients. Blacks are overrepresented among clients in social and medical detoxification programs. Minority overrepresentation in treatment facilities does not mean that treatment needs are being adequately met. Available data reflect primarily public treatment programs, not private programs in which minorities are likely to be underrepresented. Between 1982-1984, there was an increase in specialized programs for blacks offered by alcoholism treatment centers. However, between 1979-1982 there was a 9% decline in publicly funded treatment units (USDHHS, 1991). Black women appear to enter alcohol treatment at a younger age (mean = 38) than white women (mean = 44) (Gorowitz, Bahn, Warthen, & Cooper, 1970).

After entry into treatment, the counselor must help women confront survival needs including employment, health, safety, clothing, housing, legal and school-related issues. Assessment of the partner's drinking behavior, and involvement of nuclear and extended family networks are important in treating the black female alcoholic. Black women are reported to drink to make friends, therefore understanding the role of her social group in the promotion of the drinking behavior is important (Brown & Tooley, 1989). Effective treatment strategies for blacks tend to be directive, cognitive, and action-oriented (Harper, 1984).

In a study of crack cocaine users, more women (30%) than men (19%) reported that they knew no one who could assist them in stopping their drug use. It is unclear whether this sense of isolation is related to personal or environmental factors (Boyd & Mieczkowski, 1990). Women of lower socioeconomic status often have minimal educational and/or vocational skills, little or no work history, and underdeveloped life-management skills. When long-term residential treatment is indicated, family responsibilities can be a barrier to treatment or the reason for early departure. Residing in environments that are drug saturated coupled with underdeveloped life-management coping skills places them at higher risk of relapse. Identification of social support networks and development of comprehensive strategies to address poor coping skills, dependency, low self-esteem, and family and intimate relationship issues are important for successful treatment. Relapse prevention planning can assist women in developing strategies for coping with potential relapse stressors (Weiner, Wallen, & Zankowski, 1990).

HISPANIC WOMEN AND SUBSTANCE ABUSE

People of Hispanic heritage constitute the fastest growing minority group in the United States, representing approximately 9% of the U.S. population. The term "Hispanic" covers a widely heterogeneous group of people who claim ethnicity based on Latin American birth or ancestry. Genetic and cultural roots of this group come from Asian (through Native Americans), African, and European populations. The three most studied groups of Hispanics in the United States are Mexican-Americans, Puerto Ricans, and Cuban-Americans. Substance use patterns of foreign-born Hispanics resembles that of homeland compatriots, while U.S.-born Hispanics more resemble that of the dominant culture (Cervantes, Gilbert, de Snyder, & Padilla, 1991). Because patterns of substance use differ along ethnic and regional lines, it is inappropriate to generalize study findings from one subgroup of Hispanics to another.

Choice of language and literacy is considered a paramount indicator of acculturation, and more comprehensive scales also measure exposure to American culture via the acquisition of values, beliefs, behaviors, and material possessions associated with the American mainstream. Breakdown of traditional culture and loss of social supports for cultural identity affect people at all socioeconomic levels, and increase the risk of developing dangerous substance use behaviors. Substance abusers form alternative subcultures that often accept the immigrant more readily than other sectors of the dominant culture, providing social support for substance abuse rather than cultural identity.

In the case of Hispanic drinking, acculturation may result in a shift from either complete abstinence or nonproblematic, socially controlled drinking in ritual and celebration, typical of many rural Latin American societies, to alcohol abuse and dependence in the U.S. setting. Caetano's (1986-1987) finding that first-generation American-born women are least likely to be abstainers, and that succeeding generations are most likely to be high-volume, high-frequency drinkers, has important implications for the design of prevention programs for Hispanic youth.

Hispanic children, like children from other non-Anglo immigrant and minority groups, are influenced, through interaction with American institutional systems and the media, to believe that they and their culture are inferior. They come to devalue their own culture, while the mainstream offers little of positive value in replacement (Goldman, 1992). Substance abuse prevention programs aimed at Hispanic youth must not only facilitate integration into American society by helping youth to develop the tools and resources to do so, but must reinforce their pride in their Hispanic heritage.

Alcohol

Specific Hispanic female drinking patterns differ throughout the U.S., reflecting regional differences among the general population. In addition to gender differences, behaviors are mediated by sociodemographic factors such as age, education, income, marital status, and birthplace (Caetano, 1986-1987; 1990; Caetano & Mora, 1988).

Hispanic women who drink more, and more frequently, are not those in the lowest socioeconomic groups. Most Hispanic women who drink in quantity with high frequency are American-born, middle-aged, and have achieved a relatively high acculturation and socioeconomic status (i.e., better educated, less impoverished than abstainers; Caetano, 1990; Holck, Warren, Smith, & Rochat, 1984; Stroup-Behnam, Treviño, & Treviño, 1990). A distinction has been made between women in single- and dual-headed households. Traditional family values persist in American Hispanic communities, while at the same time the reality of life in the modern world reflects the impact of factors that lead to erosion of family stability. Most single heads of households in the Caetano survey are divorced or separated, with only 14.3% having never been married. Prevalence of heavy drinkers among female single heads of households who drink (46%) is almost double that of heavy drinkers among drinkers from dual-headed households (24%), although the former group is smaller. Single heads of households and women in upper socioeconomic categories would be least constrained by traditional culture and thus freer to drink liberally. Additionally, studies in Latin America have shown that those who abandon their cultural roots—by choice or by circumstance—often suffer from the stress of lost social supports and the inability to gain a clear and positively accepted social identification within the American mainstream (Lewis, 1959; Lomnitz, 1977; Safa, 1974).

Data from a national survey show that acculturation can be positively correlated with more frequent and heavier drinking (Caetano, 1989, 1990; Caetano & Mora, 1988). Mexican-American women, for example, were compared to a sample of women in a Mexican city and while rates of drinking were low in both groups, fewer Mexican-Americans than Mexicans reported abstention (46% vs. 66%), while more reported drinking at least once a week, and consuming at least five drinks at a sitting at least once a year (12% vs. < 0.5%). Abstainers make up the largest category in both groups, and the next most common pattern of drinking is less than monthly, endorsed by 24% of the Mexican-American respondents.

Drinking patterns of women in the "low acculturation" group resemble most closely those of women living in Mexico. The behavior of Mexican-born women living in the United States appears to be less affected by acculturation than is the behavior of U.S.-born women. Women for whom either parent is an abstainer are more likely to be abstainers themselves, but a father's ambivalent attitude toward a daughter's drinking correlates with a greater likelihood she will drink.

Tobacco

The prevalence of cigarette smoking is lower for Hispanics than for blacks or whites, with 51.8% of Hispanic women having ever smoked cigarettes (NCADI Update, 1989). Cohort analysis of HHANES data, however, shows that smoking rates for Puerto Rican and Cuban-American women have increased considerably in comparison to rate increases in the general U.S. female population (Escobedo & Remington, 1989).

Other Drugs

In an ethnographic study of 100 Cuban-American women in Florida, Gonzalez and Page (1981) found that almost 75% of the subjects had at some time used minor tranquilizers to aid sleep, and 20% had used them nightly. Anxiety over the immigration process, combined with the stress produced from efforts to balance the traditional Cuban women's role at the center of family life with the demands of working women in American society, were cited as reasons for taking prescription drugs. Women in this community are commonly introduced to tranquilizers informally by friends or relatives, and their use for calming nerves follows the pattern of traditional herbal remedy use.

In regard to drugs other than alcohol, one should avoid generalizing findings to Hispanics as a whole; however, women are less likely than men to use these drugs. Extreme poverty has been associated with elevated risk for drug abuse, and for Hispanics, this may be a major factor in consumption of drugs other than alcohol. Among three subgroups of Hispanics, Puerto Rican women have the highest rate of having ever tried marijuana (35.8%), followed by Mexican-American women (27.9%), and Cuban-American women (13.1%). Of those women who have ever used marijuana, more than half of the respondents had not done so in the past year. Rates of ever having used cocaine, inhalants, and sedatives are much lower than for marijuana (NCADI Update, 1989). Amaro, Whittaker, Coffman, and Heeren (1990) found that there is some relationship between women's predominant use of the English language and higher rates of marijuana and cocaine use, but the patterns differ among the Mexican-American, Cuban-American, and Puerto Rican respondents.

Among minority populations in the United States, HIV is an increasing problem, particularly for women and children. The higher rates found for Hispanics and blacks than those found for whites is attributed to sociostructural differences. Of women who have developed HIV infection, Hispanics comprise 13% of those who were put at risk through sex with a bisexual male, 27% of those whose risk was having sex with a male IVDU, and 16% of those whose risk was using IV drugs themselves (see Friedman, Sufian, & Des Jarlais, 1990). In many Latin American countries, there is a common practice of injecting family members at home with antibiotics, vitamins, and vaccines via a reused family needle and syringe which may cause some Hispanics in the United States to be accustomed to the reuse of syringes.

NATIVE AMERICAN WOMEN AND SUBSTANCE ABUSE

Specific patterns of substance use have changed historically under pressures of culture contact, migration, and other forces of modernization. The case of Native Americans is distinct from other ethnic minority groups in the United States and Canada, however, because alcohol is a substance largely nonindigenous to Native North American cultures.

Throughout the literature, alcohol abuse and its consequences are cited as the foremost health problems facing Native Americans. While Native Americans constitute less than 1% of the U.S. population, they represent more than 280 cultural groups. Exact substance use patterns and statistics vary widely from group to group, between urban areas, federal reservations, and isolated northern villages, and between men and women. Some studies have shown that alcohol-related mortality is higher on the Indian reservations than for the Native American population as a whole. This is at least partially due to other factors of reservation life—poverty, malnutrition, poor sanitation, exposure to pollutants, and poor healthcare—that put residents at greater health risk. It is important to emphasize that alcohol abuse is but one of a myriad of problems experienced by Native Americans today, and should be seen as a symptomatic of many of these other problems. The literature presents conflicting perspectives on the complex issues associated with Native American substance use based on data from small studies of individual groups that cannot adequately represent the experience of heterogeneous Native American cultures. We are thus cautioned against perpetuating popularly held, reductionistic stereotypes that lump all Native American groups together within a common stigmatized or fictionalized category with regard to alcohol use, family life, customs, and other sociocultural characteristics (Deloria, 1969).

Alcohol

Alcohol-associated mortality rates due to alcoholism, alcohol-related motor vehicle accidents, suicide, homicide, and cirrhosis of the liver are found to be higher among Native Americans than among the general U.S. population. In 1980, alcoholism (including psychosis and alcohol-related cirrhosis) accounted for a mortality rate 5.5 times greater among U.S. Indians than the rate in the general population, and deaths from accidents occurred at a rate 2.5 times greater among Indians than for the general population. Native American women generally consume less alcohol than do the men in their communities; however, women's deaths account for almost half of the deaths due to cirrhosis. The widely reported accounts of strong connections between Native American drinking and suicide, homicide, and crime (mostly public drunkenness) can be seen as largely anecdotal and otherwise inconclusive when the data is closely scrutinized for sample size, generalizability, longitudinal patterns, data collection techniques, reporting style, and other confounding factors (Heath, 1989; Leland, 1978, 1980; May, 1986).

A significant point often overlooked in discussions of alcohol use is that studies have shown that not all Native Americans are drinkers. There are both abstainers and heavy drinkers (among individuals and entire groups), with fewer numbers of those who drink in moderation (Heath, 1989). Lemert (1982) and Whittaker (1963) found that about half of the abstainers in their studies had been heavy drinkers in their younger years, a pattern that is more common for women than for men. This "maturing" out of drinking among women most often occurs in connection with the onset of family responsibilities (Leland, 1978; Whittaker, 1963), although in Leland's sample only the mild and moderate drinkers eventually switched to abstention. Stereotypes of Native American women whose drinking results in fetal alcohol damage are overstated, considering the other risk factors affecting fetal outcome (e.g., nutrition, access to health care, tobacco). Drinking patterns vary widely, and the popular perception that alcohol abuse affects all or most Native Americans arises largely from a superficial analysis of reports on the severity of alcohol's effect on this population (Heath, 1989). Following is a brief review of some statistical patterns of substance use among Native Americans (see Heath, 1989). While it is now recognized that there are differences in substance use patterns between males and females, little data is available pertaining specifically to Native American women.

Native American reservations have a young population, with the median age below 20 years old. Studies conducted among American Indian school children and youth report that beer drinking is common. While exact prevalence varies from tribe to tribe, surveys report that from 56–89% of Indian youth have experimented with alcohol. Boredom is a frequent explanation youth give for drinking, and those who claim to use alcohol for this reason drink more frequently than do others. However, peer pressure, excitement, and the desire to enhance good feelings and dull bad feelings are other common responses. Social, economic, and political marginalization also contribute to substance abuse. The factors involved include low self-esteem, family instability (25% of youth are raised outside the family of origin), and high parental and community tolerance of substance abuse (Binion, Miller, Beauvais, & Oetting, 1988; Forslund, 1979, Swanson, Bratrude, & Brown, 1971; Weibel-Orlando, 1984; Whittaker, 1963).

In a comparative study of several urban and rural American Indian groups, Weibel-Orlando (1986-1987; 1989) found that women tend to drink less than men, and that women in urban settings drink less than women in rural settings. Weibel-Orlando's one sampled group in which women claimed to drink more than men were rural-dwelling Sioux. Although this sample is small, it is instructive in that women as well as men in this group use prolonged drinking parties as a major form of recreation, especially during seasons when there is 75% unemployment among the Sioux. This situation provides both time and motivation to drink, a condition typical of idle, economically depressed communities, and not limited to Native Americans. In contrast, while binge drinking does occur in cities, Weibel-Orlando found that the common pattern of drinking in urban environments is frequent, moderate-to-heavy drinking.

Whittaker (1962), in a study of the Standing Rock Sioux reservation, found that at least 55% of the women drink, with the greatest percentage of drinkers found among women 30–39 years old. Among 15–17-year-old females, 40% reported drinking, even though 94% stated that their parents forbade them to drink at home. Thirty-six percent of the women reported drinking less than 3 times weekly, and 19% reported drinking at least three times per week. Drinking appears to have increased in younger generations of women, as a smaller percentage of the female respondents' mothers were drinkers.

Leland (1978) argues that since so few studies of alcohol use have focused specifically on women, there has been a tendency in the literature and among policy makers to adopt the popular notion that Indians "can't hold their liquor," a stereotype that Leland claims for women "is even less justified than for the men" (p. 86). Leland found that most of the women living in a Nevada Indian settlement rarely (39%) or never (36%) drink. Using ethnoscience research methods to elicit the Indians' own categories of alcohol use and related behaviors, Leland concluded that 90% of those women in the settlement who do drink follow drinking patterns categorized as "able to handle" liquor. This broad category encompasses drinking behaviors ranging from rare, occasional drinking (39% of women) to heavy weekend (12%) and party (6%) drinking. Women classified as "winos" make up 7% of women in the settlement, have the oldest average age (54 years old), and were judged more harshly by female study respondents than were the other types of heavy drinkers.

An additional issue for women is their need to cope with the effects of drinking by members of their families, often men. Leland (1978) found that the majority of women whose husbands drink have no way to effectively deal with the situation, and respond by passively making the necessary lifestyle adjustments. Similarly, 54% of the respondents in Whittaker's (1963) study felt that a woman would be wrong to leave her husband under any circumstances, including repeated alcohol-related abusive behavior.

The effect of heavy drinking on the family may vary by location. In settings where tribal culture has survived, child-rearing responsibilities are shared among many individuals in the extended family and significant others (Ho, 1987). If there are alcohol-impaired parents, the extended network tends to protect the children as long as there are unimpaired individuals present. This protective pattern breaks down in urban settings where nuclear families are the typical format.

Community responses to community-wide alcohol problems. Historically derived social and political circumstances are largely responsible for the problems of low self-esteem, cultural confusion, and marginalization that contribute to increased rates of substance abuse in Native American populations. Among Native Americans themselves, this recognition is not new, and historically has given rise to various forms of religious and cultural revitalization movements (e.g., the religion of Handsome Lake that arose among the New York State Iroquois at the end of the 18th century; Wallace, 1966, 1969). The emergence of these movements has been in response to the abuse and erosion of Indian culture, dignity, and lifeways that have occurred for almost four centuries. The movements are efforts to restore a positive sense of identity, often incorporating spiritual concepts that predate European contact. An important goal of these revitalization movements is to provide structure and encouragement for people to stop abusing alcohol and other substances (Beauvais & LeBoueff, 1985; Hall, 1985; Wallace, 1969).

Native American groups today continue to suffer the stresses of past and recent loss of lands, forced relocations, and community disruption due to economic development and political decision making (e.g., Scudder, 1982; Shkilnyk, 1985). In the 1950s, the U.S. Bureau of Indian Affairs began a long-term program to move American Indians from the rural areas into industrial cities, where half of all U.S. Indians now live (Weibel-Orlando, 1986-1987). Not all rural-to-urban migration was experienced negatively. However, often the pressures of social change that involve conflicting traditional and modern values and beliefs are combined with tensions caused by a miserable reality of poverty, discrimination, and material and ideological culture loss. This creates conditions where Native Americans lose their own cultural base without the possibility of a modern substitution, because they face tremendous social, political, and economic barriers to incorporation into the cultural mainstream. The response for many is similar now as during Handsome Lake's time: self-medication with alcohol, a substance that was initially introduced to Native Americans by white whalers, soldiers, traders, and settlers. Indeed, it has been shown that Native American alcohol use patterns have developed in tandem with regulations reflecting a wide range of legal, political, and commercial interests that have been imposed historically to facilitate or impede access to alcohol (Kelso & DuBay, 1989).

Other Drugs

The use rate of inhalants (17–22%) and marijuana (41–62%) is greater for Native American youth than for other ethnic minority youth and whites (May, 1986). Little other data are available.

Treatment

Substance abuse treatment methods that focus on the individual substance abuser have been shown to be largely unsuccessful in treating Native American men (Grobsmith & Dam, 1990). Effective treatment must be culturally competent, tailored to the specific values of the woman and her extended family. However, a community-based perspective to the problem of substance abuse is appropriate because alcoholism and other substance abuse are viewed by Native Americans as family- and community-based problems. In most Native American groups, individual autonomy is highly respected, but it is embedded in a strong sense of community-wide interdependence, hence, therapeutic counseling techniques that emphasize individual responsibility are likely to be rejected. Family therapy, though difficult for non-Indian therapists, may be more effective (Ho, 1987). For Native Americans, increased pride in their own heritage and communities is necessary to the development of individual self-esteem, a deterrent of substance abuse. In addition, studies have shown that the existing structure of resources allotted to address substance abuse prevention and treatment for Native Americans is sorely inadequate in terms of funding, training, staffing, follow-up, and overall theoretical perspective and procedures (Grobsmith & Dam, 1990; Hill, 1989; May, 1986; Parker, 1990, 1991). Substance abuse treatment and prevention programs that are generated internally by the community itself, and coordinate with the currently vital movements for Indian self-determination, have the most likelihood of providing the services that Native American communities want and need (Beauvais & LaBoueff, 1985).

FEMALE ADOLESCENT SUBSTANCE ABUSERS

The developmental tasks which adolescents face put them at particular risk of experimentation with psychoactive substances and for developing drug or alcohol dependence, especially those with the least capacity to adjust to the rapid psychological changes and stresses they experience (Tubman, Vicary, von Eye, & Lerner, 1991). Adjusting to a rapidly changing body image during puberty is especially difficult for adolescent girls in a society which values extreme thinness, but markets high-fat fast food targeted toward a teen market. They may rely on smoking, diet pills, or cocaine to avoid weight gain. Advertising associates alcohol and tobacco with sex appeal and glamour. While anabolic steroid use is less common in females than males, 1.4–2.5% of female high school athletes report having used them (Terney & McLain, 1990; Windsor, 1989). The process of separation from parents and the increasing importance placed on peer values results in susceptibility to experimentation with drugs and alcohol, the use of which is identified as "adult" privilege, a badge of maturity.

Teens adapt to the norms of group behavior, hence many smoke or drink only when with friends. Those who join formal groups (e.g., clubs, 4-H, church youth groups) tend to use substances less than those who gather with other youths in informal groups (e.g., gangs, video arcades) (Selnow & Crano, 1986). They deny being (physically) dependent, because they do not use daily and disregard their social dependence (i.e., feeling one has to conform to one's friends' behavior). Young teenagers may not foresee consequences and may believe themselves immune to consequences of risky behavior.

The mere experimentation with substances does not in itself constitute substance abuse. It is continuing involvement with substances that begins to harmfully interfere with life roles that is defined as substance abuse. Adolescents with more risk factors (e.g., family problems, low-self esteem, low law abidance, low religiosity, peer drug use, adult drug use, etc.) are more vulnerable to becoming substance abusers (Maddahian, Bentler, & Newcomb, 1988). More than four risk factors for substance abuse were reported by 6% of African-American, 8% of Asian, 12% of Hispanic, and 18% of white youth.

Epidemiological studies of teens, such as the annual National Survey of High School Seniors (Johnston & O'Malley, 1985) and the National Household Survey of Drug Abuse (NIDA, 1985, 1987, 1989, 1990) underestimate substance use, as the former excludes drop-outs and chronic truants, the latter excludes homeless youth, and both exclude incarcerated or institutionalized youth. For example, lifetime use of any intravenous drugs in the Household Survey was 0.4% for 12–17-year-olds, compared to 34.5% in a homeless population ranging from 12 years of age to young adults (Office of Technology Assessment, 1991). The substance use prevalence figures are understandably higher among seniors than among (ages 12–17) teens in the household survey.

Alcohol

Alcohol consumption remains the most widely experienced drug among high school senior girls, with a lifetime prevalence of 89.5%. Use in the past 30 days declined from 72% in 1980 to 57.1% in 1990 among seniors, and was 25.2% among 12–17-year-olds, and 65.3% for 18–25-year-olds (NIDA, 1989; 1991). Moderate-to-heavy drinkers among New York City schoolgirls were 6% of <13-year-olds, 16% of 13-year-olds, 27% of 14-year-olds, 43% of 15-year-olds, 48% of 16-year-olds, 55% of 17-year-olds, and 57% of those over 17 (Barnes & Welte, 1986). Ethnicity affected the proportion (43% of whites, 33% of Native Americans, 23% of Hispanics, 19% of blacks, 15% of West Indians, and 10% of Asians) of girls who were moderate-to-heavy drinkers. The percentage of seniors who consumed five or more drinks in a row remained about the same at 32.2%. Binge drinking is a serious problem in this age group.

Other Drugs

The High School Survey (Johnston & O'Malley, 1985) has shown few gender differences in prevalence of use of marijuana, cocaine, and amphetamines (see Table 10.1).

Prevalence of high school senior experimentation with illicit drugs has steadily declined from the 1980s (when up to 66% reported ever having used an illicit drug) to the current rate of 47.9% (9.2% of 12–17-year-olds have used an illicit drug in the last 30 days). Since the well-publicized death of basketball hopeful Len Bias, cocaine use has

Table 10.1. Substance Use by High School Seniors

Substance Used	Total	Male	Female
Cigarettes			
Ever	69%	67%	70%
Past 30 days	30%	28%	31%
Daily, > 9	12%	12%	12%
Alcohol			
Ever	92%	93%	92%
Past 30 days	66%	70%	62%
Heavy[a]	15%	21%	9%
Marijuana			
Ever	54%	57%	51%
Past 30 days	26%	29%	22%
Often[b]	5%	7%	3%
Cocaine			
Ever	17%	20%	15%
Past 30 days	7%	8%	6%
Often[c]	3%		
Amphetamines			
Ever	26%	25%	28%
Past 30 days	7%	6%	7%
Often[c]	3%		

[a]Heavy alcohol use: > 4 drinks in a row, > twice in past 2 wks.
[b]Use of marijuana often: > 19 times in the last 30 days.
[c]Heavy use of cocaine and amphetamines: > twice in the past mo.
Source: From *Adolescents at Risk: Prevalence and Prevention*, by J. Dryfoos, 1990, and *Monitoring the Future*, by L. Johnston & P. O'Malley, 1985. Reprinted by permission.

dropped to 5.3% in 1990; use at least once in the 30 days prior to the study dropped to 1.9% (1.1% of 12–17-year-olds); and daily use fell from 0.3% to 0.1%. The use of crack in the last month fell from 1.4% (1989) to 0.7% (1990). Daily use of marijuana has fallen from a 10.7% peak (1978) to 2.2% (1990), but it still is the most widely used illicit drug (other than alcohol and tobacco) among high school seniors. Although tobacco is officially considered an illicit drug, 11.8% of 12–17-year-olds smoked in the last 30 days (NIDA, 1988; 1991).

Progression from experimentation to addiction. Kandel (1980) has described a progression from use of beer or wine to cigarettes and hard liquor to marijuana, which is associated with progression to hard drugs. Caffeinated beverages, beer, and cigarettes, readily obtained and perceived as innocuous, serve as "gateway drugs" which introduce the youngster to other substances, whether by establishing a pattern of coping by chemically altering one's psychologic state or by introducing oneself to a peer group among whom other substances are used and available. The earlier and the heavier the use of the gateway drugs, the more likely is progression to polysubstance abuse. NIDA's 1988 National Household survey revealed that the percentage of 12–17-year-olds who use alcohol, marijuana, or cocaine is more than twice as great among daily cigarette smokers than among those who never or occasionally used cigarettes (Henningfield, Clayton, & Fullin, 1990; NIDA, 1991).

Substance use and high-risk behavior. Substance abuse is strongly associated with other risk-taking behaviors, to the extent that one may wonder whether it causes or results from a risk-taking temperament. Dinwiddie (1992) describes the importance of risk taking as an element of the quite heritable (80%) type-2 (youth onset) form of alcoholism proposed by Cloninger (1987; Cloninger, Sigvardsson, & Bohman, 1988). This disorder is associated with antisocial personality, problems in school, delinquency, and drug abuse. Although presumed to be genetically determined, it is not clear how many of the associated characteristics are simply consequences of early-onset alcoholism as opposed to part of the cause. Attention deficit disorder and mild neuro-cognitive deficits have been associated with alcoholism risk and family history of alcoholism (Begleiter, Projesz, Bihari, & Kissin, 1984; De Obaldia, Parsons, & Yohman, 1983; Gabrielli & Mednick, 1983; Tarter, 1988). Current thinking suggests that marginality of cognitive function may predispose youth to failure in academic settings, leading to social deviance, low self-esteem, and substance abuse.

Keller (1991) found, in studying HIV-relevant sexual behavior in a heterosexual inner-city population, that even moderate alcohol or marijuana use predicted high-risk sexual behavior. They infer that such moderate use may be a marker for an underlying pattern of risk-taking behavior; however, moderate use also may impair judgment and reduce inhibitions. A strong association between any kind of substance use (including tobacco) and sexual activity has been found, irrespective of gender.

The National Youth Survey showed a strong relationship between illicit drug use and delinquency. Of the multiple illicit drug users, one-quarter became involved in felonies and more than one-half in minor offenses. Of the 5% categorized as serious offenders, 94% used alcohol, 85% used marijuana, and 55% used other illicit drugs.

Twenty-six percent of heavy drug users reported mental health problems, as compared to 2% of nonusers. Low grades also are associated with substance use. About 11% of the 11–17-year-olds would be categorized by Dryfoos as at high risk of trouble because of heavy drug use or serious delinquency, and another 40% were at moderate risk of trouble because of marijuana or alcohol use, minor offenses, or delinquency (Dryfoos, 1990).

A 1983 cross-sectional case-control study of primarily African-American inner-city 11–19-year-old girls, some of whom were pregnant, found the only difference in substance use was that pregnant teens smoked more regularly. In perception of personal risk of substance use, pregnant teens believed regular LSD use and occasional or regular amphetamine use would be more risky (Pletch, 1988). Zuckerman, Amaro, and Beardslee (1987) reported more tobacco, alcohol, and other drug use by pregnant adolescents compared with pregnant adults. Studies have shown an association of substance use to rape (including acquaintance and date rape), frequency of sexually transmitted diseases, failure to use contraception, school failure, and teen pregnancy. Polydrug users had very high rates of sexual activity: 67% (male) and 71% (female) for delinquents, compared to 50% and 43%, respectively, for nondelinquents. The risk of pregnancy in the year of first sexual activity was nearly double in drug abusers and delinquents compared to other teens. Illicit drug use was related to the prevalence of abortion.

Adolescent Prevention Programs

Knowledge and attitude change do not necessarily predict change in drug use behaviors. Tobler's metaanalysis of prevention programs identifies those which use direct social influence and life-skills training (problem solving, decision making, communication skills, dealing with social pressure, and drug use resistance skills: e.g., Brown, Stetson, & Beatty, 1989) as the most effective. Programs which replace negative with positive activities (e.g., jobs, recreation) and which teach competency to high-risk youth are the next most effective. Programs which address knowledge alone were only 10% as effective as other types of programs.

Schools have been the primary location for most primary prevention programs. Most prevention programs have not been effectively evaluated. Evaluation research has suggested that effective programs follow certain general principles. The issue of substance abuse must be approached in a broad social and environmental context, targeting risk factors such as poor school achievement rather than specific drug behaviors. Community-wide efforts should include all major influences in institutions: schools, parents, media, police, peers, and so on. Early intervention in grades 5 and 6, before the onset of substance use, is more effective than intervention once it is established. Comprehensive health education programs for grades K through 12 are best.

Peer leaders are more effective than adults or professional leaders. Programs should be targeted to high-risk youth, providing individual intensive counseling. School-based social skills curricula, school-based counseling, and multicomponent collaborative community programs are models which have demonstrated behavioral change outcomes (Dryfoos, 1990).

OLDER WOMEN AND SUBSTANCE ABUSE

The proportion of the population that is elderly, whether defined as >54, >59, or >64, gets larger with each decade. In the classes of drugs to be discussed, alcohol use and abuse decreases with age. The use of illicit substances is minimal among the elderly. With aging, however, prescribed psychoactive medications become more of an issue. As with younger persons, males are more likely than females to use and abuse alcohol and to smoke, but the gender ratios in psychoactive drug use appear more complicated.

Alcohol

Although there are relatively few older female alcoholics, compared with younger women and with older male alcoholics, there are occasional clues that suggest that the numbers may be greater than those found in community surveys. Considering their generational attitudes, it is not surprising that older female alcoholics seem to be more "in the closet" than any other age/sex group. Moreover, a recent report of male and female differences in liver cirrhosis mortality, 1961–85 (Hasin, Grant, & Harford, 1990), concludes that there is increasing divergence in mortality rates for men and women under 55 but a trend toward *convergence* in the older age groups.

The fact that estimated prevalence of elderly alcoholism is higher for nursing and retirement home residents, as well as general hospital and psychiatric patients suggests that a closer examination of these populations might turn up more female alcohol-related problems than have been noted in the past. Several early studies conducted in general hospitals showed male-to-female ratios from 2:1 to 3:1 (Gomberg, 1982). Many nursing home residents and other elders with a prior history of alcoholism get placed on chronic prescribed sedatives.

Information about elderly female alcoholics is sparse. There are case-history presentations (Dupree & Schonfeld, 1989; Rathbone-McCuan & Triegaardt, 1979), but little research is reported. A few early studies compared older and younger female alcoholics (e.g., Schuckit, Morrissey, & O'Leary, 1978) who reported that older women came into treatment with shorter histories of alcohol abuse than younger women, describing the older women as relatively "more stable." Rathbone-McCuan and Roberds (1980) compared 41 female alcoholics, average age 49.0, with 16 female alcoholics, average age 61.3 years. There were more married or widowed women and fewer separated or divorced women in the older group. The older women had less education and were less likely to be in the workplace. The older women reported their past histories as less unhappy, and they were more likely to associate the onset of alcoholism with current family problems. Alcohol-related medical symptoms differed, the older women having experienced more hallucinations and seizures related to their drinking.

An interview study comparing 23 unremitted older female alcoholics in treatment with 27 older women currently in remission (and with 22 unremitted and 46 remitted male alcoholics) found few differences. The unremitted women in treatment facilities were older, more frequently did their drinking alone at home, were less able to express anger when drinking, and less frequently reported "talking with someone" to cope (Gomberg, Nelson, & Hill, 1991). When male and female unremitted alcoholics in treatment were compared, the 23 women were older, more often reported positive family history, were less able to express anger when drinking, showed more depression, and were more likely to use prayer to cope than the males. Among the unremitted alcoholics in treatment, there were gender differences in age at onset and duration (27.7 for males; 43.7 for females). The men reported drinking heavily for a mean of 34 years, the women for a mean of 22 years. Onset within the last 10 years was reported by 8.8% of the men and 28.6% of the women in treatment. Among the remitted subjects, the duration of sobriety was significantly less for the women. It would be of value to know if older women generally show shorter alcoholic histories and more recent onset than older men. This would indicate that the age trajectory of high-risk years from age 40 on might, at least for this particular cohort, be quite different for older men and older women.

Tobacco

Men are more likely to be smokers, although the percentage gap between the sexes has been narrowing. In 1965, the National Center for Health Statistics reported 28.5% of men and 9.6% of women, 65 and older, to be current smokers. In 1985, these figures were 19.6% of older men and 13.5% of older women (Gomberg, 1990).

Other Drugs

The 1985 data of the Drug Abuse Warning Network (NIDA, 1986) indicated that less than 0.2% of emergency room appearances of men and women aged 60 and older were related to illicit drugs. The current cohort of older women are unlikely to be abusers of banned substances.

The elderly receive a disproportionately large number of prescriptions for psychoactive drugs and are more likely to be long-term users of such drugs (Mellinger, Balter, & Uhlenhuth, 1984). When they appear at facilities and physicians' offices with psychosocial problems, older persons receive less counseling than other age groups and they are more likely to be treated only with psychoactive drugs, such as minor tranquilizers and sedatives (Glantz & Backenheimer, 1988). Benzodiazepine prescribing often occurs without documentation of an alcohol/drug history (Graham, Parran & Jaen, 1992). Although this is true for both men and women, older women are disproportionately more frequently prescribed psychoactive drugs, perhaps because they are disproportionate visitors of primary care doctors.[1]

What is happening in the area of aging and prescribed psychoactive drug use is *change*: change in the prevalence of depression and other psychiatric symptoms, changes in utilization of health resources, changes in physicians' prescribing practices, changes in sex-role behaviors, and so on. For now, it is clear that prescribed psychoactive drug use among the elderly is *a drug abuse problem*: (a) on an individual level when the older patient uses medication in a questionable way, and (b) on a societal level when psychoactive drugs are too readily prescribed as a solution to depression and other psychosocial problems (e. g., martial discord, financial problems, grief) of older persons.

PREGNANCY AND SUBSTANCE ABUSE

Pregnant women are not immune to the lures of tobacco, alcohol, and drugs. Epidemiological studies have shown an incidence of substance abuse in pregnancy approaching 11% with a range of 0.4% to 27% depending on the mode of identification and the intensity of drug screening (Chasnoff, 1989). Fetal exposure to these potential teratogens occurs regardless of maternal race or socioeconomic status

---

[1] In a recent report, Robbins and Clayton (1989) found that men 65 and older were more likely than women in the same age group to report prescribed use of sedatives, tranquilizers, and stimulants during the past year. The Veterans Administration may be a source of medications for many such men.

(Chasnoff, Landress, & Barrett, 1989). Unfortunately, awareness of such a major threat to the health of future generations is very recent, and identification and treatment strategies for this population are just being developed. A brief review of placental transfer, specific drug effects on the developing fetus, and the medico-legal concerns involved with two biologically linked human beings (mother and fetus) reveals the complexity of services required for optimal care of the pregnant user.

Biological Factors

Oxygen, nutrition, and chemicals reach the fetus through placental blood flow. Maternal health, maternal genetic factors (Gilliam & Irtenkauf, 1990), properties of the chemical (such as molecular size, lipid solubility, ionization, and protein binding), as well as fetal factors (such as fetal circulation and organ maturity) may affect the extent of transfer across the placenta and the ultimate effect on the fetus. Timing of exposure during gestation to a potentially detrimental agent is critical in producing outcomes such as reduced fertility, spontaneous abortion, specific congenital malformations, inhibition of fetal growth, or subtle brain dysfunction.

Alcohol, nicotine, carbon monoxide, and most psychoactive drugs cross the placenta readily. Because of slow fetal excretion and catabolic rates, enterohepatic recirculation, and amniotic fluid pooling, prolonged exposure to a drug may occur even with infrequent maternal ingestion (Nahar, 1976). In addition, individual genetic variations in susceptibility, poor correlation of human effects with those reported in animal studies, variations in impurity, content and dosage of "street drugs," and the presence of confounding factors such as inadequate prenatal care, multiple drug exposures, or concomitant stress and infection confound outcome and counseling about specific risks.

Given these limitations, extensive review of the potential and known fetal and maternal effects of drugs of abuse is beyond the scope of this section, but can be found elsewhere (Chasnoff, 1991; Hutchings, 1989). However, a discussion of the most frequent issues facing obstetrical and substance abuse caregivers may be helpful.

Alcohol

In 1988, it was estimated that there were 106 million current alcohol users and 12 million alcoholics in the United States (NIDA, 1988). Over 90% of women have tried alcohol and 34 million women of childbearing age currently drink (Voss, 1989). Even if a woman stops drinking during pregnancy, she would begin to abstain once pregnancy was confirmed after a missed menstrual period (2–4 weeks after conception); many women wait longer to have a pregnancy test. Such early fetal exposure may be the reason alcohol use has been associated with a higher rate of spontaneous abortion and alcohol related birth defects (Hanson, Streissguth, & Smith, 1978; Jones & Smith, 1973). Exposure later in pregnancy may contribute to the observed higher rate of low birthweight infants and increased perinatal mortality (Hanson et al., 1978). Fetal alcohol exposure has been called "the most common preventable cause of mental retardation" (Taysi, 1988).

The alcoholic woman may have confounding factors, such as lack of or inconsistent prenatal care, malnutrition, liver disease, infection, intoxication, withdrawal, trauma, and other drug exposure. Because of individual variability in susceptibility and timing of exposure, no safe lower limit has been established. Abstinence throughout pregnancy is the recommendation, but cessation of drinking as pregnancy progresses has been associated with improved perinatal outcome and can be used to encourage and support women in treatment (Alcohol Use in Pregnancy, 1982; Rosett et al., 1983).

Tobacco

Tobacco smoking is associated with profound maternal and fetal risks. Maternal smokers have a higher rate of pulmonary disease as well as lower weight gain in pregnancy and increased rates of abortion, bleeding, fetal growth retardation, premature rupture of fetal membranes, and preterm delivery (Stillman, Rosenberg, & Sachs, 1986). Fortunately, smoking cessation by mid-pregnancy seems to reduce most of these risks (Butler, Goldstein, & Ross, 1972). Infants raised in a home where either parent smokes have a higher rate of pulmonary problems, hospitalizations, and infant death (Rantakallio, 1978).

Other Drugs

Some of the effects of drug use are related to the intravenous route and the illegality of the drugs rather than to drug pharmacology. Hepatitis, sexually transmitted diseases, endocarditis, and HIV infection are only a few of the problems intravenous drug users (IVDUs) encounter. Afraid of legal sanctions or preoccupied with a drug seeking/using lifestyle, most come for little or no prenatal care. Furthermore, many drug treatment programs have been reluctant to accept pregnant clients because of concerns of medico-legal culpability for birth defects blamed on the treatment rather than the drug use.

Cocaine. Cocaine in its various forms (including crack) is rapidly becoming the most devastating illegal substance used in pregnancy. Known general health risks to the mother such as myocardial ischemia, cardiac arrhythmias, pulmonary fibrosis, intestinal ischemia, and seizures would be indirectly detrimental to fetal health (Rosenak, Diamant, Yaffe, & Hornstein, 1990). Specific maternal risks, likely secondary to vasospasm and decreased uterine blood flow (Woods, Plessinger, & Clark, 1987), may include rupture of ectopic pregnancy, spontaneous abortion, and abruptio placentae (Chasnoff, Burns, Schnoll, & Burns, 1985; Chasnoff, Bussey, Savich, & Stack, 1986). Described fetal and neonatal effects include congenital malformations, in utero stroke and seizures, possible alterations in neurobehavior and withdrawal (Chasnoff et al., 1986; Oro & Dixon, 1987; Rosenak, Diamant, Yaffe, & Hornstein, 1990). In addition, concomitant use of alcohol, tobacco, or other drugs is common, each adding unique risks. Combinations of cocaine with sedatives (e.g., alcohol, benzodiazepines) is common as a means to reduce stimulant side effects and bear the "crash" after a cocaine binge.

Opioids. Methadone maintenance has been the treatment of choice for heroin and other opioid addicts in an effort to remove the "environmental" risks, such as infection, acute withdrawal, poor nutrition, and lack of prenatal care (Zuspan, Gumpel, Megia-Zelaya, Maddem, & Davis, 1975). As one might expect, the specific fetal and neonatal effects likely to be caused by the narcotic itself, such as growth retardation, preterm delivery, increased perinatal mortality and withdrawal have been seen with methadone as well as with heroin (Edelin et al., 1988). Less clear are the long-term effects of *in utero* opioid exposure, although when evaluating these children, maternal–child interaction, stability of the home, and total environment must be taken into consideration and appear to be at least equally important (Hans, 1989).

Marijuana. Considering the widespread use of marijuana, there is a "surprising paucity of objective information" (Fried, 1989). It is known that marijuana is commonly taken with other drugs, and that because of prolonged storage in fat, intermittent usage by the mother may still cause chronic fetal exposure (Nahar, 1976). Unlike other drugs, heavy marijuana usage was least likely to change with pregnancy, and women quickly returned to prepregnancy levels postpartum (Fried, Barnes, & Drake, 1985). Preliminary studies suggest an increase in low birthweight infants and increased startle and jitteriness in the nursery which was not sustained at 12 to 24 months (Fried, 1989).

Clinical Approaches to Substance Abuse in Prenatal Care

A careful drug and alcohol history taken by the nurse or physician is the most effective screening technique to identify patients at risk, and should be obtained on all patients regardless of income, race, or type of practice. Questions less likely to trigger guilt and defensiveness should be asked first, including usage patterns by friends and before pregnancy. Most women today are aware that drug use is undesirable during pregnancy, hence they feel ashamed if they cannot cease their use. Since denial, minimizing, and rationalizing are common, these sensitive questions, if initially answered negatively, should be repeated later in pregnancy as the bond between the patient and provider grows. At subsequent visits, a woman may retrospectively admit to prior use, which then can be used to begin a counseling relationship focusing on positive aspects (e.g., "I'm glad you felt comfortable enough to tell me.") rather than guilt induction. Questionnaires also may be helpful if given in a safe, nonjudgmental way. The commonly used CAGE questionnaire has been modified to T-ACE in pregnancy with T standing for tolerance (Table 10.2), since "guilt" is a common feeling for pregnant women who do *anything* that might be risky for the fetus (Sokol, Martier, & Ager, 1989).

Some guilt and secrecy may be understandable. Several states consider substance use in pregnancy a form of child abuse punishable by imprisonment or removal of the child from the home after birth. It is important to know the laws in your community concerning substance use by pregnant women before giving advice about legal issues.

For the patient who appears at risk but denies a problem, or for ongoing evaluation of a patient who is in substance abuse treatment, urine toxicology screens and blood or breath alcohol levels may be helpful. Even when pregnant patients are not being forthright about their relapses, they often provide urine or breath samples willingly upon request. However, be careful to collect the specimen in a way that removes any doubt as to its source.

Table 10.2.   The T-ACE Questions for Alcohol Use During Pregnancy

T	How many drinks does it take to make you feel high (**TOLERANCE**)?
A	Have people **ANNOYED** you by criticizing your drinking?
C	Have you felt you ought to **CUT DOWN** on your drinking?
E	Have you ever had a drink first thing in the morning to steady your nerves or get rid of a hangover (**EYE-OPENER**)?

Source: From "The T-ACE Questions: Practical Prenatal Detection of Risk-Taking," by R.J. Sokol, S.S. Martier, & J.W. Ager, 1989, *American Journal of Obstetrics and Gynecology, 160*, 863–868. Reprinted by permission.

After the baby is born, neonatal urine toxicology screening is common in high-risk populations. Meconium (baby's first feces) testing for drug residues appears to offer some advantages over urine in that it represents exposure over the entire third trimester and is easier to collect (Maynard, Amoruso, & Oh, 1991). Hair samples also appear to give valuable information about drug exposure over time (Welch, Martier, Ager, Ostrea, & Sokol, 1990). Patients should be informed that such testing is being done; they are most likely to consent when it is presented as part of a diagnostic evaluation (i.e., looking for a reason for bleeding or growth retardation). Ultimately, the information should be used to help mother and baby by getting them substance abuse treatment and social services rather than using it punitively. As long as the mother is recovering and the baby is in a safe environment, one can keep information about prior history of substance abuse confidential (Duquette, 1981; Reed, Beschner, & Mondanaro, 1982).

Society (including healthcare professionals) can be very judgmental and lack understanding when it comes to the pregnant addict. A pregnant woman is expected to have more will power, better coping skills, and to put her child ahead of herself, often without medical or community support. For the substance abuser, whose life is frequently under stress, pregnancy may be unplanned and may add additional guilt, including concerns about the damage her current lifestyle is doing to the fetus and will do to the baby after birth. As conception often occurs during intoxication, the fetus may be unwanted, and the mother may lack social support for a maternal role. The mother may be underage or immature, hence ill prepared for a maternal role. Many drug abusing women have childhood and adult histories of having been physically, sexually, or emotionally abused; indeed the pregnancy may have resulted from an abusive relationship. Continuing use of drugs is often a way to help suppress unpleasant, overwhelming feelings associated with such problems.

An effective treatment program needs to be safe; staff must express concern for and interest in both the patient *and* her fetus. A therapy team incorporating case management, nutritional support, high-risk obstetrical evaluation, expertise in substance abuse detox and rehabilitation, and pediatric follow-up seems to offer the best approach. At times, the entire environment must be changed, and residential facilities for pregnant women and eventually their newborns and other children are ideal, though difficult to find. Unfortunately, the woman on methadone maintenance often is excluded from residential or 12-step programs, because she is not "drug free."

Many pregnant addicts respond to being cared for because this has been lacking in their current environment or their background. Guilt reduction often is more effective than guilt induction. Group support among other women in similar circumstances may help to improve self-esteem and to provide a better perspective on the situation. Similarly, confrontation by someone in a similar predicament may be accepted more easily than by someone who does not appear to understand. If the pregnant mother intimidates the staff with her paranoia and mistrust, it may indicate that she suffers from concurrent severe psychopathology requiring more sophisticated mental health services or even psychopharmocology (which is challenging under the limitations of safety to fetus and to recovering addict mother). Family support may be helpful, but at times it may introduce additional problems into therapy. Consequently, when using a family approach, staff may need additional support or lower caseloads to be effective. Services offering comprehensive care to pregnant addicts and their families also must be culturally competent to be accepted and appreciated.

Gradually, an awareness that substance abuse occurs in women, especially pregnant women, is growing. A drug and alcohol history is a standard part of most prenatal records, and slowly, specialized treatment programs are being developed. Although initially complex and costly, the long-term benefits of drug treatment to mother and infant both medically and emotionally would seem to make this a good investment.

FEMALE ATHLETES

Female athletes occupy an increasingly prominent place in our society. This is due to two factors: (a) increasing numbers of women are participating in sports, and (b) women are enjoying greater attention in society for their athletic performance at the secondary school, collegiate, Olympic, and professional levels. The first factor is a function of greater overall numbers of children participating in organized sports and the forceful gender antidiscrimination actions of the federal government in the 1960s and 1970s. The second factor is a function of prominence in the media, high-profile and highly paid female professional athletes (particularly in tennis and golf), active recruitment of women to athletic scholarships at the collegiate level, and increasing popularity of women's sports competition. Marketing commercial products to women by using famous female athletes has added to their exposure in the public media.

Women have become part of the athletic culture. Participation in sports has several benefits: (a) having fun; (b) facilitating peer relationships both within and outside the sport; (c) developing, testing, and improving one's athletic skills; (d) enhancing physical fitness; (e) participating in competition—confronting issues of winning and losing, fair play; (f) setting and achieving goals; (g) enhancing self-esteem through repeated successes; and (h) developing techniques to withstand performance stress.

Performance stress is a complicated factor. It stimulates athletes to enhance their performance (similar to the stress a student may experience in the classroom) and may lead to utilization of negative or positive coping mechanisms which may vary depending on the athlete's level of competition. Positive approaches include using biofeedback to identify and control autonomic nervous system reactions, setting goals, learning relaxation techniques, assertiveness training, imaging and mental preparation for competition (particularly individual sports such as gymnastics, golf, and tennis), and improving concentration. There are several risks associated with performance stress, however: (a) overtraining and burnout, (b) sleep disturbances, (c) depression, (d) vegetative signs of decreased appetite and increased fatigue, (e) eating disorders, and (f) substance abuse.

Functions of Substance Use

Drugs may be used in three ways by female athletes. First, drugs may be used for appropriate therapeutic purposes. These may include acute treatment of injury or infection, injury rehabilitation, pain management, management of chronic conditions, and management of the menstrual cycle. This latter use does not correlate with improved performance (Quandagno, Faquin, Um, Kuminka, & Moffatt, 1991; Schelkun, 1991) but rather is a response to unpleasant symptoms of fluid retention, mood lability, breast tenderness, and so on. Second, drugs may be used to enhance performance, despite widespread condemnation of and sanctions against this use. Anabolic or ergogenic drugs, stimulants, and relaxants are the most common substances used for this purpose. Third, drugs may be used for recreational purposes or to relax after competition (e.g., alcohol, marijuana, cocaine, and opioids).

While sports enthusiasts had been assumed to be against drug use, recent scandals have demonstrated that drug abuse has penetrated the sports culture. With greater financial purses to win, athletes have become vulnerable to temptations to exceed their natural limits through the use of anabolic steroids and stimulants to enhance performance (Kashkin & Kleber, 1989). Stimulants also are used to suppress appetite and lose weight in order to qualify for lower weight classes.

After, and even during, the sports events, athletes have increasingly come to rely upon opioids and sedatives to cope with the damage induced by overextension of their bodies. The substantial experimentation with drugs by today's adolescents makes it more likely that athletes will have prior drug experiences and perhaps will continue or resume such use during athletic careers.

Epidemiology

There is little epidemiologic data specific to female athletes and substance use or abuse. The most extensive data at the collegiate level are that of Anderson and McKeag (1985; 1989). Their data do include ergogenic and social drug use in women's sports. The most striking difference between men and women is the higher use of anabolic steroids by men and the generally higher use of weight-loss products by women. The only epidemiologic study specific to female athletes is a survey questionnaire in 1986 done by the Hazelden Center in cooperation with the Womens Sports Foundation (Hazelden, 1987). Those surveyed were athletes who competed at various levels: college varsity, Olympic, other amateur, professional, senior/masters, and retired. The survey focused on use patterns, attitudes, and behaviors. Results of this survey confirm drug use across a broad range of drugs with striking use of alcohol (see Table 10.3).

Table 10.3. Use of Substances by Elite Female Athletes

Alcohol		12% > 4 drinks in a row in past 2 wks	
		7% use prior to or during competition	
		91% in past year	76% in past month
Amphetamines		6% before competition	3% during competition
Anabolic steroids		3–5% ever	0% in past month
Cocaine		7% ever used	
	Olympic:	3% before competition	2% during competition
Marijuana		17% past year	
	Olympic:	3% prior to competition	
Narcotics		11% during sports season or off season	
Sedatives		12% past year	
	Olympic:	3% past year	
Tobacco	Olympic:	16% had smoked in past month	
		20% lifetime use smokeless tobacco	

Source: From *Elite Women Athletes Survey*, by Hazelden Health Promotion Services, 1987. Reprinted by permission.
Olympic = athletes of Olympic level competition

Consequences of Substance Use

Consequences of drug use during athletics are several: (a) social ostracism for violating rules of the sports league, (b) trauma-induced damage to the body, (c) return to athletic activities before trauma has fully and properly healed, and (d) chemical dependence. Consequences of specific chemical use, such as masculinization secondary to anabolic steroid use, and artificial weight loss secondary to stimulant use, are well-documented (Wadler & Hainline, 1989).

Treatment of Substance-Abusing Female Athletes

The treatment of women with substance abuse problems is beyond the scope of this chapter. However, we include a brief discourse on treatment of the special problems of the female athlete. Female athletes have become set apart from others, functioning in a world established by and designed for men (Birrell, 1988). Thus female athletes may find that they have little in common with other women and more in common with male athletes with respect to love of competition, self-esteem rooted in athletic performance, and a strong desire to train, keep fit, and compete. Their medical management is complicated by conditions specific to female athletes: disorders of the menstrual cycle and osteoporosis (DeCree, 1990; DeCree, Vermeulen, & Ostyn, 1991; Highet, 1989; Izzo & Labriola, 1991; Loucks, 1990; Muburgh, Watkins, & Noakes, 1992). They appear to be at particular risk of eating disorders (Selby, Weinstein, & Bird, 1990) and may be at higher risk of ectopic pregnancy (James, 1989). They may have difficulty relating to other nonathletic women in treatment programs. Finding a positive therapeutic balance between a female athlete's expressed desire to continue training while in substance abuse treatment when there is physical contraindication or the possibility that the training may represent a maladaptive coping mechanism such as an eating disorder (Yates, Leehey, & Shisslak, 1983) is a difficult issue for the treatment team to face when challenging the existing lifestyle and coping patterns. Input from other female athletes in recovery is influential.

REFERENCES

Alcohol use in pregnancy: A report by the American Council on Science and Health. (1982). *Nutrition Today, 17,* 29.

Amaro, H., Whittaker, R., Coffman, G., & Heeren, T. (1990). Acculturation and marijuana and cocaine use: Findings from the HHANES 1982-1984. *American Journal of Public Health, 80* (Suppi.), 54–60.

Anderson, W.A., & McKeag, D.B. (1985, June). *The substance use and abuse habits of college student-athletes.* East Lansing, MI: College of Human Medicine, Michigan State University.

Anderson, W.A., & McKeag, D.B. (1989, October). *Replication of the national study of the substance use and abuse habits of college student-athletes.* Final report to the National Collegiate Athletic Association by College of Human Medicine, Michigan State University, East Lansing, MI.

Barnes, G.M., & Weltz, J.W. (1986). Patterns and predictors of alcohol use among 7th-12th grade students in New York State. *Journal of Studies on Alcohol, 47,* 53–62.

Beauvais, F., & LaBoueff, S. (1985). Drug and alcohol abuse intervention in American Indian communities. *International Journal of the Addictions, 20,* 139–171.

Begleiter, H., Projesz, B., Bihari, B., & Kissin, B. (1984). Event-related brain potentials in boys at risk for alcoholism. *Science, 225,* 1493–1496.

Binion, A., Jr., Miller, C.D., Beauvais, F., & Oetting, E.R. (1988). Relationales for the use of alcohol, marijuana, and other drugs by eighth-grade Native American and Anglo youth. *The International Journal of the Addictions, 23,* 47–64.

Birrell, S.J. (1988) Discourses on the gender/sport relationship: From women in sport to gender relations. *Exercise and Sport Sciences Reviews, 16,* 459–502.

Boyd, C., & Mieczkowski, T. (1990). Drug use, health, family and social support in "crack" cocaine users. *Addictive Behaviors, 15,* 481–485.

Brown, F., & Tooley, J. (1989). Alcoholism in the black community. In G.W. Lawson & A.W. Lawson (Eds.), *Alcoholism and substance abuse in special populations.* Rockville, MD: Aspen Publishing.

Brown, L.S. (1990). Black intravenous drug users: Prospects for intervening in the transmission of human immunodeficiency virus infection. In C.G. Leukefield, R.J. Battjes, & Z. Amsel (Eds.), *AIDS and intravenous drug use: Future directions for community-based prevention research* (NIDA Research Monograph No. 93, DHHS Publ. No. (ADM) 89-1627). Rockville, MD: U.S. Government Printing Office.

Brown, S.A., Stetson, B.A., & Beatty, P.A. (1989). Cognitive and behavioral features of adolescent coping in high-risk situations. *Addictive Behaviors, 14,* 43–52.

Butler, N.R., Goldstein, H., & Ross, E.M. (1972). Cigarette smoking in pregnancy: Its influence on birth weight and perinatal mortality. *British Medical Journal, 2,* 127–130.

Cadoret, R.J., Troughton, E., O'Gorman, T.W., & Haywood, E. (1986). An adoption study of genetic and environmental factors in drug abuse. *Archives of General Psychiatry, 43,* 1131–1136.

Caetano, R. (1984). Ethnicity and drinking in Northern California: A comparison among whites, blacks and Hispanics. *Alcohol & Alcoholism, 19,* 31–44.

Caetano, R. (1986-1987). Drinking and Hispanic-American family Life: The view outside the clinic walls. *Alcohol Health & Research World, 2,* 27–35.

Caetano, R. (1989). Responding to alcohol-related problems among Hispanics. *Contemporary Drug Problems* (Special Reprint), pp. 335–363.

Caetano, R. (1990). Hispanic drinking in the U.S.: Thinking in new directions. *British Journal of Addiction, 85,* 1231–1236.

Caetano, R., & Herd, D. (1984). Black drinking practices in Northern California. *American Journal of Drug & Alcohol Abuse, 10,* 571–587.

Caetano, R., & Mora, M.E.M. (1988). Acculturation and drinking among people of Mexican descent in Mexico and the United States. *Journal of Studies on Alcohol, 49,* 462–471.

Cahalan, D., Cisin, I.H., & Crossley, H.M. (1969). *American drinking practices.* New Brunswick, NJ: Rutgers Center of Alcohol Studies.

Cervantes, R.C., Gilbert, M.J., de Snyder, N.S., & Padilla, A. (1991). Psychosocial and cognitive correlates of alcohol use in younger adult immigrant and U.S.-born Hispanics. *The International Journal of the Addictions, 25,* 687–708.

Chasnoff, I.J. (1989). Drug use and women: Establishing a standard of care. *Annals of the New York Academy of Sciences, 562,* 208–210.

Chasnoff, I.J. (1991). Chemical dependency and pregnancy. *Clinics in Perinatology, 18,* 1–191.

Chasnoff, I.J., Burns, W.J., Schnoll, S.H., & Burns, K.A. (1985). Cocaine use in pregnancy. *New England Journal of Medicine, 313,* 666–669.

Chasnoff, I.J., Bussey, M.E., Savich, R., & Stack, C.M. (1986). Perinatal cerebral infarction and maternal cocaine abuse. *Journal of Pediatrics, 108,* 456–459.

Chasnoff, I.J., Landress, H.J., & Barrett, M.C. (1989). The prevalence of illicit drug or alcohol use during pregnancy and discrepancies in mandatory reporting in Pinellas County, Florida. *New England Journal of Medicine, 322,* 1202–1206.

Cloninger, C.R. (1987). Neurogenetic adaptive mechanisms in alcoholism. *Science, 236,* 410–416.

Cloninger, C.R., Sigvardsson, S., & Bohman, M. (1988). Childhood personality predicts alcohol abuse in young adults. *Alcoholism: Clinical and Experimental Research, 12,* 494–505.

DeCree, C. (1990). The possible involvement of endogenous opioid peptides and catecholestrogens in provoking menstrual irregularities in women athletes. *International Journal of Sports Medicine, 11,* 329–348.

DeCree, C., Vermeulen, A., & Ostyn, M. (1991). Are high-performance young women athletes doomed to become low-performance old wives? A reconsideration of the increased risk of osteoporosis in amenorrheic women. *Journal of Sports Medicine and Physical Fitness, 31,* 108–114.

Deloria, V., Jr. (1969). *Custer died for your sins: An Indian manifesto.* London: Macmillan.

De Obaldia, R., Parsons, O.A., & Yohman, R. (1983). Minimal brain dysfunction symptoms claimed by primary and secondary alcoholics: Relation to cognitive functioning. *International Journal of Neuroscience, 20,* 173–181.

DHHS (1991). *Health status of minority and low-income groups* (pp. 249–280). Washington, DC: U.S. Government Printing Office.

Dinwiddie, S.H. (1992). Patterns of alcoholism inheritance. *Journal of Substance Abuse, 4,* 155–163.

Dryfoos, J. (1990). *Adolescents at risk: Prevalence and prevention.* New York: Oxford University Press.

Dupree, L.W., & Schonfeld, L. (1989). Treating late-life-onset alcohol abusers: Demonstration through a case study. *Clinical Gerontologist, 9,* 65–68.

Duquette, D.N. (1981). *Michigan law manual on foster care and adoption.* Lansing, MI: Michigan Department of Social Services.

Edelin, K.C., Gurganious, L., Golar, K., Oellerich, D., Kyei-Aboagye, K., & Hamid, M. (1988). Methadone maintenance in pregnancy: Consequences to care and outcome. *Obstetrics and Gynecology, 71,* 399–404.

Escobedo, L., & Remington, P. (1989). Birth cohort analysis of prevalence of cigarette smoking among Hispanics in the United States. *Journal of the American Medical Association, 261,* 66–69.

Fleming, C.M., & Manson, S.M. (1990). Native American women. In R.C. Engs (Ed.), *Women: Alcohol and other drugs.* Dubuque, IA: Kendall/Hunt.

Forslund, M.A. (1979). Drinking problems of Native American and white youth. *Journal of Drug Education, 9,* 21–27.

Frezza, M., di Padova, C., Pozzato, G., Terpin, M., Baraona, E., & Lieber, C.S. (1990). High blood alcohol levels in women: The role of gastric alcohol dehydrogenase activity and first-pass metabolism. *The New England Journal of Medicine, 322,* 95–99.

Fried, P.A. (1989). Postnatal consequences of maternal marijuana use in humans. *Annals of the New York Academy of Sciences, 562,* 123–132.

Fried, P.A., Barnes, M.V., & Drake, E.R. (1985). Soft drug usage after pregnancy compared to use before and during pregnancy. *Obstetrics and Gynecology, 151,* 787–792.

Friedman, S., Sufian, M., & Des Jarlais, D.C. (1990). The AIDS epidemic among Latino intravenous drug users. In R. Glick & J. Moore (Eds.), *Drugs in Hispanic Communities* (pp. 45–54). New Brunswick, NJ: Rutgers University Press.

Gabrielli, W., & Mednick, S. (1983). Intellectual performance in children of alcoholics. *Journal of Nervous and Mental Disease, 171,* 444–447.

Gilliam, D.M., & Irtenkauf, K.T. (1990). Maternal genetic effects on ethanol teratogenesis and dominance of relative embryonic resistance to malformations. *Alcoholism: Clinical and Experimental Research, 14,* 539–545.

Glantz, M.D., & Backenheimer, M.S. (1988). Substance abuse among elderly women. *Clinical Gerontologist, 8,* 3–26.

Goldman, R., (1992, February). *Qualitative data collection among ethnic minority health center patients.* Paper presented at the Office of Substance Abuse Prevention PPWI Training Conference, Washington, DC.

Gomberg, E.S.L. (1982). Alcohol use and alcohol problems among the elderly. *Alcohol and Health Monograph 4. Special Population Issues* (DHHS Publ. No. (ADM) 82-1193, pp. 263–290). Rockville, MD: National Institute on Alcohol Abuse and Alcoholism.

Gomberg, E.S.L. (1990). Drugs, alcohol and aging. In L.T. Kozlowski, H.M. Annis, H.D. Cappell, F.B. Glaser, M.D. Goodstadt, Y. Israel, H. Kalant, E.M. Sellers, & E.R. Vingilis (Eds.), *Research advances in alcohol and drug problems* (Vol. 10, pp. 171–213). New York: Plenum.

Gomberg, E.S.L., Nelson, B., & Hill, E.M. (1991). Treatment of alcoholism in elderly persons: Preliminary report. *Alcoholism: Clinical and Experimental Research, 15,* 383.

Gonzalez, D., & Page J.B. (1981). Cuban women, sex role conflicts and the use of prescription drugs. *Journal of Psychoactive Drugs, 13,* 47–51.

Gorowitz, K., Bahn, A., Warthen, F., & Cooper, M. (1970). Some epidemiological data on alcoholism in Maryland, based on admissions to psychiatric facilities. *Quarterly Journal of Studies on Alcohol, 31,* 423–443.

Graham, A.V., Parran, T.V., & Jaen, C.R. (1992). Physician failure to record alcohol use history when prescribing benzodiazepines. *Journal of Substance Abuse, 4,* 179–185.

Grobsmith, E.S., & Dam, J. (1990). The revolving door: Substance abuse treatment and criminal sanctions for Native American offenders. *Journal of Substance Abuse, 4,* 405–425.

Hahn, R.A. (1992). The state of federal health statistics on racial and ethnic groups. *Journal of the American Medical Association, 267,* 268–271.

Hall, R. (1985). Distribution of the Sweat Lodge in alcohol treatment programs. *Current Anthropology, 26,* 134–135.

Hans, S.L. (1989). Developmental consequences of prenatal exposure to methadone. *Annals of the New York Academy of Sciences, 562,* 195–207.

Hanson, J.W., Streissguth, A.P., & Smith, D.W. (1978). The effects of moderate alcohol consumption on fetal growth and morphogenesis. *Journal of Pediatrics, 92,* 457–460.

Harford, T., & Lowman, C. (1989). Alcohol use among black and white teenagers. In L. Spiegler, D. A. Tate, S. Aitken, & M. Christian (Eds.), *Alcohol use among U. S. ethnic minorities.* (pp. 51–61; NIAAA Research Monograph No. 18, DHHS Publ. No. (ADM) 89-1435). Rockville, MD: U. S. Department of Health and Human Services.

Harper, F. D. (1984). Group strategies with black alcoholics. *Journal for Specialists in Group Work, 9,* 38–43.

Hasin, D.S., Grant, B., & Harford, T.C. (1990). Male and female differences in liver cirrhosis mortality in the United States, 1961–1985. *Journal of Studies on Alcohol, 51,* 123–129.

Hazelden Health Promotion Services. (1987). *Elite women athletes survey.* Minneapolis, MN: author.

Heath, D. (1989). American Indians and alcohol: Epidemiological and sociocultural relevance. In L. Spiegler, D. A. Tate, S. Aitken, & M. Christian (Eds.), *Alcohol use among U. S. ethnic minorities* (pp. 207–222, NIAAA

Research Monograph 18, DHHS Publ. No. (ADM) 89–1435). Rockville, MD: U. S. Department of Health and Human Services.

Henningfield, J. E., Clayton, R., & Fullin, W. (1990). Involvement of tobacco in alcohol and illicit drug use. *British Journal of Addiction, 85,* 292–297.

Herd, D. (1989). The epidemiology of drinking patterns and alcohol-related problems among U. S. Blacks. In L. Spiegler, D. A. Tate, S. Aitken, & M. Christian (Eds.), *Alcohol use among U.S. ethnic minorities* (pp. 3–50; NIAAA Research Monograph 18, DHHS Publ. No. (ADM) 89–1435). Rockville, MD: U. S. Department of Health and Human Services.

Highet, R. (1989). Athletic amenorrhoea: An update on aetiology, complications and management. *Sports Medicine, 7,* 82–108.

Hill, A. (1989). Treatment and prevention of alcoholism in the Native American family. In G. Lawson & A. Lawson (Eds.), *Alcoholism and substance abuse in special populations* (pp. 247–272). Rockville, MD: Aspen Publishers.

Hill, S. Y., Steinhauer, S. R., Smith, T. R., & Locke, J. (1991). Risk markers for alcoholism in high-density families. *Journal of Substance Abuse, 3,* 351–368.

Ho, K. H. (1987). *Family therapy with ethnic minorities.* Newbury Park, CA: Sage.

Holck, S., Warren, C., Smith, J., & Rochat, W. (1984). Alcohol consumption among Mexican American and Anglo women: Results of survey along the U. S.-Mexican border. *Journal of Studies on Alcohol, 45,* 149–154.

Honigmann, J., & Honigmann, I. (1970). *Arctic townsmen.* Ottawa: Canadian Research Centre for Anthropology, Saint Paul University.

Hutchings, D. E. (1989). Prenatal abuse of licit and illicit drugs. *Annals of the New York Academy of Sciences, 562:*1–387.

Izzo, A., & Labriola, D. (1991). Dysemenorrhea and sports activities in adolescents. *Clinical and Experimental Obstetrics and Gynecology, 18,* 109–116.

James, W. H. (1989). A hypothesis on the increasing rates of ectopic pregnancy. *Pediatric and Perinatal Epidemiology, 3,* 189–193.

Johnson, P., Armor, D., Polich, S., & Stambul, H. (1977). *U. S. drinking practices: Time trends, social correlates and sex roles.* Rockville, MD: National Institute on Alcohol Abuse and Alcoholism.

Johnson, R. C. (1985). The flushing response and alcohol use. In L. Spiegler, D. A. Tate, S. Aitken, & M. Christian (Eds.), *Alcohol use among U. S. ethnic minorities* (pp. 383–396; NIAAA Research Monograph 18, DHHS Publ. No. (ADM) 89–1435). Rockville, MD: NIAAA

Johnston, L., & O'Malley, P. (1985). *Monitoring the future.* Ann Arbor, MI: Institute for Social Research.

Jones, K.L., & Smith, D.W. (1973). Recognition of the fetal alcohol syndrome in early infancy. *Lancet, 2,* 999–1001.

Kandel, D.B. (1980). Drug and drinking behavior among youth. *Annual Review of Sociology, 6,* 235–285.

Kashkin, K.B., & Kleber, H.D. (1989). Hooked on hormones? An anabolic steroid addiction hypothesis. *Journal of the American Medical Association, 262,* 3166–3170.

Keller, S.E. (1991). HIV-relevant sexual behavior among a healthy inner-city heterosexual population in an endemic area of HIV. *Journal of Adolescent Health Care, 12,* 1–44.

Kelso, D., & DuBay, W. (1989). Alaskan natives and alcohol: A sociocultural and epidemiological review. In L. Spiegler, D.A. Tate, S. Aitken, & M. Christian (Eds.)., *Alcohol use among U.S. ethnic minorities* (pp. 223–238; NIAAA Research Monograph 18, DHHS Publ. No. (ADM) 89-1435). Rockville, MD: U.S. Department of Health and Human Services.

Knupfer, G., & Lurie, E. (1961). *Characteristics of abstainers: A comparison of drinkers and non-drinkers in a large California city* (Drinking Practices Study Report No. 3). Berkeley, CA: State Department of Public Health.

Leland, J. (1978). Women and alcohol in an Indian settlement. *Medical Anthropology, 2,* 85–119.

Leland, J. (1980). Native American alcohol use: A review of the literature. In P.D. Mail & D.R. McDonald (Eds.), *Tulapai to Tokay: A bibliography of alcohol use and abuse among Native Americans of North America.* New Haven, CT: Human Relations Area Files (HRAF) Press.

Lemart, E. (1982). Drinking among American Indians. In E.L. Gomberg, H.R. White, & J. Carpenter (Eds.), *Alcohol, science and society, revisited* (pp. 80–95). New Brunswick, NJ: Rutgers Center of Alcohol Studies.

Lewis, O. (1959). *Five families: Mexican case studies in the culture of poverty.* New York: Basic Books.

Lillie-Blanton, M., Mackenzie, E., & Anthony, J. (1991). Black-white differences in alcohol use by women: Baltimore survey findings. *Public Health Reports, 10,* 124–133.

Lomnitz, L. (1977). *Networks and marginality: Life in a Mexican shantytown.* New York: Academic.

Loucks, A.B. (1990). Effects of exercise training on the menstrual cycle: Existence and mechanisms. *Medicine and Science in Sports and Exercise, 22,* 275–280.

Maddahian, E., Bentler, P.M., & Newcomb, M.B. (1988). Risk factors for substance use: Ethnic differences among adolescents. *Journal of Substance Abuse, 1,* 11–23.

Markides, K.S., Krause, N., & Mendes de Leon, C.F. (1988). Acculturation and alcohol consumption among Mexican-Americans: A three-generation study. *American Journal of Public Health, 78,* 1178–1181.

May, P. (1986). Alcohol and drug misuse prevention programs for American Indians: Needs and opportunities. *Journal of Studies on Alcohol, 47,* 187–195.

Maynard, E.C., Amoruso, L.P., & Oh, W. (1991). Meconium for drug testing. *Substance Abuse, 12,* 99–103.

McAdoo, H. (1977). Family therapy in the Black community. *Journal of the American Orthopsychiatric Association, 47,* 74–79.

Mellinger, G., Balter, M., & Uhlenhuth, E. (1984). Prevalence and correlates of the long-term regular use of anxiolytics. *Journal of the American Medical Association, 251,* 375–379.

Muburgh, K.H., Watkins, V.A., & Noakes, T.D. (1992). Are risk factors for menstrual dysfunction cumulative? *Physicians and Sportsmedicine, 20,* 114–125.

Nahar, G.G. (1976). *Marijuana: Chemistry, biochemistry, and cellular effects.* New York: Springer-Verlag.

National Center for Health Statistics. (1989). *Health, United States 1988* (DHHS Publ. No. (PHS) 89-1232). Washington, DC: Author, U.S. Government Printing Office.

National Clearinghouse for Alcohol and Drug Information. (1989). Alcohol and other drug use in three Hispanic populations: Mexican-Americans, Puerto Ricans, and Cuban-Americans. In *NCADI Update.* Rockville, MD: Author.

Neighbors, H. (1985). Seeking professional help for personal problems: Black Americans' use of health and mental health services. *Community Mental Health Journal, 21,* 156–166.

NIDA (1985). *National Household Survey on Drug Abuse: Main findings* (DHHS Publ. No. (ADM) 88-1586). Rockville, MD: author.

NIDA (1986). *Annual data 1985 from the Drug Abuse Warning Network* (National Institute on Drug Abuse Statistical Series 1, No. 9). Rockville, MD: National Institute on Drug Abuse, Division of Epidemiology and Prevention Research.

NIDA (1987). *National Household Survey of Drug Abuse.* Washington, DC: Author.

NIDA (1989). *National Household Survey of Drug Abuse: 1988 Population Estimates.* Rockville, MD: National Institute on Drug Abuse.

NIDA (1990). *National Survey on Drug Abuse: Population Estimates.* Rockville, MD: National Institute on Drug Abuse.

NIDA (1991, Spring). *NIDA Notes, 6,* 2, 23–24, 35.

NIDA (1991, Summer/Fall). *NIDA Notes, 6,* 3.

Office of Technology Assessment. (1991). *Adolescent health.* Washington, DC: U.S. Congress.

Oro, A.S., & Dixon, D.D. (1987). Perinatal cocaine and methamphetamine exposure: Maternal and neonatal correlates. *Journal of Pediatrics, 111,* 571–578.

Parker, L. (1990). *The role of cultural traditions in alcohol and drug abuse prevention: A Native American study.* Doctoral dissertation, Department of Anthropology, Brown University.

Parker, L. (1991). Traditions and innovations: A community-based approach to substance abuse prevention. *Rhode Island Medical Journal, 6,* 281–286.

Parrish, K.M., Higuchi, S., Stinson, F.S., Towle, L.H., Dufour, M.C., & Harford, T.C. (1992). The association of drinking levels and drinking attitudes among Japanese in Japan and Japanese-Americans in Hawaii and California. *Journal of Substance Abuse, 4,* 165–177.

Pletch, P.K. (1988). Substance use and health activities of pregnant adolescents. *Journal of Adolescent Health Care, 9*, 1.

Quadagno, D., Faquin, L., Lim, G.-N., Kuminka, W., & Moffatt, R. (1991). The menstrual cycle: Does it affect performance? *Physicians and Sportsmedicine, 19*, 121–124.

Rantakallio, P. (1978). Relationship of maternal smoking to morbidity and mortality of the child up to the age of five. *Acta Paediatrica Scandinavia, 67*, 621–631.

Rathbone-McCuan, E., & Roberds, L.A. (1980). Treatment of the older female alcoholic. *Focus on Women, 1*, 104–129.

Rathbone-McCuan, E., & Triegaadt, J. (1979). The older alcoholic and the family. *Alcohol Health & Research World, 3*, 7.

Reed, B.G., Beschner, G.M., & Mondanaro, J. (1982). *Treatment services for drug dependent women* (Vol. II, pp. 519–523, USDHHS Publ. No. (ADM) 82-1219). Washington, DC: U.S. Government Printing Office.

Robbins, C., & Clayton, R.R. (1989). Gender-related differences in psychoactive drug use among older adults. *The Journal of Drug Issues, 19*, 207–219.

Romano, P.S., Bloom, J., & Syme, S.L. (1991). Smoking, social support and hassles in an urban African-American community. *American Journal of Public Health, 81*, 1415–1421.

Ronan, L. (1986-1987). Alcohol-related health risks among Black Americans. *Alcohol Health & Research World*, pp. 36–39.

Rosenak, D., Diamant, Y.Z., Yaffe, H., & Hornstein, E. (1990). Cocaine: Maternal use during pregnancy and its effect on mother, the fetus and the infant. *Obstetrics and Gynecology Survey, 45*, 348–359.

Rosett, H.L., Weiner, L., Lee, A., Zuckerman, B., Dooling, E., & Oppenheimer, E. (1983). Patterns of alcohol consumption and fetal development. *Obstetrics and Gynecology, 61*, 539–546.

Russell, M. (1989). Alcohol use and related problems among black and white gynecologic patients. In L. Spiegler, D.A. Tate, S. Aitken, & M. Christian (Eds.), *Alcohol use among U.S. ethnic minorities* (pp. 75–94; NIAAA Monograph No. 18, DHHS Publ. No. (ADM) 89-1435). Washington, DC: U.S. Department of Health and Human Services.

Russell, M., Cooper, M., & Frone, M. (1990). The influence of sociodemographic characteristics on familial alcohol problems: Data from a community sample. *Alcohol: Clinical and Experimental Research, 14*, 221–226.

Safa, H.I. (1974). *The urban poor of Puerto Rico: A study in development and inequality*. New York: Holt, Rinehart, Winston.

Schelkun, P.H. (1991). Exercise and "The Pill." *Physician and Sportsmedicine, 19*, 143–152.

Schuckit, M.A., Morrissey, E.R., & O'Leary, M.R. (1978). Alcohol problems in elderly men and women. *Addictive Diseases, 3*, 405–416.

Scudder, T. (1982). *No place to go: Effects of compulsory relocation on Navajos*. Philadelphia, PA: Institute for the Study of Human Issues (ISHI).

Selby, R., Weinstein, H.M., & Baird, T.S. (1990). The health of university athletes: Attitudes, behaviors and stressors. *Journal of American College Health, 39,* 11–18.

Shkilnyk, A.M. (1985). *A poison stronger than love: The destruction of an Ojibwa community.* New Haven, CT: Yale University Press.

Sokol, R.J., Martier, S.S., & Ager, J.W. (1989). The T-ACE questions: Practical prenatal detection of risk-drinking. *American Journal of Obstetrics and Gynecology, 160,* 863–868.

Stillman, R.J., Rosenberg, M.J., & Sachs, B.P. (1986). Smoking and reproduction. *Fertility and Sterility, 46,* 545–566.

Stroup-Benham, C., Treviño, F., Treviño, D. (1990). Alcohol consumption patterns among Mexican American mothers and among children from single- and dual-headed households: Findings from HHANES 1982–84. *American Journal of Public Health, 80*(Suppl.), 36–41.

Swan, G.E., Carmelli, D., Rosenman, R.H., Fabsitz, R.R., & Christian, J.C. (1990). Smoking and alcohol consumption in adult male twins: Genetic heritability and shared environmental influences. *Journal of Substance Abuse, 2,* 39–50.

Swanson, D.W., Bratrude, A.P., & Brown, E.M. (1971). Alcohol abuse in a population of Indian children. *Diseases of the Nervous System, 32,* 835–842.

Tarter, R.E. (1988). Are there inherited behavioral traits that predispose to substance abuse? *Journal of Consulting and Clinical Psychology, 56,* 189–196.

Taysi, K. (1988). Preconceptual counseling. *Obstetrics and Gynecology Clinics of North America, 15,* 167–178.

Terney, R., & McLain, L. (1990). The use of anabolic steroids in high school students. *American Journal of Diseases of Childhood, 144,* 99–103.

Toneatto, A., Sobell, L.C., & Sobell, M.B. (1992). Gender issues in the treatment of abusers of alcohol, nicotine, and other drugs. *Journal of Substance Abuse, 4,* 209–218.

Tubman, J.G., Vicary, J.R., von Eye, A., & Lerner, J.V. (1991). Qualitative changes in relationships between substance use and adjustment during adolescence. *Journal of Substance Abuse, 3,* 405–414.

USDHHS (1991). *Health status of minority and low income groups* (3rd ed.). Rockville, MD: U.S. Government Printing Office.

Voss, H.L. (1989). *Patterns of drug use: Data from the 1985 National Household Survey* (pp. 33–46; NIDA Research Monograph, No. 91. Publication No. (ADM) 89-1672, (ADM) 1730). Rockville, MD: National Institute of Drug Abuse.

Wadler, G.I., & Hainline, B. (1989). *Drugs and the athlete.* Philadelphia, PA: FA Davis.

Wallace, A.F.C. (1966). *Religion: An anthropological view.* New York: Random House.

Wallace, A.F.C. (1969). *The death and rebirth of the Seneca.* New York: Vintage Books.

Wechsler, H., Demone, H., & Gottlieb, N. (1980). Drinking patterns of Greater

Boston adults: Subgroup differences on the QFU index. *Journal of Studies on Alcohol, 41,* 672–681.

Weibel-Orlando, J. (1984). Substance abuse among American Indian youth: A continuing crisis. *The Journal of Drug Issues, 14,* 313–335.

Weibel-Orlando, J. (1986-1987). Drinking patterns of urban and rural American Indians. *Alcohol Health & Research World, 2,* 9–14.

Weibel-Orlando, J. (1989). Pass the bottle, bro! A comparison of urban and rural Indian drinking patterns. In L. Spiegler, D.A. Tate, S. Aitken, & M. Christian (Eds.), *Alcohol use among U.S. ethnic minorities* (pp. 269–289; NIAAA Research Monograph No. 18), DHHS Publ. No. (ADM) 89-1435. Rockville, MD: U.S. Department of Health and Human Services.

Weiner, H., Wallen, M., & Zankowski, G. (1980). Culture and social class as intervening variables in relapse prevention with chemically dependent women. *Journal of Psychoactive Drugs, 22,* 239–248.

Welch, R.A., Martier, S.S., Ager, J.W., Ostrea, E.M., & Sokol, R.J. (1990). Radioimmunoassay of hair: A valid technique for determining maternal cocaine abuse. *Substance Abuse, 11,* 214–217.

White, D.G. (1985). *Aren't I a woman?* New York: W.W. Norton.

Whittaker, J.O. (1962). Alcohol and the Standing Rock Sioux Tribe (I). *Quarterly Journal of Studies on Alcohol, 23,* 468–479.

Whittaker, J.O. (1963). Alcohol and the Standing Rock Sioux Tribe (II). *Quarterly Journal of Studies on Alcohol, 24,* 80–90.

Wilsnack, R.W. (1992, June). *Drinking among women in unwanted statuses.* Presentation at the Annual Meeting of the Research Society on Alcoholism, San Diego, CA.

Wilsnack, R.W., Wilsnack, S.C., & Klassen, A.D. (1984). Women's drinking and drinking problems: Patterns from a 1981 national survey. *American Journal of Public Health, 74,* 1231–1238.

Windsor, D. (1989). Prevalence of anabolic steroid use by male and female adolescents. *Medical Science, Sports, and Exercise, 21,* 494–497.

Wolin, S.J., Bennett, L.A., Noonan, D.L., & Teitelbaum, M.A. (1980). Disrupted family rituals: A factor in the intergenerational transmission of alcoholism. *Journal of Studies on Alcohol, 41,* 199–214.

Womble, M. (1990). Black women. In R.C. Engs (Eds.), *Women: Alcohol and other drugs.* Dubuque, IA: Kendall/Hunt.

Woods, J.R., Jr., Plessinger, M.A., & Clark, K.E. (1987). Effect of cocaine on uterine blood flow and fetal oxygenation. *Journal of the American Medical Association, 257,* 957–961.

Yates, A., Leehey, K., & Shisslak, C.M. (1983). Running—An analogue of anorexia? *New England Journal of Medicine, 308,* 251–255.

Zuckerman, B.S., Amaro, H.A., & Beardslee, W. (1987). Mental health of adolescent mothers. *Developmental and Behavioral Pediatrics, 8,* 111–116.

Zuspan, F.P., Gumpel, J.A., Megia-Zelaya, A., Maddem, J., & Davis, R. (1975). Fetal stress from methadone withdrawal. *American Journal of Obstetrics and Gynecology, 122,* 43–46.

Chapter 11

Women and Smoking: Toward the Year 2000*

Barbara A. Berman, Ph.D.

Division of Cancer Control
Jonsson Comprehensive
Cancer Center
and
Department of Community
Health Sciences
School of Public Health
University of California
Los Angeles

Ellen R. Gritz, Ph.D.

Professor in Residence
Department of Surgery
Director, Division of
Cancer Control
Jonsson Comprehensive
Cancer Center
University of California
Los Angeles

* The preparation of this chapter was supported by the following grants from the National Cancer Institute: Cancer Control Science Program, CA 43461; Smoking Cessation for Women in an HMO Population, CA 41616; and Cancer Center Core Support Supplement: Minority Enhancement Award, CA, 16042. It was also supported by the following grant from the National Heart, Lung and Blood Institute: Targeting Adult Minority Smokers Through Public Schools, HL 43608.

We thank Elisa Clements for expert word-processing assistance. We wish to acknowledge, in memoriam, the support of Dr. Joseph Cullen during whose NCI leadership a portion of this research was carried out.

INTRODUCTION

The 1980s was a decade of significant change in smoking among women. The health consequences of this behavior were documented with growing alarm, factors and forces contributing to female tobacco use were explored, and strategies for altering these trends were identified. Key issues remain. The mandate for gender-specific research and effective interventions continues to be a central public health challenge in the 1990s.

SMOKING PREVALENCE

Tobacco use by women is not an innovation of modern times. Extensive cross-cultural evidence exists that women have smoked cigarettes, pipes, cigars, and have dipped, chewed, snuffed, drunk, and licked tobacco in diverse cultures throughout history (Gritz, 1980). Women have used tobacco products for magico-religious, medicinal, hygienic, and recreational purposes (Gritz, 1980; Wilbert, 1975).

Tobacco use has existed through the nation's history, as reflected in the antitobacco movement that dates from the Civil War period (Heimann, 1960; Robert, 1952). However, during the late 19th and early 20th centuries, cultural norms in the United States discouraged female tobacco use. This began to change during the 1920s (Ernster, 1985; Gritz, 1980; Howe, 1984) and smoking among women accelerated, particularly during and after World War II. Prevalence increased from approximately 18.1% in 1935 to a peak of 33.3% in 1965 (USDHEW, 1980), and remained virtually unchanged at 31% to 32% through 1977. Despite the misconception that smoking rates among women continue to increase (Rodin & Ickovics, 1990), smoking prevalence began to decline slowly after 1977. Rates reached 25.7% in 1988, and are projected to decrease further over time (CDC, 1991; Pierce, Fiore, Novotny, Hatziandreu, & Davis, 1989a; USDHHS, 1989).

This pattern contrasts with the smoking experience of men. Cigarettes largely replaced other forms of tobacco use for men during the first half of the 20th century. Half of all adult males are estimated to have been smoking by 1925, and smoking prevalence accelerated during World War II (USDHEW, 1980). Men born between 1911 and 1930 reached 70% prevalence, the highest proportion of smokers, by the 1940s and 1950s. By 1964, unlike women, smoking prevalence for men was already declining. Smoking among men has decreased from 50.2% in 1965 to 30.8% in 1988 (CDC, 1991; USDHHS, 1989).

While the proportion of smokers is still higher for adult men than women, the rate of decline is greater among men (Fiore, Novotny,

Pierce, Hatziandreu, Patel, & Davis, 1989). If current trends continue, smoking prevalence of men and women is expected to be at parity by 1995. By the year 2000, it is anticipated that a larger proportion of women than men will be smokers, with rates estimated at 23% for women and 20% for men (Pierce et al., 1989a). Insofar as "no evidence has been found of any cultural group in which tobacco use has been substantially more common among women" (Kaplan, Carriker, & Waldron, 1990, p. 305), this would represent an important though troubling historical event regarding female substance use. However, evidence exists of a decline in smoking initiation in 1987 among 20–24-year-old women, the only group among whom initiation was increasing before 1985. This decline suggests that convergence may not be inevitable, and underscores the need to track current trends among women carefully (Pierce, Fiore, Novotny, Hatziandreu, & Davis, 1989b).

Racial/ethnic and socioeconomic variations in smoking prevalence have been identified. According to the most recent data (1988 National Health Interview Survey), smoking prevalence was higher among men than women in all age groups except 18–24-year-olds (CDC, 1991). Among women alone, smoking was more prevalent among blacks than whites (27.8% vs 25.7%) and non-Hispanic than Hispanic (26.2% vs 18.7%). However, education more than gender, race, or any other variable accounts for variations in smoking prevalence within the population (Escobedo, Anda, Smith, Remington, & Mast, 1990; Fiore et al., 1989). Women of all races with less education, like their male counterparts, are more likely to smoke (CDC, 1991; Pierce et al., 1989b). Because education is a marker for socioeconomic status, it is evident that smoking is increasingly the behavior of the socioeconomically disadvantaged (Pierce et al., 1989a).

While participation in the labor force is not seen as contributing to increased smoking prevalence among women (Waldron & Lye, 1989), occupational variations in smoking prevalence have been reported (Stellman, Boffetta, & Garfinkel, 1988). These variations are less than for men (Stellman et al., 1988), are not linked to employment in male-dominated occupations (Waldron & Lye, 1989) and are related, to a large extent, to socioeconomic status (Stellman et al., 1988). Since most smoking initiation occurs in adolescence, occupational experiences clearly are not a dominant factor (Waldron & Lye, 1989). However, insofar as data for the latest birth cohort of adults (1960–62) indicate that 18% of those who have smoked with at least a *high school* education started to smoke in their young adult years (19–24 years of age), the influence of occupational experiences cannot be ignored (Pierce, Naquin, Gilpin, Giovino, Mills, & Marcus, 1991).

Although tobacco consumption has declined in many developed nations (Canada, Great Britain, Australia) though not in all (Norway) (Pierce, 1989), global consumption has risen primarily because of increases in developing nations. Notable increases have occurred throughout Asia, Africa, and Latin America (Chandler, 1988; Crofton, 1990).

In most nations, women are less likely than men to smoke (Waldron et al., 1988). Collapsing data across variables such as type of tobacco products used can obscure the reasons for gender differences and important aspects of change in prevalence patterns (Kaplan et al., 1990). Gender differences may be large (Japan, China, Greece, Indonesia, Tunisia) or small (Canada, United Kingdom, New Guinea, Uruguay, United States) and not easily summarized in terms of westernization or industrial development (Grunberg, Winders, & Wewers, 1991; Kaplan et al., 1990). Small gender differences are not always linked to low prevalence and large gender differences are not always associated with high prevalence among men (Crofton, 1990; Grunberg, et al., 1991). Evidence suggests that in some countries where prevalence among women is traditionally low, smoking rates are increasing, particularly among women with more education (Crofton, 1990). Reflecting earlier trends in the United States and other Western nations, smoking is seen as modern and sophisticated (Crofton, 1990), and in nations such as Brazil, Chile, Uruguay, and New Guinea, more adolescent girls than boys now smoke.

HEALTH CONSEQUENCES FOR WOMEN

The health consequences of cigarette smoking are well established (USDHHS, 1989). An estimated three-fourths of a million smoking-related deaths were avoided or postponed between 1964 and 1985 as a result of decisions to stop smoking or not to start (USDHHS, 1989). Nonetheless, calculations of excess deaths attributable to smoking make clear that tobacco use remains the single major preventable cause of death and disease in the nation (Stellman & Garfinkel, 1989). Smoking was linked to an estimated 390,000 deaths for men and women from all causes in 1985 (ACS, 1990; USDHHS, 1989). This represents one out of every six deaths in the nation (USDHHS, 1989). Among women, smoking accounted for 30,000 deaths in 1965 and 106,000 in 1985 from 10 causes. These include heart disease, stroke, chronic obstructive pulmonary disease, and cancer of the lung, mouth, esophagus, larynx, pancreas, bladder, and kidney (Davis, 1990). This increase in deaths persists after adjustment for population size (Davis,

1990; USDHHS, 1989). It reflects the earlier age of smoking initiation, increased dosage, and deeper inhalation among women who smoke now than in the past (Davis, 1990; Garfinkel & Stellman, 1988).

The impact of smoking on the health of women can perhaps best be illustrated with regard to lung cancer. The incidence of this disease has leveled off among males as a result of more than 20 years of decrease in smoking (Garfinkel & Stellman, 1988; Stellman & Garfinkel, 1989). This is not the case for females. Indeed, since 1986, lung cancer has been the number one cause of cancer mortality for females. As a result of cessation trends, a decline in lung cancer rates for women under 45 years of age and a leveling off in rates for women aged 45 to 54 can be seen (Garfinkel & Stellman, 1988). However, the overall death rate from this disease among women is expected to increase over the next 10 years as a result of the age distribution of the population (DeVesa, Blot, & Fraumeni, 1989; Novotny et al., 1990).

Women are not only at risk for all of the smoking related diseases first demonstrated in males, but are also at special risk related to the female reproductive system and pregnancy (Berman & Gritz, 1988; USDHHS, 1989). Female smokers have higher rates of osteoporosis and experience earlier menopause. Smokers who use oral contraceptives face an increased risk of stroke. An association has been identified between smoking and reduced fertility (USDHHS, 1989). Women who smoke increase their risk of spontaneous abortion, perinatal mortality, and stillbirth (Chow, Daling, Weiss, & Voight, 1988; Kline, Stein, Susser, & Warburton, 1977; Wilner, 1985). A direct link has been found between smoking and abruptio placenta, bleeding during pregnancy, premature rupture of membranes, and preterm delivery (Berman & Gritz, 1988; Meyer & Tonascia, 1977; USDHHS, 1989).

Maternal smoking has significant implications for the fetus, neonate, and growing child (Abel, 1980; Berman & Gritz, 1988; USDHEW, 1980; USDHHS, 1989). There is a well-established connection to low birthweight and intrauterine growth retardation (Kramer, 1987). Research suggests that a link also may exist between smoking and other birth outcomes such as a low or depressed 1- and 5-minute Apgar Score (Garn, Jonston, Ridella, & Petzold, 1981), oral clefting (Khoury et al., 1987), and SIDS, the sudden infant death syndrome (Haglund & Cnattingius, 1990; Peterson, 1981). Maternal smoking also has been associated with lower respiratory tract illness during the first 5 years of life, which cannot be explained by passive exposure to smoking after birth (Taylor & Wadsworth, 1987). Although not conclusive, some studies also have noted a dose-related association between smoking during pregnancy and the risk of adult and childhood cancer (Buckley et al., 1986; Stjernfeldt, Lindsten, Berglund, & Ludvigsson, 1986) and with behavioral, intellectual, and emotional deficits in children (Butler & Goldstein, 1973; Naeye & Peters, 1984; Rantakallio, 1983). Finally, passive smoking is linked to bronchitis and other childhood illness and behavioral problems, as well as to an increased risk of lung cancer in adulthood (Butler & Golding, 1986; Byrd, Shapiro, & Schiedermayer, 1989; Correa, Pickle, Fontham, Lin, & Haenszell, 1983). Lower socio-economic status children are at increased risk from passive smoking, since they are more likely than other children to live in households where both parents smoke (Miller & Hunter, 1990).

Consistent with patterns observed in the United States (Yu et al., 1990), in nations where current levels of smoking have not declined or are increasing, an epidemic of smoking-related deaths is anticipated and, indeed, has already begun (Chandler, 1988; Crofton, 1990; Warner & Connolly, 1991; Yu et al., 1990). As smoking among women increases to the level of men in societies where female smoking has traditionally been lower, women are at particular risk for increased morbidity and mortality.

INITIATION, CESSATION, AND RELAPSE

In light of these significant health consequences, tobacco use among women remains a central public health concern. In order to identify effective means of intervention, an understanding of the processes that contribute to smoking prevalence—initiation, cessation, and relapse—is needed.

Initiation

Differences in initiation, rather than cessation, account for the converging smoking prevalence rates for men and women (Fiore et al., 1989; Hatziandreu et al., 1990; Pierce et al., 1989a). Approximately 1.3 million men and women stopped smoking each year between 1974 and 1985. However, in the early 1980s, approximately one million young people—an estimated 3,000 every day— became regular smokers annually (Fiore et al., 1989).

For both males and females, smoking initiation is primarily an adolescent behavior; few adults begin to smoke on a regular basis after their teenage years (DiFranza & Tye, 1990). For the cohort born between 1950 and 1959, 88% of male and 84% of female smokers began to smoke before age 20 (Smoking and Health, 1986) and there is evidence of a trend toward smoking at increasingly early ages, particularly among women (Escobedo et al., 1990; Johnston, O'Malley, & Bachman, 1989; Kandel & Logan, 1984; USDHHS, 1989). While national surveys indicate that smoking prevalence among adolescents has declined since the 1970s, smoking prevalence has remained consistently higher among teenage girls than boys. Among high school seniors, smoking prevalence declined from 30% and 28% for females and males in 1976 to 20% and 16%, respectively, by 1987 (USDHHS, 1989). Models integrating biological, psychological, and environmental variables to account for smoking initiation have been developed. Flay, d'Avernas, Best, Kersell, and Ryan (1983) stated that in *preparation or anticipation* of smoking, parents and other highly regarded adults serve as important role models (Chassin, Presson, & Sherman, 1984; Cohen, Sattler, Felix, & Brownell, 1987; Flay et al., 1983; Gritz, 1986; Mittelmark, et al., 1987). An adolescent girl is five times as likely to smoke if one or both parents or an older sibling smokes in the household (NIE, 1979; Yankelovich, Skelly, & White, Inc., 1977).

During *initiation*, peers become more important. *Experimentation* with first cigarettes most frequently occurs with friends of the same sex (Biglan, Severson, Bavry, & McConnell, 1983). Furthermore, smoking represents one aspect of a lifestyle choice. Adolescents who smoke are more likely to be from lower income backgrounds, less likely to go to college, and more likely to come from single-parent families (Covey & Tam, 1990; Gritz, 1984). They more frequently engage in delinquent behavior than nonsmokers. Supporting the "gateway" theory of substance use, these adolescent smokers are more likely to experiment with other drugs such as liquor, beer, and marijuana (Wong-McCarthy & Gritz, 1982). The accelerated development and maturation of young women may also play a role at this point (Gilchrist, Schinke, & Nurius, 1989). Teenage girls who smoke are characterized as more socially aggressive, sexually precocious, self-confident, rebellious, and rejecting of authority than their male counterparts (Gilchrist et al., 1989; Gritz, 1984; Yankelovich, Skelly, & White, 1977). Young girls are more likely than boys to be propelled into smoking in an effort to gain approval from opposite sex peers (Gilchrist et al., 1989).

The stage of *becoming* is a period in which the transition to regular smoking takes place and habituation occurs. Techniques of inhalation and nicotine/dosage regulation are mastered. The habit may become addictive, with withdrawal symptoms adding to the likelihood of continued smoking (Flay et al., 1983). Social reinforcement and the formation of a self-image which embraces smoking also takes place (Wong-McCarthy & Gritz, 1982). The dramatic, rapid changes in social roles during the past quarter century support this positive self-image for female initiates. Norms that disinhibit smoking have weakened.

Intensive, expensive advertising efforts (Davis, 1987, 1990; USDHEW, 1980; Warner, 1985) use magazines, newspapers, outdoor displays, and sponsorship of special events to underscore the social acceptability of this behavior (Davis, 1990; Ernster, 1985, 1986; Goldstein, Fischer, Richards, & Creten, 1987; Howe, 1984) and evidence suggests particular targeting to women and young people (Albright, Altman, Slater, & Maccoby, 1988). An image of female smokers as sophisticated, mature, liberated, independent, successful, poised, healthy, young, and sexy has been crafted. Recent efforts to market *Dakota* and *Uptown* brands among young minority and lower socio-economic status women reflect the sophistication of the industry's subtargeting efforts (Davis, 1990; O'Keefe, 1990).

Reflecting the concerns among young girls about their weight, particular emphasis has been placed on the desirability of being thin (Gritz, 1984, 1986; Grunberg, Winders, & Wewers, 1991; USDHEW, 1980). The belief that cigarette smoking is a means of weight control rises after age 12, and is much more prevalent in smokers than non-smokers (Charlton, 1984). Smoking rates are higher among women with eating disorders (Frank, Serdula, & Abel, 1987; Killen et al., 1987). Use of diet pills and amphetamines to control weight is greater among female than male high school seniors who smoke and among female smokers than nonsmokers (Gritz & Crane, 1991).

These advertising efforts are not surprising. Long-term profits to be derived from childhood addiction to nicotine grow as initiation occurs at increasingly early ages (DiFranza & Tye, 1990). Although a few magazines refuse cigarette advertisements, the self-censoring of many magazines with regard to information about the health consequences of smoking can be understood in the context of cigarette advertising revenues (Warner, 1985; White & Whelan, 1986).

Finally, recruitment cannot be viewed only in domestic terms. Tobacco advertisers not only seek to recruit new smokers among low-income and ethnically diverse populations in this nation, but among female populations internationally, as well. In many nations, while smoking behavior is well entrenched, it does not yet include large proportions of women (e.g., Japan), who then are vulnerable to marketing strategies (Grunberg et al., 1991; Yu et al., 1990). Current increases reflect the marketing efforts, often with U.S. government support (Taiwan, South Korea, and Thailand) of multinational tobacco companies seeking to compensate for the declining demand for their cigarettes in developed nations (Crofton, 1990; Cullen, McKenna, & Massey, 1986; Roemer, 1991; Warner & Connolly, 1991). Advertising of Western brands is in place even where such advertising is supposedly forbidden (Crofton, 1990; Yu et al., 1990). Western companies are assisting local companies, such as those in China, to increase the nicotine content of local cigarettes and cigarette production, create new jointly owned companies and brands, and adopt Western advertising and promotional strategies (Crofton, 1990; Warner & Connolly, 1991; Yu et al., 1990).

Cessation and Relapse

The 1988 Surgeon General's report summarized a large body of literature which focused on the highly addicting properties of nicotine in cigarettes (USDHHS, 1988). Nonetheless, despite the difficulties in quitting, there is ample evidence of substantial cessation among smokers. Most smokers want to quit, approximately 30% of all smokers attempt to quit each year, and about 10% of smokers who try to quit succeed each year (Fiore et al., 1990; Hatziandreu et al., 1990). As an effort to integrate such findings with theory, the 1980s have been marked by development of models for cessation (Biener & Abrams, 1991; Brownell, Marlatt, Lichtenstein, & Wilson, 1986; DiClemente et al., 1991; Prochaska & DiClemente, 1983), long- and short-term relapse (Sutton, 1989), and adherence to healthful behaviors (Gritz, DiMatteo, & Hays, 1989).

The 1980 Surgeon General's Report (USDHEW, 1980) was unequivocal in its claim that "women have more difficulty giving up smoking than men, both at the end of treatment and at long-term points of measurement" (p. 307), and there is still some evidence that women have more trouble quitting than men. However, in the decade following this report, as men and women have become more similar with regard to smoking behavior, it has become evident that their cessation behavior has become more alike, as well (Hatziandreu et al., 1990). The probability of attempting to quit and of actually quitting were virtually equivalent for women and men by 1979 and these trends have continued to the present (Fiore et al., 1989; Orlandi, 1986). Although a smaller proportion of women than men who have ever smoked have quit, perhaps more important, the quit ratio (defined as the proportion of ever smokers who are former smokers) is increasing for men and women over time and at an equal rate of change (Davis, 1990). The estimated quit ratio increased for men from 38.5% in 1974 to 45.8% in 1985 and for women from 29.9% to 39.8% (Fiore et al., 1989).

One reason for the belief that women had less success than men in quitting may have been that data from formal treatment programs were used as the basis for these conclusions, and women do not fare as well as men in such settings (Blake et al., 1989; USDHEW, 1980). However, 85% to 95% of smokers who want to quit do so on their own

(Fiore et al., 1990; Ockene, 1984; Schneider, Benya, & Singer, 1984; USDHHS, 1989) and fewer gender differences have been found among this majority of self quitters (Cohen et al., 1989).

Sustaining abstinence remains a difficult problem for many former smokers. Approximately 80% of smokers who quit relapse within a year, which is similar to the relapse rates for other dependencies (USDHHS, 1988). However, as with cessation, belief that this is a problem particularly for women is no longer supported. Whereas a higher proportion of males than females report their quitting lasted more than six months, data do not suggest a significant difference in relapse rates over longer periods of time (Orlandi, 1986).

Research is ongoing with regard to variables that are particularly relevant to cessation and relapse among women. These include social support, concerns about weight gain, and attitudes and beliefs regarding stress reduction and other issues. The place of "naturally" occurring support in cessation has been identified as particularly important for women (Coppotelli & Orleans, 1985; Fisher, Bishop, Goldmuntz, & Jacobs, 1988; Mermelstein, Cohen, Lichtenstein, Baer, & Kamarck, 1986; Mermelstein, Lichtenstein, & McIntyre, 1983). Attention is now focusing on the potential impact of diverse social networks (i.e., friends and coworkers, as well as spouse and family members) for quitting and in promoting relapse (Morgan, Ashenberg, & Fisher, 1988). Others smoking in the home has been found to be particularly important in predicting smoking for young and middle-aged men and women (Coreil, Ray, & Markides, 1991).

Concern about weight gain, an important factor in initiation, continues to affect smoking behavior, particularly among women. Women are less tolerant of even small weight gains that occur with cessation than men, and weight gain has been considered a key relapse trigger (Straeter, Sargent, & Ward, 1989; USDHHS, 1988). However, successful abstainers—both women and men—have been found to gain more than relapsers (Gritz, Carr, & Marcus, 1988; Hall, Ginsberg, & Jones, 1986). When cessation is prioritized, those quitting seem willing to sustain weight gain (Gritz, Berman, Read, Marcus, & Siau, 1990).

It is not entirely clear whether smoking actually reduces stress. However, the belief that it does may play a role in continued smoking and relapse, particularly for women (Grunberg et al., 1991; USDHHS, 1988). Women are more often than men described as "negative affect smokers," smoking in response to emotional discomfort and for tension reduction (Gilchrist et al., 1989). In several recent studies linking smoking and depression, no gender differences were identified (Anda, Williamson, Escobedo, Mast, & Giovino, 1990; Covey & Tam, 1990; Glassman et al., 1990).

Smoking and relapse may relate more to the need for stimulation than for reduction of stress. With regard to workplace stress, women who experienced greater work-related strain were *less* likely to relapse (Swan et al., 1988). Work pressure may be linked to feelings of accomplishment and job satisfaction, while lower levels of strain may be linked to underutilization and boredom. It is interesting to note that women with more leisure time and unemployed women are more likely than other women to relapse. There is also some evidence that smoking among women occurs to demarcate "break time" at home and in the workplace (Gritz et al., 1988; Orlandi, 1986).

Gender-specific attitudes, beliefs, and perceptions may also play an important role in relapse. Women are less likely than men to perceive the health benefits of quitting (Sorenson & Pechacek, 1987). Women may be less confident than men in their ability to quit (Blake et al., 1989). Although a lapse or relapse can be seen either as discouraging or as an opportunity for learning and practicing, women may respond more negatively than men to cessation failures (Blake et al., 1989). Differences in goals regarding altering smoking behavior may play an important part in gender differences relating to relapse. In one study, men reported wanting to quit entirely, while women were more likely to want to cut down on the number of cigarettes smoked (Blake et al., 1989).

IMPLICATIONS FOR INTERVENTION AND POLICY

Diverse antitobacco policy efforts, research initiatives, intervention, and programmatic activities in this and other nations during the past 25 years are well documented (Cullen, McKenna, & Massey, 1986; Epstein, Grunberg, Lichtenstein, & Evans, 1989; Sachs, 1990; Schwartz, 1987; USDHHS, 1988; USDHHS, 1989). Voluntary and government agencies, professional associations (medical, dental, nursing, pharmacists, etc.), health organizations, private industry, schools, churches, and many others are playing a part in tobacco prevention and control (Longsdon, Lazaro, & Meier, 1989; Orleans, 1985; USDHHS, 1989). Cooperative activities and action through coalitions are becoming more common (Bloch & White, 1990; Davis, 1990). Just as smoking is an evolving process, so, too, are the tobacco control movement and its activities.

Targeting Women

A comprehensive review of change strategies is beyond the scope of this chapter. However, two types of efforts targeted to women have become increasingly well established since the 1980 Surgeon General's Report (USDHEW, 1980). First, programs have focused on tailoring content and messages to women. Second, emphasis has been placed on identifying channels through which access to women can be maximized, and dissemination of the antitobacco message can be achieved with greatest effectiveness (Cullen et al., 1986).

Tailoring the Message and Treatment

Effort to design effective, tailored prevention and education materials and messages must take into account the vulnerability of young women to media images (Gritz, 1986). In spite of attempts at tailored messages, a convincing image of the nonsmoker that can rival the tobacco industry's female smoker is not yet in place (Howe, 1984). Antitobacco advocates argue that the effort to match the print, broadcast, and billboard appeal of the tobacco industry with antitobacco messages must become increasingly forceful, vigorous, and creative (Gritz, 1986).

The contents of school-based programs also need to be critically reviewed (Glynn, 1989). Evaluation of school-based studies available to date suggest that psychosocial approaches which focus on social consequences, short-term physiological effects, refusal skills, and social influences are effective (Glynn, 1989; Flay, 1985), although questions regarding why, for whom, and under what conditions have yet to be answered (Flay, 1985). Programs with a smoking-only or a multicomponent health focus have been found to have equal effect on smoking prevention, as long as the stop-smoking component receives sufficient emphasis (i.e., at least five classroom sessions in each of two years) (Glynn, 1989). Most programs now go well beyond traditional approaches which emphasized health issues and risks (Cullen et al., 1986). Many school systems have sought to involve peers and parents, and to establish a supportive organizational climate to maximize the effectiveness of smoking prevention efforts (Glynn, 1989), although the possibility that such efforts can backfire (Ellickson & Bell, 1990) also has been found. With regard to adolescent women, many programs are still inadequate in that they fail to address the particular concerns which accompany female patterns of maturation (Gilchrist et al., 1989). Specifically, those who are uninterested in school, not college bound and/or are precocious in social and sexual behaviors are at highest risk of smoking (Gritz, 1986). Materials geared to lower socioeconomic status girls in their early teens are not readily available (Escobedo et al., 1990). Appropriate materials in Spanish and other languages are also lacking.

With regard to cessation, booklets, brochures, videos, and the like have been designed which reflect the preference for self-quitting and for brief, minimal contact strategies. Describing health risks does not suffice, although assumption that all women are aware of these risks is not well supported (Gilchrist et al., 1989; Gritz, 1986). Focusing on other reasons to quit (e.g., cosmetic, declining social acceptability) brings in more immediate physical and sociocultural dimensions. Specific techniques and strategies which can help female smokers stop smoking and remain abstinent include techniques for coping with stress and smoking triggers, utilizing support, exercise, weight management, and dealing with a lapse or relapse. In each case, these strategies need to be refined and tailored on the basis of ongoing gender-specific research. For example, strategies which recommend ways to avoid weight gain are appropriate. However, evidence mounts that despite careful diet, women who stop smoking gain weight (Gritz et al., 1990; Williamson et al., 1991). Care needs to be taken with regard to the advice given. Weight-control messages should be carefully crafted so as not to create expectations which can prove to be discouraging and can lead to relapse.

Advocacy groups, including those particularly concerned with smoking among women such as the Women versus Smoking Network (Block & White, 1990), emphasize through their efforts to mold public policy that the broadest possible meaning be given to the concept of "message." Pressure on legislators to strengthen cigarette-labeling requirements illustrates concern regarding *explicit* information that smokers and potential smokers receive (Davis, Healy, & Hawk, 1990). Support of bans on smoking in schools, public buildings, and transportation not only reflect concern regarding the health consequences of passive smoking, but concern regarding the *implicit* message conveyed through tacit social approval and endorsement of smoking as well (Cullen et al., 1986; Escobedo et al., 1990; Foege, 1990; Grunberg et al., 1991).

The Issues of Access

Prevention. If the content of preventive programs remains a concern, so, too, does developing and maintaining access to adolescent women. Intervention is critical at all ages. Where this is not possible, evidence suggests that it is particularly important to focus on children in grades 6–9 (Glynn, 1989). However, prevention at the college level and at the worksite should not be overlooked in light of evidence that educational programs in secondary schools may be leading to a delay in initiation until the early adult years among a significant fraction of high school graduates (Pierce et al., 1991). Faced with pressing demands and limited resources, many schools and other agencies do not include smoking prevention as part of their curricula. Where such programs do exist, they are not necessarily targeted to low socioeconomic status adolescents or initiated at early enough ages (Escobedo et al., 1990). Agencies to which young women turn for a range of services and information need to be identified and brought into the antitobacco network. In particular, avenues for reaching school dropouts and other adolescent females at high risk for initiation need to be utilized (Glynn, 1989).

The role of the media is central. A vast audience can be reached, and such programming can be effective particularly when part of coordinated community campaigns promoting health behavior change (Farquhar et al., 1977; Pierce, Macaskill, & Hill, 1990; Salonen, Puska, Kottke, & Tuomilehto, 1981). Development of well-established, sharply focused nonsmoking media images and role models may be a way off. Nonetheless, while evidence suggests that bans on cigarette advertising in isolation are not sufficient to stem tobacco use (Chandler, 1988), antitobacco activists argue that it is entirely appropriate for women to: (a) pressure publishers, producers, and other key gatekeepers to provide the antitobacco message, especially in magazines, newspapers, and programs geared to women, and to limit or suspend tobacco advertising (Ernster, 1985); (b) remain alert to acceleration of targeted tobacco industry campaigns (Davis, 1990); and (c) encourage groups which see the health and well-being of women as their primary concern to adopt an active antitobacco commitment (Ernster, 1986).

Activists also emphasize that it is critical to reach populations of women who have not had high smoking prevalence rates in the past, but who are at high risk for recruitment (Haynes, Harvey, Montes, Nickens, & Cohen, 1990). For example, there is evidence that prevalence among Hispanic women is increasing with acculturation (Marin, Perez-Stable, & Marin, 1989). Older Hispanic women smoke less than non-Hispanic whites or blacks, but prevalence among some young Hispanic females (Puerto Rican, Cuban-American) is at parity with other ethnicities (Haynes et al., 1990). Although the prevalence is lower among young Mexican-American women, reports of their cigarette consumption may be underreported (Perez-Stable, Marin, Marin, Brody, & Benowitz, 1990). Potential health risks from increases in smoking among Hispanic women are of particular concern in light of health care barriers in this population (Haynes et al., 1990).

From an international perspective, the World Health Organization, the International Union Against Cancer, the ACS, the International Agency on Tobacco and Health, and other national and international agencies and organizations support antitobacco initiatives (Crofton, 1990). As resources and priorities allow, governments develop public policy to address this issue (Cullen et al., 1986; Yu et al., 1990). In 1990, 91 nations, including developing nations such as China, Thailand, and Morroco, had some type of legislation, in contrast to 57 nations in 1982 (Roemer, 1991), and subnational legislation is increasingly commonplace. Tobacco bans, legislation restricting advertising, and increased taxes on tobacco products are proposed (Chapman & Richardson, 1990; Roemer, 1991) and are becoming more frequent. Concern regarding enforcement of laws on the books remains an issue, as does the need for developing economically viable alternatives to tobacco production and sales. Women from many nations are joining forces to oppose targeted marketing and to prevent the smoking-related health consequences that have plagued men (Bloch & White, 1990; Jacobson, Amos, & Aghi, 1989). Pressure on our government to discourage export of tobacco products to these nations is emerging as a central prevention strategy (McLellan, 1990; Warner, 1990; Warner & Connolly, 1991).

Cessation. In terms of cessation, emphasis has shifted from clinical to public health perspectives (Epstein et al., 1989) particularly in light of the effectiveness of self-quitting strategies (Curry, Marlatt, Gordon, & Baer, 1988; Cohen et al., 1989, Davis, Faust, & Ordentlich, 1984). Nonetheless, intensive treatment and the use of formal programs remains important. These programs are more often used by heavier smokers, by those who have been unsuccessful at quitting on their own, by college-educated and middle-aged smokers, and by women (Fiore et al., 1990). Where such programs are not utilized, barriers relating to cultural sensitivity, cost, location, and literacy may be involved (Fiore et al, 1990; Meade & Byrd, 1989; Orleans, 1989). Efforts to explore their effectiveness, if appropriately modified, would be worthwhile. Recommendations that formal treatment programs be abandoned (Chapman, 1985) are unwarranted. Among clinical strategies, the use of nicotine gum would appear to be particularly promising with regard to early and late maintenance among women, insofar as women may be particularly vulnerable to fear of weight gain (Gritz, Klesges, & Meyers, 1989; Gross, Stitzer, & Maldonado, 1989). There is general support for the effectiveness of nicotine gum compared to placebo, especially when accompanied by a behavioral or psychological treatment component and used correctly (Sachs, 1990; USDHHS, 1988). The newest pharmacologic aid to smoking cessation is the nicotine patch, which may be more appealing to smokers in general and women in particular, as it bypasses both an unattractive habit (chewing) and does not require multiple daily administration (Rose, Levin,

Behm, Adivi, & Schur, 1990; Tonnesen, Norregaard, Simonsen, & Sawe, 1991). An estimated 2 million smokers still turn to clinical programs annually as a means of quitting (Fiore et al., 1990).

With regard to public health strategies, the focus is increasingly on embedding the antismoking message into community-based interactions and institutions. These include: (a) educational settings such as Head Start, public schools, and worksites; (b) community organizations such as churches and block clubs; and (c) medical and health care delivery locations, including health departments, clinics, private health care providers, WIC, family-planning clinics, and so on. Working with community agencies to recruit women to smoking-cessation programs raises particular issues for researchers and health care providers. Cultural sensitivity, involvement of community and organization members in all facets of program planning and implementation, and meshing of program requirements with the priorities and mandates of the organization becomes critical.

Worksite smoking-cessation programs hold particular promise insofar as they reflect an activity that is in the economic interest of employers as well as in the interest of employees (Glasgow & Klesges, 1985). Such programs can provide access to a considerable proportion of the adult population, and can take advantage of naturally occurring support. Smoking-cessation programs are among the most frequently offered programs where health promotion activities are provided (Fielding & Piserchia, 1989). However, although there is evidence that worksite health-promotion activities are increasing, they are not the norm (Fielding & Piserchia, 1989), and problems regarding program participation and attrition have yet to be resolved (Klesges et al., 1988). More research is needed into the effectiveness of different types of programs (i.e., group, self-help) (Bertera, Oehl, & Telepchak, 1990), assumptions regarding the impact of the work environment (i.e., partial and total smoking bans) on program effectiveness, and on the issue of the "fit" between the organization and the program (Glasgow et al., 1991; Hymowitz, Campbell, & Feuerman, 1991).

Health care settings have received particular attention because of the special influence of health care providers with their patients (Alexander, 1988; Glynn & Manley, 1989; Kottke, Battista, DeFriese, & Brekke, 1988; Kottke, Blackburn, Brekke, & Solberg, 1987; Longsdon et al., 1989; Mecklenburg, 1990; Orleans, 1985; Solberg, 1988). Physician messages are particularly relevant for women, who more frequently use physician services than men, and often serve as caretakers who access health care services for children and other family members. Physicians may continue to play an especially important role in cessation among older female smokers (Orleans, Rimer, Cristinzio, Keintz,

& Fleisher, 1991). Minimal interventions in these settings can be effective (Curry et al., 1988), training to deliver such interventions can be easily accomplished, and small increments in the message provided can make significant differences (Ockene, 1985; Orleans, 1985). Multi-component behavioral interventions can be effective (USDHHS, 1988) but must be carefully crafted (Curry et al., 1988). Bringing too many elements together can be overwhelming and counterproductive (Meichenbaum & Turk, 1987; USDHHS, 1988), and can undermine the attempt to increase access to smoking populations in diverse minimal-contact settings.

Minimal-contact strategies, tailored appropriately, may be particularly valuable for reaching high-risk populations of women. The case of pregnant women is illustrative. Programs using such approaches have been found to bolster cessation in this population (Aaronson, Ershoff, & Danaher, 1985; Ershoff, Mullen, & Quinn, 1989; Mayer, Hawkins, & Todd, 1990; Mullen, Quinn, & Ershoff, 1990; Sexton & Hebel, 1984; Windsor et al., 1985). In light of recent estimates suggesting that about 25% of U.S. women smoke throughout pregnancy (USDHHS, 1990), and that the proportion is higher for unmarried pregnant women (Williamson, Serdula, Kendrick, & Binkin, 1989) and for pregnant women with less education (USDHHS, 1990), these strategies need to be extended to reach all pregnant women. In particular, programs need to be delivered through nontraditional channels to reach lower socioeconomic status women (Kleinman & Kopstein, 1987). Issues of literacy, cultural sensitivity, and age-appropriate messages remain relevant. Finally, although pregnant women stop smoking at higher rates than do women in general (Kleinman & Kopstein, 1987), relapse rates are high following delivery (Fingerhut, Kleinman, & Kendrick, 1990; Mullen et al., 1990). Postpartum tracking and follow-up regarding smoking behavior is needed. Interventions should emphasize the dangers of postpartum recidivism to the neonate and growing child (Fingerhut et al., 1990). The new mother critically needs assistance in coping with postpartum smoking triggers that can undermine abstinence, such as the desire to lose weight gained in pregnancy and the resumption of caffeine and alcohol use (Mullen et al., 1990). Other postpartum stressors which can lead to relapse include infant care, fatigue, and return to work (Mullen et al., 1990).

CONCLUSION

Since 1980, knowledge about smoking has increased, but important research questions remain. There is a need to learn more about the behavioral and contextual factors that influence smoking behavior, and about change strategies that are effective among high-risk women. Ongoing efforts need to be made to increase awareness of the heavy burden of smoking among women, particularly among those of lower socioeconomic status. Antitobacco programs and strategies will be most effective when they grow out of the commitment and involvement of the women they are targeted to serve. Progress in the 1980s stands as an important stepping stone to increased understanding and forceful interventions in the 1990s.

REFERENCES

Aaronson, N.K., Ershoff, D.H., & Danaher, B.G. (1985). Smoking cessation in pregnancy: A self-help approach. *Addictive Behaviors, 10,* 103–108.

Abel, E.L. (1980). Smoking during pregnancy: A review of effects on growth and development of offspring. *Human Biology, 52,* 593–625.

Albright, C.L., Altman, D.G., Slater, M.D., & Maccoby, N. (1988). Cigarette advertisements in magazines: Evidence for a differential focus on women's and youth magazines. *Health Education Quarterly, 15,* 223–233.

Alexander, L.L. (1988). Patient smoking cessation—Treatment strategies. *Nurse Practitioner, 13,* 27–37.

American Cancer Society. (1990). *Cancer Facts and Figures, 1990* (Rep. 90-425M-No. 5008-Le). Atlanta, GA: Author.

Anda, R.F., Williamson, D.F., Escobedo, G., Mast, E.E., & Giovino, G.A. (1990). Depression and the dynamics of smoking. *Journal of the American Medical Association, 264,* 1541–1545.

Berman, B.A., & Gritz, E.R. (1988). Smoking and pregnancy: Present and future challenges. *Wellness Perspectives, 4,* 19–26.

Bertera, R.L., Oehl, L.K., & Telepchak, J.M. (1990). Self-help versus group approaches to smoking cessation in the workplace: Eighteen-month follow-up and cost analysis. *American Journal of Health Promotion, 4,* 187–192.

Biener, L., & Abrams, D.B. (1991). The contemplation ladder: Validation of a measure of readiness to consider smoking cessation. *Health Psychology, 10,* 360–365.

Biglan, A., Severson, H., Bavry, J., & McConnell, S. (1983). Social influence and adolescent smoking: A first look behind the barn. *Health Education, 14,* 14–18.

Blake, S.M., Klepp, K.I., Pechacek, T.F., Folsom, A.R., Luepker, R.V., Jacobs, D.R., & Mittelmark, M.B. (1989). Differences in smoking cessation strategies between men and women. *Addictive Behaviors, 14,* 409–418.

Bloch, M., & White, L.D. (1990, October). *The Women Versus Smoking Network: Mobilizing the women's community to tackle tobacco.* Paper presented at the 118th Annual Meeting of the American Public Health Association, New York.

Brownell, K.D., Marlatt, G.A., Lichtenstein, E., & Wilson, G.T. (1986). Understanding and preventing relapse. *American Psychologist, 41*, 765–782.

Buckley, J.D., Hobbie, W.L., Ruccione, K., Sather, H.N., Woods, W.G., & Hammond, G.D. (1986). Maternal smoking during pregnancy and the risk of childhood cancer [Letter to the Editor]. *Lancet, 76*, 520.

Butler, N., & Golding, J. (1986). *From birth to five*. Oxford, UK: Pergamon.

Butler, N., & Goldstein, H. (1973). Smoking in pregnancy and subsequent child development. *British Medical Journal, 4*, 573–575.

Byrd, J.C., Shapiro, R.S., & Schiedermayer, D.L. (1989). Passive smoking: A review of medical and legal issues. *American Journal of Public Health, 79*, 209–215.

CDC (1991). Cigarette smoking among adults. *Morbidity & Mortality Weekly Report, 40*(44), 757–765.

Chandler, W.V. (1988, January/February). Smoking epidemic widens. *World Watch*, Article #81(3), 39–40.

Chapman, S. (1985). Stop smoking clinics: A case for their abandoment. *Lancet, 1*, 918–920.

Chapman, S., & Richardson, J. (1990). Tobacco excise and declining tobacco consumption: The case of Papua New Guinea. *American Journal of Public Health, 80*, 537–540.

Charlton, A. (1984). Smoking and weight control in teenagers. *Public Health, 98*, 277–281.

Chassin, L., Presson, C.C., & Sherman, S.J. (1984). Cognitive and social influence factors in adolescent smoking cessation. *Addictive Behaviors, 9*, 383–390.

Chow, W.H., Daling, J.R., Weiss, N.S., & Voigt, L.A. (1988). Maternal cigarette smoking and tubal pregnancy. *Obstetrics and Gynecology, 71*, 167–170.

Cohen, R.Y., Sattler, J., Felix, M.R.J., & Brownell, K.D. (1987). Experimentation with smokeless tobacco and cigarettes by children and adolescents: Relationship to beliefs, peer use and perinatal use. *American Journal of Public Health, 77*, 1454–1456.

Cohen, S., Lichtenstein, E., Prochaska, J.O., Rossi, J.S., Gritz, E.R., Carr, C.R., Orleans, C.T., Schoenbach, V.J., Biener, L., Abrams, D., DiClemente, C., Curry, S., Marlatt, G.A., Cummings, K.M., Emont, S.L., Giovino, G., & Ossip-Klein, D. (1989). Debunking myths about self-quitting: Evidence from 10 prospective studies of persons who attempt to quit smoking by themselves. *American Psychologist, 44*, 1355–1365.

Coppotelli, H.C., & Orleans, C.T. (1985). Partner support and other determinants of smoking cessation maintenance among women. *Journal of Consulting and Clinical Psychology, 53*, 455–460.

Coreil, J., Ray, L.A., & Markides, K.S. (1991). Predictors of smoking among Mexican-Americans: Findings from the Hispanic HANES. *Preventive Medicine, 20*, 508–517.

Correa, P., Pickle, L., Fontham, G., Lin, Y., & Haenszell, W. (1983). Passive smoking and lung cancer. *Lancet, 2*, 595–597.

Covey, L.S., & Tam, D. (1990). Depressive mood, the single-parent home, and adolescent cigarette smoking. *American Journal of Public Health, 80,* 1330–1333.

Crofton, J. (1990). Tobacco and the third world. *Thorax, 45,* 164–169.

Cullen, J.W., McKenna, J.W., & Massey, M.M. (1986). International control of smoking and the U.S. experience. *Chest, 89* (Suppl.), 206s–217s.

Curry, S.J., Marlatt, G.A., Gordon, J., & Baer, J.S. (1988). A comparison of alternative theoretical approaches to smoking cessation and relapse. *Health Psychology, 7,* 545–556.

Davis, A.L., Faust, R., & Ordentlich, M. (1984). Self-help smoking cessation and maintenance programs: A comparative study with 12-month follow-up by the American Lung Association. *American Journal of Public Health, 74,* 1212–1219.

Davis, R.M. (1987). Current trends in cigarette advertising and marketing. *New England Journal of Medicine, 316,* 725–732.

Davis, R.M. (1990, April). *Women and smoking in the United States: How lung cancer became an "equal opportunity" disease.* Paper presented at the Seventh World Conference on Tobacco and Health, Perth, Australia.

Davis, R.M., Healy, P., & Hawk, S.A. (1990). Information on tar and nicotine yields on cigarette packages. *American Journal of Public Health, 80,* 551–553.

DeVesa, J.P., Blot, W.J., & Fraumeni, J.F. (1989). Declining lung cancer rates among young men and women in the United States: A cohort analysis. *Journal of the National Cancer Institute, 81,* 1568–1571.

DiClemente, C.C., Prochaska, J.O., Fairhurst, S.K., Velicer, W.F., Velasquez, M.M., & Rossi, J.S. (1991). The process of smoking cessation: An analysis of precontemplation, contemplation, and preparation stages of change. *Journal of Consulting and Clinical Psychology, 59,* 295–304.

DiFranza, J.R., & Tye, J.B. (1990). Who profits from tobacco sales to children? *Journal of the American Medical Association, 263,* 2784–2787.

Ellickson, P.L., & Bell, R.M. (1990). Drug prevention in junior high: A multi-site longitudinal test. *Science, 24,* 1299–1305.

Epstein, L.H., Grunberg, N.E., Lichtenstein, E., & Evans, R.I. (1989). Smoking research: Basic research, intervention, prevention, and new trends. *Health Psychology, 8,* 705–721.

Ernster, V.L. (1985). Mixed messages for women: A social history of cigarette smoking and advertising. *New York State Journal of Medicine, 85,* 335–340.

Ernster, V.L. (1986). Women, smoking, cigarette advertising and cancer. *Women and Health, 11,* 217–235.

Ershoff, D.H., Mullen, P.D., & Quinn, V.P. (1989). A randomized trial of a serialized self-help smoking cessation program for pregnant women in an HMO. *American Journal of Public Health, 79,* 182–187.

Escobedo, L.G., Anda, R.F., Smith, P.F., Remington, P.L., & Mast, E.E. (1990). Sociodemographic characteristics of cigarette smoking initiation in the United States: Implications for smoking prevention policy. *Journal of the American Medical Association, 264,* 1550–1555.

Farquhar, J.W., Maccoby, N., Wood, P.D., Breitrose, H., Haskell, W.L., Meyer,

A.J., Stern, M.P., Alexander, J.K., Brown, B.W., Jr., McAlister, A.L., & Nash, J.D. (1977). Community education for cardiovascular health. *Lancet, 1,* 1192–1195.

Fielding, J.E., & Piserchia, P.V. (1989). Frequency of worksite health promotion activities. *American Journal of Public Health, 79,* 16–20.

Fingerhut, L.A., Kleinman, J.C., & Kendrick, J.S. (1990). Smoking before, during, and after pregnancy. *American Journal of Public Health, 8,* 541–544.

Fiore, M.C., Novotny, T.E., Pierce, J.P., Giovino, G.A., Hatziandreu, E.J., Newcomb, P.A., Surawicz, T.S., & Davis, R.M. (1990). Methods used to quit smoking in the United States: Do cessation programs help? *Journal of the American Medical Association, 263,* 2760–2765.

Fiore, M.C., Novotny, T.E., Pierce, J.P., Hatziandreu, E.J., Patel, K.M., & Davis, R.M. (1989). Trends in cigarette smoking in the United States. The changing influence of gender and race. *Journal of the American Medical Association, 261,* 49–55.

Fisher, E.B., Jr., Bishop, D.B., Goldmuntz, J., & Jacobs, A. (1988). Implications for the practicing physician of the psychosocial dimensions of smoking. *Chest, 93,* 69S–78S.

Flay, B.F. (1985). Psychosocial approaches to smoking prevention: A review of findings. *Health Psychology, 4,* 449–488.

Flay, B.F., D'Avernas, J.R., Best, J.A., Kersell, M.W., & Ryan, K.B. (1983). Cigarette smoking: Why young people do it and ways of preventing it. In P. McGrath & P. Firestone (Eds.), *Pediatric and adolescent behavioral medicine: Treatment issues* (Volume of behavior therapy and behavioral medicine, pp. 132–183). New York: Springer.

Foege, W.H. (1990). The growing brown plague. *Journal of the American Medical Association, 264,* 1580.

Frank, R.E., Serdula, M., & Abel, G.G. (1987). Bulimic eating behaviors: Association with alcohol and tobacco [Letter to the Editor]. *Public Health, 77,* 369–370.

Garfinkel, L., & Stellman, S.D. (1988). Smoking and lung cancer in women: Findings in a prospective study. *Cancer Research, 48,* 6951–6955.

Garn, S.M., Jonston, M., Ridella, S.A., & Petzold, A.S. (1981). Effects of maternal cigarette smoking on Apgar Scores. *American Journal of Diseases of Children, 135,* 503–406.

Gilchrist, L.D., Schinke, S.R., & Nurius, P. (1989). Reducing onset of habitual smoking among women. *Prevention Medicine, 18,* 235–248.

Glasgow, R.E., Hollis, J.F., Pettigrew, L., Foster, L., Givi, M.J., & Morrisette, G. (1991). Implementing a year-long, worksite-based incentive program for smoking cessation. *American Journal of Health Promotion, 5,* 192–199.

Glasgow, R.E., & Klesges, R.C. (1985). Smoking intervention programs in the workplace. In *The health consequences of smoking, cancer and chronic lung disease in the workplace: A report of the Surgeon General* (DHHS

Publication No. PHS 85-50207, pp. 475–515). Rockville, MD: U.S. Government Printing Office.

Glassman, A.H., Helzer, J.E., Covey, L.S., Cottler, L.B., Stetner, F., Tipp, J.E., & Johnson, J. (1990). Smoking, smoking cessation and major depression. *Journal of the American Medical Association, 264,* 1546–1549.

Glynn, T.J. (1989). Essential elements of school-based smoking prevention programs. *Journal of School Health, 59,* 181–186.

Glynn, T.J., & Manley, M.W. (1989). *How to help your patients stop smoking: A National Cancer Institute Manual for physicians* (National Institutes of Health Publication 89-3064). Bethesda, MD: U.S. Department of Health and Human Services.

Goldstein, A.O., Fischer, P.M., Richards, J.W., Jr., & Creten, D. (1987). Relationship between high school student smoking and recognition of cigarette advertisements. *Journal of Pediatrics, 110,* 488–491.

Gritz, E.R. (1980). Problems related to the use of tobacco by women. In O. Kalant (Ed.), *Advances in alcohol and drug problems in women* (Vol. 5, pp. 487–544). New York: Plenum.

Gritz, E.R. (1984). Cigarette smoking by adolescent females: Implications for health and behavior. *Women and Health, 9,* 103–115.

Gritz, E.R. (1986). Gender and the teen-age smoker. In B. Ray & M. Braude (Eds.), *Women and drugs: A new era for research* (National Institute on Drug Abuse Monograph 65, pp. 70–79). Rockville, MD: U.S. Department of Health and Human Services, Public Health Service, Alcohol, Drug Abuse, and Mental Health Administration.

Gritz, E.R., Berman, B.A., Read, L.L., Marcus, A.C., & Siau, J. (1990). Weight change among registered nurses in a self-help smoking cessation program. *American Journal of Health Promotion, 5,* 115–121.

Gritz, E.R., Carr, C.R., & Marcus, A.C. (1988). Unaided smoking cessation: Great American Smokeout and New Year's Day quitters. *Journal of Psychosocial Oncology, 6,* 41–63.

Gritz, E.R., & Crane, L.A. (1991). Use of diet pills and amphetamines to lose weight among smoking and nonsmoking high school seniors. *Health Psychology, 10,* 330–336.

Gritz, E.R., DiMatteo, M.R., & Hays, R.D. (1989). Methodological issues in adherence to cancer control regimens. *Prevention Medicine, 18,* 711–720.

Gritz, E.R., Klesges, R.C., & Meyers, A.W. (1989). The smoking and body weight relationship: Implications for interventions and postcessation weight control. *Annals of Behavioral Medicine, 11,* 144–153.

Gritz, E.R., Marcus, A.C., Berman, B.A., Read, L.L., Kanim, L.E.A., & Reeder, S.J. (1988). Evaluation of a worksite self-help smoking cessation program for registered nurses. *American Journal of Health Promotion, 3,* 26–35.

Gross, J., Stitzer, M.L., & Maldonado, J. (1989). Nicotine replacement: Effects on post-cessation weight gain. *Journal of Consulting and Clinical Psychology, 57,* 87–92.

Grunberg, N.E., Winders, S.E., & Wewers, M.E. (1991). Gender differences in tobacco use. *Health Psychology, 10,* 143–153.

Haglund, B., & Cnattingius, S. (1990). Cigarette smoking as a risk factor for Sudden Infant Death Syndrome: A population-based study. *American Journal of Public Health, 80,* 29–32.

Hall, S.M., Ginsberg, D., & Jones, R.T. (1986). Smoking cessation and weight gain. *Journal of Consulting and Clinical Psychology, 54,* 342–346.

Hatziandreu, E.J., Pierce, J.P., Lefkopoulou, M., Fiore, M.C., Mills, S.L., Novotny, T.E., Giovino, G.A., & Davis, R.M. (1990). Quitting smoking in the United States in 1986. *Journal of the National Cancer Institute, 82,* 1402–1406.

Haynes, S.G., Harvey, C., Montes, H., Nickens, H., & Cohen, B.H. (1990). Patterns of cigarette smoking among Hispanics in the United States: Results from HHANES 1982–84. *American Journal of Public Health, 80,* (Suppl.), 47–53.

Heimann, R.K. (1960). *Tobacco and Americans.* New York: McGraw-Hill.

Howe, H. (1984). An historical review of women, smoking and advertising. *Health Education, 15,* 3–8.

Hymowitz, N., Campbell, K., & Feuerman, M. (1991). Long-term smoking intervention at the worksite: Effects of quit-smoking groups and an "enriched milieu" on smoking cessation in adult white-collar employees. *Health Psychology, 10,* 366–369.

Jacobson, B., Amos, A., & Aghi, M. (1989). World no tobacco day: A challenge for women's health. *The Lancet, 1* (8648), 1193–1194.

Johnston, L.D., O'Malley, P.M., & Bachman, J.G. (1989). Drug use, drinking, and smoking: National survey results from high school, college, and young adult populations 1975-1988 (DHHS Publication No. ADM 89-1638). Rockville, MD: U.S. Department of Health and Human Services, Public Health Service, Alcohol, Drug Abuse, and Mental Health Administration, National Institute on Drug Abuse.

Kandel, D.B., & Logan, J.A. (1984). Patterns of drug use from adolescence to young adulthood. I: Periods of risk for initiation, continued use, and discontinuation. *American Journal of Public Health, 74,* 660–666.

Kaplan, M., Carriker, L., & Waldron, I. (1990). Gender differences in tobacco use in Kenya. *Social Science and Medicine, 30,* 305–310.

Khoury, M.J., Weinstein, A., Panny, S., Holtzman, N.A., Lindsay, P.K., Farrel, K., & Eisenberg, M. (1987). Maternal cigarette smoking and oral clefts: A population-based study. *American Journal of Public Health, 77,* 623–625.

Killen, J.D., Taylor, C.B., Telch, M.J., Robinson, T.N., Maron, D.J., & Saylor, K.E. (1987). Depressive symptoms and substance use among adolescent binge eaters and purgers: A defined population study. *American Journal of Public Health, 77,* 1539–1541.

Kleinman, J.C., & Kopstein, A. (1987). Smoking during pregnancy, 1967-1980. *American Journal of Public Health, 77,* 823–825.

Klesges, R.C., Brown, K., Pascale, R.W., Murphy, M., Williams, E., & Cigrang, J.A. (1988). Factors associated with participation, attrition, and outcome in a smoking cessation program at the workplace. *Health Psychology, 7,* 575–589.

Kline, J., Stein, Z.A., Susser, M., & Warburton, D. (1977). Smoking: A risk factor for spontaneous abortion. *The New England Journal of Medicine, 297,* 793–796.

Kottke, T.E., Battista, R.N., DeFriese, G.H., & Brekke, M.L. (1988). Attributes of successful smoking cessation interventions in medical practice: A meta-analysis of 39 controlled trials. *Journal of the American Medical Association, 259,* 2883–2889.

Kottke, T.E., Blackburn, H., Brekke, M.L., & Solberg, L.I. (1987). The systematic practice of preventive cardiology. *The American Journal of Cardiology, 59,* 690–694.

Kramer, M.S. (1987). Intrauterine growth and gestational duration determinants. *Pediatrics, 80,* 502–511.

Longsdon, D.H., Lazaro, C.M., & Meier, R.V. (1989). The feasibility of behavioral risk reduction in primary medical care. *American Journal of Preventive Medicine, 5,* 249–256.

Marin, G., Perez-Stable, E.J., & Marin, B.V. (1989). Cigarette smoking among San Francisco Hispanics: The role of acculturation and gender. *American Journal of Public Health, 79,* 196–198.

Mayer, J.P., Hawkins, B., & Todd, R. (1990). A randomized evaluation of smoking cessation interventions for pregnant women at a WIC clinic. *American Journal of Public Health, 80,* 76–78.

McLellan, D.L. (1990, October). *The women's international network on smoking.* Paper presented at the 118th Annual Meeting of the American Public Health Association, New York.

Meade, C.D., & Byrd, J.C. (1989). Patient literacy and the readability of smoking education literature. *American Journal of Public Health, 79,* 204–296.

Mecklenburg, R.E. (1990). The National Cancer Institute's invitation to dental professionals in smoking cessation. *Journal of the American Dental Association* (January Suppl.), pp. 40S–41S.

Meichenbaum, D., & Turk, D.C. (1987). *Facilitating treatment adherence: A practitioner's guidebook.* New York: Plenum.

Mermelstein, R., Cohen, S., Lichtenstein, E., Baer, J.S., & Kamarck, D. (1986). Social support and smoking cessation and maintenance. *Journal of Consulting and Clinical Psychology, 54,* 447–453.

Mermelstein, R., Lichtenstein, E., & McIntyre, K. (1983). Partner support and relapse in smoking-cessation programs. *Journal of Consulting and Clinical Psychology, 51,* 465–466.

Meyer, M.B., & Tonascia, J.A. (1977). Maternal smoking, pregnancy complications, and perinatal mortality. *American Journal of Obstetrics and Gynecology, 128,* 494–502.

Miller, W.J., & Hunter, L. (1990). The relationship between socioeconomic status and household smoking patterns in Canada. *American Journal of Health Promotion, 5,* 36–42.

Mittelmark, M.B., Murray, D.M., Luepker, R.V., Pechacek, T.F., Pirie, P.L., & Pallonen, U.E. (1987). Predicting experimentation with cigarettes: The childhood antecedents study. *American Journal of Public Health, 77,* 206–208.

Morgan, G.D., Ashenberg, Z.S., & Fisher, E.B. (1988). Abstinence from smoking and the social environment. *Journal of Consulting and Clinical Psychology, 56,* 298–301.

Mullen, P.D., Quinn, V.P., & Ershoff, D.H. (1990). Maintenance of nonsmoking by women who stopped smoking during pregnancy. *American Journal of Public Health, 80,* 992–994.

Naeye, R.L., & Peters, E.C. (1984). Mental development of children whose mothers smoked during pregnancy. *Obstetrics and Gynecology, 64,* 601–607.

National Institute of Education. (1979). *Teen-age smoking: Immediate and long-term patterns.* Washington, DC: Author.

Novotny, T.E., Fiore, M.C., Hatziandreu, E.J., Giovino, G.A., Mills, S.L., & Pierce, J.P. (1990). Trends in smoking by age and sex, United States, 1974-1987: The implications for disease impact. *Preventive Medicine, 19,* 552–561.

Ockene, J.K. (1984). Toward a smoke-free society [Editorial]. *American Journal of Public Health, 74,* 1198–1200.

O'Keefe, A.M. (1990, October). *Targeted marketing: Selling cigarettes to women.* Paper presented at the 118th Annual Meeting of the American Public Health Association, New York.

Orlandi, M.A. (1986). Gender differences in smoking cessation. *Women and Health, 11,* 237–251.

Orleans, C.T. (1985). Understanding and promoting smoking cessation: Overview and guidelines for physician intervention. *Annual Review of Medicine, 36,* 51–61.

Orleans, C.T., Rimer, B.K., Cristinzio, S., Keintz, M.K., & Fleisher, L. (1991). A national survey of older smokers: Treatment needs of a growing population. *Health Psychology, 10,* 343–351.

Orleans, C.T., Schoenbach, V.J., Salmon, M.A., Strecher, V.J., Kalsbeek, W., Quade, D., Brooks, E.F., Konrad, R., Blackmon, C., & Watts, C.D. (1989). A survey of smoking and quitting patterns among Black Americans. *American Journal of Public Health, 79,* 176–181.

Perez-Stable, E.J., Marin, B.V., Marin, G., Brody, D.J., & Benowitz, N.L. (1990). Apparent underreporting of cigarette consumption among Mexican-American smokers. *American Journal of Public Health, 80,* 1057–1061.

Peterson, D.R. (1981). The sudden infant death syndrome—reassessment of growth retardation in relation to maternal smoking and the hypoxia hypothesis. *American Journal of Epidemiology, 113,* 583–589.

Pierce, J.P. (1989). International comparisons of trends in cigarette smoking prevalence. *American Journal of Public Health, 79,* 152–157.

Pierce, J.P., Fiore, M.C., Novotny, T.E., Hatziandreu, E.J., & Davis, R.M. (1989a). Trends in cigarette smoking in the United States: Projections to the year 2000. *Journal of the American Medical Association, 261,* 61–65.

Pierce, J.P., Fiore, M.C., Novotny, T.E., Hatziandreu, E.J., & Davis, R.M. (1989b). Trends in cigarette smoking in the United States: Educational differences are increasing. *Journal of the American Medical Association, 261,* 56–60.

Pierce, J.P., Macaskill, P., & Hill, D. (1990). Long-term effectiveness of mass media antismoking campaigns in Australia. *American Journal of Public Health, 80,* 565–569.

Pierce, J.P., Naquin, M., Gilpin, E., Giovino, G., Mills, S., & Marcus, S. (1991). Smoking initiation in the United States: A role for worksite and college smoking bans. *Journal of the National Cancer Institute, 83,* 1009–1013.

Prochaska, J.O., & DiClemente, C.C. (1983). Stages and process of self-change of smoking: Toward an integrative model of change. *Journal of Consulting and Clinical Psychology, 51,* 390–395.

Rantakallio, P. (1983). A follow-up study to the age of 14 of children whose mothers smoked during pregnancy. *Acta Paediatrica Scandinavica, 72,* 747–753.

Robert, J.C. (1952). *The story of tobacco in America.* New York: Knopf.

Rodin, J., & Ickovics, J.R. (1990). Women's health: Review and research agenda as we approach the 21st century. *American Psychologist, 45,* 1018–1034.

Roemer, R. (1991, November). *Overview of world legislation to control tobacco use.* Paper presented at the 119th Annual Meeting of the American Public Health Association, Atlanta, GA.

Rose, J., Levin, E.D., Behm, F.M., Adivi, C., & Schur, C. (1990). Transdermal nicotine facilitates smoking cessation. *Clinical and Pharmacological Therapy, 47,* 323–330.

Sachs, D.P.L. (1990). Smoking cessation strategies: What works, what doesn't. *Journal of the American Dental Association* (January Suppl.), pp. 13S–19S.

Salonen, J.T., Puska, P., Kottke, T.E., & Tuomilehto, J. (1981). Changes in smoking, serum cholesterol, and blood pressure levels during a community-based cardiovascular disease prevention program—The North Karelia Project. *American Journal of Epidemiology, 114,* 81–94.

Schneider, S.J., Benya, A., & Singer, H. (1984). Computerized direct mail to treat smokers who avoid treatment. *Computers and Biomedical Research, 17,* 409–418.

Schwartz, J.L. (1987). *Review and evaluation of smoking cessation methods: The United States and Canada, 1978–1985* (Publication No. 87-2940). Washington, DC: Division of Cancer Prevention and Control, National Cancer Institute, USDHHS, Public Health Service, National Institutes of Health.

Sexton, M., & Hebel, J.R. (1984). A clinical trial of change in maternal smoking and its effect on birth weight. *Journal of the American Medical Association, 251*, 911–915.

Smoking and Health: A National Status Report. A Report to Congress. (1987). Rockville, MD: USDHHS, Centers for Disease Control, Public Health Service, Center for Health Promotion and Education, Office on Smoking and Health.

Solberg, L.I. (1988). Implementing a tobacco cessation program in clinical practice. *Medical Times, 116*, 119–124.

Sorensen, G., & Pechacek, T.F. (1987). Attitudes toward smoking cessation among men and women. *Journal of Behavioral Medicine, 10*, 129–137.

Stellman, S.D., Boffetta, P., & Garfinkel, L. (1988). Smoking habits of 800,000 American men and women in relation to their occupations. *American Journal of Industrial Medicine, 13*, 43–58.

Stellman, S.D., & Garfinkel, L. (1989). Proportions of cancer deaths attributable to cigarette smoking in women, 1988. *Women and Health, 15*, 19–28.

Stjernfeldt, J., Lindsten, J., Berglund, K., & Ludvigsson, J. (1986). Maternal smoking during pregnancy and risk of childhood cancer. *Lancet, 1*, 1350–1352.

Straeter, J.A., Sargent, R.G., & Ward, D.S. (1989). A study of factors associated with weight change in women who attempt smoking cessation. *Addictive Behaviors, 14*, 523–530.

Sutton, S. (1989). Relapse following smoking cessation: A critical review of current theory and research. In M. Gossop (Ed.), *Relapse and addictive behavior*. London: Rutledge.

Swan, G.E., Denk, C.E., Parker, S.D., Carmelli, D., Furze, C.T., & Rosenman, R.H. (1988). Risk factors for late relapse in male and female ex-smokers. *Addictive Behaviors, 13*, 253–266.

Taylor, B., & Wadsworth, J. (1987). Maternal smoking during pregnancy and lower respiratory tract illness in early life. *Archives of Disease in Childhood, 62*, 786–791.

Tonnesen, P., Norregaard, J., Simonson, K., & Sawe, U. (1991). A double-blind trial of a 16-hour transdermal nicotine patch in smoking cessation. *New England Journal of Medicine, 325*, 311–315.

U.S. Department of Health, Education and Welfare. (1980). *The health consequences of smoking for women. A report of the Surgeon General*. Washington, DC: U.S. Government Printing Office.

U.S. Department of Health and Human Services. (1988). *The health consequences of smoking: Nicotine addiction. A report of the Surgeon General* (DHHS Publication No. CDC 88-8406) Washington, DC: U.S. Government Printing Office.

U.S. Department of Health and Human Services. (1989). *Reducing the health consequences of smoking: 25 years of progress. A report of the Surgeon General* (DHHS Publication No. CDC 90-8416). Washington, DC: U.S. Government Printing Office.

U.S. Department of Health and Human Services. (1990). *The health benefits of smoking cessation. A report of the Surgeon General* (DHHS Publication No. CDC 90-8416). Washington, DC: U.S. Government Printing Office.

Waldron, I., Bratelli, G., Carriker, L., Sung, W.C., Vogeli, C., & Waldman, E. (1988). Gender differences in tobacco use in Africa, Asia, the Pacific and Latin America. *Social Science and Medicine, 27,* 1269–1275.

Waldron, I., & Lye, D. (1989). Employment, unemployment, occupation, and smoking. *American Journal of Preventive Medicine, 5,* 142–149.

Wallett, R., & Sutton, S.R. (1988). Intervening against smoking in the workplace. *Psychology and Health, 2,* 13–29.

Warner, K.E. (1985). Cigarette advertising and media coverage of smoking and health. *New England Journal of Medicine, 312,* 384–388.

Warner, K.E. (1990). Tobacco taxation as health policy in the third world. *American Journal of Public Health, 80,* 529–531.

Warner, K.E., & Connolly, G.N. (1991). Viewpoint. The global metastasis of the Marlboro man. *American Journal of Health Promotion, 5,* 325–327.

White, L., & Whelan, E.M. (1986). How well do American magazines cover the health hazards of smoking? The 1986 survey. *ACSH News and Views, 7,* 7–10.

Wilbert, J. (1975). Magico-religious use of tobacco among Southern American Indians. In V: Rubin (Ed.), *Cannabis and culture* (pp. 439–461). The Hague: Mouton.

Williamson, D.F., Madans, J., Anda, R.F., Kleinman, J.C., Giovino, G.A., & Byers, T. (1991). Smoking cessation and severity of weight gain in a national cohort. *New England Journal of Medicine, 324,* 739–745.

Williamson, D.F., Serdula, M.K., Kendrick, J.S., & Binkin, N.J. (1989). Comparing the prevalence of smoking in pregnant and nonpregnant women, 1985 to 1986. *Journal of the American Medical Association, 261,* 70–74.

Wilner, S. (1985). Efforts to change smoking and drinking behavior in pregnant women. In Committee to Study the Prevention of Low Birth Weight, Institute of Medicine (Ed.), *Preventing low birth weight.* Washington, DC: National Academy Press.

Windsor, R.A., Cutter, G., Morris, J., Reese, Y., Manzella, B., Bartlett, E.E., Samuelson, C., & Spanos, D. (1985). The effectiveness of smoking cessation methods for smokers in public health maternity clinics: A randomized trial. *American Journal of Public Health, 75,* 1389–1392.

Wong-McCarthy, W.J., & Gritz, E.R. (1982). Preventing regular teen-age cigarette smoking. *Pediatric Annals, 11,* 683–689.

Yankelovich, Skelly, & White, Inc. (1977). *A study of cigarette smoking among teen-age girls and young women: Summary of findings* (DHEW Publication No. NIH 77-1203). Washington, DC: Department of Health, Education and Welfare, Public Health Service, National Institutes of Health, National Cancer Institute.

Yu, J.J., Mattson, M.E., Boyd, G.M., Mueller, M.D., Shopland, D.R., Pechacek, T.F., & Cullen, J.W. (1990). A comparison of smoking patterns in the People's Republic of China with the United States. An impending health catastrophe in the middle kingdom. *Journal of the American Medical Association, 264,* 1575–1579.

Chapter 12

The Relationship of Eating Disorders and Substance Abuse*

Dean D. Krahn, M.D.
Director of Research in Eating Disorders
Dept. of Psychiatry
University of Wisconsin
Madison, WI

INTRODUCTION

Initial interest in the relationship between eating disorders, which occur primarily in women, and substance abuse, which is much more frequent in men than women, stemmed from the observations of Crisp (1968) who noted that chronic anorexics who developed bulimic behavior often abused alcohol. More recently, cross-sectional studies of women with eating disorders have documented prevalences of alcohol and other substance abuse in these women which are much higher than

* This work was supported by NIDA grants 06791-01 and 06827-01.

those reported in the general female population. Conversely, women with substance abuse disorders report eating-disordered behavior more often than the general population. Identification and study of high-risk groups (such as sons of male alcoholics) has been an important strategy used in research on the pathogenesis of substance abuse in recent years (Tarter, 1988). If people (mostly women) with eating disorders or related behaviors are a high-risk group for the development of substance use disorders, then it is possible that the study of dieting women might also be fruitful. This chapter first presents a definition of eating disorders and then addresses: (a) the rate of coprevalance of eating disorders and substance abuse, (b) the mechanism of the coprevalence of these disorders, (c) the clinical similarities of these disorders, and (d) future directions.

DEFINITION OF EATING DISORDERS

Eating disorders include anorexia nervosa, bulimia nervosa, and the poorly defined, but not necessarily less severe category, eating disorders not otherwise specified. Figure 12.1 shows the DSM-IIIR criteria for diagnosis of these disorders. For the purposes of this article, obesity will not be defined as an eating disorder, although a subset of obese people are bulimic in that they are prone to the same cycles of severe deprivation followed by overconsumption seen in low-weight or normal-weight patients. The clinical features of eating disorders have been reviewed extensively elsewhere (Eckert, 1985; Mitchell, 1985), but a few points are emphasized for the purposes of this chapter.

Anorexia nervosa can be diagnosed in about 0.5–1% of young women (Crisp, Palmer, & Kalucy, 1976) while bulimia nervosa is found in 3% of this group (Drewnowski, Yee, & Krahn, 1988a). Both disorders usually begin in adolescence, but can be present at any age. Rates of these eating disorders in men are less than one-tenth of the rates in women (Anderson & Mickalide, 1983). It is important to note that the primary symptom of both disorders is a pursuit of thinness or an ideal body shape which drives the patient to employ such behaviors as rigid dieting, fasting, overexercising, and purging. Thus, self-imposed food deprivation in the pursuit of thinness is the core abnormality of eating in these patients, even though the more spectacular binging and purging behaviors often receive more attention in the popular press. As the sociocultural pressure on men to achieve thinness is arguably less, men seem to employ dieting and other weight-loss strategies less (Anderson, 1986), although pursuit of an ideal body may be in part driving a new type of substance abuse, anabolic steroid abuse (Brower,

Table 12.1.   Diagnostic Criteria for Anorexia Nervosa and Bulimia Nervosa

Anorexia Nervosa	Bulimia Nervosa
Refusal to maintain body weight over a minimal normal weight for age and height, e.g., weight loss leading to maintenance of body weight 15% below that expected; or failure to make expected weight gain during period of growth, leading to body weight 15% below that expected.	Recurrent episodes of binge eating (rapid consumption of a large amount of food in a discrete period of time).
Intense fear of gaining weight or becoming fat, even though underweight.	A feeling of lack of control over eating behavior during the eating binges.
Disturbance in the way in which one's body weight, size, or shape is experienced, e.g., the person claims to "feel fat" even when emaciated, believes that one area of the body is "too fat" even when obviously underweight.	The person regularly engages in either self-induced vomiting, use of laxatives or diuretics, strict dieting or fasting, or vigorous exercise in order to prevent weight gain.
In females, absence of at least 3 consecutive menstrual cycles when otherwise expected to occur (primary or secondary amenorrhea). (A woman is considered to have amenorrhea if her periods occur only following hormone, e.g., estrogen, administration.)	A minimum average of two binge eating episodes a week for at least 3 months.
	Persistent overconcern with body shape and weight.

Eliopulos, Blow, Catlin, & Beresford, 1990). One poorly understood part of the pathogenesis of eating disorders is the factor or factors which determine the progression of some women from dieting (which is practiced by greater than 85% of college women) (Krahn, Kurth, Demitrack, & Drewnowski, 1992) to eating disorders (which are present in the smaller numbers described above).

While some young women manage to achieve weights consistent with anorexia nervosa via simple restriction of caloric intake, far more suffer a breakdown in their rigid self-deprivation and binge-eat. This binge-eating usually involves intense cravings for "forbidden," sweet and/or high-fat foods, followed by consumption of large amounts of these foods in episodes during which patients report feeling "out-of-control." While binge-eating is an understandable and predictable response to semistarvation which has been seen in men starved under laboratory conditions (Franklin, Schiele, Brozek, & Keys, 1948), these women feel guilty about their dietary indiscretions and often purge to avoid the weight-increase consequences of binging. Unfortunately, purging only returns the patient to the state of self-deprivation marked by tension, food cravings, and hunger, which precipitated the binge, and often the patient becomes locked in a cycle of self-deprivation→binge→guilt→purge→self deprivation→binge which is reminiscent of the cyclic behavior of substance abusers (Abraham & Beumont, 1982; Garner, Rockert, Olmsted, Johnson, & Coscina, 1985). Likewise, use of diet pills and laxatives often take on cyclic, repetitive characteristics.

Both anorexia nervosa and bulimia nervosa can have chronic courses marked by remissions (Mitchell, 1985) and relapses. It is important to note, however, as did Vandereycken (1990), that such similarities in longitudinal course do not prove a relationship. Both disorders can have severe physical and psychological consequences. Mortality rates ranging from 0–22% have been reported to follow-up studies of anorexic patients (Mitchell, 1985). Most deaths result from suicide or cardiovascular collapse. The morbidity and mortality rates for bulimia nervosa without anorexia nervosa is not known. Many of these patients suffer from repeated bouts of depression as well as obsessive-compulsive and self-harmful behaviors. Furthermore, many of these patients abuse not only laxatives and diet pills, but also other substances that have been the more traditional substances of interest for those who treat chemical dependency.

THE RATE OF COPREVALENCE OF EATING DISORDERS AND SUBSTANCE ABUSE

Studies of the relationship between eating disorders and substance abuse have occurred in two main types: (a) those using a clinical population being treated for one of the two disorders and studying the prevalence of the "other" disorder, and (b) those studies which screen larger community samples for the prevalence of symptoms of each disorder. We examine the clinical studies first, then turn to those complementary studies which used the community samples.

The frequency of substance abuse in eating-disordered clinical populations has been far more extensively studied than the frequency of eating disorders in substance abuse patients. Crisp (1968) was one of the first to comment on the relationship between anorexia with bulimia and alcoholism stating that "chronic patients who have progressed to a state of overeating and vomiting not infrequently appear to become dominated by oral behavior, and may sometimes present with alcoholism" (p. 372). Numerous cross-sectional studies have since demonstrated that female patients presenting with eating disorders, including anorexia and bulimia nervosa, have high prevalences of alcohol and other drug abuse (Beary, Lacey, & Merry, 1986; Brisman & Siegel, 1984; Cantwell, Sturzenberg, Burrough, Salkin, & Green, 1977; Carroll & Leon, 1981; Eckert, Goldberg, Halmi, Casper, & Davis, 1979; Eckert, Goldberg, Halmi, Casper, & Davis, 1982; Ewing, 1987; Frank, Serdula, & Abel, 1987; Gwirtsman, Roy-Bryne, Yager, & Gerner, 1983; Hatsukami, Eckert, Mitchell, & Pyle, 1984; Hatsukami, Owen, Pyle, & Mitchell, 1982; Herzog, 1982; Hudson, Pope, Jonas, & Yurgelun-Todd, 1983; Jonas, Gold Sweeney, & Pottash, 1987; Jones, Cheshire, & Moorhouse, 1985; Johnston, O'Malley, & Bachman, 1985; Kassett et al., 1989; Killen et al., 1987; Leon, Carroll, Chernyk, & Finn, 1985; Lundholm, 1989; Marcus & Halmi, 1989; Mitchell, Hatsukami, Eckert, & Pyle, 1985; Mitchell, Hatsukami, Pyle, & Eckert, 1988; Pyle, Mitchell, & Eckert, 1981; Pyle et al., 1983; Strober, Salkin, Burroughs, & Morrell, 1982; Weiss & Ebert, 1983). Table 12.2 shows a compilation of findings from studies in which clinical eating disordered populations were assessed for substance use and abuse, and substance abuse populations were assessed for eating disorders. Almost all of these reports support the hypothesis that substance abuse occurs more often in patients with eating disorders and eating disorders occur more often in patients with substance abuse than either disorder occurs in the general population.

Cantwell et al. (1977) reported that 23% of 26 anorexic patients had developed alcoholism or alcohol abuse. Eckert et al. (1982), in a larger sample, found a 6.7% incidence of alcoholism or probable alcoholism by RDC criteria in 105 anorexics, with patients with alcohol problems being found predominantly in the group who also had problems with bulimia and kleptomania. This incidence of alcoholism is high, and is even higher when one considers that the average age of this sample was 20 years. When one looks at studies of normal-weight bulimics, even higher rates are reported. For example, Mitchell et al. (1985) reported that 49% of a large sample of 275 bulimia nervosa patients collected at a university-based clinic reported using alcohol several times per week or more. This contrasts with the 3.5% of women of similar ages who report daily alcohol use in nationwide surveys (Johnston, O'Malley & Bachman, 1985). Pyle, Mitchell, and Eckert (1981) and Beary et al. (1986) reported that 24% and 50%, respectively, of their patients with bulimia nervosa had clinically significant substance abuse problems. Pyle et al. (1981) reported in their initial description of normal-weight bulimia that 24% of their bulimic patients had significant chemical-dependency problems. At the time of evaluation, 41% were using alcohol at least several times a week and 18% were using it daily; 21% reported intermittent amphetamine abuse, while 12% admitted to daily amphetamine use. Beary et al. (1986)

compared 20 consecutive alcoholic women under age 40 with 20 age-matched patients with bulimia nervosa and 17 age-matched normal controls. Thirty-five percent of alcoholics had a previous major eating disorder while 50% of the bulimics either abused alcohol or used it to excess. Both bulimic and alcoholic subjects had a history of larger swings in weight than controls. Weiss and Ebert (1983) reported that significantly more bulimics than normal controls used marijuana, cocaine, amphetamines, and barbiturates. However, all of these reports on the abuse of substances by women with eating disorders need to be compared with the rate of substance abuse in women with other psychiatric disorders.

Conversely, cross-sectional studies of clinical populations have shown a high prevalence of eating disorders in female patients presenting with substance abuse (Beary, Lacey, & Merry, 1986; Marcus & Halmi, 1989) (see Table 12.2). As noted above, Beary et al. (1986) found that the alcoholic women studied had a 35% rate of a previous or ongoing eating disorder. Marcus and Halmi (1989) reported that slightly more than half of female patients presenting for substance abuse treatment in a psychiatric hospital met DSM-III R criteria for an eating disorder. While alcohol is the most frequent drug abused by patients with eating disorders, abusers of other substances also have eating disorders. Jonas et al. (1987) documented a high incidence of eating disorders in females calling for help with cocaine abuse and dependence. Because the eating disorder often antedated the substance abuse, these investigators did not feel that they were misdiagnosing the acute anorexia of cocaine intoxication and the overeating of cocaine withdrawal as an eating disorder.

Thus, it is clear that there is an association between clinical eating disorders and substance abuse in women. Anderson (1986) has reported that men with eating disorders also display a high incidence of alcohol and other drug abuse but, given the much smaller numbers of males with eating disorders, there are no large studies documenting the actual frequencies of this coprevalence.

One could explain the increased coprevalence of alcohol and other substance abuse as an example of a more general phenomenon of psychiatrically-impaired populations demonstrating a higher incidence of substance abuse than normal populations. For example, the Epidemiologic Catchment Area Study of the National Institute of Mental Health (Regier et al., 1990) found that 23.7% of subjects with anxiety disorders and 32% of subjects with affective disorders had at least one substance use disorder. While these rates are comparable to those reported for patients with eating disorders, it must be remembered that the rates reported for the Catchment study reflect the rate

Table 12.2 Studies of Comorbidity of Eating Disorders and Substance Abuse Patients

Eating Disorder Populations

Author	Year	Population	Method	Findings and Comments
Garfinkel et al.	1980	141 anorexia nervosa patients 68 with bulimia and 43 without	clinical interviews with standardized questionnaire	Bulimic anorexic patients used alcohol more frequently and had higher prevalence of street drug use than retricting anorexics.
Pyle et al.	1981	34 DSMIII female bulimic patients	self-report database and clinical interview	8/34 had previous SA treatment; 19/34 used alcohol several times a week; 11/34 used amphetamine intermittently; or more
Hatsukami	1982	53 DSMIII bulimic female patients compared to 120 females in alcohol or drug abuse treatment	MMPI/MacAndrews Scale	Some similarities in MMPI profiles; Inpatient alcohol/drug abusers more disturbed than outpatient bulimic patients.
Weiss & Ebert	1983	15 normal weight, female DSMIII bulimic subjects (not patients) compared with 15 normal weight controls	structured self-report and interview	Bulimic women had a significantly higher prevalence of cocaine, amphetamine, and barbituate use than normals.
Hatsukami et al.	1984	108 female DSMIII bulimic patients	semi-structured interview and self-report database	13.9% had history of past or current alcohol abuse; 10.2% had history of past or current drug abuse; 16.8% used alcohol at least daily.
Henzel	1984	15 (3 male, 12 female) anorexia nervosa patients	Landeen's Self-administered Drinking Problem Questionnaire	33% scored "likely" for alcoholism; 67% reported "drinking problems."
Leon et al.	1985	37 DSMIII bulimic outpatient female patients (57% participation rate)	self-report instrument, the Eating Patterns Questionnaire and MMPI	6.7% previously diagnosed as chemically dependent; 61% reported history of excessive use of alcohol.
Mitchell et al.	1985	275 DSMIII bulimic patients	semi-structured clinical interview and self-report database	34.4% reported history of problems with alcohol or other drugs; 23% had history of alcohol abuse and 17.7% prior treatment for substance abuse.

Author	Year	Population	Method	Findings and Comments
Walsh et al.	1985	50 female DSMIII bulimia patients	SADS interview	14% met criteria for alcohol abuse including 33% of patients with bulimia plus anorexia; 18% had history of drug abuse.
Bulik	1987	35 female, DSMIII bulimics compared with 35 normal controls	structured interview (DIS)	48.6% of bulimics vs. 8.6% of controls had alcohol abuse; 22.9% of bulimics were alcohol dependents and 34.3% were drug dependent.

Substance Abuse Populations

Author	Year	Population	Method	Findings and Comments
Jones et al.	1985	27 mostly female patients primarily from population in alcohol treatment	clinical interview	Authors identified 27 cases of ED and SA comorbidity and observed that ED came first.
Beary et al.	1986	20 DSMIII bulimia nervosa females compared with 20 age-matched alcohol dependent females and 17 age-matched normal controls	semi-structured interview	35% of alcoholics had previous eating disorders; 50% of bulimic patients had history of abuse or excessive use of alcohol.
Lacy & Moureli	1986	27 alcoholic women	clinical interview	40% reported history of "major binge eating"; most dated eating disorder problems earlier than alcohol problems; poorer clinical outcome suggested.
Jones et al.	1987	259 DSMIII cocaine abusers (47% men, 53% women)	structured clinical interview by phone	22% met DSMIII criteria for bulimia; 7% anorexia and bulimia; 2% anorexia: 6.5% possible anorexia.
Peveler & Fairburn	1990	31 female (between 17 and 40 years old) "first attenders" at alcohol treatment	structured self-report instrument including EDE-Q and SAD-Q	36% of subjects binge ate; 26% had probable current eating disorders; 19% had history of probable anorexia nervosa.

of substance use problems in a population of males and females, rather than the often-exclusively female populations used in eating disorders studies. Moreover, subjects drawn from community (i.e., nonclinical) populations with bulimic behaviors which did not meet diagnostic criteria for bulimia nervosa also show a close relationship with alcohol and other substance use.

Killen et al. (1987) reported that high school student subjects with either bulimia or bulimic behaviors reported higher usage rates than normals for cigarettes and marijuana and more frequent episodes of drunkenness. College freshman women who were smokers or drinkers reported higher prevalences of bulimic behaviors (Frank, Serdula, and Abel, 1987). In a study of more than 1,700 (90% response rate) college freshman women, Krahn and colleagues (Krahn, Kurth, Demitrack, & Drewnowski, 1992) found that there was a continuous, graded relationship between six dieting severity categories—ranging from non-dieters to bulimic dieters—and the frequency and intensity of alcohol use, such that the more severely dieting groups consumed alcohol more frequently and more heavily than the less severe dieting groups. Similar relationships were found between dieting severity and frequency of cigarette and marijuana use. Thus, dieting, even at levels which were very routine in this age group, was associated with increased frequency of alcohol and other drug use. Finally, another study which used a community-based sample drawn from a twin registry found that subjects who met criteria for bulimia nervosa according to a standardized interview had a much increased rate of alcohol abuse and dependence (Kendler, MacLean, Neale, Kessler, Heath, & Eaves, 1991). Not all studies using community samples have found this correlation, however.

Xinaris and Boland (Wilson, 1991) did not find a relationship between scores on scales measuring bulimic behaviors and frequency of alcohol use or drunkenness. Wilson (1991), in an extensive review on these issues, also notes that the Epidemiologic Catchment Area study by NIMH (Helzer & Pryzbeck, 1988) failed to show an association between anorexia nervosa and alcoholism. However, this study depended on a structured interview with a very high likelihood of screening out any eating disordered patient who had not met stringent criteria for anorexia nervosa. Table 12.3 shows a compilation of studies of eating and substance use behaviors in community-based samples.

A study at the University of Michigan examined the relationship between dieting behaviors and alcohol use in general psychiatric patients. Our hypothesis was that those patients with histories of frequent dieting or bulimic behaviors would answer more questions positively (i.e., pathologically) on the CAGE screening questionnaire for

Table 12.3   Studies of Relationship of Eating Disordered Behaviors Substance Use in Community Populations

Author	Year	Population	Method	Findings and Comments
Claydon	1987	1302 male and female college freshmen (62% response rate)	standardized self-report questionnaire	Children of alcoholics were more likely to report eating as well as substance abuse problems.
Frank et al.	1987	174 college women and 118 college men	questionnaire	College women who smoked or drank alcohol had higher prevalences of bulimic behavior.
Killen et at.	1991	646 tenth-grade females (100% response rate)	questionnaire	Those with bulimia or bulimia-like syndromes used more cigarettes and marijuana and were drunk more often.
Bradstock et al.	1988	12,467 women from 28 states comprised a national representative study sample	standardized telephone survey of behavioral health risks	Binge drinking occurred more in women with relatively restrictive eating patterns.
Timmerman et al.	1989	1391 male and female high school students (98.6% part).	questionnaire	A positive association between number of bulimic behaviors and alcohol abuse was found in females and a similar, but weaker association was found with boys.
Lundholm	1989	135 females in college introductory psychology classes (? part. rate)	self-report standardized instruments; EDI & Millon	Females with high alcohol use scored higher on four EDI subscales than low alcohol users.
Xinaris & Boland	1990	167 undergraduate college females (59% response rate)	standardized questionnaire including Binge Scale, Restraint Scale, and EAT	Very weak, if any, relationship between alcohol use and binging found.
Kendler et al.	1991	2163 female twins obtained from population registry	SCID interview	Significant comorbidity of alcoholism with bulimia and "bulimia-like" syndrome was found.
Krahn et al.	1992	1796 college freshman females (90% response rate)	questionnaire re: dieting behaviors and alcohol and drug use	A significant relationship between dieting severity and the frequency and intensity of alcohol use was found.

alcoholism (Ewing, 1987). We reviewed the records of 243 consecutive patients between ages 18 and 40 evaluated at the Department of Psychiatry. Patients presenting to the Eating Disorders Clinic and those patients ($n = 6$) given an eating disorder diagnosis at evaluation were excluded. Each patient completed a questionnaire assessing dieting and bulimic behaviors, as well as the CAGE questionnaire. Patients were classified as frequent dieters and as positive or negative for history of pathological weight-control efforts (i.e., purging or fasting behavior consistent with eating disorders). Results showed that 98 of the 236 patients reported a positive history for pathological weight control efforts. In the 98 patients with this positive history, 41.8% responded positively to two or more CAGE questions; only 18.1% of the 138 with a negative history answered similarly. (Chi-square = 16.01, $p < .001$). In these 98 patients with positive history for pathological weight-control efforts, 51% responded positively to one or more CAGE questions, while only 29.7% of those with negative histories answered similarly (Chi-square = 10.99, $p < .001$). From these data it was concluded that, at least in the general psychiatric population, bulimic behavior which does not meet diagnostic criteria for bulimia nervosa carries with it an increased risk of pathological use of alcohol. These data also suggest that a history of bulimic behaviors is associated with a risk of alcohol abuse over and above any increased risk conferred only by being a psychiatric patient.

Obviously, further studies which would quantify alcohol use, other drug use, and a variety of dieting and bulimic behaviors are needed to clarify this relationship. These cross-sectional studies also cannot address the relationship between time of onset or changes in dieting and drug use. The fact that any history of pathologic weight-control behaviors predicts more pathologic use of alcohol supports the possibility that bulimic behaviors signify a trait of increased susceptibility to excessive alcohol and drug use rather than a state which changes with alterations in dieting behaviors.

Thus, there is some evidence that not only bulimia nervosa or anorexia nervosa, but also bulimic behaviors are related to increased alcohol and/or drug abuse. Certainly, these data suggest that eating behaviors should be assessed in all women presenting for any type of substance abuse.

The Mechanism of Coprevalence of These Disorders

There are at least two possible ways to explain the high rates of coprevalence of eating disorders and substance abuse. One possible explanation is that both of these disorders are actually different expressions of the same underlying problem. Another explanation is that one disorder leads to the other disorder (e.g., the restriction of food intake leads to increased susceptibility to drug abuse).

Data support the idea that there is a common underlying pathology for eating disorders and substance abuse. Compared to normal controls or the general population, patients with eating disorders have increased frequencies of positive family histories for alcohol and other drug abuse, as well as depression in most, but not all studies (Brisman & Siegel, 1984; Gwirtsman, Roy-Bryne, Yager, & Gerner, 1983; Herzog, 1982; Hudson, Pope, Jonas, & Yurgelun-Todd, 1983; Jones, Cheshire, & Moorhouse, 1985; Stern et al., 1984; Strober, Salkin, Burroughs, & Morrell, 1982; Wooley & Wooley, 1981). Table 12.3 provides a compilation of relevant studies on the family history of patients with eating disorders. For example, Eckert et al. (1979) found that of 105 anorexics (of whom 6.7% were alcoholic), 16.5% of fathers and 1.9% of mothers were alcoholic. Carroll and Leon (1981) investigated the substance abuse histories of 37 bulimics and their families. While 61% of patients admitted to excessive alcohol use and 46% to excessive drug use, 51% of the sample had at least one first-degree relative with substance abuse problems. However, the rates of substance abuse in the mothers and sisters of these bulimic patients were 14% and 20%, respectively. It is possible that dieting and/or eating disordered behavior in females in these genetically "at-risk" families may trigger an underlying genetic tendency to use alcohol and other drugs.

Perhaps the best study of families of bulimics was reported by Kassett et al. (1989). In a study which employed interviews of not only the patient, but also interviews of family members, Kassett and colleagues reported alcoholism in 30% of families of bulimics vs. 10% of controls. Another important observation, however, by Mitchell et al. (1988) was that the prevalence of periods of alcohol or drug abuse was not significantly different in bulimics who reported a positive family history of chemical abuse (28.4% had periods of chemical abuse) from prevalence in bulimics who reported a negative family history (19.8% had periods of chemical abuse), although the bulimics with positive family histories were more likely to have had treatment for chemical dependency (Mitchell et al., 1988). Those bulimics with a positive family history of substance abuse also reported a history of being overweight more frequently than those bulimics without a positive family history of alcoholism (Mitchell et al., 1988). As dieting is more common in overweight women (Drewnowski, Yee, & Krahn, 1988a), it is possible that women with a positive family history of substance abuse are also more frequently overweight and, therefore, are more frequently dieting. Dieting, in turn, may accentuate their predisposition to substance use/abuse. Nonetheless, while most of the above data

Table 12.4 Studies of Substance Abuse in Families of Eating Disordered Patients

Author	Year	Population	Method	Findings and Comments
Halmi & Loney	1973	94 parental pairs for 94 anorexic patients	chart review	Higher frequency of alcoholism in both fathers and mothers of anorexics than reported for general population.
Herzog et al.	1982	8 adolescent females	FH-RDC standardized method	negative FH/ positive 22% alcoholism in patients.
Strober et al.	1982	35 adolescent bulimic anorexics and 35 restrictor anorexics and families	MMPI & SADS of each patient and first degree family member were done. Indirect evaluation of 2nd degree relatives.	83% of bulimic anorexic patients and 49% of restrictor anorexics had positive FH of alcoholism. Bulimic anorexics had significantly higher + FH rate.
Hudson et al.	1983	420 first degree relatives of male and female ED patients compared to first-degree relatives of other psychiatric patients	clinical interviews with patient and available family members used	44 of 420 first degree relatives of ED patients had alcoholism.
Stern et al.	1984	27 bulimic females and their parents and 27 non-ED females and their parents	separate, semi-structured interviews of patient and parent	No difference in rate of substance use disorders between families of bulimic and non-ED probands.
Rivinus et al.	1984	545 first and second degree relatives of 40 anorexic females and 277 relatives of 23 control females	Family History FDC were applied to data from interviews of parent of subjects	Significantly more ED relatives had depression or substance abuse than non-ED relatives; The difference for substance abuse alone was not significant.

Collins et al.	1985	148 first degree relatives of bulimic anorexics; all older than 18 years old	chart review	12.2% alcoholism in first degree relatives of bulimic anorexics was found which is higher than the general population.
Leon et al.	1985	37 DSMIII bulimic females	self-report form re: family substance use	51% of sample had one or more first degree relatives diagnosed as chemically dependent.
Hudson et al.	1987	283 first-degree relatives to 69 bulimic probands; 104 first-degree relatives of depressed probands; and 149 first-degree relatives of 28 non-psychiatric controls	interviewed probands re: family using standardized methodology	19.1% of relatives of bulimics had substance use disorders versus 9.1% of relatives of depressed and 6.5% of relatives of controls.
Bulik	1987	family history study of 35 bulimic and 35 normals	standardized family history interview (FHRDC)	48.6% of bulimics had first degree relatives with alcoholism versus 20% of the controls.
Kassett et al.	1989	first-degree relatives of 40 bulimic patients compared to first-degree relatives of 24 normal controls ($n = 188$, 62% response)	direct interviews of relatives with SADS-L	33% of first-degree relatives of bulimics vs. 13.6% of relatives of controls had alcoholism. Bulimic family members also abused other drugs more often than control.
Logue et al.	1989	families of 30 ED, 16 depressed, and 20 normal controls (total $n = 340$ first-degree relat.)	DIS by phone	No increased rate of alcoholism or drug abuse in families of EDs; families of depressed patients had higher frequencies of drug abuse than ED families.

would support the hypothesis that eating disorders and alcoholism are different phenotypic expressions of the same underlying abnormality, the Mitchell et al. (1988) study, comparing bulimics with and without positive family histories of alcoholism, could be interpreted as supporting the hypothesis that food intake restriction and/or binge eating can increase the risk of chemical abuse in young women. However, none of the types of family studies which could more clearly differentiate genetic from social influences of alcoholic families have been done.

While family history data suggest that at least some common underlying factors for drug abuse and eating disorders exist, data from experiments in which animals or humans are deprived of food support the hypothesis that self-imposed food deprivation (i.e., dieting) increases drug self-administration. As food deprivation increases preferences for sweet, high-fat foods (i.e., the foods most often included in binges) in animals, and dieting antedates binge eating in bulimics, one might hypothesize that food deprivation leads to binge eating and drug abuse in these patients.

Food deprivation is one of the most potent environmental stimulants of drug self-administration in animals. Food deprivation increases the self-administration of drugs by both intravenous (Carroll, France, & Meisch, 1979, 1981) and oral (Carroll, 1982; Carroll & Meisch, 1980) routes, and this effect occurs in both rats and rhesus monkeys (Carroll & Meisch, 1979; Meisch & Kliner, 1979). The self-administration of a wide variety of drugs including alcohol (Meisch & Thompson, 1973), methohexital (Carroll, Stotz, Kliner, & Meisch, 1984), pentobarbital (Kliner & Meisch, 1989), etonitazene (Carroll, France, & Meisch, 1981), cocaine (Carroll, France, & Meisch, 1981), amphetamine (Takahashi, Singer, & Oei, 1978), phencyclidine (Carroll, 1982), heroin (Oei, Singer, Jeffreys, Lang, & Latiff, 1978), and nicotine (Oei, Singer, Jeffreys, Lang, & Latiff, 1978) is increased by food deprivation. Various forms of food restriction have become standard methods for establishing drug use in animal (Stewart & Grupp, 1984; Henningfeld & Meisch, 1975). Thus, food deprivation increases the likelihood of acquisition of the drug as a reinforcer, as well as the consumption of drugs already established as reinforcers. Food deprivation also increases the rate of electrical intracranial self-stimulation (Olds, 1985; Stellar & Gallistel, 1975). Therefore, it is likely that food deprivation alters the function of the central reward mechanism in addition to any specific effects on drug intake. Additional studies show that food deprivation increases the intake of saccharin (i.e., sweet substances) (Hursh & Beck, 1971; Sheffield & Roby, 1950) and fat (Reed, Contreras, Maggio, Greenwood, & Rodin, 1988). Increased intakes of alcohol, drugs, and sweet, high-fat foods resemble alcohol and drug use and binge-eating episodes seen in bulimics. It is interesting that rats which prefer high-fat diets drink more alcohol than those rats which prefer high-carbohydrate diets and, conversely, that rats bred for high-alcohol preference prefer diets which are sweet and/or high in fat compared to rats bred for low-alcohol preference (Krahn & Gosnell, 1991). Food deprivation may alter the dynamics of central reward mechanisms, increasing the consumption of reinforcing chemicals and palatable foods as well as perhaps increasing the reward value of other reinforcers. Thus, food deprivation may increase operant behaviors, as well as increasing reward values of previously established reinforcers. While the effect may occur for all reinforcers, it is likely that the most clinically relevant change is in the increased reward value of drugs of abuse. The converse hypothesis, that drug use significantly alters the regulation of food intake, is not as well documented. While the self-administration of some drugs with potent anorectic effects, such as cocaine, do affect patterns of food intake, alcohol drinking is compensated for calorically by laboratory animals (Richter, 1941).

Food-deprived humans also may increase their drug intake. In a classic study, normal males who were placed on half their normal caloric intake for six months dramatically increased their consumption of coffee and tobacco (which were the only drugs available to these laboratory-confined subjects) (Franklin, Schiele, Brozek, & Keys, 1948). Chewing of coca leaf increases during food deprivation and decreases when food is plentiful among Quechua Indians of Peru (Hanna & Hornick, 1977). Of note, a number of the men who were deprived of food in a laboratory setting experienced binge-eating episodes on sweet, high-fat foods in addition to the increase in drug intake (Franklin, Schiele, Brozek, & Keys, 1948). Bulimic and anorectic women (groups with high incidences of alcohol and other drug use and abuse) report hedonic responses to sweet tastants more pleasurable than do normals (Drewnowski, Halmi, Pierce, Gibbs, & Smith, 1987). Thus, it seems likely that restricted food intake in humans, like animals, simultaneously increases the intake of highly palatable, "binge" foods and the intake of drugs.

Another interpretation of these data is that deprivation of one reinforcer increases the use of other reinforcers. Interestingly, Yung, Gordis, and Holt (1983) have shown that those alcoholics who used the most sugar during their first few months of sobriety demonstrated fewer relapses to alcohol use than did those who used less sugar. It is possible that these studies document a scientific basis for the experience-derived recommendation of recovering alcoholics that the newly sober alcoholic eat sweets during periods of increased alcohol craving (Alcoholics Anonymous World Services, Inc., 1987). If food deprivation increases reward values of reinforcers like alcohol, and use of alternative reinforcers (e.g., sweets) decreases the use of alcohol and other drugs, then prescription of restrictive diets early in sobriety may be counterproductive. More study in this area is needed.

Of course, some women use drugs as anorectic agents in order to help them in their pursuit of thinness. Data from the NIDA High School Senior Survey (Johnston, O'Malley, & Bachman, 1985) show that 1.9% of high school senior females use diet pills daily and 43% of high school senior females have used diet pills at some time. Gritz suggests that "cigarette smoking provides a lifestyle crutch with a physiological basis to facilitate weight control" and that smoking is motivated, in part, by the desire to suppress appetite (Gritz, 1986). These anorectic drugs could act as gateway drugs to more widespread or severe drug use. It has been hypothesized on the basis of animal studies, however, that women who deprive themselves of food and also use anorectic agents in that deprived state are using these agents at a point of increased sensitivity to their reinforcing effects and, therefore, are at increased risk for addition to these agents (Papasava & Singer, 1985).

If one disorder predisposes to the other disorder, one might expect that there would be a characteristic order of onset of eating and drug problems. Several authors note that the development of eating disorders or problems usually antedate the onset of alcohol or other drug abuse. Jones et al. (1985) reviewed 27 cases in which the onset of an eating disorder antedated the onset of alcohol abuse. Reflecting on more than two decades of clinical work with a stable population, the authors note that "the most striking feature has been the reemergence of the same individuals with alcoholism who had suffered eating disorder in earlier years" (p. 377). Hatsukami, Mitchell, Eckert, and Pyle (1986) demonstrated that the frequency of use of alcohol by bulimic patients increased significantly after the onset of bulimic behavior (binge eating accompanied by and preceded by severe restriction of intake). In bulimic patients who were eventually diagnosed as substance abusers, daily alcohol use increased to 41.1% of patients after the onset of bulimia, compared to 14.7% before the onset of bulimia. Mitchell and Specker (1991), in a recent review, reported that the eating disorder preceded the onset of alcohol problems in about two-thirds of cases. Beary et al. (1986) also noted that 35% of alcoholic subjects reported a previous major eating disorder and that 50% of bulimic subjects reported significant alcohol abuse following the onset of their eating disorders. By age 35, 50% of bulimic patients used alcohol excessively or abused alcohol. The authors infer that ongoing eating-disordered behavior results in a gradual increase in alcohol use and that a history of previous eating disorders should alert physicians to the future diagnosis of alcoholism. Thus, the order of onset of disorders supports the idea that eating abnormalities might play a role in the onset of substance use disorders.

The two possible types of relationships between eating and substance use disorders described here need not be mutually exclusive. For example, a common type of vulnerability may be inherited for chemical dependency and eating disorders which may be relatively quiescent until triggered by self-imposed food deprivation (or perhaps deprivations of other types). Subsequent exposure to alcohol may then be especially likely to lead to pathologic consumption patterns.

The Clinical Similarities of These Disorders

While the two disorders are not necessarily identical in pathogenesis, several characteristics are similar, such as the importance of denial in the psychopathology, ambivalence regarding treatment, the tendency to act out in handling emotions, and the tendency to relapse. However, although similarities exist, these similarities do not and cannot prove a common addictive mechanism. At this point, even though opiate mechanisms may be involved in the control of food intake as well as drug intake (Vandereycken, 1990), there is no clear evidence of the induction of such signs of addiction as tolerance or dependence by food intake. (Please see a review by Wilson (1991) for a complete discussion of this point.) Furthermore, it also is important to note that an abstinence model is not a reasonable, routine approach to the treatment of eating disorders. Many of these patients can make a full recovery and can, in a gradual, progressive manner, learn to eat all foods, regardless of sugar or fat content, in a balanced, healthy diet (Mitchell, Pyle, Specker, & Hatsukami, in press). It is relatively rare to find a documented allergy to an avoided food in this population, although many patients confuse starvation-induced intolerance of high-fat foods or dairy products with allergies. In other words, "social" eating is perfectly possible for many bulimics. Furthermore, teaching these patients that they must avoid certain foods reinforces fears of foods that are unreasonable in the cases of foods which are merely usable energy sources. In contrast, teaching fears of alcohol and other drugs which are often cellular toxins or which induce abnormal brain function is consistent with medical knowledge. If one feels compelled to use abstinence terminology with eating disorder patients, then one should direct patients to abstain from the behavior of dieting or the pursuit of thinness as opposed to balanced, healthy eating. The above statements are not aimed at denying the potential usefulness of an appropriately focused 12-step abstinence-based program (described by Yeary, 1987; Yeary & Heck, 1989) in the treatment of eating disorders. However, controlled trials of the effectiveness of this approach are lacking.

While denial of physical and emotional consequences of drug use is commonly recognized as a major problem in alcohol and other drug abuse, it is less well known that denial of similar consequences is a key symptom of eating disorders (Eckert, 1985). In clinical practice, this may well be the most important commonality between these patient groups. An insidious type of denial occurs when the patient is willing to admit to only one or the other disorder, much as polysubstance abusers will admit to use of one drug but not to abuse of others. Another type of denial occurs when the eating disordered patient identifies that binging or purging is a problem and must be given up, but refuses to acknowledge the role that pursuit of thinness via food restriction plays in the disorder. Given the difficulties of challenging denial for even one disorder, it has been the author's experience that clinicians often are reluctant to identify yet another denied problem which also will require consistent confrontation. Identifying denied problems also requires that therapists of eating disorders or substance abusers also be vigilant for symptoms of the commonly comorbid disorder. Both groups of patients have frequently denied or minimized their problems, despite the fact that many people around them had called their attention to them. On the other hand, sometimes the families of the patients have been "in denial" as well, and have helped the patient "overlook" the problem. Family work aimed at confronting family, as well as enabling family to tolerate, affect, and resolve conflicts, is frequently vital in eating disorders, much as in substance abuse (Schwartz, Barrett, & Saba, 1985).

Because of denial, eating disordered patients are often as ambivalent regarding treatment as are substance abusers. As with substance abusers, recognition of positive aspects of the disorder, (from the point of view of the patient) as well as the negative consequences of the behavior, are more useful in building a therapeutic relationship with patients than is a listing of negatives. Education regarding the consequences of eating disorders and, especially, the consequences of dieting, is vitally important. Finally, in the author's experience, one of the great benefits of group-therapy settings is the ability of others with the same disorder to support while confronting fellow sufferers regarding their symptoms. The presence of other patients with eating disorders also allows patients who are ashamed of their behavior to discuss it more openly. Obviously, shame is an intense aspect of the problem of alcoholism in women as well. Occasionally, female patients with eating disorders and substance abuse problems are able to discuss the relationship between these problems in women's groups in Alcoholics Anonymous. Often these patients are surprised to find the number of other female substance abusers in the group who have been silently suffering with the same problems.

Another commonality between the two disorders is the use of a substance (food or drug) to alleviate any negative affect. Also known as acting out, this type of behavior must be stopped if any useful psychologic treatment of these negative affects is to occur. In the commonly used cognitive-behavioral treatments for eating disorders, an early emphasis is placed on stopping self-deprivation of food, as well as binging and purging. Much as in alcoholism treatment, a control of these acting-out behaviors is necessary prior to any consideration of intensive psychotherapy. If these behaviors are not under control, then the intensification of affect involved in intensive psychotherapy often will result in increased acting out.

While the point that some eating disordered patients are capable of apparently complete recovery was emphatically made above, it also is the case that a large percentage of bulimic and anorexic patients will relapse at some point in their life. Thus, like substance abusers, education and planning for appropriate behavior in the event of potential relapses is important. For patients with both disorders, it seems likely that this type of relapse prevention programming may be even more important. The fact that both of these disorders are cited among those psychiatric disorders which carry the highest risk of unemployment in a follow-up study in Edmonton (Bland, Stebelsky, Orn, & Newman, 1988) highlights the chronicity and severity of the problems likely to be seen by those suffering from both disorders.

A question which comes up frequently in clinical practice, but which has not been adequately researched at this point, is whether treatment for eating disorders or substance abuse should come first. In the author's opinion, this question is based less on what is appropriate for the patient and more on what various care providers feel comfortable with treating. In other words, most often the unstated question is really, "When should this person be transferred from chemical-dependency treatment (where I feel competent) to eating disorders treatment (where I feel incompetent) or vice versa?" In fact, I believe that, in the long run, chemical-dependency treatment providers must become skilled in treating eating disorder problems and eating disorder treatment providers must become adept at treating chemical dependency. After all, the clear results of the cross-sectional studies are that half of all female clients of either substance-abuse or eating disorder programs have the "other" problem as well.

If competence in treating the "other" problem can be developed (see Katz, 1990 and Marcus & Katz, 1990, for reviews that are helpful in "cross-training"), or if a very close relationship between eating-disorder and substance abuse programs can be developed, then one can address questions regarding timing of treatment interventions in a more appropriate, patient-centered way. For example, the first stage of treatment in either disorder is the management of severe physical consequences of the disorder (detoxification in chemical dependency or malnutrition and electrolyte problems in eating disorders).

One problem which needs to be recognized in this first stage of treatment of patients with both eating and alcohol disorders is that the comorbid disorder can accentuate physical problems seen in the primary disorder for which the patient is being treated. For example, magnesium deficiencies induced by vomiting or laxatives may aggravate seizures during alcohol withdrawal. Weakening of the esophagus secondary to wretching may make the development of GI bleeding more likely or dangerous. The use of laxatives may make the differential diagnosis of melena in the alcoholic more difficult. There are many more potential interactions, but the point is made that the two disorders can aggravate one another. The second stage involves confrontation of denial and education regarding the illnesses. It seems that it matters less whether a patient is in an eating disorder program or a chemical-dependency program than that these steps are addressed by a competent, caring clinician who has taken the time to study both disorders.

Other stages of treatment which involve developing alternative coping mechanisms and finding a new meaning in life are similar in the two disorders, yet require, optimally, a clinician with a background in both disorders. Alternatively, the author has found that a smoothly working team of clinicians who address both disorders without overloading the patient with a new therapist for every complaint can be formed. However, these arrangements should be clearly worked out in advance rather than put together in a piecemeal fashion during treatment. Most important is that the therapist and patient not fall into the trap of searching for a primary problem which will take care of both the eating disorder and chemical dependency or the similar dead end of deciding whether the chemical dependency or eating disorder is more important. Both disorders need to be addressed in an ongoing manner although one or the other may be more symptomatic on any given day or in any given therapy session. One disorder should never be given primacy, because with this comes the subtle permission to deny the importance of the "other" problem. It is comforting to note the study by Mitchell, Pyle, Eckert, and Hatsukami (1990), which showed that patients who presented for treatment of their eating disorder after at least six months of sobriety from substance abuse did not show frequent relapse to alcoholism as a result of treatment of their eating disorder.

FUTURE DIRECTIONS

The close relationship of these disorders suggests several important questions for further research. First, what is the longitudinal course of the two disorders? Do the symptoms of substance abuse, eating disorders, and also depression tend to improve or worsen together or do these syndromes actually have important differences in longitudinal course? Does treatment which is helpful for one disorder actually have important benefits for the other disorder? Is malnutrition, as opposed to the self-imposed starvation of dieting, also a risk factor for development of substance abuse? Is dieting a risk factor for relapse in recovering substance abusers? If so, is it a risk factor for both men and women and for both young and old? Is there a common psychobiologic mechanism for the cravings for drugs and the craving for sweet, high-fat binge foods? If so, can pharmacologic treatments be developed to improve treatment outcome? Can prevention programs aimed at decreasing dieting among young women actually decrease substance use among this group? Finally, should we attempt to limit the use of slim body images in the merchandising of addicting products (e.g., "light" beers, "slim" cigarettes) as they will likely encourage food-deprived individuals to use chemicals in a state in which they are vulnerable to addiction?

Obviously much more work remains to be done to understand a relatively recently discovered relationship between food deprivation, eating disorders, and substance abuse. The search for answers to these questions may result in important clinical advances as well as important advances in our understanding of the neural control of the ingestion of rewarding substances.

REFERENCES

Abraham, S., & Beumont, P.J.V. (1982). How patients describe bulimia or binge eating. *Psychological Medicine, 12,* 625–635.
Alcoholics Anonymous World Services, Inc. (1987). *Living sober: Some methods A.A. members have used for not drinking.* New York: Alcoholics Anonymous World Services, Inc.

Anderson, A.E. (1986). Males with eating disorders, In F.E.F Lavocca (Ed.), *New directions for mental health services, Vol. 31, Eating disorders* (pp. 39–46). San Francisco, CA: Jossey-Bass.

Anderson, A.E., & Mickalide, A.D. (1983). Anorexia nervosa in the male: An underdiagnosed disorder. *Psychosomatics, 24,* 1066–1075.

Beary, M.D., Lacey, J.H., & Merry, J. (1986). Alcoholism and eating disorders in women of fertile age. *British Journal of Addiction, 81,* 685–689.

Bland, R.C., Stebelsky, G., Orn, H., & Newman, S.C. (1988). Psychiatric disorders and unemployment in Edmonton. *Acta Psychiatrica Scandinavia, 77,* 72–80.

Bradstock, K., Forman, M.R., Binkin, N.J., Gentry, E.M., Hogelin, G.C., Williamson, D.F., & Trowbridge, F.L. (1988). Alcohol use and health behavior lifestyles among U.S. women: The behavioral risk factor surveys. *Addictive Behaviors, 13,* 61–71.

Brisman, J., & Siegel, M. (1984). Bulimia and alcoholism: Two sides of the same coin? *Journal of Substance Abuse Treatment, 1,* 113–118.

Brower, K.J., Eliopulos, G.A., Blow, F.C., Catlin, D.H., & Beresford, T.P. (1990). Evidence for physical and psychological dependence on anabolic androgenic steriods in eight weight lifters. *American Journal of Psychiatry, 147,* 510–512.

Bulik, C.M. (1987). Drug and alcohol abuse by bulimic women and their families. *American Journal of Psychiatry, 144,* 1604–1606.

Cantwell, D.P., Sturzenberg, S., Burrough, J. Salkin, B., & Green, J.K. (1977). Anorexia nervosa: An affective disorder? *Archives of General Psychiatry, 34,* 1087–1093.

Carroll, K., & Leon, G. (1981, October). *The bulimic-vomiting disorder within a generalized substance abuse pattern.* Paper presented at the annual meeting of the Association for the Advancement of Behavior Therapy, Toronto, Canada.

Carroll, M.E. (1982). Rapid acquisition of oral phencyclidine self-administration in food-deprived and food-satiated rhesus monkeys: Concurrent phencyclidine and water choice. *Pharmacology, Biochemistry, and Behavior, 17,* 341–346.

Carroll, M.E., France, C.P., & Meisch, R.A. (1979). Food deprivation increases oral and intravenous drug intake in rats. *Science, 205,* 319–321.

Carroll, M.E., France, C.P., & Meisch, R.A. (1981). Intravenous self-administration of etonitazene, cocaine, and phencyclidine in rats during food deprivation and starvation. *Journal of Pharmacology and Experimental Therapeutics, 217,* 241–247.

Carroll, M.E., & Meisch, R.A. (1979). Effects of food deprivation on etonitazene consumption in rats. *Pharmacology, Biochemistry, and Behavior, 10,* 155–159.

Carroll, M.E., & Meisch, R.A. (1980). Oral phencyclidine (PCP) self-administration in rhesus monkeys: Effects of feeding conditions. *Journal of Pharmacology and Experimental Therapeutics, 214,* 339–346.

Carroll, M.E., Stotz, D.C., Kliner, D.J., & Meisch, R.A. (1984). Self-administration of orally delivered methohexital in rhesus monkey with phencyclidine or pentobarbital histories: Effects of food deprivation and satiation. *Pharmacology, Biochemistry, and Behavior, 20,* 145–151.

Claydon, P. (1987). Self-reported alcohol, drug, and eating-disorder problems among male and female collegiate children of alcoholics. *Journal of American College Health, 36,* 111–116.

Collins, G.B., Kotz, M., Janesz, J.W., Matthew, M., Ferguson, T. (1985). Alcoholism in the families of bulimic anorexics. *Cleveland Clinic Quarterly, 52,* 65–67.

Crisp, A.H. (1968). Primary anorexia nervosa, *Gut, 9,* 370–372.

Crisp, A.H., Palmer, R.L., & Kalucy, R.S. (1976). How common is anorexia nervosa? A prevalence study. *British Journal of Psychiatry, 128,* 49–54.

Drewnowski, A., Halmi, K.A., Pierce, B., Gibbs, J., & Smith, G.P. (1987). Taste and eating disorders. *American Journal of Clinical Nutrition, 46,* 442–450.

Drewnowski, A., Yee, D., & Krahn, D.D. (1988a). Bulimia on campus: Incidence and recovery rates. *American Journal of Psychiatry, 6,* 753–755.

Drewnowski, A., Yee, D.K., & Krahn, D.D. (1988b, May). *Pubertal timing and diet practices in adolescence.* Paper presented at American Psychiatric Association, 141st Annual Meeting, Montreal.

Eckert, E.D. (1985). Characteristics of anorexia nervosa. In J.E. Mitchell (Ed.), *Anorexia nervosa & bulimia: Diagnosis and treatment.* Minneapolis: University of Minnesota Press.

Eckert, E.D., Goldberg, S.C., Halmi, K.A., Casper, R.C., & Davis, J.M. (1979). Alcoholism in anorexia nervosa. In R.W. Pickens & L.L. Heston (Eds.), *Psychiatric factors in drug abuse* (pp. 267–283). New York: Grune & Stratton.

Eckert, E.D., Goldberg, S.C., Halmi, K.A., Casper, R.C., & Davis, J.M. (1982). Depression in anorexia nervosa. *Psychological Medicine, 12,* 115–122.

Ewing, J.A. (1987). Detecting alcoholism, the CAGE questionnaire. *Journal of the American Medical Association, 252,* 111–121.

Frank, R.E., Serdula, M., & Abel, G.G. (1987). Bulimic eating behaviors: Association with alcohol and tobacco. *American Journal of Public Health, 77,* 369–370.

Franklin, J.C., Schiele, B.C., Brozek, J., & Keys, A. (1948). Observations on human behavior in experimental semistarvation and rehabilitation. *Journal of Clinical Psychology, 4,* 28–45.

Garfinkel, P.E., Moldofsky, H., & Garner, D.M. (1980). The heterogeneity of anorexia nervosa: Bulimia as a distinct subgroup. *Arch of General Psychiatry, 37,* 1036–1040.

Garner, D.M., Rockert, W., Olmsted, M.P., Johnson, C., & Coscina, D.V. (1985). Psychoeducational principles in the treatment of bulimia and anorexia nervosa. In D.M. Garner & P.E. Garfinkel (Eds.), *Handbook of psychotherapy for anorexia and bulimia.* New York: Guilford Press.

Gritz, E.R. (1986). Gender and the teenage smoker. In *Women and drugs: A new era for research* (NIDA Research Monograph Series No. 65, pp. 70–79).

Gwirtsman, H.E., Roy-Bryne, P., Yager, J., & Gerner, R.H. (1983). Neuroendocrine abnormalities in bulimia. *American Journal of Psychiatry, 140*, 559–563.

Halmi K.A., & Loney, J. (1973). Familial alcoholism in anorexia nervosa. *British Journal of Psychiatry, 123*, 53–54.

Hanna, J.M., & Hornick, C.A. (1977). Use of coca leaf in southern Peru: Adaptation or addiction. *Bulletin on Narcotics, 29*, 63–74.

Hatsukami, D., Mitchell, J.E., Eckert, E.D., & Pyle, R. (1986). Characteristics of patients with bulimia only, bulimia with affective disorder, and bulimia with substance abuse problems. *Addictive Behaviors, 11*, 399–406.

Hatsukami, D., Owen, P., Pyle, R., & Mitchell, J. (1982). Similarities and differences on the MMPI between women with bulimia and women with alcohol or drug abuse problems. *Addictive Behaviors, 7*, 435–439.

Hatsukami, D.K., Eckert, E.D., Mitchell, J.E., & Pyle, R.L. (1984). Affective disorder and substance abuse among women with bulimia. *Psychological Medicine, 14*, 701–704.

Helzer J.E., & Prybeck, T.R. (1988). The co-occurrence of alcoholism with other psychiatric disorders in the general population and its impact on treatment. *Journal of Studies on Alcohol, 49*, 219–224.

Henningfeld, J.E., & Meisch, R.A. (1975). Ethanol-reinforced responding and intake as a function of volume per reinforcement. *Pharmacology, Biochemistry, and Behavior, 3*, 437–441.

Henzel, H.A. (1984). Diagnosing alcoholism in patients with anorexia nervosa. *American Journal of Drug Alcohol Abuse, 10*, 461–466.

Herzog, D.B. (1982). Bulimia in the adolescent. *American Journal of Diseases of Children, 136*, 985–989.

Hudson, J.I., Pope, H.G., Jonas, J.M., & Yurgelun-Todd, D. (1983). Family history study of anorexia nervosa and bulimia. *British Journal of Psychiatry, 142*, 133–138.

Hudson, J.I., Pope, H.G., Jonas, J.M., Yurgeltun-Todd, D., & Frankenburg, F.R. (1987). A controlled family history study of bulimia. *Psychological Medicine, 17*, 883–890.

Hursh, S.R., & Beck, R.C. (1971). Bitter and sweet saccharin preference as a function of food deprivation. *Psychological Reports, 29*, 419–422.

Johnston, L.D., O'Malley, P.M., & Bachman, J.G. (1985). *Use of licit and illicit drugs by America's high school students, 1975–1984* (DHHS Publication No. ADM 85-1394, 159).

Jonas, J.M., Gold, M.S., Sweeney, D., & Pottash, A.L.C. (1987). Eating disorders and cocaine abuse: A survey of 259 cocaine abusers. *Journal of Clinical Psychiatry, 48*, 47–50.

Jones, D.A., Cheshire, N., & Moorhouse, H. (1985). Anorexia nervosa, bulimia and alcoholism-association of eating disorder and alcohol. *Journal of Psychiatric Research, 19*(2/3), 377–380.

Kassett, J.A., Gershon, E.S., Maxwell, M.E., Guroff, J.J., Kazuba, D.M., Smith, A.L., Brandt, H.A., & Jimerson, D.C. (1989). Psychiatric disorders in the first-degree relatives of probands with bulimia nervosa. *American Journal of Psychiatry, 146*, 1468–1471.

Katz, J.L. (1990). Eating disorders: A primer for the substance abuse specialist: 1. Clinical features. *Journal of Substance Abuse Treatment*, *7*, 143–149.

Katz, J.L. (1990). Eating disorders: A primer for the substance abuse specialist 2. Theories of etiology, treatment approaches, and considerations during co-morbidity with substance abuse. *Journal of Substance Abuse Treatment*, *7*, 211–217.

Kendler, K.S., MacLean, C., Neale, M., Kessler, R., Heath, A., & Eaves, L. (1991). The genetic epidemiology of bulimia nervosa. *The American Journal of Psychiatry*, *148*, 1627–1637.

Killen, J.D., Taylor, C.B., Telch, M.J., Robinson, T.N., Maron, D.J., & Saylor, K.E. (1987). Depressive symptoms and substance use among adolescent binge eaters and purgers: A defined population study. *American Journal of Public Health*, *77*, 1539–1541.

Kliner, D.J., & Meisch, R.A. (1989). Oral pentobarbital intake in rhesus monkeys: Effects of drug concentration under conditions of food deprivation and satiation. *Pharmacology, Biochemistry, and Behavior*, *32*, 347–354.

Krahn, D.D., & Gosnell, B.A. (1991). Fat-preferring rats consume more alcohol than carbohydrate preferring rats. *Alcohol*, *8*, 313–316.

Krahn, D.D., Kurth, C., Demitrack, M.A., & Drewnowski, A. (1992, April). Abstract presented at the Society of Biological Psychiatry Annual Meeting, Washington, DC.

Lacey, J.H., & Moureli, E. (1986). Bulimic alcoholics: Some features of a colinical sub-group. *British Journal of Addiction*, *81*, 389–393.

Leon, G.R., Carroll, K., Chernyk, B., & Finn, S. (1985). Binge eating and associated habit patterns within college student and identified bulimic populations. *International Journal of Eating Disorders*, *4*, 43–57.

Logue, C.M., Crowe, R.R., & Bean, J.A. (1989). A family study of anorexia nervosa and bulimia. *Comprehensive Psychiatry*, *30*, 179–188.

Lundholm, J.K. (1989). Alcohol use among university females: Relationship to eating disordered behavior. *Addictive Behaviors*, *11*, 181–185.

Marcus, R.N., & Katz, J.L. (1990). Inpatient care of the substance-abusing patient with a concomitan eating disorder. *Hospital and Community Psychiatry*, *41*, 59–63.

Marcus, R.N., & Halmi, K.A. (1989, May). *Eating disorders in substance abuse patients*. Paper presented at the American Psychiatric Association, San Francisco.

Meisch, R.A., & Kliner, D.J. (1979). Etonitazene as a reinforcer for rats: Increased etonitazene-reinforced behavior due to food deprivation. *Psychopharmacology*, *63*, 97–98.

Meisch, R.A., & Thompson, T. (1973). Ethanol as a reinforcer: Effects of fixed-ratio size and food deprivation. *Psychopharmacologia*, *28*, 171–183.

Mitchell, J.E. (Ed.). (1985). *Anorexia nervosa & bulimia: Diagnosis and treatment*. Minneapolis: University of Minnesota Press.

Mitchell, J.E., Hatsukami, D., Eckert, E.D., & Pyle, R.L. (1985). Characteristics of 275 patients with bulimia. *American Journal of Psychiatry*, *142*, 482–485.

Mitchell, J.E., Hatsukami, D., Pyle, R., & Eckert, E. (1988). Bulimia with and without a family history of drug abuse. *Addictive Behaviors, 13,* 245–251.

Mitchell, J.E., Pyle, R., Eckert, E.D., & Hatsukami, D. (1990). The influence of prior alcohol and drug abuse problems on bulimia nervosa treatment outcome. *Addictive Behaviors, 15,* 169–173.

Mitchell, J.E., Pyle, R.L., Specker, S., & Hatsukami, D. (in press). The relationship between eating disorders and chemical dependency.

Oei, T.P.S., Singer, G., Jeffreys, D., Lang, W., & Latiff, A. (1978). Schedule-induced self-injection of nicotine, heroin, and methadone by naive animals. In F.C. Colpaert, & J.A. Rosecrans (Eds.), *Stimulus properties of drugs: Ten years of progress* (pp. 503–516) Amsterdam: Elsevier/North-Holland, Biomedical Press.

Olds, J. (1958). Effects of hunger and male sex hormones on self-stimulation of the brain. *Journal of Comparative and Physiological Psychology, 51,* 320–324.

Papasava, M., & Singer, G. (1985). Self-administration of low-dose cocaine by rats at reduced and recovered body weight. *Psychopharmacology, 85,* 419–425.

Peveler, R., & Fairburn, C. (1990). Eating disorders in women who abuse alcohol. *British Journal of Addictions, 85,* 1633–1638.

Pyle, R.L., Mitchell, J.E., & Eckert, E.D. (1981). Bulimia: A report of 34 cases. *Journal of Clinical Psychiatry, 42,* 60–64.

Pyle, R.L., Mitchell, J.E., Eckert, E.D., Halvorson, P.A., Neuman, P.A., & Goff, G.M. (1983). The incidence of bulimia in freshmen college students. *International Journal of Eating Disorders, 2,* 75–85.

Reed, D.R., Contreras, R.J., Maggio, C., Greenwood, M.R.C., & Rodin, J. (1988) Weight cycling in female rats increases dietary fat selection and adiposity. *Physiology and Behavior, 42,* 389–395.

Regier, D.A., Farmer, M.E., Rae, D.S., Locke, B.Z., Keith, S.J., Judd, L.L., & Goodwin, F.K. (1990). Comorbidity of mental disorders with alcohol and other drug abuse: Results from the epidemiologic catchment area (ECA) study. Journal of the American Medical Association, *264,* (19), 2511–2518.

Richter, C.P. (1941). Alcohol as a food. *Quarterly Journal of the Study of Alcohol, 1,* 650–662.

Rivinus, T.M., Biederman, J., Herzog, D.B., Kemper, K., Harper, G.P., Harmatz, J.S., & Houseworth, S. (1984). Anorexia nervosa and affective disorders: A controlled family history study. *American Journal of Psychiatry, 141,* 1414–1418.

Schwartz, R.C., Barrett, M.J., & Saba, G. (1985). Family therapy for bulimia. In D.M. Garner & P.E. Garfinkel (Eds.), *Handbook of psychotherapy for anorexia nervosa and bulimia.* New York: Guilford Press.

Sheffield, F.D., & Roby, T.B. (1950). Reward value of a nonnutritive sweet taste. *Journal of Comparative and Physiological Psychology, 43,* 471–481.

Stellar, J.R., & Gallistel, C.R. (1975). Runway performance of rats for brain-stimulation or food reward: Effects of hunger and priming. *Journal of Comparative and Physiological Psychology, 89*, 590–599.

Stern, S.L., Dixon, K.N., Nemzer, E., Lake, M.D., Sansone, R.A., Smeltzer, D.J., Lantz, S., & Schrier, S.S. (1984). Affective disorder in the families of women with normal weight bulimia. *American Journal of Psychiatry, 141*, 1224–1227.

Stewart, R.B., & Grupp, L.A. (1984). A simplified procedure for producing ethanol self-selection in rats. *Pharmacology, Biochemistry, and Behavior, 21*, 255–258.

Strober, M., Salkin, B., Burroughs, J., & Morrell, W. (1982). Validity of the bulimia-restrictor distinction in anorexia nervosa. *The Journal of Nervous and Mental Disease, 170*, 345–351.

Takahashi, R.N., Singer, G., & Oei, T.P.S. (1978). Schedule-induced self-injection of d-amphetamine by naive animals. *Pharmacology, Biochemistry, and Behavior, 9*, 857–861.

Tarter, R.E., (1988). The high-risk paradigm in alcohol and drug abuse research. *NIDA Research Monograph 89*, 73–86.

Timmerman, M.G., Wells, L.A., & Chen, S. (1989). Bulimia nervosa and associated alcohol abuse among secondary school students. *Journal of American Academic Child Adolescent Psychiatry, 29*, 118–121.

Vandereycken, W. (1990). The addiction model in eating disorders: Some critical remarks and a selected bibliography. *International Journal of Eating Disorders, 9*, 95–101.

Walsh, B.T., Roose, S.P., Glassman, A.H., Gladis, M., & Sadik, C. (1985). Bulimia and depression. *Psychosomatic Medication, 47*, 123–131.

Weiss, S., & Ebert, M. (1983). Psychological and behavioral characteristics of normal-weight bulimics and normal-weight controls. *Psychosomatic Medicine, 45*, 293–303.

Wilson, T.G. (1991). The addiction model of eating disorders: A critical analysis. *Advance Behavior Research Theory, 13*, 27–72.

Wooley, S.C., & Wooley, O.W. (1981). Overeating as substance abuse. *Advances in Substance Abuses, 2*, 41–67.

Yeary, J. (1987). The use of overeaters anonymous in the treatment of eating disorders. *Journal of Psychiatric Drugs, 19*, 303–309.

Yeary, J.R., & Heck, C.L. (1989). Dual diagnosis: Eating disorders and psychoactive substance dependence. *Journal of Psychoactive Drugs, 21*, 239–249.

Yung, L., Gordis, E., & Holt, J. (1983). Dietary choices and likelihood of abstinence among alcoholic patients in an outpatient clinic. *Drug and Alcohol Dependency, 12*, 355–362.

Chapter 13

Women and Substance Abuse: Treatment Modalities and Outcomes*

Barbara S. McCrady
Helen Raytek

Rutgers—The State University of New Jersey

In 1984, Vannicelli published a comprehensive review of research on the outcomes of treatment for alcoholic women. In her review, she reported that more than half the studies published up to 1980 had used all-male samples, less than 5% used all-female samples, and about 10% included both sexes and reported results separately by gender. In reviewing studies that did analyze data separately for males and females, she concluded that there were no data that suggested different treatment outcomes for men and women with drinking problems. Further, no studies had examined the effectiveness of marital or family therapy for women, or the comparative effectiveness of individual

---

* Preparation of this manuscript was supported in part by grants AA07070 and AA08747.

versus group therapy or sex-segregated versus sex-integrated treatment programs. Vannicelli (1984) concluded, "strong beliefs notwithstanding, there are relatively few solidly established facts about the outcomes of treated female alcoholics" (Vannicelli, 1984, p. 393).

Has the state of research on treatment for women changed in the last decade? What do we know now about the treatment of alcoholic women? In this chapter, we will address a number of questions related to the treatment of women with drinking problems. We will examine current knowledge about the nature of women's drinking problems, and will discuss how this knowledge has been applied to the development of clinical treatment programs for women. We will then consider the state of treatment-outcome research for this population, reporting current findings. Finally, we will examine the gaps between the general body of treatment-outcome research on alcoholism and research on treatment for female alcoholics, and between clinical practice and research knowledge. Given the complexity of the research on women and substance abuse, and the page limitations for the chapter, the review will be limited to research on women and alcohol, rather than to other substances of abuse.

NATURE OF THE POPULATION

Alcoholic women are a heterogeneous group in terms of age, socioeconomic status, race and ethnicity, sexual orientation, physical health status, relationship status, and other variables. These factors affect the onset and course of alcoholism and are important to take into account in identifying and treating individual alcoholic women. Services developed with sensitivity to these factors should be likely to involve and maintain women in treatment.

Age

There have been a number of trends in the drinking behavior of women of different ages over the last several decades. The percentage of adolescent girls who consumed alcohol increased sharply between the 1940s and the 1960s, with further increases through the mid-1970s in urban and suburban populations (Thompson & Wilsnack, 1984). Since then, there has been a leveling off in the national percentage of adolescent girls who drink or get drunk, although there is some evidence of an increasing number of episodes of heavy drinking in girls who do drink (Thompson & Wilsnack, 1984). There is also evidence of a trend for middle-aged women (35–64 years) to do more heavy drinking

(Hilton, 1988). There is little research on the prevalence of alcoholism in elderly women (Williams & Klerman, 1984), although the data that do exist suggest that lifetime prevalence is lowest in females 65 and older as compared to other age groups (Robins, 1989).

In addition to different drinking trends in women of different ages, the situations in which drinking takes place vary. Adolescent girls often drink with opposite-sex peers and drink as a result of peer pressure (Harford, 1976). Elderly female alcoholics are often widows living alone or in institutions who drink to relieve depression (Gomberg, 1980). These differences point to the need to address different issues in the treatment of women of different ages. For example, the adolescent girl might need to learn to cope with peer pressure, while the elderly woman might need to learn to cope with loss.

Socioeconomic Issues

In the past, females of higher socioeconomic status were more likely to remain "hidden" alcoholics than were females of lower socioeconomic status (Beckman, 1975). For example, Lisansky (1957) found that many of the females in a state correctional institution were of lower socioeconomic status and were identified as alcoholic as a result of conflict with the law and resulting institutionalization. The females of higher socioeconomic status in Lisansky's sample were more concealed from public view. These differences in the rates of identification of drinking problems among women of different socioeconomic status seem to have diminished (Wilsnack, Wilsnack, & Klassen, 1984). One exception appears to be homeless women, of whom as many as one-fourth may be alcoholic (Harris & Bachrach, 1990). Women of different socioeconomic levels have different levels of social supports and economic resources, with poorer women having less access to treatment facilities. For example, in Massachusetts, only nine shelters for the homeless have alcohol or drug programs (Women's Alcoholism Program of CASPAR, 1990). The different economic and social support needs of women of differing socioeconomic backgrounds suggest the need for different treatment elements for women of different backgrounds.

Racial and Ethnic Diversity

Drinking patterns and drinking problems vary among different racial and ethnic groups. In a national survey, Herd (1989) found that nearly half of the African-American women surveyed abstained from alcohol consumption, compared to one-third of white females. Among women who drank, African-American females were somewhat more likely than white women to be infrequent or lighter drinkers. African-American females reported fewer alcohol-related problems such as driving while intoxicated, belligerence, and financial problems, than did white females. However, the mortality rate for African-American female alcoholics is twice the rate for white alcoholic females (Smith, Cloninger, & Bradford, 1983).

Hispanic females are less likely than non-Hispanic females to drink heavily or report having problems (Burnam, 1989). Surveys of Native American females have been too small to yield definitive results (Heath, 1989). Though there is evidence that a high percentage of Native American females are abstainers, it appears that among Native American females who do drink, the rates of heavy drinking are high (Heath, 1989). The high rate of heavy drinking is accompanied by extremely high rates of Fetal Alcohol Syndrome and a death rate from cirrhosis among Native American females that is about six times greater than the rate for white females (Heath, 1989).

Some researchers are questioning whether these variations among racial and ethnic groups are related to variables other than membership in a particular racial or ethnic group. For example, other demographic variables such as age, education, family income, marital status, and geographic region may be underlying variables influencing drinking patterns (Wilson & Williams, 1989).

Sexual Orientation

Historically, much of lesbian socializing has centered around gay bars (McGirr, 1975). It has been hypothesized that bar-centered socializing and the stress of living in a society which is often oppressive of homosexuals has led to an increased incidence of alcoholism in the lesbian community. Studies have found about one-third of lesbians in both urban and smaller nonurban communities to be alcoholics (Lewis, Saghir, & Robins, 1982; Lohrenz, Connelly, & Spare, 1978). These findings have implications for identification and treatment of alcoholism in lesbian clients. Clinicians need to be sensitive to the possibility of drinking problems in lesbian clients, the need to help lesbian alcoholics utilize extended support networks in treatment, and to find alternate ways of socializing.

Physical Health Status

Women reach higher peak blood alcohol levels than men from equal doses of ethanol per pound of body weight. There also appears to be an

318 MCCRADY & RAYTEK

accelerated rate of development in women of health-related complications from alcohol consumption, including gastrointestinal (cirrhosis and pancreatitis), neuromuscular, cardiovascular, and gynecological disorders (Blume, 1986). Although women generally have been drinking to excess for a significantly shorter time than men their age, their rates of alcohol-related disease are comparable. Studies have found the mortality rate of female alcoholics to be as high as seven times that of the general population (Smith, Cloninger, & Bradford, 1983). This female rate is twice the morality rate for male alcoholics, which is about three times that of the general population.

Pregnant alcoholic women have received increasing attention from researchers and legal institutions as concern about fetal alcohol syndrome (FAS) and fetal alcohol effects (FAE) has grown (see Little & Wendt, this volume). FAS has a currently estimated incidence of 1 to 3 cases per 1,000 births. The incidence of FAE is estimated to be three times higher than that of FAS (Blume, 1986). The FAS literature has been used to stigmatize women (Gomberg, 1979). Recently, pregnant women who are substance abusers have been convicted of child abuse for delivering alcohol and drugs to children *in utero* (Pollitt, 1990).

Women's unique vulnerability to the physical consequences of heavy alcohol consumption, and the risks the heavy drinking creates during pregnancy also suggest the need for specialized attention to physical health issues and pregnancy issues during women's alcoholism treatment.

Relationship Status

Married alcoholic women report more marital difficulties and are more likely to be divorced by their spouses during the course of their alcoholism than married alcoholic men (Perodeau, 1984). Many of the husbands of alcoholic women have serious drinking or psychiatric problems themselves. Not only may this preclude an alcoholic woman's husband from being supportive of her while she is in treatment, but he also may be invested in her continuing to drink (Gomberg, Nelson, & Hatchett, 1991). Many single and married alcoholic women also have primary responsibility for childcare. All of these relationship factors complicate treatment for alcoholic women.

PROBLEMS OF WOMEN ALCOHOLICS

Patterns of Substance Use

Women show certain patterns of alcohol consumption that have significant implications for treatment. Women are more likely to drink alone and at home than men (Braiker, 1984), making it less likely that their drinking problems will be noticed by their family and friends and less likely that they will be referred for treatment. Alcoholic women's drinking often is complicated by the concomitant use of prescription drugs. Physicians prescribe two-thirds of all legal psychoactive drugs to women, and it is estimated that more than one million women are dependent on those drugs (Sandmaier, 1984). Celantano and McQueen (1984) report that almost half of women alcoholics abuse minor tranquilizers or sedatives, twice the rate found in male alcoholics. The presence of sedative abuse raises significant clinical issues, such as possible accidental overdoses from2 the drugs' synergistic pharmacologic interaction with alcohol, or the development of dependency on a prescription drug when a woman stops drinking. In fact, physicians often prescribe tranquilizers to treat complaints of anxiety and depression that may be caused by heavy alcohol consumption, thus delaying the female alcoholic's entry into appropriate alcoholism treatment. Delaying entry into alcoholism treatment may be especially dangerous for women because of their greater vulnerability to the negative physical effects of alcohol.

Comorbidity of Other Psychiatric Problems

There has been a growing awareness that alcoholics frequently experience concomitant psychiatric disorders (see Hesselbrock, this volume). As many as half of female alcoholics also may fit the diagnostic criteria for another psychiatric disorder such as depression, anxiety, eating disorders, or posttraumatic stress, often resulting from sexual abuse as a child or an adult (Bedi & Halikas, 1985; Helzer & Pryzbeck, 1988). These psychiatric disorders may begin before, concurrently with, or after the onset of alcoholism.

Female alcoholics report experiencing more depressive symptoms than male alcoholics (Bedi & Halikas, 1985; Schuckit, 1986). More than half of hospitalized alcoholic women experience a diagnosable depression (Hesselbrock, Meyer, & Keener, 1985). Alcoholic women in the community are twice as likely to experience depression or dysthymia as nonalcoholic women (Helzer & Pryzbeck, 1988). Some researchers argue that most depression in female alcoholics precedes their abuse of alcohol (Hesselbrock et al., 1985). Other researchers focus on the depressant effect of alcohol on the central nervous system and argue that for the majority of alcoholic women who experience depression, it is secondary to their alcoholism (Turnbull & Gomberg, 1988). Whether the depression is primary or secondary, if untreated, the depressive symptoms may persist even after extended periods of sobriety (Turnbull & Gomberg, 1988). Female alcoholics are also at higher risk than male alcoholics for both attempted and completed suicides (Murray, 1989). Suicide prevention techniques and treatment for depression therefore are necessary for those alcoholic women whose depressive symptoms persist after abstinence.

Many alcoholic women also experience anxiety or have anxiety disorders (Helzer & Pryzbeck, 1988). As with depression, anxiety disorders may have begun before or after the onset of alcoholism. Women with anxiety disorders may drink to self-medicate. As well, the after-effects of heavy drinking such as sleeping problems, restlessness, and anxiety may be a result of overarousal of the woman's central nervous system. Alcoholic women in a community sample are two to three times as likely as nonalcoholic women to have diagnosable panic and phobic disorders (Helzer & Pryzbeck, 1988). In a study of hospitalized female alcoholics (Hesselbrock, Meyer, & Keener, 1985), 44% of the women were found to have phobias (including agoraphobia, social, simple, and mixed phobias), and 14% of the women were experiencing panic disorders.

Eating disorders, particularly bulimia, also may occur concurrently with alcoholism. Almost a third of women in treatment for bulimia report a history of drug and alcohol abuse (Brisman & Siegel, 1984; Peveler & Fairburn, 1990). The growing public awareness of eating disorders may help bring bulimic women who are alcoholics into treatment where both problems can be addressed.

A history of sexual abuse as a child or adult may put some women at higher risk for developing alcoholism. Researchers have estimated that more than half of alcoholic women studied have a history of childhood sexual abuse, with more than 80% of those women being survivors of incest (Benward & Densen-Gerber, 1975; Schaefer & Evans, 1987). Up to 74% of alcoholic and drug-dependent women report either childhood or adult sexual abuse, including rape and incest (Wilsnack, 1984). These experiences may complicate recovery from alcoholism. With abstinence, memories of childhood and adult sexual abuse may arise or become more vivid, which may lead to relapses (Evans & Schaefer, 1980). As with the other concomitant emotional issues discussed above, concurrent treatment for posttraumatic stress disorder resulting from sexual abuse may be an important part of treatment for many alcoholic women.

Social Complications

Various aspects of female alcoholics' social networks affect their utilization of treatment resources, both in terms of the identification of their alcoholism and the social support they receive if they do seek treatment. As discussed above, alcoholic women often drink alone and at home, decreasing the likelihood that their drinking problems will be identified by friends or family. Alcoholic women may present to their physician with complaints of depression or anxiety and may receive medication for these symptoms instead of appropriate treatment for the underlying alcoholism. Both the alcoholic woman's reluctance to report her drinking and the physician's reluctance to label women as alcoholic probably contribute to physicians' underdiagnosis of alcoholism in women. Alcoholic women may seek treatment for marital difficulties and family problems that result from their alcoholism but not address the alcohol abuse that contributes to these interpersonal problems. All of these factors decrease the likelihood of a female alcoholic being identified and referred to treatment.

Female alcoholics in treatment receive less support from their spouses than do male alcoholics. This lack of support may be due both to women traditionally assuming a supportive and nurturing role in marriage and to the greater likelihood that the alcoholic woman's spouse is alcoholic or has other psychiatric problems. Lack of childcare arrangements can also impede an alcoholic woman's involvement in treatment.

Subjective Experience of Female Substance Abusers

Female alcoholics usually report poorer self-concept and lower self-esteem than alcoholic men or nonalcoholic women (Beckman, 1978; Graham & Strenger, 1988). Many alcoholic women come from families in which one or both parents are alcoholics themselves (Schaefer & Evans, 1987). Growing up in an alcoholic family could create feelings of unworthiness and low self-esteem (Schaefer & Evans, 1987), which are exacerbated by the shame that accompanies being an alcoholic woman.

Alcoholism appears to have more of a social stigma for women than for men (Hanna, 1978). Female drunkenness is judged more negatively than male drunkenness (Gomberg, 1981). This stigma contributes to the already low self-esteem of female alcoholics. It would seem that the low self-esteem and possibly a resultant lack of assertiveness are issues that need to be addressed in treatment.

Implications for Treatment Models and Programs

Female alcoholics are a heterogeneous group in terms of demographics, patterns of substance abuse, and concomitant physical, emotional, and practical problems. The best treatment models and programs for alcoholic women should be sensitive to the specific subpopulation they address, both in terms of general characteristics and individual variations within that subpopulation. An alcoholic woman may not initiate or continue treatment in a program that misunderstands or ignores important aspects of her life, whether it be her race or ethnicity, sexual orientation, health, financial needs, or social support network. An alcoholic woman will not be able to stay in treatment if pressing practical needs, such as medical care, childcare, employment, or shelter are not addressed. The preceding sections examined the range of issues that could be considered in developing treatment models and programs for alcoholic women. The next section examines how this knowledge has been translated into existing treatment programs.

CLINICAL MODELS FOR TREATING WOMEN: THE CLINICIAN'S PERSPECTIVE ON TREATMENT

In recent years, a growing number of treatment programs have been developed to provide comprehensive services to women alcoholics. Examples include the Alcoholism Center for Women in Los Angeles and The Women's Alcoholism Program of CASPAR (Cambridge and Somerville Program for Alcoholism and Drug Abuse Rehabilitation) in Massachusetts. These and other programs have taken into account the complexities of the lives of female alcoholics and attempt to address these women's practical and emotional needs in a holistic and organized fashion (Underhill, 1986; Women's Alcohol Program of CASPAR, 1990).

These programs offer a range of services including inpatient treatment, emergency counseling, residential treatment, aftercare, and outpatient treatment. An inpatient program may be utilized for the woman who is suicidal or in need of detoxification. The Women's Alcoholism Program of CASPAR offers a residential program for pregnant women. The women and their newborn children are eligible to remain in the program for up to six months after the birth.

Close working relationships with community referral sources and ancillary services are another important characteristic of these programs. Battered women may be referred to domestic violence shelters. Women in need of clothing, shelter, or childcare that cannot be provided by the alcoholism program are informed of other community resources. Women with special medical needs such as prenatal care or dependence on prescription medication are referred to physicians who are knowledgeable about alcoholism treatment. Referrals to job training programs, employment counselors, and financial advisors are also available.

The alcoholism treatment programs also help women build constructive support networks. Use of group modalities for treatment and incorporation of AA and other 12-step programs in the treatment represent methods of helping the women build support networks.

A constructive relationship with a therapist that is based on support, trust, and nonjudgmental care is another essential element of these treatment programs. Alcoholic women are seen as entering treatment with feelings of hopelessness, guilt, and self-hatred, and the feeling that they do not deserve treatment. Therapists are trained to help clients increase their self-esteem and self-acceptance and build new coping skills as alternatives to drinking. Therapists also help clients through the various crises experienced by alcoholic women. After the client has been abstinent for a period, the therapist may begin to address other emotional issues, such as depression or sexual abuse.

Many therapists report that treating alcoholic women can be frustrating at times. Practical and emotional barriers to treatment and the lack of social supports may lead to lack of progress or early termination. Therapists working in specialized treatment programs for women use relationships with other clinicians and regular supervision to prevent therapist burnout.

Research and clinical experience have provided information on the heterogeneous nature of the population of female alcoholics and the complexities of concomitant issues such as lack of social support, comorbidity of other psychiatric problems, low self-esteem, stigmatization of female alcoholics, and dependence on prescription medications. It would be helpful to clinicians to have research on how these factors affect treatment variables such as case identification, remaining in treatment, and treatment outcome. Are there more and less effective ways to address the concomitant issues as alcoholism treatment proceeds? To what kinds of treatment are specific subpopulations of alcoholic women most responsive? The following sections examine what current research has been done to explore these areas.

RESEARCH ON THE TREATMENT OF WOMEN ALCOHOLICS

In considering the state of current research, three questions are examined: (a) To what degree are researchers studying women as subjects in treatment outcome studies? (b) On what treatment issues are research data on women available? (c) What major treatment research issues are not being studied with female subjects?

Women as Subjects in Treatment Outcome Research

We conducted a selective review of treatment outcome studies published since 1980. This review included treatment process and outcome studies reviewed in the Institute of Medicine (1989) report, published research on treatment listed in the Center of Alcohol Studies bibliography series on women, and selected new treatment-outcome studies not yet indexed in these sources. While this review was not intended to be fully comprehensive, major research studies were selected from throughout this period.

Of 78 treatment outcome studies[1] that used objective measures of outcome and followed subjects for at least 6 months, 21 (26.9%) reported on male subjects only ($n = 2,665$), 8 (10.3%) reported on females only ($n = 897$), 2 studies (2.6%) did not specify gender ($n = 324$), 33 (42.3%) included both male and female subjects, but did not report outcomes separately by gender ($n = 3,114$ males, 911 females), and 14 (17.9%) included both males and females and reported outcomes separately by gender ($n = 5,438$ males, 1,360 females). Among studies that had male and female subjects but did not report analyses by sex, 10 (30%) had less than 20% female subjects. These statistics, although based on a less complete sample of studies than Vannicelli (1984), suggest increased research attention to women in treatment, reflected in an increase in the proportion of studies analyzing data separately by gender (from approximately 10% to 18%), and a decrease in male-only studies (from 55% to 27%). Women with drinking problems, however, continue to be studied in a minority of studies.

Treatment Research Data on Women

This section examines major studies on the identification of women with drinking problems, the selection of treatment goals, the level and intensity of treatment, and the effectiveness of specific types of treatments.

Identification and referral. Contemporary alcoholism treatment is fed by large numbers of clients who have been identified through

---

[1] A complete list of the articles reviewed for these summary statistics is available from the first author.

active case-finding procedures in various settings. Underlying identification and referral programs is the assumption that most persons with drinking problems do not readily identify or acknowledge these problems, and are not motivated to seek treatment on their own. Major sites (outside the family) for identifying people with drinking problems include the employment setting, medical settings, and the legal system.

Research on the identification of women alcoholics through employment settings has examined supervisor attitudes and the effects of training programs. In a study of referral patterns of supervisors, Young, Reichman, and Levy (1987) found that the best predictors of employee assistance program (EAP) referrals were the number of employees supervised and the supervisor's judgment of the effectiveness of the EAP. Egalitarian attitudes towards women's rights and roles, and holding a less stigmatized view of women's drinking were marginally related to supervisors' referral patterns. Cahill, Volicer and Neuberger (1982) studied the impact of supervisor training on referrals of women employees, using an experimental design that introduced specialized training into some companies while using others as controls. Over the three years of training, there was a significant increase in referrals of women employees from the companies that had received training, but no comparable increase in the control companies.

Research on the identification of women through medical information has studied the value of brief screening interviews and laboratory findings in identifying women who are heavy drinkers or alcoholics. These studies find that asking detailed questions about women's alcohol intake, and asking these questions by beverage type (beer, wine, hard liquor) is more likely to identify heavy or problem drinkers than are screening interviews such as the CAGE (Mayfield, McLeod, & Hall, 1974) or the Michigan Alcoholism Screening Test (MAST, Selzer, 1971; Russell & Bigler, 1979; Waterson & Murray-Lyon, 1989). Several laboratory values have been examined for their utility in identifying drinking problems among medical populations. Mean corpuscular value (MCV) and gamma-glutamyl-transferate (GGTP) have been reported to be the most sensitive and specific single laboratory tests for identifying male alcoholics. In an extension of this work to pregnant alcohol abusers, Ylikorkara, Stenman, and Halmesmaki (1987) reported 59.1% sensitivity for GGTP and 40.2% sensitivity for MCV in identifying alcoholics in their population. The overall predictive value of these tests (in identifying alcoholics as alcoholics and nonalcoholics as nonalcoholics) was quite high, at 88.7% for GGTP and 84.8% for MCV.

Few data are available about the role of the legal system in identify-ing women alcoholics and referring them to treatment. A study of referral sources for 550 programs that report to the National Alcohol-ism Program Information System (NAPIS) reported significantly dif-ferent referral patterns for men and women. Women were much more likely to have come to treatment through a personal referral from self, family, friends, an employer, or a clergy person, or through a medical referral, and were much less likely than men to be referred to treat-ment from the legal system (Dunham, 1986).

Data on the identification and referral of women with drinking problems suggest a number of positive methods of identifying women in diverse settings, and some differences between effective methods for identifying men and women. Specialized training for supervisors, training medical personnel to conduct detailed interviews about drink-ing patterns, and examination of specific blood chemistries are empiri-cally supported approaches. Once women are identified as in need of treatment, what goals are they seeking, and how successful are they in achieving different treatment goals?

Selection of treatment goals. A major controversy in the alcohol field has been the appropriateness of teaching clients to control their drinking rather than to abstain. Theoretical and empirical arguments on both sides of the issue abound (see, for example, McCrady, in press, a; Peele, in press). Several studies have examined drinking goals of women clients, and have examined the outcomes of treatment when moderation training has been provided. Sanchez-Craig, Leigh, Spivak, and Lei (1989) provided treatment to men and women who responded to an advertisement offering brief treatment to people who wished to reduce their alcohol intake. Thirty-seven women and 53 men re-sponded and were admitted to the study. Although clients were pro-vided a choice of abstinence or moderation, 80% selected a moderation goal. Orford and Keddie (1986) selected patients from the outpatient department of a psychiatric hospital. Subjects who expressed a strong preference for abstinence or moderation were provided treatment in accord with their stated preference. Although no data are provided, Orford and Keddie (1986) reported, "There was an almost significant tendency for men to adopt continued drinking and women to adopt abstinence" (p. 501).

Duckert and Johnsen (1987), in a study of use of disulfiram in be-havioral treatment, reported that 65% of male subjects and 69% of female subjects selected controlled drinking as a treatment goal. In a clinical trial in which subjects were randomly assigned to moderation or abstinence goals, Graber and Miller (1988) reported that, among five women assigned to abstinence, none had maintained abstinence over a 3.5-year follow-up, but that four out of the five were either asymptomatic or somewhat improved. Only two female subjects were assigned to controlled-drinking treatment, and no results of that treatment were reported by gender.

Data on the selection of drinking goals are quite limited. From Sanchez-Craig's (Sanchez-Craig et al., 1989) and Duckert and Johnsen's (1987) data, it appears that there are women who want to moderate their drinking rather than abstain, although Orford and Keddie's (1986) data seem to imply that women presenting for treatment may be more likely to prefer abstinence.

Outcomes of inpatient treatment. Inpatient rehabilitation programs are common in the United States. Several well-designed evaluations of such programs have been reported in recent years, with several examining differential outcomes for male and female patients. Alford (1980) evaluated treatment outcomes among a sample of 56 patients receiving inpatient alcohol rehabilitation, in which the treatment was based on the philosophy of 12-step programs. The 27 men and 29 women were followed for two years after treatment. Outcomes for women were markedly better than for men, with 72% of the women and 41% of the men having good outcomes (abstinence or light-moderate drinking, employed or in other productive roles, and socially stable). In contrast, Filstead (1990) reported no gender differences in outcome among a sample of 1,675 men and 684 women followed for one year after inpatient rehabilitation. Among adolescents, two studies report significantly better outcomes for female than male patients (Alford, Koehler, & Leonard, 1991; Filstead, 1990).

These well-controlled evaluation studies suggest that inpatient adolescent alcohol rehabilitation is differentially effective for young women, but that comparable treatment for adults does not consistently produce better treatment outcomes for women or men.

Level or intensity of treatment. The 1970s and 1980s saw a proliferation of residential rehabilitation facilities for the treatment of alcoholism. A number of investigators questioned the necessity for inpatient treatment, rather than less costly and less disruptive ambulatory alternatives. Even more radical have been suggestions that treatment in any formal sense is unnecessary, and that advice, bibliotherapy, or very brief treatment might yield outcomes equal to those of more extensive forms of treatment. McLachlan and Stein (1982) reported the results of a comparison of inpatient and day treatment for alcoholics. Of the 100 subjects in the study, 18 were women (9 per treatment group). They found no overall differences in drinking outcome between the treatment settings, and found no differences between settings for male or female clients. Chapman and Huygens

(1988) randomly assigned subjects (90 men and 23 women) to inpatient treatment, outpatient treatment, or a single confrontational interview. They found no differences in the proportion of subjects who were abstinent at either 6 or 18 months after treatment. At the longer term follow-up, they found that women drank less than men in the sample, but did not report analyses of treatment outcome by gender for the three treatment conditions. Sanchez-Craig and her colleagues (Sanchez-Craig et al., 1989) randomly assigned subjects to one of three treatments: (a) "Guidelines": a two-page pamphlet outlining ways to reduce or stop drinking and three 30–45-minute sessions with a therapist; (b) "Manual": a 40-page self-help booklet outlining ways to decrease or stop drinking and three 30–45-minute sessions with a therapist; or (c) "Therapist": training in the procedures in the self-help manual during six, 60-minute treatment sessions. Subjects in all treatment conditions successfully reduced their drinking, and women had significantly greater reductions in heavy and problem drinking than did men, regardless of treatment condition (among women, 50% of those receiving "Guidelines," 69% receiving "Manual," and 58% receiving "Therapist" treatment were problem-free 12 months after treatment. For men, 28%, 53%, and 41%, respectively, were problem-free 12 months after treatment).

The results of research on treatment intensity that includes women subjects parallels the larger body of research on this topic (reviewed in Miller & Hester, 1986). Only one recent study (Walsh et al., 1991) has reported superior effectiveness for inpatient treatment when compared to ambulatory care—referral to Alcoholics Anonymous with no other treatment services. No other data support the superior effectiveness of inpatient treatment over less intensive forms of treatment, and Walsh and her colleagues included only 9 women among the 227 subjects, and did not report outcomes separately by sex. In addition, two of the studies of treatment intensity that did analyze data separately by sex found that women had significantly better treatment outcomes than men. Clearly, definitive conclusions about treatment intensity cannot be drawn from two studies that included only 41 women, but the results are consistent with the larger outcome literature on this issue.

Specialized treatment programs for women. One of the most common themes in the literature on treatment of female alcoholics is the assertion that sex-segregated treatment should be preferable to treatment that includes men and women. Recently, Dahlgren and Willander (1989) reported a controlled study of 200 female patients randomly assigned to a specialty treatment program for women only (the Early Treatment of women with Alcohol Addiction program [EWA]), or to a coeducational alcoholism treatment center at the same facility. Patients were followed two years after treatment. Results uniformly favored the EWA program over the control treatment, in terms of several measures of drinking outcome—job stability, relationships with children, maintenance of custody of children, and symptoms associated with drinking.

Other studies of specialized services for women have not utilized comparison control groups, but rather have reported evaluations of the outcomes of treatment for a single sample. In two studies, pregnant problem drinkers received advice to cut down, counseling, and education. One-half to two-thirds of these patients abstained or substantially reduced their drinking (Halmesmaki, 1988; Rosett, Weiner, & Edelin, 1983).

A specialized treatment program for inner-city female alcoholics addressed the multiple health, vocational, legal, and financial needs of these patients, as well as their needs for alcoholism treatment (Bander, Stilwell, Fein, & Bishop, 1983). The authors report their experiences with 167 urban women, reporting a fairly high rate of continuation with treatment (44% for at least 6 months), and a 19% abstinence rate. They did not include a comparison of these results with patients treated in conventional treatment programs.

Rist and Watzl (1983) developed and evaluated a behavioral assertiveness-training program provided to 145 women being treated in an inpatient women's treatment program. Results at 18 months included 32% abstinent and an additional 18% improved. They also reported that the best predictor of short-term (3-month) treatment success was a positive response to the question, "Do you believe that you will ever be able to stop drinking completely?" Without a comparison group, it is not possible to assess the impact of the assertiveness training on treatment outcome, separate from the other elements of the treatment program.

Other treatment approaches. Disulfiram (Antabuse) is a medication that blocks the metabolic breakdown of alcohol, and is used as a deterrent to alcohol consumption. Only one study of disulfiram has examined the experiences of female subjects. Duckert and Johnsen (1987) used disulfiram as part of a behavioral treatment program. In contrast to most studies of disulfiram, in which it is administered on a regular basis, these investigators educated clients to use disulfiram in any of four different situations: (a) to end a binge or drinking slip, (b) to use disulfiram on a longer term, continuous basis, (c) to use disulfiram in specific situations that would be considered as high-risk for drinking, (d) to use it to attain a period of abstinence after exceeding controlled drinking goals. Duckert and Johnsen (1987) found that 30% of men and 30% of women used disulfiram at some point during the treatment or 21-month follow-up, but that reasons for using the medication appeared to be different for men and women, although no statistical analyses were reported. Women were more likely to use disulfiram to achieve abstinence when they had been exceeding their controlled drinking goals, to end a binge, or in specific high-risk situations. Men were more likely to use disulfiram on a long-term basis.

Fitzgerald and Mulford (1985) studied the impact of providing biweekly telephone aftercare contacts to 208 men and 80 women who had received inpatient alcoholism treatment. They found no differences in outcome between men and women who received the aftercare contacts, but did not report analyses of experimental versus control treatments by gender.

Predictors of treatment outcome. This section examines factors that predict more or less successful treatment outcome for women with drinking problems. Two studies that included only female subjects found several factors associated with poor outcome, including marital problems prior to treatment, a dysfunctional relationship with an important person, few primary relationships prior to treatment, multiple life problems (MacDonald, 1987), history of delirium tremens, loss of control drinking, early onset of alcoholism, lack of employment, diagnosis of antisocial personality disorder, and being unmarried/not living with husband (Smith & Cloninger, 1984). In contrast to these female-limited samples, Cronkite and Moos (1984) reported that being unmarried predicted better treatment outcome for women (while being married predicted better male outcome), as did attendance at lectures and films during treatment. Rounsaville, Dolinsky, Babor, and Meyer (1987) examined the relationships between psychiatric diagnoses and treatment outcomes. They found that women with diagnoses of major depressive disorders had better outcomes than women with no concomitant psychiatric diagnosis. In contrast, males with a depression diagnosis had worse outcomes. Also, men and women with diagnoses of antisocial personality disorder or other drug abuse had poorer outcomes.

It is clear that important treatment topics are being researched in regard to female patients. Identification of women with problems, examination of drinking goals, studies of specialized treatments for women, studies of intensity of treatment, evaluations of traditional treatment programs, and evaluation of certain behavioral approaches have all included women as unique subjects of study. Notably absent are studies that address the heterogeneity of the female alcoholic population or that study any of the clinical issues believed to be important in women's alcoholism treatment. In addition, there are a number of important lines of treatment research that have not been applied to women.

Treatment Research Not Including Women

In the last decade many areas of alcoholism treatment research have not addressed women as subjects at all. Two major reviews of treatment-outcome research (Institute of Medicine, 1989; McCrady, in press-b) describe several innovative approaches that will be briefly enumerated here. Details and references are available in the two treatment-outcome review articles cited above.

Treatment process research. Despite clinical writings pointing to the significance of the therapeutic relationship, no controlled research addresses these issues with female clients. With male or mixed samples, researchers have addressed therapist variables such as experience level, personal recovery status, and therapist skills. Treatment process research also has examined ways to motivate clients to recognize problems or seek treatment, and has examined the impact of mandating treatment involvement.

Behavior therapy. Although a number of behavioral approaches have been evaluated for female clients, other approaches have been male limited. These have included community reinforcement therapy, covert sensitization, behavioral approaches to couples or family therapy, relapse prevention, and cue exposure.

Pharmacotherapies. With the exception of one behavioral study of disulfiram (Duckert & Johnsen, 1987), no controlled evaluations of disulfiram in the last decade have systematically included women. And, despite the high comorbidity of alcoholism and other psychiatric disorders in women, no controlled studies of the effectiveness of lithium carbonate or antidepressants for female alcoholics have been reported in the last ten years.

Other treatments. Other therapies that have received some attention in the empirical literature include insight-oriented therapies, Alcoholics Anonymous, and acupuncture. In addition, some researchers have begun to systematically study the impact of matching subtypes of patients to different treatments. None of these advances have yet been applied to women.

SUMMARY AND CONCLUSIONS

Knowledge about women's alcoholism has increased in the last decade. The population of women with alcohol problems is heterogeneous in terms of age, socioeconomic status, race and ethnicity, sexual orientation, relationship status, substance-use patterns and problems, concomitant psychopathology, social supports, and self-esteem. A body of clinical wisdom has developed about how best to address the needs of female alcoholics in treatment, and specialized treatment programs have been developed. Research on treatment has pointed to a number of sensitive methods to identify women with drinking problems, and has found: (a) that women select both abstinence and controlled-drinking goals, (b) that adolescent females appear to have a better response to treatment than adolescent males, (c) that adult women may have a better response to behavioral outpatient treatment than adult males, (d) that women use disulfiram differently when provided as part of behavioral treatment than do men, (e) that specialized treatment programs for women seem to result in better treatment outcomes than mixed-sex units, and (f) that there is no evidence to date for the superiority of inpatient treatment over outpatient treatment for women. Additionally, several predictors of positive treatment outcome have been identified, including having less conflict with intimate others, a more extensive social support system, less severe alcohol problems, and experiencing a depressive disorder along with alcoholism.

Despite these advances in research, there are many gaps. First, there are still too few studies that include women as subjects, or that include them in numbers sufficient to allow for separate analyses by gender. Second, there is essentially no research that studies patient-treatment matching issues within female populations. In essence, the rich literature on the heterogeneous nature of the female alcoholic population and the numerous hypotheses about the differing treatment needs of different subpopulations of women are completely unexamined in the research literature. Third, when new treatments are developed and researched, the early research generally uses all-male populations, or makes no special attempts to recruit female subjects in sufficient numbers.

Why do these discrepancies exist? Vannicelli (1984) suggested sex bias in research. Although it is possible that sex bias is operating, there are a number of research design issues that also contribute. For example, the numbers of women in alcoholism treatment are smaller than the numbers of men, both because of the greater rates of male drinking problems and because of the barriers to women seeking treatment. To design and complete a treatment outcome study requires an enormous commitment of time and resources. If males can be recruited into a study three times as quickly as females, the researcher who wants to complete a study will be inclined to use the most available population. If both males and females are recruited into the study, and analyses by gender suggest different treatment responses, then the data from males and females cannot be combined, and the researcher loses statistical power to detect treatment effects unless a larger sample is recruited. If further analyses by subgroup within the female sample are planned, the size of the whole sample must grow even further.

The discrepancy between research and clinical practice is not unique to female alcoholics. In general, the dissemination and application of treatment research findings has been slow in the alcohol field. The National Institute on Alcohol Abuse and Alcoholism (NIAAA) held a workshop in November 1990 to address issues of research dissemination, and a number of papers related to that workshop will be appearing (e.g., McCrady, in press-b). Many clinicians, however, are suspicious of research, or find research too constraining of clinical practice, and therefore may not be willing to participate in research.

There are a number of possible ways to address the problems associated with conducting treatment research with female alcoholic populations. First, researchers need to develop designs that allow for the recruitment of larger samples of women. Accessing large clinical facilities and developing multisite studies would create a larger subject pool for research. Clinicians would have to be willing to allow researchers into their facilities, and would have to be willing to provide treatments within defined experimental protocols. If clinicians were involved in the definition and design of those protocols, they might be more amenable to collaboration. Researchers need to pay closer attention to the concerns of clinicians, and need to examine current clinical models of treatment with women.

NIAAA now requires that all studies either include female subjects, or provide a compelling justification for not including women. Reviewers and editors of journals should complement NIAAA's efforts by requiring that analyses of sex differences in treatment outcome be reported in all studies that include male and female subjects.

Finally, we would suggest a moratorium on review articles on women, substance abuse, and the treatment (including our own reviews). Too many creative scholars are putting their energy into reviewing the field rather than generating new knowledge. If some of the many creative ideas generated by researchers and scholars would be tested through serious research programs, the next review of the literature on the treatment of women alcoholics will be much richer in results.

REFERENCES

Alford, G.S. (1980). Alcoholics Anonymous: An empirical outcome study. *Addictive Behaviors*, 5, 359–370.

Alford, G.S., Koehler, R.A., & Leonard, J. (1991). Alcoholics Anonymous-Narcotics Anonymous model inpatient treatment of chemically dependent adolescents: A 2-year outcome study. *Journal of Studies on Alcohol, 52*, 118–126.

Bander, K.W., Stilwell, N.A., Fein, E., & Bishop, G. (1983). Relationship of patient characteristics to program attendance by women alcoholics. *Journal of Studies on Alcohol, 44*, 318–327.

Beckman, L.J. (1975). Women alcoholics: A review of social and psychological studies. *Journal of Studies on Alcohol, 36*, 797–824.

Beckman, L.J. (1978). The self-esteem of women alcoholics. *Journal of Studies on Alcohol, 39*, 98–109.

Bedi, A., & Halikas, J.A. (1985). Alcoholism and affective disorder. *Alcohol: Clinical and Experimental Research, 8*, 48–51.

Benward, J., & Densen-Gerber, J. (1975). Incest as a causative factor in antisocial behavior: An exploratory study. *Contemporary Drug Problems, 4*, 323–340.

Blume, S.B. (1986). Women and alcohol. *Journal of the American Medical Association, 256*, 1467–1469.

Braiker, H.B. (1984). Therapeutic issues in the treatment of alcoholic women. In S.C. Wilsnack & L. J. Beckman (Eds.), *Alcohol problems in women* (pp. 349–368). New York: Guilford Press.

Brisman, J., & Siegel, M. (1984). Bulimia and alcoholics: Two sides of the same coin? *Journal of Substance Abuse Treatment, 2*, 113–118.

Burnam, M.A. (1989). Prevalence of alcohol abuse and dependence among Mexican Americans and non-Hispanic whites in the community. In D.L. Spiegler, D.A. Tate, S.A. Aitken, & C.M. Christian (Eds.), *Alcohol use among U.S. ethnic minorities* (pp. 163–177). Rockville, MD: U.S. Department of Health and Human Services.

Cahill, M.H., Volicer, B.J., & Neuberger, E. (1982). Female referral to employees assistance programs: The impact of specialized intervention. *Drug and Alcohol Dependence, 10*, 223–233.

Celentano, D.D., & McQueen, D.V. (1984). Multiple substance abuse among women with alcohol-related problems. In S.C. Wilsnack & L.J. Beckman (Eds.), *Alcohol problems in women* (pp. 97–116). New York: Guilford Press.

Chapman, P.L.H., & Huygens, I. (1988). An evaluation of three treatment programmes for alcoholism: An experimental study with 6- and 18-month follow-ups. *British Journal of Addiction, 83*, 67–81.

Cronkite, R.C., & Moos, R.H. (1984). Sex and marital status in relation to the treatment and outcome of alcoholic patients. *Sex roles, 11*, 93–112.

Dahlgren, L., & Willander, A. (1989). Are special treatment facilities for female alcoholics needed? A controlled 2-year study from a specialized female unit (EWA) versus a mixed male/female treatment facility. *Alcoholism: Clinical and Experimental Research, 13*, 499–504.

Duckert, F., & Johnsen, J. (1987). Behavioral use of disulfiram in the treatment of problem drinking. *International Journal of the Addictions, 22*, 445–454.

Dunham, R.G. (1986). Noticing alcoholism in the elderly and women: A nationwide examination of referral behavior. *Journal of Drug Issues, 16*, 397–406.

Evans, S., & Schaefer, S. (1980, September). Why women's sexuality is important to address in chemical dependency treatment programs. *Grassroots—Treatment and Rehabilitation*, pp. 37–39.

Filstead, W.J. (1990). *Treatment outcome: An evaluation of adult and youth treatment services*. Park Ridge, IL: Parkside Medical Services Corporation.

Fitzgerald, J.L., & Mulford, H.A. (1985). An experimental test of telephone aftercare contacts with alcoholics. *Journal of Studies on Alcohol, 46*, 418–424.

Gomberg, E.S.L. (1979). Drinking patterns of women alcoholics. In V. Burtle (Ed.), *Women who drink*. Springfield, MA: Thomas.

Gomberg, E.S.L. (1980). *Drinking and problem drinking among the elderly*. Ann Arbor: Institute of Gerontology, University of Michigan.

Gomberg, E.S.L. (1981). Women, sex roles, and alcohol problems. *Professional Psychology, 12*, 146–152.

Gomberg, E.S.L., Nelson, B.W., & Hatchett, B.F. (1991). Women, alcoholism, and family therapy. *Family Community Health, 13*, 61–71.

Graham, J.R., & Strenger, V.E. (1988). MMPI characteristics of alcoholics: A review. *Journal of Consulting and Clinical Psychology, 56*, 197–205.

Graber, R.A., & Miller, W.R. (1988). Abstinence or controlled drinking goals for problem drinkers: A randomized clinical trial. *Psychology of Addictive Behaviors, 2*, 20–33.

Halmesmaki, E. (1988). Alcohol counselling of 85 pregnant problem drinkers: Effect on drinking and fetal outcome. *British Journal of Obstetrics and Gynaecology, 95*, 243–247.

Hanna, E. (1978). Attitudes toward problem drinkers. *Journal of Studies on Alcohol, 39*, 98–109.

Harford, T. C. (1976). Teenage alcohol use. *Postgraduate Medicine, 60*, 73–76.

Harris, M., & Bachrach, L.L. (1990). Perspectives on homeless mentally ill women. *Hospital and Community Psychiatry, 41*, 253–254.

Heath, D.B. (1989). American Indians and alcohol: Epidemiological and sociocultural revelance. In D.L. Spiegler, D.A. Tate, S.A. Aitken, & C.M. Christian (Eds.), *Alcohol use among U.S. ethnic minorities* (pp. 207–222). Rockville, MD: US Department of Health and Human Services.

Helzer, J.E., & Pryzbeck, T.R. (1988). The co-occurrence of alcoholism with other psychiatric disorders in the general population with its impact on treatment. *Journal of Studies on Alcohol, 49*, 219–224.

Herd, D. (1989). The epidemiology of drinking patterns and alcohol-related problems among U.S. Blacks. In D.L. Spiegler, D.A. Tate, S.A. Aitken & C.M. Christian (Eds.), *Alcohol use among U.S. ethnic minorities* (pp. 3–50). Rockville, MD: US Department of Health and Human Services.

Hesselbrock, M.N., Meyer, R.E., & Keener, J.J. (1985). Psychopathology in hospitalized alcoholics. *Archives of General Psychiatry, 42*, 1050–1055.

Hilton, M.E. (1988). Trends in U.S. drinking patterns: Further evidence from the past twenty years. *British Journal of Addiction, 83*, 269–278.

Institute of Medicine. (1989). *Prevention and treatment of alcohol problems. Research opportunities*. Washington, DC: National Academy Press.

Lewis, C.E., Saghir, J.T., & Robins, E. (1982). Drinking patterns in homosexual and heterosexual women. *Journal of Clinical Psychiatry, 43,* 277–279.

Lisansky, E.S. (1957). Alcoholism in women: Social and psychological concomitants. *Quarterly Journal of Studies on Alcohol, 18,* 588–623.

Lohrenz, L.J., Connelly, J.C., & Spare, K.E. (1978). Alcohol problems in several midwestern homosexual communities. *Journal of Studies on Alcohol, 39,* 1959–1963.

MacDonald, J.G. (1987). Predictors of treatment outcome for alcoholic women. *International Journal of the Addictions, 22,* 235–248.

Mayfield, D., McLeod, G., & Hall, P. (1974). The CAGE questionnaire: Validation of a new alcoholism screening instrument. *American Journal of Psychiatry, 131,* 1121–1123.

McCrady, B.S. (in press-a). A reply to Peele: Is this how you treat your friends? *Addictive Behaviors.*

McCrady, B.S. (in press-b). Promising but underutilized treatment approaches. *Alcohol, Health and Research World.*

McCrady, B.S., Noel, N.E., Abrams, D.B., Stout, R.L., Nelson, H.F., & Hay, W. (1986). Comparative effectiveness of three types of spouse involvement in outpatient behavioral alcoholism treatment. *Journal of Studies on Alcohol, 47,* 459–467.

McGirr, K.J. (1975). Alcohol use and abuse in the gay community: A view toward alienation. In K. Jay & A. Youth (Eds.), *After you're out.* New York: Pyramid Books.

McLachlan, J.F.C., & Stein, R.L. (1982). Evaluation of a day clinic for alcoholics. *Journal of Studies on Alcohol, 43,* 261–272.

Miller, W.R., & Hester, R. (1986). Inpatient alcoholism treatment: Who benefits? *American Psychologist, 41,* 794–805.

Murray, J.B. (1989). Psychologists and alcoholic women. *Psychological Reports, 64,* 627–644.

Orford, J., & Keddie, A. (1986). Abstinence or controlled drinking in clinical practice: A test of the dependence and persuasion hypotheses. *British Journal of Addiction, 81,* 495–504.

Peele, S. (in press). Alcoholism, politics, and bureaucracy: The consensus against controlled-drinking therapy in America. *Addictive Behaviors.*

Perodeau, G.A. (1984). Married alcoholic women: A review. *Journal of Drug Issues, 14,* 703–719.

Peveler, R., & Fairburn, C. (1990). Eating disorders in women who abuse alcohol. *British Journal of Addiction, 85,* 1633–1638.

Pollitt, K. (1990). A new assault on feminism. *The Nation,* March 26, 1990, 409–418.

Rist, F., & Watzl, H. (1983). Self-assessment of relapse risk and assertiveness in relation to treatment outcome of female alcoholics. *Addictive Behaviors, 8,* 121–127.

Robins, L.N. (1989). Alcohol abuse in Blacks and Whites as indicated in the Epidemiological Catchment Area Program. In D.L. Spiegler, D.A. Tate, S.A. Aitken, & C.M. Christian (Eds.), *Alcohol use among U.S. ethnic minorities* (pp. 63–73). Rockville, MD: US Department of Health and Human Services.

Rosett, H.L., Weiner, L. & Edelin, K.C. (1983). Treatment experience with pregnant problem drinkers. *Journal of the American Medical Association, 249*, 2029–2033.

Rounsaville, B.J., Dolinsky, Z.S., Babor, T.F., & Meyer, R.E. (1987). Psychopathology as a predictor of treatment outcome in alcoholics. *Archives of General Psychiatry, 44*, 505–513.

Russell, M., & Bigler, L. (1979). Screening for alcohol-related problems in an outpatient obstetric-gynecologic clinic. *American Journal of Obstetrics and Gynecology, 134*, 4–12.

Sanchez-Craig, M., Leigh, G., Spivak, K., & Lei, H. (1989). Superior outcome of females over males after brief treatment for the reduction of heavy drinking. *British Journal of Addiction, 84*, 395–404.

Sandmaier, M. (1984). Alcohol, mood-altering drugs, and smoking. In Boston Women's Health Collective (Eds.), *The new our bodies, ourselves*. New York: Simon & Schuster.

Schaefer, S., & Evans, S. (1987). Women, sexuality, and the process of recovery. *Journal of Chemical Dependency Treatment, 1*, 91–120.

Schuckit, M.A. (1986). Genetic and clinical implications of alcoholism and affective disorder. *American Journal of Psychiatry, 143*, 140–147.

Selzer, M. (1971). The Michigan Alcoholism Screening Test: The quest for a new diagnostic instrument. *American Journal of Psychiatry, 127*, 1653–1658.

Smith, E.M., & Cloninger, C.R. (1984). A prospective twelve-year follow-up of alcoholic women: A prognostic scale for long-term outcome. *National Institute of Drug Abuse Research Monograph Series, 55*, 245–251.

Smith, E.M., Cloninger, R., & Bradford, S. (1983). Predictors of mortality in alcoholic women: A prospective follow-up study. *Alcohol: Clinical and Experimental Research, 7*, 237–241.

Thompson, K.M., & Wilsnack, R.W. (1984). Drinking and drinking problems among female adolescents: Patterns and influences. In S.C. Wilsnack & L.J. Beckman (Eds.), *Alcohol problems in women* (pp. 37–65). New York: Guilford Press.

Turnbull, J.E., & Gomberg, E.S.L. (1988). Impact of depressive symptomatology on alcohol problems in women. *Alcoholism: Clinical and Experimental Research, 12*, 374–381.

Underhill, B.L. (1986). Issues relevant to aftercare programs for women. *Alcohol Health and Research World, 11*, 46–47.

Vannicelli, M. (1984). Treatment outcome of alcoholic women: The state of the art in relation to sex bias and expectancy effects. In S. Wilsnack & L. Beckman (Eds.), *Alcohol problems in women* (pp. 369–412). New York: Guilford Press.

Walsh, D.C., Hingson, R.W., Merrigan, D.M., Levenson, S.M., Cupples, A., Heeren, T., Coffman, G.A., Becker, C.A., Barker, T.A., Hamilton, S.K., McGuire, T.G., & Kelly, C.A. (1991). A randomized trial of treatment options for alcohol-abusing workers. *New England Journal of Medicine,* *325,* 775–782.

Waterson, E.J., & Murray-Lyon, E.M. (1989). Screening for alcohol-related problems in the antenatal clinic: An assessment of different methods. *Alcohol and Alcoholism, 24,* 21–30.

Williams, C.N., & Klerman, L.V. (1984). Female alcohol abuse: Its effects on the family. In S.C. Wilsnack & L.J. Beckman (Eds.), *Alcohol problems in women* (pp. 280–312). New York: Guilford Press.

Wilsnack, S. (1984). Drinking, sexuality, and sexual dysfunction in women. In S.C. Wilsnack & L.J. Beckman (Eds.), *Alcohol problems in women* (pp. 189–227). New York: Guilford Press.

Wilsnack, R.W., Wilsnack, S.C., & Klassen, A.D. (1984). Women's drinking and drinking problems: Patterns from a 1981 national survey. *American Journal of Public Health, 74,* 11.

Wilson, R.W., & Williams, G.D. (1989). Alcohol use and abuse among U.S. minority groups: Results from the 1983 National Health Interview Survey. In D.L. Spiegler, D.A. Tate, S.A. Aitken, & C.M. Christian (Eds.), *Alcohol use among U.S. ethnic minorities* (pp. 399–410). Rockville, MD: U.S. Department of Health and Human Services.

Women's Alcoholism Program of CASPAR. (1990). *Getting sober, getting well.* Cambridge, MA: CASPAR.

Ylikorkara, O., Stenman, U.-H., & Halmesmaki, E. (1987). [Gamma]-glutamyl transferase and mean cell volume reveal maternal alcohol abuse and fetal alcohol effects. *American Journal of Obstetrics and Gynecology, 157,* 344–348.

Young, D.W., Reichman, W.R., & Levy, M.F. (1987). Differential referral of women and men to employee assistance programs: The role of supervisory attitudes. *Journal of Studies on Alcohol, 48,* 22–28.

Chapter 14

Prevention of Alcohol and Drug Problems Among Women

Ted D. Nirenberg

Department of Psychiatry and
Human Behavior
Center for Alcohol and
Addiction Studies
Brown University
and
Roger Williams Medical Center
Providence, RI

Edith S. Lisansky Gomberg

University of Michigan

INTRODUCTION

There are different models of prevention and they lead to different emphases in prevention strategy. A useful distinction is one made between primary and secondary prevention (Nirenberg & Miller, 1984). *Primary* prevention may be seen as targeted to those who manifest no signs of substance abuse and may not even use a particular substance, for example, campaigns directed toward nonsmokers to prevent the use of nicotine. *Secondary* prevention is directed toward those individuals who are considered high-risk in terms of their backgrounds and demographic characteristics or who are in early stages of use, for example alcohol/drug education for those who are children of alcoholics, experimenting with a drug, or beginning to drink heavily. In primary and secondary prevention, we are not dealing with drug-dependent or alcohol-dependent people but are rather working to head off the development of such dependence. *Tertiary* prevention involves the treatment of the consequences of drug abuse and drug dependence and, in essence, the prevention of continued abuse.

The importance of prevention efforts lies in the well-founded assumption that it is less difficult to prevent further movement on the road to alcohol and drug dependence than it is to deal with dependence, once developed. Economically, prevention makes sense because treatment is usually prolonged and expensive, and for many individuals ineffective. From the viewpoint of costs, prevention or "wellness" campaigns are less costly than the healthcare costs of treating substance abuse and addiction. Prevention has, in the past, simply consisted of lectures to school-aged children, some public health warnings, and religious injunctions. However, our knowledge base has increased significantly and it is quite clear that effective prevention is much more complex and involves, for example, peer role models, parental guidance, media messages, alternative activities, goal setting, treatment of other psychological problems, and even awareness of biological markers.

One of the many issues which face primary prevention programs is the goal or objective of the program. This will vary from one substance to another. It is simply against the law to use heroin, marijuana, cocaine, and other banned substances, so most prevention programs are directed toward *No Use*. For nicotine, although it is not an illegal substance, the goal is not to get started, because smoking cessation is quite difficult once the person is nicotine dependent. What about alcoholic beverages? The messages are very confusing. Moderate drinking in small quantities is okay (for adults); intoxication is not. Social drinking is acceptable, but not if a woman is pregnant or when one drives a car. The usual objective of primary prevention of use of alcoholic beverages by adults is not self-imposed prohibition (i.e., *no* drinking) but rather the abolition of excessive drinking, problem drinking, and alcohol abuse. It is with alcoholism per se and problem drinking that prevention, which seeks to reduce the incidence of problems, is concerned (Wallack, 1984). It is *not* the right to drink, but the social damage and consequences, including medical and family problems, which are the target of prevention strategies. The one exception is during pregnancy, because the "safe limits" are not known and women are advised not to drink any alcoholic beverages while they are pregnant. This is a matter of expediency: Fetal alcohol effects tend to occur when a pregnant woman drinks heavily and/or steadily, but it has been argued that moderate drinking, too, may impair the fetus, so to avoid any teratogenic effects, obstetricians and prenatal clinics advise abstinence during pregnancy.

Secondary prevention strategies are directed toward *early* intervention with emphasis on "danger signals" (e.g., The ABC's of Alcohol Education for Women, 1987; Roth, 1991b). The objective is to head off further development of alcohol or drug abuse. Here we cannot simply say to people, "Just Say No," because they may have already said "Yes," and they may be in the early stages of developing abuse or dependence. Sometimes secondary prevention strategies are defined to also target those who are not in the early stages of substance abuse but are particularly vulnerable to or likely to develop such problems. If, for example, a woman has grown up in an alcoholic family, responds to stress with maladaptive coping mechanisms, is involved in a divorce, has been abandoned by her spouse, is left with young children to raise, and/or is moving toward a social environment of heavy drinkers, she is a high-risk person toward whom secondary prevention strategies should be directed. Secondary prevention raises many questions. For instance, if one is to target high-risk subgroups of women, who are these high-risk women? How can we link alcohol- and drug-related problems in family relationships, health, occupational adjustment, and legal complications to secondary prevention? What useful knowledge do we have about high-risk factors for women and the consequences which appear early on the road to dependence? Should any prevention efforts be targeted directly toward women or should we assume that general prevention campaigns will work with them? There is a good deal of evidence which shows clear gender differences in the antecedents, the onset, drinking behaviors, and drinking consequences of men and women. Gender-specific programs clearly are justified and programs for women need development.

MODELS

Several models of prevention have been suggested and the selection of one model over another may have a significant influence on the type of prevention program selected (Nirenberg & Miller, 1984). For example, the *socialization or sociocultural model* is based on the assumption that people learn to use alcohol and other drugs in particular ways on particular occasions in social groups (e.g., family, neighborhood, peers, coworkers) in which they grew up. Norms are learned, and actions are based on these norms—sometimes conforming, sometimes deviating. The model increases in complexity as the different memberships and groups to which a person belongs are considered: family, church, ethnic group, neighborhood, continuing education, employment, region, etc. A young person may be both conforming and deviant at the same time, for example, conforming to peer norms and defying parental norms. Behavior relating to alcohol may change over time. For example, elderly persons may discontinue drinking as they mature, or they may begin to drink more heavily after they move into a retirement colony in which "happy hour" and social-life drinking is relatively heavy and drinking in leisure time activities is normative (Gomberg, 1990). There also is a body of research on different rates of alcohol problems among different national/ethnic/religious groups, which includes study of drinking customs or norms of these groups (Bennett & Ames, 1985). Reasoning from these data, recommendations for normative change in American alcohol use are derived, for example, that wine be drunk with meals or that pubs ("bright cherry taverns") be encouraged as community centers (Whitehead, 1975; Wilkinson, 1970).

A variant of the sociocultural model is the *social-psychological model* (Jessor & Jessor, 1975; Miller & Nirenberg, 1984; Zucker, 1979), which views problem drinking and drug abuse as a result of the interaction between the person and environmental factors. Parental and peer influences are considered primary, and the objective of strategies based on the social-psychological model is improvement of relationships and the development of more adaptive coping skills.

Finally, there is a model which is based on modification of the agent itself. This *distribution-of-consumption model* assumes a direct relationship between per capita consumption of alcoholic beverages and alcohol abuse and has as an objective a reduction in the availability of alcoholic beverages. Measures derived from this model include manipulation of price, purchase age, hours of sale and the like. The evidence of efficacy as prevention methods, however, is mixed (Bruun et al., 1975; Cook & Tauchen, 1982; DuMouchel, Williams & Zador, 1985; Parker & Harmon, 1978).

PREVENTION DESIGN

Strategies in prevention efforts range from the "individualistic" to the "situational" (Gusfield, 1976; Liepman & Nirenberg, 1984; Moser, 1980). Although the ultimate end is always to affect individual behavior to modify alcohol or drug habits, the end may be sought through attempts to control demand or to control supply. One set of strategies is primarily focused on individual behavior changes ("individualistic" or "personological") and another set on legal and economic changes ("situational" or "environmental"). An example of an individual behavior change strategy is an educational campaign or a media campaign about the destructive effects of alcohol and other drugs, or work directed toward improvements of mental health in general. Legal and economic changes take the form of raising prices or taxes, changing the hours for selling alcoholic beverages, banning the sale of alcoholic beverages to persons below a particular age, increasing the negative consequences of possession or sale of illegal substances or driving under the influence of alcohol or other drugs, and so on (Gomberg, 1980b).

There is a burgeoning literature on principles and strategies in prevention of alcohol problems. While prevention has always been a major focus in public health concerns, it is only in recent years that the biosocial sciences have developed interest in prevention of alcohol and drug problems (Blane, 1976; Gerstein, 1984; Gordis, 1988; Gusfield, 1976; Gusfield, 1982; Miller & Nirenberg, 1984; Moore & Gerstein, 1981; Wallack, 1981). The temperance movement and prohibition itself were attempts at primary prevention, just as federal laws which ban some drug substances are directed toward preventing the use of drugs which are socially disapproved (Musto, 1987). Most reviews accept the triad of host, agent, and environment. The *host* is translated as the vulnerable person or the "high-risk group"; the *agent* is the alcohol or drugs; and the *environment* includes family, neighborhood, peers, ethnic and religious groups, region, and society. Most frequently, attempts to control *supply* are directed toward the agent and attempts to control *demand* are host or environmental programs.

Historically, it is true that most prevention effort has focused on self-initiated behavior (Wallack, 1981), whether such efforts take the form of Women's Christian Temperance Union tracts or school education programs. It is also true that there have been some governmental and community controls exercised from the earliest days of the American republic, for example, licensing of taverns and taxes on whiskey. Alcohol education has a long history and there has been a naive faith that knowing facts about the effects of alcohol or other drugs would make people less likely to abuse either substance. Studies of the effectiveness of such educational efforts, culminating in a recent meta-analysis of alcohol and drug education studies (Bangert-Drowns, 1986), show that educational programs increase the recipient's store of information and frequently modify attitudes about drug and alcohol use. However, educational programs do not appear to have modified *behavior* relating to alcohol and drugs to any appreciable extent.

A number of reviews have addressed prevention viewpoints and strategies to minimize alcohol problems among *women* (Bry, 1984;

Ferrence, 1984; Morrissey, 1986; Noel & McCrady, 1984; Wilsnack, 1980). Most of these reviews cover similar ground and the points raised will be discussed, as follows:

1. Why special prevention approaches for women?
2. Which alcohol-related problems are specific to or maximally found among women?
3. Who are the high-risk subpopulations toward whom prevention efforts should have priority?
4. What are some strategies, techniques and programs used, and which seem to be the most effective?

WHY SPECIAL PREVENTION APPROACHES FOR WOMEN?

A rationale for special prevention approaches for women by Ferrence (1984) focuses on sex differences in physiology and social roles. Physiological differences include gender differences in weight, body composition, hormones, and so on. The health-related consequences of heavy drinking are different, for example, women showing greater vulnerability to hepatic disorder (Frezza et al., 1990). Heavy alcohol intake and sexual/reproductive dysfunction are linked. Women's drinking patterns are different from men's in terms of quantity/ frequency of use, settings, and visibility. Women are more frequently prescribed psychoactive drugs and are at greater risk for drug interactions; the reasons why they initiate and maintain smoking are different (Gilchrist, Schinke, & Nurius, 1989); and male heavy drinkers are more likely than female heavy drinkers to be involved in accidents. Overall, a woman's involvement with the health-care system is generally greater than a man's. The sexes differ in employment patterns, economic status, and role definition in marriage and parenting.

The gender differences seem obvious but it is important to emphasize, too, the wide-ranging heterogeneity within each gender: There are subpopulations of women in terms of age, ethnicity, socioeconomic class, occupational status, and other demographic factors. A single message directed toward *all* women is a message directed toward a very diffuse population.

ALCOHOL-RELATED PROBLEMS OF WOMEN

What are the problems to be prevented? To speak of preventing alcohol abuse or alcoholism may be too broad; alcohol abuse and alcoholism may include deviant use of alcohol, the development of tolerance, withdrawal syndrome, and a host of family, occupational, legal, and social problems. Furthermore, do "alcohol-related problems" include problems which preexist the development of alcohol abuse, which are antecedent, possibly etiological? Or should prevention efforts be concentrated on the consequences of heavy drinking and alcohol abuse?

Noel and McCrady (1984) have made a very useful distinction between primary and secondary intervention in which primary intervention is linked to antecedents and secondary intervention is linked to consequences of excessive drinking. Most of the writings about prevention programs among women define *primary* prevention, yet list as targets for programs the alcohol-related problems of women which *follow* from their excessive drinking. We will distinguish between antecedent problems, targeted for primary prevention, and the consequences of excessive drinking, targeted for secondary or tertiary prevention (see Chapter 6, this volume).

Family Problems

In the analysis proposed by Noel and McCrady (1984), family history of alcoholism, peer group encouragement and modeling of excessive drinking, the ready availability of alcohol, a lack of alternative behaviors, and life stresses are listed as antecedents. There is some empirical evidence that these are relevant antecedents (Gomberg, 1986), although questions have been raised about "life stress" as a precipitant (Allan & Cooke, 1985). Williams and Klerman (1984) describe early family life of problem drinking females as "one in which parent-child relationships are impaired and family life is destabilized by separation, neglect, erratic discipline, and poor parenting" (p. 290). While childhood, adolescent, and young adulthood antecedents are described as more inclusive than "family problems," they have been summed up by Gomberg and Lisansky (1984) as including biological/genetic factors, personality and coping mechanisms, sociocultural norms and roles, and the influence of family/peers on drinking behaviors.

Family consequences of heavy drinking include marital disruption and disturbed relationships with parents, siblings, and children. The clinical literature reports that female alcohol abusers report marital disruption more frequently than male alcohol abusers. Although the evidence is mixed, there is strong belief that maternal alcoholism has worse effects on children than paternal alcoholism (Gomberg, 1988a). While it is true that women still carry more childbearing responsibility than men, it is also true that alcoholic women display more concern and more guilt about parenting (Gomberg, 1988b).

Health Problems

The absence of longitudinal studies means that we have no evidence of antecedent health problems which predict problem drinking. There are reports of an association between premenstrual syndrome and heavy drinking but the reliability of the association is not clear. There is research evidence of an association between heavy drinking and reproductive dysfunction, although which is antecedent and which consequential is unclear. There are two health issues which have not been adequately considered in primary prevention: the use of drugs other than alcohol, and the presence of depression. First, there are consistent reports that women are more frequently users of prescribed psychoactive drugs than are men (Clayton, Voss, Robbins, & Skinner, 1986; Cooperstock, 1976). There also are indications of age differences among alcoholic persons, younger alcoholics being more likely to use illegal drugs and older alcoholics more likely to use psychoactive medication (Gomberg, 1982; Gomberg, 1989b). One of the best predictors for early onset of alcoholism among women is use of marijuana and other drugs starting at about age 13 (Gomberg, 1988c). Smoking patterns also differ. Alcoholic women are not only more frequently smokers and heavier smokers than a comparable nonalcoholic group of women, but the alcoholic women report smoking earlier in life as well (Gomberg, 1988c).

The role of depression as an antecedent to female alcoholism has produced a typology of female alcoholism (Schuckit, Pitts, Reich, King, & Winokur, 1968) and comorbidity studies show a significant association between female alcoholism and depression (Hesselbrock, this volume; Turnbull & Gomberg, 1988). The significance of depression as a consequence of heavy drinking is clear and it is difficult to determine when a woman is seen clinically to what extent depression antedates the heavy drinking. In gender comparisons of psychiatric symptomatology, there is consistent evidence that depression is reported more frequently by women than by men in the general population. As a predictor of heavy drinking, depression per se is questionable, but depression coupled with positive family history, heavy drinking by people close to the women, and similar indices, make the likelihood of female alcoholism greater. In the development of primary prevention programs for women, the significance of depression must be considered.

The health consequences of heavy drinking for women are well known (Hill, 1986; Lieber, this volume). Fetal alcohol effects, automobile accidents, liver damage, and other health consequences have been discussed in prevention reviews dealing with women (Ferrence,

1984; Noel & McCrady, 1984). In addition to acute and chronic health problems, suicide attempts and completed suicides are a significant health risk for women alcoholics (Gomberg, 1989a).

Occupational Problems

The relationship between women and employment outside the home and heavy drinking is far from clear. One study reports employed married women to have significantly higher rates of problem drinking than single working women or housewives (Johnson, 1982). Wilsnack, Wilsnack, and Klassen (1984) report highest rates of problem drinking among single working women and unemployed women seeking work. Celentano and McQueen (1984) report more heavy drinking among employed women. A recent study, comparing 301 alcoholic women in treatment with a matched sample of nonalcoholic women found that in spite of similar socioeconomic backgrounds, the women who became alcoholic had dropped out of school significantly earlier than the controls, and the occupational level of the same women, as employed adults, was significantly lower (Gomberg, 1986). These findings suggest that school and work records may show difficulties *before* the heavy drinking begins.

There is relatively little study of women, alcoholic or not, as workers. Reports usually involve percentages of women in the workplace, proportion of skilled and unskilled, utilization of employee assistance programs, and so on. Anecdotal reports suggest that women in higher status jobs are probably less likely to present workplace drinking problems than women in lower status jobs. Workplace stresses seem more likely to be associated with monotony and boredom, but in the absence of data, workplace supervisors who might be utilized in secondary prevention programs should receive advice, as well as some consciousness raising in noting work-related difficulties, such as frequent absences, sicknesses, and/or decrease in productivity (Gomberg, 1977).

Legal Problems

By the time a woman is ticketed for driving under the influence, it is questionable to describe drunken driving as antecedent behavior. There is a different line of inquiry which few have pursued: What is the nature of the relationship between female delinquency, criminal behavior, and alcohol/drug abuse? Regardless of whether a generalized tendency toward deviant behavior is viable as an explanatory concept, or whether other explanations are required, there does seem to be a strong association between alcohol/drug abuse and criminal behavior. This suggests a potential focus for primary prevention programs directed toward women in the criminal justice system.

The legal consequences of excessive drinking usually involve public drunkenness and are manifested much more frequently among male alcoholics than female alcoholics. Young female alcoholics are more likely to be drinking in public places, are more publicly visible, and are more likely to suffer legal consequences than older women alcoholics. The relationship between public visibility of drinking and legal consequences needs study.

HIGH-RISK SUBPOPULATIONS

Although each review of prevention programs chooses a somewhat different list of "high-risk women" to target for prevention programs, the different lists do overlap. In an early review of proneness and vulnerability factors, Gomberg (1980a) described women at highest risk as young, involved in a pressure-to-drink peer group, married to or living with a heavy drinker, experiencing a life crisis or loss, and frequently drinking to escape daily problems. Wilsnack's (1980) high-risk list included daughters and wives of alcoholics, women who are depressed and/or experiencing "life crises or transitions," lesbians, women in military service, and women in the criminal justice system.

The high-risk group was listed by Ferrence (1984) as including young women, those in the labor force, those experiencing marital disruption, "pregnant and potentially pregnant women," and women who manifest depression or other psychiatric conditions. Ferrence also lists "genetic and physiological factors" but the latter are not defined. Morrissey (1986) provides a profile of a woman who drinks heavily and uses alcohol to relieve stress. It is not altogether clear whether this is a description of a high-risk woman, although that is implied in the following profile:

> She is under 45, in the labor force, most probably in a higher status occupation, and unmarried. She is more likely than other women to accept a function of alcohol valued by men: the use of alcohol to relieve tension, anxiety or solve problems. (Morrissey, 1986, p. 248).

A composite then of the high-risk women would include: a positive family history of alcohol problems, a young woman who is probably in the workforce (employed or unemployed), heavy-drinking companions, and perception of alcohol as tension reducer.

A number of other points made about high-risk women should be noted. Brown and Harris (1978) emphasized in their work on the social origins of depression among women that young women at home, with young children, and with little emotional support, are at high risk for depression, and presumably for problem drinking. Another group, unconventional women, those cohabiting in "quasimarital relationships" (Wilsnack et al., 1984) or in "out of role" lifestyles (Johnson, 1982) are more likely to drink unconventionally (i.e., heavily), and to experience adverse drinking consequences. Women who report, retrospectively, a lack of childhood supports and feelings of deprivation (Schilit & Gomberg, 1987), as well as feelings of powerlessness and inadequacy (Fellios, 1989), also may show a proneness to heavy drinking, although this tends to be reported after the development of problem drinking.

One problem with these high-risk lists in their overinclusiveness. Women, for example, who are pregnant or potentially pregnant, constitute a very large percentage of young women of childbearing age. Perhaps it would be wise to estimate greater and lesser risk and to give priority to prevention programs among those at greatest risk. It is interesting that current findings suggest that younger women are more likely to develop alcohol-related drinking problems than are middle-aged women but the younger group apparently move in and out of the problem-drinking population more readily than the older group (Wilsnack, Klassen, Schur, & Wilsnack 1991). For women in the 35- to 49-year age group, once they have developed patterns of alcohol abuse, the abuse is more likely to persist. These differences may relate to the rapid changes which occur in the lives of young women, changes in terms of marital status, career, and parenting. There also may be different characteristic behaviors at different stages of the lifespan. Prevention programs must take into account these lifespan differences.

SOME PREVENTION STRATEGIES FOR WOMEN

As noted earlier, prevention programs range from the environmental to the personological. Programs for prevention may involve *strategies to change the law* in an effort to reduce access to alcohol or other drugs, for example, establishing minimum drinking age, licensing liquor outlets, or increasing penalties for drug dealers; and *economic strategies* designed to increase the cost of alcohol and drugs, for example, raising the tax on alcoholic beverages. *Strategies may be community-based*, but oriented toward *individual behavior change*, for example, coping-with-stress education, drink-refusal skill training, or self-esteem-building exercises, in which the goal is prevention through self-initiated behaviors. In a sense, all strategies seek to effect behavior change. The legal, economic, and community programs work through social controls and the establishment of rules or messages which reach out to the whole community. In individual behavior change strategies, the message is that it is up to the person toward whom the program is directed to modify or control his/her behavior. While strategies to change the law usually are directed toward both sexes, there have been past legal restrictions specific to women, for example, regulating their presence at a bar.

Prevention strategies may also be differentiated in terms of specificity. An example of an alcohol- and drug-specific message is "good friends don't let their friends drive drunk." A nonspecific program is usually oriented toward improving mental health, for example, managing stress effectively. The reasoning is clear: Heavy drinking is related to poor mental health and alcohol abuse can be prevented by improving mental health. An *alcohol-specific* program for women is "Reflections in a Glass," developed by the National Center for Alcohol Education (NCAE, 1977), an eight-session course containing information and exercises designed to make women more aware of their drinking behavior. This program also helps develop decision-making skills. "Woman to Woman," which is sponsored by the Junior Leagues, focuses on alcohol's effect on health (Pond, 1988). This program has served as the impetus for some companies to initiate alcohol-awareness programs specifically for their female employees. Other alcohol-specific programs are the numerous educational campaigns about fetal alcohol effects (Prugh, 1986). *Nonspecific* prevention programs are directed toward low self-esteem, psychological distress, stress, depression, etc. A nonspecific prevention program has been developed in California (Project Breakthrough, 1984), directed toward women who have experienced recent marital disruption, and consisting primarily of classes on stress management and career planning. "Project Opportunity," a prevention program directed at women who were experiencing "major life transitions," focuses on increasing a woman's self-esteem (Bitonti, 1989). Preliminary results of the program suggest that increases in self-esteem led to a decrease in participants' use of psychoactive substances. Other nonspecific prevention strategies (Alcohol Programs for Women, 1980) include consciousness-raising groups, body awareness workshops, assertiveness training, sports and exercise, job counseling, and parent-effectiveness training. The broad "health promotion" campaigns are the ultimate nonspecific programs: reduce hypertension, eliminate smoking, eat right. A question has been raised as to whether such diffuse "health promotion" is effective at all (Burros, 1988).

Anti-smoking campaigns often are directed toward the young because it is during the early adolescent years smoking begins. There has been some proliferation of educational and organizational campaigns directed against adolescent drinking. "Just Say No" campaigns begin even earlier than adolescence, and organizations like Students Against Drunk Driving also work toward prevention. There are not many programs directed toward young women, although it is apparent that it would be wise to combine issues of alcohol abuse, drug abuse, smoking, sexually transmitted disease, rape, and unwanted pregnancies as targeted behaviors.

There is evidence that "a multiple prevention" approach is a good one (Bry, 1984). A multiple approach combines interpersonal and community approaches, for example, a small-group program combined with community education. There is some evidence that women are more responsive to small-group approaches and that community education reinforces the positive response. Maccoby, Fahrquhar, Wood, & Alexander (1977) have described a campaign to reduce cardiovascular disease, a campaign which included media programming, billboards, posters, and mailings about behavior measures to reduce heart attacks in two California communities. In one, the program also included workshops dealing with smoking and obesity. Outcome measures show the greatest impact in the community which received both the educational campaigns *and* workshops.

SOME LIMITATIONS OF PREVENTION EFFORTS

In all prevention work, there are problems with evaluating effectiveness. Ferrence (1984) noted in her review that there are many available prevention programs for women but evaluation components are minimal. In measuring effectiveness, the question arises: Should evaluation be done immediately after the program, six months later, or a year later? Programs often have an immediate impact which diminishes rapidly. Thus, while an educational program designed to discourage teenage pregnancy lowered the rates during its first twelve months, the rates returned to preprogram levels a year later (Telsch, 1985). The benefits of frequent "booster sessions" to prolong the initial behavioral changes needs to be explored.

It has been argued that research on antecedents of alcohol abuse is more readily applicable to prevention than to treatment (Gomberg, 1980a). As noted earlier, Noel and McCrady (1984) made an important distinction between first-stage or primary prevention based on *antecedents* of problem drinking, and second-stage or secondary prevention directed toward the problems which are the *consequences* of alcoholic drinking. Clearly, the weight of evidence shows a positive family history occurring more frequently among those who develop alcohol problems than among those who do not, but not all who are born into positive history develop into problem drinkers. A critical research question is which life events and patterns of behavior militate against the development of alcohol or drug abuse, even in a vulnerable population? There are data which suggest that the nature of a parent's drinking (daily versus unpredictable) or the presence of family rituals influence the offspring's future drinking behavior (Harford, 1984; Spiegler & Harford, 1987). Antecedents which have been well studied—for example, losses, impulsive behaviors, or marital disruption—can be the basis of prevention efforts.

Prevention work presupposes some knowledge of the earlier- and later-stage behaviors in alcohol or drug abuse. Early-stage alcohol- or drug-related behaviors need to be known because primary prevention is *preonset* intervention and secondary intervention is *early-stage* intervention. Without necessarily accepting Jellinek's phases of alcoholism (1962), it seems wise to accept the concept of phasic development of alcohol or drug abuse. It is likely that different phasic development schemes need to be described for male and female alcohol and drug abusers, but a primary task is some mapping of earlier and later alcohol-related behaviors. A brief report describes earlier- and later-stage symptoms of men and women in the "prodromal stage" (James, 1975). Early behaviors reported by male members of Alcoholics Anonymous include blackouts, guilt feelings, and gulping and sneaking drinks. Women reported personality changes, feeling more adequate when drinking, and drinking more during premenstrual days. Both men and women reported, as early signs, increased tolerance for alcohol and unwillingness to discuss their drinking. Information like that is relevant in planning primary and secondary prevention interventions.

Most alcohol prevention programs focus on alcohol use per se. Heavy drinkers, however, tend to be heavy smokers and frequently are users of other drugs. Therefore it is essential to study the relative effectiveness of alcohol-specific or drug-specific programs versus a generalized "don't-use-any-drugs" program.

SOME IDEAS FOR PREVENTION FOR WOMEN

It has already been noted that multiple strategies, individual and community, are probably more effective than either strategy alone. It seems clear that the attention paid to smoking by physicians and other health workers, combined with public information campaigns, have been effective in reducing the number of smokers.

Further information about the pre-substance abuse behaviors which distinguish female abusers from nonabusers is needed. A current research study of alcoholic women in treatment has compared these women with nonalcoholic women of the same age and social class (Gomberg, 1986). Early behaviors which distinguish the two groups of women include childhood temper tantrums, cool relationship with mother, early use of marijuana, and unsatisfactory relationships with other girls during adolescence. It is difficult to predict who, in a group of female adolescents, will develop drinking problems in their 40s, but early-onset female problem drinkers show many early signs of impulse-control difficulties. An impulsive, depressed adolescent girl with a family history of alcoholism who drinks, at times, to intoxication and already is using marijuana, clearly needs help before the problem worsens.

When high-risk adolescent girls are identified, what kinds of interventions are needed? The use of volunteers, particularly from self-help organizations, may be helpful. Some schools do present programs with recovered young people talking about their experiences, but it is important, too, with adolescent girls to develop one-to-one programs so that a recovered young person may act like an older sibling to the youngster at risk. Many alcoholism programs do involve the family in the treatment process whenever possible and family members should be involved in prevention as well. The emphasis needs to be on interpersonal interaction, whether the helping person is a relative, a peer, a recovered alcoholic volunteer or a professional therapist. Outreach programs are more workable while young people are still in school, but some imagination is called for in trying to reach those who have dropped out of school.

We have mentioned above the wisdom of combining issues in programs and dealing with alcohol, drugs, sexually transmitted disease, rape, and unwanted pregnancies in combined programs. With adolescents, sexuality is a primary concern and the task is to convince impulsive and insecure adolescent girls that the use of alcohol and other drugs often is linked with unsafe sex. It is a challenge to convey the information that there is a double standard in rape and that drinking by the rapists is viewed by the public quite differently than is drinking by the victim.

Some limited effort has been made in the direction of prevention programs for minority women. They and other populations of women, such as those that are homeless, on welfare, or living in slum housing, still are significantly underserved. Some fresh ideas are called for, ideas which should be sought among the women to be served. Most prevention strategies are, presumably, colorblind but are they equally effective with minority-group women? What would come out of meetings and interviews with unreached groups of women in public housing, welfare offices, and on the street? Working with minority women, the prevention worker needs a few ethnographic techniques to find out where the women take their troubles (Kail, 1989; Lambert, 1990; Rosenbaum & Murphy, 1990). The prevention worker, for example, who wants to develop programs for Hispanic and Native American women needs to know something of curanderismo, espiritismo, and shamanism (Gross, 1987).

Legal and economic moves which make alcoholic beverages less available impact on both men and women. Limiting the hours during which bars and cocktail lounges may serve alcoholic beverages or increasing punishments for drunken driving or possession of illegal drugs impinge on both sexes. Since driving under the influence is becoming a female as well as a male alcohol-related problem (Popkin, 1989), laws which come down harder on drunk driving will presumably affect young female drivers as well as young male drivers. It would be of interest to study whether changes in law such as recent changes in minimum purchase age affect the alcohol-related behavior of one sex more than the other.

Would feminists be disturbed if a prevention campaign directed toward female adolescents emphasized the relationship between alcohol consumption and the health-and-beauty fantasies of young women? Since cosmetics and clothing are primary interests to many female adolescents, how can this interest be capitalized in primary prevention strategies?

Effective prevention strategies call for new ideas. Can the message be delivered that moderate drinking is acceptable but abusive drinking is not? Can we perhaps turn things about so that the double standard attitude and the stigma attached to female intoxication in public be of use in preventing such intoxication? Can we turn a "Just Say No" campaign into an antirape, antidrunkenness and antidrug campaign?

REFERENCES

Alcohol programs for women: Issues, strategies and resources. (1980). Washington, DC: National Clearinghouse for Alcohol Information, National Institute on Alcohol Abuse and Alcoholism.

Allan, C.A., & Cooke, D.J. (1985). Stress life events and alcohol misuse in women: A critical review. *Journal of Studies on Alcohol, 46,* 147–152.

Bangert-Drowns, R.L. (1986). *Meta-analysis on the effects of alcohol and drug education*. Doctoral dissertation, University of Michigan.

Bennett, L.A., Ames, G.M. (Eds.). (1985). *The American experience with alcohol: Contrasting cultural perspectives*. New York: Plenum.

Bitonti, C. (1989). *Evaluation of project opportunity: Primary prevention program for women in major life transition* (pp. 1–197). Sonora, CA: Project Opportunity.

Blane, H.T. (1976). Issues in preventing alcohol problems. *Preventive Medicine, 5*, 176–186.

Brown, G.W., & Harris, T. (1978). *Social origins of depression: A study of psychiatric disorder in women*. New York: The Free Press.

Bruun, K., Edwards, G., Lumio, M., Makela, K., Pan, L., Popham, R.E., Room, R., Schmidt, W., Skog, O.M., Sulkunen, P., & Osterberg, E. (1975). *Alcohol control policies in public health perspective*. Helsinki: Finnish Foundation for Alcohol Studies.

Bry, B.H. (1984). Substance abuse in women: Etiology and prevention. In A.U. Rickel, M. Gerrard, & I. Iscoe (Eds.), *Social and psychological problems of women: Prevention and crisis intervention* (pp. 253–272). Washington, DC: Hemisphere Publishing.

Burros, M. (1988, January). What Americans eat: Nutrition can wait, survey finds. *The New York Times*, pp. 15–16.

Celentano, D.D., & McQueen, D.V. (1984). Alcohol consumption patterns among women in Baltimore. *Journal of Studies on Alcohol, 45*, 355–358.

Clayton, R.R., Voss, H.L., Robbins, C., & Skinner, W.F. (1986). Gender differences in drug use: An epidemiological perspective. In B.A. Ray & M.D. Braude (Eds.), *Women and drugs: A new era for research* (National Institute on Drug Abuse Research Monograph 65, DHHS Publ. No. (ADM) 87-1447, pp. 80–98). Washington, DC: National Institute on Drug Abuse.

Cook, P., & Tauchen, G. (1982). The effect of liquor taxes on heavy drinking. *Bell Journal of Economics, 13*, 379–390.

Cooperstock, R. (1976). Psychotropic drug use among women. *Canadian Medical Association Journal, 115*, 760–763.

DuMouchel, W., Williams, A., & Zador, P. (1985). *Raising the alcohol purchase age: Its effects on fatal motor vehicle crashes in 26 states*. Washington, DC: *Insurance Institute for Highway Safety*.

Fellios, P.G. (1989). Alcoholism in women: Causes, treatment, and prevention. In G.W. Lawson & A.W. Lawson (Eds.), *Alcoholism and substance abuse in special populations* (pp. 11–36). Rockville, MD: Aspen Publishers.

Ferrence, R.G. (1984). Prevention of alcohol problems in women. In S.C. Wilsnack & L.J. Beckman (Eds.), *Alcohol problems in women* (pp. 413–442). New York: Guilford.

Frezza, M., diPadova, C., Pozzato, G., Terpin, M., Baraona, E., & Lieber, C.S. (1990). High blood alcohol levels in women: The role of decreased gastric alcohol dehydrogenease activity and first-pass metabolism. *The New England Journal of Medicine, 322*, 95–99.

Gerstein, D.R. (1984). *Toward the prevention of alcohol problems—government, business, and community action.* Washington, DC: National Academy Press.

Gerstein, D.R. (1990). *Treating drug problems.* Washington, DC: National Academy Press.

Gilchrist, L.D., Schinke, S.P., & Nurius, P. (1989). Reducing onset of habitual smoking among women. *Preventive Medicine, 18*(2), 235–248.

Gomberg, E.S. (1977). Women, work, and alcohol: A disturbing trend. *Supervisory Management, 22*, 16–20.

Gomberg, E.S. (1980a). Risk factors related to alcohol problems among women: Proneness and vulnerability. Institute on Alcohol Abuse and Alcoholism. *Alcoholism and alcohol abuse among women: Research Issues.* (Research Monograph No. 1, DHEW Publication No. (ADM) 80-835, pp. 83–106.) Washington, DC: National Institute on Alcohol Abuse and Alcoholism.

Gomberg, E.S. (1980b). *Prevention issues: Report of a study: Alcoholism and related problems: Opportunity for research* (Publ. 10M 80-04, pp. 103–138). Washington, DC: National Academy of Sciences.

Gomberg, E.S.L. (1982). The young male alcoholic: A pilot study. *Journal of Studies on Alcohol, 43*, 683–701.

Gomberg, E.S.L. (1986). Women and alcoholism: Psychosocial issues. *Women and alcohol: Health-related issues* (Research Monograph 16, DHHS Publ. No. (ADM) 86-1139. pp.78–120). Washington, DC: National Institute on Alcohol Abuse and Alcoholism.

Gomberg, E.S.L. (1988a). Alcoholic women in treatment: The question of stigma and age. *Alcohol & Alcoholism, 23*, 507–514.

Gomberg, E.S.L. (1988b). Shame and guilt issues among women alcoholics. *Alcoholism Treatment Quarterly, 4*, 139–155.

Gomberg, E.S.L. (1988c). Alcoholism in women: Predicting age at onset. *Alcoholism: Clinical and Experimental Research, 12*, 337 (abstract).

Gomberg, E.S.L. (1989a). Suicide risk among women with alcohol problems. *American Journal of Public Health, 79*, 1363–1365.

Gomberg, E.S.L. (1989b). Alcoholism in women: Use of other drugs. *Alcoholism: Clinical and Experimental Research, 13*, 338 (abstract).

Gomberg, E.S.L. (1990). Drugs, alcohol and aging. In L.T. Kozlowski et al. (Eds.), *Research advances in alcohol and drug problems* (Volume 10, pp. 178–213). Toronto: Addiction Research Foundation.

Gomberg, E.S.L., & Lisansky, J.M. (1984). Antecedents of alcohol problems in women. In S.C. Wilsnack & L.J. Beckman (Eds.), *Alcohol problems in women* (pp. 233–259). New York: Guilford.

Gordis, E. (1988). A perspective on science and public health policy. Public Health Reports, *Journal of the U.S. Public Health Service, 103*, 575–578.

Gross, E.R. (1987). *Curanderismo, espiritismo, shamanism and social work practice* (Working papers). Ann Arbor: School of Social Work, University of Michigan.

Gusfield, J.R. (1976). The prevention of drinking problems. In W.J. Filstead, J. Rossi, & M. Keller (Eds.), *Alcohol and alcohol problems: New thinking and new directions* (pp. 267–291). Cambridge, MA: Ballinger/Lippincott.

Gusfield, J.R. (1982). Prevention: Rise, decline and renaissance. In E.L. Gomberg, H.R. White, & J.A. Carpenter (Eds.), *Alcohol, science and society revisited* (pp. 402–425). Ann Arbor, MI: University of Michigan Press.

Harford, T.C. (1984). Situational factors in drinking: A developmental perspective on drinking contexts. In P.M. Miller, & T.D. Nirenberg (Eds.), *Prevention of alcohol abuse* (pp. 119–156). New York: Plenum Press.

Hill, S.Y. (1986). Physiological effects of alcohol in women. *Women and alcohol: Health-related issues* (Research Monograph No. 16, DHHS Publication No. (ADM) 86-1139, pp. 199–214). Washington, DC: National Institute on Alcohol Abuse and Alcoholism.

James, J.E. (1975). Symptoms of alcoholism in women: A preliminary survey of A.A. members. *Journal of Studies on Alcohol, 36*, 1564–1569.

Jellinek, E.M. (1962). Phases of alcohol addiction. In D.J. Pittman & C.R. Snyder (Eds.), *Society, culture and drinking patterns* (pp. 356–368). New York: Wiley.

Jessor, R., & Jessor, S.L. (1975) Adolescent development and the onset of drinking. *Journal of Studies on Alcohol, 36*, 27–51.

Johnson, P.B. (1982). Sex differences, women's roles and alcohol use: Preliminary national data. *Journal of Social Issues, 38*, 93–116.

Kail, B.L. (1989). Drugs, gender and ethnicity: Is the older minority woman at risk? *Journal of Drug Issues, 19*(2), 171–179.

Lambert, E.Y. (Ed.). (1990). *The collection and interpretation of data from hidden populations*. Rockville, MD: NIDA Research Monograph 98.

Liepman, M.R., & Nirenberg, T.D. (1984). Prevention of substance abuse problems. In M.R. Liepman, R.C. Anderson, & J.V. Fisher (Eds.), *Family Medicine Curriculum Guide to Substance Abuse* (pp. 1–30). Kansas City, Missouri: *The Society of Teachers of Family Medicine*.

Maccoby, N., Farquhar, J.W., Wood, P.D., & Alexander, J. (1977). Reducing the risk of cardiovascular disease: Effects of a community-based campaign on knowledge and behavior. *Journal of Community Health, 3*, 100–114.

Miller, P.M., & Nirenberg, T.D. (Eds.). (1981). *Prevention of alcohol abuse*. New York: Plenum Press.

Miller, S.I. (Ed.). (1992). *The American Journal on Addictions. 1*, 1–92.

Moore, M.H., & Gerstein, D.R. (Eds.). (1984). *Alcohol and public policy: Beyond the shadow of prohibition*. Washington, DC: National Academy Press.

Morrissey, E.R. (1986). Of women, by women or for women? Selected issues in the primary prevention of drinking problems. *Women and alcohol: Health-related issues* (Research Monograph No. 16, DHHS Publication No. (ADM) 86-1139, pp. 226–259). Washington, DC: National Institute on Alcohol Abuse and Alcoholism.

Moser, J. (Ed.). (1980). *Prevention of alcohol-related problems: An international review of preventive measures, policies and programmes*. Toronto, Canada: Addiction Research Foundation.

Musto, D.F. (1987). *The American disease, origins of narcotic control*. New York: Oxford University Press.

National Center for Alcohol Education. (1977). *Program overviews of the decisions and drinking series*. Arlington, VA: Author.

National Institute on Alcohol Abuse and Alcoholism. (1981). *NIAAA public education campaign evaluation.* Rockville, MD: NIAAA Division of Prevention.

Nirenberg, T.D., & Maisto, S.A. (Eds.). (1987). *Developments in the assessment and treatment of addictive behaviors.* Norwood, NJ: Ablex Publishing.

Nirenberg, T.D., & Miller, P.M. (1984). History and overview of the prevention of alcohol abuse. In P.M. Miller & T.D. Nirenberg (Eds.), *Prevention of alcohol abuse* (pp. 3–14). New York. Plenum Press.

Noel, N.E., & McCrady, B.S. (1984). Target populations for alcohol abuse prevention. In P.M. Miller & T.D. Nirenberg (Eds.), *Prevention of alcohol abuse* (pp. 55–94). New York: Plenum Press.

Parker, D.A., & Harmon, M.S. (1978). The distribution of consumption model of prevention of alcohol problems: A critical assessment. *Journal of Studies on Alcohol, 39,* 377–399.

Pond, M. (1988). Woman to woman: Alcoholism prevention in the workplace. *EAP Digest, 9*(1), 70–71.

Popkin, C.L. (1989). Drinking and driving by young females. *33rd Annual Proceedings, Association for the Advancement of Automotive Medicine* (pp. 29–40). Baltimore, MD: Association for the Advancement of Automotive Medicine.

Project Breakthrough: Executive Summary. (1984). Inglewood, CA: California Women's Commission on Alcoholism.

Prugh, T. (1986). Point-of-purchase health warning notices. *Alcohol Health and Research World, 10,* 36–37.

Rosenbaum, M., & Murphy, S. (1990). Women and addiction: Process, treatment, and outcome. In E.Y. Lambert (Ed.), *The collection and interpretation of data from hidden populations* (pp. 120–127). Rockville, MD: NIDA Research Monograph 98.

Roth, P. (Ed.). (1991a). *Alcohol and drugs are women's issues (Volume one: A review of issues)* Metuchen, NJ: The ScareCrow Press.

Roth, P. (Ed.). (1991b). *Alcohol and drugs are women's issues (Volume two: The model program guide).* Metuchen, NJ: The Scarecrow Press.

Schilit, R., & Gomberg, E.S.L. (1987). Social support structures of women in treatment for alcoholism. *Health and Social Work, 12,* 187–196.

Schuckit, M., Pitts, F.N., Reich, T., King, L.J., & Winokur, G. (1968). Alcoholism. I. Two types of alcoholism in women. *Archives of Environmental Health, 18,* 301–306.

Spiegler, D.L., & Harford, T.C. (1987). Addictive behaviors among youth. In T.D. Nirenberg, & S.A. Maisto, (Eds.), *Developments in the assessment and treatment of addictive behaviors* (pp. 305–318). Norwood, NJ: Ablex Publishing.

Teltsch, K. (1985, May 19). Results mixed on curbing teenage pregnancies. *The New York Times.*

The ABC's of alcohol education for women. (1987). New York: The Association of Junior Leagues.

Turnbull, J.E., & Gomberg, E.S.L. (1988). Impact of depressive symptomatology on alcohol problems in women. *Alcoholism: Clinical and experimental research, 12,* 374–381.

Wallack, L.M. (1981). The problems of preventing problems: Barriers to policy and program. In A.M. Newman & W.E. Ford (Eds.), *Opportunities for prevention in treatment agency and settings: A conference on alcohol-related issues* (pp. 7–25). Lincoln, NB: Nebraska Center for Alcohol and Drug Abuse.

Wallack, L.M. (1984). Practical issues, ethical concerns and future directions in the prevention of alcohol-related problems. *Journal of Primary Prevention, 4*, 199–224.

Whitehead, P.C. (1975). The prevention of alcoholism: Divergences and convergences of two approaches. *Addictive Diseases, 1*, 431–443.

Wilkinson, R. (1970). *The prevention of drinking problems: Legal controls and cultural influences.* New York: Oxford University Press.

Williams, C.N., & Klerman, L.V. (1984). Female alcohol abuse: Its effects on the family. In S.C. Wilsnack & L.J. Beckman (Eds.), *Alcohol problems in women* (pp. 280–312). New York: Guilford.

Wilsnack, R.W., Wilsnack, S.C., & Klassen, A.D. (1984). Women's drinking and drinking problems: Patterns from a 1981 national survey. *American Journal of Public Health, 74*, 1231–1238.

Wilsnack, S.C. (1980). Prevention and education research. National Institute on Alcohol Abuse and Alcoholism Research Monograph 1. *Alcoholism and alcohol abuse among women: Research issues* (DHEW Publ. No. (ADM) 80–835. pp. 163–186).

Wilsnack, S.C., Klassen, A.D., Schur, B.E., & Wilsnack, R.W. (1991). Predicting onset and chronicity of women's problem drinking: A 5-year longitudinal analysis. *American Journal of Public Health, 81*, 305–318.

Zucker, R.A. (1979). Developmental aspects of drinking through the young adult years. In H.T. Blane & M.E. Chafetz (Eds.), *Youth, Alcohol, and Social Policy* (pp. 91–146). New York: Plenum Press.

Author Index

A

Aaronson, N.K. 274, *275*
Aase, J.M. 194, *210*
Abd-el-Hay, M.M. 10, *16*
Abel, E.L. 136, *137*, 192, 194, *207*, 262, 275
Abel, G.G. 265, *278*, 290, 294, 295, *309*
Ablon, J. 109, *112*
Abraham, S. 289, *307*
Abraham, W.W. 194, 195, 206, *207*
Abrams, D.B. 266, 267, 272, *275*, *276*, *336*
Adams, W.L. 71, *92*
Adelmann, P.K. 74, *92*
Adivi, C. 273, *283*
Adlercreutz, H. 34, *36*
Ager, J.W. 105, *113*, 194, *208*, *212*, 242, 243, *256*, *257*
Aghi, M. 272, *280*
Albright, C.L. 265, *275*
Alexander, J.K. 271, *278*, 351, *357*
Alexander, L.L. 273, *275*
Alford, G.S. 327, *333*
Allan, C.A. 126, 128, *137*, 345, *354*
Allan, J.S. 10, *12*
Allen, C.J. 103, 111, *112*
Alpert, J.J. 193, 194, 196, 198, *208*, *213*
Alterman, A.I. 151, *157*
Altman, D.G. 265, *275*
Altman, K. 25, *39*

Altmann, M.W. 56, *59*
Amaro, H.A. 134, *137*, 168, *185*, 225, 235, *247*, *257*
Ames, G. 67, 81, 82, 86, 93, *95*, *97*, 129, *140*, 147, *160*, 342, *355*
Amoruso, L.P. 243, *253*
Amos, A. 272, *280*
Anda, R.F. 260, 264, 267, 269, 270, 271, *275*, *277*, *285*
Anderson, A.E. 287, 291, *308*
Anderson, G.D. 177, *186*
Anderson, H.R. 201, 205, *207*, *208*
Anderson, J. 30, *38*
Anderson, K.W. 202, *209*
Anderson, W.A. 246, *248*
Andres, R. 8, *17*
Angel, E. 199, *208*
Anglin, M.D. 172, 173, *185*, *187*
Ankouute, C.C. 196, 198, *207*
Anthony, J.C. 44, *60*, 67, *96*, 218, 219, 220, *253*
Antonucci, T.C. 74, *92*
Archer, L. 63, *93*
Argeriou, M. 164, *186*
Armor, D. 218, *252*
Armstrong, B.K. 35, *36*
Armstrong, R.W. 102, *113*
Aronson, M. 197, *207*, *209*
Arthur, M.J. 2, *12*, 20, *41*
Ashenberg, Z.S. 267, *282*

Asker, R.L. 193, 200, *209*
Aston, C.E. 47, 48, 56, *58*

B

Babor, T.F. 150, 151, 152, 155, *156, 158, 159, 160*, 168, 169, *186*, 330, *337*
Bachman, J.G. 65, *95*, 264, *280*, 290, 302, *310*
Bachrach, L.L. 316, *335*
Backenheimer, M.S. 238, *250*
Bacon, M.K. 102, 103, 110, *113*
Bacon, S.D. 125, *138*
Baer, J.S. 267, 272, 274, *277, 281*
Bahn, A. 222, *251*
Bahr, H. 103, *113*
Bailey, N.C. 10, *15*
Baird, T.S. *256*
Balter, M. 238, *253*
Bander, K. 150, *156*, 329, *334*
Bangert-Drowns, R.L. 343, *355*
Bannwart, C. 34, *36*
Baraona, E. 2, 3, 4, 5n, 6, 9, 10, 11, *12, 13, 14, 15, 16*, 105, *114*, 215, *250*, 344, *355*
Barbano, H. 72, 81, *93*
Barker, T.A. *337*
Barnes, G.M. 232, *248*
Barnes, M.V. 241, *250*
Barr, H.M. 195, 196, 197, 198, 200, 201, *207, 210, 212*
Barrett, M.C. 239, *249*
Barrett, M.J. 304, *312*
Barrett-Conner, E. 20, *37*
Barrison, I.G. 193, 200, *213*
Barry, H. 102, 103, 110, *113*
Bavry, J. 264, *275*
Bartlett, E.E. 274, *285*
Bateman, D.A. 174, 175, 179, *189*
Battista, R.N. 273, *281*
Bawol, R.D. 30, *39*
Bean, J.A. 299, *311*
Beardslee, W. 235, *257*
Beary, M.D. 290, 291, 293, 302, *308*
Beatty, P.A. 235, *248*
Beauchamp, G.K. 206, *210*
Beaumont, P.J.V. 289, *307*
Beauvais, F. 228, 229, 231, *248*
Becerra, J.E. 194, 198, *207*
Beck, A.T. 181, *186*
Beck, R.C. 300, *310*
Becker, C.A. *337*
Becker, F.F. 4, *12*

Beckman, L.J. 104, *113, 117*, 127, 134, *137, 141*, 316, 321, *334*
Bedi, A. 319, *334*
Bednar, I.J. 34, *41*
Begleiter, H. 234, *248*
Behar, D. 150, *156*
Behm, F.M. 273, *283*
Belfer, M.L. 105, *113*
Bell, R.M. 269, *277*
Belle, S. 29, *38*
Benaventura, L.M. 177, *186*
Bennett, L.A. 215, *257*, 342, *355*
Benowitz, N.L. 271, *282*
Bentler, P.M. 231, *253*
Benward, J. 320, *334*
Benya, A. 267, *283*
Beral, V. 193, 201, *208*
Berendes, H.W. 193, *210*
Berenson, A. 177, *186*
Beresford, T.P. 288, *308*
Berg, C.J. 150, *156*
Berglund, K. 262, *284*
Berkowitz, A.D. 63, *92*
Berkowitz, G.S. 196, *207*
Berlin, J.A. 11, *14*
Berman, B.A. 262, 267, 268, 270, *275, 279*
Berner, P. 101, *113*
Berner, R. 148, *156*
Berta, J.L. 10, *15*
Bertera, R.L. 273, *275*
Beschner, G.M. 243, *255*
Best, J.A. 264, *278*
Bhandari, P.R. 34, *36*
Bickoff, E.M. 34, *37, 39*
Biederman, J. 298, *312*
Biener, L. 266, 267, 272, *275, 276*
Biggers, J.D. 33, *37*
Biglan, A. 264, *275*
Bigler, L. 193, 198, *211*, 325, *337*
Bihari, B. 234, *248*
Billings, A.G. 103, *113*
Bingel, A.S. 35, *38*
Bingham, S. 151, *159*
Binion, A., Jr. 228, *248*
Binkin, N.J. 274, *285*, 295, *308*
Birnbaum, I.M. 146, *156*
Birnbaum, L.M. 183, *186*
Birrell, S.J. 247, *248*
Bishop, D.B. 267, *278*
Bishop, G. 329, *334*
Bitonti, C. 350, *355*

Blackard, C. 193, 194, 196, 198, *213*
Blackburn, H. 273, *281*
Blackmon, C. *282*
Black-Sandler, R. 30, *37*
Blake, S.M. 266, 268, *275*
Bland, J.M. 201, 205, *207, 208*
Bland, R.C. 305, *308*
Blane, H.T. 118, *138*, 343, *355*
Bloch, M. 268, 270, 272, *275*
Block, J.H. 123, *138*
Bloom, J. 220, *255*
Blot, W.J. 262, *277*
Blow, F.C. 288, *308*
Blum, T. 134, *139*
Blume, S.B. 100, *113*, 183, *189*, 318, *334*
Boffetta, P. 201, *207*, 260, *284*
Bohlin, A.B. 194, 197, 200, 206, *209*
Bohman, B. *186*
Bohman, M. 44, 49, 50, 53, 54, 56, 57,
       58, *58, 59, 61*, 154, 155, *157*, 183,
       184, *187*, 234, *249*
Bolelli, G.F. 19, *40*
Bonavia, M. 19, *40*
Bookstein, F.L. 197, 200, *212*
Booth, A.N. 34, *37*
Booth, M.W. 172, *185, 187*
Borowsky, S.A. 10, *12*
Borstein, M.H. 179, *188*
Boss, M. 2, 6, *14*
Bottoms, S. 197, *208*
Bower, T. 44, *60*, 164, 184, *188*
Boyd, C. 222, *248*
Boyd, G.M. 263, 265, 266, 272, *285*
Boyd, J.H. 44, *60*, 67, *96*
Bradford, S. 317, 318, *337*
Bradley, H. 76, *92*
Bradstock, K. 295, *308*
Brady, M. 111, *113*
Braiker, H.B. 319, *334*
Brandt, H.A. 290, 297, 299, *310*
Bratelli, G. 261, *285*
Bratrude, A.P. 228, *256*
Breitrose, H. 271, *277*
Brekke, M.L. 273, *281*
Bremer, D.A. 86, *95*
Brill, N.J. 196, 199, *210*
Brinton, L.A. 30, *41*
Brisman, J. 290, 297, *308*, 320, *334*
Brody, D.J. 271, *282*
Brooke, O.G. 201, 205, *207, 208*
Brooks, E.F. *282*
Brower, K.J. 287, *308*

Brown, B.W., Jr. 271, *278*
Brown, C.H. 153, *157*
Brown, E.M. 228, *256*
Brown, F. 222, *248*
Brown, G.W. 349, *355*
Brown, J.B. 35, *36*
Brown, K. 148, 149, *161*, 273, *281*
Brown, L.S. 220, *248*
Brown, S.A. 235, *248*
Brownell, K.D. 264, 266, *276*
Brozek, J. 288, 301, *309*
Brunn, K. 51, *60*
Bruns, C. 172, *186*
Brunswick, A.F. 182, *186*
Bruun, K. 342, *355*
Bry, B.H. 343, 351, *355*
Buckley, J.D. 262, *276*
Buhler, R. 2, *15*
Bulik, C.M. 299, *308*
Bulletti, C. 19, *40*
Burch, R.E. 8, *13*
Burger, H.G. 35, *41*
Buring, J.E. 30, *37*
Burke, J.D. 44, *60,* 67, *96*
Burnam, M.A. 81, *93*, 317, *334*
Burns, K.A. 241, *249*
Burns, W.J. 241, *249*
Burros, M. 350, *355*
Burroughs, J. 290, 297, 298, *308, 313*
Busch, D. 177, *186*
Bussey, M.E. 241, *249*
Butler, N.R. 240, *248*, 263, *276*
Butler, S. 163, *187*
Buttner, H. 7, *12*
Byers, T. 270, *285*
Byrd, J.C. 263, 272, *276, 281*

C

Cabelleria, J. 4, 6, *12, 13*
Cadoret, R.J. 49, 50, *58*, 143, 151, 153,
       157, 215, *248*
Caetano, R. 82, 83, *92*, 218, 219, 220,
       223, 224, *248, 249*
Cahalan, D. x, *xi*, 22, *37*, 77, *92*, 124,
       129, *138*, 216, *249*
Cahill, M.H. 325, *334*
Campbell, I.M. 34, *38, 40, 41*
Campbell, K. 273, *280*
Canestrini, K. 164, 175, 176, *186*
Cantwell, D.P. 290, *308*
Carmelli, D. 215, *256*, 268, *284*
Carr, C.R. 267, 272, *276, 279*

Carr, D. 149, *161*
Carriker, L. 260, 261, *280, 285*
Carroll, B. 148, *159*
Carroll, K. 290, 292, 297, 299, *308, 311*
Carroll, M.E. 300, *308*
Carter, C.L. 30, *41*
Carter, E.A. 2, *12*
Casper, R.C. 290, 297, *309*
Catlin, D.H. 288, 308
Cauley, J.A. 29, 30, *37, 38*
Cederbaum, A.I. 4, *12*
Celentano, D.D. 319, *334*, 347, *355*
Cervantes, R.C. 222, *249*
Chabert, C. 10, *15*
Chaffee, F.L. 35, *40*
Chalmers, T.C. 11, *14*
Chan, A.W. 163, *186*
Chandler, W.V. 261, 263, 271, *276*
Chang, H.H.S. 34, *37*
Chapman, P.L.H. 327, *334*
Chapman, S. 272, *276*
Charlton, A. 265, *276*
Chasnoff, I.J. 238, 239, 241, *249*
Chassin, L. 264, *276*
Chaudron, C.D. 118, *138*
Chavez, G.F. 194, 198, *207*
Cheitman, E.A. 80, *92*
Cheloha, R. 70, 74, 85, *98*
Chen, S. 295, *313*
Chernick, V. *208*
Chernyk, B. 290, 292, 299, *311*
Cheshire, N. 290, 293, 297, 302, *310*
Chi, I. 81, 88, *92*
Child, I.L. 102, 103, 110, *113*
Childiaeva, R. *208*
Chou, P. 67, 68, 69, 71, 81, 82, *94*
Chow, W.H. 262, *276*
Christian, J.C. 215, *256*
Christiansen, K.O. 46, 47, *59*
Christiansen, R.C. 153, *157*
Christie, S. 149, *159*
Cigrang, J.A. 273, *281*
Ciotte, P. 19, *40*
Cisin, I.H. x, *xi*, 22, 37, 77, *92*, 124, 129, *138*, 216, *249*
Clapp, T.A. 7, *15*
Clare, A. 148, *159*
Clark, K.E. 241, *257*
Clark, W.B. 24, *37, 39*, 65, 66, 70, 77, *92*, 124, *138*
Clarke, H.T. 35, *36*
Clarren, S.K. 192, 196, 202, 205, *207, 209, 210, 212*

Claydon, P. 295, *309*
Clayton, P.J. 43, 51, 52, 58, *59, 60*, 149, *161*
Clayton, R.L. 164, *186*, 234, *252*
Clayton, R.R. 238n, *255*, 346, *355*
Clifford, C.A. 43, 51, *59, 60*
Cloninger, C.R. 44, 45, 46, 47, 48, 49, 50, 53, 54, 56, 57, 58, *58, 60, 61*, 68, *96*, 153, 154, 155, *157*, 183, 184, *186, 187, 189*, 234, *249*, 317, 318, 330, *337*
Cnattingius, S. 262, *280*
Cobb, C.F. 25, *37*
Coble, P. 195, *211*
Cochin, J. 178, 184, *190*
Coffman, G.A. 225, *247, 337*
Cohen, B.H. 271, *280*
Cohen, J. 55, *59*
Cohen, M.E. 56, *59*
Cohen, R.D. 79, *97*
Cohen, R.Y. 264, *276*
Cohen, S. 267, 272, *276, 281*
Coie, J.D. 128, *138*
Colditz, G.A. 20, 22, 30, *37, 39, 41*
Cole-Harding, S. 6, *12*
Coleman, L.M. 74, *92*
Coles, C.D. 179, *187*, 195, 206, *207, 211*
Collins, B.G. 299, *309*
Colliver, J. 72, 81, *93*
Colsher, P.L. 200, *207*
Colson, E. 107, *113*
Common, R.H. 34, *37*
Connelly, J.C. 317, *336*
Connolly, G.N. 263, 265, 266, 272, *285*
Conry, J.L. 192, *211*
Conry, R.F. 192, *211*
Conton-Ortega, T. 25, *39*
Contreras, R.J. 300, *312*
Cook, P. 342, *355*
Cooke, D.J. 126, 128, *137*, 345, *354*
Cooney, J. 148, *159*
Cooper, A.M. 101, *115*
Cooper, M.L. 77, 81, 83, *93, 97*, 219, 222, *251, 255*
Cooperstock, R. 110, *113*, 346, *355*
Coppotelli, H.C. 267, *276*
Corbett, K. 81, 82, 86, *93*
Corbett, R. 85, *96*
Corcowl, M.A. 10, *15*
Cordell, G.A. 35, *38*
Cordero, J.F. 194, 198, *207*
Coreil, J. 267, *276*
Cornelius, M. 194, 197, *207*

Correa, P. 263, *276*
Correy, J.F. 196, 198, 201, *209, 210*
Corrigan, E.M. 133, *138*, 163, *187*
Corti, B. 1, *12*
Coscina, D.V. 289, *309*
Coste, G. 19, *39*
Costanzo, P.R. 128, *138*
Cottler, L.B. 267, *279*
Courtney, Y.R. 4, *13*
Covey, L.S. 264, 267, *276, 279*
Cox, R.I. 34, *41*
Cozzolino, P. 11, *15*
Crabb, D.W. 7, 8, *14, 16*
Crane, F.A. 35, *38*
Crane, L.A. 265, *279*
Creten, D. 265, *279*
Cripps, A.W. 8, *12*
Criqui, M.H. 20, *37*
Crisp, A.H. 286, 287, 289, *309*
Cristinzio, S. 273, *282*
Crofton, J. 261, 263, 265, 266, 272, *277*
Crohan, S.E. 74, *92*
Cronkite, R.C. 330, *334*
Crooke, D.K. 35, *36*
Crossley, H.M. x, *xi*, 77, *92*, 124, 129, *138*, 216, *249*
Croughan, J. 167, *189*
Crowe, R.R. 299, *311*
Csemy, L. 75, 90, *95*
Cuervas-Mons, V. 25, *39*
Cullen, J.W. 263, 265, 266, 268, 269, 270, 272, *277, 285*
Cullen, K. 20, *37*
Cummings, K.M. 267, 272, *276*
Cupples, A. *337*
Curnow, D.H. 33, *37, 38*
Curran, J.T. 196, 198, 201, *209, 210*
Curren, F.I. 101, *113*
Curry, S.J. 267, 272, 274, *276, 277*
Curtis, R. 175, *188*
Cutter, G. 274, *285*
Czeizel, A. 196, *213*
Czeizel, E. *213*

D

Dackis, C.A. 147, *157*
Dahlgren, L. 86, *93*, 328, *334*
Daino, L. 11, *15*
Daling, J.R. 262, *276*
Daly, M. 148, *159*
Dam, J. 230, 231, *251*
Danaher, B.G. 274, *275*
Darby, B.L. 194, 196, 197, 198, *208, 212*

Darrowy, S.L. 77, 81, 83, *93*
Datta, S. 8, 12
D'Avernas, J.R. 264, *278*
Davidson, B.J. 30, *38*
Davidson, R.S. 148, *159*
Davies, M. 166, 169, *188*
Davis, A.L. 272, *277*
Davis, J.M. 290, 297, *309*
Davis, R.M. 241, 257, 259, 260, 261, 262, 265, 266, 267, 268, 270, 271, 273, *277, 278, 280, 283*
Davis, W.N. 103, *115*
Dawson, D.A. 63, 67, 68, 69, 71, 81, 82, *93, 94*
Day, N.L. 193, 194, 195, 196, 197, 200, *207, 208*
Debakey, S.F. 64, 72, 81, 88, *93, 98*
DeBanne, S. 194, *212*
DeCree, C. 247, *249*
DeEds, F. 34, *37*
DeFriese, G.H. 273, *281*
Deitz, S.R. 85, *97*
DelBoca, F.K. 155, *156*
Delgado, I.M. 129, *141*
Deloria, V., Jr. 226, *249*
Demitrack, M.A. 288, 294, 295, *311*
Demone, H. 218, *256*
Denk, C.E. 268, *284*
Densen-Gerber, J. 320, *334*
DeObaldia, R. 234, *249*
Derache, R. 2, *14*
DeSaint Blanquat, G. 2, *14*
Des Jarlais, D.C. 225, *250*
deSnyder, N.S. 222, *249*
DeVesa, J.P. 262, *277*
Devine, D. 85, *96*
Diamant, Y.Z. 241, *255*
DiClemente, C.C. 266, 267, 272, *276, 277, 283*
Diehl, A.M. 7, *15*
DiFranza, J.R. 263, 265, *277*
DiMatteo, M.R. 266, *279*
Dindzans, V. 11, *15*
Dinwiddie, S.H. 215, 234, *250*
DiPadova, C. 2, 3, 4, 5n, 6, 9, 11, *12, 13, 14*, 105, *114*, 215, *250*
Dixon, D.D. 241, *254*
Dixon, K.N. 297, 298, *313*
Dolinsky, Z. 150, *160*, 330, *337*
Donovan, J. 193, 201, *208*
Dooling, E. 193, 194, 196, *208, 211*, 240, *255*
Dorus, W. 147, *157*

Downs, W.R. 85, *95, 96*, 127, *139*
Drake, E.R. 241, *250*
Drewnowski, A. 287, 288, 294, 295, 297, 301, *309, 311*
Druley, K.A. 143, *159*
Dryfoos, J. 234, 236, *250*
DuBay, W. 230, *253*
Duckert, F. 326, 327, 329, 331, *334*
Duffy, E.L. *161*
Dufour, M.C. 2, *15*, 30, *41*, 72, 81, *93*, 216, *254*
DuMouchel, W. 342, *355*
Dunham, R.G. 326, *334*
Dupreee, L.W. 236, *250*
Duquette, D.N. 243, *250*

E

Eagon, P.K. 34, *38, 40*
Eames, A. 106, *113*
Eaves, L.J. 121, *139*, 294, 295, *311*
Ebert, M. 290, 291, 292, *313*
Eckert, E.D. 287, 290, 292, 297, 300, 302, 304, 306, *309, 310, 311*
Edelin, K.C. 194, 196, 198, 200, 206, *211, 213*, 241, *250*, 329, *337*
Edgerton, R.B. 102, *115*
Edwards, G. 342, *355*
Egerer, G. 9, *16*
Eisenberg, M. 262, *280*
Eliopulos, G.A. 288, *308*
Ellickson, P.L. 264, *277*
ElMougy, S.A. 34, *38*
El Samannoudy, F.A. 34, *38*
Emont, S.L. 267, 272, *276*
Endicott, J. 55, *59*, 69, *94*, 150, *159*, 174, *190*
Engel, J.A. 8, *13*
Engs, R.C. 100, *113*
Ensminger, M. 153, *157*
Epstein, L.H. 268, 272, *277*
Ernhart, C.B. 105, *113*, 194, 195, 198, 200, 206, *207, 208, 212*
Ernster, V.L. 259, 265, 271, *277*
Ershoff, D.H. 274, *275, 277, 282*
Ervin, C.H. 106, *115*, 202, 205, *209*
Escobedo, G. 267, *275*
Escobedo, L.G. 225, *250*, 260, 264, 269, 270, 271, *277*
Estaugh, V. 79, *96*
Estes, N.J. 127, *138*
Evans, R.I. 268, 272, *277*

Evans, S. 320, 321, *335, 337*
Eward, A.M. 205, *208*
Ewing, J.A. 290, 296, *309*
Eydoux, H. 10, *15*
vonEye, A. 231, *256*

F

Fabsitz, R.R. 215, *256*
Faden, V. 79, 80, *94*, 125, *139*
Fagal, S.M. 35, *40*
Fairburn, C. 293, *312*, 320, *336*
Fairhurst, S.K. 266, *277*
Falconer, D.S. 46, *59*
Falek, A. 179, *187*, 195, 206, *207*
Faquin, L. 245, *255*
Farholt, S. 25, *39*
Farmer, M.E. 291, *312*
Farnsworth, N.R. 35, *38*
Farquhar, J.W. 271, *277*, 351, *357*
Farrel, K. 262, *280*
Farres, J. 4, *13*
Farrington, D.P. 152, *157*
Faust, R. 272, *277*
Feighner, J.P. 53, 55, *59*
Fein, E. 329, *334*
Felix, M.R.J. 264, *276*
Fellios, P.G. 349, *355*
Felson, D.T. 30, *38*
Fenselau, C. 34, *38*
Feo, F. 11, *15*
Fereidoon, F. 25, *39*
Ferguson, T. 299, *309*
Fernhoff, P.M. 195, 206, *207*
Ferrence, R.G. *93*, 164, *187*, 344, 346, 348, 351, *355*
Feuerman, M. 273, *280*
Fielding, J.E. 273, *278*
Filipovich, H.F. 194, 195, 206, *207*
Fillmore, K.M. 63, 71, 91, *93*, 108, 112, *113, 114*, 125, *138*
Filstead, W.J. 327, *335*
Fineberg, E. 25, *40*
Fingerhut, L.A. 274, *278*
Finn, S. 290, 292, 299, *311*
Fiore, M.C. 259, 260, 262, 263, 266, 267, 272, 273, *278, 280, 282*
Fischer, P.M. 265, *279*
Fishbein, D.H. 152, *159*
Fisher, E.B. 267, *282*
Fisher, E.B., Jr. 267, *278*
Fisher, S. 171, *189*
Fitzgerald, J.L. 68, *96*, 330, *335*

Flamignni, C. 19, *40*
Flay, B.F. 264, 269, *278*
Fleisher, L. 274, *282*
Fleming, C.M. *250*
Florey, C.D. 193, 196, 198, *213*
Foege, W.H. 270, *278*
Fogg, C. 164, *187*
Folsom, A.R. 266, 268, *275*
Fong, H.H.S. 35, *38*
Fontham, G. 263, *276*
Ford, R. 153, *157*
Forman, M.R. 295, *308*
Forslund, M.A. 228, *250*
Fort, T. 128, *138*
Foster, L. 273, *278*
Fotsis, T. 34, *36*
Fowler, R.C. 146, 149, *157*
Fox, H.E. 199, *208*
Franc, M. 194, 196, *209*
France, C.P. 300, *308*
Franceschetti, F. 19, *40*
Frank, R.E. 265, *278*, 290, 294, 295, *309*
Frankenburg, F.R. 299, *310*
Franklin, J.C. 288, 301, *309*
Frassetto, S. 11, *15*
Fraumeni, J.F. 262, *277*
Frezza, M. 2, 4, 5n, 6, 9, 11, *12, 13*, 105,
    114, 215, *250*, 344, *355*
Fried, L.E. 168, *185*
Fried, P.A. 193, 196, 198, *208, 212*, 241,
    250
Friedman, G.D. 20, *40*
Friedman, S. 225, *250*
Froberg, D. 74, *93*
Frone, M.R. 77, 81, 83, *93, 97*, 219, *255*
Fullin, W. 234, *252*
Furze, C.T. 268, *284*

G
Gabral, H. 168, *185*
Gabrielli, W. 234, *250*
Gallistel, C.R. 300, *313*
Galvao-Teles, A. 25, 35, 36, *39, 41*
Garcea, R. 11, *15*
Garfinkel, L. 201, 207, 260, 261, 262,
    278, 284
Garfinkel, P.E. 292, *309*
Garland, C. 20, *37*
Garn, S.M. 262, *278*
Garner, D.M. 289, 292, *309*
Garrett, G.R. 103, *113*
Garry, P.J. 24, *39*, 71, *92*

Gavaler, J.S. 8, 11, *15, 16, 17*, 19, 20, 24,
    25, 28, 29, 34, 35, 36, *37, 38, 39,
    40, 41*
Gefou-Madianou, D. 110, 111, *114*
Geist, C. 172, *186*
Gentry, E.M. 295, *308*
Gentry, R.T. 4, 6, *13, 16*
Gerkins, V.R. 30, *40*
Gerok, W. 10, *14*
Gerner, R.H. 290, 297, *309*
Gershon, E.S. 290, 297, 299, *310*
Gerstein, D.R. 179, *187*, 343, *356, 357*
Gerstley, L.J. 151, *157*
Ghannudi, S.A. 34, *38*
Gibbons, R.D. 147, *157*
Gibbs, J. 301, *309*
Gilbert, M.J. 81, 82, 83, *93, 96*, 110,
    114, 249
Gilchrist, L.D. 264, 267, 269, 270, *278*,
    344, *356*
Gillaly, G.A. 34, *38*
Gilliam, D.M. 239, *250*
Gilligan, S.B. 47, 48, *59*
Gilpin, E. 260, 271, *283*
Ginsberg, D. 267, *280*
Giovino, G.A. 260, 262, 263, 266, 267,
    270, 271, 272, 273, *275, 276, 278,
    280, 282, 283, 285*
Givi, M.J. 273, *278*
Gjerdingen, D. 74, *93*
Gladis, M. 293, *313*
Glantz, M.D. 238, *250*
Glaser, F. 145, *160*, 167, 183, *189*
Glasgow, R.E. 273, *278*
Glassman, A.H. 267, *279*, 293, *313*
Glenn, S.W. 45, *59*, 155, *157*
Gluud, C. 25, *39*
Glynn, T.J. 269, 270, 271, 273, *279*
Goff, G.M. 290, *312*
Goist, K.C., Jr. 7, *16*
Golar, K. 241, *250*
Gold, E.O. 7, *16*
Gold, M.S. 147, *157*, 290, 291, *310*
Goldberg, S.C. 290, 297, *309*
Golden, N.L. 197, *208*
Golding, J.M. 81, *93*, 202, *208*, 263, *276*
Goldman, R. 223, *250*
Goldmuntz, J. 267, *278*
Goldstein, A.O. 265, *279*
Goldstein, H. 240, *248*, 263, *276*
Goldstein, M.S. 180, *187*
Gomberg, C.A. 103, *113*

Gomberg, E.S.L. ix, *xi*, 24, *39*, 71, 86, *93*, 112, *114*, 120, 121, 123, 124, 125, 126, 129, 131, 133, 134, 135, 136, *138, 139, 140, 141*, 143, 148, 149, 152, *158, 161*, 166, *187*, 236, 237, *251*, 316, 318, 319, 321, *335*, 337, 342, 345, 346, 347, 348, 349, 351, 353, *356, 358*
Gonczy, E. *213*
Gondoli, D.M. 85, *95*, 127, *139*
Gonzalez, D. 225, *251*
Goodall, A. 19, *39*
Goodwin, D.W. 48, 50, 54, *59*, 121, *139*, 148, *158*
Goodwin, F.K. 143, *160*, 291, *312*
Goodwin, J.M. *39*
Goodwin, J.S. 24, *39*, 71, *92*
Gordis, E. 301, *313*, 343, *356*
Gordon, G.D. *39*
Gordon, G.G. 25, *39*
Gordon, J. 272, 274, *277*
Gordon, M.G. 193, 200, *213*
Gordon, T. 22, *39*, 71, *94*
Gorowitz, K. 222, *251*
Gosnell, B.A. 301, *311*
Gottesman, I.I. 46, 47, *59*, 153, *157*
Gottlieb, N. 218, *256*
Gould, J.B. 196, *211*
Graber, R.A. 326, *335*
Graham, A.V. 238, *251*
Graham, J.M., Jr. 194, 196, 197, *208*
Graham, J.R. 321, *335*
Granger, R.H. 179, *188*
Grant, B.F. 67, 68, 69, 71, 81, 82, *94, 98*, 236, *251*
Grathwohl, H.L. 196, *210*
Graubard, B.I. 193, 194, 198, *210*
Graves, G. 22, *40*
Graves, T.D. 193, *209*
Green, J.K. 290, *308*
Green, J.R.B. 19, *39*
Greenberg, I. 168, 169, *186*
Greenblatt, M. 100, *114*
Greenstein, R. 4, *13*
Greenwald, N.E. 170, 171, 183, *188*
Greenwood, M.R.C. 300, *312*
Griffin, M.L. 164, 170, 171, 172, 176, 177, 183, *187, 188*
Grigson, M.B. 72, 81, *93*
Grisso, J.A. 193, 201, *208*
Gritz, E.R. 259, 262, 264, 265, 266, 267, 268, 269, 270, 272, *275, 276, 279*, *285*, 302, *309*

Grobsmith, E.S. 230, 231, *251*
Gross, E.R. 354, *356*
Gross, J. 272, *279*
Gruenberg, E. 44, *61*
Grunberg, H. 150, *156*
Grunberg, N.E. 261, 265, 267, 268, 270, 272, *277, 280*
Grupp, L.A. 300, *313*
Guggolz, J. 34, *39*
Gultekin, A. 149, *159*
Gumpel, J.A. 241, *257*
Gurganious, L. 241, *250*
Gurling, H.M.D. 43, 51, *59, 60*
Guroff, J.J. 290, 297, 299, *310*
Gusella, J.L. 193, 196, 198, *208*
Gusfield, J.R. 342, 343, *356, 357*
Gutai, J.P. 30, *37*
Guze, S.B. 48, 50, 53, 54, 55, 58, *59*, 121, *139*, 148, 149, 153, *157, 158*, *161*
Guzinski, G.M. 196, *210*
Gwirtsman, H.E. 290, 297, *309*

H

Haag, S.G. 10, *14*
Haavio-Mannila, E. 75, 86, *94*, 100, *114*
Haenszell, W. 263, *276*
Hagaman, B.L. 107, *114*
Haglund, B. 262, *280*
Hahn, H.K.J. 8, *13*
Hahn, R.A. 215, *251*
Hahnel, R. 35, *36*
Hainline, B. 247, *256*
Halbreich, U. 55, *59*
Halikas, J.A. 319, *334*
Hall, P. 325, *336*
Hall, R. 229, *251*
Hall, S.M. 267, *280*
Hallen, J. 9, *13*
Hallstrom, T. 90, *97*
Halmesmaki, E. 194, 196, *208*, 325, 329, *335*, 338
Halmi, K.A. 290, 291, 297, 298, 301, *309, 310, 311*
Halsted, C.H. 4, *13*
Halvorson, P.A. 290, *312*
Hamalainen, E. 34, *36*
Hamid, M. 241, *250*
Hamilton, S.K. *337*
Hammer, T. 69, 74, 76, 86, *94*
Hammond, G.D. 30, *38*, 262, *276*
Hanna, E. 79, 80, *94*, 125, *139*, 321, *335*
Hanna, J.M. 301, *310*

Hans, S.L. 241, *251*
Hansen, E.H. 110, *114*
Hanson, J.W. 192, 194, 196, 197, 199, 208, 240, *251*
Hanson, R.C. 193, *209*
Harburg, E. 205, *208*
Harding, P. 145, *161*
Harford, T.C. 67, 68, 69, 71, 79, 80, 81, 82, *94, 98*, 125, *139*, 216, 218, 236, *251, 254*, 316, *335*, 352, *357, 358*
Harlap, S. 196, *208*
Harley, E. 193, *210*
Harmatz, J.S. 298, *312*
Harmon, M.S. 342, *358*
Harper, F.D. 222, *251*
Harper, F.F. 106, *114*
Harper, G.P. 298, *312*
Harris, M. 316, *335*
Harris, T.R. 80, *95*, 349, *355*
Hartka, E. 63, 71, 91, *93*
Harvey, C. 271, *280*
Harvey, E.B. 30, *41*
Harwood, H.J. 179, *187*
Hasegawa, T. 34, *36*
Hasin, D.S. 69, *94*, 236, *251*
Haskell, W.L. 271, *277*
Hatchett, B.F. 134, *139*, 318, *335*
Hatsukami, D. 290, 292, 297, 300, 302, 303, 306, *310, 311, 312*
Hatziandreu, E.J. 259, 260, 262, 263, 266, 267, 272, 273, *278, 280, 282*, 283
Hawk, S.A. 270, *277*
Hawkins, B. 274, *281*
Hay, V.M. 8, *12*
Hay, W. *336*
Haynes, S.G. 271, *280*
Hays, R.D. 266, *279*
Haywood, E. 215, *248*
Healy, P. 270, *277*
Heath, A.C. 51, *59*, 121, *139*, 294, 295, *311*
Heath, D.B. 101, 103, 105, 112, *114, 115*, 227, *251*, 317, *335*
Hebel, J.R. 274, *284*
Heck, C.L. 304, *313*
Heeren, T. 225, *247, 337*
Heikkinen, R. 34, *36*
Heimann, R.K. 259, *280*
Heinemann, M.E. 127, *138*
Heller, J. 205, *208*
Hellmann, E. 107, *115*

Helzer, J.E. 44, *61*, 67, 68, 69, *96*, 145, 147, 151, 152, *158, 159*, 167, *189*, 267, *279*, 294, *310*, 319, 320, *335*
Hemenway, D. 30, *39*
Hempel, J.D. 2, 4, *12, 13*
Henderson, B.E. 20, 30, *40, 41*
Henderson, C. 183, *189*
Hendrickson, A.P. 34, *37*
Hennekens, C.H. 20, 22, 30, *37, 41*
Henningfield, J.E. 234, *252*, 300, *310*
Henzel, H.A. 292, *310*
Herd, D. 82, *94*, 217, 218, 219, 220, *249, 252*, 316, *385*
Herman, C.S. 196, 200, *207, 210, 212*
Hermansen, L. 121, *139*
Hernandez, R. 4, 6, *12*
Hernandez-Munoz, R. 4, *13*
Herrera, E. 7, *17*
Hershon, H.I. 147, *158*
Herskowitz, J. 164, *187*
Herzog, D.B. 290, 297, 298, *310, 312*
Hess, M. 2, *15*
Hesselbrock, M.N. 143, 144, 145, 147, 149, 150, 151, 152, 155, 156, *158*, 177, *187*, 319, 320, *335*
Hesselbrock, V.M. 143, 144, 149, 151, 152, 155, 156, *156, 158*
Hester, R. *336*
Heston, L.L. 43, 51, 52, *60*
Heywood, E. 49, 50, *58*, 153, *157*
Hiatt, R.A. 30, *39*
Higashi, A. 34, *36*
Highnet, R. 247, *252*
Higuchi, S. 2, *15*, 216, *254*
Hill, A. 231, *252*
Hill, D. 271, *283*
Hill, E.M. 237, *251*
Hill, J.L. 34, *40*
Hill, S.Y. 42, 47, 48, 56, *58, 59*, 106, *115*, 215, *252*, 346, *357*
Hilton, M.E. 24, *39*, 64, 65, 69, 70, 78, *92, 94*, 316, *335*
Hingson, R. 193, 194, 196, *208, 337*
Hirschfeld, R.M.A. 150, *159*
Ho, K.H. 221, 229, 230, *252*
Hobbie, W.L. 262, *276*
Hoechstetter, L. 8, *17*
Hofmann, M. 155, *156*
Hogelin, G.C. 295, *308*
Holck, S. 224, *252*
Hollis, J.F. 273, *278*
Holmes, R. 4, ·*13*
Holmila, M. 111, *115*

Holt, J. 301, *313*
Holt, L. 164, *186*
Holtzman, N.A. 262, *280*
Holzer, C.E. 44, *60*, 67, *96*
Honigmann, I. *252*
Honigmann, J. *252*
Honjo, H. 34, *36*
Hoover, R.N. 30, *41*
Horn, J.L. 52, *60*
Hornick, C.A. 301, *310*
Hornstein, E. 241, *255*
Horwitz, A.V. 78, *94*
Houseworth, S. 298, *312*
Howe, H. 259, 265, 269, *280*
Hrubec, Z. 51, *60*
Hser, Y.I. 172, 173, *185, 187*
Hudson, J.I. 290, 297, 298, 299, *310*
Hudson, R. 22, *40*
Hugues, J.N. 19, *39*
Hui, S.L. 30, *41*
Hunt, C. 24, *39*
Hunt, G. 103, *115*
Hunt, W.C. 71, *92*
Hunter, L. 263, *282*
Hurley, D.L. 85, *95*
Hursh, S.R. 300, *310*
Hutchings, D.E. 239, *252*
Huygens, I. 327, *334*
Hyman, M. 125, *138*
Hymbaugh, K.J. 194, *210*
Hymowitz, N. 273, *280*

I
Ibrahim, J. 1, *12*
Ickovics, J.R. 259, *283*
Imhoff, A.F. 34, *38*
Inglis, J. 199, 208
Inskip, H. 193, 201, *208*
Irtenkauf, K.T. 239, *250*
Isaac, N. *97*
Isselbacher, K.J. 2, *12*
Izzo, A. 247, *252*

J
Jackson, B. 77, 81, 83, *97*
Jackson, J.K. x, *xi*
Jackson, J.O. 143, *160*
Jacob, T. 86, *95*
Jacobs, A. 266, 267, *278*
Jacobs, D.R. 268, *275*
Jacobson, B. 272, *280*
Jacobson, G. 147, *159*

Jaen, C.R. 238, *251*
Jaffe, J.H. 152, 159
James, J.E. 352, *357*
James, M.E. 179, *187*
James, V.H.T. 19, *39*
James, W.H. 247, *252*
Janesz, J.W. 299, *309*
Jardine, R. 51, *59*
Jarvinen, M. 111, *115*
Jasonni, V.M. 19, *40*
Jasperese, D. 194, 197, 200, *207*
Jayle, M.F. 19, *39*
Jeffreys, D. 300, *312*
Jellinek, E.M. x, *xi*, 9, *13*, 52, *60*, 352,
    357
Jessor, R. 119, *139, 209*, 342, 357
Jessor, S.L. 119, *139*, 193, *209*, 342, *357*
Jimerson, D.C. 290, 297, 299, *310*
Joffe, S. *208*
Johnsen, J. 326, 327, 329, 331, *334*
Johnson, C. 289, *309*
Johnson, J. 267, *279*
Johnson, P.B. 73, 77, *95*, 218, *252*, 347,
    349, *357*
Johnson, P.R. 124, *139*
Johnson, R.C. 215, *252*
Johnston, C.C. 30, *41*
Johnston, L.D. 65, *95*, 232, *252*, 264,
    280, 290, 302, *310*
Johnstone, B.M. 63, 71, 91, *93*
Jolliffe, N. 9, *13*
Jonas, J.M. 290, 291, 297, 298, 299, *310*
Jones, B.M. 2, 11, *13*, 105, *115*
Jones, D.A. 293, 297, 302, *310*
Jones, D.L. 19, 30, *39, 40*
Jones, D.Y. *41*
Jones, K.L. 136, *139*, 193, 194, *209*, 240,
    252
Jones, M.K. 2, 11, *13*, 105, *115*
Jones, R.T. 267, *280*
Jonsson, E. 51, *60*
Jonston, M. 262, *278*
Joshi, S.H. 8, *17*
Judd, H.L. 30, *38*
Judd, L.L. 143, *160*, 291, *312*
Julia, P. 4, *13*
Julkunen, R.J.K. 3, 4, 6, *13, 14*

K
Kahn, J.H. 33, *40*
Kaij, L. 51, *60*
Kail, B.L. 354, *357*

Kalin, R. 103, *115*
Kalsbeek, W. *282*
Kalucy, R.S. 287, *309*
Kamarck, D. 267, *281*
Kaminski, M. 193, 194, 196, *209*
Kandel, D.B. 166, 167, 168, 169, *187,*
    188, 233, *252*, 264, *280*
Kandell, D. 168, *189*
Kanim, L.E.A. 268, *279*
Kannel, W.B. 22, *38, 39*, 71, *94*
Kantor, G.K. 168, *188*
Kaplan, G.A, 79, *97*
Kaplan, M. 260, 261, *280*
Kappas, A. 10, *14*
Kaprio, J. 51, *60*
Karlberg, E. 197, *209*
Karpman, B. 101, *115*
Karus, D. 166, 169, *188*
Kashkin, K.B. 245, *252*
Kassett, J.A. 279, 299, *310*
Katz, J.L. 306, *310, 311*
Kayne, H. 193, 194, 196, *208*
Kazuba, D.M. 290, 297, 299, *310*
Keddie, A. 129, 135, *140*, 326, 327, *336*
Keeler, M.H. *159*
Keener, J.J. 143, 144, 145, 147, *158*, 177,
    187, 319, 320, *335*
Keil, A. *95*, 127, *139*
Keintz, M.K. 273, *282*
Keith, S.J. 143, *160*, 291, *312*
Kellam, S. 153, *157*
Keller, L.S. 195, *209*
Keller, M.B. 150, *159*
Keller, S.E. 234, *253*
Kelly, C.A. *337*
Kelly, R.H. 29, *38*
Kelly, R.W. 34, *40*
Kelso, D. 230, *253*
Kemper, K. 298, *312*
Kendler, K.S. 121, *139*, 294, 295, *311*
Kendrick, J.S. 274, *278, 285*
Kennard, M.J. 194, 195, 206, *207*
Kennedy, J.G. 103, *115*, 147, *157*
Kera, K. 10, *15*
Kersell, M.W. 264, *278*
Kessler, M. 103, *113*
Kessler, R.C. 121, *139*, 168, *189*, 294,
    295, *311*
Keyes, S. 123, *138*
Keys, A. 288, 301, *309*
Khavari, K.A. 1, *15*
Khoury, M.J. 262, *280*

Kiel, D.P. 30, *38*
Killen, J.D. 265, *280*, 290, 294, 295, *311*
King, A.R. 7, *16*
King, L.J. 50, *61*, 147, *160*, 346, *358*
Kingstone, D. 2, 6, *14*
Kirchner, G.L. 196, 197, *212*
Kissin, B. 234, *248*
Kitano, H.H.L. 81, 88, *92*
Klassen, A.D. 44, *61*, 63, 66, 69, 70, 72,
    74, 76, 77, 78, 80, 82, 84, 86, 90,
    91, *95, 98, 99*, 109, *117*, 122, 124,
    126, 127, *140, 141*, 178, *190*, 218,
    257, 316, *338*, 347, 349, *359*
Klassen, R.W. 136, *139*
Klatsky, A.L. 20, *40*
Klebanoff, M.A. 196, 201, *211*
Kleber, H.D. 147, *161*, 173, 174, 177,
    188, 245, *252*
Klee, L. 67, *95, 97*, 129, *140*, 147, *160*
Kleinman, J.C. 270, 274, *278, 280, 285*
Klepp, K.I. 266, 268, *275*
Klerman, L.V. 134, *140*, 316, *338*, 345,
    359
Klesges, R.C. 272, 273, *278, 279, 281*
Kline, J. 196, *209*, 262, *281*
Kliner, D.J. 300, *308, 311*
Knop, J. 48, 50, 54, *59*, 121, *139*, 148,
    158
von Knorring, A.L. 53, 54, 56, 57, 58,
    59, 61, 184, *187*
Knupfer, G. 66, *95*, 112, *115*, 218, *253*
Koehler, R.A. 327, *333*
Kohler, G.O. 34, *37*
Kolonel, L.N. 86, *95*
Konrad, R. *282*
Kopstein, A. 274, *280*
Koranyi, G. *213*
Korsten, M.A. 4, 6, *12*
Kosier, T. 150, *159*
Koskenvuo, M. 51, *60*
Kosten, T.R. 173, 174, 177, *188*
Kottke, T.E. 271, 273, *281, 283*
Kotz, M. 299, *309*
Kozel, N.J. 163, *188*
Kozeny, J. 75, 90, *95*
Krahn, D.D. 287, 288, 294, 295, 297,
    301, *309, 311*
Kramer, M.S. 44, *60*, 67, *96*, 262, 281
Krause, N. 216, *253*
Krook, H. 9, *13*
Kubicka, L. 75, 90, *95*
Kuehnle, J.C. 168, 169, *186*

Kuhnert, B.R. 197, *208*
Kuller, L.H. 30, *37*
Kuminka, W. 245, *255*
Kuntz, E.J. 164, *190*
Kurth, C. 288, 294, 295, *311*
Kuzma, J.W. 193, 194, *209, 212*
Kwok, P. 198, *209*
Kyei-Aboagye, K. 241, *250*
Kyllerman, M. 197, *207, 209*

L
LaBoueff, S. 229, 231, *248*
Labriola, D. 247, *252*
Lacey, J.H. 290, 291, 293, 302, *308, 311*
LaDroitte, P. 2, *14*
LaDue, R.A. 197, 199, *212*
Lagomasino, I. 164, 166, 179, 184, *188*
Lake, M.D. 297, 298, *313*
Lambert, E.Y. 354, *357*
Lambert, M.D. 198, *210*
Lambouef, Y. 2, *14*
Lammer, E.J. 194, *213*
Lancaster, J. 195, 206, *211*
Landesman-Dwyer, S. 195, 197, *209*
Landress, H.J. 239, *249*
Lang, W. 300, *312*
Lange, U. 164, 176, 177, 183, *187*
Lantz, S. 297, 298, *313*
LaPorte, D.J. 143, *159*
LaPorte, R.E. 30, *37*
LaRosa, J.H. 75, 76, *95*
Larsen, O. 145, 148, *161*
Larson, D.B. 30, *41*
Larsson, G. 194, 197, 200, 206, *209*
Larsson-Cohn, U. 10, *14*
Latiff, A. 300, *312*
Lavori, P.W. 150, *159*
Lazaro, C.M. 268, 273, *281*
Lazarus, N.B. 79, *97*
Leaf, P.J. 44, *60, 67, 96*
Lebouvier, M. 194, 196, *209*
Lee, A. 2, *12, 196, 211, 240, 255*
Lee, J. 86, *95*
Leehey, K. 247, *257*
Lefkopoulou, M. 263, 266, *280*
Lei, H. 326, 327, 328, *337*
Leigh, B.C. *115, 136, 139*
Leigh, G. 326, 327, 328, *337*
Leino, E.V. 63, 71, 91, *93*
Leland, J. 81, 88, *95, 227, 228, 229, 253*
Lemart, E. 227, *253*

Leo, M.A. 10, *12*
Leon, G.R. 290, 292, 297, 299, *308, 311*
Leonard, J. 327, *333*
Leonard, K.E. 118, *138*
Lerner, J.V. 231, *256*
Lesch, O.M. 148, *156*
Lester, D. 2, *14*
Lester, R. 8, *16*
Levenson, S.M. *337*
Levin, E.D. 272, *283*
Levy, M.F. 325, *338*
Lewin, K. 119, *139*
Lewis, C.E. 151, 152, *159*, 317, *335*
Lewis, I.G. 193, 200, *213*
Lewis, O. 224, *253*
Lex, B.W. 7, *14, 44, 60, 164, 165, 166,*
    168, 169, 170, 171, 172, 173, 178,
    179, 183, 184, *188, 190*
Lichtenstein, E. 266, 267, 268, 272, *276,*
    277, 281
Licitra, L.M. 30, *41*
Lieber, C.S. 2, 3, 4, 5n, 6, 7, 8, 9, 10, 11,
    12, 13, 14, 15, 16, 17, 25, *39,* 105,
    215, *250,* 344, *355*
Liepman, M.R. 127, *140,* 342, *357*
Lillie-Blanton, M. 218, 219, 220, *253*
Lim, G.N. *255*
Lim, R.T., Jr. 4, *16*
Lin, G.W.J. 2, *14*
Lin, Y. 263, *276*
Lindsay, D.R. 34, *40*
Lindsay, P.K. 262, *280*
Lindsten, J. *284*
Link, M. 30, *37*
Linn, P.L. 195, 206, *207*
Linn, S. 193, 194, *210*
Lipnick, R.J. 30, *37*
Lippmann, S. 149, *159*
Lisansky, E.S. 101, *115,* 126, *139,* 316,
    336
Lisansky, J.M. *139,* 345, *356*
Liskow, B.I. 143, 146, 149, *157, 160*
Lisman, S.A. 146, *159*
Little, R.E. 106, *115,* 136, *139,* 193, 196,
    197, 198, 200, 202, 205, 206, *209,*
    210, 212
Livingston, A.L. 34, *37, 39*
Lloyd, C.W. 19, *40*
Locke, B.Z. 143, *160,* 291, *312*
Locke, J. 215, *252*
Loeber, R. 152, *159*
Logan, J.A. 264, *280*

Logue, C.M. 299, *311*
Lohrenz, L.J. 317, *336*
Lomnitz, L. 224, *253*
Loney, J. 298, *310*
Longcope, C. 25, 30, *40, 41*
Longnecker, M.P. 11, *14*
Longsdon, D.H. 268, 273, *281*
Loucks, A.B. 247, *253*
Love, K. 25, 28, 29, *38, 39*
Lowendorf, F. 7, *16*
Lowenfels, A.B. 11, *14*
Lowman, C. 218, *251*
Lubben, J.E. 81, 88, *92*
Luborsky, L. 143, *159*, 173, 181, *188*
Ludvigsson, J. 262, *284*
Luepker, R.V. 266, 268, *275, 282*
Lukas, S.E. 170, 171, 183, *188*
Lumeng, L. 8, *14*
Lumio, M. 342, *355*
Lumley, J. 196, 201, *210*
Lund, C.A. 195, *210*
Lundholm, J.K. 290, 295, *311*
Lurie, E. 218, *253*
Lye, D. 260, *285*
Lykken, D.T. 43, 51, 52, *60*
Lyman, R.I. 34, *37*

M

Ma, X.L. 10, *16*
Macaskill, P. 271, *283*
MacAndrew, C. 102, *115*
Maccoby, N. 265, 271, *275, 277*, 351, *357*
MacDonald, J.A. 7, *15*
MacDonald, J.G. 150, *159*, 330, *336*
Mack, A.M. 30, *40*
Mack, T.M. 20, *41*
Mackenzie, E. 218, 219, 220, *253*
MacLean, C. 294, 295, *311*
MacLennan, A. 100, *115*
MacRae, K.D. 193, 200, *213*
Madans, J. 270, *285*
Maddahian, E. 231, *253*
Maddem, J. 241, *257*
Maeda, T. 10, *15*
Maggio, C. 300, *312*
Magura, M. 79, *95*
Maher, L. 175, *188*
Maier, K.P. 10, *14*
Maisto, S.A. *358*
Majewski, F. 206, *210*
Mak, K.M. 11, *17*
Makela, K. 135, 136, *139*, 342, *355*

Makin, D. 164, *187*
Maldonado, J. 272, *279*
Malin, H. 72, 81, *93*
Maly, P.I. 7, *14*
Mandell, W. 197, 198, *209, 210*
Manley, M.W. 273, *279*
Mann, S.L. 196, *210*
Manshadi, M. 149, *159*
Manson, S.M. *250*
Manzella, B. 274, *285*
Marbury, M.C. 193, 194, *210*
Marcus, A.C. 267, 270, *279*
Marcus, R.N. 290, 291, 306, *311*
Marcus, S. 260, 271, *283*
Marin, B.V. 271, *281, 282*
Marin, G. 271, *281, 282*
Markides, K.S. 216, *253*, 267, *276*
Markkanen, T. 51, *60*
Marlatt, G.A. 266, 267, 272, 274, *276,*
   277
Marmer, M.E. 143, *160*
Maron, D.J. 265, *280*, 290, 294, 295, *311*
Marsh, A.G. 35, *40*
Marshall, A.W. 2, 6, *14*
Marshall, J.R. 143, *159*
Marshall, M. 102, *115*
Martier, S. 105, *113*, 194, 198, 200, *208,*
   212, 242, 243, *256, 257*
Martin, D.C. 195, 196, 197, 198, 201,
   207, 210, 212
Martin, J.C. 195, 196, 198, 201, *210*
Martin, N.G. 51, *59*
Masarei, J.R. 35, *36*
Massey, M.M. 265, 268, 269, 270, 272,
   277
Mast, E.E. 260, 264, 267, 269, 270, 271,
   275, 277
Matthew, M. 299, *309*
Mattson, M.E. 263, 265, 266, 272, *285*
May, P.A. 194, *210*, 227, 230, 231, *253*
Mayer, J.P. 274, *281*
Mayfield, D. 325, *336*
Maynard, E.C. 243, *253*
Maynes, L.C. 179, *188*
Maxwell, M.E. 290, 297, 299, *310*
du Mazaubrun, C. 194, 196, *209*
McAdoo, H. 221, *253*
McAlister, A.L. 271, *278*
McBride, A.B. 177, *186*
McCarty, D. 164, *186*
McClelland, D.C. 103, *115*
McConnell, S. 264, *275*

McCoy, M.L. 164, *190*
McCrady, B.S. 326, 331, 333, *336*, 344, 345, 347, 351, *358*
McGirr, K.J. 317, *336*
McGlothlin, W.H. 172, 173, *185*, *187*
McGue, M. 43, 51, 52, *60*
McGuire, E. 8, *17*
McGuire, T.G. *337*
McIntyre, K. 267, *281*
McKay, C. 109, *116*
McKeag, D.B. 246, *248*
McKenna, J.W. 265, 268, 269, 270, 272, 277
McKenna, T. 54, *60*
McKernon, J. 150, *160*
McKinlay, S. 194, 196, 200, 206, *211*
McKinney, J. 50, *59*
McLachlan, J.F.C. 327, *336*
McLain, L. 231, *256*
McLellan, A.T. 143, 151, *157*, *159*, 173, 181, *188*
McLellan, D.L. 272, *281*
McLeod, G. 325, *336*
McMahon, R.C. 148, *159*
McPhillips, J. 20, *37*
McQueen, D.V. 319, *334*, 347, *355*
Meade, C.D. 272, *281*
Mecklenburg, R.E. 273, *281*
Medina Mora, M.E. 83, *92*
Medley, G. 35, *41*
Mednick, S. 48, 50, 54, *59*, 121, *139*, 148, *158*, 234, *250*
Medvid, L. 199, *208*
Megia-Zelaya, A. 241, *257*
Meichenbaum, D. 274, *281*
Meier, R.V. 267, 273, *281*
Meisch, R.A. 300, *308*, *310*, *311*
Mellinger, G. 238, *253*
Mello, N.K. 164, 166, 168, 169, 170, 171, 172, 178, 179, 183, 184, *186. 188*, *189*, *190*
Mendelson, J.H. 44, *60*, 146, *161*, 164, 166, 168, 169, 170, 171, 172, 178, 179, 183, 184, *186*, *188*, *189*, *190*
Mendes de Leon, C.F. 216, *253*
Mennella, J.A. 206, *210*
Mercer, P.W. 1, *15*
Mermelstein, R. 267, *281*
Merrigan, D.M. *337*
Merry, J. 290, 291, 293, 302, *308*
Messeri, P.A. 182, *186*
Meyer, A.J. 271, *277*

Meyer, M.B. 262, *281*
Meyer, R.E. 143, 144, 145, 147, 150, 151, 152, 155, 156, *158*, *160*, 171, 177, *187*, *189*, 319, 320, 330, *335*, *337*
Meyers, A.W. 272, *279*
Mezey, E. 4, 6, 7, 8, *13*, *15*, *17*
Michelson, O. 35, *40*
Mickalide, A.D. 287, *308*
Midanik, L. 24, *37*, 54, *60*, 66, 77, *92*, 124, *138*, 166, 183, *189*
Mieczkowski, T. 222, *248*
Miller, B.A. 85, *95*, *96*, 127, *139*, 144, 145, *161*
Miller, C.D. 228, *248*
Miller, P.M. 339, 341, 342, 343, *357*, *358*
Miller, S.I. 193, 194, 196, *212*, *357*
Miller, W.C. *159*
Miller, W.J. 263, *282*
Miller, W.R. 326, *335*, *336*
Mills, J.L. 193, 194, 198, *210*
Mills, S.L. 260, 262, 263, 266, 271, *280*, *282*, *283*
Milne, S.H. 134, *139*
Mirin, S.M. 164, 171, 176, 177, 183, *187*, *189*
Mishra, L. 6, *15*
Mitchell, A.A. 194, *213*
Mitchell, J.E. 287, 289, 290, 292, 297, 300, 302, 303, 306, *310*, *311*, *312*
Mittelmark, M.B. 264, 266, 268, *275*, *282*
Modigliani, E. 19, *39*
Moffatt, R. 245, *255*
Moldofsky, H. 292, *309*
Moll, P. 205, *208*
Mondanaro, J. 243, *255*
Monson, R. 193, 194, *210*
Monteiro, E. 25, 35, 36, *39*, *41*
Monteiro, M.G. 144, 146, 147, 148, *160*
Montes, H. 271, *280*
Moore, C. 136, *137*
Moore, M.H. 343, *357*
Moorhouse, H. 290, 293, 297, 302, *310*
Moos, R.H. 330, *334*
Mora, J. 81, 82, 83, 86, *93*, *96*
Mora, M.E.M. 223, 224, *249*
Morelock, S. 193, 194, 196, *208*
Morgan, G.D. 267, *282*
Morgan, M.Y. 2, 6, 10, *14*, *15*
Moron, P. 194, *208*
Morrell, W. 290, 297, 298, *313*
Morris, J. 274, *285*

Morris, N.F. 193, 200, *213*
Morrisette, G. 273, *278*
Morrissey, E.R. 76, *96*, 104, 109, *116*, 236, *255*, 344, 348, *357*
Morrow-Tlucak, M. 105, *113*, 198, *208*
Moser, J. 342, *357*
Motoyoshi, M. 63, 71, 91, *93*
Moureli, E. 293, *311*
Muburgh, K.H. 247, *254*
Mudar, P.J. 77, 81, 83, *93, 97*
Mueller, M.D. 263, 265, 266, 272, *285*
Mulford, H.A. 68, *96,* 330
Mulinski, P. 144, *159*
Mullaney, J. 45, *60,* 68, *96,* 184, *189*
Mullen, P.D. 274, 277, *282*
Munoz, R. 53, 55, *59*
Murphy, M. 273, *281*
Murphy, S. 354, *358*
Murray, D.M. *282*
Murray, J.B. 320, *336*
Murray, R.M. 43, 51, *59, 60*
Murray-Lyon, E.M. 325, *338*
Murray-Lyon, I.M. 193, 200, *213*
Musto, D.F. 343, *357*
Myers, J.K. 44, *60,* 67, *96,* 145, *161*
Myrianthopoulous, N.C. 194, *209*

N
Nadler, D. 194, *208*
Naeye, R.L. 263, *282*
Nahar, G.G. 239, 241, *254*
Nakamura, S. 10, *15*
Naquin, M. 260, 271, *283*
Nash, J.D. 271, *278*
Nathan, P.E. 146, *159*
Neale, M.C. 121, *139*, 294, 295, *311*
Nee, J. 55, *59*
Neighbors, H. 221, *254*
Nelson, B.W. 134, *139*, 237, *251*, 318, *335*
Nelson, H.F. *336*
Nemzer, E. 297, 298, *313*
Neuberger, E. 325, *334*
Neuman, P.A. 290, *312*
Newberry, P. 150, *160*
Newcomb, M.B. 231, *253*
Newcomb, P.A. 266, 267, 272, 273, *278*
Newman, N.M. 196, 198, 201, *209, 210*
Newman, S.C. 305, *308*
Nickel, E.J. 143, *160*
Nickens, H. 271, *280*
Nilsson, A. 34, *40*

Nilsson, T. 51, *60*
Nirenberg, T.D. ix, *xi*, 339, 340, 342, 343, *357, 358*
Nixon, S.J. 45, *59*, 155, *157*
Noakes, T.D. 247, *254*
Noble, J. 67, 68, 69, 71, 81, 82, *94, 98*
Noel, C.T. 19, *40*
Noel, N.E. *336*, 344, 345, 347, 351, *358*
Noonan, D.L. 215, *257*
Norregaard, J. 273, *284*
Norris, A.H. 8, *17*
Novotny, T.E. 259, 260, 262, 263, 266, 267, 272, 273, *278, 280, 282, 283*
Nurius, P. 264, 267, 269, 270, *278*, 344, *356*

O
O'Brien, C.P. 143, *159*, 173, 181, *188*
Ockene, J.K. 267, 274, *282*
O'Connell, B. 22, *40*
O'Connor, M.J. 196, 199, *210*
Oehl, L.K. 273, *275*
Oei, T.P.S. 300, *312, 313*
Oellerich, D. 241, *250*
Oetting, E.R. 228, *248*
O'Gorman, T.W. 49, 50, *58*, 153, *157*, 215, *248*
Ogston, S.A. 193, 196, 198, *213*
Oh, W. 243, *253*
Okada, H. 34, *36*
O'Keefe, A.M. 265, *282*
Olds, J. 300, *312*
O'Leary, M.R. 236, *255*
Olegard, R. 197, *207, 209*
Olivo, J. 25, *39*
Olmsted, M.P. 289, *309*
Olsen, J. *211*
O'Malley, P.M. 65, *95*, 232, *252*, 264, *280*, 290, 302, *310*
Omenn, G.S. 51, *60*
Oppenheimer, E. 193, 194, 196, *208, 211*, 240, *255*
Ordentlich, M. 272, *277*
Orford, J. 129, 135, *140*, 326, 327, *336*
Orlandi, M.A. 266, 268, *282*
Orleans, C.T. 267, 268, 272, 273, 274, *276, 282*
Orn, H. 305, *308*
Oro, A.S. 241, *254*
Orvaschel, H. 44, *60, 61*, 67, *96*
Orza, M.J. 11, *14*
Osgood, S. 164, *187*

Ossip-Klein, D. 267, 272, *276*
Osterberg, E. 342, *355*
Ostrea, E.M. 243, *257*
Ostyn, M. 247, *249*
O'Sullivan, K. 148, *159*
Othmer, E. 151, *159*
Ouellette, E.M. 195, 196, *211*
Owen, P. 290, *310*

P

Padilla, A. 222, *249*
di Padova, C. 344, *355*
Paganini-Hill, A. 20, 30, *38, 40, 41*
Page, J.B. 109, *116*, 225, *251*
Pallonen, U.E. *282*
Palmer, R.L. 287, *309*
Palmieri, S.L. 169, *188*
Pan, L. 342, *355*
Panny, S. 262, *280*
Papasava, M. 302, *312*
Pares, X. 4, *13*
Park, J. 101, 110, *116*
Parker, D.A. 342, *358*
Parker, E.S. 146, *156*, 183, *186*
Parker, L. 231, *254*
Parker, S.D. 268, *284*
Parran, T.V. 238, *251*
Parrish, K.M. 2, *15*, 216, *254*
Parsons, O.A. 234, *249*
Partanen, J. 51, *60*
Pascale, R.W. 11, *15*, 273, *281*
Patel, K.M. 260, 263, 266, *278*
Paton, S. 168, *189*
Paulozzi, L. 196, *210*
Peacock, J.L. 201, 205, *207, 208*
Pechacek, T.F. 263, 265, 266, 268, 272, *275, 282, 284, 285*
Peele, S. 43, *60*, 326, *336*
Pellegrin, F. 20, *40*
Penick, E. 143, 151, *159, 160*
Pequignot, G. 10, *15*
Perez-Stable, E.J. 271, *281, 282*
Perkins, H.W. 63, 65, *92, 96*, 135, *140*
Perodeau, G.A. 318, *336*
Perodeau, G.M. 133, *140*
Perret, T. 19, *39*
Persaud, T.V.N. 136, *139*
Peskar, B.M. 10, *14*
Pessel, D. 199, *208*
Pestalozzi, D.M. 2, *15*
Peters, E.C. 263, *282*
Peterson, D.R. 262, *282*
Petitti, D.B. 20, *40*

Peto, R. 30, *37*
Petrie, L. 150, *160*
Pettigrew, L. 273, *278*
Petty, F. 148, 149, *161*
Petzold, A.S. 262, *278*
Peveler, R. 293, *312*, 320, *336*
Phibbs, C.S. 174, 175, 179, *189*
Pickens, R.W. 43, 51, 52, 54, *60*
Pickering, R. 67, 68, 69, 71, 81, 82, *94*
Pickle, L. 263, *276*
Pierce, B. 301, *309*
Pierce, J.P. 259, 260, 261, 262, 263, 266, 267, 271, 272, 273, *278, 280, 282, 283*
Pietruszko, R. 2, 4, *12, 13*
Pignon, J.P. 10, *15, 16*
Pihl, E. 10, *15*
Pikkarainen, P. 10, *16*
Pillard, R. 171, *189*
Pirie, P.L. *282*
Pirola, R.C. 33, *40*
Piserchia, P.V. 273, *278*
Pitts, F.N. 50, 53, *61*, 147, 149, *160, 161*, 346, *358*
Pitts, F.N., Jr. 147, *160*
Placek, P.J. 202, *211*
Platzman, K.A. 179, *187*
Plessinger, M.A. 241, *257*
Pletch, P.K. 235, *255*
Pleuvry, B.J. 8, *12*
Pohl, C.R. 34, *38*
Polich, S. 218, *252*
Pollitt, K. 318, *336*
Pond, M. 350, *358*
Pope, H.G. 290, 297, 298, 299, *310*
Popham, R.E. 342, *355*
Popkin, C.L. 70, *96*, 354, *358*
Porterfield, A.L. 128, *138*
Pottash, A.L.C. 147, *157*, 290, 291, *310*
Pottenger, M. 147, 150, *160, 161*
Potter, D. 164, *186*
Potter, J.J. 6, 7, 8, *15*
Powell, B. 143, 151, *159, 160*
Power, C. 79, *96*
Powers, J. 164, *187*
Pozzato, G. 2, 5n, 6, 9, 11, *13*, 105, *114*, 215, *250*, 344, *355*
Pratt, J.H. 25, *40*
Presson, C.C. 264, *276*
Preston, M. 74, *93*
Prochaska, J.O. 266, 267, 272, *276, 277, 283*
Projesz, B. 234, *248*

Prugh, T. 350, *358*
Prybeck, T.R. 294, *310*
Przybeck, T.R. 67, 68, 69, *96,* 145, 147, *158,* 319, 320, *335*
Purtell, J.J. 56, *59*
Puska, P. 271, *283*
Pyle, R.L. 290, 292, 297, 300, 302, 303, 306, *310, 311, 312*

Q

Quadagno, D. 245, *255*
Quade, D. *282*
Quinn, V.P. 274, 277, *282*
Qulali, R. 7, *16*

R

Rabinovitz, M. 11, *15*
Rabinowitz, E. 150, *156*
Rachmamin, G. 7, *15*
Rachootin, P. *211*
Rae, D.S. 143, *160,* 291, *312*
Ragozin, A.S. 197, *209*
Rais, O. 10, *15*
Raivio, K.O. 194, 196, *208*
Ramcharan, S. 20, *40*
Rankin, G. 10, *17*
Rankin, J.G. 9, *16*
Rantakallio, P. 240, *255,* 263, *283*
Raphael, B. 155, *161*
Ratajczak, T. 35, *36*
Ratcliff, K.S. 167, *189*
Rathbone-McCuan, E. 236, 237, *255*
Ravi, S.D. 147, *157*
Ray, L.A. 267, *276*
Read, L.L. 267, 268, 270, *279*
Reed, B.G. 243, *255*
Reed, D.R. 300, *312*
Reed, G. 193, 196, *212*
Reed, M.J. 19, *40*
Reeder, S.J. 268, *279*
Reese, Y. 274, *285*
Regier, D.A. 67, 68, 69, *96,* 143, *160,* 291, *312*
Reich, T. 45, 46, 47, 48, 50, 53, *59, 60, 61,* 68, *96,* 147, 153, *157, 160, 161,* 183, 184, *187, 189,* 346, *358*
Reichman, W.R. 325, *338*
Reid, D.E. 56, *59*
Reiss, J.P. 45, *60*
Remington, P.L. 225, *250,* 260, 264, 269, 270, 271, *277*
Renwick, J.H. 193, 200, *209*
Rhoads, G.G. 193, 196, 201, *210, 211*

Rhyne, R. 70, *92*
Rice, A. 151, *159*
Rice, J.P. 68, *96,* 151, 152, *159,* 184, *189*
Richards, J.W., Jr. 265, *279*
Richardson, G. 194, 195, 197, 200, *207, 211*
Richardson, J. 272, *276*
Richter, C.P. 301, *312*
Ridella, S.A. 262, *278*
Ridlon, F.V. 104, *116*
Rimer, B.K. 273, *282*
Rimmer, J. 53, *61,* 147, *160, 161*
Rio, L. 109, *116*
Risch, S.C. 7, *16*
Rist, F. 329, *336*
Rivinus, T.M. 298, *312*
Roberds, L.A. 237, *255*
Robert, J.C. 259, *283*
Robbins, C. 63, 65, 66, *96,* 129, *140,* 164, 165, 166, *186, 189,* 238n, *255,* 346, *355*
Robins, E. 44, 53, 55, *59,* 167, 174, *190, 335*
Robins, L.N. 56, *61,* 67, 68, 69, *96,* 122, *140, 189,* 317, *336*
Robinson, A.B. 34, *37*
Robinson, G.C. 192, *211*
Robinson, T.N. 265, *280,* 290, 294, 295, *311*
Robles, E.A. 4, *13*
Robles, N. 194, 197, 200, *207*
Roby, T.B. 300, *312*
Rochat, W. 224, *252*
Rockert, W. 289, *309*
Rodin, J. 259, *283,* 300, *312*
Roemer, R. 265, 272, *283*
Rohsenow, D.J. 85, *96*
Roine, R. 4, 6, *13, 16*
Roman, E. 193, 201, *208*
Roman, P.M. 134, *139*
Romano, P.S. 220, *255*
Romelsjo, A. 79, *97*
Ronan, L. 218, *255*
Room, R. 69, *97,* 342, *355*
Roose, S.P. 293, *313*
Rose, J. 272, *283*
Rosenak, D. 241, *255*
Rosenbaum. M. 354, *358*
Rosenberg, L. 194, *213*
Rosenberg, M.J. 240, *256*
Rosenblum, E.R. 11, *17,* 34, 35, 36, *38, 39, 40, 41*
Rosenman, R.H. 215, *256,* 268, *284*

Rosett, H.L. 105, *116*, 194, 195, 196, 198, 200, 206, *211, 213,* 240, *255,* 329, *337*
Rosman, N.P. 195, *211*
Rosner, B. 20, 30, *37, 41*
Ross, E.M. 240, *248*
Ross, H. 145, *160,* 167, 183, *189*
Ross, R.A. 7, *16*
Ross, R.K. 20, 30, *38, 40, 41*
Rossi, J.S. 266, 267, 272, *276, 277*
Roth, P. 341, *358*
Rounsaville, B.J. 150, *160,* 173, 174, 177, *188,* 330, *337*
Roy-Bryne, P. 290, 297, *309*
Ruben, H.L. 147, 150, *160, 161*
Rubin, E. 4, *12,* 25, *39*
Ruccione, K. 262, *276*
Rudas, T. *213*
Ruggiu, M.E. 11, *15*
Rumeau-Rouquette, C. 193, 194, 196, *209*
Russell, D.E.H. 86, *97*
Russell, M. 77, 81, 83, *93, 97,* 183, *189,* 191, 193, 198, 199, 200, *211,* 218, 219, *255,* 325, *337*
Russell, S.A. 85, *97*
Ryan, K.B. 264, *278*
Ryan, K.J. 193, 194, *210*

S
Saba, G. 304, *312*
Sabel, K.G. 197, *207, 209*
Sachs, B.P. 240, *256*
Sachs, D.P.L. 268, 272, *283*
Sadava, S.W. 119, 127, *140*
Sadik, C. 293, *313*
Safa, H.I. 224, *255*
Saghir, J.T. 317, *335*
Saleh, F.M. 10, *16*
Salkin, B. 290, 297, 298, *308, 313*
Salmon, M.A. *282*
Salonen, J.T. 271, *283*
Sambamoorthi, U. 194, 197, 200, *207*
Samet, J.M. 194, *210*
Sampson, P.D. 193, 197, 200, *209, 212*
Sanchez, C.J. 24, *39*
Sanchez, T.V. 35, *40*
Sanchez-Craig, M. 326, 327, 328, *337*
Sander, L.W. 196, *211*
Sandin, B. 197, *207, 209*
Sandmaier, M. 319, *337*

Sandman, B.M. 196, 197, *212*
Sanghvi, A. 29, *38*
Sansone, R.A. 297, 298, *313*
Santamaria, J.N. 9, *17*
Sargent, R.G. 267, *284*
Sarna, S. 51, *60*
Sashin, D. 30, *37*
Sasse, D. 7, *14*
Sather, H.N. 262, *276*
Sato, T. 10, *15*
Satterlee, S. 103, *115*
Sattler, J. 264, *276*
Savich, R. 241, *249*
Savolainen, M.J. 10, *16*
Sawe, U. 273, *284*
Saylor, K.E. 265, *280,* 290, 294, 295, *311*
Schaefer, S. 320, 321, *335, 337*
Schamaling, D.B. 152, *159*
Schatzkin, A. 30, *41*
Schelkun, P.H. 245, *255*
Scher, M. 194, 195, 197, 200, *207, 211*
Schiedermayer, D.L. 263, *276*
Schiele, B.C. 288, 301, *309*
Schilit, R. 134, 135, *139, 140,* 349, *358*
Schinke, S.R. 264, 267, 269, 270, *278*
Schinko, S.P. 344, *356*
Schiodt, A.V. *211*
Schmidt, C. 67, *95, 97,* 129, *140*
Schmidt, W. 342, *355*
Schneider, S.J. 25, *40,* 267, *283*
Schnoll, S.H. 241, *249*
Schoenbach, V.J. 267, 272, *276, 282*
Schoenbaum, S. 193, 194, *210*
Schonfeld, L. 236, *250*
Schrier, S.S. 297, 298, *313*
Schuckit, M.A. 7, *16,* 50, *61,* 100, 104, *114, 116,* 143, 144, 146, 147, 148, 150, 151, *160,* 183, *189,* 236, *255,* 319, *337,* 346, *358*
Schulsinger, F. 48, 50, 54, *59,* 148, *158*
Schulsinger, R. 121, *139*
Schultz, F.A. 197, 198, *209, 210*
Schur, B.E. 72, 77, 84, 90, *98,* 178, *190,* 349, *359*
Schur, C. 273, *283*
Schwartz, D. 193, 196, *209*
Schwartz, J.L. 268, *283*
Schwartz, R.C. 304, *312*
Schwartz, R.M. 174, 175, 179, *189*
Scott, L.D. 8, *16*
Scudder, T. 107, *113,* 229, *255*
Sebaoun, J. 19, *39*

Seck, M. 164, *187*
Seitz, H.K. 9, *16*
Selby, R. 247, *256*
Selzer, M.L. 177, *189*, 325, *337*
Serdula, M.K. 265, 274, *278, 285*, 290, 294, 295, *309*
Severson, H. 264, *275*
Sexton, M. 274, *284*
Shader, R.I. 105, *113*
Shapiro, E. 79, *95*
Shapiro, L. 171, *189*
Shapiro, R.S. 263, *276*
Shareha, A.M. 34, *38*
Sharma, S. 6, *15*
Shaw, S. 126, *140*, 180, *186*
Sheffield, F.D. 300, *312*
Sherlock, S. 10, *15*
Sherman, S.J. 264, *276*
Shevchuk, O. 10, *16*
Shiono, P.H. 196, 201, *208, 211*
Shisslak, C.M. 247, *257*
Shkilnyk, A.M. 229, *256*
Sholar, J.W. 44, *60,* 164, 184, *188*
Shopland, D.R. 263, 265, 266, 272, *285*
Shore, E.R. 164, *190*
Short, F. 19, *39*
Shrout, P. 196, *209*
Shutt, D.A. 34, *41*
Siau, J. 267, 270, *279*
Siegel, M. 290, 297, *308*, 320, *334*
Siegelaub, A.B. 20, *40*
Sigman, M. 196, 199, *210*
Sigvardsson, S. 44, 49, 50, 53, 54, 56, 57, 58, *58, 59, 61,* 154, 155, *157,* 183, 184, *186, 187,* 234, *249*
Siiteri, P.K. 30, *38*
Simanowski, U.A. 9, *16*
Simonson, K. 273, *284*
Simpura, J. 135, 136, *139*
Sing, C.F. 206, *210*
Singer, G. 300, 302, *312, 313*
Singer, H. 267, *283*
Skinner, J.B. 200, *211*
Skinner, W.F. 164, *186*, 346, *355*
Skog, O.M. 342, *355*
Slater, M.D. 265, *275*
Slemenda, C.W. 30, *41*
Smeltzer, D.J. 297, 298, *313*
Smith, A.L. 290, 297. 299, *310*
Smith, D.W. 136, *139*, 192, 194, 199, *207, 208, 209,* 240, *251, 252*
Smith, E.M. 318, 330, *337*

Smith, G.P. 301, *309*
Smith, I.E. 179, *187*, 195, 206, *207, 211*
Smith, J.R. 198, *212*, 224, *252*
Smith, P.F. 260, 264, 269, 270, 271, *277*
Smith, T.R. 215, *252*
Snyder, P. 196, *211*
Sobell, L.C. 217, *256*
Sobell, M.B. 217, *256*
Sokol, R.J. 105, *113,* 192, 193, 194, 195, 196, 197, 198, 200, 206, *207, 208, 209, 212,* 242, 243, *256, 257*
Solberg, L.I. 273, *281, 284*
Solms, W. 101, *113*
Solomon, J. 148, 149, *160*
Sorensen, G. 268, *284*
Sorrell, M.F. 10, *17*
Southren, A.L. 25, *39*
Spak, F. 90, *97*
Spare, K.E. 317, *336*
Specker, S. 302, 303, *312*
Speizer, F.E. 20, 22, 30, *37, 39, 41*
Spiegler, D.L. 352, *358*
Spitzer, R.L. 174, *190*
Spivak, K. 326, 327, 328, *337*
Stabenau, J. 151, 152, *158*
Stack, C.M. 241, *249*
Staden, H. 111, *116*
Staisey, N.L. 196, *212*
Stambul, H. 218, *252*
Stampfer, M.J. 20, 22, 30, *37, 39, 41*
Stebelsky, G. 305, *308*
Steer, R.A. 180, *186*
Stein, R.L. 327, *336*
Stein, Z.A. 196, *209,* 262, *281*
Steinbrecher, M. 199, *208*
Steinhauer, S.R. 215, *252*
Stellar, J.R. 300, *313*
Stellman, S.D. 260, 261, 262, *278, 284*
Stenhouse, N.S. 20, *37*
Stenman, U.H. 325, *338*
Stern, M.P. 271, *278*
Stern, S.L. 297, 298, *313*
Sternglass, E. 30, *37*
Stetner, F. 267, *279*
Stetson, B.A. 235, *248*
Stewart, C.M. 201, 205, *207, 208*
Stewart, R.B. 300, *313*
Stiasny, S. 145, *160,* 167, 183, *189*
Stiglich, N.J. 177, *186*
Stillman, R.J. 240, *256*
Stilwell, N.A. 329, *334*
Stimmel, B. 100, *116*

Stinson, F.S. 67, 68, 69, 71, 81, 82, *94*, 216, *254*
Stitzer, M.L. 272, *279*
Stjernfeldt, J. 262, *284*
Stoffer, D.S. 194, 195, 197, 200, *207, 211*
Stoltzman, R. 44, *60*, 67, *96*
Stotz, D.C. 300, *308*
Stout, R.L. *336*
Straeter, J.A. *284*
Strecher, V.J. 267, *282*
Streissguth, A.P. 136, *139*, 192, 194, 195, 196, 197, 198, 199, 200, 206, *207, 208, 209, 210*, 240, *251*
Stremple, J.R. 8, *16*
Strempler, J.F. *17*
Strenger, V.E. 321, *335*
Strober, M. 290, 297, 298, *313*
Strohmeyer, G. 7, *16*
Stroup-Benham, C. 224, *256*
Stubblefield, P.G. 193, 194, *210*
Sturzenberg, S. 290, *308*
Suarez, L. 20, *37*
Sufian, M. 225, *250*
Sulaiman, N.D. 193, 196, 198, *213*
Sulkunen, P. 342, *355*
Sung, W.C. 261, *285*
Surawicz, T.S. 266, 267, 272, 273, *278*
Surber, M. 180, *187*
Susser, M. 196, *209*, 262, *281*
Sutker, P.B. 7, *16*
Sutton, S.R. 266, *284, 285*
Svikis, D.S. 43, 51, 52, *60*
Swan, G.E. 215, *256*, 268, *284*
Swanson, D.W. 228, *256*
Sweeney, D.R. 147, *157*, 291, *310*
Sweeney, J. 109, *116*
Syme, S.L. 220, *255*
Syzmanski, K. 149, *158*

T
Takahashi, R.N. 300, *313*
Takezawa, Y. 10, *15*
Talalay, P. 34, *38*
Tam, D. 264, 267, *276*
Tamerin, J.S. 146, *161*
Tanna, V.L. 146, 149, *157*
Tannenbaum, L. 3, *14*
Tarter, R.E. 11, *17*, 234, *256*, 287, *313*
Tauchen, G. 342, *355*
Taylor, B. 262, *284*
Taylor, C.B. 265, *280*, 290, 294, 295, *311*
Taylor, C.J. *159*

Taylor, D.J. 193, 196, 198, *213*
Taylor, J. 77, 81, 83, *97*
Taylor, P. 194, 197, 200, *207*
Taylor, T.H. 146, *156*, 183, *186*
Taylor, T.P. 30, *41*
Taysi, K. 240, *256*
Teitelbaum, M.A. 215, *257*
Telch, M.J. 265, *280*, 290, 294, 295, *311*
Telepchak, J.M. 273, *275*
Teltsch, K. 351, *358*
Temple, M.T. 63, 71, 91, *93*
Tennen, H. 143, 156, *158*
Tennes, K. 193, 194, 196, 198, *213*
Teoh, S.K. 164, 166, 178, 179, 183, 184, *188, 189, 190*
Terney, R. 231, *256*
Terpin, M. 2, 5n, 6, 9, 11, *13*, 105, *114*, 215, *250*, 344, *355*
Teschke, R. 7, *16*
Testa, M. 85, *96*
Thomas, P. 24, *39*
Thompson, C.R. 34, *37*
Thompson, K.M. 315, *337*
Thompson, T. 300, *311*
Thompson, W.D. 147, *161*
Timmerman, M.G. 295, *313*
Tipp, J.E. 267, *279*
Tischler, G.L. 44, *60*, 67, *96*
Todd, R. 274, *281*
Tokin, J.D. 8, *17*
Tonascia, J.A. 262, *281*
Toneatto, A. 217, *256*
Tonnesen, P. 273, *284*
Tooley, J. 222, *248*
Toonen, L.A. 164, *190*
Toplis, P.J. 193, 200, *213*
Topper, M.D. *116*
Towle, L.H. 216, *254*
Trevino, D. 224, *256*
Trevino, F. 224, *256*
Triegaadt, J. 236, *255*
Troughton, E. 49, 50, *58*, 151, 153, *157*, 215, *248*
Trowbridge, F.L. 295, *308*
Tubman, J.G. 231, *256*
Tuma, D.J. 10, *17*
Tunell, R. 194, 197, 200, 206, *209*
Tuomilehto, J. 271, *283*
Turk, D.C. 274, *281*
Turnbull, J.E. 131, *140*, 148, *158, 161*, 183, *190*, 319, *337*, 346, *358*
Turner, S. 150, *156*

Tuyns, A.J. 10, *15*
Tye, J.B. 263, 265, *277*
Tyler, E.T. 10, *12*

U

Uhl, C.N. 196, 206, *210*
Uhlenhuth, E. 238, *253*
Ulleland, C.N. 136, *139*
Underhill, B.L. 164, 182, *190*, 322, *337*

V

Vaglum, P. 70, 74, 76, 86, *94*, 145, 148, *161*
Vaglum, S. 145, 148, *161*
Vanclay, F.M. 155, *161*
VandeBerg, J.L. 4, *13*
Vandereycken, W. 289, 303, *313*
VanEerdewegh, P. 45, *60*, 68, *96*, 184, *189*
Vannicelli, M. 315, 324, 332, *337*
Vannini, M.G. 11, *15*
Van Thiel, D.H. 2, 8, 11, *15, 16, 17,* 20, 25, 29, 34, 35, 36, *37, 38, 39, 40, 41*
Velasquez, M.M. 266, *277*
Velicer, W.F. 266, *277*
Verbrugge, L.M. 74, *97*
Vermeulen, A. 247, *249*
Vestal, R.E. 8, *17*
Vicary, J.R. 231, *256*
Vitez, M. 196, *213*
Vittek, J. 25, *39*
Vogeli, C. 261, *285*
Voigt, L.A. 262, *276*
Volentine, G.D. 10, *17*
Volicer, B.J. 325, *334*
Voss, H.L. 164, *186*, 240, *256*, 346, *355*

W

Wadler, G.I. 247, *256*
Wadsworth, J. 262, *284*
Wagner, J.G. 2, *17*
Wahid, S. 7, *15*
Wahlqvist, M.L. 35, *41*
Wald, A. 8, *17*
Waldman, E. 261, *285*
Waldron, I. 260, 261, *280, 285*
Walker, J.B. 19, *39*
Wall, J.H. 101, *116,* 126, *140*
Wallace, A.F.C. 229, *256*
Wallace, B. 174, *190*
Wallace, R.B. 200, *207*

Wallack, L.M. 340, 343, *359*
Wallen, M. 222, *257*
Wallett, R. *285*
Walsh, B.T. 293, *313*
Walsh, D.C. 337
Walter, H. 148, *156*
Wanberg, K.W. 52, *60*
Wannagat, F.J. 7, *16*
Wanner, E. 103, *115*
Warburton, D. 196, *209*, 262, *281*
Ward, D.S. 267, *284*
Warner, K.E. 263, 265, 266, 272, *285*
Warren, C. 224, *252*
von Wartburg, J.P. 2, *15*
Wartenberg, A.A. 127, *140*
Warthen, F. 222, *251*
Waterson, E.J. 193, 200, *213*, 325, *338*
Watkins, V.A. 247, *254*
Watts, C.D. *282*
Watzl, H. 329, *336*
Wearne, K.L. 20, *37*
Wechsler, H. 22, *41*, 97, 218, *256*
Weibel-Orlando, J. 88, *97*, 102, *116*, 228, 229, *257*
Weidenman, M. 143, 149, 151, 152, 156, *158*
Weiner, H. 222, *257*
Weiner, L. 105, *116*, 194, 195, 196, 198, 200, 206, *211, 213*, 240, *255*, 329, *337*
Weiner, S. 103, *113*, 146, *161*
Weinstein, A. 262, *280*
Weinstein, H.M. 247, *256*
Weiss, N.S. 262, *276*
Weiss, R.D. 164, 176, 177, 183, *187*
Weiss, S. 290, 291, 292, *313*
Weissman, M.M. 44, *60*, 67, *96*, 145, 147, 150, *160, 161*
Weissman, M.N. 44, *61*
Welch, R.A. 243, *257*
Wellman, H. *41*
Wells, K.B. 81, *93*
Wells, L.A. 295, *313*
Weltz, J.W. 232, *248*
Wendt, J.K. 136, *139*
Werler, M.M. 194, *213*
Wewers, M.E. 261, 265, 267, 270, *280*
Whelan, E.M. 265, *285*
Whillans, P. 148, *159*
White, D.G. 217, *257*
White, H.R. 78, *94*
White, L.D. 265, 268, 270, 272, *275, 285*

Whitehead, P.C. 164, *187*, 342, *359*
Whittaker, J.O. 227, 228, 229, *257*
Whittaker, R. 225, *247*
Widiger, T.A. 154, *157*
Widmer, R. 151, *157*
Wiese, B. 7, *16*
Wight, C. 29, *38*
Wilbert, J. 259, *285*
Wilcox, G. 35, *41*
Wilkinson, D.A. 118, *138*
Wilkinson, G.S. 177, *186*
Wilkinson, P. 9, *17*
Wilkinson, R. 342, *359*
Willander, A. 328, *334*
Willett, W.C. 20, 22, 30, *37, 39, 41*
Williams, A. 342, *355*
Williams, C.N. 134, *140*, 316, 317, *338*, 345, *359*
Williams, D. 147, *161*
Williams, E. 273, *281*
Williams, G.D. 64, 67, 72, 81, 88, *93, 98, 99, 338*
Williams, R.H. 19, *40*
Williams, V.J. 8, *12*
Williamson, D.F. 267, 270, 274, *275, 285*, 295, *308*
Wilner, D.M. 180, *187*
Wilner, S. 262, *285*
Wilsnack, R.W. 44, *61,* 62n, 63, 66, 69, 70, 72, 74, 76, 77, 78, 79, 80, 82, 84, 85, 86, 87, 90, 91, *98,* 99, 109, 122, 124, 125, 126, *140,* 141, 178, *190,* 216, 218, 219, 257, 315, 316, *337, 338,* 347, 349, *359*
Wilsnack, S.C. 44, *61,* 62n, 63, 66, 69, 70, 72, 74, 76, 77, 78, 80, 82, 84, 85, 86, 87, 90, 91, *95, 98, 99,* 100, 103, 104, 109, *116, 117,* 122, 124, 125, 126, 127, 135, *140, 141,* 178, *190,* 218, 257, 316, 320, *338,* 344, 347, 348, 349, *359*
Wilson, G.T. 266, *276*
Wilson, J.R. 6, *12*
Wilson, R.W. 81, *99,* 317, *338*
Wilson, T.G. 294, 303, *313*
Winders, S.E. 261, 265, 267, 270, *280*
Windle, M. 144, 145, 153, *161*
Windsor, D. 231, *257*
Windsor, R.A. 274, *285*
Wingard, D.L. 20, *37*
Wingerd, J. 20, *40*

Winokur, G. 50, 53, 55, *59, 61,* 121, *139,* 143, 147, 149, 150, *156, 157, 160, 161,* 346, *358*
Wofgram, E. 50, *59*
Wolf, A. 194, *208*
Wolfe, R. 205, *208*
Wolin, S.J. 215, *257*
Womble, M. 221, *257*
Wong, T.H. 88, *99*
Wong-McCarthy, W.J. 264, *285*
Wood, H.P. *161*
Wood, P.D. 271, *277,* 315, *357*
Woodell, S. 200, *212*
Woodruff, R.A. 53, 55, *59,* 149, *161*
Woodruff, R.A., Jr. 58, *59*
Woods, C.P. 103, 117
Woods, J.R., Jr. 241, *257*
Woods, W.G. 262, *276*
Woodside, M. 183, *190*
Woody, G.E. 143, 151, *157, 159,* 173, *188*
Wooley, O.W. 297, *313*
Wooley, S.C. 297, *313*
Workman-Daniels, K.L. 149, 151, *158*
Worner, T.M. 3, 6, *13,* 129, *141*
Worthington-Roberts, B. 198, 202, 205, *209, 210*
Wright, J.T. 193, 200, *213*
Wright, R. 2, *12*
Wright, S.I. 74, 76, 79, *98*
Wyatt, G.E. 86, *99*

Y

Yaffe, H. 241, *255*
Yager, J. 290, 297, *309*
Yamada, S. 11, *17*
Yamaguchi, K. 166, 169, *188*
Yates, A. 247, *257*
Yates, W.R. 148, 149, *161*
Yeary, J.R. 304, *313*
Yee, D. 287, 297, *309*
Ylikorkara, O. 194, 196, *208,* 325, *338*
Yohman, R. 234, *249*
Youcha, G. 101, 109, *117*
Young, A. 196, 206, *210*
Young, D.W. 325, *338*
Yu, J.J. 263, 265, 266, 272, *285*
Yung, L. 301, *313*
Yurgelun-Todd, D. 290, 297, 298, 299, *310*

Z

Zador, P. 342, *355*
Zankowski, G. 222, *257*
Zenisek, A. 34, *41*
Zeuchner, E. 10, *15*
Zevola, S.A. 11, *14*
Ziegler, R.G. 30, *41*

Zorzano, A. 7, *17*
Zucker, R.A. 119, *141*, 342, *359*
Zuckerman, B.S. 168, 179, *185*, *188*, 193,
    194, 196, 198, 200, 206, *208*, *211*,
    213, 235, 240, *255*, *257*
Zuspan, F.P. 241, *257*

Subject Index

A

Adolescents, substance abuse among, 231–236
  alcohol, 232
  cigarette smoking, 263–266
  drug use, 232–235
  prevention programs, 235–266
Advertising of tobacco industry, 265–266
Affective disorder, *see* Depression
African-American women, substance abuse among, 217–222
  alcohol, 218–220
  cigarette smoking, 220
  drug use, 220
  treatment of, 221–222
Alcohol dehydrogenase (ADH) activity, 4–9
Alcohol disorders, *see* Drinking-related problems; Alcoholism
Alcoholism
  among elderly women, 236–237
  antisocial personality disorder (ASP) and, 150–155
  availability of alcohol and, 107
  differentiating between depression and, 145–149; *see also* Depression and alcoholism
  early-onset vs. late-onset, 44–45
  genetic heterogeneity in, 52–58
    Pittsburgh family study, 54–57
  genetic models of, 45–52
    adoption studies, 48–50, 154–155
    family history data, 46–48
    twin studies, 51–52
  rates of by age, 44
Anabolic steroid use, 245–247
Antecedents to alcohol use/abuse, 119–127
  biological/genetic variables, 120–122
  current behavior with substances, 125–126
  personality variables, 122–124
  sociocultural variables, 124–125
Antisocial personality disorder (ASP)
  and cocaine use, 176
  and consequences of alcoholism, 151–153
  expression of, 153–154
  and gender, 143, 150–151
  and transmission of alcoholism, 154–155
Athletes, substance abuse among, 244–247
  treatment of, 247

B

Birth defects, 193–195; *see also* Fetal alcohol syndrome
Breast cancer, effects of moderate alcohol use on, 30

C

Cigarette smoking
  advertising and, 265–266
  among African Americans, 220
  among the elderly, 237
  among Hispanics, 224–225
  cessation and relapse of, 266–268
  during pregnancy, 235, 240, 274
  and eating disorders, 294, 302
  health consequences, 261–263
  initiation of, 263–266
  intervention programs, 268–274
  prevalence of, 259–261
Cocaine use, 174–177
  and crime, 175–176
  fetal exposure, 175, 241
  and prostitution, 175
Consequences of alcohol use/abuse,
      127–137; see also Drinking-related
      problems
  biopsychosocial factors influencing,
      128–129
  comorbidity, 133
  employment/economic status, 134, 347
  family problems, 133–134, 345
  gender differences in, 129–130
  legal problems, 135, 347–348
  medical/physical, 132–133, 346–347
  reproductive problems, 136
  sexuality and sexual dysfunction,
      135–136
  social supports and social networks,
      134–135
  stigma and social attitudes, 136,
      320–321
Coronary heart disease, beneficial effects
      of moderate alcohol use on, 20–24
Cross-cultural studies on alcohol use,
      100–112; see also Women's
      drinking, among special
      populations
  control by women using alcohol,
      110–111
  control of women using alcohol,
      108–110
  gender differences, 101–104
  women's access to alcohol, 106–107

D

Depression and alcoholism, 53, 55–56,
      319–320
  and cocaine use, 176

differentiating between, 145–149
gender and, 144–149
relationship of antisocial personality
      disorder to, 149
Drinking levels, gender differences in,
      63–65
Drinking-related problems, see also
      Consequences of alcohol use/abuse
  alcohol abuse/alcohol dependence,
      67–68
  gender differences in, 65–67
  variations in among women, see
      Women's drinking, variations in

E

Eating disorders
  defined, 287–289
  family history data, 297–300
  food deprivation and drug self-
      administration, 300–302
  and substance abuse, 289–307, 320
    alcohol, 290–291, 294
    clinical similarities between,
        303–307
    cocaine, 291
    cigarette/marijuana smoking, 294
    explanation of coprevalence of,
        296–303
Elderly women, substance abuse among,
      236–238; see also Postmenopausal
      women
  alcohol, 236–237
  cigarette smoking, 237
  drug use, 238
Employment and drinking, 73–76
Estrogen
  natural sources of, 33–36
  postmenopausal levels of, 25–29
Ethanol metabolism, gender differences
      in, 2–9
Ethnicity and drinking, 81–83

F

Fetal alcohol syndrome (FAS), 105–106,
      192–193

G

Gender differences
  in consequences of alcohol use/abuse,
      129–130
  in drinking levels, 63–65
    cross-culturally, 101–104

Gender differences (*continued*)
  in drinking problems, 65–67
  in liver disease, 9–12
  in marijuana use, 168–169
  in psychosocial problems, 165–166
Genetic predisposition to substance
    abuse, 45–52, 120–122, 215–216

H
Heavy drinking, definition of, 22
Heroin use, *see* Opiate use
Hispanic women, substance abuse
    among, 222–226
  alcohol, 223–224
  cigarette smoking, 224–225
  drug use, 225–226

I
Illicit drug use, 163–185
  cocaine, 174–177
  marijuana, 167–172
  opiates, 172–174
  polysubstance use, 164–167
  prevention of, 182–184
  social and biological consequences of,
      177–179
  treatment of, 179–182
Infertility and drug use, 177–178

J
J-shaped risk curve, 200–202

L
Liver disease
  effects of moderate alcohol use on,
      29–30
  gender differences in, 9–12
  increased estrogen levels in
      postmenopausal women with,
      24, 25

M
Marijuana use, 167–172
  and drinking, 170–171
  during pregnancy, 241
  and eating disorders, 294
  gender differences in, 168–169
Marital status and drinking, 76–81, 318
  cohabitation, 77
  divorce and separation, 77–81
  spouse's influence, 86–87, 88–89

Menstrual cycle, *see also*
    Postmenopausal women
  effect of on gastric emptying, 8
  premenstural syndrome, 55–57, 121
Moderate alcohol use
  among postmenopausal women, 22–24
  benefits of, 20–24
  possible negative effects of, 29–33
  and postmenopausal estrogen levels,
      25–29
  as source of estrogenic substances,
      33–36

N
Native American women, substance
    abuse among, 226–231
  alcohol, 226–230
  drug use, 230
  treatment of, 230–231

O
Opiate use, 172–174
  during pregnancy, 241
Osteoporosis, effects of moderate alcohol
    use on, 30

P
Postmenopausal women
  effects of plant estrogens on, 34–35
  estrogen levels of, 24–29
  moderate alcohol consumption among,
      22–24
Pregnancy, substance abuse and,
    238–244
  alcohol, 192–199, 239–240
    anomalies and, 193–195
    before conception, 199–205
    CNS and, 195
    fetal growth and, 193
    follow-up studies of, 196–197
  biological factors, 239
  cigarette smoking, 235, 240
  clinical approaches to in prenatal care,
      242–244
  drug use, 240–241
Premenstrual Assessment Form and
    alcoholism, 55–57
Prevention strategies, 182–184, 339–354
  for adolescents, 235–236
  ideas for, 352–354
  limitations of, 351–352

models of, 341–342
  distribution-of-consumption, 342
  social-psychological, 342
  sociocultural, 341–342
  vs. secondary, 339–341
  for women, 344, 348–351
Prostitution and cocaine use, 175
Psychotropic drugs, 110

R
Reproductive problems, 136, 177–179

S
Sexual abuse as predictor of problem
    drinking, 85–86, 320
Sexual arousal and alcohol, 103–104,
    135–136
Smoking cessation, 266–268, 272–274;
    see also Cigarette smoking
Sociopathy and alcoholism, 53, 57–58
Somatization disorder and alcoholism,
    53, 56–57
Substance abuse treatment programs,
    179–182
  for African-American women, 221–222
  for alcoholic women, 322–323
  identification and referral, 324–326
  inpatient treatment, 327
  level of treatment, 327–328
  for Native American women, 230–231

predictors of outcome, 330
research on, 323–331
specialized programs for women,
    328–329
treatment goals, 326–327
Suicide and alcoholism, 149

W
Women's drinking
  among special populations, 218–220,
      223–224, 226–230, 232,
      236–237, 239–240
  childhood sexual abuse and, 85–86,
      320
  during pregnancy, 191–199, 239–240,
      318
  predicting onset of, 83–85
  relationship to husband's drinking,
      86–89
  risk factors of problems with, 89–90
  social contexts of, 88–89
  time trends of, 87–88
  variations in
    age, 70–73, 232, 236–237, 315–316
    employment, 73–76, 316
    ethnicity, 81–83, 218–220, 223–224,
        226–230, 316–317
    marital status, 76–81, 318
    sexual orientation, 317